Lecture Notes in Computer Science 917
Edited by G. Goos, J. Hartmanis and J. van Leeuwen

Springer
Berlin
Heidelberg
New York
Barcelona
Budapest
Hong Kong
London
Milan
Paris
Tokyo

Josef Pieprzyk
Reihanah Safavi-Naini (Eds.)

Advances in Cryptology – ASIACRYPT '94

4th International Conference on
the Theory and Applications of Cryptology
Wollongong, Australia
November 28 - December 1, 1994
Proceedings

Springer

Series Editors

Gerhard Goos
Universität Karlsruhe
Vincenz-Priessnitz-Straße 3, D-76128 Karlsruhe, Germany

Juris Hartmanis
Department of Computer Science, Cornell University
4130 Upson Hall, Ithaca, NY 14853, USA

Jan van Leeuwen
Department of Computer Science, Utrecht University
Padualaan 14, 3584 CH Utrecht, The Netherlands

Volume Editors

Josef Pieprzyk
Reihanah Safavi-Naini
Department of Computer Science, The University of Wollongong
Wollongong, N.S.W. 2500, Australia

CR Subject Classification (1991):E.3-4, G.2.1, C.2.0, F.2.2
1991 Mathematics Subject Classification: 68P25, 94A60, 11T71

ISBN 3-540-59339-X Springer-Verlag Berlin Heidelberg New York

CIP data applied for

Typesetting: Camera-ready by author
SPIN: 10485870 06/3142-543210 - Printed on acid-free paper

PREFACE

The ASIACRYPT'94 was the fourth conference in the Asia-Pacific region and was a continuation of AUSCRYPT'90, ASIACRYPT'91 and AUSCRYPT'92 series of workshops devoted to the Theory and Application of Cryptology. The conference was held on the campus of the University of Wollongong, New South Wales, Australia. It started on November 28, 1994 and ended on December 1, 1994. The conference was organized by the Center for Computer Security Research and the Department of Computer Science, University of Wollongong, in co-operation with the International Association for Cryptologic Research (IACR). The sponsor of the conference was the Center for Computer Security Research, University of Wollongong.

The conference ran very smoothly and with a relaxed atmosphere. The credit for this goes to the General Chair, Professor Jennifer Seberry of the University of Wollongong, Mrs Margot Hall (the Conference Secretary) and graduate students of the Department of Computer Science.

The Program Chair received 99 submissions from 20 countries. The Program Committee reviewed 94 papers - the remaining five were not considered as they arrived too late. After a rigorous blind review process, 30 papers were accepted. Program Committee members' submissions were anonymous and went through exactly the same refereeing procedure as all other papers. From the accepted papers, Japan has 8, Australia 6, USA 3, France and Israel 2 each, and China, Finland, Germany, Korea, New Zealand, Saudi Arabia, Spain, UK, Yugoslavia a single paper each. The Committee chose three invited speakers: Thomas Beth, the Director of European Institute for System Security, University of Karlsruhe, Germany, Catherine Meadows, Center for High Assurance Computer Systems, Naval Research Laboratory, USA, and Hideki Imai, Institute of Industrial Science, University of Tokyo, Japan. These invited talks were not refereed and the authors bear full responsibility for their contents.

The traditional Rump Session was organized by Dr Reihanah Safavi-Naini with the help of Bill Forsyth. There were 13 submissions, all of which were presented. After a review 4 of them were accepted and placed in the proceedings.

We are pleased to thank all the members of the Program Committee: Don Beaver (Pennsylvania State University, USA), Eli Biham (Technion, Israel), Chin-Chen Chang (Chung Cheng University, Taiwan), Zong-Duo Dai (Academia Sinica, PROC), Yvo Desmedt (University of Wisconsin, USA), Toshiya Itoh (Tokyo Institute of Technology, Japan), Tsutomu Matsumoto (Yokohama National University, Japan), Andrew Odlyzko (AT&T Bell Laboratories, USA), Tatsuaki

Okamoto (NTT, Japan), Bart Preneel (Katholieke Universiteit Leuven, Belgium), Rainer Rueppel (R^3 Security Engineering AG, Switzerland), Yuliang Zheng (University of Wollongong, Australia). Thanks also go to the reviewers nominated by Program Committee members.

The conference also gave an opportunity for participants from Australia and New Zealand to get together and establish the Australasian Society for Electronic Security (ASES). The aim of ASES are to promote research and development in all areas of information security in the region.

We wish to thank all the authors for sending their submissions (successful or otherwise), the speakers, and all the participants of Asiacrypt'94 conference.

Wollongong, New South Wales, Australia
January 1995

Josef Pieprzyk
Reihanah Safavi-Naini

ASIACRYPT'94

THE 4th CONFERENCE ON THE THEORY AND APPLICATIONS OF CRYPTOLOGY

Sponsored by

Center for Computer Security Research
University of Wollongong, Australia

In co-operation with

The International Association for Cryptologic Research (IACR)

General Chair

Jennifer Seberry *(University of Wollongong, Australia)*

Program Chair

Josef Pieprzyk *(University of Wollongong, Australia)*

Program Committee

Donald Beaver *(Pennsylvania State University, USA)*
Eli Biham *(Technion, Israel)*
Chin-Chen Chang *(Chung-Cheng University, Taiwan)*
Zong-Duo Dai *(Academia Sinica, PROC)*
Yvo Desmedt *(University of Wisconsin-Milwaukee, USA)*
Toshiya Itoh *(Tokyo Institute of Technology, Japan)*
Tsutomu Matsumoto *(Yokohama National University, Japan)*
Andrew Odlyzko *(AT&T Bell Laboratories, USA)*
Tatsuaki Okamoto *(NTT, Japan)*
Bart Preneel *(Katholieke Universiteit Leuven, Belgium)*
Rainer Rueppel *(R^3 Security Engineering AG, Switzerland)*
Reihanah Safavi-Naini *(University of Wollongong, Australia)*
Yuliang Zheng *(University of Wollongong, Australia)*

Referees

Ross Anderson *(Cambridge University)*, Donald Beaver *(Pennsylvania State University)*, Amos Beimel *(Technion)*, Charles Bennett *(IBM Watson Research Center)*, Eli Biham *(Technion)*, Mike Burmester *(University of London)*, Chin-Chen Chang *(Chung-Cheng University)*, Yvo Desmedt *(University of Wisconsin-Milwaukee)*, Toshiya Itoh *(Tokyo Institute of Technology)*, Kaoru Kurosawa *(Tokyo Institute of Technology)*, Xuejia Lai *(R^3 Security Engineering AG)*, Keith Martin *(University of Adelaide)*, Tsutomu Matsumoto *(Yokohama National University)*, Yi Mu *(University of Wollongong)*, Andrew Odlyzko *(AT&T Bell Laboratories)*, Tatsuaki Okamoto *(NTT)*, Josef Pieprzyk *(University of Wollongong)*, Bart Preneel *(Katholieke Universiteit Leuven)*, Jim Reeds *(AT&T Bell Laboratories)*, Rainer Rueppel *(R^3 Security Engineering AG)*, Reihanah Safavi-Naini *(University of Wollongong)*, Peter Shor *(AT&T Bell Laboratories)*, Yuliang Zheng *(University of Wollongong)*.

Organizing Committee *(all from University of Wollongong, Australia)*

Margot Hall *(Conference Secretary)*, Mark Arnold, Shahram Bakhtiari, Ahmad Baraani-Dastjerdi, Ghulam Rasool Chaudhry, Nitin Devikar, Mansour Esmaili, Bill Forsyth, Hossein Ghodosi, Justin Lister, Anish Mathuria, Viswanathan Narain, Colin Spargo

CONTENTS

INVITED LECTURE 1

Thomas Beth

(Universität Karlsruhe, Germany)

Multifeature Security through Homomorphic Encryption *

Thomas Beth

Universität Karlsruhe, Europäisches Institut für Systemsicherheit, Am Fasanengarten 5, D-76128 Karlsruhe, Germany

Abstract. After the announcement of a U.S. digital signature standard by NIST, the role of the Exponential One Way Function - which had been used in the initial illustration of public key cryptography - has again received proper recognition as being another security primitive in addition to the RSA-scheme.

In this paper we present the exponential security system TESS developed at the European Institute for System Security (E.I.S.S.) embedded in a package of freeware. The system has meanwhile been applied to some TCP/IP based services such as `telnet`, `rsh` and `rcp` supplementing these services with additional security features. TESS is based on the use of the one way function *exp* that had originally been described by Pohlig and Hellman and is the central feature in the well-known Diffie-Hellman key exchange protocol. The subsequent contributions by El-Gamal have indicated the multifeature capabilities of this proper one way function. Based on these results, the invention of the Beth-Schnorr-Zero-Knowledge Protocols in extension of the Chaum-Evertse-van de Graaf-Zero Knowledge Scheme has made authentication and signature procedures available, which support the view that the exponential one way function is a security primitive suited for supporting practically all mechanisms needed for the design of secure systems.

The implementation of the authenticated key exchange protocol KATHY within the Network Security System SELANE developed at E.I.S.S., Karlsruhe, based on the Günther-Bauspieß-Knobloch scheme forms an integral part of TESS, providing a universal security toolbox for access control, authentication, key exchange, confidentiality protection, digital signatures and verifiable distributed network security management. Its suitability for the incorporation in the X.509 Directory Authentication Framework as well as its free availability make it an interesting system to extend the features of KERBEROS or DSSA towards a proposed Open System Security Architecture.

A further mechanisms composed from TESS primitives is the Electronic Exponential Signature (EES) scheme. It had been developed for EDI

---

* In order to ensure a wider dissemination in the Network Community this article will also be published in the Network Security Observations entitled: Security Systems based on Exponentiation Primitives

purposes and banking applications already in 1989, when after an in-depth study of up-to-date signature procedures, prior to the new U.S. standard, the superiority of the exponential scheme became apparent.

1 The Exponentiation Primitive

Exponentiation is the basis of the Diffie-Hellman key exchange scheme [DiHe76], the first example of a public key cryptosystem. In the original presentation, exponentiation was performed modulo a prime number p, i.e.

$$x \longrightarrow g^x \bmod p$$

was the main security primitive. It takes a nonzero element $g \in Z_p$ to the power $x \in \{1, \ldots, p-1\}$, where Z_p denotes the field of integers modulo a prime p. This mapping had been suggested as a one way function by Pohlig and Hellman [PoHe78]. The cryptographic property that a one way function serves as a 'logical' diode for information flow will be indicated by the notation

$$x \;\rightarrow\!\!\!\!\triangleright\!\!\!\!\mid\; g^x .$$

Exponentiation modulo p is, however, only an instance of a more general primitive $x \longrightarrow g^x$, which maps a bit string x, interpreted as a binary number x, to the xth power of an element $g \in G$, where G is a finite multiplicative group.

Above, we have used the multiplicative group Z_p^* of the finite field $GF(p) = Z_p$. Alternatives are the multiplicative group $GF(q)^*$ of a finite field $GF(q) = GF(p^n)$, and also many other finite groups such as $GEC(q)$, the group of rational points on an elliptic curve over $GF(q)$ (see Beth and Schaefer [BeSc91]). It is desirable to find groups where exponentiation can be implemented efficiently while achieving a high degree of security at the same time. A comparison of these options has been given by Beth, Agnew and Vanstone [BeAV90].

1.1 Security

The security of the exponentiation function over Z_p lies in the hardness of the discrete logarithm problem

$$\mathrm{Dlog}_{GF(p)} \equiv \{x : y = g^x \bmod p \mid p, g, y\},$$

i.e. of computing x when $y = g^x \bmod p$, g, and p are given. To the best of today's knowledge, the complexity κ of this problem seems to be of the size

$$\kappa(\mathrm{Dlog}_{GF(p)}) = e^{c\sqrt[3]{\log p\,(\log\log p)^2}}$$

making it at least as hard as factoring an RSA-number of the same size. The current estimate of the security the discrete logarithm problem in $GF(p^n)$ is governed by a similar result [Odly84]. Resent results have shown that there exist subexponential algorithms for computing the discrete logarithm in an arbitrary finite field $GF(p^n)$. Due to Adleman and DeMarrais the complexity of these algorithms is bounded by

$$\kappa(\mathrm{Dlog}_{GF(p^n)}) = e^{c\sqrt{\log(p^n)\log\log(p^n)}}$$

for some suitable constant $c > 0$ [AdMa93].

Exponentiation over $GEC(q)$ is expected to provide even better security. For some types of elliptic curves the fastest known approach to figure out discrete logarithms is the well known giant step – baby step algorithm that leads to a complexity

$$\kappa(\mathrm{Dlog}_{DEC}) = \sqrt{|GEC(q)|}$$

so $|GEC(q)|$ should be in the order of magnitude of 2^{160}, an order of magnitude that fits to smart card applications when suitable hardware, that supports the arithmetic needed, is available. Details and algorithms for exponentiation on elliptic curves – including hardware layout – can be found in [Scha93].

1.2 Implementation

The computation $x \to g^x \bmod p$ can be decomposed according to the law

$$g^{x+1} = g^x \cdot g \quad \text{in } G$$

and can be performed in $O(\log p)$ multiplication steps by the well-known Square-and-Multiply-Algorithm. The implementation of this algorithm for sufficiently large p is possible with high efficiency on the CPU of any modern workstation. Implementations for high-speed throughput are discussed by Beth and Gollmann [BeGo89]. The homomorphism property

$$g^{\lambda x+\mu y} = (g^x)^\lambda \cdot (g^y)^\mu$$

and the commutativity

$$(g^x)^y = (g^y)^x$$

are the basic properties for the proof of the correctness of the protocols of Section 2. The essential feature of the exponential scheme is that its cryptographic security combined with the algebraic homomorphism properties allows for the verification of features hidden by the one way function. It should be noted that by this the trapdoor feature $N = pq$ of the RSA function

$$x \to x^e \bmod N$$

is circumvented giving an essential security gain in many applications.

1.3 Alternative Exponential Primitives

The exponential primitive has the advantage of being applicable in groups, in which the Dlog-problem is hard. By employing seemingly complicated groups it is possible to design schemes which

- require very little memory in identification tokens such as smart cards, and
- allow for high-speed implementation of the exp-function.

Furthermore the choice of the General-Exp function (see below) gives even more possibilities for one way functions with special features such as the Trace-Exp function which has been designed to overcome the well known homomorphism attacks e.g. against RSA signatures. A short list of options is given by the following table.

Oneway function	System
$x \longmapsto x^e \bmod N$	RSA with trapdoor
$x \longmapsto g^x \bmod p$	proper EXP
$x \longmapsto x^x \bmod p$	Trace EXP
$x \longmapsto G(x)^{E(x)}$	General EXP

2 Examples for EXP-based Protocols

The fundamental primitive 'exponentiation' has been used ever since the invention of the public key concept [DiHe76]. In the following, we discuss two-party protocols where the secret of participant A is denoted by $SK(A)$ whereas the corresponding public value generated by the one way function is denoted by $PK(A)$. We now focus on four examples for the use of exponentiation in cryptographic protocol design. The examples cover a wide range of needs in achieving system security: Key exchange, encryption, signatures, and zero knowledge proof techniques.

2.1 Commutative Key Exchange Protocol of Diffie and Hellman

Figure 1 shows the well known Diffie-Hellman key exchange mechanism using the discrete exponentiation as its particular commutative one way function [DiHe76].

2.2 Signature and Encryption Protocol of ElGamal

In 1985 ElGamal presented a cryptosystem which – like RSA – allows both message signing and encryption [ElGa85]. In contrary to RSA, it is not based on the difficulty of factoring large integers but on the discrete logarithm assumption. Figures 2 and 3 show the basic protocols for message signing and encryption via exponentiation. It should be noted that the security of these schemes also depends on the mode of generating the random values r.

	Alice	Channel	Bob
	choose $SK(A) \in \mathbb{Z}_{p-1}$ $SK(A) \mathrel{-\!\!\triangleright\!\!+} PK(A)$ $PK(A)$	$\Longrightarrow$	Parameter g, p and $PK(A)$
	Parameter $PK(B)$	$\Longleftarrow$	choose $SK(B) \in \mathbb{Z}_{p-1}$ $SK(B) \mathrel{-\!\!\triangleright\!\!+} PK(B)$ $PK(B)$
	$KEY := PK(B)^{SK(A)} \bmod p$		$KEY := PK(A)^{SK(B)} \bmod p$

Fig. 1. Diffie-Hellman Key Exchange

2.3 Zero-Knowledge Authentication and Identification

The authentication protocols of Beth [Beth88] and Schnorr [Schn89] are based on the fact that it is possible to prove the knowledge of a special discrete logarithm without revealing its concrete value. A special passport authority (SKIA) sends to the prover one or more ID related secrets while signatures of the passport authority are known to the verifier. The main idea is to prove knowledge of the ID related secrets without revealing it. The following protocol of Chaum, Evertse and van de Graaf [ChEG87] in figure 4 allows proving possession of a secret logarithm a for some number z with $a \mathrel{-\!\!\triangleright\!\!+} z$. The value z is known to the verifier before the protocol starts. Repeating steps 1 and 2 for m times, the prover can have successfully cheated with probability 2^{-m}. The verifier gains no knowledge about a.

2.4 Verifiable Secret Sharing in Geometry based Schemes

Recent results have shown how efficiently the homomorphic properties of discrete exponentiation for suitable finite fields can be exploited. Here we give a short description of a protocol for verifiable secret sharing dealing with general monotone access structures [Otte92, BeKO93]. The protocol is the first scheme for verifiable secret sharing that can be used with more complicated access structures than the commonly known threshold access structures. It is based on secret sharing with geometrical schemes such as the Simmons–Jackson–Martin scheme [SiJM91]. The scheme consists of a secret variety V_i of some n dimensional affine geometry $AG(n, q)$ over some finite field $GF(q)$, and a public known variety V_d.

	Alice	Channel	Bob
K	choose $SK(A) \in \mathbb{Z}_{p-1}$ $SK(A) \dashrightarrow PK(A)$ $PK(A)$	$\Longrightarrow$	Parameter g, p and $PK(A)$
S	Message $m \in \mathbb{Z}_{p-1}$ choose $r \in \mathbb{Z}^*_{p-1} \setminus \{1\}$ $r \dashrightarrow z$ Solve $m = hr + SK(A) \cdot z$ $\bmod p - 1$ for h (m, z, h)	$\Longrightarrow$	Verification of $g^m = z^h \cdot PK(A)^z \bmod p$

Fig. 2. ElGamal Signature with key generation (K) and signature (S)

The secret to be distributed is the intersection of these two varieties

$$\{p\} = V_i \cap V_d$$

(see figure 5 for an illustration). Each shareholder possesses one or more points p_i in V_i in such a manner, that every designated subset of shareholders is able to construct V_i and therefore to derive the secret point p.

The main idea how to prove the claim, that a secret p was distributed according to a monotone access structure is to check the vector valued equations

$$p = p_0 + \sum_{i=i}^{m} \lambda_i (p_i - p_0) = y_0 + \sum_{j=1}^{r} \rho_j (y_j - y_0)$$

for $V_d = \langle y_0, \ldots, y_r \rangle$ and $V_i = \langle p_0, \ldots, p_m \rangle$ with coefficients λ_i and $\rho_j \in GF(q)$ under a suitable one way function. Using discrete exponentiation the last equations change to the form

$$g^p = \prod_{i=i}^{m} \left(\frac{g^{p_i}}{g^{p_0}} \right)^{\lambda_i} = \prod_{j=1}^{r} (g^{\rho_j})^{y_j - y_0} \quad (1)$$

By broadcasting the values g^p, λ_i, g^{p_i}, y_j and g^{ρ_j} each participant can check whether he has received on the one hand a valid share, and on the other hand if equation (1) holds (this implies that p lies in the intersection of V_i and V_d). A few other protocol steps ensure each participant, that $V_i \cap V_d$ has dimension 0 (that means p is the only point belonging to both varieties). Details of the solution

	Alice	Channel	Bob
	 B	 $\Leftarrow$	$b \mathrel{-\!\!\triangleright\!\!\!+} B$ B
	Message $m \in \mathbb{Z}_{p-1}$ choose $r \in \mathbb{Z}_{p-1}^{*} r$ $r \mathrel{-\!\!\triangleright\!\!\!+} R$ Encryption: $C := m + B^r \bmod p$ (C, R)	 $\Rightarrow$	 Decryption: $m := C - R^b \bmod p$

Fig. 3. Symmetric Encryption protocol of ElGamal

	Prover	Channel	Verifier
	Choose random numbers $r_1, \ldots, r_n$ $s_j := g^{r_j} \bmod p$	 $\Rightarrow$	 receives $\{s_1, \ldots, s_n\}$
1	receive challenge (k, ϵ)	$\Leftarrow$	choose $k \in \{1, \ldots, n\}, \epsilon \in \{0, 1\}$
2	$t_k := \epsilon a + r_k \bmod p$	$\Rightarrow$	receives t_k and checks $g^{t_k} = z^{\epsilon} \cdot s_k \bmod p$

Fig. 4. Zero Knowledge Proof of Chaum, Evertse, van de Graaf

can be found in the papers cited above; [Otte92] contains also a generalization of the shown approach dealing with a wider class of geometry based secret sharing schemes.

3 The KATHY Protocol

With the basic primitives mentioned above, a provably secure Key-Exchange-cum-Authentication protocol has been developed by Günther [Günt89] and by Bauspieß and Knobloch [BaKn89], incorporating an authenticated Diffie-Hellman-Scheme, whose correctness can be based on the Dlog-security assump-

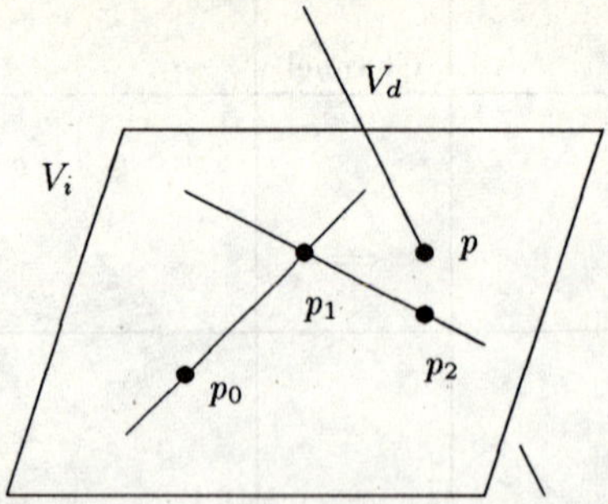

Fig. 5. Realization of a monotone access structure in a geometry based secret sharing scheme: Giving Participant A the point p_0, participant B the point p_1 and giving p_2 to both participants C and D, we have found a solution for the access structure $ABC \vee ABD$.

tion. The acronym KATHY expresses the central feature of this protocol, which embeds authentication within the key exchange. KATHY provides real-time authenticated log-in for a trusted session between any two participants, based on the following assumptions:

1. It is assumed that the system environment has (access to) a trusted authority SKIA (Secure Key Issuing Authority) in the role of a passport-office (not necessarily being online).
2. Every participant will be installed by the SKIA (once in a life-time).

The basic protocol steps are

1. **Setup of SKIA**
   SKIA chooses a prime p together with a primitive element g of $GF(p)$. It publishes $y_S \mathrel{-\!\!\mid\!\!\lhd\!\!-} x_S$ for some secret value x_S.
2. **Registration of a Participant A by SKIA**
   The name m_A of the participant is combined with the SKIA's secret. The participant receives values r_A and s_A together with m_A. It keeps s_A as its secret.
3. **Exchange of authentic keys between A and B**
   The participants generate a key depending on the secret key s_A of A, the name m_B of B, and the public key y_S of the SKIA, as well as a second key from s_B, m_A, and y_S.
4. **Interlock Procedure**
   To ensure A about B's authenticity, B has to prove that he was able to compute the two keys, and vice versa. Each participant can compute one of the keys only if he was registered by the SKIA and knows his secret key which corresponds to his name. Encryption and decryption of nonces (random challenges) R_A and R_B is used to verify the knowledge of the keys.

Figure 6 shows a realization of the first three steps. Further details of the solution can be found in [BaKn89] and [Günt89]. KATHY will be used as a building block of the SELANE protocol which is described in the next section.

S	**SKIA** chooses $x_S \in Z^*_{p-1}$, computes $y_S := g^{x_S}$, and publishes p, g and y_S

C	chooses $k_A \in Z^*_{p-1}$, computes $r_A := g^{k_A}$ and $s_A := (m_A - x_S \cdot r_A)k_A^{-1} \bmod p-1$ (m_A, r_A, s_A) , p, g, y_S	chooses $k_B \in Z^*_{p-1}$, chooses $r_B := g^{k_B}$ and $s_B := (m_B - x_S \cdot r_B)k_B^{-1} \bmod p-1$ (m_B, r_B, s_B), p, g, y_S

$\Vert$ secret $\Downarrow$ | $\Vert$ authentic public $\Downarrow$ | $\Vert$ secret $\Downarrow$ | $\Vert$ authentic public $\Downarrow$

A K	**Participant** A	Channel	**Participant** B
	(m_A, r_A)	public $\Longleftrightarrow$	(m_B, r_B)
	chooses $t_A \in Z_{p-1}$ $v_A := r_B^{t_A}$		chooses $t_B \in Z_{p-1}$ $v_B := r_A^{t_B}$
	$K_B := (g^{m_B} \cdot y_S^{-r_B})^{t_A}$		$K_A := (g^{m_A} \cdot y_S^{-r_A})^{t_B}$
	v_A	$\Longleftrightarrow$	v_B
	$K_A := v_B^{s_A}$		$K_B := v_A^{s_B}$

Fig. 6. KATHY protocol with setup (S), certification (C) and authentication / key exchange (A, K) phase

4 SELANE

SELANE was initially conceived as a LANSEC environment (see Bauspieß [Baus88]). Based on the KATHY Protocol, which guarantees a trusted path from participant to participant in a local network where the SKIA acts as an authentication server, the SELANE System consists of

- Authenticated Access based on the Protocol KATHY
- Confidential Session Communication according to independent Encipherment Algorithms
- Synchronization, Escape and End-of-Session management
- Automatic Reauthentication and Key Progression after the guaranteed security bounds of the Session-Encryption has been reached.

4.1 Implementations

SELANE has been implemented on common processors such as MC680xx, Intel 80x86 and SPARC processors, under UNIX, MS/DOS and the MacIntosh Operating System. Using the CPUs of SUN SPARCstation 10/30 authentication requires less than 250 milliseconds and is therefore practically invisible in the login procedure. Using SELANE some TCP/IP based services such as `telnet`, `rsh` or `rcp` have be supplemented with additional security features.

The encipherment algorithm is designed to run with additional hardware at network transmission speed. Reauthentication is carried out in the background, practically invisible. Special hardware modules have been developed at the E.I.S.S. to meet the higher performance requirements of central host CPUs serving a large number of clients at bulk traffic rate [Otto90]. This high-speed hardware modules are available as PCBs with suitable bus adapters and system interfaces for IBM PCs and SCSI.

4.2 Essential features

It should be noted that owing to the features of the KATHY protocol the SKIA

- does not need to keep any secret database after users have been issued their certificates
- can be operated off-line
- rather plays the role of a reference witness than that of a system monitor with need-to-know-everything.

These latter properties arose out of the original requirements of a large open distributed university computing environment regulated by national data privacy legislation. They provide features which make SELANE an interesting option for an truly Open Distributed System Security Environment.

5 SELANE as Open Distributed System Security Environment

Although SELANE primarily has been designed as a LANSEC System with the essential goal of authenticated access control and end-to-end user confidentiality at high performance rates, its architecture is well suited to provide system security throughout open distributed systems, (see Horster and Knobloch [HoKn91]).

5.1 Naming, Key Management and Authentication

The protocol has effectively been implemented using the format of Internet packets thus fully using the world-wide accepted naming tree. The role of a local network SKIA is fully compatible with that of the X.509 Directory Authentication Framework.

5.2 Transitivity and Delegation through a Network

The special structure of the authentication protocol not only allows a direct implementation of the X.500 recommendations. It is especially suited to authenticate participants in such a way that the validity of an authentication chain can be recomputed without exposing the private secret of each authenticator node. This fact not only provides an additional security feature, but also an unprecedented compressibility of authentication data to make feasible the use of smart cards as identification and authentication tokens. With this special construction SELANE supports the X.509 feature allowing an authentication through already 'known' sub-nodes of another branch of the network.

A token can hold the necessary authenticator information for each participant's 'acquaintances'. Also, the compressibility of authentication data allows a rather decentralized network management as a high degree of transitivity will be reached through delegation. The arithmetic structure of the SELANE protocol in particular supports the establishment of two independent directed authentication chains. This so called Bipolar Authentication allows participants to authenticate their partner through a reference point ('acquaintance') of their own choice, rather than trusting a single authority.

6 Advantages over Established Protocols

6.1 Network Authentication Management

As described above, the use of the exponential one way function provides transitivity throughout the network without large amounts of directory and authentication path information. SELANE fully incorporates the idea of a passport-token oriented network security system requiring the availability of authentication servers only at the time of installation, but not for real time operation, while KERBEROS [Kerb89] or CHIMAERA [Chim90] do require this latter property.

The security defects of X.509 as for instance described by I'Anson and Mitchell [AnMi90] are overcome in SELANE by the use of the proper one way exponential function. Problems arising in KERBEROS [Kerb89] due to the centralized role of the authentication servers do not exist in SELANE as it has been designed for open systems without central servers. This was recently carried out by Klein [Klei93].

6.2 Encryption

Authentication and key exchange have been uncoupled from the session-communication confidentiality through the use of independent enciphering algorithms. KATHY can provide an authenticated session key private to both participants only. The twin role of the KERBEROS head node as authentication server and system monitor, with the ability to act as a Big Brother as it knows the session keys, is not present in SELANE.

6.3 Security

Basing TESS on the Dlog-problem, which is considered as being even harder than factoring, gives this toolbox the highest security amongst all public key systems known today. The non-existence of an a-priori trapdoor for this system provides some superior features with respect to undeniable signatures or non-repudiable proofs of identity.

6.4 Provable Correctness and Completeness

The clear algebraic structure of proper one way functions (rather than trapdoor functions) facilitate a proper evaluation of the SELANE protocol. A correctness proof is essentially reduced to the proof of correct implementation of arithmetics. Completeness proofs also pose well defined problems, as the protocol is based on algebraic equations over conventional algebraic structures. An additional correctness proof using an extension of the logic of authentication of Burrows, Abadi, and Needham [BuAN89], which includes rules dealing with the algebraic structure of SELANE, is actually under consideration. An analysis of the SELANE protocol considering the different trust aspects of authentication protocols can be found in [YaKB93].

6.5 Portability and Migration to SELANE

With the option of a switch-on/off confidentiality module to be chosen for each application, the SELANE-System is freely available. It could therefore be adopted for any Open Information System or Open System Environment Standard without restriction. The portability is guaranteed, as the authentication part only comprises integer arithmetics (C-source code is available from E.I.S.S., cf. [Stem90]) while the optional encryption could be agreed upon in each single application.

Conventional security protocols such as KERBEROS and DSSA resting on both public key algorithms (such as Diffie-Hellman or RSA) and symmetric encryption via DES can easily be extended to implement SELANE. Note that RSA is based on taking powers modulo the RSA-integer N

$$x \to x^e \bmod N$$

while TESS uses exponentiation modulo a prime p

$$x \to g^x \bmod p$$

so the same basic algorithm is the core of either protocol. As the SELANE-session confidentiality is provided by a fast symmetric cipher, DES could serve in this role as well. A migration to SELANE therefore is only an evolutionary step at system level.

7 Conclusion

TESS is being developed by the E.I.S.S. as a toolbox of security kernel primitives for confidentiality, authenticity, and integrity. The SELANE-System is the package most advanced at present. Further applications are the Electronic Exponential Signature (EES) developed for EDI purposes and banking applications.

The exponential security system can also be a building block in establishing a mechanism called *Democratic REference MONitor* (DREMON), providing a system engineering tool for the purposes of confidentiality, integrity, authenticity as well as audit and control for Verifiable Open Distributed System Security Environments.

The structure of SELANE is based on the modular separation of key management and authentication from confidentiality algorithms. For the implementation of the former task, commutative one way functions are needed, while for the latter conventional symmetric ciphers suffice. In basing the authentication procedure on the concept of the ElGamal signature scheme, SELANE is well suited to provide one of the first implementations of the new U.S. digital signature standard independently of the decision on the encryption algorithm to be chosen. The strong algebraic theory of the underlying data types makes this system to be amongst the few Computer Security Systems that will be able to comply with the European IT-Security Evaluation Criteria [ITSE91].

References

[AdMa93] L. M. Adleman, J. DeMarrais: *A Subexponential Algorithm for Discrete Logarithms over all Finite Fields*, Santa Barbara, Crypto '93, Preprints

[AnMi90] C. I'Anson, C. J. Mitchell: *Security Defects in CCITT Recommendation X.509*, Technical Memo, HP Labs, Bristol, Jan. 1990

[Baus88] F. Bauspieß: *SELANE*, Studienarbeit, Fakultät für Informatik, Universität Karlsruhe, 1988

[BaKn89] F. Bauspieß, H.-J. Knobloch: *How to keep Authenticity Alive in a Computer Network*, Eurocrypt '89, Advances in Cryptology, LNCS 434, Springer-Verlag, Berlin, 1989, pp. 38–46

[Beth88] Th. Beth: *Efficient Zero-Knowledge Identification Scheme for Smart Cards*, Eurocrypt '88, Advances in Cryptology, LNCS 330, Springer-Verlag, Berlin, 1988, pp. 77–84

[BeAV90] Th. Beth, G. Agnew, S. A. Vanstone: *What one should know about Public Key Algorithms – Today!*, Proceedings SECURICOM '90.

[BeGo89] Th. Beth, D. Gollmann: *Algorithm Engineering for Public Key Algorithms*, IEEE JSAC, Vol. 7, No. 4, pp. 458–466, 1989

[BeKO93] Th. Beth, H.-J. Knobloch, M. Otten: *Verifiable Secret Sharing for Monotone Access Structures*, Proceedings of the 1st ACM Conference on Computer and Communications Security, Fairfax, USA, November 1993, to be published

[BeSc91] Th. Beth, F. Schaefer: *Non-Supersingular Elliptic Curves for Public Key Cryptosystems*, Eurocrypt '91, Advances in Cryptology, LNCS 547, Springer-Verlag, Berlin, 1991 pp. 316–327

[BuAN89] M. Burrows, M. Abadi, R. Needham: *A Logic of Authentication*, DEC-SRC, Research Report Series No. 39, 1989

[ChEG87] D. Chaum, J.-H. Evertse, J. van de Graaf: *An Improved Protocol for Demonstrating Possession of a Discrete Logarithm and Some Generalizations*, Eurocrypt '87, Advances in Cryptology, LNCS 304, Springer-Verlag, Berlin, 1988, pp. 127–141

[Chim90] A. Tarah, C. Huitema: *CHIMAERA: A Network Security Model*, Proc. ESORICS '90, afcet, 1990, pp. 127–145

[DiHe76] W. Diffie, M. E. Hellman: *New Directions in Cryptography*, IEEE Trans. Inf. Theory, IT-22, 1976, pp. 664–654

[ElGa85] T. ElGamal: *A public key crypto-system and signature scheme based on discrete logarithms*, IEEE Trans. Inf. Theory, IT-31, 1985, 469–472,

[Günt89] C. Günther: *Diffie-Hellman and El-Gamal Protocols With One Single Authentication Key*, Eurocrypt '89, Advances in Cryptology, LNCS 434, Springer-Verlag, Berlin, 1989, pp. 29–37

[HoKn91] P. Horster, H.-J. Knobloch: *Discrete Logarithm Based Protocols*, Eurocrypt '91, Advances in Cryptology, LNCS 547, Springer-Verlag, Berlin, 1991, pp. 399–408

[ITSE91] ITSEC: *Harmonised Criteria of France, Germany, the Netherlands, the United Kingdom*, Brussels, 1991

[Kerb89] Network Working Group J. Kohl, B. C. Neumann, J. Steiner: *MIT Project Athena: The Kerberos Network Authentication Service*, Draft 2, MIT, November 1989

[Klei93] B. Klein: *Authentifikationsdienste für sichere Informationssysteme*, Dissertation, Universität Karlsruhe, 1993, to be published

[Odly84] A. M. Odlyzko: *Discrete logarithms in finite fields and their cryptographic significance*, Eurocrypt '84, Advances in Cryptology, LNCS 209, Springer-Verlag, Berlin, 1985, pp. 224–314

[Otte92] M. Otten: *Mehrparteienprotokolle und Korrektes Verteilen von Geheimnissen*, Diplomarbeit, Fakultät für Informatik, Universität Karlsruhe, 1992

[Otto90] C. Otto: *SELANE-Hardwareentwicklung*, Diplomarbeit, Fakultät für Informatik, Universität Karlsruhe, 1990

[PoHe78] S. C. Pohlig, M. E. Hellman: *An improved algorithm for computing logarithms in GF(p) and its cryptographic significance*, IEEE Trans. Inf. Theory, IT-24, 1978, pp. 106–111

[Scha93] F. Schaefer-Lorinser: *Arithmetik auf elliptischen Kurven zur Konstruktion kryptographischer Einwegfunktionen*, Dissertation, Universität Karlsruhe, 1993

[Schn89] C. P. Schnorr: *Efficient Identification and Signatures for Smart Cards*, Crypto '89, Advances in Cryptology, LNCS 435, Springer-Verlag, Berlin, 1989, pp. 239–252

[SiJM91] G. J. Simmons, W.-A. Jackson, K. Martin: *The Geometry of Shared Secret Schemes*, Bulletin of the Institute of Combinatorics, Winnipeg Canada, January 1991

[Stem90] S. Stempel: *SELANE Pilot-Implementierung*, Diplomarbeit, Fakultät für Informatik, Universität Karlsruhe, 1990

[YaKB93] R. Yahalom, B. Klein, Th. Beth: *Trust Relationships in Secure Systems – A Distributed Authentication Perspective*, Proceedings of the IEEE Conference on Research in Security and Privacy, 1993.

SESSION 1

SECRET SHARING

Chair: Ed Dawson

(Queensland University of Technology, Australia)

Multiplicative non-abelian sharing schemes and their application to threshold cryptography

Yvo Desmedt[1] * and Giovanni Di Crescenzo[2] and Mike Burmester[3]

[1] Department of Electrical Engineering and Computer Science, University of Wisconsin–Milwaukee, WI 53201-0784, U.S.A., e-mail: desmedt@cs.uwm.edu
[2] Dipartimento di Informatica ed Applicazioni, Università di Salerno, 84081 Baronissi (SA), Italy, e-mail: giodic@udsab.dia.unisa.it
[3] Department of Mathematics, RH – University of London, Egham, Surrey TW20 OEX, U.K., e-mail: uhah205@vax.rhbnc.ac.uk

Abstract. We show how to construct a perfect zero-knowledge threshold proof of knowledge of an isomorphism between two graphs, and extend this result to general access structures. The provers work sequentially and are not allowed to interact among themselves, so the number of message communications each prover sends is the same as with the Goldreich-Micali-Wigderson [12] scheme. Our construction is based on multiplicative sharing schemes in which the secret belongs to a group which is not necessarily Abelian.

1 Introduction

The idea to combine zero-knowledge [13] and threshold schemes [3, 18] into zero-knowledge threshold proofs came independently from Pedersen [15] and Desmedt-Frankel [7]. In these schemes a threshold of provers share knowledge of a secret and prove jointly this knowledge to a verifier. In Pedersen's case the provers are known and any threshold of them prove joint knowledge for the simultaneous discrete log problem [4]. In Desmedt-Frankel the provers form a set of which membership is anonymous and a threshold of them prove jointly knowledge of a square root.

Pedersen's scheme allows a threshold of "secretaries" to prove jointly the validity of an undeniable signature. The purpose of Desmedt-Frankel's scheme is to obtain one-time-valid threshold authentication.

One of the main features of zero-knowledge threshold proofs is that the provers do not interact among themselves when communicating with the verifier (by interaction we mean that at least one participant sends data, receives data and then replies). For example in [7], all provers execute the same protocol in parallel and forward their part to a combiner (e.g. one of the provers) who talks with the verifier. The reply from the verifier is broadcast to all provers.

* A part of this work has been supported by NSF Grant NCR-9106327. Partly carried out while visiting Royal Holloway, University of London and the Università di Salerno, Italy, respectively, and supported in part by NSF Grant INT-9123464 and in part by CNR AI n.94.00011.

In his overview paper Desmedt [6] observed that several languages in NP for which the secret belongs to an Abelian group have zero-knowledge threshold proofs. He also observed that no threshold zero-knowledge proof for graph isomorphism has been presented so far (the secret belongs to a *non*-Abelian group).

Organization of the paper. In Section 2 we recall some background results, such as the graph isomorphism protocol of [12], and the concept of zero-knowledge secret sharing schemes given in [8]. In Section 3 we introduce our model and define perfect zero-knowledge shared proofs. In Section 4 we give a perfect zero-knowledge proof of knowledge of graph isomorphism for a simple 2-out-of-2 access structure. In Section 5 we overview the concept of multiplicative secret sharing schemes and prove that it is possible to construct zero-knowledge shared proofs using such schemes. In Section 6 we construct and analyze a multiplicative threshold scheme for (non-Abelian) groups, and discuss its applications to threshold cryptography. In Section 7 we construct a multiplicative sharing scheme for general access structures. In Section 8 we conclude with some open problems.

2 Preliminaries

2.1 Notation

Let m be a natural number and S_m be the symmetric group on m objects. If G is an m-node (vertices) graph and π is a permutation of S_m, then $H = \pi(G)$ denotes the graph H obtained by applying the permutation π to the nodes of G. We call the permutation π an isomorphism of G to H. We denote by $\circ$ the composition operation over S_m; more precisely, if $G_1 = \pi_1(G_0)$ and $G_2 = \pi_2(G_1)$ then $G_2 = (\pi_2 \circ \pi_1)(G_0) = \pi_2(\pi_1(G_0))$. A relation R is a subset of $\{0,1\}^* \times \{0,1\}^*$.

2.2 The graph isomorphism protocol of GMW

We briefly recall the zero-knowledge proof for graph isomorphism given in [12], as it will be our basis for the constructions in the next sections. On input a pair of graphs (G_0, G_1), each having m nodes, the protocol consists of m independent repetitions of the following atomic steps. First the prover P uniformly chooses a permutation $\pi \in S_m$, computes a graph $G = \pi(G_0)$ and sends it to the verifier V, who replies with a uniformly chosen question $b \in \{0,1\}$. Then P answers in the following way: if $b = 0$ he sends to V the permutation $\psi = \pi$ (thus proving that the graph G has been correctly constructed); on the other hand, if $b = 1$ he sends to V the permutation $\psi = \pi \circ \phi$, where ϕ is the isomorphism $G_0 = \phi(G_1)$ (thus proving that if the graph G has been correctly constructed, then graphs G_0 and G_1 are isomorphic). Finally V verifies that $G = \psi(G_b)$. At the end of the m iterations, V accepts if and only if all the verifications have been satisfied. This scheme is also a proof of knowledge for graph isomorphism.

2.3 Zero-knowledge secret sharing schemes

Let us briefly remind the reader the concept of zero-knowledge secret sharing introduced in [8]. A secret sharing scheme is zero-knowledge if the view in the distribution phase of the participants that are not in the access structure can be efficiently simulated. In [8] a zero-knowledge secret sharing scheme was given for secrets in Abelian groups. This scheme does not apply to graph isomorphism for which the group of permutations S_m is not Abelian when $m > 2$, and cannot be used for threshold zero-knowledge proofs of Graph Isomorphism.

3 The model for zero-knowledge shared proofs

The model we consider is the following: there are n provers $P_1, \ldots, P_n$ and a verifier V such that: a) $P_1, \ldots, P_n$ and V are probabilistic Turing machines running in polynomial-time in m, the size of the common input x; b) there is no interaction between the provers, only one prover can send messages to V, and the verifier V can broadcast his messages to all provers; c) each prover P_i has a knowledge tape on which there is written an auxiliary input w_i. The following definition can be skipped by the reader who is familiar with the topic.

Let Γ be an access structure over $P_1, \ldots, P_n$ for a relation $R \subseteq \{0,1\}^m \times \{0,1\}^m$. That is, Γ is a set of subsets $B \subseteq \{1, \ldots, n\}$ such that for each $x \in \mathrm{dom}R$ there exists an efficiently computable function f which returns w with $(x, w) \in R$, when given the share set $\{w_{i_j} | i_j \in B\}$ as input.

We use the following convention: P_i, V, represent 'honest' machines which adhere to the designated program, while P'_i, V', represent possibly 'dishonest' machines. Based on [6] we define informally a perfect *zero-knowledge shared proof* of knowledge for the relation R and the access structure Γ as a protocol $(P_1, \ldots, P_n, V)$ for which,

- *Completeness.* For any set $\{i_1, \ldots, i_l\} \in \Gamma$: given $x \in \mathrm{dom}R$ V will accept with overwhelming probability in the execution of $(P_{i_1}, \ldots, P_{i_l}, V)$.
- *Soundness.* For any input x and provers $P'_{i_1}, \ldots, P'_{i_h}$: if V accepts with overwhelming probability in the execution of $(P'_{i_1}, \ldots, P'_{i_h}, V)$, then there exists an efficient extractor E which can compute a w such that $(x, w) \in R$ with overwhelming probability by using $P'_{i_1}, \ldots, P'_{i_h}$ as a black box.
- *Perfect Zero-Knowledge.* For any $x \in \mathrm{dom}R$ and any subset $A = \{j_1, \ldots j_k\} \notin \Gamma$ and any polynomial time provers $P'_{j_1}, \ldots, P'_{j_k}$, for any V', for any subset $B = \{i_1, \ldots, i_l\} \in \Gamma$ and provers $P'_{i_1}, \ldots, P'_{i_l}$ with $P'_i = P_i$ if $i \in B \backslash A$, the joint view of $P'_{j_1}, \ldots, P'_{j_k}$ and V' in the execution of $(P'_{i_1}, \ldots, P'_{i_l}, V')$ can be simulated efficiently and perfectly. The view of a prover P'_i is given by its random, knowledge and communication tapes (if the last are used) and the view of the verifier V' is given by its random and communication tapes.

The completeness and soundness conditions refer to the 'proof of knowledge' aspect of the protocol. We require that on input $x \in \mathrm{dom}R$, the verifier will accept with overwhelming probability any authorized set of provers who know shares of w such that $(x, w) \in R$. Furthermore, if V accepts on input x, then the provers must jointly know a w such that $(x, w) \in R$. Finally for zero-knowledge, when $x \in \text{dom}R$, in any execution of the protocol by an authorized set, no knowledge leaks to a dishonest verifier who may conspire with an unauthorized set of (possibly dishonest) provers, even if some of these belong to the authorized set. This requirement addresses a very strong adversarial scenario: e.g. it could be that a subset of an authorized set conspires with a dishonest verifier to obtain some knowledge about the shares of the others in the authorized set.

In the sequel we only consider perfect zero-knowledge shared proofs. So if the relation R and the access structure Γ are clear from the context, we just use the term zero-knowledge shared proof. Our formal definition is built on the definitions of proofs of knowledge in [21, 10, 1].

4 ZK proofs of knowledge for simple access structures

In this section we discuss the problem of constructing a zero-knowledge proof of knowledge of graph isomorphism for a simple access structure Γ. In particular we consider the case when Γ is a 2-out-of-2 threshold structure for two participants P_1, P_2 who share knowledge of an isomorphism ϕ of the input graphs G_0, G_1 and who want to prove to V that they can compute ϕ together.

A center distributes the shares of the isomorphism ϕ to the provers. Let G_0, G_1 be two m-node graphs with $G_0 = \phi(G_1)$. The center uniformly chooses a permutation $\phi_1 \in S_m$, computes $\phi_2 = \phi_1^{-1} \circ \phi$ and distributes ϕ_i to P_i, $i = 1, 2$. The protocol (P_1,P_2,V) to prove knowledge of a permutation ϕ such that $G_0 = \phi(G_1)$ is given by m independent executions of the following atomic steps.

Step 1 P_1 uniformly chooses a $\pi_1 \in S_m$, and sends $G = \pi_1(G_0)$ to P_2.
Step 2 P_2 uniformly chooses a $\pi_2 \in S_m$, and sends $H = \pi_2(G)$ to V.
Step 3 V broadcasts a uniformly chosen query $q \in \{0, 1\}$ to P_1 and P_2.
Step 4 If $q = 0$ then P_1 sends $\psi_1 = \pi_1$ to P_2, else he sends $\psi_1 = \pi_1 \circ \phi_1$.
Step 5 If $q = 0$ then P_2 sends $\psi = \pi_2 \circ \psi_1$ to V, else he sends $\psi = \pi_2 \circ \psi_1 \circ \phi_2$.
Step 6 V verifies that $H = \psi(G_q)$.

We have the following

Theorem 1. *The protocol (P_1,P_2, V) is a perfect zero-knowledge shared proof of knowledge of graph isomorphism for a 2-out-of-2 threshold structure.*

Proof. See final paper.

5 Multiplicative sharing schemes: an introduction

5.1 Motivation and definition

It is easy to generalize the protocol of the previous section in order to obtain a zero-knowledge shared proof for an n-out-of-n access structure. In this section we consider multiplicative [6] secret sharing schemes. As we shall see such schemes are useful to obtain zero-knowledge shared proofs. We assume that the reader is familiar with secret sharing schemes.

Definition 2. [6] Let $\mathcal{G}$ be a set from which the secrets are chosen and $\mathcal{S}_i$ (e.g. $\mathcal{G}^{a_i}$) be a set from which the shares are chosen. From now on, we will consider $\mathcal{G}$ as a (non-Abelian) group. Also, let $\mathrm{P}_1, \ldots, \mathrm{P}_n$ be a set of participants, and Γ be an access structure over $\mathrm{P}_1, \ldots, \mathrm{P}_n$. A *multiplicative* sharing scheme for $\mathcal{G}$ is a secret sharing scheme in which the dealer distributes the shares in such a way that if P_i gets s_i, $i = 1, \ldots, n$, then for each $B = \{\mathrm{P}_{i_1}, \ldots, \mathrm{P}_{i_{|B|}}\} \in \Gamma$, any secret $k \in \mathcal{G}$ can be expressed as

$$k = f_{i_1,B}(s_{i_1}) \cdot f_{i_2,B}(s_{i_2}) \cdot \cdots f_{i_{|B|},B}(s_{i_{|B|}}) \,, \tag{1}$$

where the $f_{j,B}$, $j \in B$, are functions from $\mathcal{S}_j$ to $\mathcal{G}$ which any P_j can compute. So if the participants P_j run in polynomial time, as in our case, then it should be feasible for them to compute all the $f_{i,B}(s_j)$, $j \in B$.

5.2 Applications: ZK shared proofs from multiplicative sharing schemes

It is possible to construct zero-knowledge shared proofs for graph isomorphism using multiplicative secret sharing schemes. Informally, there are two phases, the distribution phase and the proof phase. In the first, on input a pair (G_0, G_1) of m-node graphs and an isomorphism $\phi \in S_m$ with $G_0 = \phi(G_1)$, a center distributes share $s_i \in \mathcal{S}_i$ to prover P_i, for $i = 1, \ldots, n$, where the shares s_i constitute multiplicative shares of the secret ϕ. In the second phase, on input (G_0, G_1), any subset $B \in \Gamma$ of provers $\mathrm{P}_{i_1}, \ldots, \mathrm{P}_{i_l}$ can, by using their shares (which are now on their knowledge tape), prove non-interactively to a verifier V that they know an isomorphism ϕ such that $G_0 = \phi(G_1)$. If the multiplicative sharing scheme is zero-knowledge, then the shared proof obtained is also zero-knowledge. Let Γ be an access structure over n participants $\mathrm{P}_1, \ldots, \mathrm{P}_n$. From our discussion above we get the following result.

Lemma 3. *Given a zero-knowledge multiplicative sharing scheme for S_m and the access structure Γ, it is possible to construct a zero-knowledge shared proof of knowledge for graph isomorphism and the access structure Γ.*

Remark. In many applications there is no need for a center. For instance, in the 2-out-of-2 access structure of the previous section, provers P_1, P_2 can generate a pair of isomorphic graphs and two shares of their isomorphism without the help of a center. They do this in the following way. P_1 chooses a graph G_0, then uniformly chooses a permutation $\phi_1 \in S_n$, computes the graph $H = \phi_1(G_0)$ and sends H to P_2. Similarly P_2 uniformly chooses a permutation $\phi_2 \in S_n$ and then computes the graph $G_1 = \phi_2(H)$. The common input will be the pair (G_0, G_1).

6 Multiplicative threshold schemes

The aim of this section is to construct a multiplicative threshold scheme. We observe that Shamir's threshold scheme is multiplicative for Abelian groups, but does not work for non-Abelian groups.

6.1 The construction

The multiplicative threshold scheme we give is of recursive nature. For the sake of description, we will describe it for a number n of participants, where $n = 2^t$, for some natural number t.

An informal description. Our scheme is based on *Vandermonde's convolution* equation (see [22] and [14, pp. 169-170]):

$$\sum_l \binom{r}{l}\binom{s}{h-l} = \binom{r+s}{h}, \tag{2}$$

that has the following combinatorial interpretation: the right side is the number of ways to choose h people among r men and s women, and the left side is the number of ways to choose l men and $h-l$ women, for each possible l. We use it for the case $r = s = n/2$ and make the following observation: the way of choosing h participants out of n to recover a secret is exactly the way of choosing l participants out of the first group of $n/2$ participants and $h-l$ out of the second group of $n/2$ participants.

In order to share a secret k in an (h, n)-threshold structure over participants $P_1, \ldots, P_n$, we write $k = k_1 \cdot k_2$ and share k_1 in an $(l, n/2)$-threshold structure over $P_1, \ldots, P_{n/2}$, and k_2 in an $(h-l, n/2)$-threshold structure over $P_{n/2+1}, \ldots, P_n$, where l is such that $\max(0, h-n/2) \leq l \leq \min(h, n/2)$.

Formal description. Let $k \in \mathcal{G}$ be a secret to be shared among $P_1, \ldots, P_n$, and let h be a threshold. The center will run the procedure SHARE with parameters $(k; 1, n; h; list)$ where *list* is initially empty. During the course of the execution of procedure SHARE, *list* will contain a trace of all recursive executions of SHARE already run. Later we see that this information will be useful to a participant receiving a pair $(list, k)$ as a sub-share in order to run the recovering protocol. Now we formally describe the procedure SHARE, which on input $(k; i, j; h; list)$ distributes the secret k to participants $P_i, \ldots, P_j$ such that at least h of them can recover it.

Procedure: SHARE$(k; i, j; h; list)$.

> If $i = j$ and $h = 1$ then give the pair $(list, k)$ to participant P_i. P_i stores k at (virtual) address *list*, so sets SUB-SHARE$[list] := k$.
> If $i < j$ then
>> set $m = j-i+1$, $m_1 = \max(0, h-m/2)$ and $m_2 = \min(h, m/2)$;
>> for $l = m_1, \ldots, m_2$,

if $l \neq 0$ then
 if $l \neq h$ then
  uniformly choose intermediate share $k_{1,l} \in \mathcal{G}$;
  compute intermediate share $k_{2,l} = k_{1,l}^{-1} \cdot k$;
  set list1=list $\cup\{(i, i-1+m/2; l)\}$;
  run SHARE($k_{1,l}$; $i, i-1+m/2$; l ; *list*1);
  set list2=list $\cup\{(i+m/2, j; h-l)\}$;
  run SHARE($k_{2,l}$; $i+m/2, j$; $h-l$; *list*2);
 else run SHARE(k ; $i, i-1+m/2$; h ; *list*1);
else run SHARE(k ; $i+m/2, j$; h ; *list*2);
Return.

Remark. After execution of the procedure SHARE a participant may receive many pairs (*list*, k). We call each of these k a *sub-share*.

Let B be a subset of h participants that have to recover the secret k. To the subset B we associate the n-tuple of bits $b_1, \ldots, b_n$ such that $b_i = 1$ if and only if $\mathrm{P}_i \in B$. Now we describe a procedure RECOVER that, when executed by participant P_a on input B, allows him to recompute the *list* associated to the sub-share k_a received in the distribution phase, and such that $k = \prod_{P_a \in B} k_a$.

An informal description. First of all we observe that each *list* associated with a sub-share k_a is a list of $\log n$ triples $(i, j\,;\, h)$, such that for each triple at least h participants between $\mathrm{P}_i, \mathrm{P}_{i+1}, \ldots, \mathrm{P}_j$ recover an intermediate share (or if $i = j$, a sub-share) k_a. While running procedure RECOVER, P_a computes a list of $\log n$ triples $(i, j\,;\, h)$, and then he can output the sub-share k_a associated with that list. At each iteration participant P_a computes a new triple in the following way. If $(i, j\,;\, h)$ is the last triple computed then P_a divides interval $[i, j]$ into two equal subintervals $[i, m]$ and $[m+1, j]$. Now if $a \in [i, m]$, the new triple is $(i, m\,;\, h')$, where $h' = \sum_{t=i}^{m} b_t$, otherwise it is $(m+1, j\,;\, h')$, where $h' = \sum_{t=m+1}^{j} b_t$. It is easy to see that *list* is correctly generated in this way.

Formal description. Participant $\mathrm{P}_a \in B$, for $a \in \{1, \ldots, n\}$, will run the procedure RECOVER on input $(a\,;\, 1, n\,;\, b_1, \ldots, b_n\,;\, list)$, where *list* is an empty list and the Hamming weight of $(b_1, \ldots, b_n)$ is h. Now we formally describe the procedure RECOVER.

Procedure: RECOVER(l ; i, j ; $b_i, \ldots, b_j$; *list*).

Set $m = j - i + 1$.
If $m = 1$ then
 set $list = list \cup (i, i\,;\, b_i)$;
 output k_l :=SUB-SHARE[*list*] and halt.
If $l \leq m/2$ then
 set $h_1 = \sum_{t=i}^{i-1+m/2} b_t$ and $list = list \cup \{(i, i-1+m/2\,;\, h_1)\}$;
 run RECOVER (k ; $i, i-1+m/2$; $b_i, \ldots, b_{i-1+m/2}$; *list*);
else set $h_2 = \sum_{t=i+m/2}^{j} b_t$ and $list = list \cup \{(i+m/2, j\,;\, h_2)\}$;
 run RECOVER (i ; $i+m/2, j$; $b_{i+m/2}, \ldots, b_j$; *list*).
Return.

Theorem 4. (SHARE,RECOVER) *is a multiplicative (h,n)-threshold scheme.*

Proof. See final paper for a formal proof.

6.2 Analysis of the scheme

Now we analyze the efficiency of our multiplicative threshold scheme by computing the asymptotic total number of sub-shares distributed to participants. We define $S(h,n)$ as the number of sub-shares distributed to n participants in our multiplicative (h,n)-threshold scheme. From the code of procedure SHARE, we derive the following:

$$S(h,n) = \sum_{l=0}^{h} (\, S(h-l,n/2) + S(l,n/2)\,), \qquad \text{for } 2 \le h \le n/2;$$

$$S(h,n) = \sum_{l=h-n/2}^{n/2} (\, S(h-l,n/2) + S(l,n/2)\,), \qquad \text{for } n/2+1 \le h \le n-1;$$

$$S(h,n) = n\,, \quad \text{for } h=1,n; \qquad S(h,n) = 0\,, \quad \text{for } h \le 0 \text{ or } h > n.$$

Lemma 5. $S(h,n) = O\left(\frac{n^{1+\log e}}{\sqrt{\log n}} \cdot \left(\frac{h}{\log n}\right)^{\log n}\right)$.

Proof. Observe that,

$$\sum_{l=h-n/2}^{n/2} (\, S(h-l,n/2) + S(l,n/2)\,) \le \sum_{l=0}^{h} (\, S(h-l,n/2) + S(l,n/2)\,), \qquad \text{if } h > n/2.$$

Using this equation repeatedly we get the following reduction for $2 \le h \le n/2$,

$$\begin{aligned} S(h,n) &= 2 \cdot \sum_{i=0}^{h} S(i,n/2) \;\le\; 2^2 \cdot \sum_{i_1=0}^{h} \sum_{i_2=0}^{i_1} S(i_2, n/2^2) \;\le\; \cdots \;\le \\ &\le\; 2^{\log n} \cdot \sum_{i_1=0}^{h} \sum_{i_2=0}^{i_1} \cdots \sum_{i_{\log n}=0}^{i_{\log n-1}} S(i_{\log n}, n/2^{\log n}) \\ &\le\; n \cdot \sum_{i_1=0}^{h} \sum_{i_2=0}^{i_1} \cdots \sum_{i_{\log n}=0}^{i_{\log n-1}} 1 \;\le\; O\left(n \cdot \frac{h^{\log n}}{(\log n)!}\right) \\ &\le\; O\left(\frac{n^{1+\log e}}{\sqrt{\log n}} \cdot \left(\frac{h}{\log n}\right)^{\log n}\right). \end{aligned}$$

Lemma 6. *If $h=2$ and $n \ge 2$ then $S(h,n) = n\log n$.*

Proof. $S(2,n) = 2(S(1,n/2)+S(2,n/2)) = n+2S(2,n/2) = \cdots = n(\log n - 1) + S(2,2)\,n/2 = n\log n$.

Lemma 6 implies that for our scheme the shares are shorter than for the Simmons-Jackson-Martin scheme [20], which is also multiplicative (for non-Abelian groups) in the case of 2-out-of-n threshold.

Also the 2-out-of-n case can be used with Abelian groups and then we get a homomorphic scheme for which the shares are much shorter than in [9] (each share is only $\lceil \log_2 n \rceil$ instead of $O(n)$ in [9]). From [11] and [5] it follows immediately that if there are more optimal 2-out-of-n zero-knowledge multiplicative sharing schemes, then 2-out-of-n RSA threshold-signatures and RSA threshold-decryption can be implemented more efficiently. This also applies to generalizations of RSA and proven secure schemes that rely on functions similar to RSA discussed in [5].

Let us briefly mention a trivial multiplicative threshold scheme in order to compare its efficiency with that of our scheme. Consider the set of all subsets B of $\{P_1, \ldots, P_n\}$ of cardinality equal to h. For each $B = \{P_{i_1}, \ldots, P_{i_h}\}$ the secret k can be written as $\prod_{j=1}^{h} k_{i_j}$, where k_{i_j} is the sub-share to be distributed to participant P_{i_j}. It is easy to see that the total number of sub-shares distributed to participants $P_1, \ldots, P_n$ is in this case $h \cdot \binom{n}{h}$.

6.3 An application to threshold cryptography

We observe that the multiplicative threshold scheme described in the previous section is not zero-knowledge in general. In this case, a proof similar to Lemma 3 cannot be applied since the provers are probabilistic polynomial time and may not be able to store in their knowledge tape all the sub-shares received in the distribution phase. However, when $h = O(\log n)$, all the participants receive in the distribution phase a number of sub-shares polynomial in n, where n is the number of participants. Then we have the following:

Theorem 7. *Let $\{G_m\}$ be a family of samplable groups. If $h = O(\log n)$ and $n = O(m^c)$, c constant, the multiplicative (h,n)-threshold scheme* (SHARE,RECOVER) *for $\{G_m\}$ is zero-knowledge.*

Proof. See final paper for a formal proof.

The above theorem, together with Lemma 6, proves the following:

Corollary 8. *If $n = O(m^c)$, c constant, and $h = O(\log n)$, then there is a perfect zero-knowledge (h,n)-threshold proof of knowledge for graph isomorphism.*

Furthermore if $n = O(\log m)$ then there is a perfect zero-knowledge proof of knowledge for graph isomorphism and for the access structure Γ, regardless of h.

7 Multiplicative general sharing schemes

In this section we consider the problem of constructing multiplicative secret sharing schemes for access structures more general than those based on threshold. First of all we observe that the sharing schemes of [20] and [2] for arbitrary access structures are not multiplicative for non-Abelian groups. In fact, it is possible to construct examples of access structures for which their schemes do not satisfy equation (1) of Section 5.1.

7.1 The construction

In this section we construct a multiplicative secret sharing scheme for any access structure. Recall that for perfect secret sharing schemes the access structure Γ must be monotone. That is, if A and B are subsets of participants with $A \subseteq B$, then $A \in \Gamma$ implies $B \in \Gamma$. Then, to the access structure Γ we can associate the monotone boolean function $F_\Gamma : \{0,1\}^n \longrightarrow \{0,1\}$ such that for each $(b_1, \ldots, b_n) \in \{0,1\}^n$, $F_\Gamma(b_1, \ldots, b_n) = 1$ if and only if the subset $B = \{ \mathrm{P}_{i_j} \mid b_{i_j} = 1\}$ belongs to Γ. We call F_Γ the boolean description of Γ.

An informal description. The scheme is based on the *Fundamental theorem of Boolean algebra* (see [16]):

$$f(x_1, \ldots, x_{n-1}, x_n) = (x_n \wedge f(x_1, \ldots, x_{n-1}, 1)) \vee (\overline{x_n} \wedge f(x_1, \ldots, x_{n-1}, 0)),$$

where f is a boolean formula in n variables and $x_1, \ldots, x_{n-1}, x_n$ are n binary variables. Let Γ_1 be an access structure associated with the monotone boolean function $g(x_1, \ldots, x_{n-1}) = F_\Gamma(x_1, \ldots, x_{n-1}, 1)$ with $n-1$ variables, and Γ_0 be an access structure associated with the monotone boolean function $h(x_1, \ldots, x_{n-1}) = F_\Gamma(x_1, \ldots, x_{n-1}, 0)$ with $n-1$ variables. The scheme is based on the following observation: if we write our secret $k = k_1 \cdot k_2$, a set of participant $\mathrm{P}_1, \ldots, \mathrm{P}_n$ in Γ is able to recover the secret k if and only if one of the following two events is true: a) the participant P_n has received as subshare k_2 and the subset of participants $\mathrm{P}_1, \ldots, \mathrm{P}_{n-1}$ is in Γ_1 and k_1 is a secret $\mathrm{P}_1, \ldots, \mathrm{P}_{n-1}$ can recover, or b) the subset of participants $\mathrm{P}_1, \ldots, \mathrm{P}_{n-1}$ in Γ_0 can recover the secret k. Using this observation, as for threshold structures, we can give a recursive construction of a multiplicative secret sharing scheme for any access structure. Now, we let Γ to be an access structure for which this scheme allows participants to receive polynomially long shares.

8 Open problems and conclusion

8.1 Open problems

In Section 6 we gave an upper bound for the number of sub-shares distributed in our multiplicative threshold scheme which is only slightly exponential in the number of participants. Is it possible to improve this bound? More interestingly, is it possible to construct a multiplicative threshold scheme in which the size of the shares distributed is polynomial in the number of participants? Finally, if the boolean description of Γ is polynomial space in the number of participants, does a multiplicative sharing scheme exist which is polynomial space?

8.2 Conclusion

The problem of making a zero-knowledge shared proof for graph isomorphism was posed in [6]. We solved it for several access structures. For this purpose we used a multiplicative secret sharing scheme for non-Abelian groups. Our multiplicative secret sharing schemes may also be useful in other (than zero-knowledge shared proofs) threshold cryptosystems relying on non-Abelian groups. Although most modern cryptosystems have an Abelian group as underlying structure (as RSA [17] and most discrete log schemes), some research towards schemes relying on non-Abelian groups is emerging (see for example [19]).

The multiplicative secret sharing scheme we discussed for general access structures has some similarity with our threshold scheme. Indeed, for each set in the access structure a participant will use at maximum *one* sub-share, while in other schemes a participant may use more than one sub-share (called "points" in [20]). Whether the shares we obtain are shorter (in general) than in competing schemes is difficult to analyze. However, although the shares in our threshold sharing scheme are large, for $h = 2$ they are shorter than in the Simmons-Jackson-Martin scheme [20], and when the group is Abelian the new schemes are the best homomorphic sharing schemes known so far. This may imply that the techniques used to achieve multiplicative sharing schemes have some value beyond the context of threshold cryptography.

Acknowledgements

The authors would like to thank Carlo Blundo and Alfredo De Santis for useful discussions. Carlo's remark made us realize that if $h = 2$ then the Simmons-Jackson-Martin scheme is multiplicative for any group (see Section 6.2).

References

1. M. Bellare, O. Goldreich: On defining proofs of knowledge. In: E. F. Brickell (ed.): Advances in Cryptology – Crypto '92, Proceedings (Lecture Notes in Computer Science 740), Berlin: Springer 1993, pp. 390–420
2. J. C. Benaloh, J. Leichter: Generalized secret sharing and monotone functions. In: S. Goldwasser (ed.): Advances in Cryptology, Proc. of Crypto'88 (Lecture Notes in Computer Science 403), Berlin: Springer 1990, pp. 27–35
3. G. R. Blakley: Safeguarding cryptographic keys. In: Proc. Nat. Computer Conf. AFIPS Conf. Proc., vol.48, 1979, pp. 313–317
4. D. Chaum, J.-H. Evertse, J. van de Graaf: An improved protocol for demonstrating possession of discrete logarithms and some generalizations. In: D. Chaum and W. L. Price (eds.): Advances in Cryptology – Eurocrypt '87 (Lecture Notes in Computer Science 304), Berlin: Springer, Berlin 1988, pp. 127–141

5. A. De Santis, Y. Desmedt, Y. Frankel, M. Yung: How to Share a Function Securely. Proceedings of the twenty-sixth annual ACM Symp. Theory of Computing (STOC), May 23–25, 1994, pp. 522–533 (full paper in preparation)
6. Y. Desmedt: Threshold cryptosystems. In: J. Seberry, Y. Zheng (eds.): Advances in Cryptology – Auscrypt '92 (Lecture Notes in Computer Science 718), Berlin: Springer 1993, pp. 3–14
7. Y. Desmedt, Y. Frankel: Shared generation of authenticators and signatures. In: J. Feigenbaum (ed.): Advances in Cryptology – Crypto '91, Proceedings (Lecture Notes in Computer Science 576), Berlin: Springer 1992, pp. 457–469
8. Y. Desmedt, Y. Frankel: Perfect zero-knowledge sharing schemes over any finite Abelian group. In: R. Capocelli, A. De Santis, and U. Vaccaro (eds.): Sequences II (Methods in Communication, Security, and Computer Science), Berlin: Springer 1993, pp. 369–378
9. Y. G. Desmedt, Y. Frankel: Homomorphic Zero-Knowledge Threshold Schemes over any Finite Abelian Group. SIAM Journal on Discrete Mathematics, 7(4), pp. 667–67 (1994)
10. U. Feige, A. Fiat, A. Shamir: Zero knowledge proofs of identity. Journal of Cryptology, 1(2), pp. 77–94 (1988)
11. Y. Frankel, Y. Desmedt: Parallel reliable threshold multisignature. Technical Report #TR-92-04-02, April 1992, Dept. of EE & CS, Univ. of Wisconsin–Milwaukee
12. O. Goldreich, S. Micali, A. Wigderson: Proofs that yield nothing but their validity or all languages in NP have zero-knowledge proof systems. Journal of the ACM, 38(1), pp. 691–729, (1991)
13. S. Goldwasser, S. Micali, C. Rackoff: The knowledge complexity of interactive proof systems. Siam J. Comput., 18(1), pp. 186–208 (1989)
14. R. Graham, D. E. Knuth, O. Patashnik: Concrete Mathematics – A foundation for computer science. Addison-Wesley, Reading, MA (1989)
15. T. P. Pedersen: Distributed provers with applications to undeniable signatures. In: D. W. Davies (ed.): Advances in Cryptology, Proc. of Eurocrypt '91 (Lecture Notes in Computer Science 547), Berlin: Springer April 1991, pp. 221–242
16. F. P. Preparata: Introduction to computer engineering. Harper & Row, New York (1985)
17. R. L. Rivest, A. Shamir, L. Adleman: A method for obtaining digital signatures and public key cryptosystems. Commun. ACM, 21, pp. 294–299 (1978)
18. A. Shamir: How to share a secret. Commun. ACM, 22, pp. 612–613 (1979)
19. V. M. Sidelnikov: Exponentiation-based key generation using noncommutative groups. In: Proceedings 1994 IEEE International Symposium on Information Theory, p. 497, Trondheim, Norway, June 27–July 1, 1994
20. G. J. Simmons, W. Jackson, K. Martin: The geometry of shared secret schemes. Bulletin of the Institute of Combinatorics and its Applications, 1, pp. 71–88 (1991)
21. M. Tompa, H. Woll: Random self-reducibility and zero-knowledge interactive proofs of possession of information. In: 28th Annual Symp. on Foundations of Computer Science (FOCS), pp. 472–482, IEEE Computer Society Press (1987)
22. A. Vandermonde: Mémoire sur des irrationnelles de différens ordres avac une application au cercle, 1772. Histoire de l'Académie Royale des Sciences, part 1, pp. 71–72; Mémoires de Mathématique et de Physique, Tirés des Registres de l'Academie Royale des Sciences, pp. 489–498

Lower Bound on the Size of Shares of Nonperfect Secret Sharing Schemes

Koji OKADA and Kaoru KUROSAWA

Department of Electrical and Electronic Engineering,
Faculty of Engineering, Tokyo Institute of Technology
2–12–1 O-okayama, Meguro-ku, Tokyo 152, Japan

Abstract. In a secret sharing scheme (SS), a dealer D distributes a piece of information V_i of a secret S to each participant P_i. If we desire that $|V_i| < |S|$, a nonperfct SS must be used, in which there exists a semi-access set C that has some information on S, but cannot recover S. This paper first presents a general lower bound on $|V_i|$ which includes the previous lower bounds for perfect SSs and nonperfect SSs as special cases. There exist, however, access hierarchies in which $|V_i|$ must be larger than the general lower bound, of course. As our second contribution, we determine the optimum size of V_i for such a certain access hierarchy.

1 Introduction

A secret sharing scheme (SS) is a technique to distribute a secret s among a set of participants $\mathcal{P} = \{P_i\}$. It is useful for the management of cryptographic keys and fault tolerant multiparty protocols. In such a scheme, a dealer D gives v_i (called a share) to P_i, where v_i is a piece of information of s [1, 2]. $A \subseteq \mathcal{P}$ is called an access set if A can recover s. In other words, $H(S|A) = 0$, where S is a random variable induced by s and $H(X)$ denotes the entropy of X. $B \subseteq \mathcal{P}$ is called a non-access set if C has absolutely no information on s, or $H(S|C) = H(S)$. An SS is called perfect if any subset of $\mathcal{P}$ is an access set or a non-access set. A family of all the access sets of $\mathcal{P}$ is called an access structure, usually denoted by Γ. [3] showed that there exists a perfect SS for Γ if and only if Γ is monotone. Let V_i be the domain of v_i. Let S be the domain of s (as well as the random variable). $|V_i|$ should be small as possible because the security of a system degrades if $|V_i|$ is large. [5] and [8] showed that $|\forall V_i| \geq |S|$ in any perfect SS if S is uniformly distributed. A perfect SS is called ideal if $|V_i| = |S|$ for any participant P_i. [7] showed that an ideal perfect SS has a matroid structure. However, it is a very hard problem to determine the optimum size of V_i for a given access structure in general, which is a major concern of recent studies in this area. [8, 9, 10, 11, 12] showed (optimum) lower bounds on $|V_i|$ for some specific access structures. Let Γ^- denote a family of minimal access sets. Especially, [8] showed the optimum lower bound for $\Gamma^- = \{\{P_1, P_2\}, \{P_2, P_3\}, \{P_3, P_4\}\}$ such that $\max\{\log_2 |V_2|, \log_2 |V_3|\} \geq 3 \log_2 |S|$.

On the other hand, a nonperfct SS must be used [6] if we desire that $|V_i| < |S|$. In a nonperfect SS, there exists a semi-access set B such that $0 < H(S|B) <$

$H(S)$. B has some information on s, but cannot recover s. Let $\Gamma_1 \triangleq \{\text{access set}\}$, $\Gamma_2 \triangleq \{\text{semi-access set}\}$ and $\Gamma_3 \triangleq \{\text{non-access set}\}$. Ogata, Kurosawa and Tsujii showed that $\max_i \log_2 |V_i| \geq \log_2 |S|/(\min |A \setminus B|)$ for nonperfect SSs, where the minimum is taken over $A \in \Gamma_1$ and $B \in \Gamma_3$ [15].

We say that a nonperfect SS has a level d access hierarchy if $H(S|A) = (k/d)H(S)$ $(0 \leq k \leq d)$ for $\forall A \subseteq \mathcal{P}$. Kurosawa *et al* showed that $\log_2 |\forall V_i| \geq \log_2 |S|/d$ for any level d nonperfect SS [16]. We say that a level d nonperfect SS is ideal if $\log_2 |V_i| = \log_2 |S|/d$ for any participant P_i. Kurosawa *et al* showed that an ideal nonperfect SS also has a matroid structure [16].

This paper first shows an improvement of the lower bound on $|V_i|$ of [16]. We call it a general lower bound because it includes the previous bound for perfect SSs such that $|\forall V_i| \geq |S|$ and that for nonperfect SSs such that $\log_2 |\forall V_i| \geq \log_2 |S|/d$ as special cases. There exist, however, access hierarchies in which $|V_i|$ must be larger than the general lower bound, of course. As in perfect SSs, it is very hard to determine the optimum size of V_i for a given access hierarchy in general. As our second contribution, we determine the optimum size of V_i for a certain level 2 access hierarchy and show its extension.

2 Preliminaries

2.1 Notation

- $|A|$ denotes the cardinality of a set A. $A \backslash B \triangleq \{x | \, x \in A, x \notin B\}$.
- $H(X)$ denotes the entropy of a random variable X. $H(X|Y)$ denotes the conditional entropy for two random variables X and Y. $I(X;Y)$ denotes the mutual entropy. See appendix. Also, for the details of entropy, see [17], for example.
- For a random variable X, we define $\hat{X} \triangleq \{x | \Pr(X = x) > 0\}$.
- Γ^- denotes the family of minimal sets of Γ.

2.2 Secret Sharing Scheme

In a secret sharing scheme, there is a probabilistic Turing machine D, called a dealer, whose input is a random variable S. $\hat{S}$ is called a set of secrets. On input $s \in \hat{S}$, the dealer randomly produces $(v_1, v_2, \ldots, v_n)$, where v_i is called a share. Let $V_1, \ldots, V_n$ be the random variables induced by $v_1, \ldots, v_n$, respectively. Let $P \triangleq \{1, 2, \cdots, n\}$.

Definition 1. A secret sharing scheme (SS) is a triple (S, D, P).

Definition 2. For $A \subseteq P$, define $V_A \triangleq \{V_i | i \in A\}$.

An access set is a qualified subset which can recover s. More formally,

Definition 3. A is an access set if $H(S|V_A) = 0$.

Definition 4. We say that C has no information on S if $H(S|V_C) = H(S)$.

Definition 5. A secret sharing scheme (S, D, P) is perfect on Γ if the following conditions are satisfied, where $\Gamma \subseteq 2^P$.

1. If $A \in \Gamma$, then A is an access set.
2. If $C \notin \Gamma$, then C has no information on S.

That is, $\Gamma = \{A|\ A \text{ is an access set}\}$ and $\Gamma^- = \{A|\ A \text{ is a minimal access set}\}$. We say that Γ is the access structure. Γ^- is the minimal access structure.

Definition 6. $\Gamma \subseteq 2^P$ is said to be monotone if $A \in \Gamma, A \subseteq A' \Rightarrow A' \in \Gamma$.

Proposition 7. *[3, 4] There exists a perfect SS on Γ if and only if Γ is monotone.*

Definition 8. We say that $i \in P$ is independent in Γ if $i \in A$ for some $A \in \Gamma^-$.

Suppose that S is uniformly distributed.

Proposition 9. *[5, 8] In a perfect SS, $|\hat{V}_i| \geq |\hat{S}|$ for any independent i in Γ.*

Definition 10. We say that a perfect SS is ideal if $|\hat{V}_i| = |\hat{S}|$ for any i.

Proposition 11. *[7] If (S, D, P) is an ideal perfect SS, it has a matroid structure.*

Proposition 12. *[8] Suppose that $\Gamma^- = \{\{1,2\},\{2,3\},\{3,4\}\}$. In any perfect SS on Γ,*

$$\max\{\log|\hat{V}_2|, \log|\hat{V}_3|\} \geq (3/2)\log|\hat{S}| \ .$$

3 Nonperfect secret sharing scheme

Definition 13. We say that an SS (S, D, P) is nonperfect on $(\Gamma_1, \Gamma_2, \Gamma_3)$ if $2^P = \Gamma_1 \cup \Gamma_2 \cup \Gamma_3$, $\Gamma_1 = \{A|\ H(S|V_A) = 0\}$, $\Gamma_2 = \{B|\ 0 < H(S|V_B) < H(S)\}$, $\Gamma_3 = \{C|\ H(S|V_C) = H(S)\}$.

Proposition 14. *[15] Suppose that $|\hat{S}|$ is not a prime. There exists a nonperfect SS on $(\Gamma_1, \Gamma_2, \Gamma_3)$ if and only if Γ_1 is monotone and $\Gamma_1 \cup \Gamma_2$ is monotone.*

Proposition 15. *[15]*

$$\max_i \log|\hat{V}_i| \geq \log|\hat{S}| / \min|A \backslash C|$$

where the minimum is taken over $A \in \Gamma_1$ and $C \in \Gamma_3$.

Definition 16. Let d be a positive integer. We say that an SS (S, D, P) has a level d access hierarchy $(\Sigma_0, \Sigma_1, \ldots, \Sigma_d)$ if

1. $\Sigma_k = \{A|H(S|A) = (k/d)H(S)\}$ where $k = 0, 1, \ldots, d$,
2. $2^P = \Sigma_0 \cup \Sigma_1 \cup \ldots \cup \Sigma_d$.

Definition 17. Suppose that a nonperfect SS has a level d access hierarchy $(\Sigma_0, \Sigma_1, \ldots, \Sigma_d)$. We say that $i \in P$ is independent in Σ_k if $i \in A$ for some $A \in \Sigma_k^-$. We say that i is independent if i is independent in Σ_k for some k $(0 \leq k < d)$.

If i is not independent, i is useless clearly. Suppose that S is uniformly distributed.

Proposition 18. *[16] In level d nonperfect SS,* $\log|\hat{V}_i| \geq \log|\hat{S}|/d$ *for any independent i.*

Definition 19. We say that a level d nonperfect SS is ideal if $\log|\hat{V}_i| = \log|\hat{S}|/d$ for any i.

Proposition 20. *[16] Suppose that $|\hat{S}|$ is a prime power. There exists a level d nonperfect SS for $(\Sigma_0, \Sigma_1, \cdots, \Sigma_d)$ if and only if $\bigcup_{i=0}^{k} \Sigma_i$ is monotone for $0 \leq \forall k \leq d-1$, respectively.*

4 General lower bound on $|V_i|$

In this section, we show an improvement of Proposition 18. We call it a general lower bound because it includes Proposition 9 for perfect SSs and Proposition 18 for nonperfect SSs as special cases. For simplicity, we denote $V_{\{X\}}$ by X.

Lemma 21. *If $Y \in \Sigma_l$ and $X \cup Y \in \Sigma_k$ $(k \leq l)$, then*

$$H(X|Y) = \frac{l-k}{d}H(S) + H(X|YS) \ .$$

Proof.

$$\begin{aligned} H(X|Y) &= I(X;S|Y) + H(X|YS) \qquad \text{(from eq.(8))} \\ &= H(S|Y) - H(S|XY) + H(X|YS) \qquad \text{(from eq.(9))} \\ &= \frac{l}{d}H(S) - \frac{k}{d}H(S) + H(X|YS) \qquad \text{(from Def.16)} \\ &= \frac{l-k}{d}H(S) + H(X|YS) \ . \end{aligned}$$

□

Theorem 22. *Let $(\Sigma_0, \Sigma_1, \cdots, \Sigma_d)$ be a level d access hierarchy. Suppose that S is uniformly distributed. If $A \cup \{i\} \in \Sigma_k$ and $A \in \Sigma_l$ for some A, then*

$$\log_2|\hat{V}_i| \geq \max_A\,(l-k)/d \times \log_2|\hat{S}|$$

in any nonperfect SS for $(\Sigma_0, \Sigma_1, \cdots, \Sigma_d)$.

Proof. In Lemma 21, let $Y = A, X = \{i\}$. Then,

$$\begin{aligned}\log_2 |V_i| \geq H(V_i) &\geq H(V_i|V_A) \quad \text{(from eq.(10))} \\ &= (l-k)/d \times H(S) + H(V_i|V_A S) \quad \text{(from Lemma 21)} \\ &\geq (l-k)/d \times H(S) \quad \text{(from eq.(10))} \ .\end{aligned}$$

Since S is uniformly distributed, $H(S) = \log_2 |\hat{S}|$. Thus, Theorem 22 is obtained. □

We can consider that, in a perfect SS, $\Gamma = \Sigma_0$ and $2^P \setminus \Gamma = \Sigma_d$. If i is independent in Γ, there exists A such that $A \cup \{i\} \in \Sigma_0$ and $A \in \Sigma_d$. Then, Theorem 22 becomes $\log_2 |\hat{V}_i| \geq \log_2 |\hat{S}|$. Thus, Proposition 9 is obtained as a special case. Similarly, Proposition 18 is obtained from Theorem 22.

5 Access hierarchy where $|V_i|$ must be larger

5.1 More tight lower bound for a certain $(\Sigma_0, \Sigma_1, \Sigma_2)$

In this section, we show a level 2 access hierarchy in which $|V_i|$ must be strictly larger than the bound of Theorem 22 and determine the optimum size of V_i for this access hierarchy.

¿From Proposition 20, it is enough to specify (Σ_0^-, Σ_1^-) for $(\Sigma_0, \Sigma_1, \Sigma_2)$, where Σ_i^- denotes the family of minimal sets of Σ_i.

Theorem 23. *Consider a level 2 access hierarchy $(\Sigma_0, \Sigma_1, \Sigma_2)$ such that*

$$P = \{1,\ 2,\ 3,\ 4\},\ \Sigma_0^- = \{\{1,\ 2,\ 3\}\},\ \Sigma_1^- = \{\{4,\ 1\},\ \{4,\ 2\}\} \ .$$

Suppose that S is uniformly distributed. Then,

$$\log_2 |\hat{V}_1| + \log_2 |\hat{V}_4| \geq 2 \log_2 |\hat{S}| \ , \tag{1}$$

$$\log_2 |\hat{V}_2| + \log_2 |\hat{V}_4| \geq 2 \log_2 |\hat{S}| \tag{2}$$

in any nonperfect SS for $(\Sigma_0, \Sigma_1, \Sigma_2)$.

Remark. The corresponding bound derived from Theorem 22 is that

$$\log_2 |\hat{V}_1| + \log_2 |\hat{V}_4| \geq (3/2) \log_2 |\hat{S}| \ . \tag{3}$$

Thus, Theorem 23 gives a more tight lower bound. (From Theorem 22, we have

$$\log_2 |\hat{V}_1| \geq \log_2 |\hat{S}|,\ \log_2 |\hat{V}_4| \geq (1/2) \log_2 |\hat{S}|$$

because $\{2,3\} \cup \{1\} \in \Sigma_0$, $\{2,3\} \in \Sigma_2$ and $\{1\} \cup \{4\} \in \Sigma_1$, $\{1\} \in \Sigma_2$. Thus, eq.(3) is obtained.)

The proof of Theorem 23 will be given in subsection 5.2. In subsection 5.3, we show a scheme which satisfies the equalities of eq.(1) and eq.(2).

5.2 Proof of Theorem 23

Lemma 24. $H(V_1|V_2) \geq H(S)$.

Proof. Note that $\{2,3\} \in \Sigma_2$, and $\{1,2,3\} \in \Sigma_0$. Then,

$$\begin{aligned} H(V_1|V_2) &\geq H(V_1|V_2V_3) \quad \text{(from eq.(11))} \\ &= H(S) + H(V_1|V_2V_3S) \quad \text{(from Lemma 21)} \\ &\geq H(S) \quad \text{(from eq.(10))} \ . \end{aligned}$$

□

Lemma 25. $H(V_1|V_2) \leq \log|\hat{V}_1| + \log|\hat{V}_4| - H(S)$.

Proof. Note that $\{2\},\{1,2\} \in \Sigma_2$ and $\{1,4\},\{2,4\} \in \Sigma_1^-$. Then,

$$\begin{aligned} H(V_1|V_2) &= H(V_1|V_2S) \quad \text{(from Lemma 21)} \\ &\leq H(V_1V_4|V_2S) \quad \text{(from eq.(11))} \\ &= H(V_4|V_2S) + H(V_1|V_4V_2S) \quad \text{(from eq.(12))} \\ &\leq H(V_4|V_2S) + H(V_1|V_4S) \quad \text{(from eq.(11))} \\ &= H(V_4|V_2) - H(S)/2 + H(V_1|V_4) - H(S)/2 \quad \text{(from Lemma 21)} \\ &\leq H(V_4) + H(V_1) - H(S) \quad \text{(from eq.(10))} \\ &\leq \log|\hat{V}_4| + \log|\hat{V}_1| - H(S) \quad \text{(from eq.(10))} \ . \end{aligned}$$

□

Proof of Theorem 23. ¿From Lemma 24 and Lemma 25, we have

$$H(S) \leq \log|\hat{V}_1| + \log|\hat{V}_4| - H(S) \ .$$

Then,

$$\log|\hat{V}_1| + \log|\hat{V}_4| \geq 2H(S) \ .$$

Since we assume that S is uniformly distributed, $H(S) = |\hat{S}|$. Therefore, eq.(1) is obtained. Eq.(2) is proved similarly. □

5.3 Realization

Let s be

$$s = (s_1, s_2), \text{ where } \log|\hat{S}_1| = \log|\hat{S}_2| = \log|\hat{S}|/2 \ . \tag{4}$$

(S_1 and S_2 are random variables induced by s_1 and s_2, respectively.)
Let $v_1, \ldots, v_4$ be

$$\begin{aligned} v_1 &= (r_1, r_3) \ , \\ v_2 &= (r_2, r_4) \ , \\ v_3 &= (r_1 \oplus r_4 \oplus s_1, \ r_2 \oplus r_3 \oplus s_2) \ , \\ v_4 &= (r_1 \oplus s_1, \ r_2 \oplus s_1) \end{aligned}$$

where $r_1, \ldots, r_4$ are random numbers and $\oplus$ denotes bitwise exclusive or. It is easy to see that this is a level 2 nonperfect SS for $(\Sigma_0, \Sigma_1, \Sigma_2)$ and the scheme satisfies the equalities of Theorem 23.

6 Extension

Theorem 26. *Consider a level 2 access hierarchy $(\Sigma_0, \Sigma_1, \Sigma_2)$ such that*

$$\begin{aligned} P &= \{1,\ 2,\ 3,\ 4,\ 5\}\ , \\ \Sigma_0^- &= \{\{1,\ 5\},\ \{2,\ 5\},\ \{3,\ 5\},\ \{1,\ 2,\ 3,\ 4\}\}\ , \\ \Sigma_1^- &= \{\{1\},\ \{5\}\}\ . \end{aligned}$$

Suppose that S is uniformly distributed. Then,

$$\log_2 |\hat{V}_1| + \log_2 |\hat{V}_2| + \log_2 |\hat{V}_5| \geq 3 \log_2 |\hat{S}|$$

in any nonperfect SS for $(\Sigma_0, \Sigma_1, \Sigma_2)$. Further, there exists a scheme which meets the equality.

Lemma 27. $H(V_1V_2|V_3) \geq (3/2)H(S)$.

Proof.

$$\begin{aligned} H(V_1V_2|V_3) &\geq H(V_1|V_3) + H(V_2|V_1V_3) \qquad \text{(from eq.(12))} \\ &\geq H(V_1|V_2V_3V_4) + H(V_2|V_1V_3V_4) \qquad \text{(from eq.(11))} \\ &= H(S) + H(V_1|V_2V_3V_4S) + H(S)/2 + H(V_2|V_1V_3V_4) \\ &\qquad \text{(from Lemma 21)} \\ &\geq (3/2)H(S) \qquad \text{(from eq.(10))}\ . \end{aligned}$$

□

Lemma 28. $H(V_1V_2|V_3) \leq \log |\hat{V}_1| + \log |\hat{V}_2| + \log |\hat{V}_5| - (3/2)H(S)$.

Proof.

$$\begin{aligned} H(V_1V_2|V_3) &= H(V_1V_2|V_3S) + H(S)/2 \qquad \text{(from Lemma 21)} \\ &\leq H(V_1V_2V_5|V_3S) + H(S)/2 \qquad \text{(from eq.(11))} \\ &= H(V_5|V_3S) + H(V_1|V_5V_3S) + H(V_2|V_5V_3V_1S) + H(S)/2 \\ &\qquad \text{(from eq.(12))} \\ &\leq H(V_5|V_3S) + H(V_1|V_5S) + H(V_2|V_5S) + H(S)/2 \\ &\qquad \text{(from eq.(11))} \\ &= H(V_5|V_3) - H(S) + H(V_1|V_5) - H(S)/2 \\ &\qquad + H(V_2|V_5) - H(S)/2 + H(S)/2 \quad \text{(from Lemma 21)} \\ &\leq H(V_5) + H(V_1) + H(V_2) - (3/2)H(S) \qquad \text{(from eq.(10))} \\ &\leq \log |\hat{V}_5| + \log |\hat{V}_1| + \log |\hat{V}_2| - (3/2)H(S) \qquad \text{(from eq.(10))}\ . \end{aligned}$$

□

Proof of Theorem 26. ¿From Lemma 27 and Lemma 28, we have

$$(3/2)H(S) \le \log|\hat{V}_1| + \log|\hat{V}_2| + \log|\hat{V}_5| - (3/2)H(S) \ .$$

Then,

$$\log|\hat{V}_1| + \log|\hat{V}_2| + \log|\hat{V}_5| \ge 3H(S) \ .$$

Since we assume that S is uniformly distributed, $H(S) = \log|\hat{S}|$. Therefore,

$$|\hat{V}_1| + |\hat{V}_2| + |\hat{V}_5| \ge 3|\hat{S}| \ .$$

Let $s = (s_1, s_2)$ be as in eq.(4). Let $v_1, \ldots, v_5$ be

$$\begin{aligned} v_1 &= (s_1, r_1) \ , \\ v_2 &= (r_2) \ , \\ v_3 &= (r_3) \ , \\ v_4 &= (r_1 \oplus r_2 \oplus r_3 \oplus s_2) \ , \\ v_5 &= (s_2,\ r_2 \oplus s_1,\ r_3 \oplus s_1) \end{aligned}$$

where $r_1, \ldots, r_3$ are random numbers. It is easy to see that this is a level 2 nonperfect SS for $(\Sigma_0, \Sigma_1, \Sigma_2)$ and the scheme satisfies the equality. □

Appendix

$$H(X) \triangleq -\sum_x \Pr(X = x) \log_2 \Pr(X = x). \tag{5}$$

$$\begin{aligned} I(X;Y) &= H(X) - H(X|Y) && (6)\\ &= H(Y) - H(Y|X) = I(Y;X). && (7)\\ I(X;Y|Z) &= H(X|Z) - H(X|YZ) && (8)\\ &= H(Y|Z) - H(Y|XZ) = I(Y,X|Z). && (9)\\ 0 \le H(X|Y) &\le H(X) \le \log_2|\hat{X}|. && (10)\\ 0 \le H(X|ZW) &\le H(X|Z) \le H(XY|Z). && (11)\\ H(XY|Z) &= H(X|Z) + H(Y|XZ). && (12) \end{aligned}$$

References

1. G.R.Blakley : Safeguarding cryptographic keys. Proc. of the AFIPS 1979 National Computer Conference, vol.48, pp.313-317 (1979)
2. A.Shamir : How to share a secret. Journal of Cryptology, vol.6, No.1, pp.15-20 (1993)
3. M.Itoh, A.Saito and T.Nishizeki : Secret sharing scheme realizing general access structure. Proc. of IEEE Globecom '87, Tokyo, pp.99-102 (1987)
   Also, Multiple assignment scheme for sharing secret. Journal of Cryptology, vol.6, No.1, pp.15-20 (1993)

4. J.C.Benaloh and J.Leichter : Generalized secret sharing and monotone functions. Crypto'88, pp.27-36 (1990)
5. E.D.Karnin, J.W.Green and M.E.Hellman : On secret sharing systems. IEEE Trans. IT-29, No.1, pp.35-41 (1982)
6. G.R.Blakeley and C.Meadows : Security of ramp schemes. Crypto'84, pp.242-268 (1984)
7. E.F.Brickell and D.M.Davenport : On the classification of ideal secret sharing schemes. Journal of Cryptology, vol.4, No.2, pp.123-134 (1991)
8. R.M.Capocelli, A.De Santis, L.Gargano and U.Vaccaro : On the size of shares for secret sharing schemes. Crypto'91, pp.101-113 (1991)
9. E.F.Brickell and D.R.Stinson : Some improved bounds on the information rate of perfect secret sharing schemes. Crypto'90, pp.242-252 (1990)
10. C.Blund, A.De Santis, D.R.Stinson and U.Vaccaro : Graph decomposition and secret sharing schemes. Eurocrypt'92, pp.1-20 (1992)
11. C.Blund, A.De Santis, L.Gargano and U.Vaccaro : On the information rate of secret sharing schemes. Crypto'92 (1992)
12. D.R.Stinson : New general bounds on the information rate of secret sharing schemes. Crypto'92 (1992)
13. M.Franklin and M.Yung : Communication complexity of secure computation. STOC'92, pp.699-710 (1992)
14. C.Blund, A.De Santis and U.Vaccaro : Efficient sharing of many secrets. STACS'93, pp.692-703 (1993)
15. W.Ogata, K.Kurosawa and S.Tsujii : Nonperfect secret sharing schemes. Auscrypt'92 (1992)
16. K.Kurosawa, K.Okada, K.Sakano, W.Ogata and S.Tsujii : Nonperfect secret sharing schemes and matroids. Eurocrypt'93 (1993)
17. R.G.Gallager : Information Theory and Reliable Communications. John Wiley & Sons, New York, NY (1968)

On Sharing Many Secrets
(Extended Abstract)

Wen-Ai Jackson, Keith M. Martin* and Christine M. O'Keefe*

Department of Pure Mathematics, The University of Adelaide, Adelaide SA 5005, Australia

Abstract. We consider secret sharing schemes which, through an initial issuing of shares to a group of participants, permit a number of different secrets to be protected. Each secret is associated with a (potentially different) access structure and a particular secret can be reconstructed by any group of participants from its associated access structure without the need for further broadcast information. Two distinct problems are addressed. Firstly we consider ideal secret sharing schemes in this more general environment. In particular, we classify the collections of access structures that can be combined in such an ideal secret sharing scheme and we provide a general method of construction for such schemes. We also explore the extent to which the results that connect ideal secret sharing schemes to matroids can be appropriately generalised. Secondly we consider secret sharing schemes that can be used more than once. This problem can be considered as a type of secret sharing scheme wi! th different secrets but with the same access structure for each of the secrets.

1 Introduction

The basic idea behind secret sharing schemes and their relevance to cryptology is well documented (see [25]). Informally a *secret sharing scheme* permits a group of *participants* to jointly protect a *secret* through the issue of a related *share* of the secret to each participant. The scheme is designed so that if a set of participants pool their shares then only those sets that are specified to be in the *access structure* of the scheme will be able to use their shares to reconstruct the secret.

Many secret sharing applications, particularly those associated with key management and key distribution problems, require the protection of more than one secret, possibly with different access structures associated with each secret. The precise generalisation of a secret sharing scheme to include the option of protecting more than one secret is not immediately apparent. For instance,

- Should all the secrets be available for potential reconstruction during the lifetime of the scheme, or should the access of secrets be further controlled by enabling the reconstruction of a particular secret only after extra information has been broadcast to the participants?

* This work was supported by the Australian Research Council

- Should a scheme be used just once, to reconstruct one or all of the secrets, or should the scheme be designed to enable multiple use?
- If a scheme is to be used more than once: in the event that a particular secret has been 'reconstructed' by a group of participants, does the exact value of the secret remain undisclosed or is it known by the participants who enabled its reconstruction, or indeed, is it known by all of the participants?

The desirable properties of a particular scheme depend on both the requirements of the application and also on the implementation. We deal with two completely different scenarios in this abstract. Firstly we consider perhaps the most straightforward definition of a secret sharing scheme with multiple secrets. In this model all of the secrets are available for reconstruction without the need for additional broadcast information and the schemes are designed for one-time use only (of course, if an implementation is done in such a way that the value of the secret is not revealed to any of the participants then such a scheme can be used repeatedly). Schemes of this type which have *threshold* access structures (see later) have been studied in [5, 8, 16, 17, 21] (we note that the schemes in [5, 8, 21] can be used repeatedly as the threshold access structures are trivial). We extend the notion of an ideal secret sharing scheme to this situation and classify such schemes.

Secondly we consider schemes that are designed for multiple use. We study schemes that allow several secrets to be protected by a fixed access structure under the assumption that once a secret has been reconstructed its value becomes public knowledge. We will present constructions for such schemes that are minimal with respect to the size of each participant's share.

Multiple secret sharing schemes that require broadcast information have been studied in [6, 7].

Note that schemes that we study offer *unconditional security*. This means that their security is independent of the time and resources available to any opponent who is trying to interfere with the procedure.

2 Single Secret Sharing Schemes

For finite sets A and B we write AB for $A \cup B$, and $B \setminus A$ for B (set) minus A. For all singleton sets $\{x\}$ we omit the brackets and write x. All of the access structures under consideration in this paper are monotone. An access structure Γ defined on a participant set $\mathcal{P}$ is *monotone* if for all $A \subseteq B \subseteq \mathcal{P}$, if $A \in \Gamma$ then $B \in \Gamma$. We can describe Γ uniquely by the collection Γ^- of *minimal sets* of Γ, that is, the sets $A \subseteq \mathcal{P}$ such that $A \in \Gamma$ but $A \setminus a \notin \Gamma$ for all $a \in A$. We let core $\Gamma = \{p \in \mathcal{P} : p \in A$ for some $A \in \Gamma^-\}$ and say that Γ is *connected* if core $\Gamma = \mathcal{P}$. Let $A \subseteq \mathcal{P}$. The *restriction* $\Gamma|A$ of Γ at A is the access structure defined on $\mathcal{P}\setminus A$ as $\Gamma|A = \{B \subseteq \mathcal{P}\setminus A : B \in \Gamma\}$. The *contraction* $\Gamma \cdot A$ of Γ at A is the access structure defined on $\mathcal{P}\setminus A$ as $\Gamma \cdot A = \{B \subseteq \mathcal{P}\setminus A : AB \in \Gamma\}$. Note that if $A \in \Gamma$ then $(\Gamma \cdot A)^- = \{\emptyset\}$. If $|\mathcal{P}| = n$ then for $1 \leq k \leq n$, the (k,n)-*threshold* access structure Γ is such that $\Gamma = \{A \subseteq \mathcal{P} : |A| \geq k\}$. If $k = 1$ then we say that the threshold access structure is *trivial*.

Now we review some notation and the definition of entropy, noting that all logarithms used in this paper have base 2.

Let X be a finite set and let $\langle X\rangle$ be a finite collection of tuples, such that the entries of each $\pi \in \langle X\rangle$ are indexed by the elements of X. For example, if $X = \{a,b,c\}$ then $\pi = (\pi_a, \pi_b, \pi_c) \in \langle X\rangle$ for some values π_a, π_b, π_c. For $\pi = (\pi_x)_{x\in X} \in \langle X\rangle$ and for $A \subseteq X$, let π_A denote the tuple $(\pi_x)_{x\in A}$ and let $\langle A\rangle = \{\pi_A : \pi \in \langle X\rangle\}$. Let ρ be a probability measure on $\langle X\rangle$, and let $\theta(A)$ be the random variable defined by the projection $\langle X\rangle \to \langle A\rangle$. The measure ρ induces a probability mass function ρ_A of $\theta(A)$ on $\langle A\rangle$, such that for each $\alpha \in \langle A\rangle$, we have $\rho_A(\alpha) = \sum_{\{\pi\in\langle X\rangle : \pi_A=\alpha\}} \rho(\pi)$. Let $[A]_\rho = \{\alpha \in \langle A\rangle : \rho_A(\alpha) > 0\}$. The *entropy* $H_\rho(A)$ of $\theta(A)$ is

$$H_\rho(A) = -\sum_{\alpha\in[A]_\rho} \rho_A(\alpha)\log\rho_A(\alpha).$$

When there is no ambiguity, we write $[A]$ for $[A]_\rho$ and $H(A)$ for $H_\rho(A)$. For $A, B \subseteq X$, $\alpha \in [A]$ and $\beta \in [B]$, let $\rho_{A,B}(\alpha,\beta) = \sum_{\{\pi\in[X] : \pi_A=\alpha, \pi_B=\beta\}} \rho(\pi)$. The measure ρ induces the conditional probability mass function $\rho_{A|B}$ such that for each $\alpha \in [A]$ and $\beta \in [B]$, $\rho_{A|B}(\alpha,\beta) = \frac{\rho_{A,B}(\alpha,\beta)}{\rho_B(\beta)}$. The *conditional entropy* $H(A \mid B = \beta)$ of $\theta(A)$ given that $\theta(B) = \beta$ is $H(A \mid B = \beta) = -\sum_{\alpha\in[A]} \rho_{A|B}(\alpha,\beta)\log\rho_{A|B}(\alpha,\beta)$, and the *conditional entropy* $H(A \mid B)$ of $\theta(A)$ given $\theta(B)$ is

$$H(A \mid B) = \sum_{\beta\in[B]} \rho_B(\beta)H(A \mid B = \beta).$$

Let $\mathcal{P}$ be a (finite) set of participants, let Γ denote a monotone access structure on $\mathcal{P}$ and let s ($s \notin \mathcal{P}$) denote the secret variable. Further, let ρ be a probability measure on $\langle s\mathcal{P}\rangle$. Then $M = (\mathcal{P}, s, \rho)$ is a *secret sharing scheme* for Γ if for $A \subseteq \mathcal{P}$,
(1) if $A \in \Gamma$ then $H(s \mid A) = 0$, and
(2) if $A \notin \Gamma$ then $H(s \mid A) = H(s)$.
If Γ is connected then we say that M is *connected.* It is straightforward to show that if $p \in \operatorname{core}\Gamma$ then $H(p) \geq H(s)$. Since it is desirable to minimise the *size* $H(p)$ of the share of each participant p in a secret sharing scheme, we say that M is *ideal* if $H(p) = H(s)$ for every $p \in \operatorname{core}\Gamma$. Hence the set of shares participant p can be assigned is $[p]$ and the set of possible secrets is $[s]$. From a lemma in [15] it follows that if M is ideal then $|[p]| = |[s]|$ for all $p \in \mathcal{P}$. We refer to $H(s)$ as the *size* of the secret s and call an access structure Γ *ideal* if there is an ideal secret sharing scheme M for Γ.

To implement a secret sharing scheme, a trusted *dealer* selects a tuple $\pi \in [s\mathcal{P}]$ with probability $\rho(\pi)$. Participant $p \in \mathcal{P}$ is given share π_p and the secret value is π_s. Any subset $A \in \Gamma$ is able to determine the value of s since the probability that the secret is π_s, given the pooled shares π_A, is 1. Further, if any subset $A \notin \Gamma$ pools their shares to form π_A, then the probability that any $\sigma \in [s]$ is the secret is exactly the same as for someone outside the scheme who knows M but not the value of any shares.

2.1 Ideal Secret Sharing Schemes and Matroids

For a basic introduction to the theory of matroids, see [22]. A combinatorial equivalent of the following result first appeared in [11]. This version appeared in [15] and similar versions (under slightly different definitions of 'ideal') have appeared in [2, 19].

Result 1. *Let $M = (\mathcal{P}, s, \rho)$ be an ideal secret sharing scheme for Γ. If Γ is connected, then associated with M there is a connected matroid $T(M) = (s\mathcal{P}, \mathcal{I})$ satisfying*
(1) if $A \subseteq s\mathcal{P}$ then $\operatorname{rank}(A) = H(A)/H(s)$*;*
(2) the dependent sets of $T(M)$ are precisely the sets $A \subseteq s\mathcal{P}$ such that there exists $a \in A$ satisfying $H(a \mid A\backslash a) = 0$;
(3) the circuits of $T(M)$ containing s are precisely the sets sA for $A \in \Gamma^{-}$.

We say that $T(M)$ is the *matroid associated with M*. It follows ([15]) that the matroid $T(M)$ associated with an ideal secret sharing scheme $M = (\mathcal{P}, s, \rho)$ for Γ depends only on Γ. Thus, for any ideal secret sharing scheme M for Γ, we may refer to the matroid associated with M as the *matroid associated with Γ*. Conversely, let $T = (s\mathcal{P}, \mathcal{I})$ be a matroid with distinguished point s, and let $\Gamma^{-} = \{A \subseteq \mathcal{P} : sA \text{ is a circuit of } T\}$. Now let $\Gamma(T) = \{B \subseteq \mathcal{P} : B \supseteq A \text{ for some } A \in \Gamma^{-}\}$. Then $\Gamma(T)$ is a monotone access structure, called the *monotone access structure associated with T*. Given a matroid T, it is an open problem as to when $\Gamma(T)$ is ideal. It was shown in [11] that if T is representable then $\Gamma(T)$ is ideal, however in [23] it was shown that the access structure associated with the (non-representable) Vamos matroid is not ideal.

We will need the following slight extension of the idea of the matroid associated with an ideal secret sharing scheme to the case of a finite set with a probability measure. Let Z be a finite set and let ρ be a probability measure on $\langle Z \rangle$, such that $H_\rho(a)$ is a constant h for all $a \in Z$. Suppose that for all $A \subseteq Z$ and for all $a \in Z$ we have $H(a \mid A) = 0$ or $H(a)$ (and hence for any $A \subseteq Z$, $H_\rho(A)$ is a multiple of h). Then by a similar proof to that of Result 1, the pair (Z, ρ) has an *associated* matroid $T = (Z, \mathcal{I})$ satisfying:
(1) if $A \subseteq Z$ then $\operatorname{rank}(A) = H(A)/h$;
(2) the dependent sets of T are precisely the sets $A \subseteq Z$ such that there exists $a \in A$ satisfying $H(a \mid A\backslash a) = 0$.

3 Ideal Secret Sharing Schemes with Multiple Secrets

Let $\mathcal{P}$ be a finite set of participants, and let $\mathcal{S}$ be a finite set of secrets. Let $\Gamma = (\Gamma_s)_{s \in \mathcal{S}}$ be a tuple of monotone access structures on $\mathcal{P}$. Note that Γ will continue to represent an access structure associated with a single secret. Let ρ be a probability measure on $\langle \mathcal{S}\mathcal{P} \rangle$. Then $M = (\mathcal{P}, \mathcal{S}, \rho)$ is a *secret sharing scheme* for Γ if, for each $s \in \mathcal{S}$, the scheme $M_s = (\mathcal{P}, s, \rho_{s\mathcal{P}})$ is a secret sharing scheme for Γ_s. For $s \in \mathcal{S}$, let $\mathcal{P}_s = \operatorname{core} \Gamma_s$, and note that $(\mathcal{P}_s, s, \rho_{s\mathcal{P}_s})$ is a connected secret sharing scheme for Γ_s.

We call M_s a *component* scheme of M, and we remark that M_s is not necessarily connected. We say that M is *connected* if $\mathcal{P} = \bigcup_{s \in \mathcal{S}} \mathcal{P}_s$, that is, each participant is in the core of some access structure Γ_s. Further, M is *ideal* if there exists a constant $h > 0$ such that $H(x) = h$ for every $x \in \mathcal{SP}$ (or, equivalently, if each component scheme is ideal and all the components schemes have the same secret size).

We now extend the definitions of restriction and contraction of a single secret sharing scheme to the case of a secret sharing scheme with one or more secrets. In particular, we will sometimes wish to restrict or contract at a subset of $\mathcal{SP}$, not just at a subset of $\mathcal{P}$. Let $\Gamma = (\Gamma_s)_{s \in \mathcal{S}}$ be a collection of access structures on a participant set $\mathcal{P}$, and let $A \subseteq \mathcal{SP}$. Let $\mathcal{R} = \mathcal{S} \backslash A$. The *restriction* $\Gamma | A$ of Γ at A is the access structure $\Gamma | A = (\Gamma_s | (A \cap \mathcal{P}))_{s \in \mathcal{R}}$ defined on $\mathcal{P} \backslash A$. The *contraction* $\Gamma \cdot A$ of Γ at A is the access structure $\Gamma \cdot A = (\Gamma_s \cdot (A \cap \mathcal{P}))_{s \in \mathcal{R}}$ defined on $\mathcal{P} \backslash A$.

Theorem 2. *Let $M = (\mathcal{P}, \mathcal{S}, \rho)$ be a secret sharing scheme for $\Gamma = (\Gamma_s)_{s \in \mathcal{S}}$. Let $A \subseteq \mathcal{SP}$ and let $\mathcal{Q} = \mathcal{P} \backslash A$ and $\mathcal{R} = \mathcal{S} \backslash A$.*
(a) There exists a secret sharing scheme $M | A = (\mathcal{Q}, \mathcal{R}, \mu)$ for $\Gamma | A$, with $\mu = \rho_{\mathcal{RQ}}$. Further, if M is ideal then $M | A$ is ideal.
(b) There exists a secret sharing scheme $M \cdot A = (\mathcal{Q}, \mathcal{R}, \mu)$ for $\Gamma \cdot A$, where for a given $\alpha \in [A \cap \mathcal{P}]$ we have $\mu(\omega) = \rho_{\mathcal{RQ}|(A \cap \mathcal{P})}(\omega, \alpha)$, for each $\omega \in [\mathcal{RQ}]$. Further, if M is ideal then $M \cdot A$ is ideal.

3.1 Separators of Matroids and Probability Measures

In this section we discuss the concept of *separators*, both of matroids and of probability measures. The results shown here are used to establish our main result.

Let $T = (\mathcal{E}, \mathcal{I})$ be a matroid, and let $A \subseteq \mathcal{E}$. The set A is a *separator* of T if $\operatorname{rank} A + \operatorname{rank} \mathcal{E} \backslash A = \operatorname{rank} \mathcal{E}$. We note that A is a separator of T if and only if each circuit of T lies either in A or in $\mathcal{E} \backslash A$ (see [22, Proposition 4.2.1]).

Let ρ be a probability measure on a finite set $\langle Z \rangle$, and let $A \subseteq B \subseteq Z$. We say that A is a *separator* of (B, ρ) if $H(A \mid B \backslash A) = H(A)$, which holds if and only if $H(B \backslash A \mid A) = H(B \backslash A)$ which is if and only if $H(B) = H(A) + H(B \backslash A)$. So A is a separator of B if and only if $B \backslash A$ is a separator of B, which is if and only if $\theta(A)$ and $\theta(B \backslash A)$ are independent random variables. Note that A is a separator of (B, ρ) if and only if A is a separator of (B, ρ_B).

Lemma 3. *Let ρ be a probability measure on a finite set $\langle Z \rangle$ for which there exists an associated matroid $T = (Z, \mathcal{I})$. Then the separators of (Z, ρ) are precisely the separators of T.*

3.2 Construction and Classification of Ideal Secret Sharing Schemes

In this section we give a complete classification of the collections of secret sharing schemes which occur as the components of an ideal secret sharing scheme. In doing so, we show explicitly how to construct a secret sharing scheme from such a collection of components.

For the remainder of this section, let $M = (\mathcal{P}, \mathcal{S}, \rho)$ be a connected, ideal secret sharing scheme for $\Gamma = (\Gamma_s)_{s \in \mathcal{S}}$, and let $\mathcal{P}_s = \operatorname{core} \Gamma_s$ (for $s \in \mathcal{S}$). For each $X \subseteq \mathcal{S}$, let

$$\mathcal{P}^X = \left(\bigcap_{s \in X} \mathcal{P}_s \right) \cap \left(\bigcap_{s \notin X} \mathcal{P} \backslash \mathcal{P}_s \right).$$

That is, $\mathcal{P}^X$ is the set of participants which are in $\mathcal{P}_s$ for all $s \in X$ and not in $\mathcal{P}_s$ for any $s \notin X$. We note that the non-empty sets $\mathcal{P}^X$, for $X \subseteq \mathcal{S}$, partition $\mathcal{P}$.

The next result gives necessary and sufficient conditions on a collection of ideal single secret sharing schemes in order that it can occur as the collection of components of an ideal secret sharing scheme. These conditions are that each access structure is a product of access structures on the subsets $\mathcal{P}^X$ of participants, and that the respective probability mass functions agree on the subsets $\mathcal{P}^X$. Our theorem shows explicitly the construction of an ideal secret sharing scheme from its component schemes. We write $\Gamma = \Delta_1 \Delta_2$ to mean that $\Gamma = \{A_1 A_2 : A_1 \in \Delta_1, A_2 \in \Delta_2\}$.

Theorem 4. *Let $h > 0$. Let $\Gamma = (\Gamma_s)_{s \in \mathcal{S}}$ be a collection of ideal access structures on a participant set $\mathcal{P}$, with set $\mathcal{S}$ of secrets. For $s \in \mathcal{S}$, let $\mathcal{P}_s = \operatorname{core} \Gamma_s$ and let $T_s = (s\mathcal{P}_s, \mathcal{I}_s)$ be the matroid associated with Γ_s. Suppose that $\mathcal{P} = \cup_{s \in \mathcal{S}} \mathcal{P}_s$. There exists a connected ideal secret sharing scheme $M = (\mathcal{P}, \mathcal{S}, \rho)$ for Γ with $H(s) = h$ for $s \in \mathcal{S}$ if and only if the following conditions hold:*
(a) for each $s \in \mathcal{S}$ and each $X \subseteq \mathcal{S}$ with $s \in X$, then $\mathcal{P}^X$ is a separator of $T_s|s$, (equivalently, for each $s \in \mathcal{S}$ we have $\Gamma_s = \prod_{s \in X \subseteq \mathcal{S}} \Delta_s^X$ where each Δ_s^X is a (possibly empty) access structure on $\mathcal{P}^X$), and
(b) for each $s \in \mathcal{S}$ there exist ideal secret sharing schemes $M_s = (\mathcal{P}_s, s, \rho^s)$ for Γ_s satisfying $H_{\rho^s}(s) = h$ and such that for each s, t with $s, t \in \mathcal{S}$ and each $X \subseteq \mathcal{S}$ with $s, t \in X$ we have $(\rho^s)_{\mathcal{P}^X} = (\rho^t)_{\mathcal{P}^X}$.

3.3 Extending the Connection with Matroids

The matroid associated with an ideal single secret sharing scheme has proved to be an extremely important tool in the attempt to characterise such schemes. It is natural to ask whether an ideal secret sharing scheme (with more than one secret) determines a matroid in the same way. Let $M = (\mathcal{P}, \mathcal{S}, \rho)$ be a secret sharing scheme for $\Gamma = (\Gamma_s)_{s \in \mathcal{S}}$. We say that M is *associated* with a matroid T if $(\mathcal{SP}, \rho)$ is associated with T. In this case, $H(a \mid A) = H(a)$ or 0 for all $a \in \mathcal{SP}$, and $A \subseteq \mathcal{SP}$ (since the rank function is integer-valued, and so every $H(a \mid A)$ is a multiple of $H(a)$). However, an ideal secret sharing scheme does not necessarily have an associated matroid, defined on $\mathcal{SP}$, associated in the same way as in the single secret case.

We now investigate to what extent we can guarantee an associated matroid. First we recall the following definition. Let $T_1 = (\mathcal{E}_1, \mathcal{I}_1)$ and $T_2 = (\mathcal{E}_2, \mathcal{I}_2)$ be matroids, satisfying $\mathcal{E}_1 \cap \mathcal{E}_2 = \emptyset$. The *direct sum* of T_1 and T_2 is the matroid $T_1 \oplus T_2 = (\mathcal{E}_1\mathcal{E}_2, \mathcal{I})$ where $\mathcal{I} = \{I_1 I_2 : I_1 \in \mathcal{I}_1, I_2 \in \mathcal{I}_2\}$. It follows that $\mathcal{E}_1$ and $\mathcal{E}_2$ are separators of $T_1 \oplus T_2$ and that $T|\mathcal{E}_1 = T_2$ and $T|\mathcal{E}_2 = T_1$. Similarly, we can define the direct sum of a finite number of matroids, provided they are defined on disjoint sets. Conversely, given any matroid $T = (\mathcal{E}, \mathcal{I})$ with a separator A, and $B = \mathcal{E}\backslash A$ we have $T = (T|A) \oplus (T|B)$.

Theorem 5. *Let $M = (\mathcal{P}, \mathcal{S}, \rho)$ be a connected ideal secret sharing scheme for Γ. For each $s \in \mathcal{S}$ let $T_s = (s\mathcal{P}_s, \mathcal{I}_s)$ be the matroid associated with the (connected ideal) secret sharing scheme $M_s = (\mathcal{P}_s, s, \rho_{s\mathcal{P}_s})$, where $\mathcal{P}_s = \text{core}\,\Gamma_s$. For each $X \subseteq \mathcal{S}$, there exists a matroid $(T_X, \mathcal{I}_X)$ with $T_X = T_s|(\mathcal{S}\mathcal{P}\backslash\mathcal{P}^X)$, for $s \in X$. Further,*
(a) $(\mathcal{P}, \rho_{\mathcal{P}})$ is associated with the matroid $T = \oplus_{X\subseteq\mathcal{S}} T_X$;
(b) for each $s \in \mathcal{S}$, $(s\mathcal{P}, \rho_{s\mathcal{P}})$ is associated with $T = T_s \oplus (\oplus_{\{X\subseteq\mathcal{S}\,:\,s\notin X\}} T_X)$;
(c) if there exists $X \subseteq \mathcal{S}$ such that for each $s \in X$ there exists a set $X_s \subseteq \mathcal{S}$ with $H(s \mid \mathcal{P}^{X_s}) = 0$, then $(X\mathcal{P}, \rho_{X\mathcal{P}})$ is associated with matroid $T = (\oplus_{s\in X} T_s) \oplus (\oplus_{Y\subseteq\mathcal{S}\backslash X} T_Y)$.

Note that the existence of suitable sets X and X_s $(s \in X)$ in Theorem 5 (c) is equivalent to the existence of $X \subseteq \mathcal{S}$ with the properties: (1) $\mathcal{P}_s \cap \mathcal{P}_t = \emptyset$ for each $s, t \in X$ with $s \neq t$, and (2) for each $s \in X$ and each $u \in \mathcal{S}\backslash X$ either $\mathcal{P}_s \cap \mathcal{P}_u = \emptyset$ or $\mathcal{P}_s \subseteq \mathcal{P}_u$.

4 Efficient Constructions for one Sharing of many Secrets

We now consider the situation where a secret sharing scheme is to be used several times. We assume that throughout the lifetime of a scheme the integrity of the shares is preserved but the value of a reconstructed secret becomes public knowledge. For instance, let the participants be members of a military unit and the secrets be a set of one-time use passwords to be issued only in emergency situations. In the event of such an emergency an authorised set of members of the unit can use their shares to determine a password which can then be broadcast to the whole unit. During a subsequent alert a new password will be needed. The design of the scheme must take into consideration the fact that the old password is now known by all the participants. In most traditional models it is necessary to redistribute fresh shares to each participant once a particular secret has been reconstructed. This can be a costly process with respect to both time and resources. We would like to extend ! the potential lifetime of a particular set of shares by allowing them to be used in the recovery of more than one secret.

Threshold schemes that permitted shares to be re-used several times were studied in [13]. The security of these schemes was not unconditional since it relied on the difficulty of computing discrete logarithms modulo a large prime (we say that schemes of this type offer *conditional security*). Conditionally secure schemes with re-usable shares for the more general class of monotone access structures were studied in [14]. Unconditionally secure threshold schemes that protected more than one secret were first discussed in [18]. These scheme were not optimal in the sense that we will discuss later. Unconditionally secure schemes for general monotone access structures were studied in [9] and some lower bounds on the size of share that each participant holds in such schemes were shown. The size of a participant's share in a scheme reflects the efficiency of the scheme as larger shares are more costly to store and process. We will present two ! families of constructions for schemes that meet the main lower bound given in [9].

4.1 Modelling Schemes for Multiple Use

Let $\mathcal{P}$ denote a collection of m participants and let $\mathcal{S}$ denote a collection of n secrets. We say that $\mathcal{M} = (\mathcal{P}, \mathcal{S}, \rho)$ form an *n-secret sharing scheme* for Γ if the following conditions are satisfied:

1. For all $A \subseteq \mathcal{P}$ with $A \in \Gamma$ we have that $H(S|A) = 0$, for all $S \in \mathcal{S}$.
2. There exists a non-negative non-increasing sequence $(1, \alpha_1, \ldots, \alpha_{n-1})$ with the property that for all $A \subseteq \mathcal{P}$ such that $A \notin \Gamma$ and for all j $(0 \leq j \leq n-1)$,

$$H(S|S_J A) \geq \alpha_j H(S),$$

for all j-subsets $S_J \subseteq \mathcal{S}$ and all $S \in \mathcal{S} \setminus S_J$ (we assume throughout the paper that $\alpha_0 = 1$).

Note that for all $A \subseteq \mathcal{P}$ with $A \notin \Gamma$ this implies that $H(S|A) = H(S)$, for all $S \in \mathcal{S}$. Thus an n-secret sharing scheme has the following properties. If a set A is in the access structure then it can recover all the secrets $S \in \mathcal{S}$. If A is not in the access structure then the participants of A obtain no additional information about *any* of the secrets by pooling their shares. Further for each j $(1 \leq j \leq n-1)$ there is a lower bound on the amount of information that a set A not in the access structure can obtain about a particular secret, even if A has already determined the values of j previous secrets. Where appropriate we refer to such a scheme as an n-secret sharing scheme *with respect to* $(1, \alpha_1, \ldots, \alpha_{n-1})$.

Our definition of an n-secret sharing scheme is essentially the same as that of a *multisecret sharing scheme* in [9]. The definition of a multisecret sharing scheme in [9] had the less general requirement that $H(S|S_J A) = \alpha_j H(S)$ in property 2. We also note that in [14] the secrets were ordered and necessarily accessed in sequence. In our model (and that of [9]) the order of reconstruction of the secrets is not important. In [9] the following result was proved.

Result 6. *Let Γ be a monotone access structure and $P \in \mathcal{P}$. Then in an n-secret sharing scheme with respect to $(1, \alpha_1, \ldots, \alpha_{n-1})$ and for any ordering $S_0, \ldots, S_{n-1}$ of the members of $\mathcal{S}$ we have that*

$$H(P) \geq \sum_{j=0}^{n-1} \alpha_j H(S_j). \tag{1}$$

We would like to construct n-secret sharing schemes that meet (1) with equality for all $P \in \mathcal{P}$. We refer to such schemes as *n-optimal.* Unless otherwise stated we assume that $H(S)$ is a constant value for all $S \in \mathcal{S}$.

Note that 1-optimal secret sharing schemes are ideal. We refer to a 1-optimal scheme $(\mathcal{P}, S, \rho)$ such that both ρ and ρ_S are uniform on $[\mathcal{P}S]$ and $[S]$ respectively, and such that $|[S]| = q$, as a *uniform ideal* scheme for Γ with *secret length* q.

Let n, q be positive integers and let $X = \{X_1, \ldots, X_n\}$ be a set of indices and Q a finite set of size q. Let $k \leq n$ and let Ω be a set of n-tuples over Q, indexed by X, such that for every k-subset K of X and every k-tuple z over Q^k there is a unique $w \in \Omega$ such that $w_K = z$. We say that (X, ρ) is a (k, n, q)-transversal system if $[X] = \Omega$ and ρ is uniform on $[X]$.

Note that (X, ρ) is a (k, n, q)-transversal system if and only if the tuples in $[X]$ form the blocks of a combinatorial structure known as a *transversal design.* Further if $1 \leq k \leq n-1$ then (X, ρ) is equivalent to a uniform ideal (k, n)-threshold scheme with secret length q (see [15]).

4.2 A General Construction Method for n-Optimal Schemes

In this section we present a general method for the construction of n-optimal schemes. Throughout this section let Γ be an ideal access structure and let n be a positive integer. Let $(1, \alpha_1, \cdots, \alpha_{n-1})$ be a non-negative non-increasing sequence. Let $\mathcal{S}$ be a set of n secrets and with each $S \in \mathcal{S}$ associate a set $\langle S \rangle$. Let μ be a probability measure defined on $\langle \mathcal{S} \rangle$ such that μ is uniform on $[\mathcal{S}]$. We say that $(\mathcal{S}, \mu)$ forms an *n-secret distribution with respect to* $(1, \alpha_1, \ldots, \alpha_{n-1})$ if for every j $(1 \leq j \leq n-1)$, every j-subset S_J of $\mathcal{S}$ and every $S \in \mathcal{S} \setminus S_J$ we have that $H_\mu(S|S_J) = \alpha_j H_\mu(S)$. We say that $\lambda = |[\mathcal{S}]|$ is the *length* of the n-secret distribution.

Theorem 7. *Let Γ be an ideal access structure, let n be a positive integer and let $(1, \alpha_1, \ldots, \alpha_{n-1})$ be a non-negative non-increasing sequence. If there exists a uniform ideal scheme for Γ with secret length λ and there exists an n-secret distribution with respect to $(1, \alpha_1, \ldots, \alpha_{n-1})$ of length λ then there exists an n-optimal secret sharing scheme for Γ with respect to $(1, \alpha_1, \ldots \alpha_{n-1})$.*

Notice that an n-secret distribution can be used to construct n-optimal secret sharing schemes for different monotone access structures Γ. The only condition is that there must exist a uniform ideal scheme for each Γ with secret length equal to the length of the n-secret distribution.

A General n-Secret Distribution Construction. Let Γ and n be as defined previously. Let $(1, \alpha_1, \ldots, \alpha_{n-1})$ be a sequence of non-negative non-increasing rationals and let $u_0, u_1, \ldots, u_{n-1}$ be such that $\alpha_i = \frac{u_i}{u_0}$ for all i $(0 \leq i \leq n-1)$. Let $u_n = 0$ and for each i $(1 \leq i \leq n)$ let $d_i = u_{i-1} - u_i$. Let $\delta = \sum_{i=1}^{n} i d_i$. Let q be a prime power such that $q \geq n-1$ and such that there exists a uniform ideal scheme for Γ with secret length q^δ (it suffices that there exists a uniform ideal scheme for Γ with secret length q). Thus for any $1 \leq t \leq n$ there exists a (t,n,q)-transversal system ([3]). We proceed by 'multiplying' together d_i copies of an (i,n,q)-transversal system, for all i $(1 \leq i \leq n)$.

Let $\mathcal{S}$ be a set of n elements and let $S \in \mathcal{S}$. For each i $(1 \leq i \leq n)$ and each j $(1 \leq j \leq d_i)$, let $\mathcal{M}_{ij} = (\mathcal{S}, \rho^{ij})$ be a (i,n,q)-transversal system. Now define a set Ω of tuples indexed by $\mathcal{S}$ and a probability measure ρ on Ω as follows. For each set $\{w^{ij} \in [\mathcal{S}]_{\rho^{ij}} \,|\, 1 \leq i \leq n, 1 \leq j \leq d_i\}$, define a distribution rule $w = (w_S)_{S\in\mathcal{S}}$ such that $w_S = (w_S^{ij})_{1\leq i\leq n, 1\leq j\leq d_i}$. Let $\rho(w) = \Pi_{i=1}^n \Pi_{j=1}^{d_i} \rho^{ij}(w^{ij})$. In other words w is an n-tuple, each entry of which is a tuple consisting of $(\sum_{i=1}^n d_i) = u_0$ entries, one from each of the transversal systems $\mathcal{M}_{ij}$. Notice that for any $X, Y \subseteq \mathcal{S}$ we have

$$H_\rho(X|Y) = \sum_{i=1}^{n}\sum_{j=1}^{d_i} H_{\rho^{ij}}(X|Y). \tag{2}$$

We can then show that $(\mathcal{S}, \rho)$ form an n-secret distribution with respect to $(1, \alpha_1, \ldots, \alpha_{n-1})$ of length q^δ and hence by applying Theorem 7 we get the following.

Theorem 8. *For every ideal access structure Γ, every $n \geq 1$ and every non-increasing sequence of non-negative rationals $(1, \alpha_1, \ldots, \alpha_{n-1})$ there exists an n-optimal secret sharing scheme for Γ with respect to $(\alpha_1, \ldots \alpha_{n-1})$.*

The result in Theorem 8 is extremely powerful since it applies to any sequence of non-negative non-increasing rationals $(1, \alpha_1, \ldots, \alpha_{n-1})$. We note that the n-optimal schemes produced have very large secret lengths. For instance if $n = 6$ and $(\alpha_1, \alpha_2, \alpha_3, \alpha_4, \alpha_5) = (\frac{13}{22}, \frac{8}{22}, \frac{5}{22}, \frac{3}{22}, \frac{1}{22})$ then setting $u_0 = 22$ we use nine copies of a $(1,6,q)$-transversal system, five copies of a $(2,6,q)$-transversal system, three copies of a $(3,6,q)$-transversal system, two copies of a $(4,6,q)$-transversal system, two copies of a $(5,6,q)$-transversal system and one copy of a $(6,6,q)$-transversal system. The smallest known q for which there exists a $(2,6,q)$-transversal system is $q = 5$ (see [3]) and thus for this particular example we would need to base any construction on a uniform ideal scheme for Γ with secret length at least $\lambda = 5^{52} \simeq 2.22 \times 10^{36}$. We now des! cribe an alternative construction for an n-secret mapping which only works for certain sequences $(1, \alpha_1, \ldots, \alpha_{n-1})$, but which can involve smaller secret lengths. Note also that for many choices of $(1, \alpha_1, \ldots, \alpha_{n-1})$, the smallest possible secret length will be significantly smaller than in this illustration of the general technique.

An Alternative Construction. We construct an n-secret distribution by finding a mapping f that associates each secret $S \in \mathcal{S}$ with a subset of a set of ω independent random variables. Let W be the collection of u_0-subsets of the set $\{1, \ldots, \omega\}$. If we can find $f\colon \mathcal{S} \to W$ such that

$$|f(S') \setminus (\cup_{S\in S_J} f(S))| = u_j, \tag{3}$$

for every j $(1 \leq j \leq n-1)$, every j-subset S_J of $\mathcal{S}$ and every $S' \in \mathcal{S} \setminus S_J$, then we can construct an n-secret distribution with respect to $(1, \alpha_1, \ldots, \alpha_{n-1})$. We call such a pair (ω, f) a *secret allocation mapping with respect to* $(1, \alpha_1, \ldots, \alpha_{n-1})$.

Theorem 9. *Let $(1, \alpha_1, \ldots, \alpha_{n-1})$ be a non-increasing sequence of non-negative rationals and let $q \geq 2$ be an integer. If there exists a secret allocation mapping (ω, f) with respect to $(1, \alpha_1, \ldots, \alpha_{n-1})$ then there exists an n-secret distribution with respect to $(1, \alpha_1, \ldots, \alpha_{n-1})$ of length q^ω.*

Corollary 10. *Let Γ be a monotone access structure and let $(1, \alpha_1, \ldots, \alpha_{n-1})$ be a non-increasing sequence of non-negative rationals. If there exists a secret allocation mapping (ω, f) with respect to $(1, \alpha_1, \ldots, \alpha_{n-1})$ then there exists an n-optimal scheme for Γ with respect to $(1, \alpha_1, \ldots, \alpha_{n-1})$.*

We present a sufficient condition for the existence of a secret allocation mapping with respect to $(1, \alpha_1, \ldots, \alpha_{n-1})$. For each i $(1 \leq i \leq n)$ define β_i as follows:

$$\beta_i = \sum_{j=n-i}^{n-1} (-1)^{j-n+i} \binom{i-1}{n-j-1} u_j. \tag{4}$$

We say that the non-increasing sequence $(1, \alpha_1, \ldots, \alpha_{n-1})$ of non-negative rationals is *suitable* if $\beta_i \geq 0$ $(1 \leq i \leq n)$, where β_i is calculated from (4).

Theorem 11. *If $(1, \alpha_1, \ldots, \alpha_{n-1})$ is suitable then there exists a secret allocation mapping with respect to $(1, \alpha_1, \ldots, \alpha_{n-1})$.*

Combining Theorems 7, 9 and 11 we have:

Corollary 12. *Let Γ be a monotone access structure and $(1, \alpha_1, \ldots, \alpha_{n-1})$ be a non-increasing sequence of non-negative rationals. If Γ is ideal and the sequence $(1, \alpha_1, \ldots, \alpha_{n-1})$ is suitable then there exists an optimal n-secret sharing scheme for Γ with respect to $(1, \alpha_1, \ldots, \alpha_{n-1})$.*

This alternative construction can be used to show, for example, that for any ideal access structure for which there exists a uniform ideal scheme with secret length 2^{52}, there exists a 6-secret sharing scheme for Γ with respect to $(1, \frac{13}{22}, \frac{8}{22}, \frac{5}{22}, \frac{3}{22}, \frac{1}{22})$ with secret length $2^{52} \simeq 4.50 \times 10^{15}$.

References

1. I. Anderson: A first course in combinatorial mathematics, Clarendon Press, Oxford, 1989.
2. A. Beimel and B. Chor: Universally ideal secret sharing schemes. Adv. in Cryptology - CRYPTO'92, Lecture Notes in Comput. Sci,740:183–195, 1993.
3. Th. Beth, D. Jungnickel and H. Lenz: Design Theory, Bibliographisches Institut, Mannheim, 1985.

4. G. R. Blakley: Safeguarding cryptographic keys. Proceedings of AFIPS 1979 National Computer Conference **48** 313–317, 1979.
5. R. Blom: An optimal class of symmetric key generation systems. Adv. in Cryptology – EUROCRYPT'84, Lecture Notes in Comput. Sci., 209:335–338, 1984.
6. C. Blundo and A. Cresti: Space requirements for broadcast encryption. Presented at EUROCRYPT'94, 1994.
7. C. Blundo, A. Cresti, A. De Santis, and U. Vaccaro: Fully dynamic secret sharing schemes. Adv. in Cryptology – CRYPTO'93, Lecture Notes in Comput. Sci., 773:110–125, 1994.
8. C. Blundo, A. De Santis, A. Herzberg, S. Kutten, Perfectly-secure key distribution for dynamic conferences. Adv. in Cryptology – CRYPTO'92, Lecture Notes in Comput. Sci., 740:471–486, 1993.
9. C. Blundo, A. De Santis and U. Vaccaro: Efficient Sharing of Many Secrets. Proceedings of STACS '93, Lecture Notes in Comput. Sci. **665** 692–703, 1993.
10. E. F. Brickell: Some ideal secret sharing schemes. J. Combin. Math. Combin. Comput., 9:105–113, 1989.
11. E. F. Brickell and D. M. Davenport: On the Classification of Ideal Secret Sharing Schemes. J. Cryptology **2** 123–134, 1991.
12. E. F. Brickell and D. R. Stinson: Some Improved Bounds on the Information Rate of Perfect Secret Sharing Schemes. J. Cryptology **2** 153–166, 1992.
13. R. A. Croft and S. P. Harris: Public-Key Cryptography and Re-usable Shared Secrets. Cryptography and Coding, H. J. Beker and F. C. Piper, Eds. Clarendon Press 255–268, 1989.
14. L. Harn and H.-Y. Lin: An l-Span Generalized Secret Sharing Scheme. Proceedings of Crypto '92, Lecture Notes in Comput. Sci.,740:558–565, 1993.
15. W.-A. Jackson and K. M. Martin: Combinatorial Models for Perfect Secret Sharing Schemes. J. Comb. Math. Comb. Comput., to appear.
16. W.-A. Jackson, K. M. Martin, and C. M. O'Keefe: A construction for multisecret threshold schemes. Submitted, 1993.
17. W.-A. Jackson, K. M. Martin, and C. M. O'Keefe: Multisecret threshold schemes. Adv. in Cryptology – CRYPTO'93, Lecture Notes in Comput. Sci., 773:126–135, 1994.
18. E. D. Karnin, J. W. Greene and M. E. Hellman: On Secret Sharing Systems. IEEE Trans. Inf. Theory Vol IT-29 **1** 35–41, 1983.
19. K. Kurosawa, K. Okada, K. Sakano, W. Ogata and S. Tsujii: Nonperfect Secret Sharing Schemes and Matroids. Adv. in Cryptology – EUROCRYPT'93, Lecture Notes in Comput. Sci., 765:126–141, 1994.
20. K. M. Martin: New Secret Sharing Schemes from Old. J. Comb. Math. Comb. Comput. **14** 65–77, 1993.
21. T. Matsumoto and H. Imai: On the key predistribution system: a practical solution to the key distribution problem. Adv. in Cryptology – CRYPTO'87, Lecture Notes in Comput. Sci., 293:185–193, 1988.
22. J. G. Oxley: Matroid Theory. Oxford University Press, Oxford, 1992.
23. P. D. Seymour: On secret-sharing matroids. J. Combin. Theory Ser B, 56:69–73, 1992.
24. A. Shamir: How to Share a Secret. Comm. ACM Vol 22 **11** 612–613, 1979.
25. G. J. Simmons: An Introduction to Shared Secret and/or Shared Control Schemes and their Application. Contemporary Cryptology: The Science of Information Integrity, IEEE Press, 1992.

26. D. R. Stinson: An Explication of Secret Sharing Schemes. Des. Codes Cryptogr. **2** 357–390, 1992.
27. T. Uehara, T. Nishizeki, and K. Nakamura: A secret sharing system with matroidal access structure. Trans. IECE Japan, J69-A 9:1124–1132, 1986.
28. D. Welsh: Codes and Cryptography. Clarendon Press, Oxford, 1988.

Combinatorial Interpretation of Secret Sharing Schemes

Kaoru KUROSAWA and Koji OKADA

Department of Electrical and Electronic Engineering,
Faculty of Engineering, Tokyo Institute of Technology
2-12-1 O-okayama, Meguro-ku, Tokyo 152, Japan

Abstract. In a perfect secret sharing scheme, it is known that $\log_2 |\hat{V}_i| \geq H(S)$, where S is a secret and $\hat{V}_i$ is the share of user i. On the other hand, $\log_2 |\hat{S}| \geq H(S)$, where $\hat{S}$ is the domain of S. The equality holds if and only if S is uniformly distributed. Therefore, if S is uniformly distributed, we have $|\hat{V}_i| \geq |\hat{S}|$. However, if S is not uniformly distributed, $\log_2 |\hat{S}| > H(S)$. In this case, we have

$$\log_2 |\hat{V}_i| \geq H(S) < \log_2 |\hat{S}| \ .$$

Then, which is bigger, $|\hat{V}_i|$ or $|\hat{S}|$? The answer is not known.
In this paper, we first prove that $|\hat{V}_i| \geq |\hat{S}|$ for any distribution of S by using a combinatorial argument. This is a more sharp lower bound on $|\hat{V}_i|$ for not uniformly distributed S. Our proof makes it intuitively clear why $|\hat{V}_i|$ must be so large, also. Further, we show an extension of our combinatorial technique for some access structures.

1 Introduction

A secret sharing scheme [1][2] is a method in which a dealer distributes a secret s to a set of users in such a way that only qualified subsets of users can recover the secret s. The scheme is called perfect if any non-qualified subset has absolutely no information on s. A piece v_i given to user i is called a share. Let S denote the random variable induced by s. Let V_i denote the random variable induced by v_i. Let $\hat{S}$ be the domain of S. Let $\hat{V}_i$ be the domain of V_i. Let $|X|$ denote the cardinality of a set X.

[4] and [3] showed that $\log_2 |\hat{V}_i| \geq H(S)$ for any perfect secret sharing scheme by using entropy. On the other hand, it holds that $\log_2 |\hat{S}| \geq H(S)$. The equality holds if and only if S is uniformly distributed. Therefore, if S is uniformly distributed, we have $|\hat{V}_i| \geq |\hat{S}|$. However, if S is not uniformly distributed, $\log_2 |\hat{S}| > H(S)$. In this case, we have

$$\log_2 |\hat{V}_i| \geq H(S) < \log_2 |\hat{S}| \ .$$

Then, which is bigger, $|\hat{V}_i|$ or $|\hat{S}|$? The answer is not known.

In this paper, we first prove that $|\hat{V}_i| \geq |\hat{S}|$ for any distribution of S by using a combinatorial argument. This is a more sharp lower bound on $|\hat{V}_i|$ for not uniformly distributed S. Our proof makes it intuitively clear why $|\hat{V}_i|$ must be so large, also.

Further, we extend our combinatorial technique in such as follows. Let Γ_m denote the family of minimal access sets. For $\Gamma_m = \{\{V_1, V_2\}, \{V_2, V_3\}, \{V_3, V_4\}\}$, [3] showed that $\log_2 |\hat{V}_2| + \log_2 |\hat{V}_3| \geq 3H(S)$ by using entropy. This is the smallest access structure in which some $\log_2 |\hat{V}_i|$ is strictly larger than $H(S)$. If S is uniformly distributed, we have $\log_2 |\hat{V}_2| + \log_2 |\hat{V}_3| \geq 3 \log_2 |\hat{S}|$. However, this doesn't imply that $\log_2 |\hat{V}_2| + \log_2 |\hat{V}_3| \geq 3 \log_2 |\hat{S}|$ for not uniformly distributed S. We prove that $\log_2 |\hat{V}_2| + \log_2 |\hat{V}_3| \geq 3 \log_2 |\hat{S}|$ for any distribution of S if $|\hat{V}_1| = |\hat{V}_4| = |\hat{S}|$. This is a more sharp lower bound for not uniformly distribution of S. Intuitive understanding will make it easy to develop the next research, also.

Finally, suppose that user $1, \ldots, l$ have small memories and user $l+1, \ldots, n$ have large memories. In this case, it is important to find a lower bound of $|\hat{V}_{l+i}|$ under the condition that $|\hat{V}_1| = \cdots = |\hat{V}_l| = |\hat{S}|$. We show such a lower bound for some Γ_m.

2 Preliminaries

2.1 Notation and Definitions

$|A|$ denotes the cardinality of a set A. $A \backslash B \triangleq \{x | \, x \in A, x \notin B\}$. $H(X)$ denotes the entropy of a random variable X. $H(X|Y)$ denotes the conditional entropy for two random variables X and Y. For X, we define

$$\hat{X} \triangleq \{x | \Pr(X = x) > 0\} .$$

For $T = \{X_1, \ldots, X_l\}$, define

$$\hat{T} \triangleq \{(x_1, \ldots, x_l) | \Pr(X_1 = x_1, \ldots, X_l = x_l) > 0\} .$$

In a secret sharing scheme, there is a dealer whose input is a random variable S. $\hat{S}$ is called a set of secrets. On input $s \in \hat{S}$, the dealer randomly produces $(v_1, v_2, \ldots, v_n)$, where v_i is called a share. Then the joint probability $\Pr(s, v_1, \ldots, v_n)$ is determined. Let $V_1, \ldots, V_n$ be random variables induced by $v_1, \ldots, v_n$, respectively. An access set is a qualified subset of $\{V_1, \ldots, V_n\}$ which can recover s.

Definition 1.

1. $A \subseteq \{V_1, \ldots, V_m\}$ is an access set if, for $\forall a \in \hat{A}$, there exists a unique $s \in S$ such that
$$\Pr(S = s | A = a) = 1 .$$
2. $B \subseteq \{V_1, \ldots, V_m\}$ is a non-access set if, for $\forall b \in \hat{B}$ and $\forall s \in S$,
$$\Pr(S = s | B = b) = \Pr(S = s) . \tag{1}$$

For convenience, we say that $(S, V_1, \ldots, V_n)$ is a secret sharing scheme (SS).

Definition 2. $(S, V_1, \ldots, V_m)$ is a perfect SS if any subset of $\{V_1, \ldots, V_m\}$ is an access set or a non-access set.

Let

$$\Gamma \triangleq \{A|\ A \text{ is an access set}\}\ ,$$
$$\Gamma_m \triangleq \{A|\ A \text{ is a minimal access set}\}\ ,$$
$$\Delta \triangleq \{B|\ B \text{ is a non-access set}\}\ .$$

We say that Γ is an access structure. Γ_m is a minimal access structure. Δ is the family of non-access sets.

Definition 3. V_i is independent if $V_i \in A$ for some $A \in \Gamma_m$.

2.2 Known Results

Proposition 4. *[3] In a perfect SS,* $\log_2 |\hat{V}_i| \geq H(S)$ *if* V_i *is independent.*

Proposition 5. *[3] In a perfect SS such that* $\Gamma_m = \{\{V_1, V_2\}, \{V_2, V_3\}, \{V_3, V_4\}\}$, *it holds that* $\log_2 |\hat{V}_2| + \log_2 |\hat{V}_3| \geq 3H(S)$.

3 $|\widehat{V_i}|$ must be Larger

We show more sharp lower bounds on $|\hat{V}_i|$ than Proposition 4 and 5. In this section, we make it intuitively clear why $|\hat{V}_i|$ must be so large. Formal proofs will be given in Section 5. Let $\hat{S} = \{s_1, \ldots, s_n\}$.

3.1 $|\hat{V}_i| \geq |\hat{S}|$ $(\geq 2^{H(S)})$

Theorem 6. *In a perfect SS,* $|\hat{V}_i| \geq |\hat{S}|$ *for any distribution of* S *if* V_i *is independent.*

Sketch of proof. Suppose that $\{V_1, V_2, \ldots, V_k\} \in \Gamma_m$. Assume that $v_2, \ldots, v_k$ are made open. Then,

1. $\Pr(S = s_i) > 0$ for $\forall i$ because $\{V_2, \ldots, V_m\} \in \Delta$ and the scheme is perfect.
2. At this moment, V_1 alone must be able to reconstruct each s_i.

Therefore, $|\hat{V}_1| \geq |\hat{S}|$.

3.2 $|\hat{V}_2||\hat{V}_3| \geq |\hat{S}|^3 (\geq 2^{3H(S)})$

Theorem 7. *Consider a perfect SS such that*

1. $\Gamma_m = \{\{V_1, V_2\}, \{V_2, V_3\}, \{V_3, V_4\}\}$,
2. $|\hat{V}_1| = |\hat{V}_4| = |\hat{S}|$.

Then, $|\hat{V}_2||\hat{V}_3| \geq |\hat{S}|^3$ $(\geq 2^{3H(S)})$ *for any distribution of* S.

In other words,

$$|\hat{V}_2| \geq |\hat{S}|^{1.5} \text{ or } |\hat{V}_3| \geq |\hat{S}|^{1.5} \ .$$

Sketch of proof. Define $Y \stackrel{\Delta}{=} \{V_2, V_3\}$ and $Z \stackrel{\Delta}{=} \{V_1, V_4, S\}$. Then,

$$\hat{Y} = \{(v_2, v_3) | \Pr(V_2 = v_2, V_3 = v_3) > 0\} \ ,$$
$$\hat{Z} = \{(v_1, v_4, s) | \Pr(V_1 = v_1, V_4 = v_4, S = s) > 0\} \ .$$

First, we show that $|\hat{Z}| = |\hat{S}|^3$. Next, we show that $|\hat{Y}| \geq |\hat{Z}|$. Then, we have $|\hat{V}_2||\hat{V}_3| \geq |\hat{Y}| \geq |\hat{Z}| = |\hat{S}|^3$.

Lemma 8. $|\hat{Z}| = |\hat{S}|^3$.

Sketch of proof. Suppose that $\forall v_1 \in V_1$ is made open. Then, the minimal access structure becomes $\{\{V_2\}, \{V_3, V_4\}\}$. Thus, V_4 is still independent. Hence, even in this situation, $|\hat{V}_4| = |\hat{S}|$ from Theorem 6 and the assumption (2) of Theorem 7. This means that

$$\forall v_1 \in \hat{V}_1, \ \forall v_4 \in \hat{V}_4, \ \Pr(V_1 = v_1, V_4 = v_4) > 0 \ .$$

Further, since $\{V_1, V_4\} \in \Delta$,

$$\forall v_1 \in \hat{V}_1, \ \forall v_4 \in \hat{V}_4, \ \forall s \in \hat{S}, \ \Pr(V_1 = v_1, V_4 = v_4, S = s) > 0 \ .$$

Therefore, $|\hat{Z}| = |\hat{V}_1||\hat{V}_4||\hat{S}| = |\hat{S}|^3$.

Lemma 9. $|\hat{Y}| \geq |\hat{Z}|$.

Sketch of proof. For $\forall (v_1, v_4, s) \in \hat{Z}$, define

$$X(v_1, v_4, s) \stackrel{\Delta}{=} \{(v_2, v_3) | \Pr(S = s, V_1 = v_1, \ldots, V_4 = v_4) > 0\} \ .$$

Clearly, $|X(v_1, v_4, s)| \geq 1$. We show that, if $(v_1, v_4, s) \neq (v_1', v_4', s')$, then $X(v_1, v_4, s)$ $\cap X(v_1', v_4', s') = \phi$. This proves that $|\hat{Y}| \geq |\hat{Z}|$. On the contrary, suppose that $(v_2, v_3) \in (X(v_1, v_4, s) \cap X(v_1', v_4', s'))$. Then,

1. $s = s'$ because $\{V_2, V_3\} \in \Gamma_m$.
2. Suppose that v_3 is made open. Then $\Pr(S = s_i) > 0$ for $\forall i$ because $\{V_3\} \in \Delta$. At this moment, each value of $\hat{V}_4$ reconstructs each s_i because $\{V_3, V_4\} \in \Gamma_m$. This correspondence determines an onto mapping from $\hat{V}_4$ to $\hat{S}$. Therefore, $|\hat{V}_4| \geq |\hat{S}|$. This mapping is also a bijection because $|\hat{V}_4| = |\hat{S}|$ from assumption 2 of Theorem 7. Therefore, there exists an inverse mapping from $\hat{S}$ to $\hat{V}_4$. In other words, each value of $\hat{S}$ determines $\hat{V}_4$. Therefore, we see that (v_3, s) determines v_4. Hence, $v_4 = v_4'$.
3. Similarly, $v_1 = v_1'$.

This is a contradiction.

4 Weakly Perfect Secret Sharing Schemes

A weakly perfect SS was introduced by [6]. A perfect SS is included as a special case in this class. In this section, we derive some properties of weakly perfect SSs.

Definition 10. $(S, V_1, \ldots, V_n)$ is a weakly perfect SS if for $\forall B \in \Delta, \forall b \in \hat{B}, \forall s \in \hat{S}$,

$$\Pr(S = s|B = b) > 0 \ . \tag{2}$$

Lemma 11. *A perfect SS is a weakly perfect SS.*

Proof. Eq.(1) implies eq.(2). □

Lemma 12. *Let $(S, V_1, \ldots, V_n)$ be a weakly perfect SS. Suppose that $B \triangleq \{V_{i+1}, \ldots, V_n\} \in \Delta$. For $\forall b \in \hat{B}$, let $U, W_1, \cdots, W_i$ be random variables such that*

$$\Pr(U = s, W_1 = v_1, \ldots, W_i = v_i) = \Pr(S = s, V_1 = v_1, \ldots, V_i = v_i|B = b) \ .$$

Then

1. *$\hat{U} = \hat{S}$,*
2. *$(U, W_1, \ldots, W_i)$ is a weakly perfect SS.*

Proof.

1. Note that $\Pr(U = s) = \Pr(S = s|B = b) > 0$ for $\forall s \in \hat{S}$ from the definition of a weakly perfect SS. Therefore, $\hat{S} \subseteq \hat{U}$. It is easy to see that $\hat{U} \subseteq \hat{S}$. Hence, $\hat{U} = \hat{S}$.
2. Suppose that $(U, W_1, \ldots, W_i)$ is not a weakly perfect SS. Let its family of non-access sets be Δ_1. Then, $\exists C \in \Delta_1, \exists c \in \hat{C}, \exists s \in \hat{U}$,

$$\Pr(U = s|C = c) = 0 \ . \tag{3}$$

For simplicity, suppose that $C = \{W_1, \ldots, W_k\}$. Let $C' \triangleq \{V_1, \ldots, V_k\}$. Then, eq.(3) is equivalent to that

$$\Pr(S = s|C' = c, B = b) = 0 \ .$$

It is clear that $C' \cup B \in \Delta$ and $\Pr(C' = c, B = b) > 0$. This contradicts to that $(S, V_1, \ldots, V_n)$ is a weakly perfect SS.

□

Lemma 13. *In a weakly perfect SS, suppose that $V_i \in A \in \Gamma_m$. Let $C \triangleq A \backslash \{V_i\}$. Then, for $\forall c \in \hat{C}$, there exists an injection f from $\hat{S}$ to $\hat{V}_i$ such that*

$$\Pr(S = s|V_i = f(s), C = c) = 1 \ . \tag{4}$$

Proof. $C \in \Delta$ since $A \in \Gamma_m$. Let $U, W, \cdots$ be random variables such that

$$\Pr(U = s, W = v_i, \cdots) = \Pr(S = s, V_i = v_i, \cdots | C = c) \ .$$

From Lemma 12, $\hat{U} = \hat{S}$. For $\forall s \in \hat{S}$, define

$$X_s \stackrel{\triangle}{=} \{v_i | \Pr(U = s, W = v_i) > 0\} \ .$$

Then, for $\forall s \in \hat{S}$,

$$\sum_{v_i} \Pr(U = s, W = v_i) = \Pr(U = s) > 0$$

because $\hat{U} = \hat{S}$ and $s \in \hat{U}$. Therefore, $|X_s| \geq 1$. Pick $x \in X_s$ arbitrarily and define $f(s) \stackrel{\triangle}{=} x$. Suppose that $f(s_1) = f(s_2) = x$ for $s_1 \neq s_2$. Then,

$$\begin{aligned} \Pr(S = s_1 | V_i = x, C = c) &= \Pr(U = s_1 | W = x) \\ &= \frac{\Pr(U = s_1, W = x)}{\Pr(W = x)} \\ &> 0 \end{aligned}$$

since $x \in X_{s_1}$. Therefore,

$$\Pr(S = s_1 | V_i = x, C = c) = 1 \tag{5}$$

because $\{V_i\} \cup C = A \in \Gamma_m$ (it is easy to see that $\Pr(V_i = x, C = c) > 0$). Similarly, $\Pr(S = s_2 | V_i = x, C = c) = 1$. This is a contradiction. Thus, f is an injection. Eq.(4) is obtained from eq.(5). □

Lemma 14. *In a weakly perfect SS, suppose that $V_i \in A \in \Gamma_m$ and $|\hat{V}_i| = |\hat{S}|$. Let $C \stackrel{\triangle}{=} A \backslash \{V_i\}$. Then, for $\forall c \in \hat{C}$ and $\forall s \in \hat{S}$, there exists a unique $v_i \in \hat{V}_i$ such that*

$$\Pr(S = s | V_i = v_i, C = c) = 1 \ .$$

Proof. The injection f from $\hat{S}_i$ to $\hat{V}_i$ in Lemma 13 becomes a bijection if $|\hat{V}_i| = |\hat{S}|$. □

Lemma 15. *In a weakly perfect SS, for $\forall B \in \Delta$; let $W \stackrel{\triangle}{=} B \cup S$. Then $|\hat{W}| = |\hat{B}||\hat{S}|$.*

Proof. ¿From the definition of a weakly perfect SS, $\forall b \in \hat{B}, \forall s \in \hat{S}, \Pr(B = b, S = s) > 0$. Therefore, $|\hat{W}| = |\{(b, s)| \Pr(B = b, S = s) > 0\}| = |\hat{B}||\hat{S}|$. □

5 More Sharp Lower Bounds of $|V_i|$

Theorem 16. *In a weakly perfect SS, $|\hat{V}_i| \geq |\hat{S}|$ if V_i is independent.*

Proof. From Lemma 13, there is an injection from $\hat{S}$ to $\hat{V}_i$. Therefore $|\hat{V}_i| \geq |\hat{S}|$. □

Remark. [5] showed that a "perfect" SS has a matroid structure if $|\hat{V}_i| = |\hat{S}|$. However, their definition of "perfect" is different from the definition of [3]. For their definition of "perfect", no lower bound on $|\hat{V}_i|$ was known. Actually, their definition is located between perfect and weakly perfect. Then, from Theorem 16, we see that $|\hat{V}_i| \geq |\hat{S}|$ for their "perfect". Thus, Theorem 16 justifies the argument of [5].

Lemma 17. *In a weakly perfect SS $(S, V_1, \ldots, V_n)$, suppose that $B = \{V_1, \ldots, V_i\} \in \Delta$. For $b \in \hat{B}$, let $U, W_{i+1}, \cdots, W_n$ be random variables such that*

$$\begin{aligned} &\Pr(U = s, W_{i+1} = v_{i+1}, \ldots, W_n = v_n) \\ &= \Pr(S = s, V_{i+1} = v_{i+1}, \ldots, V = v_n | B = b) \ . \end{aligned}$$

Suppose that W_j is independent in a weakly perfect SS $(U, W_{i+1}, \ldots, W_n)$ for $\forall b \in B$. Let $C = B \cup \{V_j\}$. Then $|\hat{C}| \geq |\hat{B}||\hat{S}|$.

Proof. Clear from Theorem 16. □

Theorem 18. *In a weakly perfect SS, suppose that $\{V_i\} \in \Delta$, $|\hat{V}_i| = |\hat{S}|$, $A \in \Gamma$ and there exists $A_i \subseteq A$ such that $A_i \cup \{V_i\} \in \Gamma_m$ for $i = 1, 2, \ldots, l$. Let $D \triangleq \{S, V_1, \ldots, V_l\}$. Then, $|\hat{A}| \geq |\hat{D}|$.*

Proof. We show an injection h from $\hat{D}$ to $\hat{A}$. For $\forall d = (s, v_1, \ldots, v_l) \in \hat{D}$, let

$$X_d \triangleq \{a | \Pr(A = a, D = d) > 0\} \ .$$

$|X_d| \geq 1$ since $\Pr(D = d) > 0$. Pick $a \in X_d$ arbitrarily and define $h(d) = a$. Suppose that $h(d_1) = h(d_2) = a$. Let $d_1 = (s_1, v_{11}, \ldots, v_{l1})$, $d_2 = (s_2, v_{12}, \ldots, v_{l2})$. Then, from the definition of X_d,

$$\begin{aligned} &\Pr(S = s_1, V_1 = v_{11}, \cdots, V_l = v_{l1}, A = a) > 0 \ , &(6) \\ &\Pr(S = s_2, V_1 = v_{12}, \cdots, V_l = v_{l2}, A = a) > 0 \ . \end{aligned}$$

From eq.(6), we have

$$\Pr(S = s_1 | A = a) > 0 \ .$$

Since $A \in \Gamma$,

$$\Pr(S = s_1 | A = a) = 1 \ .$$

Similarly, $\Pr(S = s_2 | A = a) = 1$. Therefore $s_1 = s_2$. Suppose that $A_i = a_i$ if $A = a$. Then, from eq.(6)

$$\Pr(S = s_1, V_i = v_{i1}, A_i = a_i) > 0$$

for $i = 1, 2, \ldots, l$. Since $\{V_i\} \cup A_i \in \Gamma_m$, it must be that

$$\Pr(S = s_1 | V_i = v_{i1}, A_i = a_i) = 1 \ .$$

Similarly, we have $\Pr(S = s_2 | V_i = v_{i2}, A_i = a_i) = 1$. Then, from Lemma 14, $v_{i1} = v_{i2}$ $(1 \leq i \leq l)$ because $s_1 = s_2$. Thus, $d_1 = d_2$. Therefore, h is an injection from $\hat{D}$ to $\hat{A}$. Hence, $|\hat{A}| \geq |\hat{D}|$. □

Lemma 19. *Consider a weakly perfect SS* (S, V_1, V_2, V_3, V_4) *such that* $\Gamma_m = \{\{V_1, V_2\}, \{V_2, V_3\}, \{V_3, V_4\}\}$. *Define* $Z \triangleq \{S, V_1, V_4\}$. *If* $|\hat{V}_1| = |\hat{V}_4| = |\hat{S}|$, *then* $|\hat{Z}| = |\hat{S}|^3$.

Proof. For $\forall v_1 \in \hat{V}_1$, let U, W_2, W_3, W_4 be random variables such that

$$\begin{aligned} &\Pr(U = s, W_2 = v_2, W_3 = v_3, W_4 = v_4) \\ &= \Pr(S = s, V_2 = v_2, V_3 = v_3, V_4 = v_4 | V_1 = v_1) \ . \end{aligned}$$

From Lemma 12, we have

1. $\hat{U} = \hat{S}$.
2. (U, W_2, W_3, W_4) is a weakly perfect SS.

Let Γ_1 be the minimal access structure of (U, W_2, W_3, W_4). Then, $\Gamma_1 = \{\{W_2\}, \{W_3, W_4\}\}$. Thus, W_4 is independent. Let $E \triangleq \{V_1, V_4\}$. Then, from Lemma 17, $|\hat{E}| \geq |\hat{V}_1||\hat{S}| = |\hat{S}|^2$. Clearly, $|\hat{E}| \leq |\hat{V}_1||\hat{V}_4| = |\hat{S}|^2$. Hence, $|\hat{E}| = |\hat{S}|^2$. Now, from Lemma 15, $|\hat{Z}| = |\hat{E}||\hat{S}| = |\hat{S}|^3$. □

Theorem 20. *In a weakly perfect SS such that* $\Gamma_m = \{\{V_1, V_2\}, \{V_2, V_3\}, \{V_3, V_4\}\}$,

$$|\hat{V}_2||\hat{V}_3| \geq |\hat{S}|^3$$

if $|\hat{V}_1| = |\hat{V}_4| = |\hat{S}|$.

Proof. In Theorem 18, let $A = \{V_2, V_3\}$ and $D = \{S, V_1, V_4\}$. Then the assumption of Theorem 18 is satisfied. Now

$$\begin{aligned} |\hat{A}| &\geq |\hat{D}| \quad \text{(from Theorem 18)} \\ &= |\hat{S}|^3 \quad \text{(from Lemma 19)} \ . \end{aligned}$$

It is clear that $|\hat{V}_2||\hat{V}_3| \geq |\hat{A}|$. Therefore, $|\hat{V}_2||\hat{V}_3| \geq |\hat{S}|^3$. □

6 Extension

In this section, we consider a case such that user $1, \ldots, l$ have small memories and user $l+1, \ldots, n$ have large memories. We show a lower bound of $|\hat{V}_{l+i}|$ under the condition that $|\hat{V}_1| = \cdots = |\hat{V}_l| = |\hat{S}|$ for some Γ_m. It will be easy to extend our technique to find such a lower bound for other Γ_m.

Lemma 21. *Suppose that $(S, V_1, \ldots, V_n)$ is a weakly perfect (n,k)-threshold scheme. Let $G_i \triangleq \{V_1, \ldots, V_i\}$. Then, $|\hat{G}_i| \geq |\hat{S}|^i$ if $1 \leq i \leq k$.*

Proof. $|\hat{G}_1| \geq |\hat{S}|$ from Theorem 16. Suppose that $|\hat{G}_i| \geq |\hat{S}|^i$ for $1 \leq i < k$. Note that $G_i \in \Delta$. For $\forall g \in \hat{G}_i$, let $U, W_{i+1}, \ldots, W_n$ be random variables such that

$$\begin{aligned} &\Pr(U = s, W_{i+1} = v_{i+1}, \ldots, W_n = v_n) \\ &= \Pr(S = s, V_{i+1} = v_{i+1}, \ldots, V_n = v_n | G_i = g) \; . \end{aligned}$$

Then $\{W_{i+1}, \ldots, W_k\}$ is an minimal access set in a weakly perfect SS $(U, W_{i+1}, \ldots, W_n)$, clearly. Thus, W_{i+1} is independent. Now, from Lemma 17,

$$|\hat{G}_{i+1}| \geq |\hat{G}_i||\hat{S}| \geq |\hat{S}|^{i+1} \; .$$

□

Theorem 22. *Suppose that $(S, V_1, \ldots, V_n)$ is a weakly perfect SS such that $\Gamma_m = \{H | H \subseteq \{V_1, \ldots, V_{n-1}\}, |H| = k\} \cup \{(V_n, V_i) | 1 \leq i \leq n-1\}$ and $|\hat{V}_1| = \cdots = |\hat{V}_{k-1}| = |\hat{S}|$. Then, $|\hat{V}_n||\hat{V}_{n-1}| \geq |\hat{S}|^k$.*

Proof. In Theorem 18, let $A = \{V_n, V_{n-1}\}, D = \{S, V_1, \ldots, V_{k-1}\}$. Then, the assumption of Theorem 18 is satisfied. Now,

$$\begin{aligned} |\hat{V}_n||\hat{V}_{n-1}| \geq |\hat{A}| \geq |\hat{D}| & \qquad \text{(from Theorem 18)} \\ = |\hat{S}|^{k-1}|\hat{S}| & \qquad \text{(from Lemma 21 and Lemma 15)} \\ = |\hat{S}|^k \; . & \end{aligned}$$

□

We show a scheme which meets the bound of Theorem 22. Let $p(x)$ be a random polynomial of order $k-1$ over $GF(q)$ such that $p(0) = s$. Let $v_i = p(i)$ for $1 \leq i \leq n-1$ and $v_n = \{p(n), \ldots, p(n+k-2)\}$. Then, this is a perfect SS which satisfies the condition of Theorem 22 and $|\hat{V}_n| = |\hat{S}|^{k-1}$.

Theorem 23. *In a weakly perfect SS such that $\Gamma_m = \{\{V_1, V_2\}, \{V_2, V_3\}, \{V_1, V_3, V_4\}\}$, $|\hat{V}_2||\hat{V}_3| \geq |\hat{S}|^3$ if $|\hat{V}_1| = |\hat{V}_4| = |\hat{S}|$, or $|\hat{V}_1||\hat{V}_2| \geq |\hat{S}|^3$ if $|\hat{V}_3| = |\hat{V}_4| = |\hat{S}|$.*

The proof will be given in the final paper.

References

1. G.R.Blakley : Safeguarding cryptographic keys. Proc. of the AFIPS 1979 National Computer Conference, vol.48, pp.313-317 (1979)
2. A.Shamir : How to share a secret. Communications of the ACM, 22, (11), pp.612-613 (1979)

3. R.M.Capocelli, A.De Santis, L.Gargano, U.Vaccaro : On the size of shares for secret sharing schemes. Crypto'91, pp.101-113 (1991)
4. E.D.Karnin, J.W.Green, M.E.Hellman : On secret sharing systems. IEEE Trans. IT-29, No.1, pp.35-41 (1982)
5. E.F.Brickell, D.M.Davenport : On the classification of ideal secret sharing schemes. Journal of Cryptology, vol.4, No.2, pp.123-134 (1991)
6. E.F.Brickell, D.R.Stinson : Some improved bounds on the information rate of perfect secret sharing schemes. Journal of Cryptology, vol.5, No.3, pp.153-166 (1992)
7. C.Blund, A.De Santis, D.R.Stinson, U.Vaccaro : Graph decomposition and secret sharing schemes. Eurocrypt'92, pp.1-20 (1992)
8. Y.Frankel, Y.Desmedt : Classification of ideal homomorphic threshold schemes over finite Abelian groups. Eurocrypt'92, pp.21-29 (1992)
9. C.Blund, A.De Santis, L.Gargano, U.Vaccaro : On the information rate of secret sharing schemes. Crypto'92 (1992)
10. D.R.Stinson : New general bounds on the information rate of secret sharing schemes. Crypto'92 (1992)

SESSION 2

STREAM CIPHERS

Chair: Eli Biham

(Technion, Israel)

A Correlation Attack on the Binary Sequence Generators with Time-Varying Output Function

Miodrag J. Mihaljević *

Institute of Applied Mathematics and Electronics,
Institute of Mathematics, Academy of Arts and Sciences,
Belgrade, Yugoslavia

Abstract. A binary sequence generator (BSG) consisting of three regularly clocked linear feedback shift registers combined by a time-varying memoryless function is cryptanalysed. A novel distance measure for the binary sequences comparison relevant for the crypanalysis is proposed, its main characteristics are derived, and the divide and conquer correlation attack based on this distance is presented. It is pointed out that the novel distance based approach to cryptanalysis could be applied for attacking the binary MacLaren-Marsaglia shuffler, for signficant improvement of the correlation attack on the multiplexer BSG, and for attacking a wide class of BSG's in which the output binary sequence is a time-varying function of certain subgenerator output binary sequence.

Key words and phrases: Binary sequence generators, MacLaren-Marsaglia shuffler, Cryptanalysis, Correlation attack, Distance measures.

1 Introduction

A number of shift registers based binary sequence generators (BSG's) is proposed and considered in the literature. Shift registers can have linear or nonlinear feedback, can be clocked regularly or irregularly, and can be combined by a time independent or dependent memoryless functions or functions with memory. Some of the generators are analyzed from the cryptanalytic point of view. The problem is to find out the conditions under which it is possible to reconstruct the initial contents of indvidual shift registers knowing a segment of the keystream sequence, based on the correlation/statistical dependence between the keystream sequence and a set of the shift register sequences.

For example, when the shift registers are combined by time independent memoryless function some important cryptanalytic results are given in [1], [2], [3], [4], when the shift registers are clocked regularly, and in [5], when the shift regsters are clocked irregularly. A comprehensive survey of the relevant results published in the literature related to crptanalysis of shift register based BSG's

* Mailing Address: Šolina 4, 11040 Belgrade, Yugoslavia.

with regularly and irregularly clocked shift registers combined by time-constant memoryless or functions with memory is presented in [6].

On the other hand, a well known method for combining shift registers by a memoryless time-varying function is the MacLaren-Marsaglia shuffler [7], [8], and more generally, the MacLaren-Marsaglia algorithm [7], [9], [10], is a somewhat more complex method of combining two pseudo-random number generators. One pseudo-random generator is used to produce the values for the final keystream sequence, but the values are first saved in a table. The second generator is used to produce pointers into the table. At each cycle, the pointer generator produces a new pointer into table, and the value at that location is output. Then the value generator produces a new value, which is inserted into the table, replacing the value that was just removed. The random delaying of the values in the table has the effect of shuffling the sequence elements. When the table values are elements of an large alphabet a cryptanalysis of the MacLaren-Marsaglia generator based on the divide and conquer principle is presented in [11]. The procedure is summarized by the following: for each possible key of the value generator, generate a portion of the value sequence sufficient to find the nearest match for each value in the known keystream sequence; calculate the average of the delay between each of these numbers in the value sequence and the keystream sequence; if the average of these calculated delays is less than a threshold, then the key is very likely to be correct; in that case, begin searching for the key to the pointer generator; for each possible pointer key, generate a sequence of pointers; the difference in time between a given pointer and the next occurrence of the same pointer is the length of time that some value must stay in the table; by comparing the known value in the previously determined value sequence with the value at this delay in the keystream sequence, each delay can be verified; in this way, if the key to the value generator was correct, the key to the pointer generator can be found; if not, the key to the value generator was incorrect, and we have to continue searching; naturally the threshold should be chosen in such a way as to minimize the number of false alarms, while ensuring that the correct key is not missed. But it is, also, pointed out in [11] that the method of attack will fail if a large table is used to store relatively small values, so that, for example it would not work against a large table of single bits, and it is noted in [8] that the attack requires that the range of values to be shuffled be comparable in size with the table size.

In this paper a cryptanalytical approach will be proposed which can be also used for cryptanalysis of the binary MacLaren-Marsaglia shuffler in which the value subgenerator output is a binary sequence.

The main objective of this paper is cryptanalysis of a BSG presented in [12] which is an extension of similar structures from [13] (the BSG consisting of two LFSR's and a variable memory), [7], [10]. This generator consists of three regularly clocked linear feedback shift registers (LFSR's) combined by a time-varying memoryless function. Some characteristics of this generator are presented in [12] and [14], where minimal linear complexity of the generator output sequence and the number of different output sequences, respectively, are analyzed. Recently, a cryptographic weakness of the BSG [12] is presented in [15]. The substance of this weakness is the correlation existing between the output sequence of the generator and the sequence used to load the memory, that is the correlation between the output of the time-varying memoryless function and its input in the previous clock. Accordingly, the corresponding cryptanalytic attack could be considered as an equivalent to the Hamming distance correlation attack [1] on the well-known BSG with two LFSR's and the multiplexer, [16]. In this paper, a different and more efficient approach to the cryptanalysis of the BSG [12] is proposed.

Also, in this paper, for BSG with two LFSR's and a multiplexer [16], a modified cryptanalytic attack is proposed, and its advantage over the standard divide and conquer correlation attack [1] is shown.

Finally, it is pointed out that the cryptanalytic procedure proposed for the BSG [12] could be applied to a wide class of binary sequences generators in which the output sequence is read out from a time-varying memory loaded by a certain subgenerator.

In Section 2, a novel distance measure relevant for the correlation attack is proposed and its main characteristics are derived. A cryptanalysis of the BSG [12] is presented in Section 3, and a modified attack on the multiplexer BSG is considered in Section 4. Conclusions are given in Section 5.

2 Preliminaries

In this section a novel distance measure relevant for the considered cryptanalytical problems is proposed and its main characteristics are derived.

As the first, a general classification problem relevant for the considered cryptanalysis is stated. Suppose that $\{a_n\}_{n=1}^{L+N}$ and $\{b_n\}_{n=1}^{N}$, $L>0$, $N>L$, are two arbitrary binary sequences. The problem is acceptance one of the following two hypothesis.

H_0: $\{a_n\}$ and $\{b_n\}$ are generated by the mutually independent truly random binary sources.

H_1: $\{b_n\}$ is generated based on $\{a_n\}$ according to the following:

- *with probability* p

$$b_n = a_{n+L-\ell} \ \ for\ some\ \ell=\ell(n)\ ,\ \ell\in\{1,2,...,L\}, \tag{1}$$

- *with probability* $1-p$

$$b_n = a_i \ \ for\ some\ i=i(n)\ ,\ i<n, \tag{2}$$

where $n=1,2,...,N$, and $0<p\leq 1$.

Obviously, for acceptance of H_0 or H_1 we have to measure the similarity (dissimilarity) between the binary sequences $\{a_n\}_{n=1}^{L+N}$ and $\{b_n\}_{n=1}^{N}$. This problem could be solved employing the sequence comparison concept. Recall that in many situations there is a natural correspondence between the elements in one sequence and those in the other and the only sensible comparison is between corresponding elements. Sequence comparison deals with the complex comparisons that arise when the correspondence between sequences elements is not known in advance. A review of the sequence comparison techniques and applications is presented in [17]. Finally, note that any sequence comparison approach is based on some measure of similarity/dissimilarity or distance measure.

2.1 A Novel Distance Measure

Suppose that a distance measure d between two binary sequences is an outcome of a stochastic variable D with two probability distributions $\{Pr(D \mid H_0)\}$ and $\{Pr(D \mid H_1)\}$. According to [17] one of the widely used distances for the sequence comparison is the Levenshtein distance (LD) [18]. Let the edit operations that transform one sequence into another be substitution, deletion, and insertion. Then the LD between two sequences is defined as the minimum number of edit operations required to transform one sequence into another.

For the acceptance of H_0 or H_1 based on d we have to know relevant characteristics of $\{Pr(D \mid H_0)\}$ and $\{Pr(D \mid H_1)\}$. One approach is experimental estimation of the distributions relevant characteristics, and the other is analytical approach, for example. An open problem related to the LD is that only few weak analytical results are known about the expected value of $D^{(LD)}$ when H_0 is valid and no one analytical result is known for the case when H_1 is valid. A similar situation is with other standard distance measures.

So, for some applications more convenient distance measures are desirable.

In this subsection, a novel distance measure is proposed, relevant for the H_0 / H_1 decision problem, which ensures analytical derivation of the expected values and variances for the corresponding stochastic variable when H_0 and H_1 are valid. The distance measures the similarity (correlation) by counting the nonaccidental and accidental coincidences in the way appropriate to the relationship between $\{a_n\}$ and $\{b_n\}$ when the hypothesis H_1 is valid.

Definition 1. A novel distance measure d^* between two arbitrary binary sequences $\{a_n\}_{n=1}^{L+N}$ and $\{b_n\}_{n=1}^{N}$ is defined by the following:

$$d^* = \sum_{n=1}^{N} \sum_{\ell=1}^{L} (b_n \oplus a_{n+L-\ell}) \ . \tag{3}$$

Obviously, $0 \leq d^* \leq NL$.

Note that a set of distances d^* for different pairs $(\{a_n\}, \{b_n\})$ could be considered as the set of realizations of a stochastic integer variable D^*.

2.2 Main Characteristics of the Novel Distance Measure

Let the binary sequences $\{a_n\}$ and $\{b_n\}$ are realizations of sequences of binary stochastic variables $\{A_n\}$ and $\{B_n\}$, respectively.

Assuming that a hypothesis H is valid, denote by m_H and σ_H^2 the expected value and variance of the variable D^*, and let $E_H\{\cdot\}$ denotes the expected value operator.

$$m_H = E_H\{D^*\} = \sum_{n=1}^{N}\sum_{\ell=1}^{L} Pr(B_n \oplus A_{n+L-\ell} = 1) \tag{4}$$

$$\sigma_H^2 = E_H\{(D^*)^2\} - (E_H\{D^*\})^2 \tag{5}$$

$$E_H\{(D^*)^2\} = \sum_{n=1}^{N}\sum_{\ell=1}^{L}\sum_{i=1}^{N}\sum_{j=1}^{L} Pr(B_n \oplus A_{n+L-\ell} = 1)\cdot$$

$$\cdot\, Pr(B_i \oplus A_{i+L-j} = 1 \mid B_n \oplus A_{n+L-\ell} = 1) \tag{6}$$

Accordingly, we can show that the following theorems hold.

Assuming that the sequences $\{a_n\}_{n=1}^{L+N}$ and $\{b_n\}_{n=1}^{N}$ are realizations of the mutually independent binary truly random variables, the main statistical characteristics of the distance d^* are stated by the following theorem.

Theorem 1. When the hypothesis H_0 is valid the expected value m_{H_0} and variance $\sigma_{H_0}^2$ of the variable D^* are given by the following:

$$m_{H_0} = 0.5NL\ , \quad \sigma_{H_0}^2 = 0.25NL\ . \tag{7}$$

When the sequence $\{b_n\}_{n=1}^{N}$ is produced from the sequence $\{a_n\}_{n=1}^{L+N}$ assuming the generating model underlying the hypothesis H_1, the main statistical characteristics of the distance d^* are stated by the following theorem.

Theorem 2. When the hypothesis H_1 is valid the expected value m_{H_1}, and with probability arbitrarily close to 1 an upper bound on the variance $\sigma_{H_1}^2$ of the variable D^* are given by the following:

$$m_{H_1} = 0.5N(L-p)\ , \tag{8}$$

$$\sigma_{H_1}^2 \le c\, 0.25\, NL\ , \tag{9}$$

where c is a constant, $c << L$, and sufficiently large N is assumed.

Note that experimental results show that, for a large range of the parameters values, $c = 3$ can be used.

A quantitative illustration of the results given by the Theorems 1 and 2 is presented by the selfexplained Tables 1 and 2.

Continuing analysis of the novel distance measure we consider a separability measure between $\{Pr(D^* \mid H_0)\}$ and $\{Pr(D^* \mid H_1\}$, a probability of error related to the H_0 / H_1 acceptance based on the distance d^*, and the critical value of N, $N >> L$, which, with high probability, ensures acceptance of the correct hypothesis.

A standard measure of separability of the posterior probability distributions is the Mahalanobis separability measure (see, [19], p.38, for example). In here considered case, the Mahalanobis measure Δ_{D^*} is given by the following

$$\Delta_{D^*} = \frac{(m_{H_0} - m_{H_1})^2}{\sigma_{H_0}^2 + \sigma_{H_1}^2}\ . \tag{10}$$

Table 1. Typical examples, by the Theorem 2 calculated, and experimentally estimated values of m_{H_1} and σ_{H_1}, when $L = 8$ and $c = 3$.

N	p	m_{H_1} *theoretical value*	m_{H_1} *experimental estimation*	σ_{H_1} *theoretical upper bound*	σ_{H_1} *experimental estimation*
1000	1.	3500.	3499.8	77.46	62.3
10000	1.	35000.	35011.5	244.95	193.7
1000	0.75	3625.	3624.3	77.46	63.5
10000	0.75	36250.	36261.2	244.95	197.4

Table 2. Typical examples, by the Theorems 1 and 2 calculated, and experimentally estimated values of the differences $m_{H_0} - m_{H_1}$, when $L = 8$.

N	p	$m_{H_0} - m_{H_1}$ *theoretical value*	$m_{H_0} - m_{H_1}$ *experimental estimation*
1000	1.	500.	502.4
10000	1.	5000.	4985.3
1000	0.75	375.	372.6
10000	0.75	3750.	3730.1

According to (10) and the Theorem 1 - 2 we can show that the following lemma is valid.

Lemma 1. Δ_{D^*} is, with probability arbitrarily close to 1, lower bounded by $\frac{Np^2}{(c+1)L}$ assuming sufficiently large N and $N > L$, $c << L$.

On the other hand, the Mahalanobis measure yields the following upper bound on the Bayes probability of error P_e related to the H_0 / H_1 decision (see [19], pp. 56-57, for example):

$$P_e \leq \frac{2P_0P_1}{1 + P_0P_1\Delta_{D^*}}, \tag{11}$$

where P_0 and P_1 are the prior probabilities of H_0 and H_1, respectively.

According to (11) and the Lemma 1 we can show that the following lemma is valid.

Lemma 2. $P_e \leq \frac{2(c+1)L}{Np^2}$ with probability arbitrarily close to 1, assuming sufficiently large N and $N > L$, $[Np^2/(c+1)L]P_0P_1 >> 1$, $c << L$.

According to Lemma 2, when $p = 1$ we have the error free H_0 / H_1 decision based on d^* when N tends to ∞.

Finally, note that the critical value of N, which ensures the correct hypothesis acceptance with small decision error, could be estimated employing an approach similar to that applied for the equivalent problem in [1]. Estimation of the critical value of N is based, following [1], on the assumption that D^* is normally distributed, due to the central limit theorem, with the expected values and variances given by the Theorems 1 and 2.

3 Cryptanalysis of a Varying Memory BSG

In this section, as the first the BSG from [12] is described and the assumptions for cryptanalysis are given. Then, a novel algorithm for the cryptanalysis is proposed. Also, it is pointed out that this algorithm can be used for attacking the MacLaren-Marsaglia binary shuffler.

The considered generator consists of three binary linear feedback shift registers, $LFSR_i$, $i = 1,2,3$, and a binary memory. The length of $LFSR_i$ is ℓ_i, $i = 1,2,3$, and the memory dimension is 2^k. All the LFSR's have primitive characteristic polynomials, nonnull initial states, and they are clocked by the same clock. The read and write address for the memory are the binary k-tuples taken from any k stages of $LFSR_2$ and $LFSR_3$, respectively, whereas the binary output of $LFSR_1$ is used to load the memory. At any clock, $n = 1,2,...$, the following two operations are carried out. First, the generator output bit b_n is read out of the memory location addressed by the k-bit read address given by $LFSR_2$. Second, the $LFSR_1$ output bit a_{n+L} is written into the memory location addressed by the write address given by $LFSR_3$. Note that described BSG realizes a time-varying nonlinear function of the phase shifts of a maximum-length sequence.

According to the generator description it is directly evident that the output sequence $\{b_n\}$ depends of the variable memory initial state, especially at the begining of $\{b_n\}$. The following lemma shows that for sufficiently great n the influence of initial memory content becomes negligible.

Lemma 3. The probability p_0 that the content of an arbitrary location of the variable memory is not touched in the writing phase during N_0 succesive clocks is given by

$$p_0 = (1 - 2^{-k})^{N_0} \ . \tag{12}$$

The lemma implies that with probability arbitralily close to 1, assuming sufficiently large N_0, the output generator sequence elements b_n , $n = N_0 + 1, N_0 + 2, ..., N$, are independent of the variable memory initial content.

The following lemma describes a relationship between the $LFSR_1$ output sequence and the generator output sequence.

Lemma 4. The probability p that the $n-th$ generator output bit is equal to a $LFSR_1$ output bit with index from the set $\{n, n+1, ..., n+L-1\}$, assuming that $n >> 1$, is given by:

$$p = 1 - (1 - 2^{-k})^L . \tag{13}$$

Secret key determines the initial states of $LFSR_i$, $i = 1, 2, 3$. The memory initial content is arbitrary. We assume that the following conditions relevant for the cryptanalysis are valid: $\ell_1 > \ell_2 + \ell_3$, 2^{ℓ_1} hypothesis can be checked in the given time, and a segment $\{b_n\}_{n=N_0+1}^{N_0+N}$ of the BSG output sequence is available.

3.1 Algorithm for the Cryptanalysis

A main phase of the algorithm is reconstruction of the $LFSR_1$ initial state, that is a part of the secret key. This reconstruction employs a correlation attack based on the novel distance measure proposed in Section 2. Given an observed segment $\{b_n\}_{n=1}^{N_0+N}$ of the generator output sequence, the optimal decision strategy (yielding the mimimum probability of error) is to decide on the initial state with maximum posterior probability. Let $\{\tilde{a}_n\}$ be an $LFSR_1$ sequence corresponding to an initial state $\tilde{A}_0$. Then two hypothetical cases are possible:
- the observed sequence $\{b_n\}_{n=N_0+1}^{N_0+N}$ *is not* produced by $\tilde{A}_0$;
- the observed sequence $\{b_n\}_{n=N_0+1}^{N_0+N}$ *is* produced by $\tilde{A}_0$.

Note that, assuming p and L given by the Lemma 4, the hypothesis H_0 and H_1 considered in Section 2 are equivalent with the given two hypothetical cases, so that the proposed distance d^* could be appropriate for the H_0/H_1 decision. The acceptance of H_0 or H_1 is based on the value of d^* and the relevant threshold t^*. Following the results from [1], and due to the central limit theorem the variable D^* can be assumed to be normally distributed with the expected values and variances given by the Theorems 1 and 2. So, the threshold t^* could be determined using a standard procedure (see, [1], for example) assuming that the *probability of the missing event* P_m is chosen close to zero (for example 10^{-3}), and the *probability of the false alarm* P_f is as small as possible for given N (when $P_f = 2^{-\ell_1}$ the expected number of false alarms is equal 1). Also, using the approach from [1] we can calculate the critical value of N such that P_m and P_f have desired values. Finally, based on the previous and the experiments, note that approximate value of the threshold t^* can be calculated according to the following formula:

$$t^* = m_{H_1} + 3\sqrt{3\,0.25\,NL} \ , \tag{14}$$

where m_{H_1} is determined by the Theorem 2.

Accordingly, the $LFSR_1$ initial state reconstruction goes through the following steps for every possible initial state $\tilde{A}_0$:
- generate $\{\tilde{a}_n\}$,
- calculate the distance d^* between $\{\tilde{a}_n\}$ and $\{b_n\}$,
- using the threshold t^* accept H_0 and H_1.

The whole cryptanalytic algorithm consists of the following three phases: initialization, $LFSR_1$ initial state reconstruction, and joint reconstruction of the $LFSR_2$ and $LFSR_3$ initial states.

So, the algorithm for cryptanalysis of the varying memory BSG [12], which is an implementation of the general divide and conquer attack based on the novel distance d^*, is given by the following.

Algorithm for Cryptanalysis of the Varying Memory BSG

Input: $\{b_n\}_{n=1}^{N_{max}}$, and the $LFSR_i$, $i = 1,2,3$, characteristics polynomials.

Phase I - Initialization

Based on the Lemma 3 and Lemma 4, for given p_0 and p, calculate N_0 and L, respectively. Set $N = N_{max} - N_0$. For given N, p, L, and adopted P_m, employing the Theorems 1 - 2, and the standard procedure determine the threshold t^*.

Phase II - Reconstruction of the secret key part corresponding to $LFSR_1$

For every possible $LFSR_1$ initial state repeat the following *Step 1 - Step 3*.

Step 1: Assume a new initial state $\tilde{A}_0$ for the $LFSR_1$ different from those previously considered and generate the corresponding sequence $\{\tilde{a}_n\}_{n=1}^{N_0+L+N}$.

Step 2: Calculate the distance d^* between $\{\tilde{a}_n\}_{n=N_0+1}^{N_0+L+N}$ and $\{b_n\}_{n=N_0+1}^{N_0+N}$.

Step 3: If $d^* < t^*$ preserve the current $LFSR_1$ initial state $\tilde{A}_0$ as possible candidate for the solution.

Phase III - Reconstruction of the whole secret key

For every possible combination of $LFSR_2$ and $LFSR_3$ initial states, and the $LFSR_1$ initial states preserved in the *Step 3* repeat the following *Step 4* and *Step 5*.

Step 4: Assume a new initial states combination for $LFSR_i$, $i = 1,2,3$, different from those previously considered, and generate the corresponding output sequence $\{\tilde{b}_n\}_{n=N_0+1}^{N_0+N}$.

Step 5: If $\tilde{b}_n = b_n$ for $n = N_0+1, N_0+2, ..., N_0+N$, stop the procedure and addopt the current combination of the inital states as the secret key solution.

Output: The secret key solution or the decision that the secret key solution was missed in the *Phase II* because of non-null value of P_m.

Note that a similar one, to the proposed algorithm for cryptanalysis, can be used for attacking the MacLaren-Marsaglia binary shuffler assuming that the $LFSR_1$ plays role of the "value subgenerator", while $LFSR_2$ and $LFSR_3$ play role of the "pointer subgenerator". The previous conclusion directly yields from the fact that the MacLaren-Marsaglia binary shuffler is, looking from the cryptanalyst point of view, a simplified version of the variable memory BSG in which the read and write addresses are identical.

4 Cryptanalysis of a Multiplexer BSG

A BSG consisting of two regularly clocked LFSR's and a multiplexer was presented and analyzed in [16]. The 2^k multiplexer inputs are taken from any 2^k different stages of $LFSR_1$. The output of the multiplexer is output of the BSG. At any clock, the $k-bit$ multiplexer address is taken from $LFSR_2$ and the corresponding multiplexer input is proceeded to its output. The length of $LFSR_i$ is ℓ_i, $i = 1,2$. For simplicity we assme that $\ell_1 = 2^k$. Denote by $\{a_n\}$ the $LFSR_1$ output binary sequence, and by $\{b_n\}$ the output binary sequence from BSG. The secret key determines the initial states of $LFSR_1$ and $LFSR_2$. We assume that: $2^{\ell_1} + 2^{\ell_2}$ hypothesis can be checked in the given time, and a segment $\{b_n\}_{n=1}^N$ of the BSG output sequence is available.

Let d be a distance measure between two arbitrary binary sequences $\{a_n\}$ and $\{b_n\}$ such that a relevant threshold t can be determined which enables discrimination between the following two cases:
H_0: $\{a_n\}$ and $\{b_n\}$ are mutually independent random binary sequences,
$\hat{H}_1$: $\{b_n\}$ is the BSG output when $\{a_n\}$ is the $LFSR_1$ output.

Obviously, the threshold t is a function of the relevant posterior probability distributions and adopted value of the *missing event probability* P_m.

Note that $\hat{H}_1$ is equivalent with H_1 when $p = 1$ and $L = 2^k$.

Assuming that d is a realization of a variable D the previous two cases yield the following two probability distributions: $\{Pr(D \mid H_0)\}$ and $\Pr(D \mid \hat{H}_1)\}$. It is well known that the separability of these distributions determines the performances of the algorithm for cryptanalysis.

Accordingly, in this section we consider the following algorithm for the multiplexer BSG cryptanalysis which follows the same ideas as the algorithm for cryptanalysis of the variable-memory BSG.

Algorithm for Cryptanalysis of the Multiplexer BSG

Input: $\{b_n\}_{n=1}^N$, and the $LFSR_i$, $i = 1,2$, characteristics polynomials.

Phase I - Initialization

For given N and addopted P_m determine the threshold t.

Phase II - Reconstruction of the secret key part corresponding to $LFSR_1$

For every possible $LFSR_1$ initial state repeat the following *Step 1 - Step 3*.

Step 1: Assume a new initial state for the $LFSR_1$ different from those previously considered and generate the corresponding sequence $\{\tilde{a}_n\}_{n=1}^{\ell_1+N}$.
Step 2: Calculate the distance d between $\{\tilde{a}_n\}_{n=1}^{\ell_1+N}$ and $\{b_n\}_{n=1}^N$.
Step 3: If $d < t$ preserve the current $LFSR_1$ initial state as possible candidate for the solution.

Phase III - Reconstruction of the whole secret key

For every possible combination of $LFSR_2$ initial states and the $LFSR_1$ initial states preserved in the *Step 3* repeat the following *Step 4* and *Step 5*.

Step 4: Assume a new initial states combination for $LFSR_i$, $i = 1,2$, differ-

ent from those previously considered, and generate the corresponding output sequence $\{\tilde{b}_n\}_{n=1}^N$.
Step 5: If $\tilde{b}_n = b_n$ for $n = 1, 2, ..., N$, stop the procedure and addopt the current combination of the inital states as the secret key solution.

Output: The secret key solution or the decissin that the secret key solution was missed in the *Phase II* because of non-null value of P_m.

When the distance d is a variant of the Hamming distance defined by the following:

$$d = \sum_{n=1}^{N} (b_n \oplus a_{n+\ell_1-s}) , \tag{15}$$

where s is a constant, $s \in \{1, 2, ..., \ell_1\}$, the algorithm for cryptanalysis is a variant of the standard divide and conquer correlation attack [1]. In this attack, the first phase is reconstruction of the $LFSR_1$ initial state, and the next is reconstruction of the $LFSR_2$ initial state. So, the attack employs $2^{\ell_1} + 2^{\ell_2}$ tests assuming appropriate value of N.

Another cryptanalytic attack on the multiplexer BSG based on the linear consistency tests is proposed in [20]. As the first phase, this attack assumes reconstruction of the $LFSR_2$ initial state so that the multiplexer BSG can be broken by no more than $2^{\ell_2+min[\ell_2,\lfloor log_2\ell_1\rfloor]}$ tests assumig that $N \geq \ell_2+\ell_1 2^{min[\ell_2,\lfloor log_2\ell_1\rfloor]}$. So, in a number of situations when $\ell_1 < \ell_2$ the divide and conquer attack [1] based on (15) is more efficient than the attack based on the linear consistency tests.

The main objective of this section is to propose employment of the distance d^*, defined in Section 2, and to show its advantage over d given by (15). So, the following discussion shows the advantage of d^* over d.

The distance d could be considered as a realization of a stochastic integer variable D. According to [1] it can be shown that the expected values and variances of D under H_0 and $\hat{H}_1$ are given by the following:

$$m_{H_0} = 0.5N \ , \ \ \sigma^2_{H_0} = 0.25N \ , \tag{16}$$

$$m_{\hat{H}_1} = 0.5N(1 - 2^{-k}) \ , \ \ \sigma^2_{\hat{H}_1} = 0.25N(1 - 2^{-k}) \ . \tag{17}$$

On the other hand, when $p = 1$ and $L = \ell_1 = 2^k$, the hypothesis H_1 is equivalent with $\hat{H}_1$, and Theorem 2 yields, assuming $c = 3$, the following expected value and the variance bound of D^* when $\hat{H}_1$ is valid

$$m_{\hat{H}_1} = 0.5N(2^k - 1) \ , \ \ \sigma^2_{\hat{H}_1} \leq 3 \cdot 0.25N2^k \ . \tag{18}$$

Denote by Δ_D and Δ_{D^*} the Mahalanobis separability measure between the relevant probability distributions when the distances d and d^* are considered, respectively.

Accordingly, we can directly prove the following lemma which implies a significant gain obtained by using d^* instead of d.

Lemma 5. For $2^k >> 1$ and assuming sufficiently large N, with probability arbitrarily close to 1,

$$\frac{\Delta_{D^*}}{\Delta_D} \geq 2^{k-1} . \tag{19}$$

The lemma shows that d^* enables better separability than d of relevant probability distributions for a factor greater than 2^{k-1}. A direct consequence of the Lemma 5 is that a shorter output sequence from the multiplexer BSG is needed for the cyptanalysis, or, assuming a fix length of the output sequence, the posterior uncertainty about the key (if exists) could be eliminated when d^* is used instead d. For example, if N is the required length when d is employed than the required length could be estimated as $N/2^{k-1}$ when d^* is employed, or if the number of false alarms is of the order 100 when d is employed this uncertainty could be eliminated by employment of d^*, assuming the same value of N and that $\ell_1 >> 1$.

Finally, recall that the attack on the BSG [12] which employes the weakness [15] could be considered as an equivalent to the standard correlation attack on the multiplexer BSG based on the distance d. So, according to the Lemma 5, it can be shown that the attack based on the novel distance d^* is more efficient than the attack proposed in [15] for a factor approximately equal to half of the variable memory dimension.

5 Conclusions

The main objective of this paper was the cryptanalysis of a binary sequence generator (BSG) consisting of three regularly clocked linear feedback shift registers combined by a time-varying memoryless function realized by the time-varying memory. A novel distance measure for the binary sequences comparison relevant for the crypanalysis is proposed, its main characteristics are derived, and the divide and conquer correlation attack based on this distance is presented. Note that the novel distance based approach to cryptanalysis could be applied for attacking the binary MacLaren-Marsaglia shuffler, for signficant improvement of the correlation attack on the multiplexer BSG, and for attacking a wide class of BSG's in which the output binary sequence is a time-varying function of certain subgenerator output binary sequence. The main limitation of the proposed attack is its underlying on the exaustive search for the secret-key parts. So, when the shift regsters lengths are large the procedure is not feasible. Also, the required length of the BSG output sequence is an increasing function of the time-varying memory dimension.

References

1. T. Siegenthaler, "Decrypting a class of stream ciphers using ciphertext only", *IEEE Trans. Comput.*, vol. 34, pp.81-85, Jan. 1985.

2. W. Meier and O. Staffelbach, "Fast correlation attacks on certain stream ciphers", *Journal of Cryptology,* vol. 1, pp. 159-176, 1989.
3. K.C. Zeng and M. Huang, "On the linear syndrome algorithm in cryptanalysis with applications", Advances in Cryptology - CRYPTO '88, *Lecture Notes in Computer Science*, vol. 403, pp. 469-478, 1990.
4. M.J. Mihaljević and J.Dj. Golić, "Convergence of a Bayesian iterative error-correction procedure on a noisy shift register sequence", Advances in Cryptology - EUROCRYPT '92, *Lecture Notes in Computer Science*, vol. 658, pp. 124-137, 1993.
5. J.Dj. Golić and M.J. Mihaljević, "A generalized correlation attack on a class of stream ciphers based on the Levenshtein distance", *Journal of Cryptology,* vol. 3, pp. 201-212, 1991.
6. J.Dj. Golić, "On the security of shift register based keystream generators", Fast Software Encryption, *Lecture Notes in Computer Science*, vol. 809, pp. 91-101, 1994.
7. M.D. MacLaren and G. Marsaglia, "Uniform random number generators", *Jour. Ass. Comput. Machnery,* vol. 12, pp. 93-89, 1968.
8. W.G. Chambers, "Clock-controlled shift registers in binary sequence generators", *IEE Proceedings, Pt. E,* vol. 135, pp. 17-23, 1988.
9. G. Marsaglia and T.A. Bray, "One-line random number generators and their use in combinations", *Comm. Ass. Comput. Machinery,* vol. 11, pp. 757-759, 1968.
10. D.E. Knuth, *The art of computer programming Vol.2: Seminumerical algorithms.* Reading, MA: Addison-Wesley, 1981.
11. C.T. Retter, "A key-search attack on MacLaren-Marsaglia system", *Cryptologia,* vol. 9, pp. 114-130, 1985.
12. J.Dj. Golić and M.J. Mihaljević, "Minimal linear equivalent analysis of a variable memory binary sequences generator", *IEEE Trans. Inform. Theory,* vol. 36, pp. 190-192, 1990.
13. P.R. Geffe, "How to protect data with ciphers that are really hard to break", *Electronics,* pp. 99-101, Jan. 1973.
14. J.Dj. Golić, "The number of output sequences of a binary sequence generator", Advances in Cryptology - EUROCRYPT '91, *Lecture Notes in Computer Science,* vol. 547, pp. 160-167, 1991.
15. R. Menicocci, "Intrinsic weakness of variable-memory keystream generators", *Electronics Letters,* vol. 30, No. 11, pp. 850-851, 1994.
16. S.M. Jennings, "Multiplexed sequences: Some properties of the minimum polynomial", Proc. Workshop on Cryptography, *Lecture Notes in Computer Science*, vol. 149, pp. 189-206, 1982.
17. D.Sankoff and J.B.Kruskal, *Time warps, string edits and macromolecules: The theory and practice of sequence comparison.* Reading, MA: Addison-Wesley, 1983.
18. A.Levenshtein, "Binary codes capable of correcting deletions, insertions, and reversals", *Sov. Phy. Dokl.,* vol. 10, pp. 707-710, 1966.
19. P.A. Devijver and J. Kittler, *Pattern recognition: A statistical approach.* London: Prentice Hall, 1982.
20. K.C. Zeng, C.H. Yang, and T.R.N. Rao, "On the linear consistency test (LCT) in cryptanalysis and its applications", Advances in Cryptology - CRYPTO '90, *Lecture Notes in Computer Science*, vol. 537, pp. 34-47, 1991.

On the Linear Complexity of Nonlinearly Filtered PN-sequences

Amparo Fúster-Sabater* and Pino Caballero-Gil**

* Laboratory of Cryptography, Institute of Electronics of Communications (CSIC), Serrano 144, 28006 Madrid, Spain (amparo@iec.csic.es).
** Department of Statistics, Operations Research and Computation, Faculty of Maths, University of La Laguna, 38271 La Laguna, Spain (pcaballero@ull.es).

Abstract

A method of analysis for the linear complexity of nonlinearly filtered PN-sequences is presented. The procedure provides a general lower bound for the linear complexity and an algorithm to improve it. The results obtained are valid for any nonlinear function with a unique term of maximum order and for any maximal-length LFSR. This work, which has as starting point "the root presence test" by Rueppel, is based on the handling of binary strings instead of determinants in a finite field.

1 Introduction

A kind of running-key generator commonly used in stream ciphers is obtained by applying a nonlinear function F to the stages of a maximal-length LFSR. Generally speaking, the obtained sequence must satisfy several cryptographic properties: the period of the keystream has to be taken very large, the output sequence must appear to be random, the output bits should be easy to generate, the knowledge of part of the sequence should not enable a cryptoanalist to generate the whole sequence.

According to the last requirement, the linear complexity of the produced sequence can be computed in two different ways:

(a) Analysing the digits of the output sequence by means of the Berlekamp-Massey LFSR synthesis algorithm [4].

(b) Studying the characteristics of the nonlinear function F applied to the LFSR's stages.

In the second case several fundamental contributions must be quoted:

Groth [1] presented the linear complexity as a controllable parameter which increases with the order of F. Nevertheless, in his work there is no explicit mention to the degeneracies which may occur in the linear complexity of the produced sequence.

This work was supported by R&D Spanish Program TIC91-0386.

Key [2] established the relationship between the minimal polynomial roots required to represent the keystream generator and the linear complexity of the generated sequence. This result let Rueppel [7] state the so called "*root presence test*" for the product of distinct phases of a PN-sequence.

Independently, Kumar et al. [3] derived upper and lower bounds for the linear complexity of bent-function sequences, though they imposed some restrictive conditions on the choice of the PN-sequence phases and the LFSR's length.

The present work takes as starting point *the root presence test* by Rueppel, which is based on the computation of determinants in a finite field. In contrast to Rueppel's method, this paper proposes an algorithm to compute a lower bound for the complexity by using exclusively logic operations (OR, AND). In fact, the kind of linear systems we are dealing with, can be reduced to binary strings and their compatibility can be checked by means of logic operations.

As the algorithm INPUTS are L (LFSR's length) and k (order of the function), then the lower bound obtained is valid for any kth-order function with a unique term of maximum order and for any L-degree primitive polynomial. Thus the procedure here presented is more general than the previous proposals and can be applied to a wider class of functions.

The paper is organized as follows. In section 2 some notation and basic concepts, which will be used throughout the work, are given. Section 3 includes the main results to obtain a lower bound for the linear complexity. An algorithm to improve the above mentioned lower bound is proposed in section 4. At the end of this section a simple example is given for illustrative purposes. Finally, conclusions in section 5 end the work.

2 Notation and Basic Concepts

The following notation and basic concepts are used throughout the work.

S is the output sequence of a LFSR whose minimal polynomial $m_s(x) \in GF(2)[x]$ is primitive.

L is the length of the LFSR.

$\alpha \in GF(2^L)$ is one root of $m_s(x)$.

F is a nonlinear kth-order function with a unique maximum order term, denoted by f, which is the product of k distinct phases of S,

$$f = s_{n+t_0}\, s_{n+t_1} \cdots s_{n+t_{k-1}}$$

where k is taken $k \leq \lceil \frac{L}{2} \rceil$ in the recommended range [5] and the symbols t_j (j=0,1,...,k-1) are integers verifying

$$0 \leq t_0 < t_1 < \ldots < t_{k-1} < 2^L - 1$$

In this work only the contribution of f to the linear complexity of the resulting sequence will be studied.

The root presence test for the product of distinct phases of a PN-sequence can be stated as follows:

$\alpha^e \in GF(2^L)$ is a root of the minimal polynomial of the generated sequence if and only if

$$A_e = \begin{vmatrix} \alpha^{t_0 2^{e_0}} & \ldots & \alpha^{t_{k-1} 2^{e_0}} \\ \alpha^{t_0 2^{e_1}} & \ldots & \alpha^{t_{k-1} 2^{e_1}} \\ \vdots & \vdots & \vdots \\ \alpha^{t_0 2^{e_{k-1}}} & \ldots & \alpha^{t_{k-1} 2^{e_{k-1}}} \end{vmatrix} \neq 0 \qquad \textbf{(1)}$$

Here $\alpha^{t_j} \in GF(2^L)$ (j=0,...,k-1) correspond respectively to the k phases (s_{n+t_j}) of the PN-sequence and e, a representative element of a cyclotomic coset, is a positive integer of the form $e = 2^{e_0} + 2^{e_1} + \ldots + 2^{e_{k-1}}$ with the e_i (i=0,..,k-1) all different running in the interval [0,L). Under these conditions, α^e and its conjugate roots contribute to the linear complexity of the nonlinearly filtered sequence. The value of this contribution is equal to the number of elements in such a cyclotomic coset.

We will denote the coset containing the element e by *coset e*. We will say that the coset e is *degenerate* when the determinant (1) associated to α^e equals zero.

Considering a general function F defined as before, the present paper is concerned with two basic ideas:

(I1) For an arbitrary choice of the phases (s_{n+t_j}) and the LFSR primitive polynomial, some cosets will never be degenerate.

(I2) If certain cosets are degenerate, then other cosets cannot be so.

(I1) provides a general lower bound for the linear complexity of the generated sequence, while (I2) is used to increase that bound. Both ideas are justified in the following sections.

3 A Lower Bound for the Linear Complexity of an Arbitrary Kth-order Function

(I1) is related to the following results.

Lemma 1 Let f be the product of k distinct phases (s_{n+t_j}) of a PN-sequence. Then f is a kth-order function if and only if the powers $\alpha^{t_j} \in GF(2^L)$ (j=0,...,k-1) are linearly independent over GF(2).

Proof The result follows immediately from the fact that, according to Key´s expressions [2], any α^{t_l} verifies

$$\alpha^{t_l} = \sum_{\substack{j=0 \\ j\neq l}}^{k-1} c_j \, \alpha^{t_j}, \qquad c_j \in GF(2)$$

if and only if s_{n+t_l} can be written as

$$s_{n+t_l} = \sum_{j=0}^{k-1} c_j \, s_{n+t_j}$$

consequently f can be expressed as

$$f = s_{n+t_0} \cdots s_{n+t_l} \cdots s_{n+t_{k-1}} = s_{n+t_0} \cdots \sum_{\substack{j=0 \\ j\neq l}}^{k-1} c_j \, s_{n+t_j} \cdots s_{n+}$$

Thus, if the powers α^{t_j} (j=0,...,k-1) were linearly dependent over GF(2) then f would be either a (k-1)th-order function or the identically zero function. Reciprocally, if f were a kth-order function then the powers α^{t_j} (j=0,...,k-1) should be linearly independent over GF(2).

□

An easy way to guarantee the condition of Lemma 1 is to take the k phases (s_{n+t_j}) inside the LFSR length, since the α^{t_i} (i=0,...,L-1) are a basis of GF(2^L) over GF(2), [6].

Definition We will call *d fixed-distance coset* to any cyclotomic coset e such that e is of the form

$$e = 2^{e_0} + 2^{e_1} + \ldots + 2^{e_{k-1}}$$
$$e_i \equiv d \cdot i \pmod{L} \quad (i = 0, \ldots, k-1) \qquad \textbf{(2)}$$

where d is a positive integer less than L such that (d,L)=1.

The name of fixed-distance coset is due to the fixed distance d among the positions of the 1's in the binary representation of the number e.

Main Theorem f is a kth-order function if and only if all the d fixed-distance cosets are nondegenerate.

Proof "⇒" We proceed by induction. It is shown that if the result is true for k-1 and false for k, then we reach a contradiction. In fact, if the determinant A_e for e defined as in (2) equals zero, then the homogeneous linear system (S1)

$$\begin{cases} 0 = c_0\,\alpha^{t_0 2^{e_0}} + c_1\,\alpha^{t_1 2^{e_0}} + \ldots + c_{k-1}\,\alpha^{t_{k-1} 2^{e_0}} \\ \vdots \\ 0 = c_0\,\alpha^{t_0 2^{e_{k-1}}} + c_1\,\alpha^{t_1 2^{e_{k-1}}} + \ldots + c_{k-1}\,\alpha^{t_{k-1} 2^{e_{k-1}}} \end{cases} \qquad \textbf{(S1)}$$

is compatible with nontrivial solutions $c_i \in GF(2^L)$ (i=0,...,k-1). Now we raise every equation of (S1) to the power 2^d and we get a new homogeneous linear system where the (k-1) first equations coincide with the (k-1) last equations of (S1). Using the induction hypothesis and solving by Cramer´s rule, we derive that the solutions of (S1) must be of the form

$$c_i = (\,c_i\,)^{2^d} \quad (i = 0, \ldots, k-1)$$

This means that the order of c_i divides 2^d-1. As 2^L-1 and 2^d-1 are relatively prime, we conclude that the c_i must be binary coefficients. Then, according to Lemma 1, f cannot be a kth-order function.

"⇐" We proceed by contradiction. In fact, if f were not a kth-order function then, according to Lemma 1, the powers α^{t_j} (j=0,...,k-1) would be linearly dependent over GF(2). That is, ∃ l 0≤l≤k-1 such that,

$$\alpha^{t_l} = \sum_{\substack{j=0 \\ j \neq l}}^{k-1} c_j \, \alpha^{t_j}, \quad c_j \in GF(2) \, .$$

Since $(c_j)^{2^d} = c_j$, $\forall e_i \in [0,...,L)$, then for every arbitrary coset e, the system (S1) would always be a compatible system with nontrivial binary solutions (c_j) (j=0,...,k-1). Consequently, all the cosets with the same Hamming weight k would be degenerate, in particular all the d fixed-distance cosets.

□

Two corollaries follow immediately from this theorem.

Corollary 1 The linear complexity Λ of the sequence produced by the kth-order function f is lowerbound by

$$\Lambda \geq N_L \cdot L$$

where $N_L = \Phi(L)/2$ ($\Phi(L)$ being the Euler function). Here N_L represents the number of fixed-distance cosets and L the number of elements in each coset.

Corollary 2 If L is prime, then the linear complexity Λ is lowerbound by

$$\Lambda \geq \binom{L}{2}$$

Note that the lower bounds depend exclusively on L, e.g. they are independent of the particular form of f, the order of F (for 2≤k≤L-2) and the LFSR primitive polynomial.

Both corollaries can be easily proved by using standard results in the theory of finite fields.

4 Improvement of the Lower Bound for the Linear Complexity

(I2), in section 2, is related to the following algorithm.

4.1 General Features of the Algorithm

The algorithm here proposed is based on the previous theorem and corollaries.

For a given group of cosets, the algorithm computes:

(a) The maximum number of cosets in this group which can be simultaneously degenerate.
(b) The contribution to the linear complexity of the remaining cosets in this group.

The following notation and basic principles are used throughout the procedure:

fdc(l) ($l=1,\ldots,N_L$) denote the different fixed-distance cosets. Each fdc(l) takes its corresponding value e defined as in (2). The binary content of any fdc(l) can be interpreted as the representation of an homogeneous linear system (see (S1) in section 3) with k equations. In fact, the ith-1 in fdc(l) represents the ith-equation

$$0 = c_0\, \alpha^{t_0\, 2^{e_i}} + \ldots + c_{k-1}\, \alpha^{t_{k-1}\, 2^{e_i}}$$

of this system. According to the main theorem, such system is non-compatible (except for the trivial solution).

[Remark that throughout the algorithm either the fdc(l) initial content (e) or the shifted content (any other element in the coset) will be used].

$C_d(i)$ ($i=1,\ldots,L-(k+1)$) denote the different cosets to be studied. For every d, they are obtained from the corresponding d fixed-distance coset with (k-1) 1's plus an additional 1. Therefore, all of them have (k-1) 1's placed at the same positions. Every $C_d(i)$ can also be interpreted as an homogeneous linear system with k equations. If $C_d(i)$ is a degenerate coset, then its corresponding system of equations is compatible.

The cosets $C_d(i)$ are put into groups of n ($n=L-(k+1)-1,\ldots,2$).

$R_n(j)$ ($j=1,\ldots,\binom{L-(k+1)}{n}$) denote the OR of the n cosets $C_d(i)$ in each group.

As before, any $R_n(j)$ can be interpreted as an homogeneous linear system with (k-1+n) equations. If the n cosets are simultaneously degenerate, then the corresponding system of equations in $R_n(j)$ is compatible.

$G_n(j)$ ($j=1,\ldots,\binom{L-(k+1)}{n}$) are auxiliary variables which take as values 1 or 0.

Assumed that the n cosets $C_d(i)$ of a group are simultaneously degenerate, we realize the operation AND between the corresponding $R_n(j)$ and all the fixed-distance cosets fdc(l) $(l=1,\ldots,N_L)$. If some logic product has k 1's, then it means that a compatible system of (k-1+n) equations has a non-compatible sub-system of k equations, which is a contradiction.

If every logic product verifies this condition, then at most (n-1) cosets of the set $\{C_d(i),\ i=1,\ldots,L-(k+1)\}$ can be simultaneously degenerate. Now the cosets $C_d(i)$ must be put into groups of (n-1) and the process repeated.

If some logic product did not verify this condition, then n would be the maximum number of cosets in this group which could be simultaneously degenerate; the remaining (L-(k+1)-n) would contribute to the linear complexity.

All these considerations give raise to the following algorithm.

4.2 Algorithm

INPUT: L, k ($k \leq \lceil \frac{L}{2} \rceil$).

Step 1 Compute the N_L values of d.
Generate the fdc(l) $(l=1,\ldots,N_L)$.
Initialize the lower bound: $\Delta = L \bullet N_L$

For each value of d separately:

Step 2 Generate the cosets $C_d(i)$ $(i=1,\ldots,L-(k+1))$.
$n = L-(k+1)-1$.

Step 3 Put the cosets $C_d(i)$ into groups of n.
Realize the OR of the n cosets of each group, obtaining

$R_n(j)$ $(j=1,\ldots,\binom{L-(k+1)}{n})$.

Step 4 (For each $R_n(j)$).
Realize the AND between $R_n(j)$ and every fixed-distance coset fdc(l) $(l=1,\ldots,N_L)$.
If some logic product coincides with fdc(l), then $G_n(j)=1$,
else $G_n(j)=0$.

Step 5 If $\exists j$: $G_n(j)=0$, then $\Delta = \Delta + (L-k-n-1) \bullet L$, next d,
else if (n>2) then $n = n - 1$, go to step 3,
else $\Delta = \Delta + (L-k-n) \bullet L$, next d.

OUTPUT: The lower bound Δ.

4.3 An Illustrative Example

For $L = 9$, $k = 5$, $d = 1, 2$ or 4, $N_L = 3$, Number of cosets due to $f = 14$

d fixed-distance cosets with k 1's:

(d=1) fdc(1) = 000011111

(d=2) fdc(2) = 101010101

(d=4) fdc(3) = 110011001

fdc(i)*: a shifted version of fdc(i)

lower bound for the complexity: $\Delta = 9 \bullet 3 = 27$,

For d = 1, n = 2,

$C_1(1) = 000101111$ $C_1(2) = 001001111$ $C_1(3) = 010001111$

OR [$C_1(1)$, $C_1(2)$] = 001101111 = $R_2(1)$,

OR [$C_1(1)$, $C_1(3)$] = 010101111 = $R_2(2)$,

OR [$C_1(2)$, $C_1(3)$] = 011001111 = $R_2(3)$;

AND [$R_2(1)$, fdc(3)*] = fdc(3)* ⇒ $G_2(1) = 1$,

AND [$R_2(2)$, fdc(2)*] = fdc(2)* ⇒ $G_2(2) = 1$,

AND [$R_2(3)$, fdc(3)*] = fdc(3)* ⇒ $G_2(3) = 1$,

Therefore just 1 out of 3 cosets $C_1(i)$ can be degenerate. Thus,

$\Delta = 27 + (2 \bullet 9) = 45$.

For d = 2, n = 2,

$C_2(1) = 001010111$ $C_2(2) = 001011101$ $C_2(3) = 001110101$

OR [$C_2(1)$, $C_2(2)$] = 001011111 = $R_2(1)$,

OR [$C_2(1)$, $C_2(3)$] = 001110111 = $R_2(2)$,

OR [$C_2(2)$, $C_2(3)$] = 001111101 = $R_2(3)$;

AND [$R_2(1)$, fdc(1)] = fdc(1) ⇒ $G_2(1) = 1$,

AND [$R_2(2)$, fdc(3)*] = fdc(3)* ⇒ $G_2(2) = 1$,

AND [$R_2(3)$, fdc(1)*] = fdc(1)* ⇒ $G_2(3) = 1$,

Therefore just 1 out of 3 cosets $C_2(i)$ can be degenerate. Thus,

$\Delta = 45 + (2 \bullet 9) = 63$.

For d = 4, n = 2,

$C_3(1) = 100011011$ $C_3(2) = 100011101$ $C_3(3) = 101011001$

OR [$C_3(1)$, $C_3(2)$] = 100011111 = $R_2(1)$,

OR [$C_3(1)$, $C_3(3)$] = 101011011 = $R_2(2)$,

OR [$C_3(2)$, $C_3(3)$] = 101011101 = $R_2(3)$;

AND [$R_2(1)$, fdc(1)] = fdc(1) ⇒ $G_2(1) = 1$,

AND [$R_2(2)$, fdc(2)*] = fdc(2)* ⇒ $G_2(2) = 1$,

AND [$R_2(3)$, fdc(2)] = fdc(2) ⇒ $G_2(3) = 1$,

Therefore just 1 out of 3 cosets $C_3(i)$ can be degenerate. Thus,

$\Delta = 63 + (2 \bullet 9) = 81$.

It has been shown that 9 out of 14 cosets due to f are nondegenerate. According to *the root presence test*, for each specific choice of the function and the polynomial at least 9 determinants of order 5 should have been computed. By comparison, the result obtained by means of the proposed method is completely general for any 5th-order function and polynomial of degree 9.

4.4 Discussion of the Proposed Algorithm and Open Problems

In spite of the fact that the maximum computational complexity of the proposed algorithm is exponential in the length of the LFSR, three basic considerations must be pointed out:

a) This complexity is never reached in real cases.

b) The actual length of the LFSRs used in practice is not greater than a relatively small value (120-250).

c) The proposed algorithm has to be applied just once for every LFSR´s length (not for every sequence). In fact, the lower bound obtained is valid for every nonlinear function f and for every LFSR with primitive polynomial.

In the following table, several lower bounds for the linear complexity for different values of L are shown.

L	k	N_1	N_2	N_3	lower bound
17	9	1430	64	32	544
29	15	$2{,}67\cdot10^{6}$	196	70	2030
61	31	$3{,}81\cdot10^{15}$	900	180	10980
73	37	$1{,}19\cdot10^{19}$	1296	216	15768
109	55	$4{,}51\cdot10^{29}$	2916	324	35316
127	64	$9{,}42\cdot10^{34}$	3969	378	48006

N_1: number of cosets due to f, N_2: number of analyzed cosets,
N_3: number of cosets guaranteed to be nondegenerate.

The groups of cosets $C_d(i)$ here studied have been obtained exclusively from the d fixed-distance cosets with (k-1) 1´s. In fact, the contribution to the linear complexity from each group of cosets is small although the number of groups is large. Clearly the algorithm can be applied to other groups of cosets $C_d(i)$ in order to increase the lower bound given in this work. The elements of these new groups must all have (k-1) 1´s coincident.

The question of how to control the degeneration of the remaining cosets, e.g. those cosets that do not verify the above mentioned condition, is a problem which needs further investigation.

5 Conclusions

In this paper a general lower bound for the linear complexity of nonlinearly filtered sequences has been given and an algorithm to improve it has been proposed.

Unlike the existing proposals, this procedure is based on the handling of binary strings. Furthermore, the method is independent of the specific function and the LFSR to whose stages the nonlinear function is applied.

As the procedure improves the bound by means of independent additive increments, this algorithm is optimal for parallel implementation.

References

[1] E.J. Groth, Generation of binary sequences with controllable complexity, IEEE Trans. Inform. Theory, vol. IT-17, pp. 288-296, May 1971.

[2] E.L. Key, An analysis of the structure and complexity of nonlinear binary sequence generators, IEEE Trans. Inform. Theory, vol. IT-22, pp.732-736, Nov. 1976.

[3] P.V. Kumar and R.A. Scholtz, Bounds on the linear span of bent sequences, IEEE Trans. Inform. Theory, vol. IT-29, pp. 854-862, Nov. 1983.

[4] J.L. Massey, Shift-Register synthesis and BCH decoding, IEEE Trans. Inform. Theory, vol. IT-15, Jan. 1969.

[5] J.L. Massey, Seminar *Cryptography: Fundamentals and applications*, Zurich, 1990.

[6] W.W. Peterson and E.J. Weldon, *Error-Correcting Codes*, Cambridge, MA: MIT Press, 1972.

[7] R.A Rueppel, *Analysis and design of stream ciphers*, Springer-Verlag, New York, 1986.

Intrinsic Statistical Weakness of Keystream Generators

Jovan Dj. Golić *

Information Security Research Centre, Queensland University of Technology
GPO Box 2434, Brisbane Q 4001, Australia
School of Electrical Engineering, University of Belgrade
Email: golic@fit.qut.edu.au

Abstract. It is shown that an arbitrary binary keystream generator with M bits of memory can be linearly modelled as a non-autonomous linear feedback shift register of length at most M with an additive input sequence of nonbalanced identically distributed binary random variables. An effective method for the linear model determination based on the linear sequential circuit approximation of autonomous finite-state machines is developed. Linear models for clock-controlled shift registers and arbitrary shift register based keystream generators are derived. Several examples including the time-variant memoryless combiner, the basic summation generator, the stop-and-go cascade, and the shrinking generator are presented. Linear models are the basis for a general structure-dependent and initial-state-independent statistical test and they may also be used for correlation attacks on the initial-state. Theoretical security against the introduced statistical attack appears hard to control in practice and hard to achieve with simple schemes.

1 Introduction

Keystream generators for stream cipher applications can generally be realized as autonomous finite-state machines whose initial state and possibly structure as well depend on a secret key. Their practical security can be defined as immunity to various types of divide and conquer attacks on secret key based on known plaintext or ciphertext only, such as the Hamming distance correlation attack [19], the probabilistic decoding fast correlation attack [15], the linear consistency test [20], the collision test [1], the lock-in effect [2], the Levenshtein-like distance correlation attack [7], the probabilistic correlation attack [9], the linear sequential circuit approximation attack [8], and the embedding attack [21], see [18] and [10]. Also, keystream pseudorandom sequences should have large period and high linear complexity, which can be regarded as the resistance against the Berlekamp-Massey algorithm [13] based on known plaintext. They should also satisfy the standard key-independent statistical tests, which should prevent the reconstruction of statistically redundant plaintext from known ciphertext.

* This research was supported in part by the Science Fund of Serbia, grant #0403, through the Institute of Mathematics, Serbian Academy of Arts and Sciences.

In this paper, a general structure-dependent and initial-state-independent statistical weakness of arbitrary binary keystream generators is pointed out as well as an effective method for its practical determination. If the structure is key-independent, that is, known, then the corresponding statistical test can be used for the reconstruction of a statistically redundant plaintext from known ciphertext. If the structure is key-dependent, then the same test can also be used to determine the corresponding unknown key, that is, the structure of the keystream generator which presents a specific divide and conquer attack. Although such a weakness is intrinsic to all binary keystream generators, there exist the generators for which the corresponding statistical test is not practically effective. However, for any particular keystream generator this property generally seems to be very difficult or even practically impossible to verify.

The main results are now explained in more detail. Assume that a binary keystream generator is defined as an autonomous finite-state machine whose initial state is chosen uniformly at random. Let M denote the size of memory, that is, let 2^M be the cardinality of the state space. We first show that there exists a linear function of at most $M+1$ consecutive output bits $L(y_t, \ldots, y_{t-M})$ that is a nonbalanced function of the initial state variables. Its probability distribution is independent of time t if the next-state function is balanced. The probability distribution of a Boolean function can be expressed in terms of the correlation coefficient to the constant zero function which is the difference between the relative numbers of zeros and ones in its truth table. Accordingly, the keystream generator can be statistically modelled as a non-autonomous linear feedback shift register of length at most M, whose state at time t consists of at most M consecutive output bits $(y_{t-1}, \ldots, y_{t-M})$, with the additive input sequence of nonbalanced identically distributed binary random variables. The linear function L of consecutive output bits produces a nonbalanced sequence to which one can apply the standard chi-square frequency statistical test. The test is successful if and only if the length of the sequence is chosen to be inversely proportional to the square of the correlation coefficient. Since the period of the keystream sequences is upper-bounded by 2^M, the statistical weakness is effective only if the absolute value of the correlation coefficient is greater than $2^{-M/2}$.

We then develop an efficient procedure for finding nonbalanced linear functions of the output which is based on the *linear sequential circuit approximation* (LSCA) approach to combiners with memory introduced in [8]. More precisely, one first decomposes the output Boolean function and each of the Boolean functions in the next-state function of a keystream generator into the sum of a linear function and a nonbalanced Boolean function. The outputs of these nonlinear nonbalanced functions are then considered as the inputs so that the autonomous finite-state machine is reduced to a non-autonomous linear sequential circuit with nonbalanced input sequences. By using the generating function technique one then solves the linear recurrence equations and thus obtains almost exactly what is desired: a linear function of at most $M + 1$ consecutive output bits that is expressed as a sum of nonbalanced functions of the initial state variables. The linear function corresponds to the characteristic polynomial of the state-transition matrix of the linear sequential circuit. In general, the sum of nonbalanced Boolean functions can be balanced. However, we prove that if the functions are picked independently at random, then with high probability their sum is nonbalanced with the correlation coefficient very close to the product of the individual correlation coefficients.

Our next goal is to analyze irregularly clocked shift registers whose description as finite-state machines is complicated, because of the repetitions and/or deletions of symbols that occur in a non-synchronous manner. We show that the LSCA method is feasible even in this case and thus derive linear models for the clock-controlled shift registers with or without repetitions of symbols. We then establish a linear model for an arbitrary binary keystream generator based on regularly or irregularly clocked shift registers combined by a function with or without memory.

The organization of the paper is as follows. In Section 2, we deal with arbitrary keystream generators defined as autonomous finite-state machines and establish their intrinsic statistical weakness. In Section 3, we describe the linear sequential circuit approximation method for obtaining the corresponding linear models for these generators. In Section 4, we derive linear models for clock-controlled shift registers with or without repetition of symbols. A linear model for an arbitrary shift register based binary keystream generator is determined in Section 5. Several examples including the memoryless combiner [19], the time-variant memoryless combiner [6, 12], the basic summation generator [14, 18], the stop-and-go Gollmann cascade generator [11], and the shrinking generator [3] are also examined. Conclusions and open problems are presented in Section 6.

2 Statistical Weakness of Finite-State Machines

A binary autonomous finite-state machine or sequential circuit is defined by

$$S_{t+1} = \mathcal{F}(S_t), \quad t \geq 0 \tag{1}$$

$$y_t = f(S_t), \quad t \geq 0 \tag{2}$$

where $\mathcal{F}$: GF$(2)^M \rightarrow$ GF$(2)^M$ is a next-state vector Boolean function, f : GF$(2)^M \rightarrow$ GF(2) is an output Boolean function, $S_t = (s_{1t}, \ldots, s_{Mt})$ is the state vector at time t, M is the number of memory bits, y_t is the output bit at time t, and $S_0 = (s_{1,0}, \ldots, s_{M,0})$ is the initial state. A binary keystream generator can be defined as a binary autonomous finite-state machine whose initial state and the next-state and output functions are controlled by a secret key.

Given $\mathcal{F}$ and f, each output bit is a Boolean function of the initial state variables, that is, $y_t = f(\mathcal{F}^t(S_0))$ where $\mathcal{F}^t$ denotes the t-fold self-composition of $\mathcal{F}$ and $\mathcal{F}^0$ is the identity function, $t \geq 0$. If S_0 is assumed to be a uniformly distributed random variable, then the output bits become binary random variables. A basic design criterion for f and $\mathcal{F}$, related to the statistics of the output sequence, is that each bit y_t should be a balanced function of S_0. This is clearly satisfied if both $\mathcal{F}$ and f are balanced. A more restrictive criterion is that any M consecutive output bits constitute a balanced function of S_0. However, the vector of $M+1$ consecutive output bits $(y_t, \ldots, y_{t-M})$ can not be a balanced function of S_0 for any $t \geq M$, since S_0 has dimension only M. Therefore, there must exist a linear function $L(y_t, \ldots, y_{t-M})$ that is a nonbalanced function of S_0 for each $t \geq M$. Furthermore, when the next-state function is balanced, it is easy to prove that the probability distribution of this linear function is the same for each $t \geq M$ and that there exists such a linear function that effectively depends on y_t. Thus we have

Theorem 1 Let the next-state function of a binary autonomous finite-state machine with M bits of memory be balanced. Then there exists a linear function L of $M+1$ binary variables effectively depending on the first variable such that the function $L(y_t, \ldots, y_{t-M})$ of at most $M+1$ consecutive output bits is a nonbalanced function of the initial state variables for each $t \geq M$. Moreover, the correlation coefficient between $L(y_t, \ldots, y_{t-M})$ and the constant zero function is the same for each $t \geq M$. □

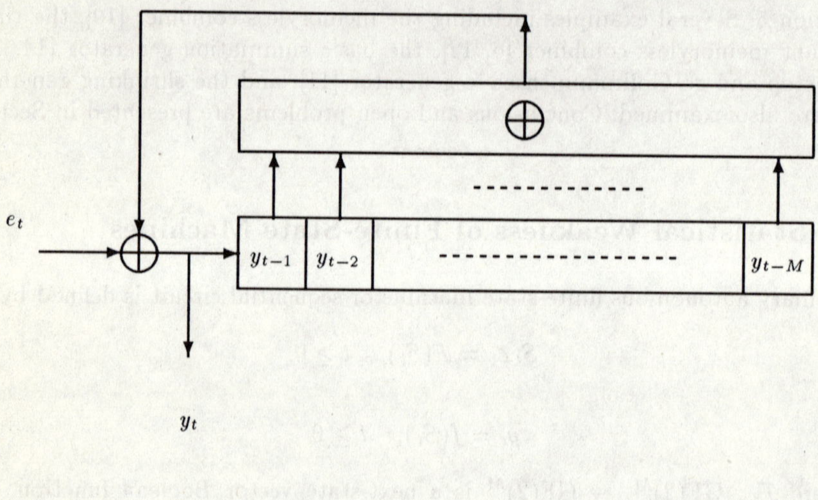

Fig. 1. Linear model for a keystream generator.

Theorem 1 essentially claims that an autonomous finite-state machine can equivalently be represented as a non-autonomous linear feedback shift register of length at most M, shown in Fig. 1, with an additive input sequence of nonbalanced identically distributed binary random variables. The variables are not independent. The linear function L specified by the feedback polynomial applied to the output sequence $\{y_t\}$ produces a nonbalanced sequence $\{e_t\}$. The standard chi-square frequency statistical test can then be applied to $\{e_t\}$. To distinguish this sequence from a purely random binary sequence with error probability less than about 10^{-3}, one needs a segment whose length is $10/c^2$ where $c = 1 - 2\Pr\{e_t = 1\}$ is the correlation coefficient of $\{e_t\}$. The same length is required for each additional bit of uncertainty to be resolved. Since the linear function L is not unique in general, the maximum effect will be achieved when the linear function with the correlation coefficient of maximum magnitude is used. If this value is smaller than or close to $2^{-M/2}$, then the keystream generator is not vulnerable to this statistical test. However, for large M, which is often the case in practice, it appears very difficult, if not impossible, to determine the value of the maximum correlation coefficient.

Another fact is even more discouraging from the cryptographer's viewpoint. Namely, one could simultaneously use different linear functions including the ones depending on more than $M + 1$ consecutive output bits, thus reducing the necessary length of the observed keystream sequence. In particular, since every linear function can be defined as a polynomial in the generating function domain which is the feedback polynomial from Fig. 1, it follows that one may also consider the polynomial multiples of the polynomials corresponding to linear functions of at most $M + 1$ variables. It appears very difficult to control all the corresponding correlation coefficients.

3 Linear Sequential Circuit Approximation Method

In order to find all the nonbalanced linear functions of at most $M+1$ consecutive output bits whose existence is established by Theorem 1, one should determine the correlation coefficients for 2^M Boolean functions of M variables. Exhaustive search method has $O(2^{2M})$ computational complexity, which is not feasible for large M.

Taking the linear sequential circuit approximation (LSCA) approach introduced in [8] for combiners with memory, we propose a LSCA method for autonomous finite-state machines which is a feasible procedure that with high probability yields nonbalanced linear functions of at most $M + 1$ consecutive output bits with comparatively large correlation coefficients. The LSCA method consists of two stages. First, find a linear (affine) approximation of the output function f and each of the component functions of the next-state function $\mathcal{F}$. This enables us to express each of these $M + 1$ functions as the sum of a linear function and a nonbalanced function. The degree of approximation is measured by the corresponding correlation coefficients, which should be different from zero. Note that to determine all the linear approximations of a Boolean function effectively depending on n variables, one may use the Walsh transform technique [18] which has $O(n2^n)$ computational complexity. In practice, both the output function and the component next-state functions effectively depend on small numbers of variables or can be expressed in terms of such functions. Therefore, the computational complexity of obtaining all the linear approximations along with the corresponding correlation coefficients is considerably smaller than $O((M+1)M2^M)$.

Second, by virtue of the obtained linear approximations, put the basic equations (1) and (2) into the form

$$S_{t+1} = \mathbf{A}S_t + \Delta(S_t), \quad t \geq 0 \tag{3}$$

$$y_t = \mathbf{B}S_t + \varepsilon(S_t), \quad t \geq 0 \tag{4}$$

where the vectors are regarded as one-column matrices, $\mathbf{A}$ and $\mathbf{B}$ are binary matrices, and ε and all the components of $\Delta = (\delta_1, \ldots, \delta_M)$ are nonbalanced Boolean functions, called the noise functions. The main point now is to treat $\{\varepsilon(S_t)\}$ and $\{\delta_i(S_t)\}$, $1 \leq i \leq M$, as the input sequences so that (3) and (4) define a non-autonomous linear sequential circuit (LSC), see [8]. Then solve the LSC using the generating function (D-transform) technique and thus obtain

$$\sum_{i=0}^{M} \varphi_i\, y_{t-i} = \sum_{i=0}^{M} \varphi_i\, \varepsilon(S_{t-i}) + \sum_{j=1}^{M} \sum_{i=0}^{M-1} a_{ji}\, \delta_j(S_{t-1-i}) \stackrel{\text{def}}{=} e_t(S_0), \quad t \geq M \tag{5}$$

where $\varphi_0 = 1$ and all the coefficients are binary. The polynomial $\varphi(z) = \sum_{i=0}^{M} \varphi_i z^i$ representing the linear function on the left-hand side of (5) is the reciprocal of the characteristic polynomial of the state-transition matrix $\mathbf{A}$ whose degree satisfies $\deg \varphi(z) \leq \operatorname{rank} \mathbf{A} \leq M$. The computational complexity to obtain (5) is only $O(M^3)$. For each $t \geq M$, the noise function e_t is a sum of individual noise functions that are nonbalanced if $S_{t-i}, 0 \leq i \leq M$, are balanced. In general, for random $\mathcal{F}$ and f, one should expect that the individual noise functions remain nonbalanced even if $S_{t-i}, 0 \leq i \leq M$, are not balanced functions of S_0 and that the resulting noise function e_t is also nonbalanced, for almost all $t \geq M$. This conclusion is justified by the following probabilistic result, which can be proved by combinatorial arguments, Stirling's approximation, and some functional analysis.

Lemma 1 Let the two Boolean functions f_1 and f_2 of the same n variables be chosen uniformly and independently at random provided that the correlation coefficient of f_i is equal to c_i, $-1 < c_i < 1, i = 1, 2$. Then, the probability distribution of the correlation coefficient c of the sum $f = f_1 + f_2$ is for large $N = 2^n$ given by

$$\begin{aligned} P(c) \sim \frac{1}{4^N \sqrt{2\pi N}} \prod_{i=1}^{2} (1-c_i)^{\frac{N(1-c_i)}{2}} (1+c_i)^{\frac{N(1+c_i)}{2}} \cdot \\ (1-c_1-c_2+c)^{-\frac{N(1-c_1-c_2+c)}{4}} (1+c_1+c_2+c)^{-\frac{N(1+c_1+c_2+c)}{4}} \cdot \\ (1+c_1-c_2-c)^{-\frac{N(1+c_1-c_2-c)}{4}} (1-c_1+c_2-c)^{-\frac{N(1-c_1+c_2-c)}{4}} \end{aligned} \tag{6}$$

for $-1+\max(c_1+c_2, 0) < c < 1-|c_1-c_2|$, which is itself asymptotically equal to the normal distribution with the expected value c_1c_2 and the standard deviation $\sigma = O(\frac{1}{\sqrt{N}})$.

□

The analogous result holds for more than two Boolean functions. By applying Chebyshev's inequality we then conclude that with probability arbitrarily close to one the correlation coefficient of the sum of Boolean functions f_i of n variables with the correlation coefficients c_i, $1 \leq i \leq k$, is $c = \prod_{i=1}^{k} c_i + O(\frac{k}{\sqrt{N}})$, $N = 2^n$. Note that $c = \prod_{i=1}^{k} c_i$ always holds if f_i are mutually independent [4].

If as in Theorem 1 one assumes that the next-state function $\mathcal{F}$ is balanced, then it follows that each of the individual noise functions in (5) is nonbalanced and identically distributed for every $t \geq M$, meaning that the corresponding correlation coefficients are nonzero and independent of t. In view of Lemma 1 we then get

Theorem 2 For a binary autonomous finite-state machine with M bits of memory, the linear sequential circuit approximation method gives a linear function L of at most $M+1$ consecutive output bits which is determined by the characteristic polynomial of the state-transition matrix of the corresponding linear sequential circuit. If the next-state function is balanced, then the correlation coefficient of L, as a function of the initial state variables, is time-independent. If it is in addition assumed that the individual noise functions in the solution equation (5) are chosen uniformly and independently at random, then L is nonbalanced with the correlation coefficient differing from the product of individual correlation coefficients by no more than $O(2^{-M/2})$, with probability arbitrarily close to one. □

For some particular finite-state machines the probabilistic assumption from Theorem 2 needed to apply Lemma 1 might not be appropriate. In that case one could group the noise functions into suitable categories, calculate the correlation coefficients for the categories, and then use Lemma 1. The main idea here is to estimate the overall correlation coefficient starting from the correlation coefficients for which the computation is feasible, by using reasonable probabilistic assumptions. Note that the direct calculation of the overall correlation coefficient has $O(2^M)$ computational complexity.

The ideal objective of the LSCA method would be to find a linear function/model with the maximum absolute value of the correlation coefficient. To this end, the number of noise terms in (5) should be small and their correlation coefficients should be large in magnitude. A reasonable approach is to repeat the procedure several times starting from the best linear approximations of the output and next-state functions. Another important point is related to linear functions of more than $M+1$ consecutive output bits. Namely, polynomial multiples of each determined characteristic polynomial also yield potentially nonbalanced linear functions of consecutive output bits. It may happen that the number of noise terms in (5) can be reduced by multiplying each side of it in the generating function domain by an appropriate polynomial, thus increasing the magnitude of the correlation coefficient. Finally, the power of the chi-square statistical test can be considerably improved by running the test on all the obtained linear models with large correlation coefficients, rather than on a single one. This also reduces the required length of the keystream sequence.

As for the design criteria for binary keystream generators with respect to the described LSCA attack, it is necessary that the memory size is large and it appears to be good if the output and the component next-state functions have large distance from linear functions and effectively depend on large subsets of the state variables.

4 Linear Models for Clock-Controlled Shift Registers

A clock-controlled shift register is a keystream generator consisting of a linear or nonlinear feedback shift register that is irregularly clocked according to an integer decimation sequence, which defines the number of clocks per output symbol and which is itself produced by a pseudorandom sequence generator, see [11] and [5]. More precisely, if $X = \{x_t\}_{t=0}^{\infty}$ denotes a regularly clocked shift register sequence and $D = \{d_t\}_{t=0}^{\infty}$ a decimation sequence, then the output sequence $Y = \{y_t\}_{t=0}^{\infty}$ is defined as a decimated sequence $y_t = x(\sum_{i=0}^{t} d_i)$, $t \geq 0$.

A clock-controlled shift register can be described as an autonomous finite-state machine by using the next-state functions of the regularly clocked shift register and of the generator producing the decimation sequence. We will show that the LSCA method is still applicable and thus obtain a linear model of the form shown in Fig. 1. First observe that nonlinear feedback can in principle be treated in the same way as linear, except for the additive noise function. Second, assume a realistic probabilistic model for the decimation sequence, for example, assume that D is a sequence of identically distributed nonnegative integer random variables with a probability distribution $\mathcal{P} = \{P(d)\}_{d\in\mathcal{D}}$ where $\mathcal{D}$ is the set of integers with positive probability. When $\mathcal{D}$ contains the positive integers only, one can define the deletion rate p_* as $1 - \frac{1}{\bar{d}}$, $\bar{d} = \sum_{d\in\mathcal{D}} dP(d)$.

We will distinguish between the two cases: the case with possible repetitions ($0 \in \mathcal{D}$) and the case without repetitions ($0 \notin \mathcal{D}$). In the first case, it is clear that regardless of the feedback polynomial

$$y_t + y_{t-1} = e_t, \quad t \geq 1 \tag{7}$$

where the correlation coefficient of e_t is equal to $P(0)$, that is, $\Pr\{e_t = 1\} = 1/2 - P(0)/2$, for any $t \geq 1$. The linear model is good if $P(0)$ is not very small. For the stop-and-go registers [2], for which $\mathcal{D} = \{0, 1\}$, $P(0) = 1/2$.

A linear model for the case without repetitions is more difficult to derive. Consider a clock-controlled linear feedback shift register of length r with the feedback polynomial $f(z) = 1 + \sum_{i=1}^{r} f_i z^i$. For the j-th stage of the register, $1 \leq j \leq r$, one may use the following linear approximation of the stage next-state function

$$s_j(t+1) = s_{j-d}(t) + e_j(t), \quad t \geq 0 \tag{8}$$

where the correlation coefficient of $e_j(t)$ is equal to $P(d)$, for an arbitrary d such that $j - d \geq 1$. If $j - d < 1$, then instead of $s_{j-d}(t)$ one should use

$$s_j(t+1) = \sum_{i=1}^{r} f_i s_{i+j-d}(t) + e_j(t), \quad t \geq 0 \tag{9}$$

for an arbitrary d such that $i_1 + j - d \geq 1$, where i_1 is the position of the first feedback tap. In general, let $f(z) = 1 + \sum_{k=1}^{w} z^{i_k}$, $1 \leq i_1 < \ldots < i_w = r$, where $W = w + 1$ is the weight of $f(z)$. By (8) and (9) using possibly different values of d for different stages one may obtain different linear models for the clock-controlled shift register, which may not include all the stages. Note that due to the specific structure of the shift register the noise sequences are statistically dependent, which makes the estimation of the overall correlation coefficient difficult. However, this is possible for a particular type of the linear approximation of the stage next-state functions. Namely, for each of the feedback tap positions $i_k, 2 \leq k \leq w$, write (8) iteratively for $j = i_k, i_k - d, \ldots, i_{k-1} + d$ using possibly different d at each step. For i_1 write (8) for $j = i_1, i_1 - d, \ldots, j_0 + d$ and for $j = j_0$ write (9) for $d = j_0$. It is not difficult to see that in this way one essentially obtains a linear model of the form

$$y_t + \sum_{k=1}^{w} y_{t-\hat{i}_k} = e_t, \quad t \geq r' \tag{10}$$

where the polynomial $\hat{f}(z) = 1 + \sum_{i=1}^{r'} \hat{f}_i z^i = 1 + \sum_{k=1}^{w} z^{\hat{i}_k}$, $1 \leq \hat{i}_1 < \ldots < \hat{i}_w = r'$, satisfies $\hat{i}_k - \hat{i}_{k-1} \leq i_k - i_{k-1}, 1 \leq k \leq w$, where $\hat{i}_0 = i_0 = 0$. Call $\hat{f}(z)$ a *shrunk polynomial* of $f(z)$. A shrunk polynomial of $f(z)$ is not unique but has the same weight as $f(z)$. It is possible to obtain an expression for the correlation coefficient of e_t for an arbitrary probability distribution $\mathcal{P} = \{P(d)\}_{d \in \mathcal{D}}$. For simplicity, we give only the expression for the geometric distribution $P(d) = p^{d-1}(1-p), d \geq 1$, which corresponds to the case of independent deletions with probability p. Note that an arbitrary $\mathcal{P}$ can be approximated by this distribution by setting $p = p_*$ where p_* is the deletion rate. It follows that the correlation coefficient in this case is given by

$$c = p^{r-r'}(1-p)^{r'+1} \prod_{k=1}^{w} \binom{\Delta_k}{\hat{\Delta}_k} \tag{11}$$

where $\Delta_k = i_k - i_{k-1} - 1$ and $\hat{\Delta}_k = \hat{i}_k - \hat{i}_{k-1} - 1$, $1 \leq k \leq w$. Equation (11) has a clear combinatorial meaning in terms of the probability of decimation sequences. Namely, the correlation coefficient is the probability of the event that the bits satisfying the feedback polynomial in the shift register sequence remain undeleted in such a way that they satisfy the shrunk feedback polynomial in the decimated sequence. It is assumed that the conditional correlation coefficient is equal to one when the event occurs and to zero otherwise. The coefficient is maximized if $\hat{\Delta}_k = \lfloor (1-p)(\Delta_k + 1) \rfloor$, $1 \leq k \leq w$. It follows that $c = 1$ if $p = 0$ and $c = 0$ if $p = 1$, which is natural. To get a feeling about the magnitude of c, suppose that all Δ_k, $p\Delta_k$, and $(1-p)\Delta_k$ are large. It follows that r/w must then be large. Then Stirling's approximation gives

$$c \sim (1-p) \left(\frac{2\pi p}{1-p} \right)^{-\frac{w}{2}} \left(\prod_{k=1}^{w} \Delta_k \right)^{-\frac{1}{2}} \tag{12}$$

which shows that the magnitude of c may be considerably larger than $2^{-r/2}$, let alone $2^{-M/2}$, M being the memory size of the whole generator. The smallest magnitude of c is obtained when the feedback taps are approximately equidistant. In this case $c \sim (1-p)(2\pi p/(1-p))^{-w/2}((r-w)/w)^{-w/2}$ so that the required length of the keystream sequence to detect the weakness is then $(10/(1-p)^2)$ $(2\pi p/(1-p))^w((r-w)/w)^w$. Given w, the larger the values of r and p the smaller the correlation coefficient, respectively. Given r and p, there exists an optimal value of w that minimizes the correlation coefficient.

For a given feedback polynomial, one may simultaneously use different shrunk polynomials or their polynomial multiples and thus obtain different linear models. In addition to that, one may also use different polynomial multiples of the feedback polynomial, especially the ones with low weight, possibly much lower than for the original polynomial. So, in general, the weakness is easily detected when the feedback polynomial is known. If the feedback polynomial is key-dependent, as is suggested in [3], then the weakness can be used to reconstruct the corresponding part of the secret key.

5 Linear Models for Shift Register Based Keystream Generators

In this section, the LSCA method is applied to an arbitrary binary keystream generator consisting of regularly or irregularly clocked shift registers (SRs) combined by a function with or without memory. Clock control sequences are produced either within the generator or by separate generators. First, one should form the linear models for individual SRs: regularly clocked linear feedback SRs stay as they are, linear models for regularly clocked nonlinear feedback SRs are made by linearizing the feedback functions, and linear models for irregularly clocked SRs are formed by using the shrunk polynomials as explained in Section 4. Second, by using the LSCA method from Section 3 one then develops a linear model for the function with memory, which is treated as a non-autonomous finite-state machine with purely random input sequences, see [8]. Consequently, one obtains a linear equation of the form (5) whose right-hand side contains the additional input sequences as well. The linear function on the left-hand side of (5) corresponds to the reciprocal $\varphi(z)$ of the characteristic polynomial of the state-transition matrix. Finally, one substitutes the outputs of the linearized SRs for the inputs to the linear sequential circuit and thus gets a linear model with the feedback polynomial being equal to the least common multiple of $\varphi(z)$ and the feedback polynomials of all the linearized SRs. For estimating the overall correlation coefficient, a reasonable assumption is that the noise sequences from the linearized SRs are mutually independent and independent from the noise sequences in the linear sequential circuit, unless the SRs are connected in a very special way. Various linear models are obtained by varying the linear models for irregularly clocked and nonlinear feedback SRs and the linear model for the function with memory. Polynomial multiples may also be used especially if they reduce the magnitude of the overall correlation coefficient. In fact, it is the polynomial multiples that make it very difficult to achieve the security against the LSCA attack. Simultaneous use of different linear models is possible.

Several well-known shift register based binary keystream generators are now examined in more detail, for illustration. It follows that they are potentially vulnerable to the proposed LSCA statistical attack if the number of shift registers is not very large.

Memoryless combiner [19]:

Take a linear approximation of the memoryless function with the correlation coefficient c. The feedback polynomial of a linear model is the least common multiple of the feedback polynomials of all the input SRs involved in the linear function, or any polynomial multiple of this polynomial. The overall correlation coefficient is c^W where W is the weight of the feedback polynomial of the linear model.

Time-variant memoryless combiner [12, 6]:

Consider a memoryless combiner with n inputs whose combining function slowly changes in time under the control of another generator, see [12] or [6], for example. This destroys the termwise correlation between the output and inputs. However, the LSCA method then yields that the linear transform $1+z$ of the output is correlated to the same transform of any linear combination of the inputs, with the correlation coefficient very close to $1/2^n$. By considering the correlation to a single input, one obtains a linear model whose feedback polynomial is equal to the product of $1+z$ and the feedback polynomial of weight W of the chosen input SR, with the overall correlation coefficient $1/2^{nW}$.

Basic summation generator [14, 18]:

The basic summation generator is a combiner with one bit of memory and two regularly clocked linear feedback SRs. Its output function is already linear, whereas its next-state function can be linearized in several ways with large correlation coefficients. By taking a linear function depending on a single input with the correlation coefficient 1/2, we obtain a linear model whose feedback polynomial is just the least common multiple of the feedback polynomials of the two input SRs, or any of its polynomial multiples. The overall correlation coefficient is $1/2^W$ where W is the weight of this polynomial. Besides, the output is correlated to the sum of one input and the linear transform $1+z$ of the other with the correlation coefficient only 1/2.

Stop-and-go cascade generator [11]:

This is a cascade of K stop-and-go linear feedback SRs with the same feedback polynomial $f(z)$, where the first SR is regularly clocked. Using the model from Section 4 for a single stop-and-go shift register and the approach described at the beginning of this section, one obtains a linear model with the feedback polynomial $(1+z)f(z)$ and the overall correlation coefficient $1/2^{(K-1)W}$ where W is the weight of $f(z)$. Instead of $f(z)$ one may also take any of its polynomial multiples. Also, the linear transform $1+z$ of the cascade output is correlated to the same linear transform of the first shift register output, with the correlation coefficient $1/2^{K-1}$. This is in accordance with the analysis from [16].

Shrinking generator [3, 17]:

This is a single irregularly clocked linear feedback SR whose clock is controlled by another linear feedback SR in a manner that corresponds to independent deletions with probability $p = 1/2$. Direct application of the model from Section 4 then yields a linear model with the feedback polynomial equal to a shrunk polynomial of the feedback polynomial of the irregularly clocked SR or of any of its polynomial multiples. The correlation coefficient is given by (11) or (12) for $p = 1/2$. If one considers a trinomial multiple of the feedback polynomial, then $w = 2$ and the weakness is easily detectable.

6 Conclusion

An intrinsic statistical weakness of keystream generators is pointed out. It is shown that a binary keystream generator realized as an autonomous finite-state machine with M bits of memory can be linearly modelled as a non-autonomous linear feedback shift register of length at most M with an additive input sequence of nonbalanced identically distributed binary random variables. An effective method based on the linear sequential circuit approximation of finite-state machines is developed for determining the feedback polynomials of linear models with comparatively large correlation coefficients of input sequences. The corresponding statistical test can be used to reduce the uncertainty of unknown plaintext and to reconstruct the unknown structure of a keystream generator, regardless of the initial state. For practical schemes, the required length of the known keystream sequence may be considerably smaller than the period.

In particular, linear models for irregularly clocked shift registers as well as for arbitrary shift register based keystream generators are derived. Illustrative examples including the time-variant memoryless combiner, the basic summation generator, the stop-and-go cascade, and the shrinking generator are presented.

Interesting open problems are to analyze the magnitude of the correlation coefficients for the introduced linear models and also to investigate the application of the linear sequential circuit approximation method for the divide and conquer attacks on the initial state of autonomous finite-state machines.

References

1. R. J. Anderson, "Solving a class of stream ciphers," *Cryptologia*, 14(3):285–288, 1990.
2. W. G. Chambers and D. Gollmann, "Lock-in effect in cascades of clock-controlled shift registers," Advances in Cryptology - EUROCRYPT '88, *Lecture Notes in Computer Science*, vol. 330, C. G. Günther ed., Springer-Verlag, pp. 331–342, 1988.
3. D. Coppersmith, H. Krawczyk, and Y. Mansour, "The shrinking generator," Advances in Cryptology – CRYPTO '93, *Lecture Notes in Computer Science*, vol. 773, D. R. Stinson ed., Springer-Verlag, pp. 22–39, 1994.
4. R. G. Gallager, "Low-density parity-check codes," *IRE Trans. Inform. Theory*, 8:21–28, Jan. 1962.

5. J. Dj. Golić and M. V. Živković, "On the linear complexity of nonuniformly decimated PN-sequences," *IEEE Trans. Inform. Theory*, 34:1077–1079, Sep. 1988.
6. J. Dj. Golić and M. J. Mihaljević, "Minimal linear equivalent analysis of a variable-memory binary sequence generator," *IEEE Trans. Inform. Theory*, 36:190–192, Jan. 1990.
7. J. Dj. Golić and M. J. Mihaljević, "A generalized correlation attack on a class of stream ciphers based on the Levenshtein distance," *Journal of Cryptology*, 3(3):201–212, 1991.
8. J. Dj. Golić, "Correlation via linear sequential circuit approximation of combiners with memory," Advances in Cryptology - EUROCRYPT '92, *Lecture Notes in Computer Science*, vol. 658, R. A Rueppel ed., Springer-Verlag, pp. 113–123, 1993.
9. J. Dj. Golić and S. V. Petrović, "A generalized correlation attack with a probabilistic constrained edit distance," Advances in Cryptology - EUROCRYPT '92, *Lecture Notes in Computer Science*, vol. 658, R. A. Rueppel ed., Springer-Verlag, pp. 472–476, 1992.
10. J. Dj. Golić, "On the security of shift register based keystream generators," Fast Software Encryption '93, *Lecture Notes of Computer Science*, vol. 809, R. J. Anderson ed., Springer-Verlag, pp. 90–100, 1994.
11. D. Gollmann and W. G. Chambers, "Clock controlled shift registers: a review," *IEEE J. Sel. Ar. Commun.*, 7(4):525–533, 1989.
12. M. D. MacLaren and G. Marsaglia, "Uniform random number generators," *J. Ass. Comput. Machinery*, 12:83–89, 1965.
13. J. L. Massey, "Shift register sequences and BCH decoding," *IEEE Trans. Inform. Theory*, 15:122-127, 1969.
14. J. L. Massey and R. A. Rueppel, "Method of, and apparatus for, transforming a digital sequence into an encoded form" U. S. Patent No. 4,797,922, 1989.
15. W. Meier and O. Staffelbach, "Fast correlation attacks on certain stream ciphers," *Journal of Cryptology*, 1(3):159–176, 1989.
16. R. Menicocci, "Short Gollmann cascade generators may be insecure," *Abstracts of the Fourth IMA Conference on Coding and Cryptography*, Cirencester, 1993, to appear in the *Proceedings*, Oxford University Press.
17. M. J. Mihaljević, "An approach to the initial state reconstruction of a clock-controlled shift register based on a novel distance measure," Advances in Cryptology - AUSCRYPT '92, *Lecture Notes in Computer Science*, vol. 718, J. Seberry and Y. Zheng eds., Springer-Verlag, pp. 349–356, 1993.
18. R. A. Rueppel, "Stream ciphers," in *Contemporary Cryptology: The Science of Information Integrity*, G. Simmons ed., pp. 65–134. New York: IEEE Press, 1991.
19. T. Siegenthaler, "Decrypting a class of stream ciphers using ciphertext only," *IEEE Trans. Comput.*, 34:81–85, Jan. 1985.
20. K. C. Zeng, C. H. Yang, and T. R. N. Rao, "On the linear consistency test (LCT) in cryptanalysis and its applications," Advances in Cryptology - CRYPTO '89, *Lecture Notes in Computer Science*, vol. 218, G. Brassard ed., Springer-Verlag, pp. 164–174, 1990.
21. M. V. Živković, "An algorithm for the initial state reconstruction of the clock-controlled shift register," *IEEE Trans. Inform. Theory*, 37:1488–1490, Sep. 1991.

SESSION 3

CRYPTOGRAPHIC FUNCTIONS

Chair: Zong-Duo Dai

(Academia Sinica, China)

Semi-bent functions

Seongtaek Chee, Sangjin Lee, Kwangjo Kim

Electronics and Telecommunications Research Institute
Taejon, 305-600, KOREA
E-mail : {chee,sjlee,kkj}@dingo.etri.re.kr

Abstract. Highly nonlinear balanced Boolean functions both satisfying the propagation criterion and having almost uniform correlation values with all linear functions are very important in the design of hash functions, stream and block ciphers. In particular, the output uncorrelated properties between two Boolean functions are required to design permutations. We present, so called, *semi-bent functions* which satisfy all of these properties.

1 Introduction

Cryptographic Boolean functions play an important role in the design of hash functions, stream and block ciphers. Recently, various criteria related to cryptographically desirable Boolean functions have been proposed, such as balancedness, high nonlinearity, correlation immunity and satisfiability of the propagation criterion.

Seberry *et al.* [16] proposed a method for constructing highly nonlinear balanced functions which are correlation immune. Camion *et al.* [3] also suggested a recursive method for constructing correlation immune functions. Such functions are very useful in many cryptographic fields. Due to Parseval's theorem [14], however, there must be correlations between correlation immune functions and some set of linear functions. This problem can be overcome by introducing a bent function [13]. Bent functions, except for the fact that they are never balanced, exhibit ideal cryptographic properties. In particular, bent functions have uniform correlation values to all linear functions.

The goal of this paper is to design a new class of cryptographically desirable Boolean functions, so called *semi-bent functions.* They are balanced, have the maximal nonlinearity that balanced functions could have, exhibit almost uniform correlation values to all linear functions, and satisfy the propagation criterion. The output uncorrelatedness between two Boolean functions are required in some applications, especially in designing permutations [7, 8, 9]. We also show that a pair of *semi-bent functions* satisfy this requirement.

The relations among the Walsh-Hadamard transformations, autocorrelation functions, nonlinearities, correlation properties, and propagation characteristics are used in this paper. Almost of these relations are well-studied by Preneel [11].

This paper is organized as follows : Section 2 introduces basic notations and definitions. Section 3 describes bent functions, the Walsh-Hadamard transformations and their properties used in this paper. Our main results are discussed in

Sections 4 and 5. In Section 4, we introduce *semi-bent functions* and study their cryptographical properties. In Section 5, we present a concept of two Boolean functions with regard to mutually output uncorrelatedness, and we discuss its cryptographic relevance to Differential [2] and Linear Cryptanalysis [5].

2 Basic notations and definitions

Let $\mathbb{Z}_2^n$ be the n-dimensional vector space($n \geq 3$) with the binary n-tuples of elements $\mathbf{x} = (x_1, \cdots, x_n)$. A Boolean function f is a function whose domain is $\mathbb{Z}_2^n$ and takes the values 0 and 1. The set of all Boolean functions on $\mathbb{Z}_2^n$ will be denoted as $\mathcal{B}_n$. In most cases it will be more convenient to deal with $\hat{f}(\mathbf{x}) = (-1)^{f(\mathbf{x})}$ that takes the values in $\{-1, 1\}$.

A function f is said to be affine if there is a vector $\mathbf{w} \in \mathbb{Z}_2^n$ and $c \in \mathbb{Z}_2$ such that $f(\mathbf{x}) = l_{\mathbf{w}}(\mathbf{x}) \oplus c = (\mathbf{x}, \mathbf{w}) \oplus c = x_1 w_1 \oplus \cdots \oplus x_n w_n \oplus c$. In particular, f will be called linear if $c = 0$. The set of all affine and linear functions on $\mathbb{Z}_2^n$ will be denoted by Λ_n and $\mathcal{L}_n$, respectively.

The Hamming weight of $\mathbf{x} \in \mathbb{Z}_2^n$, denoted by $wt(\mathbf{x})$, is the number of ones in $\mathbf{x}$ and the Hamming weight of $f \in \mathcal{B}_n$, $wt(f)$, is the number of function values equal to one. The Hamming distance $d(f, g)$ between two functions f and g is the number of function values in which they differ. If $wt(\mathbf{x}) = 1$, then $\mathbf{x}$ is called a unit vector.

Let $f \oplus g$ be a function on $\mathbb{Z}_2^n$ obtained by bit-wise exclusive-or (XOR) of two function values of f and g, and $f \mid\mid g$ be a function on $\mathbb{Z}_2^{n+1}$ whose truth table is the concatenation of the truth tables of f and g. That is,

$$(f \oplus g)(\mathbf{x}) = f(\mathbf{x}) \oplus g(\mathbf{x})$$

$$(f \mid\mid g)(\mathbf{x}^*) = (f \mid\mid g)(\mathbf{x}, x_{n+1}) = (1 \oplus x_{n+1}) f(\mathbf{x}) \oplus x_{n+1} g(\mathbf{x}).$$

Now, we define the essential criteria for cryptographic Boolean functions.

Definition 1. A function $f \in \mathcal{B}_n$ is balanced if

$$\#\{\mathbf{x} \in \mathbb{Z}_2^n \mid f(\mathbf{x}) = 0\} = \#\{\mathbf{x} \in \mathbb{Z}_2^n \mid f(\mathbf{x}) = 1\}.$$

The balancedness is a basic requirement to guarantee good statistical properties. Nonlinearity is a desirable property in cryptography, for linear cryptosystems are known to be weak. There are various ways to measure nonlinearity of Boolean functions [6, 11, 14]. Among them, we use the following definitions.

Definition 2. The nonlinearity of $f \in \mathcal{B}_n$ is defined by

$$\mathcal{N}_f = \min_{\lambda_n \in \Lambda_n} d(f, \lambda_n).$$

The propagation criterion was first introduced by Preneel [12].

Definition 3. A function $f \in \mathcal{B}_n$ satisfies the propagation criterion (PC) with respect to a non-zero $\alpha \in \mathbb{Z}_2^n$ if

$$\sum_{\mathbf{x} \in \mathbb{Z}_2^n} f(\mathbf{x}) \oplus f(\mathbf{x} \oplus \alpha) = 2^{n-1}.$$

f is said to satisfy the propagation criterion of degree k (PC(k)), if it satisfies the propagation criterion with respect to all $\alpha \in \mathbb{Z}_2^n$ such that $1 \leq wt(\alpha) \leq k$.

In fact, the propagation criterion is an extended concept of the strict avalanche criterion (SAC) which has been widely studied during last decade, and is regarded as a measure of dynamic behavior of Boolean functions when the inputs are changed. Seberry *et al.* [17] proposed a recursive method for constructing PC(k)-fulfilling Boolean functions.

Most stream ciphers employ the method for combining shift registers with nonlinear Boolean functions. In order to immunize them against a correlation attack [18], the Boolean function must be well chosen. Siegenthaler [18] introduced a correlation immune function which became an active research area in cryptology. Two methods are proposed to generate the correlation immune function by a direct or recursive method [3, 16]. However, considering the well-known Parseval's theorem [14], the correlation immune function is not the sufficient solution against a correlation attack. ¿From the global point of view, there always exists any correlation between correlation immune functions and some linear functions. So, in practical applications, some correlation immune functions may be useless. Bent functions are the best ones with respect to this property. The following is the formal definition of the m-th order correlation immune function.

Definition 4. A function $f \in \mathcal{B}_n$ is said to be m-th order correlation immune, $1 \leq m \leq n$, if

$$d(f, l_{\mathbf{w}}) = 2^{n-1}$$

holds for any $\mathbf{w} \in \mathbb{Z}_2^n$ with $1 \leq wt(\mathbf{w}) \leq m$. Furthermore, the correlation value between f and g is defined by

$$c(f, g) = 1 - \frac{d(f, g)}{2^{n-1}}.$$

3 Bent functions and Walsh-Hadamard transformations

Bent functions have been introduced by Rothaus [13]. The following definitions are used to drive our main results.

Definition 5. For $f \in \mathcal{B}_n$, the Walsh-Hadamard transformation $\hat{\mathcal{F}}_f : \mathbb{Z}_2^n \longrightarrow \mathbb{R}$ of $\hat{f}$, is defined as

$$\hat{\mathcal{F}}_f(\mathbf{w}) = \sum_{\mathbf{x} \in \mathbb{Z}_2^n} \hat{f}(\mathbf{x}) \cdot (-1)^{(\mathbf{w}, \mathbf{x})},$$

where $\mathbb{R}$ denotes the set of all real numbers.

Theorem 6 (Parseval's Theorem). *For $f \in \mathcal{B}_n$, we have*

$$\sum_{\mathbf{w} \in \mathbb{Z}_2^n} \hat{\mathcal{F}}_{\hat{f}}^2(\mathbf{w}) = 2^{2n}.$$

Definition 7. For $f \in \mathcal{B}_n$, the autocorrelation function $\hat{\mathcal{A}}_{\hat{f}} : \mathbb{Z}_2^n \longrightarrow \mathbb{R}$ of $\hat{f}$, is defined as

$$\hat{\mathcal{A}}_{\hat{f}}(\mathbf{s}) = \sum_{\mathbf{x} \in \mathbb{Z}_2^n} \hat{f}(\mathbf{x}) \cdot \hat{f}(\mathbf{x} \oplus \mathbf{s}).$$

A more general concept is the crosscorrelation between two functions.

Definition 8. For $f_0, f_1 \in \mathcal{B}_n$, the crosscorrelation function $\hat{\mathcal{C}}_{\hat{f}_0, \hat{f}_1} : \mathbb{Z}_2^n \longrightarrow \mathbb{R}$ of $\hat{f}_0$ and $\hat{f}_1$, is defined as

$$\hat{\mathcal{C}}_{\hat{f}_0, \hat{f}_1}(\mathbf{s}) = \sum_{\mathbf{x} \in \mathbb{Z}_2^n} \hat{f}_0(\mathbf{x}) \cdot \hat{f}_1(\mathbf{x} \oplus \mathbf{s}).$$

By the well-known *convolution theorem* [11], the following lemma can be obtained.

Lemma 9. *For $f_0, f_1 \in \mathcal{B}_n$, we have*

$$\hat{\mathcal{C}}_{\hat{f}_0, \hat{f}_1}(\mathbf{x}) = \frac{1}{2^n} \sum_{\mathbf{w} \in \mathbb{Z}_2^n} \hat{\mathcal{F}}_{\hat{f}_0}(\mathbf{w}) \cdot \hat{\mathcal{F}}_{\hat{f}_1}(\mathbf{w}) \cdot (-1)^{\langle \mathbf{x}, \mathbf{w} \rangle}.$$

Propagation criterion can be characterized in terms of the autocorrelation functions.

Theorem 10 [11]. *Let $f \in \mathcal{B}_n$. Then f satisfies PC(k) if and only if*

$$\hat{\mathcal{A}}_{\hat{f}}(\mathbf{s}) = 0$$

holds for all $\mathbf{s} \in \mathbb{Z}_2^n$ with $1 \leq wt(\mathbf{s}) \leq k$.

Using Lemma 9 and Theorem 10, we can easily obtain the following.

Corollary 11 [11]. *Let $f \in \mathcal{B}_n$. Then f satisfies PC(k) if and only if*

$$\sum_{\mathbf{w} \in \mathbb{Z}_2^n} \hat{\mathcal{F}}_{\hat{f}}^2(\mathbf{w}) \cdot (-1)^{\langle \mathbf{s}, \mathbf{w} \rangle} = 0$$

holds for all $\mathbf{s} \in \mathbb{Z}_2^n$ with $1 \leq wt(\mathbf{s}) \leq k$.

A bent function can be defined in a formal way as :

Definition 12. A function $f \in \mathcal{B}_n$ is called a bent function if

$$|\hat{\mathcal{F}}_{\hat{f}}(\mathbf{w})| = 2^{\frac{n}{2}}$$

holds for any $\mathbf{w} \in \mathbb{Z}_2^n$.

The following properties of the bent functions are widely known [16, 17].

Theorem 13. *Let $f \in \mathcal{B}_n$ be a bent function. Then*

1) *f exists only for the case of even n.*
2) *f is never balanced and the difference between the number of ones and the number of zeros equals $\pm 2^{\frac{n}{2}}$.*
3) $\mathcal{N}_f = 2^{n-1} - 2^{\frac{n}{2}-1}$.
4) *f satisfies $PC(n)$.*
5) *f has uniform correlation values to all linear functions, i.e., for any $\mathbf{w} \in \mathbb{Z}_2^n$, the correlation value between f and $l_{\mathbf{w}}$ is $\pm 2^{-\frac{n}{2}}$.*

Except for the facts that bent functions are not balanced and exist only on the even dimensional vector space, bent functions have ideal properties from a cryptographical point of view.

Meier and Staffelbach [6] proposed a method to randomly select a bent function and to complement an arbitrary set of $2^{\frac{n}{2}-1}$ ones (or zeros) in the truth table of bent function in order to overcome the unbalancedness of bent functions. They claimed that the modified function still has cryptographically desirable properties, and also generated a function on the odd dimensional vector space by concatenating a bent function to its complement. Later, their method was extended by Seberry *et al.* [17].

The following is an immediate consequence from the definition of Walsh-Hadamard transformation.

Lemma 14. *For $f \in \mathcal{B}_n$, we have*

$$\mathcal{N}_f = 2^{n-1} - \frac{1}{2} \max_{\mathbf{w} \in \mathbb{Z}_2^n} |\hat{\mathcal{F}}_f(\mathbf{w})|,$$

and f is balanced if and only if $\hat{\mathcal{F}}_f(\mathbf{0}) = 0$.

The following theorems tell us that, for a given Boolean function $f(\mathbf{x})$, its Walsh-Hadamard transformation and autocorrelation function are very useful tools to analyse its cryptographic behavior when employing the affine transformation of $\mathbf{x}$ and an addition of an affine function to $f(\mathbf{x})$.

Theorem 15 [11]. *For $f \in \mathcal{B}_n, \mathbf{a}, \mathbf{b} \in \mathbb{Z}_2^n, c \in \mathbb{Z}_2$ and an $2n \times 2n$ nonsingular matrix A, define $g \in \mathcal{B}_n$ by*

$$g(\mathbf{x}) = f(A\mathbf{x} \oplus \mathbf{a}) \oplus l_{\mathbf{b}}(\mathbf{x}) \oplus c.$$

Then we have

$$\hat{\mathcal{F}}_{\hat{g}}(\mathbf{w}) = (-1)^c (-1)^{(A^{-1}\mathbf{a}, \mathbf{w} \oplus \mathbf{b})} \hat{\mathcal{F}}_f((A^{-1})^t (\mathbf{w} \oplus \mathbf{b}))$$

and

$$\hat{\mathcal{A}}_{\hat{g}}(\mathbf{s}) = (-1)^{(\mathbf{s}, (A^{-1})^t \mathbf{b})} \hat{\mathcal{A}}_f(A\mathbf{s}).$$

Theorem 16 [11]. *For* $f_0, f_1 \in B_n$, $\mathbf{w}^*, \mathbf{s}^* \in \mathbb{Z}_2^{n+1}$ *and* $\mathbf{w}, \mathbf{s} \in \mathbb{Z}_2^n$, *let* $g = f_0 \parallel f_1$, *then we have*

$$\hat{\mathcal{F}}_{\hat{g}}(\mathbf{w}^*) = \hat{\mathcal{F}}_{\hat{f}_0}(\mathbf{w}) + (-1)^{w_{n+1}} \hat{\mathcal{F}}_{\hat{f}_1}(\mathbf{w})$$

and

$$\hat{\mathcal{A}}_{\hat{g}}(\mathbf{s}^*) = \begin{cases} \hat{\mathcal{A}}_{\hat{f}_0}(\mathbf{s}) + \hat{\mathcal{A}}_{\hat{f}_1}(\mathbf{s}) & \text{if } s_{n+1} = 0 \\ 2 \cdot \hat{\mathcal{C}}_{\hat{f}_0,\hat{f}_1}(\mathbf{s}) & \text{if } s_{n+1} = 1. \end{cases}$$

4 Semi-bent functions

We now define a new function defined on the odd dimensional vector sapce by concatenation of two bent functions, applying affine transformation to the input of a bent function, and complementing of the output of a bent function.

Definition 17. Let $f_0 \in \mathcal{B}_{2n}$ be a bent function, $\mathbf{a} \in \mathbb{Z}_2^{2n}$ and A be a $2n \times 2n$ nonsingular matrix. Define $f_1 \in \mathcal{B}_{2n}$ by

$$f_1(\mathbf{x}) = f_0(A\mathbf{x} \oplus \mathbf{a}) \oplus 1,$$

and $g \in \mathcal{B}_{2n+1}$ by

$$g = f_0 \parallel f_1,$$

i.e.,

$$\begin{aligned} g(\mathbf{x}^*) &= (1 \oplus x_{2n+1}) f_0(\mathbf{x}) \oplus x_{2n+1} f_1(\mathbf{x}) \\ &= f_0(\mathbf{x}) \oplus x_{2n+1} f_0(\mathbf{x}) \oplus x_{2n+1} \oplus x_{2n+1} f_0(A\mathbf{x} \oplus \mathbf{a}). \end{aligned} \tag{1}$$

We call $g \in \mathcal{B}_{2n+1}$ to be a semi-bent function.

Theorem 18. *Let* $g \in \mathcal{B}_{2n+1}$ *be a semi-bent function. Then* g *has the following properties.*

1) *g is balanced.*
2) $\mathcal{N}_g = 2^{2n} - 2^n$.
3) *For any* $\mathbf{w}^* \in \mathbb{Z}_2^{2n+1}$, *the correlation value between* g *and* $l_{\mathbf{w}^*}$ *is 0 or* $\pm 2^{-n}$, *and*

$$\#\{\mathbf{w}^* \in \mathbb{Z}_2^{2n+1} \mid c(g, l_{\mathbf{w}^*}) = 0\} = 2^{2n} = \#\{\mathbf{w}^* \in \mathbb{Z}_2^{2n+1} \mid c(g, l_{\mathbf{w}^*}) = \pm 2^{-n}\}.$$

Proof. Since f_0 is a bent function, by Definition 12 and Theorem 10, we have

$$|\hat{\mathcal{F}}_{\hat{f}_0}(\mathbf{w})| = 2^n$$

for any $\mathbf{w} \in \mathbb{Z}_2^{2n}$, and

$$\hat{\mathcal{A}}_{\hat{f}_0}(\mathbf{s}) = 0$$

for any $\mathbf{s} \in \mathbb{Z}_2^{2n}$ with $1 \leq wt(\mathbf{s}) \leq n$. Therefore, by Theorems 15 and 16, we have

$$\begin{aligned}|\hat{\mathcal{F}}_{\hat{g}}(\mathbf{w}^*)| &= |\hat{\mathcal{F}}_{\hat{f}_0}(\mathbf{w}) + (-1)^{w_{n+1}}\hat{\mathcal{F}}_{\hat{f}_1}(\mathbf{w})| \\ &= | \pm 2^n \mp (-1)^{\langle (A^{-1})^t \mathbf{a}, \mathbf{w}\rangle} 2^n | \\ &= 0 \text{ or } 2^{n+1}. \end{aligned} \tag{2}$$

By Lemma 14, since $\hat{\mathcal{F}}_{\hat{g}}(\mathbf{0}) = 0$, g is balanced, and we have

$$\mathcal{N}_g = 2^{2n} - 2^n.$$

By Eq. (2), for any $\mathbf{w}^* \in \mathbb{Z}_2^{2n+1}$, we have

$$\begin{aligned}c(g, l_{\mathbf{w}^*}) &= \frac{\hat{\mathcal{F}}_{\hat{g}}(\mathbf{w}^*)}{2^{2n+1}} \\ &= 0 \text{ or } \pm 2^{-n}.\end{aligned}$$

Let k be the number of $\mathbf{w}^* \in \mathbb{Z}_2^{2n+1}$ such that

$$c(g, l_{\mathbf{w}^*}) = \pm 2^{-n}.$$

Then by Parseval's theorem, $k = 2^{2n} = \frac{2^{2n+1}}{2}$.

Pieprzyk and Finkelstein [10] claimed that $\mathcal{N}_g = 2^{2n} - 2^n$ is the maximal nonlinearity that balanced functions in $\mathcal{B}_{2n+1}$ could have. And g has almost uniform correlation values in the sense that g is correlation immune to the half of all linear functions, and has uniform correlation values to others.

Let $\mathbf{s}^* = (\mathbf{s}, s_{2n+1})$ be a non-zero element in $\mathbb{Z}_2^{2n+1}$ with $s_{2n+1} = 0$. Then, by 4) of Theorem 13 and Theorem 15, we have

$$\hat{\mathcal{A}}_{\hat{f}_0}(\mathbf{s}) = \hat{\mathcal{A}}_{\hat{f}_1}(\mathbf{s}) = 0.$$

So, by Theorem 16, we have

$$\hat{\mathcal{A}}_{\hat{g}}(\mathbf{s}^*) = 0. \tag{3}$$

Theorem 19. *Let $g \in \mathcal{B}_{2n+1}$ be a semi-bent function. Then g satisfies the PC with respect to all non-zero $\mathbf{s}^* \in \mathbb{Z}_2^{2n+1}$ with $s_{2n+1} = 0$.*

If the matrix A equals to the identity matrix I, then we have the following

Theorem 20. *Let $g \in \mathcal{B}_{2n+1}$ be a semi-bent function with $A = I$. Then g satisfies the PC with respect to all non-zero $\mathbf{s}^* \in \mathbb{Z}_2^{2n+1}$ with $\mathbf{s} \neq \mathbf{a}$.*

Proof. Let $\mathbf{s}^* = (\mathbf{s}, s_{2n+1})$ be a non-zero element in $\mathbb{Z}_2^{2n+1}$ with $\mathbf{s} \neq \mathbf{a}$. If $s_{2n+1} = 0$, then Theorem holds by Eq. (3). Suppose that $s_{2n+1} = 1$. By Lemma 9 and Theorem 15, we have

$$\begin{aligned}
\hat{\mathcal{A}}_{\hat{g}}(\mathbf{s}^*) &= 2 \cdot \hat{\mathcal{C}}_{\hat{f}_0,\hat{f}_1}(\mathbf{s}) \\
&= 2 \cdot \frac{1}{2^{2n}} \sum_{\mathbf{w} \in \mathbb{Z}_2^{2n}} \hat{\mathcal{F}}_{\hat{f}_0}(\mathbf{w}) \cdot \hat{\mathcal{F}}_{\hat{f}_1}(\mathbf{w}) \cdot (-1)^{(\mathbf{s},\mathbf{w})} \\
&= \frac{-1}{2^{2n-1}} \sum_{\mathbf{w} \in \mathbb{Z}_2^{2n}} \hat{\mathcal{F}}^2_{\hat{f}_0}(\mathbf{w}) \cdot (-1)^{(\mathbf{a}\oplus\mathbf{s},\mathbf{w})} \\
&= -2 \sum_{\mathbf{w} \in \mathbb{Z}_2^{2n}} (-1)^{(\mathbf{a}\oplus\mathbf{s},\mathbf{w})} \\
&= 0.
\end{aligned}$$

Functions satisfying PC(k) with respect to all non-zero elements are often necessary.

Corollary 21. *Let $g \in \mathcal{B}_{2n+1}$ be a semi-bent function with $A = I$ and $\mathbf{a} = (1, \cdots, 1)$. Then g satisfies PC(2n).*

In [17], Seberry *et al.* proposed a method to generate the highly nonlinear balanced Boolean functions satisfying PC(k). Their method is based on a special type of *semi-bent function* in Theorem 20. It is possible to apply their methods (employing linear transformation on input vectors of the *semi-bent function*) to our *semi-bent function* in Eq. (1). It is also possible to generate *semi-bent functions* in $\mathcal{B}_{2n+2}$ from bent functions in $\mathcal{B}_{2n}$, such methods have already been proposed in [6, 17].

5 Strict Uncorrelated Criterion

A single Boolean function is sufficient to design a nonlinear combiner in stream ciphers. However, in most hash functions and block ciphers, more than two Boolean functions are used. Thus correlation problems among Boolean functions may occur. f and g are said to be (output) uncorrelated if $f \oplus g$ is balanced and nonlinear [15]. But this condition is not sufficient to totally output uncorrelated between two functions. Therefore, we propose a new cryptographic definition as:

Definition 22. Two functions f and g in $\mathcal{B}_n$ are said to satisfy the strict uncorrelated criterion (SUC) if f, g, and $f \oplus g$ are all balanced and satisfy PC(1).

Example 1. Let

- $f_1(x_1, x_2, x_3, x_4) = x_1x_3 \oplus x_2x_3 \oplus x_4 \oplus x_1x_4 \oplus x_2x_4$
- $f_2(x_1, x_2, x_3, x_4) = x_1x_2 \oplus x_3 \oplus x_1x_3 \oplus x_2x_4 \oplus x_3x_4$
- $f_3(x_1, x_2, x_3, x_4) = x_2 \oplus x_1x_2 \oplus x_2x_3 \oplus x_4 \oplus x_2x_4$

– $f_4(x_1, x_2, x_3, x_4) = x_1 \oplus x_1x_2 \oplus x_3 \oplus x_1x_3 \oplus x_4 \oplus x_1x_4$.

Then for $1 \leq i, j \leq 4, i \neq j$, f_i and f_j satisfy the SUC on $\mathbb{Z}_2^4$. In fact (f_1, f_2, f_3, f_4) forms a permutation on $\mathbb{Z}_2^4$.

Theorem 23. *Let g_1 and g_2 be semi-bent functions with a permutation matrix A in Eq. (1) which are generated from bent functions f_1 and f_2, respectively, such that $f_1 \oplus f_2$ is balanced and satisfies PC(1)*[1]. *Then g_1 and g_2 satisfy the SUC except for one unit vector $\mathbf{s}^* = (0, \cdots, 0, 1)$.*

Proof. By Theorems 18 and 19, g_1 and g_2 are balanced and satisfy the PC(1) with respect to all unit vectors $\mathbf{s}^*$ with $\mathbf{s}^* \neq (0, \cdots, 0, 1)$. Since g_1 and g_2 are of the forms

$$g_1(\mathbf{x}, x_{2n+1}) = f_1(\mathbf{x}) \oplus x_{2n+1} \oplus x_{2n+1}f_1(\mathbf{x}) \oplus x_{2n+1}f_1(A\mathbf{x} \oplus \mathbf{a})$$

and

$$g_2(\mathbf{x}, x_{2n+1}) = f_2(\mathbf{x}) \oplus x_{2n+1} \oplus x_{2n+1}f_2(\mathbf{x}) \oplus x_{2n+1}f_2(A\mathbf{x} \oplus \mathbf{a})$$

for any x_{2n+1}, we have

$$g_1(\mathbf{x}, x_{2n+1}) \oplus g_2(\mathbf{x}, x_{2n+1}) = f_1(\mathbf{x}) \oplus f_2(\mathbf{x}) \oplus x_{2n+1}(f_1(\mathbf{x}) \oplus f_2(\mathbf{x}) \oplus f_1(A\mathbf{x} \oplus \mathbf{a}) \oplus f_2(A\mathbf{x} \oplus \mathbf{a})).$$

This implies that

$$(g_1 \oplus g_2)(\mathbf{x}^*) = (f_1 \oplus f_2)(\mathbf{x}) \mid\mid (f_1 \oplus f_2)(A\mathbf{x} \oplus \mathbf{a}).$$

Hence $wt(g_1 \oplus g_2) = 2 \cdot wt(f_1 \oplus f_2)$. Since $f_1 \oplus f_2$ is balanced, so is $g_1 \oplus g_2$. Let $\mathbf{s}^* = (\mathbf{s}, s_{2n+1}) \in \mathbb{Z}_2^{2n+1}$ be any unit vector with $\mathbf{s}^* \neq (0, \cdots, 0, 1)$. Since A is a permutation matrix, we have $wt(\mathbf{s}) = 1 = wt(A\mathbf{s})$. Since $f_1 \oplus f_2$ satisfies PC(1), by Theorems 15 and 16, we have

$$\hat{A}_{\widehat{g_1 \oplus g_2}}(\mathbf{s}^*) = 0.$$

Therefore, $g_1 \oplus g_2$ satisfies PC(1) with respect to all unit vectors $\mathbf{s}^*$ not equal to $(0, \cdots, 0, 1)$. In all, g_1 and g_2 satisfy the SUC except for one unit vector $\mathbf{s}^* = (0, \cdots, 0, 1)$.

Corollary 24. *If $A = I$ and $wt(\mathbf{a}) = 1$ in Theorem 23, then g_1 and g_2 satisfy the SUC.*

Proof. It is enough to show that $g_1 \oplus g_2$ satisfies PC(1). Let $\mathbf{s}^* = (\mathbf{s}, s_{2n+1})$ be a unit vector in $\mathbb{Z}_2^{2n+1}$. If $s_{2n+1} = 0$, then $g_1 \oplus g_2$ satisfy PC(1) by Theorem

[1] Such functions can be easily such that $f_1 \oplus f_2$ is balanced and satisfies PC(1) among 400,960 possible pairs of bent functions.

23. Suppose that $s_{2n+1} = 1$, then $\mathbf{s} = \mathbf{0}$. Since $wt(\mathbf{a}) = 1$, by Theorems 15, 16, Lemma 9 and Corollary 11, we have

$$\begin{aligned}\hat{\mathcal{A}}_{\widehat{g_1 \oplus g_2}}(\mathbf{s}^*) &= 2 \cdot \hat{\mathcal{C}}_{\widehat{(f_1\oplus f_2)}(\mathbf{x}),\widehat{(f_1\oplus f_2)}(\mathbf{x}\oplus\mathbf{a})}(\mathbf{0}) \\ &= 2 \cdot \frac{1}{2^{2n}} \sum_{\mathbf{w}\in\mathbb{Z}_2^{2n}} \hat{\mathcal{F}}^2_{\widehat{f_1\oplus f_2}}(\mathbf{w}) \cdot (-1)^{\langle\mathbf{a},\mathbf{w}\rangle} \\ &= 0.\end{aligned}$$

Therefore, g_1 and g_2 satisfy the SUC.

Example 2. Consider two bent functions

$$f_1(x_1, x_2, x_3, x_4) = 1 \oplus x_1 \oplus x_3 \oplus x_1x_3 \oplus x_2x_4 \oplus x_3x_4$$

and

$$f_2(x_1, x_2, x_3, x_4) = 1 \oplus x_3 \oplus x_2x_3 \oplus x_4 \oplus x_1x_4 \oplus x_3x_4.$$

Then $f_1 \oplus f_2$ is balanced and satisfies PC(1).
Let g_1 and g_2 be semi-bent functions in Corollary 24 with $\mathbf{a} = (0, \cdots, 0, 1)$. Then

$$g_1(x_1, x_2, x_3, x_4, x_5) = 1 \oplus x_1 \oplus x_3 \oplus x_1x_3 \oplus x_2x_4 \oplus x_3x_4 \oplus x_5 \oplus x_2x_5 \oplus x_3x_5$$

and

$$g_2(x_1, x_2, x_3, x_4, x_5) = 1 \oplus x_3 \oplus x_2x_3 \oplus x_4 \oplus x_1x_4 \oplus x_3x_4 \oplus x_1x_5 \oplus x_3x_5.$$

Note that g_1, g_2, and $g_1 \oplus g_2$ are balanced and satisfy PC(1). That is, g_1 and g_2 satisfy the SUC on $\mathbb{Z}_2^5$.

In [15], the relationships between PC(1) and XOR distribution table are discussed. We can also see that if each Boolean function of a permutation satisfies PC(1), then the i-th row with $wt(i) = 1$ in XOR distribution table is distributed uniformly to some range. The uniformity would be increased if we consider the SUC fulfilling Boolean functions. If we extend the definition of SUC for k ($k < n$) Boolean functions (as an example, in case of even n, extend to $\frac{n}{2}$ Boolean functions), then the XOR distribution table would become close to uniform[2].

Furthermore, if we extend PC(1) to PC(k) in defining the SUC, we could get the same results for each k-th row with $1 \leq wt(i) \leq k$ of XOR distribution table. However, since the degree of the PC of a balanced Boolean function in $\mathcal{B}_n$ is controlled by the integer n [4], there must be relaxations when we extend the concept of SUC.

On the other hand, a Boolean function satisfying PC(1) is also nonlinear. Hence we can conclude that SUC fulfilling Boolean functions could have a consequence against Differential and Linear Cryptanalysis[3].

[2] This kind of permutation is not always good as we expect [15].

[3] In that case, a requirement of high nonlinearity for arbitrary linear combinations of Boolean functions is essential.

6 Conclusions

We have presented highly nonlinear balanced functions which have almost uniform correlation values to all linear functions and satisfy the propagation criterion. The methods of obtaining pairs of strict output uncorrelated Boolean functions (SUC fulfilling functions) are presented. Though we have studied independently to Seberry *et al.*'s works [15, 16, 17], there are similar results between our work and those of Seberry *et al.* The main differences among them are :

- *Semi-bent functions* include the basic functions in [17], and it is possible to adapt "*moving vectors around*" technique in [17] to our functions.
- Our approach, using Walsh-Hadamard transformations, is easy to analyse cryptographic properties, especially correlation property, which is not mentioned in [17].
- We also deal with the cryptographical properties of more than two Boolean functions which are essential to construct a permutation and useful to analyse Differential and Linear characteristics.

We believe that *semi-bent functions* are useful to design hash functions, stream ciphers and block ciphers, since there are many varieties to apply them. We shall apply *semi-bent functions* to the even dimensional vector spaces and extend the notion of SUC not only by including nonlinearity and PC(k) ($k \geq 2$), but also by considering possible linear combinations of Boolean functions.

Acknowledgement : The authors would like to thank anonymous refrees for their helpful comments.

References

1. C. Adams and S. Tavares, *"The structured design of cryptographically good S-boxes"*, Journal of Cryptology **3**, no. 1, pp. 27–43, 1990.
2. E. Biham and A. Shamir, *"Differential cryptanalysis of DES-like cryptosystems"*, Journal of Cryptology **4**, no. 1, pp. 3–72, 1991.
3. P. Camion, C. Carlet, P. Charpin and N. Sendrier, *"On correlation-immune functions"*, Advances in Cryptology - CRYPTO'91, Springer-Verlag, pp. 87–100, 1992.
4. S. Hirose and K. Ikeda, *"A note on the propagation characteristics and the strict avalanche criteria"*, The 1994 Symposium on Cryptography and Information Security, 1994.
5. M. Matsui, *"Linear cryptanalysis method for DES cipher"*, Advances in Cryptology - EUROCRYPT'93, Springer-Verlag, pp. 386–397, 1994.
6. W. Meier and O.Staffelbach, *"Nonlinearity criteria for cryptographic functions"*, Advances in Cryptology - EUROCRYPT'89, Springer-Verlag, pp. 549–562, 1990.
7. K. Nyberg, *"On the construction of highly nonlinear permutations"*, Advances in Cryptology - EUROCRYPT'92, Springer-Verlag, pp. 92–98, 1993.
8. K. Nyberg, *"Differentially uniform mappings for cryptography"*, Advances in Cryptology - EUROCRYPT'93, Springer-Verlag, pp. 55–64, 1994.
9. K. Nyberg and L.R. Knudsen, *"Provable Security against Differential Cryptanalysis"*, Advances in Cryptology - CRYPTO'92, Springer-Verlag, pp. 566–574, 1993.

10. J. Pieprzyk and G. Finkelstein, *"Towards effective nonlinear cryptosystem design"*, IEE Proceedings, Part E : Computers and Digital Techniques, Vol. 135, pp. 325–335, 1988.
11. B. Preneel, *"Analysis and design of cryptographic hash functions"*, Ph.D. Dissertation, Katholieke Universiteit Leuven, 1993.
12. B. Preneel, W. Van Leekwijck and L. Van Linden, *"Propagation characteristics of Boolean functions"*, Advances in Cryptology - EUROCRYPT'90, Springer-Verlag, pp. 161–173, 1991.
13. O.S. Rothaus, *"On "bent" functions"*, Journal of Combinatorial Theory (A), Vol.20, pp. 300–305, 1976.
14. R.A. Rueppel, Stream Ciphers, in *"Contemporary Cryptology : The Science of Information Integrity"*, G.J. Simmons, Ed., IEEE Press, pp. 65–134, 1992.
15. J. Seberry, X. M. Zhang and Y. Zheng, *"Systematic generation of cryptographically robust S-boxes"*, In Proceedings of the first ACM Conference on Computer and Communications Security, pp. 172–182, 1993.
16. J. Seberry, X. M. Zhang and Y. Zheng, *"On constructions and nonlinearity of correlation immune functions"*, Advances in Cryptology - EUROCRYPT'93, Springer-Verlag, pp. 181–199, 1994.
17. J. Seberry, X. M. Zhang and Y. Zheng, *"Nonlinearly balanced Boolean functions and their propagation characteristics"*, Advances in Cryptology - CRYPTO'93, Springer-Verlag, pp. 49–60, 1994.
18. T. Siegenthaler, *"Correlation immunity of non-linear combining functions for cryptographic applications"*, IEEE Trans. Inform. Theory IT-30, pp. 776–780, 1984.

Structures of Cryptographic Functions with Strong Avalanche Characteristics (Extended Abstract)

Jennifer Seberry, Xian-Mo Zhang and Yuliang Zheng

Department of Computer Science
University of Wollongong, Wollongong, NSW 2522, Australia
{jennie, xianmo, yuliang}@cs.uow.edu.au

Abstract. This paper studies the properties and constructions of nonlinear functions, which are a core component of cryptographic primitives including data encryption algorithms and one-way hash functions. A main contribution of this paper is to reveal the relationship between nonlinearity and propagation characteristic, two critical indicators of the cryptographic strength of a Boolean function. In particular, we prove that

(i) if f, a Boolean function on V_n, satisfies the propagation criterion with respect to all but a subset $\Re$ of vectors in V_n, then the nonlinearity of f satisfies $N_f \geq 2^{n-1} - 2^{\frac{1}{2}(n+t)-1}$, where t is the rank of $\Re$, and

(ii) When $|\Re| > 2$, the nonzero vectors in $\Re$ are linearly dependent.

Furthermore we show that

(iii) if $|\Re| = 2$ then n must be odd, the nonlinearity of f satisfies $N_f = 2^{n-1} - 2^{\frac{1}{2}(n-1)}$, and the nonzero vector in $\Re$ must be a linear structure of f.

(iv) there exists no function on V_n such that $|\Re| = 3$.

(v) if $|\Re| = 4$ then n must be even, the nonlinearity of f satisfies $N_f = 2^{n-1} - 2^{\frac{1}{2}n}$, and the nonzero vectors in $\Re$ must be linear structures of f.

(vi) if $|\Re| = 5$ then n must be odd, the nonlinearity of f is $N_f = 2^{n-1} - 2^{\frac{1}{2}(n-1)}$, the four nonzero vectors in $\Re$, denoted by β_1, β_2, β_3 and β_4, are related by the equation $\beta_1 \oplus \beta_2 \oplus \beta_3 \oplus \beta_4 = 0$, and *none* of the four vectors is a linear structure of f.

(vii) there exists no function on V_n such that $|\Re| = 6$.

We also discuss the structures of functions with $|\Re| = 2, 4, 5$. In particular we show that these functions have close relationships with bent functions, and can be easily constructed from the latter.

1 Introduction

Cryptographic techniques for information authentication and data encryption require Boolean functions with a number of critical properties that distinguish them from linear (or affine) functions. Among the properties are high nonlinearity, high degree of propagation, few linear structures, high algebraic degree etc. These properties are often called *nonlinearity criteria*. An important topic is to investigate relationships among the various nonlinearity criteria. Progress in this direction has been made in [9], where connections have been revealed among the strict avalanche characteristic (SAC), differential characteristics, linear structures and nonlinearity, of *quadratic* functions.

In this paper we carry on the investigation initiated in [9] and bring together nonlinearity and propagation characteristic of a Boolean function (quadratic or non-quadratic). These two cryptographic criteria are seemly quite separate, in the sense that the former indicates the minimum distance between a Boolean function and all the affine functions whereas the latter forecasts the avalanche behavior of the function when some input bits to the function are complemented.

We further extend our investigation into the structures of cryptographic functions. A short summary of the results is presented in Table 1.

Due to the limit on space, detailed proofs will be left to the full version of the paper.

2 Basic Definitions

We consider Boolean functions from V_n to $GF(2)$ (or simply functions on V_n), V_n is the vector space of n tuples of elements from $GF(2)$. The *truth table* of a function f on V_n is a $(0,1)$-sequence defined by $(f(\alpha_0), f(\alpha_1), \ldots, f(\alpha_{2^n-1}))$, and the *sequence* of f is a $(1,-1)$-sequence defined by $((-1)^{f(\alpha_0)}, (-1)^{f(\alpha_1)}, \ldots, (-1)^{f(\alpha_{2^n-1})})$, where $\alpha_0 = (0,\ldots,0,0)$, $\alpha_1 = (0,\ldots,0,1)$, …, $\alpha_{2^{n-1}-1} = (1,\ldots,1,1)$. The *matrix* of f is a $(1,-1)$-matrix of order 2^n defined by $M = ((-1)^{f(\alpha_i \oplus \alpha_j)})$. f is said to be *balanced* if its truth table contains an equal number of ones and zeros.

An *affine* function f on V_n is a function that takes the form of $f(x_1,\ldots,x_n) = a_1x_1 \oplus \cdots \oplus a_nx_n \oplus c$, where $a_j, c \in GF(2)$, $j = 1,2,\ldots,n$. Furthermore f is called a *linear* function if $c = 0$.

Definition 1. The *Hamming weight* of a $(0,1)$-sequence s, denoted by $W(s)$, is the number of ones in the sequence. Given two functions f and g on V_n, the *Hamming distance* $d(f,g)$ between them is defined as the Hamming weight of the truth table of $f(x) \oplus g(x)$, where $x = (x_1,\ldots,x_n)$. The *nonlinearity* of f, denoted by N_f, is the minimal Hamming distance between f and all affine functions on V_n, i.e., $N_f = \min_{i=1,2,\ldots,2^{n+1}} d(f,\varphi_i)$ where φ_1, φ_2, …, $\varphi_{2^{n+1}}$ are all the affine functions on V_n.

Now we introduce the definition of propagation criterion.

Definition 2. Let f be a function on V_n. We say that f satisfies

1. the *propagation criterion with respect to* α if $f(x) \oplus f(x \oplus \alpha)$ is a balanced function, where $x = (x_1,\ldots,x_n)$ and α is a vector in V_n.
2. the *propagation criterion of degree* k if it satisfies the propagation criterion with respect to all $\alpha \in V_n$ with $1 \le W(\alpha) \le k$.

The above definition for propagation criterion is from [7]. Further work on the topic can be found in [6]. Note that the strict avalanche criterion (SAC) introduced by Webster and Tavares [10, 11] is equivalent to the propagation criterion of degree 1 and that the perfect nonlinearity studied by Meier and Staffelbach [4] is equivalent to the propagation criterion of degree n where n is the number of the coordinates of the function.

While the propagation characteristic measures the avalanche effect of a function, the linear structure is a concept that in a sense complements the former, namely, it indicates the straightness of a function.

Definition 3. Let f be a function on V_n. A vector $\alpha \in V_n$ is called a *linear structure* of f if $f(x) \oplus f(x \oplus \alpha)$ is a constant.

By definition, the zero vector in V_n is a linear structure of all functions on V_n. It is not hard to see that the linear structures of a function f form a linear subspace of V_n. The dimension of the subspace is called the *linearity dimension* of f. We note that it was Evertse who first introduced the notion of linear structure (in a sense broader than ours) and studied its implication on the security of encryption algorithms [3].

A $(1,-1)$-matrix H of order m is called a *Hadamard* matrix if $HH^t = mI_m$, where H^t is the transpose of H and I_m is the identity matrix of order m. A Sylvester-Hadamard matrix of order 2^n, denoted by H_n, is generated by the following recursive relation

$$H_0 = 1,\ H_n = \begin{bmatrix} H_{n-1} & H_{n-1} \\ H_{n-1} & -H_{n-1} \end{bmatrix},\ n = 1, 2, \ldots.$$

Definition 4. A function f on V_n is called a *bent* function if

$$2^{-\frac{n}{2}} \sum_{x \in V_n} (-1)^{f(x) \oplus \langle \beta, x \rangle} = \pm 1,$$

for all $\beta \in V_n$. Here $\langle \beta, x \rangle$ is the scalar product of β and x, namely, $\langle \beta, x \rangle = \sum_{i=1}^{n} b_i x_i$, and $f(x) \oplus \langle \beta, x \rangle$ is regarded as a real-valued function.

Bent functions can be characterized in various ways [1, 2, 8, 12]. In particular the following four statements are equivalent:

(i) f is bent.
(ii) $\langle \xi, \ell \rangle = \pm 2^{\frac{1}{2}n}$ for any affine sequence ℓ of length 2^n, where ξ is the sequence of f.
(iii) f satisfies the propagation criterion with respect to all non-zero vectors in V_n.
(iv) M, the matrix of f, is a Hadamard matrix.

Bent functions on V_n exist only when n is even. Another important property of bent functions is that they achieve the highest possible nonlinearity $2^{n-1} - 2^{\frac{1}{2}n-1}$.

3 Propagation Characteristic and Nonlinearity

Given two sequences $a = (a_1, \ldots, a_m)$ and $b = (b_1, \ldots, b_m)$, their component-wise product is defined by $a * b = (a_1 b_1, \ldots, a_m b_m)$. Let f be a function on V_n. For a vector $\alpha \in V_n$, denote by $\xi(\alpha)$ the sequence of $f(x \oplus \alpha)$. Thus $\xi(0)$ is the sequence of f itself and $\xi(0) * \xi(\alpha)$ is the sequence of $f(x) \oplus f(x \oplus \alpha)$.

Set

$$\Delta(\alpha) = \langle \xi(0), \xi(\alpha) \rangle,$$

the scalar product of $\xi(0)$ and $\xi(\alpha)$. Obviously, $\Delta(\alpha) = 0$ if and only if $f(x) \oplus f(x \oplus \alpha)$ is balanced, i.e., f satisfies the propagation criterion with respect to α. On the other hand, if $|\Delta(\alpha)| = 2^n$, then $f(x) \oplus f(x \oplus \alpha)$ is a constant and hence α is a linear structure of f.

Let $M = ((-1)^{f(\alpha_i \oplus \alpha_j)})$ be the matrix of f and ξ be the sequence of f. Due to a very pretty result by R. L. McFarland (see Theorem 3.3 of [2]), M can be decomposed into

$$M = 2^{-n} H_n \operatorname{diag}(\langle \xi, \ell_0 \rangle, \cdots, \langle \xi, \ell_{2^n-1} \rangle) H_n$$

where ℓ_i is the ith row of H_n, a Sylvester-Hadamard matrix of order 2^n. By Lemma 2 of [8], ℓ_i is the sequence of a linear function defined by $\varphi_i(x) = \langle \alpha_i, x \rangle$, where α_i is the ith vector in V_n according to the ascending alphabetical order.

Clearly

$$MM^T = 2^{-n} H_n \operatorname{diag}(\langle \xi, \ell_0 \rangle^2, \cdots, \langle \xi, \ell_{2^n-1} \rangle^2) H_n. \qquad (1)$$

On the other hand, we always have

$$MM^T = (\Delta(\alpha_i \oplus \alpha_j)),$$

where $i, j = 0, 1, \ldots, 2^n - 1$.

Let S be a set of vectors in V_n. The *rank* of S is the maximum number of linearly independent vectors in S. Note that when S forms a linear subspace of V_n, its rank coincides with its dimension.

Lemma 6 of [8] states that the distance between two functions f_1 and f_2 on V_n can be expressed as $d(f_1, f_2) = 2^{n-1} - \frac{1}{2}\langle \xi_{f_1}, \xi_{f_2} \rangle$, where ξ_{f_1} and ξ_{f_2} are the sequences of f_1 and f_2 respectively. As an immediate consequence we have:

Lemma 5. *The nonlinearity of a function f on V_n can be calculated by*

$$N_f = 2^{n-1} - \frac{1}{2} \max\{|\langle \xi, \ell_i \rangle|, 0 \le i \le 2^n - 1\}$$

where ξ is the sequence of f and ℓ_0, ..., ℓ_{2^n-1} are the sequences of the linear functions on V_n.

Now we prove a central result of this paper:

Theorem 6. *Let f be a function on V_n that satisfies the propagation criterion with respect to all but a subset $\Re$ of vectors in V_n. Then the nonlinearity of f satisfies $N_f \ge 2^{n-1} - 2^{\frac{1}{2}(n+t)-1}$, where t is the rank of $\Re$.*

It was observed by Nyberg in Proposition 3 of [5] (see also a detailed discussion in [9]) that knowing the linearity dimension, say ℓ, of a function f on V_n, the nonlinearity of the function can be expressed as $N_f = 2^{\ell} N_r$, where N_r is the nonlinearity of a function obtained by restricting f on an $(n-\ell)$-dimensional subspace of V_n. Therefore, in a sense Theorem 6 is complementary to Proposition 3 of [5].

In the next section we discuss an interesting special case where $|\Re| = 2$. More general cases where $|\Re| > 2$, which need very different proof techniques, will be fully discussed in the later part of the paper.

4 Functions with $|\Re| = 2$

Since $\Re$ consists of two vectors, a zero and a nonzero, it forms a one-dimensional subspace of V_n. The following result on splitting a power of 2 into two squares will be used in later discussions.

Lemma 7. *Let $n \geq 2$ be a positive integer and $2^n = p^2 + q^2$ where both $p \geq 0$ and $q \geq 0$ are integers. Then $p = 2^{\frac{1}{2}n}$ and $q = 0$ when n is even, and $p = q = 2^{\frac{1}{2}(n-1)}$ when n is odd.*

Now we can prove

Theorem 8. *If f, a function on V_n, satisfies the propagation criterion with respect to all but two (a zero and a nonzero) vectors in V_n, then*

(i) n must be odd,
(ii) the nonzero vector where the propagation criterion is not satisfied must be a linear structure of f and
(iii) the nonlinearity of f satisfies $N_f = 2^{n-1} - 2^{\frac{1}{2}(n-1)}$.

A further examination of the proof for Theorem 8 reveals that a function with $|\Re| = 2$ has a very simple structure as described below.

Corollary 9. *A function f on V_n satisfies the propagation criterion with respect to all but two (a zero and a nonzero) vectors in V_n, if and only if there exists a nonsingular linear matrix of order n over $GF(2)$, say B, such that $g(x) = f(xB)$ can be written as*

$$g(x) = cx_n \oplus h(x_1, \ldots, x_{n-1})$$

where h is a bent function on V_{n-1} and c is a constant in $GF(2)$.

By Theorem 8 and Corollary 9, functions on V_n that satisfy the propagation criterion with respect to all but two vectors in V_n exist only if n is odd, and such a function can always be (informally) viewed as being obtained by repeating twice a bent function on V_{n-1} (subject to a nonsingular linear transformation on the input coordinates).

When $\Re$ has more than two vectors, it does not necessarily form a linear subspace of V_n. Therefore discussions presented in this section do not directly apply to the more general case. Nevertheless, using a different technique, we show in the next section a *significant* result on the structure of $\Re$, namely, *the nonzero vectors in $\Re$ with $|\Re| > 2$ are linearly dependent.*

5 Linear Dependence in $\Re$

The following result on vectors will be used in the proof of the main result in this section.

Lemma 10. *Let $\psi_1, \ldots, \psi_k$ be linear functions on V_n which are linearly independent. Set*

$$Q = \begin{bmatrix} \sigma_1 \\ \vdots \\ \sigma_k \end{bmatrix} \quad \text{and} \quad P = \begin{bmatrix} \ell_1 \\ \vdots \\ \ell_k \end{bmatrix}$$

where σ_i is the truth table and ℓ_i is the sequence of ψ_i, $i = 1, \ldots, k$. Then

(i) each vector in V_k appears as a column in Q precisely 2^{n-k} times and
(ii) each k-dimensional $(1, -1)$-vector appears as a column in P precisely 2^{n-k} times.

Proof. Note that (i) and (ii) are equivalent. Clearly, any nonzero linear combination of $\varphi_1, \ldots, \varphi_k$ is a nonzero linear function and thus it is balanced. Consequently, this lemma is equivalent to Lemma 7 of [9]. □

Next we show the linear dependence of nonzero vectors in $\Re$.

Theorem 11. *Suppose that f, a function on V_n, satisfies the propagation criterion with respect to all but $k+1$ vectors $0, \beta_1, \ldots, \beta_k$ in V_n, where $k > 1$. Then $\beta_1, \ldots, \beta_k$ are linearly dependent, namely, there exist k constants $c_1, \ldots, c_k \in GF(2)$, not all of which are zeros, such that $c_1\beta_1 \oplus \cdots \oplus c_k\beta_k = 0$.*

Proof. The theorem is obviously true if $k > n$. Now we prove the theorem for $k \leq n$ by contradiction. Assume that $\beta_1, \ldots, \beta_k$ are linearly independent. Let ξ be the sequence of f.

Compare the first row of the two sides of (1), we have

$$(\Delta(\alpha_0), \Delta(\alpha_1), \ldots, \Delta(\alpha_{2^n-1})) = 2^{-n}(\langle\xi, \ell_0\rangle^2, \ldots, \langle\xi, \ell_{2^n-1}\rangle^2)H_n$$

where α_j is the jth vector in V_n in the ascending alphabetical order. Equivalently we have

$$(\Delta(\alpha_0), \Delta(\alpha_1), \ldots, \Delta(\alpha_{2^n-1}))H_n = (\langle\xi, \ell_0\rangle^2, \ldots, \langle\xi, \ell_{2^n-1}\rangle^2) \tag{2}$$

Now let P be a matrix that consists of the 0th, β_1th, ..., β_kth rows of H_n. Here we regard β_i as an integer. Set $a_j^2 = \langle\xi, \ell_j\rangle^2$, $j = 0, 1, \ldots, 2^n - 1$. Note that $\Delta(\alpha) = 0$ if $\alpha \notin \{0, \beta_1, \ldots, \beta_k\}$. Hence (2) can be written as

$$(\Delta(0), \Delta(\beta_1), \ldots, \Delta(\beta_k))P = (a_0^2, a_1^2, \ldots, a_{2^n-1}^2) \tag{3}$$

where 0 in (3) is identical to α_0 in (2).

Write $P = (p_{ij})$, $i = 0, 1, \dots k$, $j = 0, 1, \dots, 2^n - 1$. As the top row of P is $(1, 1, \dots, 1)$, a_j^2 in (3) can be expressed as

$$\Delta(0) + \sum_{i=1}^{k} p_{ij}\Delta(\beta_i) = a_j^2$$

$j = 0, 1, \dots, 2^n - 1$. Let P^* be the submatrix of P obtained by removing the top row from P. As was mentioned earlier, the β_ith row of H_n is the sequence of a linear function defined by $\psi_i(x) = \langle \beta_i, x\rangle$ (see Lemma 2 of [8]). The linear independence of the vectors $\beta_1, \dots, \beta_k$ implies the linear independence of the linear functions $\psi_1(x) = \langle \beta_1, x\rangle, \dots, \psi_k(x) = \langle \beta_k, x\rangle$. By Lemma 10, each k-dimensional $(1, -1)$-vector appears in P^*, as a column vector, precisely 2^{n-k} times. Thus for each fixed j there exists a j_0 such that $(p_{1j}, \dots, p_{kj}) = -(p_{1j_0}, \dots, p_{kj_0})$ and hence

$$\Delta(0) + \sum_{i=1}^{k} p_{ij_0}\Delta(\beta_i) = a_{j_0}^2.$$

Adding together both sides of the above two equations, we have $2\Delta(0) = a_j^2 + a_{j_0}^2$. Hence $a_j^2 + a_{j_0}^2 = 2^{n+1}$. There are two cases to be considered: n even and n odd.

Case 1: n is even. By Lemma 7, $a_j^2 = a_{j_0}^2 = 2^n$. This implies that $\langle \xi, \ell_j\rangle = 2^n$ for any fixed j, which in turn implies that f is bent and that it satisfies the propagation criterion with respect to every nonzero vector in V_n (see also the equivalent statements about bent functions in Section 2). This clearly contradicts the fact that f does not satisfy the propagation criterion with respect to $\beta_1, \dots, \beta_k$.

Case 2: n is odd. Again by Lemma 7, $a_j^2 = 2^{n+1}$ or 0. If $a_j^2 = 2^{n+1}$, then $\sum_{i=1}^{k} p_{ij}\Delta(\beta_i) = 2^n$. Otherwise if $a_j^2 = 0$, then $\sum_{i=1}^{k} p_{ij}\Delta(\beta_i) = -2^n$. Thus we can write

$$\sum_{i=1}^{k} p_{ij}\Delta(\beta_i) = c_j 2^n \tag{4}$$

where $c_j = \pm 1$, $j = 0, 1, \dots, 2^n - 1$. For each fixed j rewrite (4) as

$$p_{1j}\Delta(\beta_1) + \sum_{i=2}^{k} p_{ij}\Delta(\beta_i) = c_j 2^n.$$

From Lemma 10, there exists a j_1 such that $p_{ij_1} = p_{1j}$ and $p_{ij_1} = -p_{ij}$, $i = 2, \dots, k$. Note that

$$p_{1j_1}\Delta(\beta_1) + \sum_{i=2}^{k} p_{ij_1}\Delta(\beta_i) = c_{j_1} 2^n.$$

Adding the above two equations together, we have

$$2p_{1j}\Delta(\beta_1) = (c_j + c_{j_1})2^n.$$

As f does not satisfy the propagation criterion with respect to β_1, we have $\Delta(\beta_1) \neq 0$ and $c_j + c_{j_0} \neq 0$. This implies $c_j + c_{j_0} = \pm 2$, and hence $\Delta(\beta_1) = \pm 2^n$. By the same reasoning, we can prove that $\Delta(\beta_j) = \pm 2^n$, $j = 2, \ldots, k$. Thus we can write

$$(\Delta(\beta_1), \ldots, \Delta(\beta_k)) = 2^n(b_1, \ldots, b_k)$$

where each $b_j = \pm 1$. By Lemma 10, there exists an s such that

$$(p_{1s}, \ldots, p_{ks}) = (b_1, \ldots, b_k).$$

This gives us

$$\sum_{i=1}^{k} p_{is}\Delta(\beta_i) = \sum_{i=1}^{k} b_i \Delta(\beta_i) = \sum_{i=1}^{k} b_i b_i 2^n = k2^n. \tag{5}$$

Since $k > 1$, (5) contradicts (4).

Summarizing Cases 1 and 2, we conclude that the assumption that $\beta_1, \ldots, \beta_k$ are linearly independent is wrong. This proves the theorem. □

We believe that Theorem 11 is of significant importance, as it reveals for the first time the interdependence among the vectors where the propagation criterion is not satisfied by f. Of particular interest is the case when $\Re = \{0, \beta_1, \ldots, \beta_k\}$ forms a linear subspace of V_n. Recall that linear structures form a linear subspace. Therefore, when $\Re$ is a subspace, a nonzero vector in $\Re$ is a linear structure if and only if all other nonzero vectors are linear structures of f.

In the following sections we examine the cases when $|\Re| = 3, 4, 5, 6$.

6 Functions with $|\Re| = 3$

When $|\Re| = 3$, the two distinct nonzero vectors in $\Re$ can not be linearly dependent. By Theorem 11 we have

Theorem 12. *There exists no function that does not satisfy the propagation criterion with respect to only three vectors.*

7 Functions with $|\Re| = 4$

Next we consider the case when $|\Re| = 4$. Similarly to the case of $|\Re| = 2$, the first step we take is to introduce a result on splitting a power of 2 into four, but not two, squares.

Lemma 13. *Let $n \geq 3$ be a positive integer and $2^n = \sum_{j=1}^{4} p_j^2$ where each $p_j \geq 0$ is an integer. Then*

(i) $p_1^2 = p_2^2 = 2^{n-1}$, $p_3 = p_4 = 0$, if n is odd;
(ii) $p_1^2 = 2^n$, $p_2 = p_3 = p_4 = 0$ or $p_1^2 = p_2^2 = p_3^2 = p_4^2 = 2^{n-2}$, if n is even.

Now we can prove a key result on the case of $|\Re| = 4$.

Theorem 14. *If f, a function on V_n, satisfies the propagation criterion with respect to all but four vectors (0, β_1, β_2, β_3) in V_n. Then*

(i) $\Re = \{0, \beta_1, \beta_2, \beta_3\}$ forms a two-dimensional linear subspace of V_n,
(ii) n must be even,
(iii) β_1, β_2 and β_3 must be linear structures of f,
(iv) the nonlinearity of f satisfies $N_f = 2^{n-1} - 2^{\frac{1}{2}n}$.

As a result we have

Corollary 15. *A function f on V_n satisfies the propagation criterion with respect to all but four vectors in V_n if and only if there exists a nonsingular linear matrix of order n over $GF(2)$, say B, such that $g(x) = f(xB)$ can be written as*

$$g(x) = c_1 x_{n-1} \oplus c_2 x_n \oplus h(x_1, \ldots, x_{n-2})$$

where c_1 and c_2 are constants in $GF(2)$, and h is a bent function on V_{n-2}.

In [8], it has been shown that repeating twice or four times a bent function on V_n, n even, results in a function on V_{n-1} or V_{n-2} that satisfies the propagation criterion with respect to all but two or four vectors in V_{n-1} or V_{n-2}. Combining Corollaries 15 and 9 with results shown in [8], we conclude that *the methods of repeating bent functions presented in [8] generate all the functions that satisfy the propagation criterion with respect to all but two or four vectors.*

8 Functions with $|\Re| = 5$

Let f be a function on V_n with $|\Re| = 5$ and let $\Re = \{0, \beta_1, \beta_2, \beta_3, \beta_4\}$. In the full paper we show the following result:

Theorem 16. *Let f be a Boolean function on V_n that satisfies the propagation criterion with respect to all but a subset $\Re = \{0, \beta_1, \beta_2, \beta_3, \beta_4\}$. Then*

(i) n is odd,
(ii) $\beta_1 \oplus \beta_2 \oplus \beta_3 \oplus \beta_4 = 0$,
(iii) $|\Delta(\beta_j)| = 2^{n-1}$, $j = 1, 2, 3, 4$, and three $\Delta(\beta_j)$ have the same sign while the remaining has a different sign, and
(iv) the nonlinearity of f satisfies $N_f = 2^{n-1} - 2^{\frac{1}{2}(n-1)}$.

Recall that when $|\Re| = 2$ or 4, all nonzero vectors in $\Re$ are linear structures of f, and the structure of f is very simple — it can be (informally) viewed as the two- or four-repetition of a bent function on V_{n-1} or V_{n-2}. In contrast, when $|\Re| = 5$, none of the nonzero vectors in $\Re$ is a linear structure of f. Thus if a non-bent function does *not* possess linear structures, then $|\Re|$ must be at least 5. In this sense, functions with $|\Re| = 5$ occupy a very special position in our understanding of the structures of functions.

8.1 Constructing Functions with $|\Re| = 5$

The structure of a function with $|\Re| = 5$ is not as simple as thc cases when $|\Re| < 5$. Unlike the case with $|\Re| = 2$ or 4, there seem to be a number of different ways to construct functions with $|\Re| = 5$. The purpose of this section is to demonstrate one of such construction methods.

We start with $n = 5$. Let $\omega(y)$ be a mapping from V_2 into V_3, defined as follows

$$\omega(0,0) = (1,0,0), \omega(0,1) = (0,1,0), \omega(1,0) = (1,1,0), \omega(1,1) = (0,1,1).$$

Set

$$f_5(z) = f_5(y,x) = \langle \omega(y), x \rangle \tag{6}$$

where $y \in V_2$ and $x \in V_3$, $z = (y,x)$. Obviously f_5 is a function on V_5 and

$$\begin{aligned} f_5(0,0,x_1,x_2,x_3) &= x_1, \\ f_5(0,1,x_1,x_2,x_3) &= x_2, \\ f_5(1,0,x_1,x_2,x_3) &= x_1 \oplus x_2, \\ f_5(1,1,x_1,x_2,x_3) &= x_2 \oplus x_3. \end{aligned}$$

Hence f_5 can be explicitly expressed as

$$\begin{aligned} f_5(y_1,y_2,x_1,x_2,x_3) = {} & (1 \oplus y_1)(1 \oplus y_2)x_1 \oplus (1 \oplus y_1)y_2 x_2 \oplus \\ & y_1(1 \oplus y_2)(x_1 \oplus x_2) \oplus y_1 y_2 (x_2 \oplus x_3) \end{aligned} \tag{7}$$

Let $\ell_{100}, \ell_{010}, \ell_{110}, \ell_{011}$ denote the sequences of $\varphi_{100}(x_1,x_2,x_3) = x_1$, $\varphi_{010}(x_1,x_2,x_3) = x_2$, $\varphi_{110}(x_1,x_2,x_3) = x_1 \oplus x_2$, $\varphi_{011}(x_1,x_2,x_3) = x_2 \oplus x_3$ respectively, where each φ is regarded as a linear function on V_3. By Lemma 1 of [8], ℓ_{100}, ℓ_{010}, ℓ_{110}, ℓ_{011} are four different rows of H_3. By Lemma 2 of [8], the sequence of f_5 is

$$\xi = (\ell_{100}, \ell_{010}, \ell_{110}, \ell_{011}).$$

Let $\xi(\gamma)$ denote the sequence of

$$f_5(z \oplus \gamma) = \langle \omega(y \oplus \beta), x \oplus \alpha \rangle$$

where $\beta \in V_2$ and $\alpha \in V_3$, $\gamma = (\beta, \alpha)$. We now consider $\Delta(\gamma) = \langle \xi, \xi(\gamma) \rangle$.

Case 1: $\beta \neq 0$. In this case we have

$$f_5(z) \oplus f_5(z \oplus \gamma) = \langle \omega(y) \oplus \omega(y \oplus \beta), x \rangle \oplus \langle \omega(y \oplus \beta), \alpha \rangle.$$

Note that $\omega(y) \oplus \omega(y \oplus \beta)$ is a nonzero constant vector in V_3 for any fixed $y \in V_2$. Thus $f_5(z) \oplus f_5(z \oplus \gamma)$ is a nonzero linear function on V_3 for any fixed $y \in V_2$ and hence it is balanced. This proves that $\Delta(\gamma) = 0$ with $\gamma = (\beta, \alpha)$ and $\beta \neq 0$.

Case 2: $\beta = 0$. In this case

$$f_5(z) \oplus f_5(z \oplus \gamma) = \langle \omega(y), \alpha \rangle$$

is balanced for $\alpha = (0,1,1)$, $(1,0,0)$ and $(1,1,1)$. In other words, $\Delta(\gamma) = 0$, if $\gamma = (0,\alpha)$ and $\alpha = (0,1,1)$, $(1,0,0)$ or $(1,1,1)$. It is straightforward to verify that $\Delta(\gamma) = 2^4$, -2^4, -2^4 and -2^4 with $\gamma = (0,\alpha)$ and $\alpha = (0,0,1)$, $(0,1,0)$, $(1,0,1)$ and $(1,1,0)$ respectively. Obviously $\Delta(0) = 2^5$. Thus f_5 satisfies the propagation criterion with respect to all but five vectors in V_5.

With f_5 as a basis, we now construct functions with $|\Re| = 5$ over higher dimensional spaces. Let $t \geq 5$ be odd and s be even. And let g be a function on V_t that satisfies the propagation criterion with respect to all but five vectors in V_t, and h be a bent function on V_s. Set

$$f(w) = g(v) \oplus h(u) \tag{8}$$

where $w = (v,u)$, $v \in V_t$ and $u \in V_s$. Then we have

Lemma 17. *A function constructed by (8) satisfies* $|\Re| = 5$.

Proof. Let $\xi(\beta)$ and $\eta(\alpha)$ be the sequences of $g(v \oplus \beta)$ and $h(u \oplus \alpha)$ respectively. Write $\zeta(\gamma)$ as the sequence of $f(w \oplus \gamma) = g(v \oplus \beta) \oplus h(u \oplus \alpha)$, where $\gamma = (\beta,\alpha)$. By definition, $\zeta(\gamma) = \xi(\beta) \times \eta(\alpha)$, where $\times$ is the *Kronecker product.* Hence we have

$$\begin{aligned}\Delta_f(\gamma) &= \langle \zeta(0), \zeta(\gamma)\rangle = \langle \xi(0) \times \eta(0), \xi(\beta) \times \eta(\alpha)\rangle \\ &= \langle \xi(0), \xi(\beta)\rangle \langle \eta(0), \eta(\alpha)\rangle \\ &= \Delta_h(\beta)\Delta_g(\alpha)\end{aligned}$$

where Δ_f, Δ_g and Δ_h are well defined and the subscripts are used to distinguish the three different functions f, g and h.

Since $h(u)$ is a bent function, $\Delta_h(\alpha) \neq 0$ if and only if $\alpha = 0$. On the other hand, since g satisfies the propagation criterion with respect to all but five vectors $0, \beta_1, \beta_2, \beta_3$ and β_4 in V_t, $\Delta_h(\beta) = 0$ if and only if $\beta \in \{0, \beta_1, \beta_2, \beta_3, \beta_4\}$. Thus $\Delta_g(\gamma) = 0$ if and only if $\gamma = (\beta, \alpha)$ with $\alpha = 0$ and $\beta \in \{0, \beta_1, \beta_2, \beta_3, \beta_4\}$. This proves that f satisfies the propagation criterion with respect to all but five vectors in V_{t+s}. □

A function f constructed by (8) is balanced if g is balanced. As the function f_5 on V_5 defined in (7) is balanced, we have

Theorem 18. *For any odd* $n \geq 5$, *there exists a balanced function satisfying the propagation criterion with respect to all but five vectors in* V_n.

As an example, set $h(x_6, x_7) = x_6 x_7$ and

$$f_7(x_1, x_2, x_3, x_4, x_5, x_6, x_7) = f_5(x_1, x_2, x_3, x_4, x_5) \oplus h(x_6, x_7)$$

where f_5 is defined in (7). Note that $h(x_6, x_7)$ is a bent function on V_2, by Theorem 18, f_7 is a balanced function on V_7 that satisfies $|\Re| = 5$.

To close this section we note that one can also start with constructing a function f_7 on V_7 with $|\Re| = 5$ by using the same method as that for designing f_5.

9 Functions with $|\Re| = 6$

In the full paper we prove that there is *no* function with $|\Re| = 6$.

Theorem 19. *There exists no function on V_n such that $|\Re| = 6$.*

10 Degrees of Propagation

In [8] it has been shown that if f is a function on V_n with $|\Re| = 2$, then, through a nonsingular linear transformation on input coordinates, f can be converted into a function satisfying the propagation criterion of degree $n-1$. Similarly, when $|\Re| = 4$, the degree can be $\approx \frac{2}{3}n$. In this section we show that with $|\Re| = 5$, the degree can be $n-3$.

Assume that the four nonzero vectors in $\Re$ are β_1, β_2, β_3 and β_4, and that β_1, β_2 and β_3 are a basis of $\Re = \{0, \beta_1, \beta_2, \beta_3, \beta_4\}$. Let B be an $n \times n$ nonsingular matrix on $GF(2)$ with the property that

$$\beta_1 B = (1, \ldots, 1, 0, 0, 1)$$
$$\beta_2 B = (1, \ldots, 1, 0, 1, 0)$$
$$\beta_3 B = (1, \ldots, 1, 1, 0, 0)$$

As $\beta_4 = \beta_1 \oplus \beta_2 \oplus \beta_3$, we have

$$\beta_4 B = (\beta_1 \oplus \beta_2 \oplus \beta_3)B = (1, \ldots, 1, 1, 1, 1).$$

Now let $g(x) = f(xB)$. Then g satisfies the propagation criterion of degree $n-3$, as the only exceptional vectors are $(0, \ldots, 0, 0, 0, 0)$, $(1, \ldots, 1, 0, 0, 1)$, $(1, \ldots, 1, 0, 1, 0)$, $(1, \ldots, 1, 1, 0, 0)$ and $(1, \ldots, 1, 1, 1, 1)$. These discussions, together with Theorem 18, show that for any odd $n \geq 5$, there exists balanced functions on V_n that satisfy the propagation criterion of degree $n-3$ and do not possess a nonzero linear structure.

Table 1 shows structural properties of functions with $|\Re| \leq 6$.

Acknowledgments The first author was supported in part by the Australian Research Council under the reference numbers A49130102, A49131885 and A49232172, the second author by A49130102, and the third author by A49232172.

References

1. Adams, C. M., Tavares, S. E.: Generating and counting binary bent sequences. IEEE Transactions on Information Theory **IT-36 No. 5** (1990) 1170–1173
2. Dillon, J. F.: A survey of bent functions. The NSA Technical Journal (1972) 191–215

$\Re$	$\{0\}$	$\{0, \beta\}$	$\{0, \beta_1, \beta_2, \beta_3\}$	$\{0, \beta_1, \beta_2, \beta_3, \beta_4\}$
Dimension n	even	odd	even	odd
Form of function	bent	$cx_n \oplus h(x_1, \ldots, x_{n-1})$, h is bent.	$c_1 x_n \oplus c_2 x_{n-1} \oplus h(x_1, \ldots, x_{n-2})$, h is bent.	e.g. $f_5(x_1, \ldots, x_5) \oplus h(x_6, \ldots, x_n)$, f_5 is defined in (7), h is bent.
Nonzero linear structure(s)	No	β	$\beta_1, \beta_2, \beta_3$	No
Nonlinearity	$2^{n-1} - 2^{\frac{1}{2}n-1}$	$2^{n-1} - 2^{\frac{1}{2}(n-1)}$	$2^{n-1} - 2^{\frac{1}{2}n}$	$2^{n-1} - 2^{\frac{1}{2}(n-1)}$
Degree of propagation	n	$n-1$	$\approx \frac{2}{3}n$	$n-3$
Is $\Re$ a subspace ?	Yes	Yes	Yes	No. However, $\beta_1 \oplus \beta_2 \oplus \beta_3 \oplus \beta_4 = 0$.
Rank of $\Re$	0	1	2	3

Table 1. *Structural Properties of Highly Nonlinear Functions (Functions with three or six exceptional vectors do* not *exist.)*

3. Evertse, J.-H.: Linear structures in blockciphers. In Advances in Cryptology - EUROCRYPT'87 (1988) vol. 304, Lecture Notes in Computer Science Springer-Verlag, Berlin, Heidelberg, New York pp. 249–266
4. Meier, W., Staffelbach, O.: Nonlinearity criteria for cryptographic functions. In Advances in Cryptology - EUROCRYPT'89 (1990) vol. 434, Lecture Notes in Computer Science Springer-Verlag, Berlin, Heidelberg, New York pp. 549–562
5. Nyberg, K.: On the construction of highly nonlinear permutations. In Advances in Cryptology - EUROCRYPT'92 (1993) vol. 658, Lecture Notes in Computer Science Springer-Verlag, Berlin, Heidelberg, New York pp. 92–98
6. Preneel, B., Govaerts, R., Vandewalle, J.: Boolean functions satisfying higher order propagation criteria. In Advances in Cryptology - EUROCRYPT'91 (1991) vol. 547, Lecture Notes in Computer Science Springer-Verlag, Berlin, Heidelberg, New York pp. 141–152
7. Preneel, B., Leekwijck, W. V., Linden, L. V., Govaerts, R., Vandewalle, J.: Propagation characteristics of boolean functions. In Advances in Cryptology - EUROCRYPT'90 (1991) vol. 437, Lecture Notes in Computer Science Springer-Verlag, Berlin, Heidelberg, New York pp. 155–165
8. Seberry, J., Zhang, X. M., Zheng, Y.: Nonlinearity and propagation characteristics of balanced boolean functions. To appear in *Information and Computation* 1994
9. Seberry, J., Zhang, X. M., Zheng, Y.: Relationships among nonlinearity criteria. Presented at *EUROCRYPT'94* 1994
10. Webster, A. F.: Plaintext/ciphertext bit dependencies in cryptographic system. Master's Thesis, Department of Electrical Engineering, Queen's University, Ontario, Cannada 1985
11. Webster, A. F., Tavares, S. E.: On the design of S-boxes. In Advances in Cryptol-

ogy - CRYPTO'85 (1986) vol. 219, Lecture Notes in Computer Science Springer-Verlag, Berlin, Heidelberg, New York pp. 523–534
12. Yarlagadda, R., Hershey, J. E.: Analysis and synthesis of bent sequences. IEE Proceedings (Part E) **136** (1989) 112–123

INVITED LECTURE 2

Catherine Meadows

(Naval Research Laboratory, USA)

Formal Verification of Cryptographic Protocols: A Survey

Catherine A. Meadows

Catherine A. Meadows
Center for High Assurance Computer Systems
Naval Research Laboratory
Washington DC, 20375

Abstract. In this paper we give a survey of the state of the art in the application of formal methods to the analysis of cryptographic protocols. We attempt to outline some of the major threads of research in this area, and also to document some emerging trends. ...

1 Introduction

A cryptographic protocol is meant to provide secure services. However, if the protocol is not designed correctly, it may fail to do so. A hostile intruder may be able to subvert the goals of the protocol by feeding false messages to honest users of the system. If the protocol is not designed to check these false messages adequately, then the intruder's action may result in some security failure such as key compromise or false authentication. Such security flaws in a protocol can be subtle and hard to find; a number of examples exist in the literature of flaws that were not found for some time in protocols that had received extensive hand analysis. Examples include the Needham-Schroeder key distribution protocol [30], which was found by Denning and Sacco [10] to allow an intruder to pass off an old, compromised session key as a new one, the software protection scheme of Purdy, Simmons, and Studier [33], for which Simmons [35] showed how an intruder could combine previously generated messages in such a way that the system could be induced to grant unauthorized access to software, and a protocol in the CCITT X.509 draft standard [9], for which Burrows, Abadi, and Needham [6] showed that an intruder could cause an old session key to be accepted as a new one, whether or not it had been compromised. These examples describe only a few of the documented cases; numerous others exist.

These kinds of problems appear to be well suited for the application of formal methods. They are well-contained enough so that modeling and analysis should be tractable; on the other hand, they are complex enough and the flaws are counterintuitive enough so that an informal analysis may be too prone to error to be reliable. Formal methods have long been used in the analysis of communication protocols in general, and some promising work was done in the analysis of cryptographic protocols in the late 70's and early 80's [13, 12, 27]. But in general, interest in the application of formal methods to cryptographic protocols did not become widespread until the early 90's, when several researchers were able to find heretofore undiscovered security flaws in cryptographic protocols by using formal analysis techniques.

In this paper we give a survey of the state of the art in the application of formal methods to the analysis of cryptographic protocols. In general, we will avoid the discussion of methods, such as zero-knowledge and polynomial reduction, that rely on studying the complexity-theoretic properties of the cryptographic algorithms involved, and which are already well-documented in the literature (e.g. in [15]), and instead concentrate on recently developed methods devised to study properties of protocols that are for the most part independent of the properties of the cryptoalgorithms involved. We will attempt to outline some of the major threads of research in this area, and also to document some emerging trends.

The rest of this paper is organized as follows. In Sections 2 and 3 we describe the two most commonly followed approaches to the applications of formal methods to cryptographic protocol analysis: the use of methods based on communicating state machine models, and the use of logics of knowledge and belief. In Section 4 we will discuss an approach that has not been followed by as many people, but has been successful in modeling some subtle properties of cryptographic protocols, that is, the use of algebras to model the state of an individual's knowledge about words used in a protocol. In the remaining sections we will discuss some open issues and emerging trends in the formal analysis of cryptographic protocols. These include model granularity, requirements modeling, and the use of formal methods in the design of new protocols as opposed to the analysis of existing ones.

2 Methods Based on State Machines

Most versions of the state-machine approach embody at least some aspects of the work of Dolev and Yao [13] and of Dolev, Even, and Karp [12]. In the Dolev-Yao model, the network is assumed to be under the control of a intruder who can read all traffic, alter and destroy messages, create messages, and perform any operation, such as encryption, that is available to legitimate users of the system. However, it is assumed, at least initially, that the intruder does not know any information that is to be kept secret, such as encryption keys belonging to honest users of the system.

Since the intruder can prevent any message from reaching its destination, and since he can also create messages of his own, we may treat any message sent by an honest user as a message sent to the intruder and any message received by an honest user as a message received from the intruder. Thus the system becomes a machine used by the intruder to generate words. These words obey certain rewrite rules, such as the fact that encryption and decryption with the same key cancel each other out. Thus we can think of the intruder as manipulating a term-rewriting system. If the goal of the intruder is to find out a word that is meant to be secret, then the problem of proving a protocol secure becomes a word problem in a term-rewriting system. Dolev et al. use this observation to develop several algorithms to analyze restricted classes of protocols in terms of their properties as term-rewriting systems.

The Dolev-Yao model is too restricted to be useful for the analysis of most protocols. First, it can only be used to detect failures of secrecy; second, it does not allow participants to remember state information from one state to the next. Thus, most protocol analysis methods that use the intruder-based Dolev-Yao model as a basis generally augment it with more conventional protocol modelling techniques to describe the behavior of the protocol participants.

One of the earliest systems to use a Dolev-Yao approach is the Interrogator developed by Millen [28, 20]. The Interrogator is a software tool that attempts to locate protocol security flaws by an exhaustive search of the state space. In the Interrogator, protocol participants are modeled as communicating state machines whose messages to each other are intercepted by an intruder who can either destroy messages, modify them, or let them pass through unmodified. Given a final state in which the intruder knows some word which should be secret, the Interrogator will try all possible ways of constructing a path by which that state can be reached. If it finds such a path, then it has identified a security flaw. The Interrogator has not yet found a previously unknown attack on a cryptographic protocol, but it has been able to reproduce a number of known attacks [20].

Others have used approaches similar to that of the Interrogator, but have relied upon human intervention to assist in the search. For example, a search tool developed by Longley and Rigby [22] has been used to find a subtle and previously unknown flaw in a hierarchical key management scheme. The chief difference between the Longley-Rigby tool and the Interrogator is that the Longley-Rigby tool allows human intervention. Whenever the system judges that a word cannot be found by the intruder, the user can intervene and determine whether or not that is likely to be the case. If the word is judged to be accessible, this information can be inserted into the database and the search can proceed.

In a different vein, Kemmerer has shown how cryptographic protocols can be modeled in a conventional formal specification language by modeling protocols in Ina Jo [19, 20]. He has also demonstrated how attacks on protocols can be modeled in such a language, and has used a specification animation to "walk through" several such attacks. Like Millen, Kemmerer models cryptographic protocols as communicating state machines. However, because the protocols are modeled in a specification language that has a theorem prover attached to it, it is also possible to use the prover to prove theorems about the security of the specified protocols, by defining security properties as state invariants and proving that these invariants are preserved by each transition, although this has not been yet attempted to any great extent.

The NRL Protocol Analyzer [20] is also based on the Dolev-Yao model, and uses a strategy similar to the Interrogator and the Longley-Rigby tool. As in the case of Millen's Interrogator, one uses the tool to find protocol security flaws by specifying an insecure state and attempting to construct a path to that state from an initial state. Unlike Millen's Interrogator, an unlimited number of protocol rounds are allowed in a single path, so that the state space is infinite. This allows the Analyzer to discover attacks that rely on the intruder's ability to weave several different runs of a protocol together. For example, such an attack was found in [41]. Also unlike the Interrogator, the emphasis is, not only on finding paths to insecure states, but on proving that these states are unreachable. This is made possible by having the user prove that certain paths leading backwards from the insecure state go into infinite loops, never reaching an initial state. Once these paths have been eliminated, the resulting search space is often small enough to search exhaustively. The proofs that paths lead into infinite loops are largely guided by the user; thus the search is much less automated than in the Interrogator.

Although the NRL Protocol Analyzer primarily emphasizes proofs of state unreachability, it can also be used to find flaws in protocols by generating paths to insecure states, and it has been used to find several previously undiscovered security flaws in cryptographic protocols. It has been used [25] to find an authentication flaw in Simmons' Selective Broadcast Protocol [35] and has also been used [24] to find a flaw in Burns and Mitchell's Resource Sharing Protocol [5]. The Analyzer has also been used to demonstrate several flaws that were already known to exist, including one in the Tatebayashi-Matsuzaki-Newman protocol whose flaw is demonstrated in [20], and one in a draft ISO authentication protocol, whose flaw is discussed in [11].

3 Systems Based on Modal Logic

The other approach that has been followed in the application of formal methods to cryptographic protocol analysis is to use modal logics similar to those that have been developed for the analysis of the evolution of knowledge and belief in distributed systems. Such a logic consists of various statements about belief in or knowledge about messages in a distributed system, and inference rules for deriving beliefs from other beliefs andor knowledge from other knowledge and beliefs. A discussion of research in this area is given by Syverson in [42].

Perhaps the best known and most influential such logic was that developed by Burrows, Abadi, and Needham [7], commonly known as BAN logic. BAN logic builds upon statements about messages sent and received throughout the course of a protocol. For example, one such belief, stated informally, would be: "If I believe I've received a message encrypted with key K, and I believe that only Alice and I know K, then I believe that the message was originated by either Alice or me." In an analysis of a protocol, an initial set of beliefs is assumed. Each message received is then mapped to another set of beliefs. One then uses the inference rules to determine what beliefs can be derived from the initial beliefs and the beliefs gained from participating in the protocol. If the set of beliefs is adequate, according to some predefined notion of adequacy, then the protocol is assumed to have been proven correct. If the set of beliefs is not adequate, then it may lead to the discovery of a security flaw in the protocol. This logic, which is meant to be used to prove results about replay attacks in key distribution protocols, was successfully used by its authors to find previously unknown flaws in a protocol that appeared in a draft recommendation for the CCITT X.509 standard [9].

BAN logic is the best known of the modal logics developed for cryptographic protocol analysis. But there are a number of others. These include Bieber's CKT5 [4] and Syverson's KPL [38], both of which reason about knowledge, Rangan's logic of trust [34], which reasons about trust and belief, Moser's logic [29], which reasons about knowledge and belief, and the system of Yahalom, Klein, and Beth [49], which reasons about trust. Syverson's logic can be used to reason about the two kinds of knowledge an intruder may have: knowledge of the word in the sense of seeing a string of bits, versus recognition of the significance of the words. Rangan's logic can be used to reason about the effect of trust in the composition of secure communication channels, and is intended to provide a formal basis for the evolution of belief from trust. The system of Yahalom, Klein, and Beth is used to derive information about the nature of the trust that parties in a protocol must have in each other in order for a protocol to operate correctly. Moser's logic, the only nonmonotonic one considered here, can be used to reason about the way in which beliefs developed through use of cryptographic protocols can be reversed, for example, by learning that a key used in a secure communication was compromised. Bieber's logic, CKT5, can be used to reason about the evolution of knowledge about words used in a cryptographic protocol; like Syverson's logic, it makes a distinction between seeing a message and understanding its significance.

BAN logic has proved to have been by far the most widely used of these logics. Interestingly enough, BAN logic does not attempt to model a protocol in anywhere near the richness as other logics do. BAN does not attempt to model the distinction between seeing a message and understanding it; they are both treated the same way. Likewise, unlike Moser's logic, BAN does not attempt to model the revision of beliefs; the evolution of beliefs in BAN is always monotonic. Moreover, BAN does not attempt to model trust or the lack of it; in BAN logic all principals are assumed to behave according to the rules of the protocol. Finally, since BAN does not attempt to model knowledge, it can not be used to prove results about secrecy; it can be used only to reason about authentication.

BAN's avoidance of these issues is intentional, and it makes for a simple, straightforward logic that is easy to apply and still useful for detecting flaws. This simplicity, combined with its usefulness, is much of the secret of its popularity. However, it also means that the issues it avoids must be addressed in the informal mapping from protocol specification to BAN specification. This has caused some uneasiness among many. For example, Nessett [31] has constructed a counterexample that makes use of the fact that BAN does not reason about secrecy. His example is of a protocol that can be proved to be secure using BAN logic, but is fact divulges a principal's secret key because of bad protocol design. Burroughs, Abadi, and Needham [7] have responded that this example violates one of the assumptions of the logic, namely, that principals do not divulge their secret keys. However, Nessett's example makes the point that this assumption is one that needs to be verified, since keys can be leaked not only by dishonest or incompetent principals, but as the result of the protocol itself.

To show how subtle the reasoning behind the mapping from protocol specification to BAN logic can be, we consider the following protocol due to Aziz and Diffie [2], which was analyzed using BAN logic in their paper. The protocol runs as follows:

1. $A \hookrightarrow B : Cert_A, N_A, other_1$
2. $B \hookrightarrow A : Cert_B, K_A(R_B), K_B^{-1}(hash(K_A(R_B), other_2, N_A, other_1))$
3. $A \hookrightarrow B : K_B(R_A), K_A^{-1}(hash(K_B(R_A), K_A(R_B)))$

where $Cert_X$ is X's public key certificate, R_A and R_B are used to construct a session key, N_A and R_B are nonces used to guarantee freshness, $other_1$ and $other_2$ is information not relevant to this discussion, hash is a hash function, and encrypted messages are formatted in a way that is recognizable by the recipient.

In the idealization of the protocol, the second step is mapped to an assertion that B once said that R_B was a good key for communication between A and B. But, how does A arrive at this fact? A decrypts the first part of the message and verifies that it is a meaningful message, which A can do since the message has a recognizable format. From the format, and from the fact that it was encrypted with A's key, A concludes that the message was intended for her, and that it is a message saying that R_B is a good key for communication between A and B. A also verifies the signature on the encrypted message so that she knows that B sent the message. Now she is able to conclude that it was B who said that R_B is a good key for communication between himself and A.

This reasoning is subtle, and fails if the assumption that the encrypted message is formatted is violated. In that case, one can mount the following attack[1], where I is the intruder, and I_X denotes the intruder impersonating X:

1. $A \hookrightarrow B : Cert_A, N_A, other_1$
   (intercepted by I)
2. $I_C \hookrightarrow B$: $Cert_C, N_A, other_1$
3. $B \hookrightarrow C$: $Cert_B, K_C(R_B), other_2, K_B^{-1}(hash(K_C(R_B), other_2, N_A, other_2))$
4. $I_B \hookrightarrow A : Cert_B, K_C(R_B), other_2, K_B^{-1}(hash(K_C(R_B), other_2, N_A, other_1))$

A checks the signature, and applies its private key to $K_C(R_B)$ to obtain $K_A^{-1}(K_C(R_B))$, which she then thinks is the key.

We note that this attack results in at worst a denial of service, since, although the intruder convinces A that a nonkey is a key, the intruder never learns the word that A accepts as a key, and thus cannot impersonate A or B or read encrypted traffic. However, the conclusion of the BAN analysis, that A believes that the word she receives is a good key for communication with B, no longer holds. A no longer has sufficient grounds for drawing that conclusion.

BAN logic will not help its user in distinguishing between the first, correct, version of the protocol and the other, incorrect version. Cases like this and the

[1] This attack was found using the NRL Protocol Analyzer.

Nessett counterexample have caused some concern, and have resulted in various efforts to increase BAN logic's effectiveness. Basically, there are two kinds of approaches that have been taken. One, that followed by Kailar, Gligor, and Gong in [18], is to identify the assumptions that will guarantee that BAN logic is sound if they hold. These assumptions can in turn be verified informally or formally, thus allowing other formal methods and assurance techniques to come to the assistance of BAN logic. The other approach is to increase the scope of BAN logic itself. This is the approach taken by Gong, Needham, and Yahalom in their GNY logic [16], an extended version of BAN logic. This logic includes, among other things, rules for reasoning about message recognizability that makes it possible to reason about a principal's ability to recognize that a bit string is a meaningful message. However, GNY logic is complex, containing over fifty rules, many of them complicated themselves. This has led many to reject this approach as being impractical. It may be, however, that all that is needed is a more systematic approach to the problem. Syverson and van Oorschot [43], for example, have been able, by unifying a number of different logics and developing a common semantics, to simplify them so that they become more tractable, but without sacrificing expressiveness.

4 Using Algebras to Reason About Knowledge

Another approach to applying formal methods to cryptographic protocol analysis is to model the protocol as an algebraic system, similar to the way in which Dolev and Yao model protocols, but to use the algebra to express the state of the participants' (including the intruders') knowledge about the protocol. This is an area that has not received as much attention as the state-machine and logical models discussed above, but the fact that it is able to combine a detailed model as in the state machine approach with an ability to reason about evolution of knowledge comparable to that found in logics of knowledge and belief means, in the opinion of this author, that it merits a closer look.

This approach was first used by Merritt in his PhD thesis [27]. Merritt makes use of *hidden automorphisms* to express an intruder's lack of knowledge about the contents of a message. Suppose, for example, that a principal views a message e(k,m) (denoting the encryption of m with k), where that principal does not know k. Suppose furthermore that we define an automorphism h of the space of words such that h(m) = n for some n, but all other words are left invariant. Then the set of messages known by the principal is invariant under h, (in particular h(e(k,m)) = e(k,m)). Thus effects of the automorphism are invisible to the principal, and can be used to define formally the principal's ignorance of m. Merritt uses this model to prove results about secrecy that are considerably more subtle than the simple secrecy of words; for example, he is able to prove that the correspondence between votes and individual voters in a voting protocol is unknown, even when all the voters and all votes are public.

Another approach to incorporating knowledge into an algebraic model is that taken by Toussaint [44, 45, 46]. In her model the set of words used in a protocol is expressed by an isomorphism between a free algebra with operators encryption and decryption and a crypto-algebra. A participant's state of knowledge is defined by three sets, **F**, **V**, and **SV**. **F** is a set of pairs (a,b) where a is a generator of the free algebra and b is its image in the crypto-algebra. These correspond to words that the principal has seen. **V** (or variables) consists of pairs of the form (x,y) where x is a generator of the free algebra and y is a variable. These correspond to words that the principal is aware of but has not yet seen. **SV** (or semi-variables) consists of pairs of the form (z,a) where a is an element of the crypto-algebra and z belongs to some set of possible encryptions and decryptions. These correspond to such things as the enciphering of messages under unknown keys. The principal knows the structure of the message, but has only limited knowledge about the input. Toussaint shows how this model can be used to describe evolving states of knowledge, and how attacks can be detected by a principal's seeing an inconsistency between messages received and its state of knowledge of the words used in the protocol.

Another approach is to use annotation of words used in algebraic models. This is the approach used by Meadows in [23] to extend the model used by the NRL Protocol Analyzer to reason about protocols that are designed to prevent against attacks in which an intruder may have partial knowledge of the secret words used in a protocol. An example of such an attack would be the case in which a protocol makes use of a password that belongs to a very small key space. A number of protocols have been developed to minimize the bad effects of such passwords, in particular the authentication protocol of Lomas, Gong, Saltzer, and Needham [21]. In Meadows' model each word has a *type* appended to it, which represents the knowledge the intruder has about a word. Some types are subtypes of other types, and thus reflect the intruder's increasing knowledge about the word. Thus a word may be of type possible password, meaning that it belongs to the space of possible passwords, or it may be of type password, meaning that the intruder knows that it is a password. Reduction rules are defined for types as well as words, and general rules of inference for deriving types are given. It is then shown how this approach can be used to model the guessing of a password, and how the Lomas-Gong-Saltzer-Needham protocol can be modeled.

Research in this area has not been as active as research in developing and applying state-machine models and logics of knowledge and belief. However, the models' success in representing very subtle kinds of knowledge, and the fact that the objects modeled correspond strongly to entities and messages used in the tools based on state machines suggest that these models could be used to provide the state machine tools with a stronger capability of modeling the knowledge that an intruder could gain. As yet, little research has been done on this problem. In [23] Meadows attempted to incorporate her extension of NRL Protocol Analyzer model into the tool itself, but the result was considered unsatisfactory because of the difficulty of modeling rules for increasing an intruder's knowledge as the kinds of reduction rules acceptable by the NRL Protocol Analyzer. However, the general question of whether and how these algebras can be incorporated in state machine analysis tools is still an open one.

5 Model Granularity and Range

It is unlikely that any formal method will be able to model all aspects of a cryptographic protocol, and thus it is unlikely that any formal method will be able to detect or prevent all types of protocol flaws. The best we can hope for is that it will be able to guarantee that the protocol is correct given that a certain well-defined set of assumptions is satisfied. Thus, for example, most formal models make the assumption that the underlying cryptosystem is perfect, that is, that an intruder can gain no information about a message that was encrypted with a key that he does not know. However, it is not always clear what we should attempt to include in the model, and what should be included in the assumptions. As we have seen in the discussion in the section on applying logics of knowledge and belief, much of the controversy over BAN logic concerns what should be addressed by the logic and what should be left as assumptions to be verified by other means.

In general, we can state three criteria that should be satisfied when deciding whether a feature should be included in a model:

1. Is it possible to include the feature and still have the analysis be tractable?
   For instance, although nonmonoticity can be considered a feature of cryptographic protocols, most logics of knowledge and belief that are applied to these protocols are monotonic, since monotonic logics are in general more tractable than nonmonotonic ones.
2. How useful is the ability to model the feature?
   Does the feature affect security? Is the feature likely to fail? Can the feature be handled in ways that make formal analysis unnecessary, or is the feature handled by other formal methods?
3. How well defined and natural is the boundary between the features modeled and the features not modeled?
   For example, a model that included an intruder's ability or inability to take discrete logarithms but did not include the ability or inability to factor would be considered somewhat lopsided, since these two problems are closely related.

Different systems may choose the cut-off point at different places. For example, logics such as BAN can be thought of as reasoning about the *intent* of messages. The verification that a message performs its intended function is done when the user of BAN logic maps lines in a protocol specification to their idealizations. Burrows, Abadi, and Needham describe the assumptions that will help to guarantee that this idealization will be correct, but the verification that the assumptions hold, or that they guarantee the correctness of the mapping, is not part of the logic.

State-machine-based systems based on the Dolev-Yao model, such as the Interrogator or the NRL Protocol Analyzer, generally give a more detailed approach. Messages are represented as concatenations of abstract message fields, and properties of cryptographic systems that are necessary to the correct operation of a cryptographic protocol, such as the fact that encryption and decryption with the same key in a shared-key system cancel each other out, are also modeled. However, properties of cryptosystems that may affect the security of a protocol, such as the commutative-associative property of exclusive-or, or the homomorphic properties of RSA, are usually not modeled (with a few exceptions: see for example [14]). Cryptographic integrity mechanisms are also usually not explicitly modeled. It is assumed that secrecy and integrity mechanisms do their job, but it is not asked exactly how the job is done.

It is possible to construct useful models at a lower level of granularity than this. For example, In [36] Stubblebine and Gligor introduce a model that allows them to model such things as cryptographically weak checksums (in which, given a checksum of a message, it is possible to produce another message that evaluates to the same checksum) versus collision-free checksums (in which, given a message and its checksum, it is computationally infeasible to produce another message with the same checksum). Given this model, they were able to uncover a flaw in the Kerberos system that was the result of its using such a weak checksum. The flaw was subtle and involved an intruder's cutting and pasting together different messages, and disguising the fact that he had done so by his ability to produce messages that evaluated to the same checksum. Their approach was also used to find a flaw in Privacy-Enhanced Mail [37]. Stubblebine's and Gligor's success in detecting these flaws shows that we still have not reached the limits of the degree of detail which which we can model a cryptographic protocol and still have fruitful results.

One might be tempted to conclude that only the most detailed models are useful. But all these models at the various levels of abstraction have their areas of usefulness. In general, it is most helpful to use the more abstract models at earlier points in the design stage, when implementation details have not been yet decided upon. For example, a protocol designer might use BAN or one of the similar logics to determine what the role of each message of a protocol should be. He or she might then use a state-based tool when attempting to determine what the structure of messages should be. Finally, when the actual implementation, including formatting of messages, choice of encryption systems, and choice of integrity mechanisms, is in question, it would be most appropriate to use something like the Stubblebine-Gligor model to determine how these implementation decisions affect the security of the protocol. Such an approach would allow us to locate errors as early as possible with a minimum amount of work.

6 Requirements Modeling

An area that is beginning to be explored in more depth is the question of how we specify the correctness of a protocol in the first place. Early work on applying formal methods to protocol analysis concentrated on secrecy, by attempting to show that an intruder could not learn a particular word or words. This was quickly realized to be inadequate, since many cryptographic protocols provide services such as authentication, that are only indirectly related to secrecy. At this point, it becomes necessary to determine exactly what the goals of a secure protocol must be.

This problem has been approached from several different angles, some with the aim of developing a set of criteria that can be applied to protocols in general, and others with the aim of developing ways to express criteria for a number of different types of protocols. In [11] Diffie, van Oorschot, and Wiener developed informal requirements for the correctness of an authentication protocol. Briefly, they say that session keys should remain secret, and that protocol runs should match. The latter means that, if A and B participate in a run of a protocol, then A's record of messages received from B matches B's record of messages sent to A, and vice versa. This notion has been formalized by Bellare and Rogaway in [3], using a model based on communicating probabilistic Turing machines. In the Bellare-Rogaway model, certain failure events, such as the compromise of old session keys, are included, so that the protocol can still be shown to satisfy matching runs in the face of these failures. Diffie, van Oorshot, and Wiener's notion of matching runs has also been formalized by Syverson in his extension of the Abadi-Tuttle logic to include temporal formalisms [39].

In [47] Woo and Lam independently take a similar approach to defining security of key distribution protocols. In this work Woo and Lam define a semantic model characterizing protocol executions. Two basic security properties, correspondence and secrecy, are defined. Secrecy is self-explanatory, while correspondence pertains to the requirement that certain events can take place only if others have taken place previously. The notion of correspondence thus bears a resemblance to the notion of matching protocol runs, but it is broader, since the two events in question do not have to be the sending and receiving of the same message. Woo and Lam show how to specify authentication protocol requirements in terms of assertions about correspondence and secrecy. Like Bellare and Rogaway, they also specify failure events as part of their model.

Another approach to specifying protocol requirements is shown in the requirements language currently being developed for the NRL Protocol Analyzer [40]. The requirements specified in this language have a form similar to the notion of correspondence of Woo and Lam, in that the requirements are given on sequences of events. The difference is that, instead of giving a general requirement for correspondence that applies to all protocols, the user of the language specifies only the requirements that are necessary for protocols belonging to a particular class to perform their intended functions. Thus requirements will vary according to the intended function of a protocol. The notion of "event" is also somewhat broader than that of Bellare and Rogaway or Woo and Lam in that any state change can be an event. Thus an intruder's learning a word is modeled as an event. This means that it is unnecessary to define secrecy as a separate part of the model. Internal state transitions can also be modeled as events. This makes it possible to model such things as a timestamp becoming obsolete according to a principal's internal clock. As in the Woo-Lam model, failure such as key compromise can also be modeled as events. In [40] Syverson and Meadows give a set of requirements for various kinds of message authentication protocols, while in [41] they give a set of requirements for key distribution protocols with reauthentication.

In [48] Yahalom takes a similar approach to Syverson and Meadows, but with different goals. Like them, he describes the various message passing events that must take place in a key distribution protocol, and states requirements on a protocol in terms of which events must occur before others. However, he uses these requirements to determine the minimum number of messages that must be sent in order for a protocol to satisfy these requirements, and then constructs a protocol that uses this number of messages. Thus his goals are to use the formulation of protocol requirements to achieve greater performance within the bounds set forth by the requirements.

Most work on formalizing security requirements for cryptographic protocols has concentrated on key distribution protocols. However, work on applying this approach to other areas has begun to appear. In [32] Pfitzmann uses a formal specification language to specify requirements for different kinds of signature schemes. The goal of her work is provide a classification system for the various kinds of signature schemes and their security requirements.

We note that there is still much work that remains to be done on security requirements for cryptographic protocols, and that this work could have far-reaching implications. Protocols have been developed for such applications as software protection, secure sharing of resources, and secure transmission of authorization. In general, if any two components of a distributed system engage in a transaction using a hostile communication medium, then they must make use of a cryptographic protocol to enforce their security requirements. Thus the topic of security requirements for cryptographic protocols is very close to the topic of security models for distributed systems. Once we start talking about requirements for cryptographic protocols we begin to start talking about what part of the system supplies what kind of security service to the other parts, what parts trust other parts and in what way, and so on. These are the very kinds of issues that must be addressed when we consider the security requirements for distributed systems in general. Thus in future years we can probably expect the area of cryptographic protocol analysis and the area of security modeling for distributed systems to grow closer and closer together.

7 The Use of Formal Methods in the Design of Protocols

Most of the existing work in the application of formal methods to cryptographic protocols has been concentrated on applying the methods to the analysis of existing protocols. However, in the long run it would be cheaper and more effective to use the methods in the design of the protocol in the first place, and so save the expense of redesign. In general, not much research has been done in this particular area. But, we believe that this is mainly because of the youth of the field. The use of formal methods in design as well as analysis is a natural application of the technology, and we can expect to see more of it in cryptographic protocols. In this section we describe some work that has been done so far.

The incorporation of formal methods into design can be done in two ways, as is the case with the incorporation of formal methods into the design of any product. One approach is to develop methodologies for design of protocols so that they will be more amenable to analysis by formal methods. This is the approach taken by Heintze and Tygar in [17]. In that paper they develop a modular approach to designing cryptographic protocols, and set forth properties of modules that will guarantee that their composition satisfies the desired security properties.

The other approach, which can be used together with the first, is a layered approach, in which a relatively abstract model is used at the top layer, and each succeeding layer is proved to be an implementation of the layer above it, until finally either a detailed specification or the actual protocol code is produced. This would be a more formal version of the strategy of using increasingly detailed models that was discussed in the section on model granularity. Much of the work on requirements specification, such as the Syverson and Meadows work that we discussed in the last section, has this flavor. Also, for the application of BAN logic, Carlsen [8] has developed a parser that will translate members of a limited class of protocol specifications into BAN logic. The option of integrating existing tools and methods that use models of different granularity is also an attractive one. Care must be taken, however, that the models underlying the methods can be made compatible. For example, in [26] Meadows develops a model of computation for the NRL Protocol Analyzer and compares it with the one Abadi and Tuttle [1] have developed for BAN logic. This is used to point out several important differences in the assumptions made by the two models that would have to be addressed before they were integrated.

8 Conclusion

In this paper we have attempted to give an overview of the state of the art in the application of formal methods to cryptographic protocol analysis. It is still a young field, so it is not possible to draw any final conclusions about the way in which it is headed. However, we have been able to identify some major trends and subfields, as well as identify some areas in which we believe further research is needed. We hope that in future years it will continue to build on its successes, and as it matures, will become a useful part of the secure systems designer's toolbox.

References

1. Martín Abadi and Mark Tuttle. A Semantics for a Logic of Authentication. In *Proceedings of the Tenth ACM Symposium on Principles of Distributed Computing*, pages 201–216. ACM Press, August 1991.

2. A. Aziz and W. Diffie. Privacy and Authentication for Wireless Local Area Networks. *IEEE Personal Communications*, 1(1):25–31, 1994.
3. M. Bellare and P. Rogaway. Entity Authentication and Key Distribution. In *Advances in Cryptology - CRYPTO '93*, volume to appear. Springer-Verlag, 1994.
4. P. Bieber. A Logic of Communication in a Hostile Environment. In *Proceedings of the Computer Security Foundations Workshop III*, pages 14–22. IEEE Computer Society Press, June 1990.
5. J. Burns and C. J. Mitchell. A Security Scheme for Resource Sharing Over a Network. *Computers and Security*, 19:67–76, February 1990.
6. Michael Burrows, Martín Abadi, and Roger Needham. A Logic of Authentication. *ACM Transactions in Computer Systems*, 8(1):18–36, February 1990.
7. Michael Burrows, Martín Abadi, and Roger Needham. Rejoinder to Nessett. *Operating Systems Review*, 24(2):39–40, April 1990.
8. U. Carlsen. Generating Formal Cryptographic Protocol Specifications. In *Proceedings of the 1994 IEEE Computer Society Symposium on Research in Security and Privacy*, pages 137–146. IEEE Computer Society Press, May 16-18 1994.
9. CCITT. *CCITT Draft Recomendation X.509. The Directory-Authentication Framework, Version 7*, November 1987.
10. D. E. Denning and G. M. Sacco. Timestamps in Key Distribution Protocols. *Communications of the ACM*, 24(8):198–208, 1981.
11. Whitfield Diffie, Paul C. van Oorschot, and Michael J. Wiener. Authentication and Authenticated Key Exchanges. *Designs, Codes, and Cryptography*, 2:107–125, 1992.
12. D. Dolev, S. Even, and R. Karp. On the Security of Ping-Pong Protocols. *Information and Control*, pages 57–68, 1982.
13. D. Dolev and A. Yao. On the Security of Public Key Protocols. *IEEE Transactions on Information Theory*, 29(2):198–208, March 1983.
14. Shimon Even, Oded Goldreich, and Adi Shamir. On the Security of Ping-Pong Protocols When Implemented Using the RSA. In Hugh C. Williams, editor, *Advances in Cryptology - CRYPTO '85*, pages 58–72. Springer-Verlag, 1985.
15. Joan Feigenbaum. Overview of Interactive Proof Systems and Zero Knowledge. In G. J. Simmons, editor, *Contemperary Cryptology: The Science of Information Integrity*, chapter 8, pages 423–439. IEEE Press, 1991.
16. L. Gong, R. Needham, and R. Yahalom. Reasoning about belief in cryptographic protocols. In *IEEE Computer Society Symposiun in Security and Privacy*, pages 234–248. IEEE Computer Society Press, May 1990.
17. Nevin Heintze and J. D. Tygar. A Model for Secure Protocols and Their Compositions. In *1994 IEEE Computer Society Symposium on Research in Security and Privacy*, pages 2–13. IEEE Computer Society Press, May 1994.
18. R. Kailar, V. D. Gligor, and L. Gong. On the Security Effectiveness of Cryptographic Protocols. In *Proceedings of the Fourth Internation Working Conference on Dependable Computing For Critical Applications*, 1994. to appear.
19. Richard Kemmerer. Using Formal Methods to Analyze Encryption Protocols. *IEEE Journal on Selected Areas in Communication*, 7(4):448–457, 1989.
20. Richard Kemmerer, Catherine Meadows, and Jonathan Millen. Three Systems for Cryptographic Protocol Analysis. *Journal of Cryptology*, 7(2), 1994.
21. T. M. A. Lomas, L. Gong, J. H. Saltzer, and R. H. Needham. Reducing Risks From Poorly Chosen Keys. *Operating Systems Reviews*, 23(5):14–18, 1989.
22. D. Longley and S. Rigby. An Automatic Search for Security Flaws in Key Management Schemes. *Computers and Security*, 11(1):75–90, 1992.

23. C. Meadows. Representing Partial Knowledge in an Algebraic Security Model. In *Proceedings of the Computer Security Foundations Workshop III*, pages 23–31. IEEE Computer Society Press, June 1990.
24. C. Meadows. A System for the Specification and Analysis of Key Management Protocols. In *Proceedings of the 1991 IEEE Computer Society Symposium on Research in Security and Privacy*, pages 182–195. IEEE Computer Society Press, Los Alamitos, California, 1991.
25. C. Meadows. Applying Formal Methods to the Analysis of a Key Management Protocol. *Journal of Computer Security*, 1:5–53, 1992.
26. C. Meadows. A Model of Computation for the NRL Protocol Analyzer. In *Proceedings of the 7th Computer Security Foundations Workshop*. IEEE Computer Society Press, June 1994.
27. M. J. Merritt. Cryptographic Protocols. Ph.d. thesis, Georgia Institute of Technology, 1983.
28. J. K. Millen, S. C. Clark, and S. B. Freedman. The Interrogator: Protocol Security Analysis. *IEEE Transactions on Software Engineering*, SE-13(2), 1987.
29. L. Moser. A Logic of Knowledge and Belief for Reasoning About Computer Security. In *Proceedings of the Computer Security Foundations Workshop II*, pages 57–63. IEEE Computer Society Press, June 1989.
30. R. M. Needham and M. D. Schroeder. Using Encryption for Authentication in Large Networks of Computers. *Communications of the ACM*, 21(12):993–999, December 1978.
31. D. M. Nessett. A Critique of the Burrows, Abadi, and Needham Logic. *Operating Systems Review*, 24(2):35–38, April 1990.
32. Birgit Pfitzmann. Sorting Out Signature Schemes. In *Proceedings of the First ACM Conference on Computer and Communications Security*, pages 74–85. ACM SIGSAC, ACM, November 3-5 1993.
33. G. B. Purdy, G. J. Simmons, and J. A. Studier. A Software Protection Scheme. In *Proceedings of the 1982 Symposium on Security and Privacy*, pages 99–103. IEEE Computer Society Press, April 1982.
34. P. V. Rangan. An Axiomatic Basis of Trust in Distributed Systems. In *Proceedings of the 1988 Symposium on Security and Privacy*, pages 204–211. IEEE Computer Society Press, April 1988.
35. G. J. Simmons. How to (Selectively) Broadcast a Secret. In *Proceedings of the 1985 Symposium on Security and Privac*, pages 108–113. IEEE Computer Society Press, April 1985.
36. S. Stubblebine and V. Gligor. On Message Integrity in Cryptographic Protocols. In *Proceedings of the 1992 Symposium on Security and Privacy*, pages 85–104. IEEE Computer Society Press, May 1992.
37. S. Stubblebine and V. Gligor. Protecting the Integrity of Privacy-Enhanced Mail. In *PSRG Workshop on Network and Distributed System Security*, pages 75–80, February 11-12 1993.
38. P. Syverson. Formal Semantics for Logics of Cryptographic Protocols. In *Proceedings of the Computer Security Foundations Workshop III*, pages 32–41. IEEE Computer Society Press, June 1990.
39. Paul Syverson. Adding Time to a Logic of Authentication. In *Proceedings of the First ACM Conference on Computer and Communications Security*, pages 97–101. ACM SIGSAC, ACM, November 3-5 1993.
40. Paul Syverson and Catherine Meadows. A Logical Language for Specifying Cryptographic Protocol Requirements. In *Proceedings of the 1993 IEEE Computer*

Society Symposium on Research in Security and Privacy, pages 165–177. IEEE Computer Society Press, Los Alamitos, California, 1993.

41. Paul Syverson and Catherine Meadows. Formal Requirements for Key Distribution Protocols. In *Proceedings of Eurocrypt '94*, 1994. to appear.
42. Paul F. Syverson. Knowledge, Belief, and Semantics in the Analysis of Cryptographic Protocols. *Journal of Computer Security*, 1(3):317–334, 1992.
43. Paul F. Syverson and Paul C. van Oorschot. On Unifying Some Cryptographic Protocol Logics. In *1994 IEEE Computer Society Symposium on Research in Security and Privacy*, pages 14–28. IEEE Computer Society, May 1994.
44. M.-J. Toussaint. Verification of Cryptographic Protocols. Ph.d. thesis, Universite de Liege (Belgium), 1991.
45. M.-J. Toussaint. Deriving the Complete Knowledge of Participants in Cryptographic Protocols. In *CRYPTO '91 (Advances in Cryptology—CRYPTO '91)*. Springer-Verlag, 1992.
46. M.-J. Toussaint. Separating the Specification and Implementation Phases in Cryptology. In *Computer Security - ESORICS 92*, volume LMCS 638, pages 77–102. Springer-Verlag, 1992.
47. T. Y. C. Woo and S. Lam. A Semantic Model for Authentication Protocols. In *Proceedings of the 1993 Symposium on Research in Security and Privacy*, pages 178–194. IEEE Computer Society Press, May 1993.
48. R. Yahalom. Optimality of Asynchronous Two-Party Secure Data-Exchange Protocols. *Journal of Computer Security*, 2(2-3):191–209, 1994.
49. R. Yahalom, Birgit Klein, and Thomas Beth. Trust relationships in secure systems: A distributed authentication perspective. In *Proceedings of the 1993 IEEE Symposium on Security and Privacy*, pages 150–164. IEEE Computer Society Press, May 1993.

SESSION 4

PROTOCOLS

Chair: Don Beaver

(Pennsylvania State University, USA)

Efficient electronic money (Extended abstract)

Yacov Yacobi[1]

Bellcore (2Q-338), 445 South St., Morristown, NJ 07960, USA

Abstract. Current e-cash systems with off-line bank are too complex to be practical for inexpensive e-wallets. In this paper we propose a new paradigm for e-cash, that relaxes the demands from e-cash systems, and thus enables simpler schemes. One first example along these lines is presented, which is significantly simpler in terms of computation complexity than the best previously published e-cash scheme (one or three orders of magnitude, depending on situation).

1 Introduction

Current e-cash systems with off-line bank are too complex to be practical for inexpensive e-wallets. In this paper we propose a new paradigm for e-cash, that relaxes the demands from e-cash systems, and thus enables simpler schemes. One first example along these lines is presented, which is significantly simpler in terms of computation complexity than the best previously published e-cash scheme (one or three orders of magnitude, depending on situation).

We propose the following deviations from the conventional e-cash rules:

- Allow some link-ability among bills, as long as the user can break link-ability at his discretion,
- Allow the use of anonymous calls to break (user-name, bill) link-ability, without hiding the bill.
- Load balance: Allow computationally heavy rare operations, if in return on-line operations are simplified.

A first example along these lines is presented. It is based on the phenomenon that if two distinct messages are signed by the same user, using the El-Gamal (family of) signature scheme(s) with the same random element, then with high probability the secret key of the signer can be efficiently computed by anybody that has the messages, signatures, and the public information[1]. The idea is to create a secret key which is guaranteed to contain the user's name, and to have a coin that ties together a user's public key and a corresponding random element that is used in the El-Gamal signature (i.e. such that the user knows its secret discrete-log). In the payment procedure the payer El-Gamal signs some nonce,

---

[1] It is recommended to use the NIST DSS member of the EG family, since this makes this deterministic (also it is more efficient).

using the random element in the coin, so that double spending exposes the secret key of the double spender, hence it also exposes her identity.

We break the usual explicit linkage between a user and her public key, in order to achieve non-traceability. A Certification Authority (CA) is supposed to physically authenticate a user (i), and then create a certificate for her public key. This certificate is a proof that a linkage exists between a user's name and her public key (PK), however, unlike in ordinary certificates, in our system it does not explicitly show this linkage. Rather, it is exposed only upon double spending. Since CA knows i, it is not supposed to know $i's$ public key. Yet, CA is supposed to certify that the Discrete-Log (DL) of that public key contains i's ID (I_i), wherein lies the difficulty. The solution relies on the powerful theorem of Goldreich, Micali, and Wigderson [10] that states that every $\mathcal{NP}$ predicate has a Zero-Knowledge (ZK) proof. In our case user-i presents to CA a blinded candidate for certificate, and proves in ZK that she *knows* a consistent blinding element, public key, the DL of that PK, and that this DL is composed of a concatenation of the user's ID (known to CA), and some random element. The values of the blinding element, the PK, and the random part of the DL remain unknown to CA at the end of this proof. We know that such efficient proof exists because this is an $\mathcal{NP}$ statement. In addition it should be infeasible for i to create collisions. Namely, it should be infeasible for her to create a blinded candidate for a certificate for which she knows other values of its components, such that the DL of the other PK does not contain her name. This implies that before blinding a certificate a user has to apply a collision free one way hash function. Some other protocols that we use in our system require a similar treatment.

Unlike in on-line operations, usage of relatively complex ZK protocols in the initialization phases of a system, or in any other *rare* operations, is very practical. Note that, unlike on-line/off-line signatures, where part of the complexity of creating a signature is pushed to off-line operations, here we save on the complexity of on-line operations without increasing the cost of off-line operations *per signature*. We propose the term *off-off-line* for such operations. We believe that off-off line computations may open a wide variety of applications to ZK technology, which has been viewed as too complex for most practical applications.

When a paper bank-note deteriorates the holder can exchange it in a bank without authenticating herself. The same is true in our e-money. In our case an e-coin "deteriorates" after one usage (it is not transferable). The Exchange procedure is very efficient since e-coins are not blinded, yet the linkage between a user and a coin is hidden from the bank (we assume anonymous calls). The bank does not have to verify the structure of the public key to be used in the new coin, since it accepts the certificate of the CA as a guarantee to this effect. This Exchange protocol is used to provide an efficient alternative to the relatively complex Withdrawal-from-account protocol[2]. A problem seems to arise for users who do not accumulate e-coins as payees. For them a simple solution is this. User i uses e-checks (trivial to implement) to buy e-coins from any user (j)

[2] In fact, every e-cash system in this category needs efficient exchange protocol, to refresh e-notes before expiration.

(who will trade money for some small commission to be determined by the free market), then Exchange it for new e-coins. User j in such a procedure can mark the e-coins, hence in collaboration with the bank they can trace user i. This is not different from marking paper notes, and is very useful in sting operations conducted by the police against criminals. We believe that every e-money system must have this property, in order to be accepted by governments.

Our system compares favorably to the most efficient e-money system published so far [1]. In no transaction is our system less efficient than [1], except for withdrawal from account, but almost always we can use the "exchange" alternative that requires significantly less multiplications than [1] (one or three orders of magnitude, depending on the situation).

To prevent exposure of the (user-name,coin) linkage by means external to cryptography, in our system, public keys and the corresponding certificates may have to be "refreshed" (i.e. changed) periodically, at a higher rate than is common in other public key cryptosystems (probably once every few months). We have an off-off-line "refresh certificate" protocol that does it from afar.

For general background on e-money see [3], and for a benchmark secure Non-traceable e-money see [4].

Related work:
A main building block of our system is the usage of the El-Gamal phenomenon, where a coin is a blindly signed public key. To the best of my knowledge the use of this construction appeared first in [15], and then in [8] (with another member of the El-Gamal family -the Schnorr system). Note that the El-Gamal phenomenon is common to the whole family, including the NIST-DSS, that could substitute nicely for the EG system here. In the system of [12] the payer introduces some secret randomness but they do not use the El-Gamal system. The system of [9] is based on DL problem, but does not use the El-Gamal system. The system of [1] uses the group representation problem, which is an extension of the DL problem, however, Brands does not use a blindly signed public key as a coin.

In the full paper we give a "cut and choose" alternative to the ZK protocols that uses k^2 exponentiations, where k is a security parameter, and cheating probability is $O(exp(-k))$. Typically $k = 40$. We also give a short description of a simple alternative to the gradual and verifiable release of discrete-log [2] routine, that we need in our "cut and choose" protocols. Our cut and choose solutions require word size of about 1600 bits. However, ZK solutions exist for any word size.

The next section describes the El-Gamal signature scheme, and the particular property that we use. In section 3 we describe our new system, using the fact that the necessary $\mathcal{NP}$ predicates have zero-knowledge proofs of knowledge. We do not specify the explicit ZK protocols. In the appendix we demonstrate one way to avoid direct withdrawal from account.

2 ElGamal signature schemes

Let P and S be the public and secret keys of some user, where $P \equiv \alpha^S \bmod p$, where p is a prime, and α is a generator in Z_p^*. An *El-Gamal signature* [6] by that user, on message m is an ordered pair (u, v), for which $P^u \cdot u^v \equiv \alpha^m \bmod p$. Thus a recipient of a signature can easily verify it. To create a signature, the user chooses a random number r, and computes $u \equiv \alpha^r \bmod p$. It follows that $S \cdot u + r \cdot v \equiv m \bmod p - 1$,hence that user, who is the only one who knows S, can compute v, provided $gcd(r, p-1) = 1$. It seems to be hard for anybody not knowing S to forge a signature, but we have no proof that this problem is as hard as the similar Discrete-Log (DL) problem. The El-Gamal signature system has the curious property that if the signer tries to use the same r twice, to sign two different messages, then these two signatures expose her secret key S, herein lies the clue to our emoney: if *name* is included in S, then we have a method to eventually (off-line) expose a double spender. To see how double use of r exposes S, note that $S \cdot u + r \cdot v_1 \equiv m_1 \bmod p-1$, and $S \cdot u + r \cdot v_2 \equiv m_2 \bmod p-1$. Hence, $r(v_1 - v_2) \equiv (m_1 - m_2) \bmod p-1$, and if $gcd(v_1 - v_2, p-1) = 1$ anybody knowing the messages and their signatures can find r, and if $gcd(v, p-1) = 1$ then S can be computed.

3 The system

3.1 Overview

There are four generic players in the system. Certification authority (CA), Bank, Payer, and Payee. There are six basic protocols in this system. Initial-certificate, Refresh-certificate, Withdrawal (from account), Payment, Deposit, and Exchange (old money for new).

Initial-certificate and Refresh-certificate take place between a user (potential payer) and the CA. Withdrawal involves a bank and a user (potential payer). Payer and a Payee are involved in a Payment transaction. A Bank and a Payee interact in a deposit transaction. A Bank and a user (previous Payee who is a future Payer) are involved in Exchange transaction.

In Initial-certificate a user gets a certificate from the CA, that establishes a linkage between her unique name (ID), and her public key. However, unlike in ordinary certificates, this linkage is hidden. Her name is embedded in the discrete-log of the public key, and may be exposed only after double spending (using the El-Gamal phenomenon).

Certificates may have to be refreshed periodically, to prevent leaking the correlation between a user's name and her public key, through means external to cryptography (physical surveillance). This could be done from afar using the Refresh-certificate protocol.

While withdrawing money from account the user's ID is exposed to the bank. That implies that the money must be blinded. In our system a coin is a certified (by the bank) linkage between a public key and a random element whose DL is known to the potential payer. The bank repeats the process done by CA and creates a new certificate, then ties it to the random element (we use "CA certificates" in the more commonly used "Exchange").

In the Payment protocol the payer sends a coin (certified linkage between a public key and a random element, where here the certification also assures that the public key is constructed correctly). The payee, after verifying the bank's signature on the coin, challenges the payer to El-Gamal sign a random message using the public key and the random element that were embedded in the coin. The payee then verifies the signature, and accepts if correct.

A Payee may contact the bank periodically to deposit coins that he received. He then deposits the received coin together with his challenge and the payer's El-Gamal signature on the challenge. The bank checks a list of all deposited coins to see if the coin was deposited in the past. If so, it has enough information to expose the ID of the double spender; otherwise it enters the coin on the list. Lists do not grow endlessly if we build expiration dates into coins.

In the Exchange protocol a payee deposits old coins in the bank, and at the same time gets fresh coins in the same total value from the bank. She does not tell the bank who she is, hence even if the new coin is not hidden from the bank, the linkage (user,coin) is not known to the bank. So this protocol is very efficient[3].

3.2 Notations

In the remainder of this section we specify each of the components and operations of the system. For brevity of notations we sometime use $x \equiv_p y$ to denote $x \equiv y \bmod p$. We use (s, t) to denote the concatenation of the strings representing s and t. We use subscript c for variables associated with the certification authority, and subscript b for variables associated with the bank. We use p to denote El-Gamal modulus (which may or may not be universal). The bank and certification authority sign using RSA schemes, while users use El-Gamal signature schemes. For RSA schemes we use e, d, N, with proper subscripts, to denote public and secret exponents, and a modulus, respectively. Let γ be an integer, $30 < \gamma < 50$, and let 0^γ denote a run of γ zeroes. Let $l(p) = log_2(p) + \gamma$. Let $\Sigma = \{0,1\}^{l(p)}$, and $f : \Sigma \rightarrow \Sigma$ be a publicly known, collision free one way hash function (sometimes we need f for $\Sigma = \{0,1\}^{l(p^2)}$ – which will be clear from the context).

3.3 Components

Public and secret keys: S_i is the secret key of user i. It is the concatenation of the user's name, I_i, with a string R_i of random bits, known only to i, i.e. $S_i = (I_i, R_i)$ (but S_i may include multiple copies of I_i, see e.g. our cut and choose solutions, in the appendix). Let p be a large prime, and $\alpha \in Z_p^*$ be a generator of Z_p^*, where α and p are publicly known. A public key for user i is $P_i \equiv_p \alpha^{S_i}$.

[3] As always, perpetuating non-traceability is much easier than bootstrapping it.

A certificate of a public key is a linkage between a user's name and her claimed public key, signed by some trusted authority. However, unlike in ordinary certificates, this linkage is not exposed in ordinary operations. The identity of the user is hidden in the secret exponent S_i, and may be efficiently exposed only upon double spending. A certificate of public key P_i is $Cert(i) \equiv (f(P_i, 0^\gamma))^{d_c} \bmod N_c$.

Coin: Let N_b and d_b denote the bank's public modulus, and secret exponent, for a particular denomination (e.g. \$1), respectively. A coin for user i is a triple (P_i, u, c), where $c \equiv_{N_b} (f(P_i, u, 0^\gamma))^{d_b}$, $u \equiv_p \alpha^r$, r is chosen by i, and known only to i.

3.4 Operations

We present the system the way it was invented, since this may give the reader the motivation for various constructs. So we start with a payment procedure, using the El-Gamal phenomenon, and retract to the off-off-line certification procedures, etc.

On-line Payment: The payee gets from the payer a coin (P_i, u, c), where $c \equiv_{N_b} (f(P_i, u, 0^\gamma))^{d_b}$. She verifies the bank's signature, and if correct, challenges the payer to El-Gamal sign some random challenge, m, using the (P_i, u) embedded in the coin. The payee verifies this signature, and rejects the coin if the signature is invalid. Note that the payer (often the computationally weaker) need perform only one on-line multiplication here.

Deposit: The coin, c, plus the payer's El-Gamal signature $s = (u, v)$, and the challenge, m, are deposited to the bank, which compares (m, c, s) to the list of already deposited coins. Double spending is detected if a collision is found. In such event, the payer's id is computed from two signatures on two distinct messages, with the same (P_i, u) (S_i is computed, and since I_i is included in S_i, the double spender is exposed). Otherwise, the bank accepts the coin, and adds (m, c, s) to the list. To limit the size of the list we can include expiration date in the coin (omitted in this exposition).

Exchange of old money for new (perpetuate non-traceability): A user makes an anonymous call to the bank, sends used coins, and asks for new e-coins in the same total value in return (not necessarily same denominations). The bank compares the old coin to the list of used coins, and if it is not already there, adds it to the list. Otherwise, it computes the name of the double spender, like in ordinary deposit procedure. The user shows a non-blinded certificate $(P_i, f(P_i, 0^\gamma))^{d_c} \bmod N_c$, and the bank verifies (partial) structure, and CA's signature. The bank trusts that CA verified that P_i has the right structure. Per each requested coin, the user sends $u \equiv_p \alpha^r$ of her choice, for which she knows the secret r. She gets from the bank a coin $c \equiv_{N_b} (f(P_i, u, 0^\gamma))^{d_b}$ (for denomination associated with d_b). The bank can trace this coin on its way back, but cannot associate it with any user. In this process the bank does not access any individual account.

Off-off-line This section includes all operations that have to be done very rarely. They are "Initial Certificate" (once every few years) "Refresh certificate" (once every few months?), and "Withdrawal from account." The last operation is by no means a rare operation in all existing money systems, hence we need to justify our claim. A justification appears in the introduction. It points to the possibility that usually the efficient transaction of exchanging old money for new can be used instead of the less efficient transaction for withdrawing from account, which creates new e-money.

Initial Certificate: User i picks at random with uniform distribution some $R_i \in \{0,1\}^l$ (in practice $l = 200$ is currently sufficient), and creates a secret exponent $S_i = (I_i, R_i)$. She then computes $P_i \equiv_p \alpha^{S_i}$, then pick with uniform distribution $x \in_R Z^*_{N_c}$, and compute $z \equiv_{N_c} x^{e_c} \cdot f(P_i, 0^\gamma)$, and sends z to CA, together with her ID, I_i, and in some cases even comes in person to physically authenticate herself. She then proves to CA, in ZK, that I_i is included in S_i. That is, the following $\mathcal{NP}$ predicate is proven to CA in ZK.

Predicate PR_1**:**

Given: $z, \alpha, p, N_c, e_c, I_i$,

$(\exists x, P_i, R_i, S_i)[z \equiv_{N_c} x^{e_c} f(P_i, 0^\gamma); P_i \equiv_p \alpha^{S_i}; S_i = (I_i, R_i)]$.

This predicate is always true, if $gcd(e_c, \phi(N_c)) = 1$. What needs to be proved is that the prover knows x, P_i, R_i, S_i.

Remark 1:

In addition, it must be infeasible for user, i, to find a collision, namely, $x', \in Z_{N_c}, P'_i \in Z_p, R'_i, S'_i$ such that $z \equiv_{N_c} x'^{e_c} f(P'_i, 0^\gamma); P'_i \equiv_p \alpha^{S'_i}; S'_i = (w, R'_i)$, but $w \neq I_i$. To satisfy this requirement we added the function f. Since this function is collision free the issue is resolved. This issue arises in the next two off-off-line protocols as well, and we'll not elaborate any further.

If CA verifies the proof of PR_1 positively, it signs z, i.e. computes $z^{d_c} \bmod N_c$ and sends it to user i, who multiplies it by $x^{-1} \bmod p$ to get the unblinded certificate $Cert(i) \equiv (f(P_i, 0^\gamma))^{d_c} \bmod N_c$.

Refresh certificate: Unlike creation of the initial certificate, which must include proper physical identification of the user, and therefore cannot be done over the network[4], this procedure can be done over the network. We refresh certificates periodically, not because we worry that S_i leaked, but because we worry that the correspondence $P_i \leftrightarrow i$ leaked thru means external to cryptography.

The user presents an "old" certificate (all the variables associated with the old certificate are primed), and a new blinded candidate for certificate, and proves to CA in ZK, that they share the same I_i in their corresponding exponents. This is an $\mathcal{NP}$ predicate.

Let $c_1 \equiv_{N_c} (f(P_{i,1}, 0^\gamma))^{d_c}$ be an old certificate, and $c_2^{e_c} \equiv_{N_c} x^{e_c} \cdot f(P_{i,2}, 0^\gamma)$ a new blinded candidate for certificate, not yet signed by CA. The $\mathcal{NP}$ predicate is:

[4] Under the assumption that not all communication with a user is tapped, and that a correct user is associated with a certain address, and certain phone number, we can avoid physical identification. However, these assumptions have a limited validity.

Predicate PR_2:
Given: $c_1, c_2^{e_c}, p, N_c, \alpha, e,$
$(\exists I_i, P_{i,1}, P_{i,2}, R_1, R_2, x)$
$[P_{i,1} \equiv_p \alpha^{(I_i,R_1)}, P_{i,2} \equiv_p \alpha^{(I_i,R_2)},$
$c_1 \equiv_{N_c} (f(P_{i,1}, 0^\gamma))^{d_c}, c_2^{e_c} \equiv_{N_c} x^{e_c} f(P_{i,2}, 0^\gamma)].$

This procedure would not have to be executed very frequently if each user maintains a distinct public key per subject[5] (each of us is very unique when viewed globally, but when we are "projected" on any single dimension we blend in the crowd).

After CA verifies the proof of PR_2 positively, it computes $c_2 \equiv (c_2^{e_c})^{d_c} \bmod N_c$, and sends it to user i, who now un-blinds it to find the new certificate $Cert(i) \equiv c_2 \cdot x^{-1} \bmod N_c$.

Withdrawal from account: This is a relatively painful[6] ZK protocol, but we predict that it will not be done frequently, see discussion in the introduction (and the appendix). The user contacts the bank, authenticates herself, and presents a candidate blinded coin $w \equiv_{N_b} x^{e_b} \cdot f(P_i, u, 0^\gamma)$ on which she wants the bank's RSA signature. The bank, after deducting the money from the user's balance, returns $w^{d_b} \bmod N_b$, from which the user can compute a coin $(f(P_i, u, 0^\gamma))^{d_b} \bmod N_b$. Before this is done the user proves to the bank in ZK that P_i is properly structured, i.e. that $PR_3 = true$, where

Predicate PR_3:
Given: $\alpha, p, N_b, e_b, I_i, w$
$(\exists x, P_i, u, S_i, R_i)$
$[w \equiv_{N_b} x^{e_b} \cdot f(P_i, u, 0^\gamma); P_i \equiv_p \alpha^{S_i}; S_i = (I_i, R_i)].$

After the bank verifies the ZK proof of PR_3 it signs w, i.e. computes $w^{d_b} \equiv x \cdot (f(P_i, u, 0^\gamma))^{d_b} \bmod N_b$, where d_b is the secret exponent corresponding to the required denomination, and sends it to user i, who can un blind it (i.e. multiply by the secret value $x^{-1} \bmod N_b$, known only to her) to get the coin $(f(P_i, u, 0^\gamma))^{d_b} \bmod N_b$. To use the coin, a user has to show this value together with (P_i, u).

3.5 Complexity

Note first that in El-Gamal scheme if $q|p-1$ and $ord_p(\alpha) = q$ then exponents should not exceed $log_2(q)$ in size, since we can write the congruences in the exponents modulo q. Specifically, for $log_2(p) = 512$, it currently seems sufficient to have $140 \le log_2(q) \le 170$. This idea is due to C. Schnorr, and is also used in NIST DSS.

The most dramatic complexity reduction is seen when our Exchange for payee who has old money is compared to Brands' Withdrawal (2520 multiplications). In our case a user has to do one RSA signature verification, when he verifies the new coin, i.e. two multiplications. If a user does not have old e-coins, then he has

[5] Subjects may be stock market, entertainment, sports, nuclear physics, etc.
[6] Since the user name is not "masked" the coin must be masked.

to first buy them from another user. This will take additional 280 multiplications (El-Gamal verification).

Our payment procedure requires one on-line multiplication (two in Brands').

Acknowledgement: I would like to thank Milt Anderson, Arjen Lenstra, Venkie (Venkatesan, Ramarath), and Pete Winkler for many insightful comments.

References

1. S. Brand *Electronic Cash Systems Based On The Representation Problem In Groups Of Prime Order*, Proceedings of Crypto'93, Santa Barbara 1993, pp. 26.1-26.15.
2. E.F. Brickell, D. Chaum, I.B. Damgard, and J. van de Graaf *Gradual and Verifiable Release of a Secret*, Proc. Crypto'87.
3. D. Chaum *Achieving Electronic Privacy* Scientific American, August 1992, pp. 96-101.
4. D. Chaum, A. Fiat, M. Naor *Untraceable Electronic Cash*, Proc. Crypto 1988.
5. W. Diffie, M. Hellman *New Directions in Cryptography* IEEE Trans. IT. 1976
6. T. ElGamal *A Public Key Cryptosystem and a Signature Scheme Based on Discrete Logarithms*, IEEE Trans. IT, Vol. IT-31, No. 4, July 1985, pp. 469-472.
7. S. Even, O. Goldreich, Y. Yacobi, *Electronic Wallet*, Proc. Crypto'83. A later version appeared in Proc. 1984 International Zurich Seminar on Digital Communications, pp. 199-201, IEEE cat No. 84CH1998-4.
8. T. Eng, T. Okamoto, *Single-Term Divisible Electronic Coins*, Proc. Eurocrypt'94, pp. 311-323.
9. M. Franklin, M. Yung, *Secure and Efficient Off-Line Digital Money*, Proc. ICALP 93, pp. 449-460 (1993)
10. Goldreich, Micali, and Wigderson *Proofs that yield nothing, but their validity , or All languages in NP have zero-knowledge proof systems.* J. of the ACM, 38: 691-729, 1991.
11. Goldwasser, Micali, and Rackoff, *The knowledge complexity of Interactive proof systems*, SIAM J. on Computing, 18 1, 1989, pp. 186-208.
12. T. Okamoto, K. Ohta, *Disposable Zero-Knowledge Authentication and Their Application to Untraceable Electronic Cash*, Proc. Crypto'89, pp. 481-496 (Springer-Verlag, LNCS 435, G. Brassard Ed.)
13. M.O. Rabin, *Digitalized signatures*, in Foundations of secure computation, Academic Press, NY, 1978.
14. R. Rivest, A. Shamir, and L. Adelman *A method for obtaining digital signatures and public key cryptosystems*, CACM, vol. 21, 1978, pp. 120-126.
15. Y. Yacobi, *Efficient Non-Traceable Digital Checks*, Witnessed and signed Bellcore Lab-Notebook, pp. 49-53, June 17, 1992.

4 Appendix: How to avoid direct withdrawal from account

If one has old money that he received as recipient, he may exchange it in the bank anonymously, for new money that he can spend (exchange is one of our efficient operations).

If he has in his e-wallet some un-spent balance that he wants to exchange for unlink-able new money, he must first use a "refresh-certificate" sub-protocol to create new unlink-able public key and certificate. Since "refresh-certificate" is one of our inefficient operations, one should run it off-off-line, and have the new public key and certificate ready in his wallet.

The on line operations proceed as follows:

1. First P engages in a transaction with a money trader that will buy his balance (for commission). P uses public key Pa1 here, and the trader uses Pb1 (lines 1,2 of fig-1).
2. Then P exchanges (with the bank) the old money that he got from the trader for new money, which uses his new public key Pa2 (lines 3,4 of fig-1).
3. The trader may deposit (or exchange) the money that he got from the user. The public key that the bank sees there is the old one (Pa1).[7]

Similarly, if a user has no money in his wallet, he can use e-check (we use the term "e-check" to mean the digital equivalent of ordinary personal check, namely, it contains the user's name, address, etc., the user inserts the value, and digitally signs it). Here in step (5) the bank has additional information (the personal data on the e-check), but still cannot correlate it with the data of steps (3,4). See fig-1.

Each of the above transactions may be batched for many notes at once. That's the saving in communications over on-line systems.

What the bank knows at each of the steps:
(Numbering follows the steps of fig-1.)

1. –
2. –
3. Some user, X, has e-note, that he got from user Y (both anonymous), User X, uses PK Pa2, and user Y uses Pb1.
4. I gave X e-note Ex. Y's note was Ey.
5. User B deposits a check of user A.

Correlation attacks: *Timing:* Suppose there is only one bank and one trader, and at a particular time only one user is trying to break link-ability, using the above process. If the trader deposits the money immediately after he got it, and the user exchanges money at approximately the same time, then the bank may correlate the two events, and infer the link between the old public key and the refreshed one.

Value: If there are many users engaged in processes like the above, but some user has a very unique value for his transaction, then a similar correlation attack is still possible.

Note that these attacks are feasible today with paper cash as well, if the underlying assumptions hold (notes are marked, and thereafter the bank can perpetuate the markings).

[7] Makes more sense to exchange.

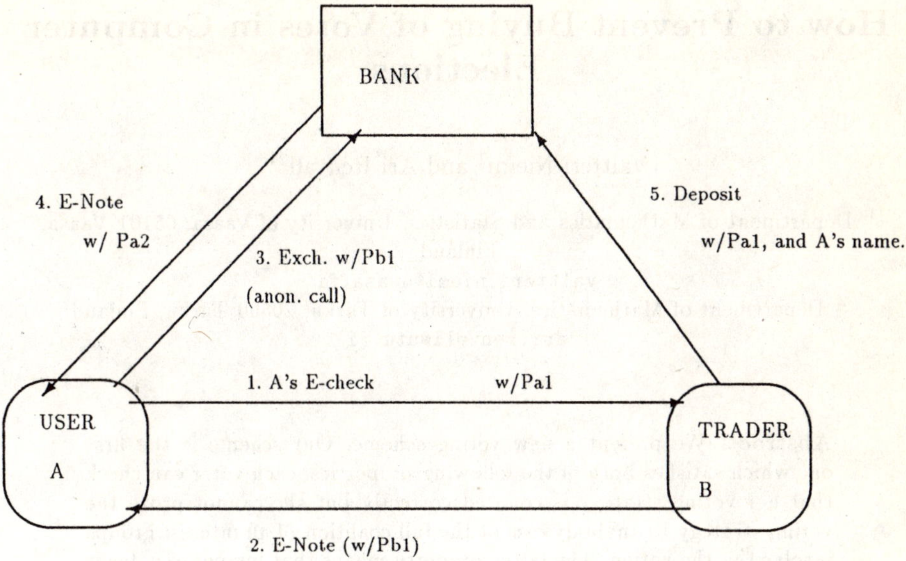

Fig. 1. Avoiding direct withdrawal

The above hypothetical conditions do not hold if there are many traders, the traders deposit in large batches, and user's are restricted to conduct transactions in certain standard values (if the old balance in a wallet does not fit a standard value it may be augmented with a check).

How to Prevent Buying of Votes in Computer Elections

Valtteri Niemi[1] and Ari Renvall[2*]

[1] Department of Mathematics and Statistics, University of Vaasa, 65101 Vaasa, Finland
valtteri.niemi@uwasa.fi

[2] Department of Mathematics, University of Turku, 20500 Turku, Finland
ari.renvall@utu.fi

Abstract. We present a new voting scheme. Our scheme is the first one which satisfies both of the following properties: each voter can check that her voting strategy is counted correctly but she cannot prove the voting strategy to anybody except the full coalition of all interest groups involved in the voting. The latter property means that buying of votes is not possible, since the potential buyer does not know whether she gets what she is paying for!

1 Introduction

Computerized elections and votings in general constitute a main application area of cryptographic protocols. Many elegant voting protocols exist [1], [2], [6], [8], [9] and they satisfy the most important requirements including secrecy of votes and correctness of results. Of course, there are many differences in type and level of security, efficiency etc.

However, all these protocols are unsatisfactory in one sense: they allow buying of votes. In traditional voting systems this is prevented in a simple manner, i.e. the voter cannot prove to a potential buyer that she/he indeed cast the vote as agreed. In all systems mentioned above any voter can invite anybody to witness casting of vote by remote terminal. The voter can even let the buyer cast the vote instead of her/him.

It can be argued how severe this problem is. Someone might have the opinion that buying of votes would be very rare and has no real impact on the result. We just want to point out that if it is believed that nobody bothers to buy votes in large scale then it might be reasonable to believe also that nobody bothers to corrupt a neutral trusted center with big money. In the latter case there is hardly any need for complicated protocols at all, a simple encryption of votes and decryption by a reliable center would be secure enough.

In [7] the problem was attacked with partial success. A detailed protocol was constructed with one essential shortcoming: it was assumed that one fixed party involved is not interested in buying votes. In the end of [7] an idea was given for

* Research supported by The Academy of Finland, grant 11281

a protocol without this shortcoming. The present paper develops the idea and we construct a protocol which prevents the voter from proving her/his voting strategy to anybody.

The basic idea is to add a preliminary registration of voters. It takes place in physically controlled circumstances and during it each voter gets some information that is needed in the actual voting. This information can, of course, be given to anybody but there is no way of checking its correctness. Indeed, the correctness is proved to the voter in zero-knowledge in a secure and private registration booth.

At first glance, it seems that a registration that requires everybody to go to some place destroys the whole idea of computerized voting. However, this is needed very seldom and only once for many different votings. Also, it is clear that some kind of physical identification of voters is needed anyway.

The paper is structured as follows. Next section gives some basic concepts and an informal description of the protocol. Section 3 contains the protocol while it is discussed in section 4.

2 An Informal Description of the Protocol

In this section we discuss the main ideas of our voting scheme. Remember that the goal is to prevent the possibility to prove one's voting strategy. Denote the voters by V_i, their votes by v_i and the corresponding voting strategy by $[v_i]$.

In traditional *balloting booth elections* connection between V_i and v_i is physically broken by scrambling v_i with a number of other votes. As a consequence V_i cannot prove which is her vote. Therefore in this setting we may choose simply $v_i = [v_i]$. In computerized secret ballot elections this is obviously not possible. In common solutions (like [1], [2], [6], [8], [9]) the voting strategy is encrypted in some way or the vote is cast anonymously together with an *eligibility token*. However, in all schemes presented so far the voter has always been able to open the encryption or to prove that a given eligibility token is the one she used. This means that the voter has been able to prove her voting strategy.

In our scheme the vote is also essentially of the form $v_i = ([v_i], e_i)$, where e_i is an eligibility token. But we construct the token in such a way that V_i can not prove the validity of e_i. In order to do this we use a special type of permutation.

Definition *A permutation f is a* zero-way permutation, *if there exists a trapdoor s and an injective function g such that*

1. *both f and f^{-1} can be efficiently computed if one knows s.*
2. *neither f nor f^{-1} can be efficiently computed if one knows only $g(s)$.*

It follows from the definition, that s cannot be computed from $g(s)$. Thus, one can commit to a zero-way permutation by disclosing $g(s)$.

It seems plausible to conjecture that zero-way permutations exist if trapdoor permutations exist. For instance, if $f = f_1 \circ f_2^{-1}$ where f_1 and f_2 are trapdoor permutations over a set X, then computing both f and f^{-1} requires to invert either f_1 or f_2. There are also other methods to obtain (candidate) zero-way permutations.

The eligibility token of our scheme is now just an element of a set $f^{-1}(Y)$ where $f : X \to X$ is a zero-way permutation chosen by the government of the voting and $Y \subseteq X$ is a suitable set. Of course, it must be computationally infeasible to generate valid tokens without the help of C. For this reason, Y should be small enough. On the other hand, Y should not be too small in order to guarantee that no two voters could get identical tokens. For example, Y could consist of all such binary strings that contain a long sequence of zeros in the middle while X contains all strings (of fixed length).

The idea of our scheme is that in a preliminary registration phase C gives each legitimate voter one valid token. The voter gets only a zero-knowledge proof of the validity of her token and can thus not transfer her conviction of the validity.

In the voting phase the voters are now allowed to cast as many votes as they wish. However, they can construct only one vote with a valid token (multiple use of same token is not allowed).

In the final phase of the scheme C computes the tally of the election. C collects the votes corresponding to the same strategy and then computes the number of valid tokens associated to them. This is done so that the the validity of any single token is never checked. Thus, the number of possible false votes with invalid tokens will be counted but no-one will find out which votes they are.

If we perform the protocol the way we described it, one severe problem arises. Even if we can not prove our voting strategy to outsiders, we can prove it to C (in fact C could find it out by itself). We solve this by dividing C to subgovernments $C_1,\ldots,C_n$. For example, all the candidates (or their representatives) might act as subgovernments, as in [6]. The basic idea is that every potential interest group can trust at least one of the subgovernments. (The reliable one may be different for each interest group.)

The zero-way fuction f must then be constructed in such a way that each C_j has a secret share s_j needed to compute f and f^{-1}. The problem of generating a valid eligibility token in the registration phase is then solved by applying a protocol for multiparty computation of [4]. The participants of the protocol are the voter V_i and every C_j. As a result V_i obtains a valid token as a private output. If we modify the protocol slightly V_i cannot prove to any proper subcollection of $\{C_1,\ldots,C_n\}$ what the output was.

In the final phase where the tally of the election is computed we need to apply similar multiparty computation protocol.

3 The Protocol

In this section we give a more detailed description of our protocol. The protocol consists of four phases. For simplicity, we call subgovernments C_j candidates in the sequel.

3.1 Preliminary Phase

This phase occurs (e.g.) once in a year. During it candidates make necessary preparations for each (possible) voting of the year. The idea is to build all the computational circuits needed later in the year.

1. Candidates agree and fix some family of zero-way and trapdoor permutations. For instance, a modulus p and a generator g of $\mathbf{Z}_p^*$ is chosen for permutations based on discrete logarithm. (This example is also used later in the protocol but other permutations like RSA-based ones could be chosen as well.)
2. For each future voting, every candidate C_j $(j = 1, ..., n)$ generates a random number s_j. They also commit to these numbers by publishing $g^{s_j} \pmod{p}$. The product $s = s_1 \cdots s_n$ serves as the secret key of the zero-way permutation $f : x \mapsto x^s \pmod{p}$, see [3], [7]. No proper subset of candidates can compute either f or f^{-1}.
3. Candidates perform a multiparty computation to obtain the element $g^s \pmod{p}$. This is used as their public key in the El Gamal cryptosystem. (For details of the system, consult [5] or some standard textbook, e.g. [10].) Also here s serves as the trapdoor information. The resulting encryption function is denoted by E and decryption function by D.

3.2 Registration Phase

In this phase each voter obtains an eligibility token for each future voting. (Of course, the set of votings for which token is given may vary with respect to, e.g. age and address of the voter.) This phase occurs also once in a year.

1. The voter is physically identified.
2. She/he goes into a physically secured booth that has private communication lines to each candidate.
3. For each voting, candidates and the voter execute a multiparty computation which gives a private output to the voter. The output is a number $f(x) = x^s \pmod{p}$ where x is of a very special form. More specifically, assume p contains $4n$ bits. Then x is OK if $x = z_1 \ldots z_{4n}$ where $z_i = 0$ for $i = n{+}1, n{+}2, \ldots, 3n\}$. (Other forms may do as well.) The number $f(x)$ is called an eligibility token. It is important that the voter cannot prove validity of the token to anybody. That means that the multiparty protocol of [4] must be modified in the following way:
(a) Each candidate chooses random numbers x_j and b_j. Her private input for the protocol consists of x_j, b_j and s_j.
(b) Each candidate sends (privately) b_j to the voter. At the same time she gives a private zero-knowledge proof that convinces the voter of the correctness of b_j. This can be easily added to the protocol of [4] since the candidate

must commit to b_j anyway using some bit commitment scheme. (We do not go into the details of this modification, since description of the protocol in [4] would be needed and it is quite lengthy.)
(c) Output of the computation is $f(x) \oplus b_1 \oplus \ldots \oplus b_n$ where x is obtained by xoring all the x_j's and adding the 0-sequence in the middle. The voter obtains the token by xoring the output by $b_1 \oplus \ldots \oplus b_n$. She has no way of proving the value of $f(x)$ to anybody (except to the full coalition of all candidates). On the other hand, the probability that a random number is a valid token is 2^{-2n}.

3.3 Voting Phase

During each voting everybody has a chance to send (possibly anonymously) messages to a public file F. Each voter sends $E([v_i], f(x))$ where a legitimate vote is encrypted by the public key of that particular voting. If the message does not show up in F the voter simply sends it again. It is worth noting that nobody is prevented from sending false messages anyhow.

3.4 Counting Phase

After every interested and legitimate voter is happy with the public file F candidates perform a multiparty computation to calculate the tally of the voting. The computation has a public input F and private inputs s_j.

1. Entries in F are decrypted and the resulting list of pairs of the form (voting strategy, token) is used as a secret input in the next step.
2. For each possible voting strategy the number of valid tokens associated to it is counted. This can be done, since all candidates together can compute f^{-1}-image of the token and check that it has the 0-sequence in the middle. It is important that the result of the validity check is solely used as an intermediate output and a secret input for the final counting circuit which gives a non-negative integer as an output.
3. Tally of the voting is the public output of the computation and anybody can check the correctness of the computation as explained in [4].

Nobody (except a full conspiracy of all candidates) obtains any information of individual entries in the public file F other than what can be derived from the tally alone.

Note that a voter may join a valid token to several voting strategies! There are several ways of preventing this. For example, all different strategies with the same token could be rejected (as a penalty for attempted misuse of the protocol). Another possibility is to check (of course, inside the multiparty computation) which of the pairs with the same token came first (or last if we want to allow a last-minute change of opinion).

4 Some Remarks

Our protocol uses heavily multiparty computations. However, operations needed are quite simple like modular exponentiations or counting of valid tokens. That means the number of gates in the circuits is not extremely large. On the other hand, the (potentially enormous) number of false votes raises the complexity of the protocol considerably although the growth is linear. Altogether, our protocol is clearly impractical. Special-purpose multiparty protocols could make a change in this matter. The main goal for future research is to construct an efficient protocol that provides the same features as our protocol.

Many minor modifications can be made in the protocol. In small scale votings it is quite possible that voters themselves act as subgovernments. Then the first two phases can be combined.

As already mentioned, there is much freedom in choosing the proper zero-way and trapdoor permutations. The main criterion is their suitability for distributed computations with private inputs. Also, it is by no means necessary that the chosen zero-way and trapdoor permutations are linked anyhow.

Encryption of (strategy,token)-pairs is needed since otherwise an active intruder could simply change the strategy and leave the token as it is. However, it could be skipped if each voter gets several tokens for each voting and these tokens are used for coding the voting strategy. More specifically, a fixed number of 0-tokens (resulting from binary strings with long 0-sequences as above) and 1-tokens (resulting from strings with 1-sequences) is given to each voter. Nobody except the whole collection of candidates can make any difference either between tokens and non-tokens or between 0-tokens and 1-tokens. The voting strategy is coded by the order of the tokens in such a way that even if the strategy of some voter is guessed the order of the tokens cannot be changed to produce a code for some other strategy. (For example, first tokens code the strategy in some straight-forward numbering system and most of the tokens are put in one of many possible orders that are associated to this particular strategy beforehand.) Thus, an active intruder could destroy the message at best and in case it happens, the voter can try again, as explained above.

References

1. J. Benaloh: Verifiable secret-ballot elections, Ph.D. thesis, Yale university, Technical report 561, (1987).
2. D. Chaum: Untraceable electronic mail, return address, and digital pseudonyms, *Comm. of ACM*, **24** (1981), pp. 84–88.
3. D. Chaum: Zero-knowledge undeniable signatures, *Proc. EUROCRYPT '90, Springer LNCS 473*, (1991), pp. 458–464.
4. D. Chaum, I. Damgård, J. van de Graaf: Multiparty computations ensuring privacy of each party's input and correctness of the result, *Proc. CRYPTO '87, Springer LNCS 293* (1988), pp. 87–119.
5. T. El Gamal: A public key cryptosystem and signature scheme based on discrete logarithms, *IEEE Transactions on Information Theory* **IT-31** (1985), pp. 469–473.

6. K. Iversen: A cryptographic scheme for computerized general elections, *Proc. CRYPTO '91, Springer LNCS 576* (1992), pp. 405–419.
7. V. Niemi, A. Renvall: Cryptographic protocols and voting, *Proc. Results and Trends in Theoretical Computer Science, Springer LNCS 812* (1994), pp. 307-316.
8. H. Nurmi, A. Salomaa, L. Santean: Secret ballot elections in computer networks, *Computers and Security* **10** (1991), pp. 553–560.
9. C. Park, K. Itoh, K. Kurosawa: Efficient anonymous channel and all/nothing election scheme, *Proc. EUROCRYPT '93, Springer LNCS 765* (1994), pp. 248–259.
10. A. Salomaa: Public-Key Cryptography, Springer-Verlag Berlin Heidelberg 1990.

Design and Analysis of Key Exchange Protocols via Secure Channel Identification*

Colin Boyd and Wenbo Mao

Communications Research Group
Electrical Engineering Laboratories
University of Manchester
Manchester M13 9PL, UK
Email: Colin.Boyd@man.ac.uk

Abstract. We suggest a new methodology for design and analysis of key exchange protocols. The basic idea is to establish the minimum cryptographic requirements in delivering a new session key, and to identify how these are achieved in the protocol under examination. The method is therefore limited to key exchange protocols and to establishing that the basic properties exist. The method is easy to carry out by hand (although some existing protocols may be difficult to handle). It allows existing protocols to be re-designed and new protocols designed in a flexible manner. A number of new protocols designed with the method are suggested.

1 Introduction

There have been great advances in recent years in the understanding of how to design and analyse cryptographic protocols for authentication and key exchange. Such protocols are typically the initial step in setting up a secure communications session; they are therefore critical in ensuring that security is maintained. Furthermore, it has been found that design of these protocols is extremely error-prone and a methodical approach is important.

The two major classes of analysis technique are algebraic state based approaches and logical approaches. While there have been successes with both approaches each has its limitations and research continues into improving them. The algebraic approach [9, 14] is to model the system as a state-based machine, to define what are the bad states and show that they cannot be reached under the assumptions of the protocol. A difficulty of this approach is how to fully define the abilities of the attacking process and what exactly constitutes a bad protocol state. In addition there is a need for a computer tool to search the state space. The logical approach [1, 13] models the beliefs and/or knowledge of each protocol principal and uses global inference rules to try and achieve the desired final beliefs after the protocol is complete. Difficulties here include

* This work is funded by the UK Engineering and Physical Sciences Research Council under research grant GR/G19787.

how to translate between the logical language and the usual manner of protocol description.

In addition to the issues mentioned above, all the existing methods are confined to protocol analysis and are of little help in re-designing a flawed protocol or designing a new one from scratch. While they may find bugs, it may or may not be obvious how the bug may be fixed, and one will certainly want to re-run the method with the altered protocol. It is therefore desirable to have methods that allow protocols to be designed in a methodical way that gives confidence that they are going to be correct. While it may be expected that such a method will restrict the domain from which such protocols may be chosen, this is likely to be out-weighed by the benefits. It is the aim of this paper to explain such a method. We will restrict ourselves here to illustrating the new method and giving an intuitive idea of the way that is works. A mathematical foundation is given in a companion paper [4].

In the remainder of this section we outline the method we are proposing. The following section examines a variety of protocols based on conventional symmetric cryptography as well as interactive key exchange. For each case we analyse a typical example and propose alternatives.

1.1 Secure Channels

Key exchange protocols make use of cryptography to ensure that the distributed keys are delivered to their destination in a manner that maintains their confidentiality and ensures their integrity. There are, however, a variety of different cryptographic functions available and it is important to select amongst them such that the correct security services are provided. Many cryptographic protocols use either conventional symmetric cryptographic algorithms or public key cryptosystems, while others make use of key agreement procedures, originally conceived by Diffie and Hellman [8]. Cryptographic security properties can broadly be classified into two types.

- **Confidentiality** allows the sender of a message to decide those users who will be able to receive it. These recipients will be defined by their possession of the required decryption key.
- **Authentication** allows the recipient of a message to decide those users who must have sent it. These senders will be defined by their possession of the required encryption key.

We can define abstract security channels, of confidentiality or authentication type, between pairs of users in possession of keys which allow cryptographic confidentiality or authentication to take place between them. These channels can be used to provide the security services needed to transport keys to be exchanged; furthermore, since these are defined in an abstract manner the particular cryptographic algorithms used can be left unspecified. We write

$$S \xrightarrow{c} A : m$$

to denote that S sends the message m on a confidentiality channel from A and

$$A \overset{a}{\longleftarrow} S : m$$

to denote that A receives the message m on an authentication channel from S. Note that the common, informal, manner of expressing protocols uses the notation $A \rightarrow B : m$ to express that the message m is transferred from A to B. However, it is *a priori* completely unknown to A who will receive m or to B who sent m. This is a quite different situation from the use of logical secure channels where confidentiality to the recipient and/or authentication from the sender is assured. In this paper we will continue to use the established notation to express concrete protocols where the security channels have been described.

In a normal key exchange protocol the aim is for two or more users to share a key for a subsequent session. It is possible for a trusted server to generate the key, or for one or more of the users to do so. Whichever of these is the case, the key needs to be passed to each user over an insecure physical channel. We will make an assumption, which is true in all practical cases, that the session key will be a shared key for use with a symmetric cryptosystem. However we will allow the methods used to exchange the session key to use either symmetric or asymmetric techniques. Whenever such an exchange takes place the following two conditions must hold.

1. The key must not be allowed to become known to any users apart from those participating in the protocol or trusted servers. Thus there must be a confidentiality channel from the generator of the key to the recipient(s).
2. Each recipient must be sure that the key comes from an authorised agent and is a new, key for use with the stated users. Thus there must be an authentication channel to each recipient of the key from the originator.

These conditions are uncontroversial and form the basis of what we will mean by a secure key exchange protocol. In practice further goals are often desired, for example that each user has confirmation that the the other users possess the new key. These additional requirements can always be achieved by additional steps independent of the actual key exchange.

To see the power of even these simple observations consider an initial example. This is the protocol of Tatebayashi, Matsuzaki and Newman (the TMN protocol) which is well known to be flawed and has been extensively analysed [9]. The protocol has the usual principals which are users A and B, who wish to share a new session key, K_{AB}, and a trusted server, S. Somewhat unusually, K_{AB} is generated by B and not S. S has a public key, K_S^{-1}, which is known to A and B. The messages exchanged in a successful protocol run may be defined as follows.

TMN Protocol

1. $A \rightarrow S$: $A, B, \{R_A\}_{K_S^{-1}}$
2. $S \rightarrow B$: A

3. $B \rightarrow S$: $\{K_{AB}\}_{K_S^{-1}}$
4. $S \rightarrow A$: $K_{AB} \oplus R_A$

Here, and throughout, the notation $\{X\}_K$ indicates the string X encrypted using the key K. It can be seen that the initial channels in the system are defined by the public key. It is implicitly assumed that the purpose of this public key is for A and B to pass messages confidentially to S. Thus the two existing channels are

$$A \xrightarrow{c} S$$

and

$$B \xrightarrow{c} S$$

(If the public key were also to be used for authentication in the form of signatures, then it would define two further channels $A \xleftarrow{a} S$ and $B \xleftarrow{a} S$. Existence of these extra channels does not alter the analysis.) By our conditions above, K_{AB} must be received by A on an authentication channel. But it can easily be seen that no such channel is used (or indeed exists), since A will accept any value sent in message 4. Thus there is no need to examine the protocol further since we can see that the correct properties have not been achieved[2]. It is not difficult to go from this observation to form a concrete attack, but even if we could not see such an attack we should still not be happy to use this protocol.

1.2 A Generic Secure Protocol

A variety of protocols may be defined by changing the way that the security channels are defined. In this paper we analyse previously published protocols by establishing how the channels are defined, even though they may not have been specifically identified by the authors of the protocols. We also define our own variations by forming these channels in the simplest way we can, with the aim of making the analysis as transparent as possible and at the same time removing all unnecessary processing. The above principles suggest a generic protocol for a key generator S to pass a key K to A, to be shared with a set of users $\mathcal{U}$, which can be abstractly defined as follows.

- $S \xrightarrow{c} A : K$
- $A \xleftarrow{a} S : K, N, \mathcal{U}$

The item N is a *nonce* which is intended to show that K is a new key and not a replayed one. N is usually either a random challenge previously sent by A, or a timestamp. A number of published protocols conform to this format and it is typical to combine both the authentication and confidentiality functions together in one cryptographic transformation. However this need not be so, and we will give examples where they are implemented separately. It should be noted that where this is done, it is implicitly expected that the key K should have its

[2] In this case it is possible to go further and show that the initial conditions are insufficient to succeed - no protocol can successfully transfer a shared key to A [2].

confidentiality protected on both channels. An obvious way to do this is via a public one way function.

It is intuitively easy to see that the generic protocol is secure in the sense that if the key generator S acts correctly then only users known to A (in other words those in $\mathcal{U}$) may end up in possession of K. S is trusted to generate a new key for each protocol run and pass it on a confidentiality channel to exactly the set of users $\mathcal{U}$. Thus we may be sure that any protocol of this format will satisfy our basic security requirements as long as the cryptographic algorithms used are confidentiality and authentication functions as required. A more formal argument is given in a companion paper [4].

The generic secure protocol is the heart of the design and analysis technique we are suggesting. Protocol design proceeds by making the generic protocol concrete through choice of specific algorithms available in the target application. Analysis works by seeking to identify the secure channels used and comparing the message fields with those of the generic protocol. As our examples illustrate, where the channels used are difficult to identify, a re-design of the protocol frequently leads to simplifications.

2 Protocols using Symmetric Cryptography

In this section we examine what may be termed classic key exchange protocols as established in the seminal paper of Needham and Schroeder [11]. The principals in these protocols are the server S and two users A and B who wish to share a new session key which will be generated by S. The key will be distributed to A and B using keys K_{AS} and K_{BS} which are initially shared by A and S, and by B and S, respectively.

2.1 Needham and Schroeder Procotol

This protocol dates from 1978 and is well known to be flawed. The messages in a successful run are as follows. R_A and R_B are random challenges chosen by A and B respectively.

Needham-Schroeder Protocol

1. $A \rightarrow S$: A, B, R_A
2. $S \rightarrow A$: $\{R_A, B, K_{AB}, \{K_{AB}, A\}_{K_{BS}}\}_{K_{AS}}$
3. $A \rightarrow B$: $\{K_{AB}, A\}_{K_{BS}}$
4. $B \rightarrow A$: $\{R_B\}_{K_{AB}}$
5. $A \rightarrow B$: $\{R_B - 1\}_{K_{AB}}$

The initial channels in the system are defined by the shared keys K_{AS} and K_{BS}. Depending on the algorithms used, these keys may define channels $A \xrightarrow{c} S$, $B \xrightarrow{c} S$, $S \xrightarrow{c} A$, $S \xrightarrow{c} B$ and $S \xleftarrow{a} A$, $S \xleftarrow{a} B$, $B \xleftarrow{a} S$ and $A \xleftarrow{a} S$. When S sends the key he encrypts it using the shared keys defining the necessary confidentiality channels. When A receives the key in message 2, she has with it a nonce and the name of B. This is similar to the generic form in section 1.2, the only difference being that the name of A is not included. In this case A can be sure that the message was intended for her as long as the algorithm used defines an authentication channel (that is, K_{AS} is required to form the message) and so we can regard A's name to be implicitly included. On the other hand, when B receives the key he has no nonce with it. Thus he cannot be sure that the key is new. Since he needs to get this assurance from the key generator, the subsequent exchange will never convince him of it. This well-known problem can be extended to a concrete attack [6].

2.2 Otway and Rees Protocol

This protocol [12] was designed to overcome the known problems of the Needham and Schroeder protocol. The steps in a successful run of the protocol are as follows, using the same notation as above.

Otway-Rees Protocol

1. $A \rightarrow B$: $M, A, B, \{R_A, M, A, B\}_{K_{AS}}$
2. $B \rightarrow S$: $M, A, B, \{R_A, M, A, B\}_{K_{AS}}, \{R_B, M, A, B\}_{K_{BS}}$
3. $S \rightarrow B$: $M, \{R_A, K_{AB}\}_{K_{AS}}, \{R_B, K_{AB}\}_{K_{BS}}$
4. $B \rightarrow A$: $M, \{R_A, K_{AB}\}_{K_{AS}}$

The value M is an extra random nonce chosen by A for practical, rather than security, purposes. It can be seen that there are many similarities with the Needham-Schroeder protocol. However, this time both A and B get to choose a nonce and have it returned with the key when it is delivered from S. The difference from the generic protocol suggested above is that the names of the recipients are not included with the key, in messages 3 and 4. A and B can therefore deduce that K_{AB} is new but cannot immediately deduce who else will know it.

Let us concentrate on message 4 received by A. As in the Needham-Schroeder protocol we may regard the name of A as implicitly included, because the authentication channel from S to A is symmetric. It is clearly intended that the returned nonce R_A is bound to the name of B, since they were sent together from A to S on an authentication channel in message 1. The exact logic by which A verifies that the key is to be used with B relies not just on the message received but also on the message sent to S and on the correct actions of S. It has been shown that the complexity of this argument is very sensitive to different interpretations of the exact actions performed [3].

We will not attempt to identify the exact authentication channel in this case, but instead note the protocol can easily be re-designed using the generic protocol. The resulting protocol is far easier to analyse since the purpose of each field is clear. At the same time the complexity of the protocol in terms of processing required is actually reduced.

Modified Otway-Rees Protocol

1. $A \rightarrow B$: A, R_A
2. $B \rightarrow S$: A, B, R_A, R_B
3. $S \rightarrow B$: $\{A, B, R_B, K_{AB}\}_{K_{BS}}, \{A, B, R_A, K_{AB}\}_{K_{AS}}$
4. $B \rightarrow A$: $\{A, B, R_A, K_{AB}\}_{K_{BS}}$

Because this conforms to the generic protocol, its security is guaranteed as long as the encryption defines both confidentiality and authentication channels from S to A and B respectively. We note that, although we show the nonces being sent to S as plaintext, there are lower level arguments that suggest they should be encrypted [10]. This would not affect the analysis at this design level.

2.3 A New Protocol

Before leaving protocols based on symmetric cryptography we examine how to design a protocol which splits the confidentiality and authentication channels. This can, of course, be done in a variety of ways. Confidentiality may be obtained by any particular encryption algorithm such as DES. There is no need to assume any particular mode of operation and since the only data encrypted is a random key the simplest choice, electronic code book [5], may as well be used. Authentication may be achieved by a key dependent message authentication code (MAC) which could also be based on a block cipher or could use a suitable one-way hash function. It is important that the MAC also provides confidentiality of the key. Thus we are led to the following protocol.

A Split Channel Protocol

1. $A \rightarrow B$: A, R_A
2. $B \rightarrow S$: A, B, R_A, R_B
3. $S \rightarrow B$: $\{K_{AB}\}_{K_{BS}}, MAC_{K_{BS}}\{A, B, R_B, K_{AB}\}$,
   $\{K_{AB}\}_{K_{AS}}, MAC_{K_{AS}}\{A, B, R_A, K_{AB}\}$
4. $B \rightarrow A$: $\{K_{AB}\}_{K_{AS}}, MAC_{K_{AS}}\{A, B, R_A, K_{AB}\}$

There is a lot of flexibility in implementing this protocol. For example, it may be that different parts of K_{AS} and K_{BS} are used for confidentiality from those used for authentication. This way confidentiality may be implemented, say, with bits from a one-time pad to give unconditional secrecy to the keys. Another variation is to alter the physical paths of the messages, since in reality there are independent parallel conversations between S and each key recipient.

3 Diffie-Hellman Type Protocols

Protocols of Diffie-Hellman type [8] have a number of potential advantages over more conventional protocols. Firstly, there is no requirement for the presence of an on-line server to aid in the key distribution. (In compensation, users need to have some mutual verification information order to provide key integrity, or provide it in terms of a public certificate.) Secondly, the users themselves participate in generation of the key. This makes it easier for them to be sure that the key chosen is new and not an old one being replayed. Finally, users do not need to share secrets with any other party, before the start of the protocol.

The generic protocol of section 1.2 does not at first appear to fit the situation of key agreement because there is not a single key generator involved, but instead the key is generated by the users themselves. However, there is no assumption that the key generator is not also a key user, and all that is required is to change the viewpoint of what messages mean in the Diffie-Hellman protocol. The Diffie-Hellman protocol uses a prime p and a primitive element $\alpha \bmod p$ which are fixed for the system.

- A chooses a random value x uniformly modulo $p-1$ and calculates $R_A = \alpha^x \bmod p$. A sends the value R_A to B.
- B chooses a random value y uniformly modulo $p-1$ and calculates $R_B = \alpha^y \bmod p$. B calculates the session key $K_{AB} = R_A^y \bmod p$. B sends R_B to A.
- A calculates the session key $K_{AB} = R_B^x \bmod p$.

In its basic form the protocol provides no authentication, to either user, of who possesses the shared key. This is a widely recognised limitation and a number of augmented protocols have been proposed to provide authentication. The station to station (STS) protocol was designed by Diffie, van Oorschot and Wiener [7] and they provided an informal analysis of the protocol security. Subsequently van Oorschot [13] analysed the protocol using an extension of an established logic which confirmed the conclusions previously reached by the original authors.

It is assumed that users can generate signatures and for this purpose certificates will need to be available either from a directory or in the protocol itself. However, we omit these in the following description. We denote the signature of user U on the message X by $Sig_U(X)$. In addition use is made of a symmetric encryption algorithm. A successful protocol run proceeds as follows, using the same notation as above.

STS Protocol

1. $A \rightarrow B$: R_A
2. $B \rightarrow A$: $R_B, \{Sig_B(R_B, R_A)\}_{K_{AB}}$
3. $A \rightarrow B$: $\{Sig_A(R_A, R_B)\}_{K_{AB}}$

When A receives message 2 she can calculate K_{AB} using R_B, and hence decrypt the second part. She checks that the result is the signature on (R_B, R_A) and if not then she aborts the protocol. Similarly B decrypts message 3 and checks that the result is (R_A, R_B). If not he aborts the protocol, otherwise he proceeds to the session.

Let us now consider what secure channels are used to deliver and authenticate the key K_{AB}. We regard the value R_A as being K_{AB} encrypted with the value y. While this may seem an odd viewpoint, it is quite clear that the value y is a secret key that is required to recover K_{AB} from R_A, which is exactly the property of a confidentiality channel. The unusual aspect is that at the time of sending, A has no idea of the value of K_{AB} or who will receive it, except that the recipient will be any user who knows the value y such that $R_B = \alpha^y$. We call this user $owner(y)$ and define the confidentiality channel as follows.

$$A \xrightarrow{c} owner(y) : K$$

means

$$A \rightarrow B : \alpha^x \bmod p$$

where $K = \alpha^{xy} \bmod p$. Note that in the concrete version we need to make some assumption about the recipient and so we write it down as B even though we cannot be sure who will get the message.

Now it is clear that for A to achieve authentication of the key it is only necessary for her to know that B knows K_{AB}, since the only user who may be in possession of K is $owner(y)$. This will therefore establish that $owner(y) = B$ and so K has been sent to B on a confidentiality channel and received from B on an authentication channel. In the STS protocol we conclude that

$$B \xleftarrow{a} A : K$$

means

$$A \rightarrow B : E_K(Sig_B\{R_B, R_A\})$$

where the values R_A and R_B are defined as above. We can now see that it is an assumption in the STS protocol that it is necessary to know K in order to form $E_K(z)$ from a given z. This is an implementation detail but it should be made clear that this property is absolutely necessary, since it is not held by all commonly used crypto-algorithms and unjustified assumptions of this sort can lead to protocol weaknesses [10]. While van Oorschot makes this assumption clear in his analysis [13] it only seems to be implicitly defined in the original definition of the STS protocol [7].

The rather complex nature of the authentication channel, which uses the signature algorithm, the key generation process and the unspecified encryption algorithm, contrasts with the simpler channel we have seen above. However, there seems to be no advantage in using this complex channel and therefore we suggest an alternative protocol with messages as follows, where h is a publicly known one-way hash function.

Modified STS Protocol

1. $A \to B$: R_A
2. $B \to A$: $R_B, Sig_B(A, B, h(K_{AB}))$
3. $A \to B$: $Sig_A(A, B, h(K_{AB}))$

While we do not believe the STS protocol is in any way unsound, we prefer the above protocol for two reasons.

- The authentication channel is much clearer. Each user receives a signed copy of the key and an acknowledgement of who the key is shared with. Notice that each user is already aware that K_{AB} is a new key since each participated in its generation using a new random value.
- The protocol is slightly simpler since the encryption algorithm is not required. Perhaps more important than efficiency is that fewer mechanisms are relied on. Note that it is usual to employ a hash function anyway when signing a message, and so the hash function h does not really require any additional processing.

4 Conclusion

We have identified the security channels used in previously published key exchange protocols. This has enabled us to suggest minor impovements and simplifications in these. We have shown how to design new protocols by using a generic protocol which can be made concrete in a number of ways. The techniques can easily be used by hand since they force a simplified representation of the protocols.

The techniques can be used in a variety of further situations. For example protocols based solely on one-way functions may be analysed and conference key protocols can also be accommodated [4]. Further research is needed to investigate extensions to multi-user and other more complex protocols.

The usefulness of the method can best be assessed by critical examination of the protocols which it is used to design. We therefore invite other researchers to assess the new designs suggested in this paper.

Acknowledgements

This paper was written while the first author was a visitor at the Computer Science Department, University of Waikato, New Zealand.

References

1. M.Burrows, M.Abadi, and R.Needham, *A Logic of Authentication*, Proceedings of the Royal Society, Vol A426,pp 233-271,1989.

2. Colin Boyd, *Security Architectures using Formal Methods*, IEEE Journal on Selected Areas in Communications, June 1993, pp.694-701.
3. Colin Boyd and Wenbo Mao, *On a Limitation of BAN logic*, Advances in Cryptology - Eurocrypt 93, Springer-Verlag, 1994, pp.240-247.
4. Colin Boyd and Wenbo Mao, *Designing Secure Key Exchange Protocols*, Proceedings of ESORICS 94, Springer-Verlag, 1994, pp.93-105.
5. D.W.Davies and W.L.Price, *Security for Computer Networks*, John Wiley and Sons, 1989
6. D.E.Denning and G.M.Sacco, *Timestamps in Key Distribution Protocols*, Communications of the ACM, 24,8,1981, pp.533-536.
7. Whitfield Diffie, Paul C. van Oorshot and Michael J. Wiener, *Authentication and Authenticated Key Exchanges*, Designs, Codes and Cryptography, 2, pp.107-125, 1992.
8. W.Diffie and M.Hellman, *New Directions in Cryptography*, IEEE Transactions on Information Theory, IT-22, 6, November 1976, pp.644-654.
9. R.Kemmerer, C.Meadows and J.Millen, *Three Systems for Cryptographic Protocol Analysis*, Journal of Cryptology, 7,2, Spring 1994, pp.79-130.
10. Wenbo Mao and Colin Boyd, *Design of Authentication Protocols: Some Misconceptions and a New Approach*, Proceedings of IEEE Computer Security Foundations Workshop VII, 1994.
11. R.M.Needham and M.D.Schroeder, *Using Encryption for Authentication in Large Networks of Computers*, Communications of the ACM, 21,12, December 1978, pp.993-999.
12. Dave Otway and Owen Rees, *Efficient and Timely Mutual Authentication*, ACM Operating Systems Review, 21,1,pp.8-10, 1987.
13. Paul C. van Oorschot, *Extending Cryptographic Logics of Belief to Key Agreement Protocols*, Proceeedings of the 1st ACM Conference on Communications and Computer Seurity, Faixfax Virginia, November 1993.
14. Darryl M. Stahl, Stafford E.Tavares and Henk Meijer, *Backward State Analysis of Cryptographic Protocols Using Coloured Petri Nets*, Workshop on Selected Areas in Cryptography, Canada, 1994.

Zero-Knowledge Proofs of Computational Power in the Shared String Model

Alfredo De Santis* Tatsuaki Okamoto† Giuseppe Persiano‡

* Dipartimento di Informatica ed Applicazioni
Università di Salerno, 84081 Baronissi (SA), Italy
Email: ads@udsab.dia.unisa.it

† NTT Laboratories
1-2356, Take, Yokosuka-shi, Kanagawa-ken, 238-03 Japan
Email: okamoto@sucaba.isl.ntt.jp

‡ Dipartimento di Matematica
Università di Catania, Catania, Italy
Email: giuper@udsab.dia.unisa.it

Abstract. Zero-knowledge proofs have several applications and come in three different flavors: to prove membership to a language [13]; to prove possession of knowledge [13, 10, 12, 16, 3]; and to prove computational power [17].
The original definition of zero-knowledge proofs was cast in an interactive setting thus making it not applicable in cases where interaction was not allowed or severly limited. In [2, 1], a non-interactive model for zero-knowledge proofs of membership, called the shared-string model, has been put forward. In [7], it was proved that the shared string model also supports proofs of knowledge.
In this paper, we formalize the concept of proofs of computational power in the shared string model and show classes of problems that admit proofs of computational power.

1 Introduction

The seminal concept of a zero-knowledge proof of membership has been introduced in [13]. It has found several applications in various fields: from Complexity Theory to Cryptography. The original definition was for *membership* problems, in which the prover proves the membership of an input string to a language. Since then, two other types of interactive zero-knowledge proofs have been proposed: proofs of *knowledge* formally introduced by Feige, Fiat, Shamir [10] (see also [13, 12, 16, 3]) in which the prover's *possession* of some information is demonstrated; and proofs of *computational power* by Yung [17], in which prover's *ability* to solve a computational problem is demonstrated.

Subsequently, the concept of a *non-interactive zero-knowledge proof* (in short NIZKP) has been introduced [2, 1]. In a NIZKP the prover and the verifier share a random string and communication is monodirectional: from the prover to the verifier only. In this non-interactive setting proofs of membership [2, 1, 5, 6, 11, 4] and proofs of knowledge [7] have been presented.

This paper makes the first contribution in formalizing the concept of proof of computational power (NIZKPP in short) in the non-interactive setting of [1] and giving implementations for it. In formalizing the concept of NIZKPP we distinguish between standard and non-standard NIZKPP's and weak and strong NIZKPP's. Hence, we have four definitions: weak standard, strong standard, weak non-standard and strong non-standard. Any standard NIZKPP is a non-standard NIZKPP, but the inverse does not necessarily hold. Similarly, any strong NIZKPP is a weak NIZKPP, but the inverse does not necessarily hold.

This paper introduces four classes of problems that admit various kinds of NIZKPP: dense random self-reducible (in short DRSR), creatable DRSR (in short CDRSR), uniform generatable (in short UG), and creatable UG (in short CUG) problems. The class of DRSR (or CDRSR) problems is included in UG (or CUG). A typical DRSR (and CDRSR) problem is the discrete logarithm problem, $R_{(p,g)} = (x, y)$ with $x = g^y \bmod p$ and $p = 2^n - a$ ($a < 2^{n/2}$) (another typical CDRSR problem is the RSA problem). A typical UG (and CUG) problem can be made from a language in NP∩co-NP.

This paper obtains the following results:

1. Any CDRSR problem has a weak standard non-interactive statistical zero-knowledge proof of computational power (standard NI-statistical-ZKPP). Moreover, this proof is very efficient.
2. Any DRSR problem whose corresponding problem has a non-interactive zero-knowledge proof of knowledge (NIZKPK) has a weak standard NIZKPP.
3. Any CUG problem has a strong non-standard non-interactive statistical zero-knowledge proofs of computational power (non-standard NI-statistical-ZKPP). Moreover, this proof is very efficient.
4. Any UG problem that has a non-interactive zero-knowledge proof of knowledge (NIZKPK) has also a strong non-standard NIZKPP.

This paper is organized as follows. Section 2 gives four types of definitions of NIZKPP's. In Section 3, we define some classes of problems related to the notion of NIZKPP. In Section 4, we present the major results, the characterization of NIZKPP's by using classes of problems which have NIZKPP's.

2 Notations

If algorithm A is a probabilistic algorithm, then for input x, the notation $A(x)$ refers to the probability space that assigns to the string σ the probability that A, on input x, outputs σ.

If S is any probability space, then $x \leftarrow S$ denotes the algorithm which assigns to x an element randomly selected according to S. If F is a finite set, then the notation "$x \leftarrow F$" denotes the algorithm which assigns to x a randomly selected element of F.

If $p(\cdot,\cdot,\cdots)$ is a predicate, the notation $\Pr[x \leftarrow S;\ y \leftarrow T;\ \ldots : p(x,y,\ldots)]$ denotes the probability that $p(x,y,\ldots)$ will be true after the ordered execution of the algorithms $x \leftarrow S;\ y \leftarrow T;\ \ldots$.

3 Non-Interactive Proofs of Computational Power

This section introduces the formal definition of a non-interactive proof of computational power (NIZKPP).

There are two types of definitions of NIZKPP's in a manner similar to those of NIZKP's of membership or knowledge (NIZKPM's or NIZKPK's): the preprocessing type and the shared-string type. An NIZKPP can be constructed through an NIZKPK, so it depends on which type of an NIZKPK is used. This paper considers only the shared-string type, since the preprocessing type is similarly defined and constructed. We can also define two types of definitions of NIZKPP's in a manner similar to those of NIZKPK's: weak type and strong type, the distinction of which depends on whether a problem is given before or after the shared-string is given (or the preprocessing is done). Moreover, there are also two types of definitions of NIZKPP's in the light of the problem solver. One is natural (standard type), and the other less natural but still reasonable (non-standard type), although the non-standard type of NIZKPP's can be applied to wider class of problems than the standard type of NIZKPP's.

Before defining NIZKPP's, we need the following concepts.

Definition 1. Let $\mathcal{N}$ be a countable infinite set. For any $N \in \mathcal{N}$, let $|N|$ denote the length of a suitable representation of N. For any $N \in \mathcal{N}$, let X_N, Y_N be finite sets, and $R_N \subseteq X_N \times Y_N$ be a relation. Let

$$\boldsymbol{dom}(R_N) = \{x \in X_N \mid (x,y) \in R_N \text{ for some } y \in Y_N\}$$

denote the *domain* of R_N,

$$R_N(x) = \{y \mid (x,y) \in R_N\}$$

the *image* of $x \in X_N$, and

$$R_N(X_N) = \{y \mid (x,y) \in R_N, x \in X_N\}$$

the *image* of R_N.

A computational problem is a family

$$\mathcal{R} = \{R_N \mid N \in \mathcal{N}\}.$$

Definition 2. A problem solver is a pair of probabilistic polynomial-time algorithms ($\boldsymbol{Sol}_0$, $\boldsymbol{Sol}_1$). Algorithm $\boldsymbol{Sol}_0$ on input 1^n (and others) outputs a pair (σ, aux), with $|\sigma| = n^c$ (c: a positive constant).

Definition 3. Let R_N be a relation. Then, by B_{R_N} we denote an oracle which, given $x \in \boldsymbol{dom}(R_N)$ outputs a randomly chosen $y \in R_N(x)$. If P is a probabilistic Turing machine then by $P(B_{R_N}; x)$ we denote the probability distribution of P's output on input x and having access to the oracle B_{R_N}.

3.1 Standard NIZKPP

A "weak and standard" non-interactive proof of computational power (NIPP, in short) can be defined as follows:

Definition 4. A pair (P, V), where P is a probabilistic Turing machine running in polynomial time and V is a deterministic polynomial-time Turing machine, is a *weak standard NIPP* for $\mathcal{R}$, if there exists a constant $c > 0$ such that:

(Completeness:) If for all constant $a > 0$, all sufficiently large n, and all $N \in \mathcal{N}$ with $n = |N|$,

$$\Pr[\sigma \leftarrow \{0,1\}^{n^c}; \Pi \leftarrow P(B_{R_N}; \sigma, N) : V(\sigma, N, \Pi) = 1] \geq 1 - n^{-a}.$$

(Soundness:) There exists a problem solver $(\boldsymbol{Sol}_0, \boldsymbol{Sol}_1)$ such that for any algorithm $\boldsymbol{Adv}$, for all constants $a > 0$, all sufficiently long N, and all $x \in \boldsymbol{dom}(R_N)$,

$$\Pr[(\sigma, aux) \leftarrow \boldsymbol{Sol}_0(x, N); \Pi \leftarrow \boldsymbol{Adv}(\sigma, N); w \leftarrow \boldsymbol{Sol}_1(\sigma, aux, x, N, \Pi)$$
$$: (x, w) \in R_N] \geq p_N(1 - |N|^{-a}),$$

where p_N denotes

$$\Pr[\sigma \leftarrow \{0,1\}^{|N|^c}; \Pi \leftarrow \boldsymbol{Adv}(\sigma, N) : V(\sigma, N, \Pi) = 1].$$

Remark: σ output by $\boldsymbol{Sol}_0$ should be uniformly distributed, or statistically close to the common string.

Next, a "strong and standard" non-interactive proof of computational power (NIPP) can be defined as follows:

Definition 5. A weak standard NIPP (P, V) is a *strong standard* NIPP for the problem $\mathcal{R}$ if there exists a constant $c > 0$ such that:
(Soundness:) There exists a problem solver $(\boldsymbol{Sol}_0, \boldsymbol{Sol}_1)$ such that for any algorithm $\boldsymbol{Adv}$ that on input a string of length n^c outputs a triplet (x, N, Π) with $x \in \boldsymbol{dom}(R_N)$ and $|N| = n$, for all constants $a > 0$, and all sufficiently long N,

$$\Pr[(\sigma, aux) \leftarrow \boldsymbol{Sol}_0(1^n); (x, N, \Pi) \leftarrow \boldsymbol{Adv}(\sigma); w \leftarrow \boldsymbol{Sol}_1(\sigma, aux, x, N, \Pi)$$
$$: (x, w) \in R_N] \geq p_N(1 - |N|^{-a}),$$

where p_N denotes

$$\Pr[\sigma \leftarrow \{0,1\}^{|N|^c}; (N, \Pi) \leftarrow \boldsymbol{Adv}(\sigma) : V(\sigma, N, \Pi) = 1].$$

Note: In the weak NIPP definition, N is chosen by the adversary before seeing the random string and thus independently from the random string. In the strong NIPP definition, we let the adversary choose N after seeing the random string. This is similar to the relationship between NIZKPK and strong NIZKPK of [7].

3.2 Non-standard NIPP

In this subsection, we define a non-standard NIPP is defined.

In the standard NIPP, the problem solver $(\boldsymbol{Sol}_0, \boldsymbol{Sol}_1)$ reading the proof string produced by the adversary $\boldsymbol{Adv}$, and given any $x \in \boldsymbol{dom}(R_N)$, can obtain y satisfying $(x, y) \in R_N$ with sufficiently high probability. Here, the success probability of obtaining y given x is "not" taken over the distribution of x. On the other hand, in the "non-standard" NIPP, problem solver $(\boldsymbol{Sol}_0, \boldsymbol{Sol}_1)$ with access to adversary $\boldsymbol{Adv}$, given $s \in \{0,1\}^*$ with uniform distribution ($x = G_{R_N}(s) \in \boldsymbol{dom}(R_N)$ with uniform distribution), can obtain y satisfying $(x, y) \in R_N$ with sufficiently high probability. Here, the success probability of obtaining y given s is taken over the uniform distribution of s and others.

Before defining a non-standard NIPP, we introduce the notion of the problem generators.

Definition 6. Let R_N denote a relation that can be verified in polynomial time in $|N|$ by a deterministic algorithm. A *uniform generator* for R_N, G_{R_N}, is a polynomial-time algorithm that, given a uniformly distributed string $s \in \{0,1\}^{|N|}$, outputs a string x with uniform probability on $\boldsymbol{dom}(R_N)$.

Definition 7. A problem $\mathcal{R} = \{R_N\}_{N \in \mathcal{N}}$ is called "uniform generation" (UG) problem, if R_N has a uniform generator G_{R_N}.

Now, a "weak and non-standard" non-interactive proof of computational power (non-standard NIPP) is defined as follows:

Definition 8. (P, V) is a *weak non-standard* NIPP for the problem $\mathcal{R}$ in UG, if there exists a constant $c > 0$ such that:

(Completeness:) Same as Definition 4.

(Soundness:) There exists a problem solver $(\boldsymbol{Sol}_0, \boldsymbol{Sol}_1)$ such that for any algorithm $\boldsymbol{Adv}$, for all constant $a > 0$, all sufficiently long N,

$$\Pr[s \leftarrow \{0,1\}^{|N|}; (\sigma, aux) \leftarrow \boldsymbol{Sol}_0(s, N); \Pi \leftarrow \boldsymbol{Adv}(\sigma, N);$$
$$w \leftarrow \boldsymbol{Sol}_1(\sigma, aux, s, N, \Pi) : (x = G_{R_N}(s), w) \in R_N] \geq p_N(1 - |N|^{-a}),$$

where p_N denotes

$$\Pr[\sigma \leftarrow \{0,1\}^{|N|^c}; \Pi \leftarrow \boldsymbol{Adv}(\sigma, N) : V(\sigma, N, \Pi) = 1].$$

We now define the concept of strong and non-standard NIPP.

Definition 9. A weak non-standard NIPP (P, V) is a *strong non-standard* NIPP for the problem $\mathcal{R} \in$ UG, if there exists a constant $c > 0$ such that:

(Soundness:) There exists a problem solver $(\boldsymbol{Sol}_0, \boldsymbol{Sol}_1)$ such that for any algorithm $\boldsymbol{Adv}$, for all constant $a > 0$, all sufficiently long N,

$$\Pr[s \leftarrow \{0,1\}^{|N|}; (\sigma, aux) \leftarrow \boldsymbol{Sol}_0(s); (N, \Pi) \leftarrow \boldsymbol{Adv}(\sigma);$$
$$w \leftarrow \boldsymbol{Sol}_1(\sigma, aux, s, N, \Pi) : (G_{R_N}(s), w) \in R_N] \geq p_N(1 - |N|^{-a}),$$

where p_N denotes

$$\Pr[\sigma \leftarrow \{0,1\}^{|N|^c}; (N, \Pi) \leftarrow \boldsymbol{Adv}(\sigma) : V(\sigma, N, \Pi) = 1].$$

3.3 Zero-knowledgeness

The zero-knowledgeness for non-interactive proofs is defined in the same manner as in [1, 7]. So, the "weak/strong" "standard/non-standard" non-interactive "zero-knowledge" proof of computational power (weak/strong standard/non-standard NIZKPP) is defined on weak/strong standard/non-standard NIPP.

4 Classes of Problems with NIZKPP

In this section, we introduce some classes of problems for which we can give NIZKPP.

Definition 10. A computational problem $\mathcal{R}$ is a *random self-reducible* (RSR) problem, if there is a polynomial time algorithm A that, given as inputs $N \in \mathcal{N}$, $x \in \boldsymbol{dom}(R_N)$, and $r \in \{0,1\}^*$, outputs $x' = A(N,x,r) \in \boldsymbol{dom}(R_N)$ satisfying the following properties.

1. If the bits of r are uniform and independent, then x' is uniformly distributed over $\boldsymbol{dom}(R_N)$.
2. There is a polynomial time algorithm that, given N, x, r, and any $y' \in R_N(A(N,x,r))$, outputs $y \in R_N(x)$.

Definition 11. A RSR problem $\mathcal{R}$ is *dense* if there exists a constant $a > 0$, such that, for any $N \in \mathcal{N}$ there exists a constant $m_N \leq |N|^a$ such that $\boldsymbol{dom}(R_N)$ is statistically close to $\{0,1\}^{m_N}$.

Definition 12. An RSR problem $\mathcal{R}$ is *creatable* if there is a polynomial time algorithm that, given N, outputs $(x,y) \in R_N$ with uniform distribution.

Definition 13. Let $\mathcal{R} = \{R_N\}$ be a UG problem and let G_{R_N} be the uniform generator for R_N. We say that $\mathcal{R}$ is *creatable* if there is a polynomial time algorithm that, on input N outputs a uniformly distributed triplet (s,x,y) such that $(x,y) \in R_N$ and $x = G_{R_N}(s)$.

Lemma 14. *If $\mathcal{R}$ is a dense problem, then $\mathcal{R}$ is a uniform generation (UG) problem.*

Therefore, if $\mathcal{R}$ is a dense RSR (DRSR) problem, then $\mathcal{R}$ is a uniform generation (UG) problem. If $\mathcal{R}$ is a creatable DRSR (CDRSR) problem, then $\mathcal{R}$ is a creatable uniform generation (CUG) problem.

$$\text{CDRSR} \subseteq \text{DRSR} \subseteq \text{UG},$$

$$\text{CDRSR} \subseteq \text{CUG} \subseteq \text{UG}.$$

Examples:

- (DRSR and CDRSR). We let $\mathcal{N}$ be the set of pairs (p, g) where p is a prime such that $p = 2^n - a$ and $a < 2^{n/2}$ and g is a generator of Z_p^*. The relation $R_{(p,g)}$ is defined as the set of pairs (x, y) such that $y \in Z_{p-1}$ and $x = g^y \bmod p$. Then, $\{R_{(p,g)}\}$ is RSR. In fact algorithm A defined by $A((p, g), x, r) = xg^r \bmod p$ satisfies the condition of the definition. Moreover, $\boldsymbol{dom}(R_{(p,g)}) = Z_p^*$ is statistically close to $\{0,1\}^n$ and thus $\{R_{(p,g)}\}$ is also dense. Finally observe that $\{R_{(p,g)}\}$ is also CDRSR, since (x, y) can be uniformly generated in polynomial time by selecting y uniformly.
- (UG and CUG). Let L be a language $\in$NP$\cap$co-NP. Then for any string $x \in \{0,1\}^*$, there exists a short (i.e. of length polynomial in $|x|$) witness w to prove either that $x \in L$ or that $x \notin L$. Let N be the parameter of L, and $(x, w) \in R_N$. Then, there exists a uniform generator G_{R_N}, which generates $x \in \{0,1\}^*$ randomly. That is, $\{R_N\}$ is UG.
  If there exists a polynomial time algorithm to generate $(x, y) \in R_N$ uniformly by selecting y uniformly, then $\{R_N\}$ is CUG.

5 Construction of NIZKPP

In this section we present non-interactive zero-knowledge proof system of computational power for the various classes of languages that we have introduced in the previous section.

5.1 Standard NISZKPP for CDRSR languages

Theorem 15. *Any creatable dense random self-reducible (CDRSR) problem $\mathcal{R} = \{R_N\}$ has a weak standard NISZKPP.*

Sketch of Proof:
Construction:

- P and V share a common random string, σ, and a common input $N \in \mathcal{N}$.
- P regards σ as $x \in \boldsymbol{dom}(R_N)$, and computes y such that $(x, y) \in R_N$.
- P sends y to V as Π.
- V accepts if $(x, y) \in R_N$ holds, otherwise rejects.

Completeness: This is trivially satisfied.
Soundness: When N and x are given, $\boldsymbol{Sol}_0$ generates a random string r and computes $x' = A(N, x, r)$. Then, $\boldsymbol{Sol}_0$ outputs x' as σ, and r as aux. If $\boldsymbol{Adv}$ outputs y' satisfying $(x', y') \in R_N$, then $\boldsymbol{Sol}_1$ can compute a y satisfying $(x, y) \in R_N$ from x, x', y', and r (from the property of RSR). The success probability that, given x, ($\boldsymbol{Sol}_0$, $\boldsymbol{Adv}$, $\boldsymbol{Sol}_1$) outputs y is almost the same as the success probability that the output of $\boldsymbol{Adv}$ is accepted.
Zero-knowledgeness: Since R_N is creatable, $(\sigma, \Pi) = (x, y) \in R_N$ can be statistically simulated by a probabilistic polynomial time machine.

□

5.2 Standard NIZKPP for DRSR languages

Theorem 16. *Any DRSR problem $\mathcal{R} = \{R_N\}$ with a non-interactive zero-knowledge proof of knowledge (NIZKPK) has a weak standard NIZKPP.*

Sketch of Proof:

Construction:

- P and V share a common random string, σ, and a common input N in $\mathcal{N}$.
- P regards a prefix of σ as $x \in \boldsymbol{dom}(R_N)$, and computes y such that $(x, y) \in R_N$. P generates a non-interactive zero-knowledge proof of knowledge (NIZKPK), Π, that P knows y. Here, the remaining part of σ is used to generate Π.
- P sends Π to V.
- V accepts if Π is valid, otherwise rejects.

Completeness: This is trivially satisfied.
Soundness: Suppose that N and x are given. Since we assume that NIZKPK exists, an extractor $(\boldsymbol{Ext}_0, \boldsymbol{Ext}_1)$ exists [7]. Then, $(\boldsymbol{Sol}_0, \boldsymbol{Sol}_1)$ is constructed as follows: First, $\boldsymbol{Sol}_0$ generates a random string r and calculates $x' = A(N, x, r)$. Then, $\boldsymbol{Sol}_0$ runs $\boldsymbol{Ext}_0$, which outputs (aux_0, σ_0). $\boldsymbol{Sol}_0$ outputs (x', σ_0) as σ, and (r, aux_0) as aux.

After $\boldsymbol{Adv}$ outputs Π, $\boldsymbol{Sol}_1$ runs $\boldsymbol{Ext}_1$, which outputs y' satisfying $(x', y') \in R_N$ with almost the same probability as $\boldsymbol{Adv}$ outputs Π, which is accepted by V. Then $\boldsymbol{Sol}_1$ can calculates y satisfying $(x, y) \in R_N$ ¿from x, x', y', and r (from the property of RSR). Therefore, the success probability that, given x, $(\boldsymbol{Sol}_0, \boldsymbol{Adv}, \boldsymbol{Sol}_1)$ outputs y is almost same as the success probability that the output of $\boldsymbol{Adv}$ is accepted.
Zero-knowledgeness: Since Π is a NIZKPK, there exists a simulator for (a part of σ, Π). Therefore, (σ, Π) can also be simulated, since the remaining part of σ is statistically close to a random string. □

5.3 Non-standard NISZKPP for CUG

Theorem 17. *Any CUG problem $\mathcal{R} = \{R_N\}$ has a "strong non-standard" non-interactive "statistical" zero-knowledge proof of computational power.*

Sketch of Proof:

Construction:

- P and V share a common random string, σ, and a common input, N in $\mathcal{N}$.
- P generates $x \in \boldsymbol{dom}(R_N)$ by $x \leftarrow G_{R_N}(s)$, where σ is regarded as s. P calculates y satisfying $(x, y) \in R_N$.
- P sends y to V as Π.
- V accepts if $(x, y) \in R_N$ holds, otherwise rejects.

Completeness: This is trivially satisfied.

Soundness: Given s, $\boldsymbol{Sol}_0$ outputs a random string s as σ. If and only if $\boldsymbol{Adv}$ outputs (R_N, y) satisfying $(x, y) \in R_N$, where $x \leftarrow G_{R_N}(s)$, it is accepted by V. $\boldsymbol{Sol}_1$ outputs y. Therefore, the success probability that, given s, ($\boldsymbol{Sol}_0$, $\boldsymbol{Adv}$, $\boldsymbol{Sol}_1$) outputs y is almost same as the success probability that the output of $\boldsymbol{Adv}$ is accepted.

Zero-knowledgeness: Since $\mathcal{R}$ is creatable, $(\sigma, \Pi) = (s, y)$ can be statistically simulated by a probabilistic polynomial time machine.

□

5.4 Non-standard NIZKPP for UG

Theorem 18. *Any UG problem $\mathcal{R} = \{R_N\}$ with a non-interactive zero-knowledge proof of knowledge (NIZKPK) has a "strong non-standard" NIZKPP.*

Sketch of Proof:

Construction:

- P and V share a common random string, $\sigma = s \circ \sigma_0$, and a common input, N in $\mathcal{N}$.
- P generates $x \in \boldsymbol{dom}(R_N)$ by $x \leftarrow G_{R_N}(s)$ and computes y satisfying $(x, y) \in R_N$.
  Here P generates a non-interactive zero-knowledge proof of knowledge, Π, that P knows y using σ_0 as reference string.
- P sends Π to V.
- V accepts if Π is valid, otherwise rejects.

Completeness: This is trivially satisfied.

Soundness: Let $(\boldsymbol{Ext}_0, \boldsymbol{Ext}_1)$ be the strong extractor for the non-interactive zero-knowledge proof of knowledge for $\mathcal{R}$. Then, $(\boldsymbol{Sol}_0, \boldsymbol{Sol}_1)$ is constructed as follows: First, given s, $\boldsymbol{Sol}_0$ runs $\boldsymbol{Ext}_0$ to obtain (aux, σ_0), and outputs $\sigma = s\circ\sigma_0$, and aux.

After receiving (N, Π) from $\boldsymbol{Adv}$, $\boldsymbol{Sol}_1$ runs $\boldsymbol{Ext}_1$ that outputs y satisfying $(x, y) \in R_N$, where $x \leftarrow G_{R_N}(s)$. The probability of success is very close to the probability that $\boldsymbol{Adv}$ output (N, Π) that is accepted by V. Then $\boldsymbol{Sol}_1$ outputs y. Therefore, the success probability that, given s, ($\boldsymbol{Sol}_0$, $\boldsymbol{Sol}_1$) outputs y is almost same as the success probability that the output of $\boldsymbol{Adv}$ is accepted.

Zero-knowledgeness: Since Π is a NIZKPK, there exists a simulator for (a part of σ_0 and Π). Therefore, (σ, Π) can also be simulated, since the remaining part of σ (i.e., s) is statistically close to a random string.

□

6 Conclusions

This paper investigated the concept of non-interactive zero-knowledge proofs of computational power (NIZKPP's), and described the first NIZKPP's. We presented the formalization of the concept of NIZKPP's, and defined four classes of problems related to the notion of NIZKPP's. This paper gave the first characterization of NIZKPP's as follows:

1. Any CDRSR problem has a "weak standard" NIZKPP.
2. Any DRSR problem whose corresponding problem has a non-interactive zero-knowledge proof of knowledge has a "weak standard" NIZKPP.
3. Any CUG problem has a "strong non-standard" NIZKPP.
4. Any UG problem whose corresponding problem has a non-interactive zero-knowledge proof of knowledge has a "strong non-standard" NIZKPP.

Acknowledgments

Authors wish to thank Giovanni Di Crescenzo and Moti Yung for their helpful comments.

References

1. M. Blum, A. De Santis, S. Micali, and G. Persiano, *Non-Interactive Zero Knowledge*, SIAM Journal of Computing, vol. 20, no. 6, pp. 1084–1118, December 1991.
2. M. Blum, P. Feldman, and S. Micali, *Non-Interactive Zero-Knowledge Proof Systems and Applications*, Proceedings of the 20th Annual ACM Symposium on Theory of Computing, Chicago, Illinois, 1988, pp. 364–383.
3. M. Bellare, and O. Goldreich, *On Defining Proofs of Knowledge*, in Proc. of Crypto '92.
4. A. De Santis, G. Di Crescenzo, and G. Persiano, *Secret Sharing and Perfect Zero Knowledge*, in Proc. of Crypto '93.
5. A. De Santis, S. Micali, and G. Persiano, *Non-Interactive Zero-Knowledge Proof Systems*, in "Advances in Cryptology – CRYPTO 87", vol. 293 of "Lecture Notes in Computer Science", Springer Verlag, pp. 52–72.
6. A. De Santis, S. Micali, and G. Persiano, *Non-Interactive Zero-Knowledge Proof-Systems with Preprocessing*, in "Advances in Cryptology - CRYPTO 88", Ed. S. Goldwasser, vol. 403 of "Lecture Notes in Computer Science", Springer-Verlag, pp. 269–282.
7. A. De Santis, and G. Persiano, *Zero-Knowledge Proofs of Knowledge Without Interaction*, Proceedings of the 33rd Annual IEEE Symposium on Foundations of Computer Science, Pittsburgh, Pennsylvania, 1992, pp. 427–436.
8. A. De Santis and M. Yung, *Cryptographic Applications of the Non-Interactive Metaproof and Many-prover Systems*, in "Advances in Cryptology - CRYPTO 90", Ed. A.J. Menezes and S.A. Vanstone, vol. 537 of "Lecture Notes in Computer Science", Springer-Verlag, pp. 366-377.
9. S. Even, O. Goldreich, and A. Lempel, *A Randomized Protocol for Signing Contracts*, CACM, vol. 28, 1985, pp. 637–647.

10. U. Feige, A. Fiat, and A. Shamir, *Zero-knowledge Proofs of Identity,* Journal of Cryptology, vol. 1, 1988, pp. 77–94. (Preliminary version in Proceedings of the 19th Annual ACM Symposium on Theory of Computing, New York, 1987, pp. 210–217.)
11. U. Feige, D. Lapidot, and A. Shamir, *Multiple Non-Interactive Zero-Knowledge Proofs Based on a Single Random String,* in Proceedings of 22nd Annual Symposium on the Theory of Computing, 1990, pp. 308–317.
12. M. Fischer, S. Micali, and C. Rackoff, *A Secure Protocol for the Oblivious Transfer,* Eurocrypt 1984.
13. S. Goldwasser, S. Micali, and C. Rackoff, *The Knowledge Complexity of Interactive Proof-Systems*, SIAM Journal on Computing, vol. 18, n. 1, February 1989.
14. O. Goldreich, S. Micali, and A. Wigderson, *Proofs that Yield Nothing but their Validity or All Languages in NP Have Zero-Knowledge Proof Systems*, Journal of the ACM, vol. 38, no. 1, July 1991, pp. 691–729.
15. T. Okamoto, D. Chaum, and K. Ohta, *Direct Zero Knowledge Proofs of Computational Power in Five Rounds,* in "Advances in Cryptology - EUROCRYPT '91', Ed. D. W. Davies, vol. 547 of "Lecture Notes in Computer Science", Springer-Verlag, pp. 96-105.
16. M. Tompa and H. Woll, *Random Self-Reducibility and Zero-knowledge Interactive Proofs of Possession of Information,* Proceedings of 28rd Symposium on Foundations of Computer Science, 1987, pp. 472–482.
17. M. Yung, *Zero-Knowledge Proofs of Computational Power*, in "Advances in Cryptology - EUROCRYPT '89', Ed. J. J. Quisquater and J. Vandewalle, vol. 434 of "Lecture Notes in Computer Science", Springer-Verlag, pp. 196-207.

INVITED LECTURE 3

Hideki Imai

(University of Tokyo, Japan)

Information Security Aspects of Spread Spectrum Systems

Hideki Imai

Institute of Industrial Science, The University of Tokyo
Roppongi, Minato-ku, Tokyo 106, Japan
E-mail: imai@iis.u-tokyo.ac.jp

Abstract. Recently spread spectrum systems have been intensively studied and developed for new commercial applications in cellular mobile communication networks and wireless personal communication networks. This is because they have some advantages such as robustness against interference and noise, low probability of intercept, anti-jamming property, high communication capacity per frequency and so on. Some of these features have given spread spectrum systems reputation that they have high information security. A purpose of this paper is to examine this reputation. It is often claimed that in some spread spectrum communication systems, noise and interference have much higher power than the desired signal so that any opponent who does not know the spreading mechanism cannot detect the signal. It is shown, however, that the knowledge of the spreading mechanism gives legitimate users at most about 5 dB advantage of signal to noise ratio over opponents. Therefore, in order to protect privacy, it is recommended to encrypt transmitting data. From the viewpoint of privacy, untraceablity is also important. We propose a registration protocol for cellular systems to keep users unidentified by opponents. From the aspects of information security, the most significant feature peculiar to spread spectrum systems is anti-jamming property. We discuss some designing methodology for spreading mechanisms to strengthen this property.

Keywords. Spread Spectrum System, Information Security, CDMA, Cellular System, Untraceability, Jamming

1 Introduction

Spread spectrum (SS) systems are not only for communications but also for ranging systems such as GPS (global positioning system). However, since the subject of this paper is information security of communications, we confine ourselves to applications of SS to CDMA (code division multiple-access) communication systems, i.e., SSMA (spread spectrum multiple-access) systems.

There are three fundamental access systems: FDMA (frequency division multiple-access), TDMA (time division multiple-access), and CDMA. For FDMA or TDMA, we assign one frequency or one time slot for one channel in which all time slots or all frequencies can be used with maximum power. On the other hand, for CDMA we assign all frequencies and time slots for one channel but with small power. Channels are separated by a spreading code or a spreading sequence assigned to each of them.

Now let us see what is SS. Unfortunately there is no clear and persuasive definition of SS systems. A most common definition is the following: "An SS system is a communication system in which the spectrum of the modulated signal is very much wider than that of the modulating signal." This definition is somewhat ambiguous, because there are various definitions of spectra and it is not very clear what the modulating signal is.

Another one is by Massey[1]: "An SS system is a communication system in which the modulated signal has a Fourier bandwidth substantially greater than its Shannon bandwidth." Here the Shannon bandwidth means one-half the minimum number of dimensions per second required to represent the modulated signal in a signal space. Massey did not use a modulating signal for his definition and specified two spectra for the modulated signal. Even by this definition, however, a TDMA system is an SS system.

There may be no use to go further into the definition problem for SS systems. We must be satisfied with the fact that SS/CDMA systems of today are either direct spreading systems or frequency hopping systems and they are clearly defined as described in the following chapter.

2 Spread Spectrum (SS) Systems

2.1 Transmitter and Receiver for SS

In this chapter we overview the SS system (Refer to [2]-[4] for more detail). Fig.1 shows the transmitter and the receiver of an SS system. The data is first modulated by a narrowband modulator and then multiplied by a spreading sequence. At the receiver, the received signal is multiplied by a despreading sequence and then demodulated by a narrowband demodulator.

2.2 Direct Spreading (DS) Systems

Fig.2 shows the direct spreading (DS) modulation. $d(t)$ is a data signal, which is the modulated signal by a data sequence. In this case narrowband modulation is BPSK (binary phase shift keying). T_d is the data bit time interval. If the data is coded by an error-control code of rate R, then T_d is the product of R and the information bit time interval T_b. The modulated data signal is multiplied by the spreading sequence $c(t)$. As a spreading sequence, we use a PN (pseudo-noise) sequence. Then we have the SS signal. Each pulse of $c(t)$ is called a chip and T_c denotes the chip time interval. For DS the spreading sequence is usually a binary sequence with values +1 and -1 and the despreading sequence is the same as the spreading sequence. In fact if we multiply the SS signal by the spreading sequence, the result is naturally the original data signal.

Fig.3 is the receiver for the DS system. In order to obtain the original binary sequence, after multiplying the PN sequence we integrate the signal over the time interval T_d, and then we estimate the original data as +1 (-1) if the integral is positive (negative). The part of multiplying the PN sequence and calculating the integral is called the correlator, since it computes correlation between the received signal and the PN sequence $c(t)$.

We now define process gain G_p for the DS system. G_p is defined as $W_c/W_d = T_d/T_c$, where W_c is the total SS signal bandwidth and W_d is the data bandwidth. The SNR (signal to noise ratio) at the correlator output is G_p times the input SNR. By the correlator, the data signal energy can exactly recovered. In other words, the desired signal energy is concentrated in the bandwidth W_d by the multiplication with the PN sequence. On the other hand, the noise is totally independent of the PN sequence $c(t)$ and hence its spectrum is not changed by the multiplication. Integrating over the time interval T_d, we can pick out the energy within the bandwidth W_d. At the input the noise energy is spread over the bandwidth W_c with uniform density and at the output only the noise energy within the bandwidth W_d appears. Thus the noise energy is reduced by W_d/W_c. The signal energy at the output is the same as that at the input. We therefore have the output SNR which is G_p times the input SNR.

For CDMA the major problem is not noise, but interference from other channels. If each user's power is controlled to give the same level at the receiver input and their interference can be treated as random noise, then the output SNR $[SNR]_O$ is written as

$$[SNR]_O = \frac{E_d G_p}{(L-1)E_d + N_0} \tag{1}$$

where E_d is the signal energy for one data bit, N_0 is the spectrum density of white Gaussian noise, and L is the number of active users. Thus the major limitation on the CDMA is the co-channel interference, while FDMA and TDMA are limited by dimension, i.e., the numbers of available frequencies and time slots.

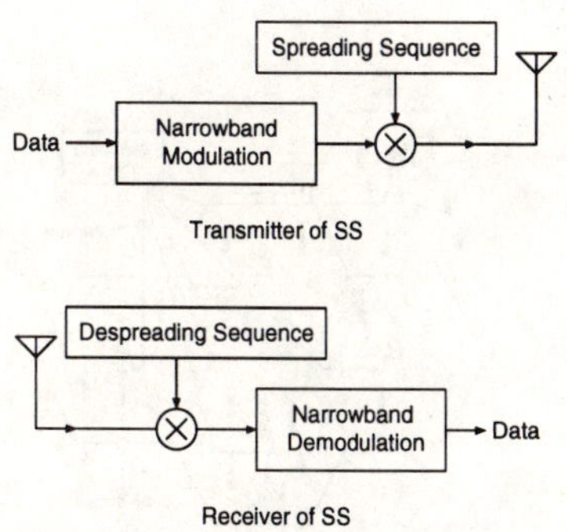

Fig. 1. Transmitter and receiver of a SS system.

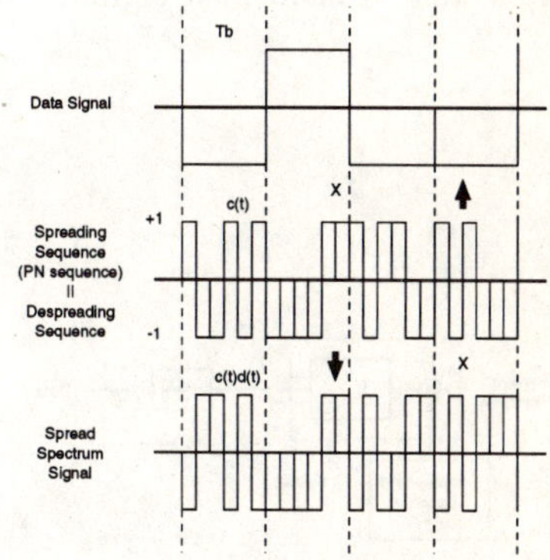

Fig. 2. DS modulation.

2.3 Frequency Hopping (FH) Systems

Now we take a brief look at frequency hopping (FH) systems. Usually FSK (frequency shift keying) is used for the narrowband modulation. After the narrowband modulation, the carrier frequency is hopped according to a PN sequence. The PN sequence is sometimes called an FH pattern. The FH system is effective for co-channel interference as the DS system and generally more effective for jamming, because it uses a lot of carrier frequencies, while the DS system uses only one carrier frequency. Therefore, for anti-jamming purposes, FH is generally adopted. However, for white Gaussian noise it works no better than the original narrowband modulation system.

There are two types of FH systems: Slow frequency hopping (SFH) and fast frequency hopping (FFH). FSK symbol rate is an integer multiple of the hop rate for SFH and vice versa for FFH. FFH used to be hard to implement, but according to the progress of the technique to fabricate frequency synthesizers, today we can realize an FFH with chip rate more than 1 MH.

2.4 Cellular Systems

In this paper we consider SS for cellular CDMA systems. For a cellular system the service area is divided into cells as shown in Fig.4. Each cell has one base station, each of which is connected to a switching office usually by wirelines. In each cell there are two kinds of communications, i.e., down link (or forward link) and up link (or reverse link). The down link means a communication link from the base station to a user (or a subscriber), and the up link means a communication link from a user in the cell to the base station. For the down link, the base station is the only one transmitter in the cell. Thus the signals for all the active users in the cell can be multiplied in an orthogonal way, and therefore they can be transmitted without mutual interference. IS-95[2][5][6], which is the US digtital cellular standard adopting CDMA, uses the 64-ary Walsh orthogonal transformation to multiply the user signals and then modulates a PN-sequence by the Walsh transformed signal. The PN sequence is an M-sequence of period

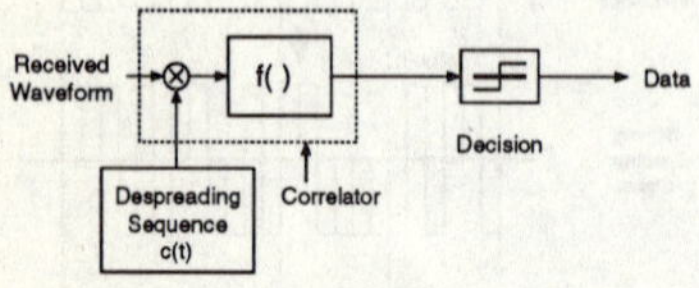

$$f() = \int_0^{T_d} ()\,dt$$

Fig. 3. Receiver for the DS system

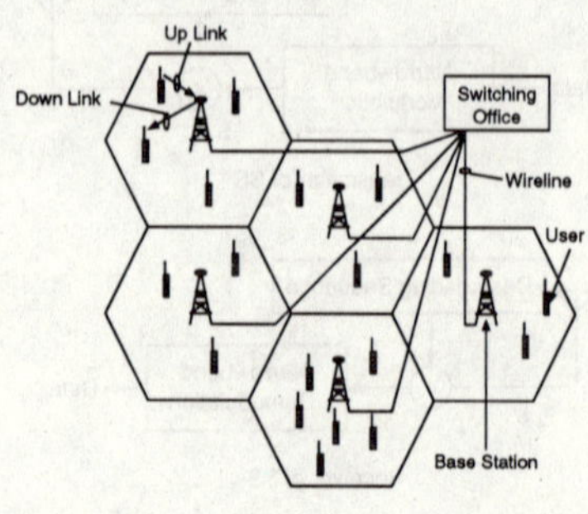

Fig. 4. Cellular System.

$2^{15}-1$ chips. Every cell uses this M-sequence, but of different phase. Therefore, each cell has its own unique PN-sequence having very low cross-correlation with that assigned to any distinct cell.

The up-link of IS-95 is very complicated[7]. Various transformations are made and finally DS modulation is performed. First, the modulating signals are spread by a unique PN sequence, which is generated by a generator of a very long M-sequence of period $2^{42}-1$. Furthermore, the waveform is multiplied by a pair of M-sequences of period $2^{15}-1$ common to all subsribers. However, the essential role to separate channels is played by the unique PN-sequence for each user. The up-link of IS-95 is an asynchronous multiple-access system, but for smaller cells such as microcells, synchronous multiple access may be practically realized. Then the interference can be reduced.

2.5 Advantage of SS Systems

Let us next consider why SS. The advantages of SS systems are listed as

(1) Low probability of intercept (LPI)
(2) Robustness against noise and interference
(3) Anti-jamming (AJ) property
(4) Less interference to other systems
(5) Flexible and easy multiple access
(6) High capacity per frequency

Most of these advantages are based on low power spectrum density of the SS signal. Sometimes the power of the signal is even 30dB below the noise and interference level so that it is difficult to detect the signal and also it will not give much interference to other systems using the same bandwidth. Thus (1) and (4) follow. The advantage (2) is mainly due to the correlation detection. Then FH is not robust against white Gaussian noise. However, FH is robust against interference that is not spread over the whole bandwidth. Further, FH has a good AJ property, because jamming tends to occur within a rather narrow bandwidth. DS is also robust against jamming if the jamming bandwidth does not include the carrier frequency, but if the carrier frequency is jammed, then DS suffers serious damage.

The advantage (5) is based on quasi-orthogonality among spreading sequences. The spreading sequences have low cross-correlation each other, even if they are asynchronously transmitted. Then each user can transmit his/her sequence at any time without giving strong interference to other users, which makes asynchronous multiple-access possible. Furthermore, if each user's spreading sequence is fixed, then the system can be run without any control by the central station. Therefore the SS system provides flexible and easy multiple access. Actually, however, co-channel interference is a critical problem for SS systems, and so at least power control is required. Further, synchronous transmission is desirable in some cases to reduce co-channel interference.

The last advantage is the high capacity of SS systems[5][8]. This was achieved for the first time by the Qualcomm's cellular communication system[5], which has become the US standard IS-95. This system is a DS communication system and uses various techniques to increase its capacity. The important techniques are power control, voice activation scheme, antenna sectorization, and reuse of the same frequency for every cell. With all these techniques, Qualcomm has claimed that its system has the capacity four times as much as the TDMA system and 20 times as much as the FDMA system. Actually, however, due to imperfection of power control, sectorization and so on, the capacity is reduced considerably, although it is still at least comparable with that of the TDMA system.

3 Spreading Sequences

Among various elements of SS systems, researchers in cryptology may be most interested in PN sequences. Desired properties of PN sequences for DS are sharp autocorrelation, low cross-correlation, randomness, and ease of generation.

In order to uniformly spread the signal spectrum to wide band, the chip rate of the sequence should be much higher than the data rate and the autocorrelation of the sequence should have a sharp main peak and low sidelobes like a white noise. This is a main reason why a PN sequence is used as a spreading sequence. Cross-correlation between arbitrary two of the spreading sequences that are assigned to individual users in CDMA should be small in a sense of absolute value for any phase shift. This is because the cross-correlation produces interference, prevents achieving synchronization, and restricts the number of simultaneously accessing users. From a viewpoint of signal processing and security, randomness of the sequences is desirable. For example, the numbers of 0's and 1's in a period of the spreading sequence should be balanced as well as the distribution of the runs of 0's and 1's. Finally, for practical purposes, the sequence should be generated easily. The generator is often required to generate various sequences. In that case the switching must be easy too. In particular, the transmitter and receiver for the user must be simple, because they are often installed in a small portable device.

Other than M-sequences, Gold, Kasami, and Bent sequences are known as representative binary sequences for DS systems (See [2] for their definitions). These sequences are good sequences with respect to correlation properties. In fact they nearly satisfy a lower bound on the maximum value of the out of phase autocorrelation function and of the cross-correlation function with equality.

However, from the security viewpoint, the number of sequences and the linear span are important. It is generally desirable to keep PN sequences secret, even if the message is encrypted, because the secrecy of assigned PN sequences prevents selective jamming, i.e., jamming to specified users. For this purpose, the number of the sequences in a class must be very large, say 2^{60}, to avoid the exhaustive attack to estimate the sequence in use. Then, for these classes of sequences, the period becomes very large, and it is impossible to compute the correlation over the whole period. Then we need to evaluate cross-correlation among partial sequences, since good correlation property is not guaranteed for partial sequences of these representative binary sequences for DS systems. However, using such partial sequences is one practical method to obtain a large class of PN sequences. Another possibility to construct a large class of sequences having good correlation properties is to use polyphase sequences[9].

Linear span (or linear complexity) of a sequence is the minimum number of stages of a linear feedback shift register generating this sequence. It should be large to prevent easy prediction of the sequence, although a large linear span does not necessarily mean that the sequence is difficult to estimate[10]. For representative binary sequences mentioned above, the linear span is small except Bent sequences. With a sequence of small linear span, we cannot have a very secure communication system unless encryption is used As a conclusion, if we use these sequences as spreading sequences, then we should encrypt the message to protect our privacy.

4 Information Security of SS Systems

Let us proceed to discuss information security of SS systems[11]. In this paper the information security of SS systems is defined as protecting information transmission in the system from intentional attack of opponents who are assumed to know everything about the communication system but the spreading sequences and the secret keys assigned to the users.

We consider here four elements of the security: confidentiality, untraceability, authenticity and integrity, and AJ property. Confidentiality means protecting the secrecy of the transmitted message from intercept. Untraceability means keeping the sender and the receiver of the message secret and preventing traffic analysis. Authenticity and integrity mean validating that the message was transmitted from an authentic sender, i.e., a properly identified sender, and was not modified in transmission. And AJ property means protecting message transmission from jamming.

As previously mentioned, the SS signal has very low power density level. Sometimes it is so lower than the power level of noise and interference as to make detection of the existence of the signal almost impossible if one does not know the spreading sequence. This is the LPI of SS systems. If this property can be perfectly trusted, then confidentiality and untraceablity are naturally realized. If not, we must use cryptography. Authenticity and integrity should be realized by cryptographic techniques. AJ property is related with LPI. If the signal cannot be detected, effective jamming is impossible. However, if the carrier frequency is jammed the DS system may suffer serious damage, while the FH system can avoid the attack to a specific frequency by hopping the frequency. Therefore, FH is an effective way to cope with jamming.

5 Confidentiality

5.1 Additive White Gaussian Noise Case

Knowing the spreading sequence, legitimate users (or base stations) have some advantage over opponents who do not know them. We consider here such advantage quantitatively. First we assume that the channel is an additive white Gaussian (AWG) channel. The spectral density of the noise and the energy of the signal per one information bit at the receiver are denoted by N_0 and E_b, respectively. From the channel capacity derived by Shannon, reliable communication is theoretically possible if and only if $E_b/N_0 > \ln 2$ [12][13]. We here assume that the opponent estimates each chip by hard decision, i.e., he / she estimates the transmitted sequence chip by chip. Then it is easily shown from the strong converse to the channel coding theorem[14] that the opponent cannot correctly estimate the transmitted information, if

$$\frac{E_b}{N_0} < \frac{H(S)\left(\frac{E_c}{N_0}\right)}{1-\mathcal{H}\left(Q\left(\left(\frac{E_c}{N_0}\right)^{\frac{1}{2}}\right)\right)} \tag{2}$$

where $H(S)$ means the entropy of the information source, $\mathcal{H}(x) = -x\log_2 x - (1-x)\log_2(1-x)$, and $Q(y) = \sqrt{1/2\pi}\int_{-\infty}^{y} e^{(-x^2/2)}dx$. When E_c/N_0 is small and $H(S) = 1$, (2) can be approximated by

$$\frac{E_b}{N_0} < \pi \cdot ln2 = 2.18 = 3.4dB. \tag{3}$$

Since legitimate users can communicate if and only if $E_b/N_0 > \ln 2$, their advantage over the opponents is approximately 5dB(=$10\log_{10}\pi$) as long as the opponent estimate the transmitted sequence chip by chip. In other words, the knowledge of the sequence gives the legitimate users the advantage of about 5dB over the opponent who estimates the sequence chip by chip.

When the opponent utilizes more sophisticated method to estimate the sequence, then it is hard to theoretically evaluate the advantage. Furthermore, one of the most difficult problem for SS systems is initial code synchronization or acquisition[15]. The acquisition essentially requires better SNR than communication after synchronization is established. Of course, the opponents have the same difficulty in synchronization. However, they may have better chance to estimate the sequence even through chip by chip estimation.

Moreover, the major obstruction to the SS systems is not AWG noise, but interference caused by mutlipath transmission and other users. Sometimes these interference can be viewed as AWG noise, then the above theory is applicable. However, a clever opponent may use the optimum detection, i.e., multi-user detection[16]-[18]. It requires exponential complexity in the number of the users, but there is a powerful sub-optimal detection such as decorrelation[16] and m-stage interference cancellation[19]. It is not known as yet how the opponent who does not know the sequences assigned to the users utilizes these schemes. Anyway, however, it is dangerous to assume the interference as AWG noise. As a conclusion, we should think that 5dB advantage may be optimistic even if the spectrum density of the signals is very low and we must use encryption to protect privacy.

6 Untraceability

6.1 Registration Protocol

Now let us consider untraceability, which is important from the viewpoint of privacy. It must be kept secret where you go and whom you are speaking to. We assume here that a huge class of PN sequences is available and the PN sequence assigned to a user is changed each time. When a user enters a cell, he/she has to make a registration at that cell, so that a call to him/her is conveyed to that base station. In this registration process, we suppose that a PN sequence is assigned to the user and also secret keys for a symmetric cryptosystem are exchanged.

Some efficient and secure protocols applicable to the registration process in cellular networks have been proposed[20]-[22]. However, these protocols do not guarantee untraceability. In Fig. 5, we present a simple registration protocol which provides for the secrecy of PN sequence and key assignment, the authenticity of communication parties, and the untraceability of users.

For communication in this protocol, a special M-sequence assigned to the base station is used. It may be common to all the base stations but the phase is different for each station. This protocol utilizes KPS (key predistribution system)[23]. KPS is a mechanism which on request brings a secret key to each member of any pair of users in a network without previous communication between the users nor access to any public key directory. The network is assumed to have one or several managing centers called KPS centers. Each user or entity has its own ID or name in a broad sense. This is called KPS-ID.

KPS is usually composed of three processes: (1)generation of center algorithms, (2)calculation and distribution of secret-algorithms, and (3)key sharing. When the system is setting up or renewed, each KPS center independently generates a special center-algorithm G_i and keeps it secret. When entity A joins the system, each KPS center applies its algorithm G_i to the KPS-ID of A to obtain a part of algorithm X_{iA}. Entity A combines all these algorithms into a secret algorithm X_A. If these processes have been set up, any pair of entities can share a secret common cryptographic key whenever they like. For example entity A can compute the secret key shared with entity B by operating A's algorithm X_A to B's KPS-ID ID_B, while entity B can compute the same key by operating B's algorithm X_B to A's KPS-ID ID_A. KPS can be implemented by using tamper resistant modules like IC-cards[24]. Then it gives a very simple and secure key distribution system.

Let us return to the registration protocol for a cellular system. The base station B broadcasts B's KPS-ID ID_B and a random number R_0 as shown in Fig.5. The random number must be changed from time to time and KPS-ID of the base station must be of special form that can be easily identified by a user and the KPS-ID of the form must not be given to any other entity. User A , after checking the validity of B's KPS-ID, computes the secret key K shared with B applying A's secret algorithm X_A to ID_B, generates a random number R_1, and encrypts R_0 and R_1 using the secret key K for a symmetric cryptosystem. Then A transmits A's pseudonym PID_A that was registered in advance and the encrypted random numbers. The base station B sends PID_A to the switching office (or the center station) by wirelines and gets necessary information including A's KPS-ID ID_A. Then B computes the secret key K common to A, decrypts the cryptogram, and checks the random number R_0. As the final stage of the registration process, B generates a random number R_2, encrypts R_1 and R_2 by the secret key K and sends out the cryptogram. Then the random number R_2 determines a PN sequence assigned to A and session keys for the symmetric crytosystem if necessary. Thus the sequence is substantially determined by the base station. We can easily modify the protocol so that both parties determine it together. It is desirable, however, that the base station has some control over the choice of PN sequences to assign a sequence having low cross-correlation with the other sequences used in the cell. The user changes his/her pseudonym during the communication.

For this protocol, the base station must communicate with the switching office, but this is necessary in a cellular system for the registration of user location, authentication of the user and so on. We can modify Aziz and Diffie protocol [22] to make another registration protocol using public key cryptosystem which does not require communication with the switching office. However, in such a

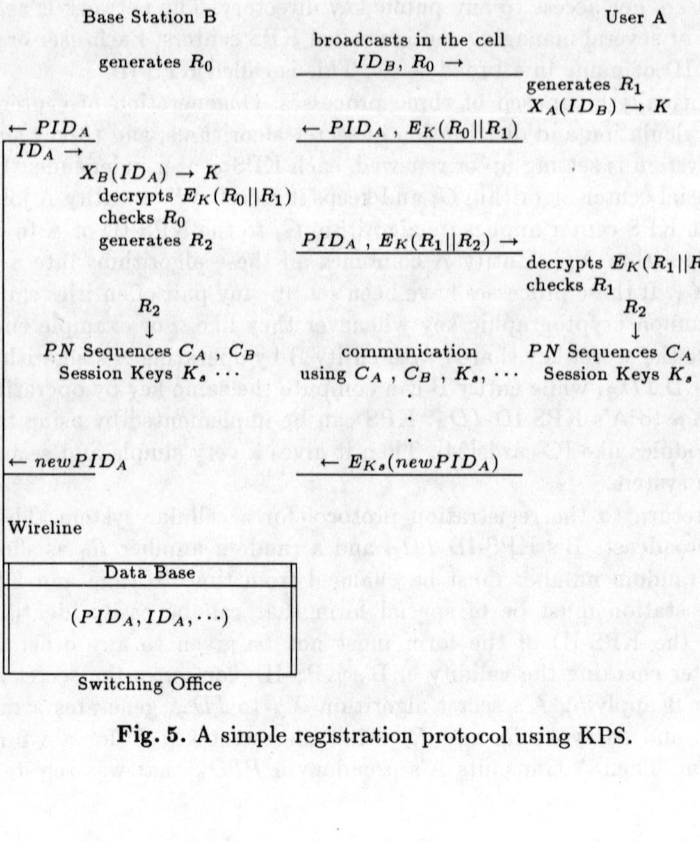

Fig. 5. A simple registration protocol using KPS.

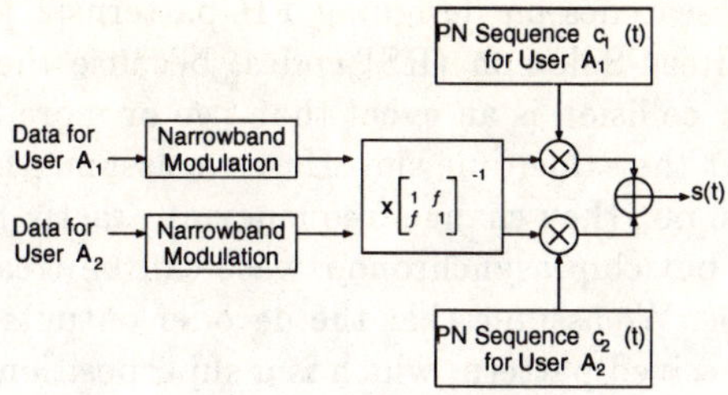

Fig. 6. Predecorrelation.

protocol mobile users perform computationally expensive secret-key operations.

The registration protocol described in this session can be applied to cellular FDMA or TDMA systems, but this protocol is more suited to cellular CDMA systems, because a lot of possible PN sequences (which correspond to channels in FDMA and TDMA) make it difficult to find any relation between the sequences and the users and prevent such attacks as selective jamming.

6.2 Predecorrelation for Down Link

After the registration, communication between the base station and the user can be initiated from either side. For down link, it is preferable to orthogonalize the sequences for the active users in the cell as in IS-95. However, it is not secure to assign a Walsh sequence to each user, since the number of Walsh sequences is very limited and it is easy for an opponent to intercept the message to any user. If the message is encrypted, it may not be a serious problem. However, it is better that the sequence assigned to each user is kept secret to the third parties. For example an opponent who may be one of the users can jam the signal for a certain user selectively. One simple way to keep the sequences secret is the predecorrelation technique[25][26].

Fig.6 shows a predecorrelation for two users A_1 and A_2. ρ is the correlation coefficient between the two PN sequences $c_1(t)$ and $c_2(t)$ assigned to A_1 and A_2, respectively. Then the base station transmits the signal $s(t)$. User A_1 correlates the received signal with $c_1(t)$. Then the co-channel interference is cancelled, because the inverse of the covariance matrix was multiplied. This is not the optimum signal design method, but it is very simple and does not reveal the other users PN sequences. Since the predecorrelation is a linear system, the PN sequences can be estimated if the data have any redundancy, although it is not very easy due to the low density of signal power spectrum.

7 Anti-Jamming (AJ) Property — FH Systems

As mentioned previously, FH systems, especially FFH systems, are desirable for AJ purposes. We consider here the design of FH patterns for FFH systems.

There are a lot of researches on designing FH patterns[27]-[29]. Almost all of them are based on Reed-Solomon (RS) codes, because the number of hits is mini- mized. A hit or collision is an event that two or more transmitters hop to the same frequency at the same time slot. Here we assume that the transmitters are chip-synchronous, i.e., they change frequency at exactly the same time. This is not very realistic, but chip-asynchronous case can be treated on the basis of chip-synchronous case. We assume that the decoder outputs all codewords that are covered by the received pattern, which is a superposition of the transmitted codewords. The maximum number of hits determines the maximum number of FH patterns that can be simultaneously transmitted without any error.

Now we show a construction method for FH patterns based on RS codes. We use a polynomial $M(x) = m_0 + m_1 x + m_2 x^2 + \cdots + m_{k-1} x^{k-1}$ with coefficients from GF(q). Then an FH pattern is given by $P = (M(1), M(\alpha), ..., M(\alpha^{q-2}))$, where α is a primitive element of GF(q) and M(α^i) is interpreted as one of q available frequencies for the FH system through a one-to-one mapping from GF(q) onto the class of q frequencies. P is a codeword of a cyclic q-ary RS code of length $q-1$ and k information symbols. The minimum distance of the RS code is $q-k$ and the number of hits between two FH patterns is no more than $k-1$.

In order to have a good AJ property, any FH pattern must not use the same frequency twice or more times, because jamming tends to occur at some frequency band for rather long time. Therefore $M(x)$ must be a permutation polynomial. A polynomial over GF(q) is called a permutation polynomial if the associated polynomial function from GF(q) into GF(q) is a permutation of GF(q). Efficient generation of permutation polynomials is being studied[30].

If the system is not frame-synchronous, then cyclic permutations of EH patterns are superimposed through the channel. Therefore, one codeword from a cyclic equivalence class of the RS code should be chosen as an FH pattern. Further, if we set $m_0 = 0$, then we have FH patterns for which every frequency is used just once. Thus if we choose a permutation polynomial of the form $M(x) = x + m_1 x + m_2 x^2 + \cdots + m_{k-1} x^{k-1}$, we have a set of efficient FH patterns having a good AJ property and small co-channel interference[29].

8 Concluding Remarks

We have seen various aspects of SS systems from the information security viewpoint. They have some physical features interesting in the viewpoint of information security such as difficulty of detecting a signal without knowledge of the spreading sequence. Examining such features we have concluded that after all cryptographic techniques must be used to keep high information security of the system. However, utilizing features of SS with cryptographic techniques, we will be able to construct very efficient and secure wireless communication systems.

References

1. J.L.Massey, "Information theory aspects of spread-spectrum communications," *Proc. ISSSTA'94*, Oulu, Finland, July 1994, pp.16-21.
2. M.K.Simon, J.K.Omura, R.A.Scholtz and B.K.Levitt, *Spread Spectrum Communications Handbook (Revised Edition)*, McGraw-Hill, Inc., New York, 1994.
3. R.C.Dixon, *Spread Spectrum Systems with Commercial Applications (Third Edition)*, John-Wiley & Sons, Inc., New York, 1994.
4. H.Imai and R.Kohno, *Advanced Spread Spectrum Communication Techniques and Applications*, Elsevier, Amsterdam, to be published.
5. K. S. Gilhousen, I. M. Jacobs, R. Padovani, A. J. Viterbi, L. A. Weaver, and C. E. Wheatley, "On the capacity of cellular CDMA system," *IEEE Trans. Vehicular Technology*, vol.40, no.2, May 1991, pp.303-312.
6. A.J.Viterbi, "The orthogonal-random waveform dichotomy for digital mobile personal commu- nication," *IEEE Personal Communications*, First Quarter 1994, pp.18-24.
7. R.Padovani, "Reverse link performance of IS-95 based cellular systems," *IEEE Personal Communications*, Third Quarter 1994, pp.28-34.
8. Y.C.Lee, "Overview of cellular CDMA," *IEEE Trans. Vehicular Technology*, vol.40, no.2, May 1991, pp.291-302.
9. N.Suehiro, "Secret sequence assignment for approximately synchronized CDMA system without co-channel interference," *Technical Report of IEICE*, IT93-104, Jan. 1994, pp.55-60.
10. K.Imamura and S.Uehara, "Relation between periodic sequences of the maximum linear complexity and m-sequences," *Proc. SITA'93*, Kanazawa, Japan, Oct. 1993, pp.255-257.
11. H.Imai, R.Kohno and T.Matsumoto, "Information security of spread spectrum systems," *IEICE Trans.*, vol.E74, no.3, March 1991, pp.488-505.
12. C.E.Shannon, "A mathematical theory of communication," *Bell System Technical Journal*, vol.27, July and Oct. 1948, pp.379-423 (Part I) and 623-656 (Part II).
13. A.J.Viterbi, "Phase-coherent communication over the continuous Gaussian channel," S.W.Golomb ed.,*Digital Communication with Space Applications*, Prentice-Hall, 1964, pp.106- 134.
14. R.G.Gallager, Information Theory and Reliable Communication, John Wiley & Sons, Inc., New York, 1986.
15. A.Polydoros and S.Glisic, "Code synchronization: A review of principle and techniques," *Proc. IEEE ISSSTA'94*, Oulu, Finland, July 1994, pp.115-137.
16. R.Kohno, H.Imai and M.Hatori, "Cancellation technique of co-channel interference in asynchronous spread spectrum multiple access systems," *IECE Trans.*, vol.J65-A, no.5, May 1983, pp.416-423.
17. S.Verdu, "Optimum multiuser asymptotic efficiency," *IEEE Trans. Communications*, vol.COM- 34, no.9, Sept. 1986, pp.85-96.
18. P.D.Alexander, A.J.Grant and M.J.Miller, "Multiuser mobile communications," presented at ISITA'94, Sydney, Australia, Nov. 1994.
19. Y.C.Yoon, R.Kohno, and H.Imai, "A spread-spectrum multiaccess system with cochannel interference cancellation for mulitipath fading channels," *IEEE J. Select. Areas Communications*, vol.11, no.7, Sept. 1993, pp.1067-1075.
20. R.Bird, I.Gopal, A.Herzberg, P.Janson, S.Kutten, R.Molve, and M.Yung, "Systematic design of two-party authentication protocols," *Advances in Cryptology—CRYPTO'91*, Springer-Verlag, 1991, pp.44-61.

21. W.Diffie, P.C.van Oorschot and M.J.Wiener, "Authentication and authenticated key exchanges," *Design, Codes and Cryptography*, Kluwer Academic Publishers, vol.2, 1992, pp.107-125.
22. A.Aziz and W.Diffie, "Privacy and authentication for wireless local area networks," *IEEE Personal Communications*, First Quarter 1994, pp.25-31.
23. T.Matsumoto and H.Imai, "On the key predistribution system: A practical solution to the key distribution problem," *Advances in Cryptology — CRYPTO'87*, Springer-Verlag, 1987, pp.185-193.
24. T.Matsumoto, Y.Takashima, H.Imai, M.Sasaki, H.Yoshikawa, and S.Watanabe, "A prototype KPS and its application: IC card based key sharing and cryptographic communication," *IEICE Trans.*, vol.E73, no.7, July 1990, pp.1092-1099.
25. Z.Tang and S.Cheng, "Pre-decorrelating single user detection for CDMA system," *Proc. IEEE VTC'94*, Stockholm, Sweden, June 1994, vol.2, pp.767-769.
26. M.Isaka and H.Imai, "A scheme of code orthogonalization in the down link of cellular CDMA (in Japanese)," *Proc. SITA'94*, Hiroshima, Japan, Dec. 1994, pp.277-280.
27. M.B.Pursley, "Reed-Solomon codes in frequency-hop communications," S.B.Wicker and V.K.Bhargava eds., *Reed-Solomon Codes and Their Applications*, Chap. 8, IEEE Press, NJ, 1994, pp.150-174.
28. D.Sarwate, "Reed-Solomon codes and the design of sequences for spread-spectrum multiple-access communications," S.B.Wicker and V.K.Bhargava eds., *Reed-Solomon Codes and Their Applications*, Chap. 9, IEEE Press, NJ, 1994, pp.175-204.
29. J.Iwatani and H.Imai, "Coding for multiple access OR channel (in Japanese)," *Proc. SITA'94*, Hiroshima, Japan, Dec. 1994, pp.389-392.
30. E.Okamoto, W.Aitken, G.R.Blakley, and I.Borosh, "Properties of permutation polynomials," *Proc. SITA'94*, Hiroshima, Japan, Dec. 1994, pp.381-384.

SESSION 5

AUTHENTICATION AND DIGITAL SIGNATURES

Chair: Jovan Golić

(Queensland University of Technology, Australia)

Combinatorial Structure of A-codes with r-fold Security

R. Safavi-Naini *
L. Tombak

Department of Computer Science University of Wollongong
Northfields Ave., Wollongong 2522, AUSTRALIA

Abstract. In this paper we prove two general characterization theorems for A-codes, that provide r-fold security, in terms of well-known combinatorial structures (t-designs and orthogonal arrays). We use Delsarte's linear programming method to find new bounds on the number of encoding rules for Cartesian A-codes with 1-fold and 2-folds security and show that in the latter case the bound is achieved by A-codes obtained from the dual of two well-studied error correcting codes: an MDS code and the extended Hamming code.

1 Introduction

Study of authentication codes (A-codes) has been an active area of research in recent years. A number of authors, for example [2], [10], [11], have characterized A-codes with the 'best' properties (in some sense) in terms of combinatorial structures. Such characterizations are highly interesting as they relate the existence and construction of such codes to combinatorial problems that are extensively studied and hence the study of A-codes can immediately benefit from them.

In this paper we prove two general theorems on A-codes, with and without secrecy that provide r-fold security against spoofing. We prove that such A-codes are equivalent to t-designs and orthogonal arrays, respectively. These results are general, as they hold for general spoofing attacks and unlike previous results we need not make restrictive assumptions such as minimality of the the number of encoding rules. Our theorems provide direct links between A-codes with the *best protection for all orders of spoofing* $\leq t$ and two well-known combinatorial structures. We will give fruitful applications of the results on these structures to the study and construction of A-codes. In particular we will give tight bounds on the number of encoding rules for A-codes with 1-fold and 2-folds security, and give constructions for such A-codes in terms of some well-known error-correcting codes.

Scobi proved [3], that if there exists a t-design then there exists an A-code with r-fold security for *uniform source*. Later Stinson [2], characterized A-codes

* Support for this project was partly provided by Australian Research Council grant A49030136.

that provide 1-fold security and have the *minimum number of encoding rules* as BIBD's and orthogonal arrays of strength two, for A-codes with secrecy and Cartesian A-codes respectively. We extend these results in two directions: the known results for impersonation and substitution are generalized to the spoofing of order r, but more importantly we can remove the restriction on the minimality of the number of encoding rules and show that *A-codes with and without secrecy, that provide r-fold protection for spoofing of order r, correspond to t-designs and orthogonal arrays respectively, in which the blocks may be repeated.* The only condition that we require, is for A-codes with secrecy where we require the source to be uniform. This is not surprising as otherwise the probability distribution of the source must be considered. It would be interesting to show that r-fold security implies uniform distribution for the source.

These results immediately make available to A-codes a wealth of results: on the existence, construction, relations among parameters and bounds on t-designs and orthogonal arrays. For example, for uniform source we can give a simple proof of a recent result of Rees and Stinson [9] using the Fisher's inequality for t-designs.

Using this equivalence we apply the elegant approach of Delsarte [8], to give a linear programming (LP) formulation of a bound on the number of encoding rules in terms of the distance distribution of A-codes (defined similar to error correcting codes). For Cartesian A-codes and for spoofing of order 1 and 2, we give explicit forms for the objective functions for the LP problem and hence obtain the bounds. We give constructions of A-codes, from error correcting codes, that achieve these bounds and hence are optimal A-codes with proven security. In particular we show that *if there exists an error correcting code with dual distance 4 and at most three non-zero distances of the form $\{v, v+1, n\}$ then we have an A-code that is 2-fold secure and has minimum number of encoding rules.* When the number of non-zero distances is 2, and of the form $\{v, n\}$, we can construct such A-codes from some known error-correcting codes. In fact the dual of a $(q+1, q-1, 4)$ MDS code and the dual of the $(\frac{q^m-1}{q-1}+1, n-(m+1), 4)$ extended Hamming code, are such optimal (least number of encoding rules) A-codes. Similar results can be obtained for A-codes with 1-fold security.

In the following section we introduce some notations and definitions that are used in the rest of the paper. In section 3 we give our characterization theorems and in section 4 give the linear programming bounds. Finally we give constructions of optimal A-codes using error correcting codes and present some concluding remarks.

2 Notations and Definitions

An (M, k, E) authentication code is a collection $\mathcal{E}$, $|\mathcal{E}| = E$, of functions called *encoding rules*, from a set $\mathcal{S}$, $|\mathcal{S}| = k$, of source states into a set $\mathcal{M}$, $|\mathcal{M}| = M$, of codewords. We consider A-codes *without splitting* where an encoding rule is a one to one function. In an authentication system, the communicants share a secret encoding rule, and the enemy tries to impersonate the transmitter or, in general, construct a fraudulent codeword after observing r codewords in the channel. This is called an *spoofing attack of order* r.

We use the following notations:

$\mathcal{M}(e_i)$: the subset of codewords authentic under the key e_i;

$A = [a_{im}]$: the *incidence matrix* of the A-code which is a zero-one matrix, of size $E \times M$, in which $a_{im} = 1$ if $m \in \mathcal{M}(e_i)$ and zero otherwise.

m^r: a sequence of r cryptograms, $m^r = m_1^r, m_2^r, ..., m_r^r$ constructed under the same key.

(m^r): the set of cryptograms in m^r.

$\mathcal{M}^r$: the collection of all sequences of the form m^r.

$\mathcal{E}(m)$: the subset of keys that are incident with $m \in \mathcal{M}$, i.e., $\mathcal{E}(m) = \{e_i \in \mathcal{E} : a_{im} = 1\}$,

$\mathcal{E}(m^r)$: the subset of keys that are incident with all codewords of (m^r).

$P(m^r)$: the probability of m^r occurring in the channel.

$\pi = (\pi_1, \cdots, \pi_E)$: communicants' strategy.

In an *spoofing attack of order* r, the enemy has access to r cryptograms generated under the same key and tries to construct a valid cryptogram $m \notin (m^r)$ which is acceptable by the receiver. We use P_i to denote the probability of the enemy's success in an spoofing attack of order i.

An A-code can be with, or without, secrecy. In an *A-code without secrecy*, also known as *Cartesian A-codes*, the knowledge of a codeword m determines a unique source state $s(m)$. For such codes if $P_0 = k/M$ then the code can be transformed into standard form in which a codeword m can be written as $s.a$ where '.' denotes concatenation and a is one of the M/k possible *authenticators*. The *authentication matrix* of such codes is an $E \times k$ matrix B, such that $B(e, s) = a$ if $e(s) = s.a$.

A t-(v, k, λ) design is a collection, of size b, of subsets of size k called *blocks* of a set X, of size v of *points*, such that every subset of size t of X occurs in exactly λ blocks. The *incidence matrix* of a t-(v, k, λ) is a $E \times v$ zero-one matrix such that an element of the matrix is one if the block indexing the corresponding row is incident with the point indexing the corresponding column.

An orthogonal array $OA_\lambda(t, k, v)$ is an array with λv^t rows, each row of size k, from the elements of set X of v symbols, such that in any t columns of the array every possible v^t ordered sequence of elements of X occurs in exactly λ rows. Usually t is referred to as the *strength* of the OA.

A q-ary (n, M, d) *error-correcting code* C (E-code) is a set of M vectors of length n over a set F of size q such that the Hamming distance between any two vectors is at least d. We assume F is an Abelian group with the neutral element 0 (zero).

The *support* of a q-ary vector of length n, denoted by $supp(x)$, is a binary vector such that $supp(x)_i = 1$ if $x_i \neq 0$ and $supp(x)_i = 0$ otherwise.

An *r-fold uniform source* is a source with

$$\begin{aligned} P(s^r) &= \frac{1}{k(k-1)\cdots(k-r+1)}, \; s_i^r \neq s_j^r, \forall i, j, \\ &= 0, \; \textit{otherwise}, \end{aligned}$$

where s^r is a sequence of r source states.

3 Perfect r-fold security and combinatorial structures

An A-code provides *perfect protection for spoofing of order i* if $P_i = \frac{k-i}{M-i}$. Perfect protection for spoofing of order i in general does not imply perfect protection for spoofing of order $i-1$. An A-code provides *r-fold security against spoofing* if

$$P_i = \frac{k-i}{M-i}, \quad 0 \leq i \leq r.$$

Providing perfect protection requires many keys and for such codes E must satisfy a lower bound [2]. Stinson characterized A-codes that provide 1-fold security against spoofing and have minimum number of encoding rules. Let $\ell = M/k$.

Theorem 1 Stinson [2], theorem 3.2. *If a Cartesian A-code provides 1-fold security against spoofing and the number of encoding rule is minimal then the authentication matrix of the code is an orthogonal array $OA(2, k, \ell)$ and the encoding rules are used with equal probability.*

Theorem 2 Stinson [2], theorem 4.2. *An A-code with minimum number of encoding rules provides 1-fold security against spoofing if and only if the incidence matrix of the code is the incidence matrix of a $(M, k, 1)$-BIBD and both source states and encoding rules are equiprobable.*

In the following we prove similar characterization theorems but *without requiring minimality of the number of encoding rules* and for the general spoofing of order r.

3.1 A-codes with secrecy

The main result of this section is a characterization theorem for A-codes with secrecy that provide r-fold security against spoofing in terms of $(r+1)$-(v, k, λ) designs. We first prove a set of necessary and sufficient conditions for such A-codes which can be seen as a generalization of theorem 8 in [7]. Next we will prove that for uniform source this set of conditions is equivalent of to the existence of $(r+1)$-(v, k, λ)-designs.

We note that for uniform source $P_r = \frac{k-r}{M-r}$ implies $P_j = \frac{k-j}{M-j}$, $0 \leq j \leq r$, and our characterization theorem, in fact, applies if the A-code provides perfect protection which is a less strict condition.

We can prove the following theorem by using a argument based on induction and theorem 8 in [7].

Theorem 3. *An A-code is r-fold secure against spoofing if and only if for all* $m^r \in \mathcal{M}$, $m' \in \mathcal{M} \backslash (m^r)$ *we have*

$$\sum_{j=1}^{E} \pi_j a_{jm_1^r} \cdots a_{jm_r^r} a_{jm'} P_S(e_j, m^r) = \frac{k-r}{M(M-1)\cdots(M-r)}. \qquad (1)$$

In this case $P(m^r) = \dfrac{1}{M(M-1)\cdots(M-r)}$.

For r-fold uniform source equation 1 becomes independent of the probability distribution of the source and we can characterize the combinatorial structure of the code.

Theorem 4. *Let the source be r-fold uniform. Then an A-code provides r-fold security against spoofing if and only if the incidence matrix of the code is the incidence matrix of a* $(r+1)$- (M,k,λ) *design.*

Proof: (sketch)

Using theorem 3 and uniform source we have, for all $m^r \in \mathcal{M}$, $m' \in \mathcal{M} \backslash (m^r)$.

$$\sum_{j=1}^{E} \pi_j a_{jm_1^r} \cdots a_{jm_r^r} a_{jm'} = \frac{k(k-1)\cdots(k-r)}{M(M-1)\cdots(M-r)}. \qquad (2)$$

This is a set of linear equation with a zero-one coefficient matrix and rational numbers as the constant values. If the set has a solution (for π_i's) then it has a solution in rational numbers. That is

$$\pi_i = \frac{\alpha_i}{\beta_i} \quad 0 \le i \le E.$$

Multiplying both sides of the equations 2 by $\prod_{i,\beta_i \neq 0} \beta_i$ we have

$$\sum_{j=1}^{E} \alpha_j \Big(\prod_{i,\beta_i \neq 0,j} \beta_i\Big) a_{jm_1^r} \cdots a_{jm_r^r} a_{jm'} = \frac{k(k-1)\cdots(k-r)}{M(M-1)\cdots(M-r)} \times \prod_{i,\beta_i \neq 0} \beta_i. \qquad (3)$$

Now we can consider $\alpha_j(\prod_{i,\beta_i \neq 0,j} \beta_i)$ as the multiplicity of the row e_j in the incidence matrix of the A-code and interpret the LHS of this equation as counting the number of rows (with the associated multiplicities) of A that cover the $supp(m^r)$. Since this is independent of m^r then we have the required result. The converse of this theorem can be proved as well.

□

An immediate corollary of this theorem is a simple proof for a special case (uniform source) of a bound recently proved by Rees and Stinson [9].

Corollary 5. *In an A-code with secrecy* $E \geq M$.

Proof:
Use Fisher's inequality for t-designs.

□

We also note that for uniform source perfect protection for spoofing of order r implies r-fold security against spoofing and hence we have the following corollary.

Corollary 6. *Let the source be r-fold uniform. Then an A-code provides perfect protection against spoofing of order r if and only if the incidence matrix of the code is the incidence matrix of a* $(r+1)$*-* (M,k,λ) *design.*

3.2 A-codes without secrecy

In the study of A-codes without secrecy we do not require any assumption on the distribution of the source. We prove the following theorem that generalizes Stinson's results (theorems 5.3 and 5.4 in [1]) and is very much in the spirit of theorem 4 proved earlier.

Theorem 7. *Let* $P_0 = P_1 = P_2 \cdots P_r = k/M$. *Then the authentication matrix is a* $OA(r+1,k,\ell)$ *where* $\ell = M/k$.

Proof: (sketch) We generalize theorem 2.2 in [2] and obtain,

$$\sum_{e \in \mathcal{E}(m^r m')} \pi_e = (\frac{k}{M})^{r+1}. \tag{4}$$

Using an argument similar to 4 we can prove that the authentication matrix is an $OA_\lambda(r+1,k,M)$.

□

We note that for $r=1$ and minimum value of E the above theorem reduces to theorem 2.3 in [2].

4 Linear programming bound for A-codes

In this section we will use an elegant approach due to Delsarte to find a bounds on E. Bierbrauer, Gopalakrishnan and Stinson [15], have recently used a similar approach in the study of resilient functions. We will only consider Cartesian A-codes while in the light of theorem 4 a similar approach can also be used for A-codes with secrecy.

In theorem 7 we showed that an A-codes with r-fold security is equivalent to an orthogonal array of strength $r+1$. Orthogonal arrays can be considered as E-codes. In fact a q-ary (n,M,d) E-code of dual distance d' is an $OA_\lambda(d'-1,n,q)$ [5] with $\lambda = \frac{M}{q^{d'-1}}$ and conversely, an $OA_\lambda(t,n,q)$ is an (n,M,d) E-code of dual distance $t+1$. We will use these equivalences to obtain tight bound on the number of encoding rules for A-codes with r-fold security and construct such A-codes with minimum number of encoding rules from E-codes. We will describe our approach for A-codes with 2-fold security and note that similar result for 1-fold security directly follows from the 2-fold security.

Let C denote the set of q-ary vectors representing the rows of an $OA_\lambda(t,n,q)$. We define the *distance distribution of an OA* to be the sequence $(B_0, B_1, ..., B_n)$ where

$$B_i = \frac{1}{M}|\{(u,v) : u,v \in C, d(u,v) = i\}|, \ 0 \le i \le n.$$

Note that $B_0 = 1$ and $B_0 + B_1 + ... + B_n = M$. The *Krawtchouk transform* of the distance distribution is a sequence $(B'_0, \cdots, B'_n)$, called *dual distance distribution*, where

$$B'_k = \frac{1}{M}\sum_{i=0}^{n} B_i P_k(i),$$

and $P_k(i)$ is the value of the Krawtchouk polynomial, $P_k(x)$, at $x = i$, i an integer, and is given by

$$P_k(i) = \sum_{j=0}^{k}(-1)^j \binom{i}{j}\binom{n-i}{k-j}.$$

If $B'_i = 0$ for $1 \le i \le d' - 1$ and $B'_{d'} \ne 0$, then d' is the *dual distance* of the code.

4.1 Linear programming bound for $OA_\lambda(t,n,q)$

Consider an $OA_\lambda(t,n,q)$. To find a lower bound on the number of rows of the OA's we form the following LP problem:

$$\text{Minimize} \quad (x_1 + x_2 + ... + x_n) \tag{5}$$

$$\text{subject to} \quad B'_1 = \sum_{i=0}^{n} x_i P_1(i) = 0, \tag{6}$$

$$B'_2 = \sum_{i=0}^{n} x_i P_2(i) = 0, \tag{7}$$

$$\cdots \tag{8}$$

$$B'_t = \sum_{i=0}^{n} x_i P_3(i) = 0, \tag{9}$$

$$x_i \ge 0, \ 0 \le i \le n, \tag{10}$$

where $x_i = B_i$'s are the components of the distance distribution. Let L be the minimum of the objective function 5. L is a lower bound on the number of rows for $OA_\lambda(t,n,q)$.

4.2 $OA_\lambda(3, n, q)$

For $OA_\lambda(3, n, q)$ we have the following **LP0** problem:

$$\text{Minimize } \left(\sum_{i=1}^{n} x_i = E - 1\right) \tag{11}$$

$$\text{subject to } \sum_{i=1}^{n} R_i x_i - D_1 = 0 \tag{12}$$

$$\sum_{i=1}^{n} (R_i^2 + D_1) x_i + D_1 + D_1^2 = 0 \tag{13}$$

$$\sum_{i=1}^{n} (R_i^3 + D_2) x_i + D_2 - D_1^3 = 0, \tag{14}$$

$$x_i' \geq 0, \text{ for } 0 \leq i \leq n, \tag{15}$$

where $R_i = (q-1)n - qi$, $D_1 = -(q-1)n$, $D_2 = -(q-1)n(q-2)$ and $x_i \geq 0$.
Consider a set of three variables, x_j, x_k, x_ℓ.
The determinant of the coefficient matrix of these variables is

$$(R_\ell - R_v)(R_\ell - R_k)(R_k - R_v)(R_\ell R_v R_k - D_1(R_\ell + R_v + R_k) + D_2),$$

which as will be shown in theorem 8, for a proper choice of the variables can be made to have a fixed sign. We use this property to find an explicit value for the minimum of the objective function and hence a bound on E. We note that a similar LP problem was considered and solved in [13].

For an orthogonal array C, let $W(C)$ be the set of indices $\{v_1, v_2, \ldots, v_s\}$ such that $x_{v_i} = B_{v_i} > 0$.

Theorem 8. *1. If $n \geq 2 + \frac{q-2}{4}$, then the number of rows in an $OA(3, n, q)$ is lower bounded by*

$$F(v, n, q) + 1 = \frac{q^3 v(v+1)}{R_v^2 - 3qR_v + 2R_v + 2q^2 - 4q + nq - n + 2},$$

where $0 < v < n$.

2. Let C be an $OA(3, n, q)$ for which

$$W(C) \subseteq W_v = \{v, v+1, n\}.$$

If $n \geq 2 + \frac{q-2}{4}$, then C has the minimum number of rows (fixed n and q).

Proof: (sketch) Let x_v, x_ℓ, x_k be three basic variables of **LP0**.
We use the following three steps to eliminate these variables from the objective function 11.

Step 1 Let

$$R_v \neq 0, R_v^2 + D_1 \neq 0, R_v^3 + D_2 \neq 0,$$

we can take the following steps.

1. Divide equation 12 by R_v and subtract from the objective function 11.

2. Multiply equation 13 by $\dfrac{R_v}{R_v^2 + D_1}$ and subtract from equation 12.

3. Multiply equation 14 by $\dfrac{R_v^2 + D_1}{R_v^3 + D_2}$ and subtract from equation 13.

The gives us the following.

$$\text{Minimise } ((\sum_{i \neq v} \frac{R_v - R_i}{R_v} x_i) + \frac{D_1}{R_v}) \tag{16}$$

$$\text{subject to } (\sum \frac{(R_v - R_i)(R_v R_i - D_1)}{R_v^2 + D_1} x_i) - \frac{D_1(R_v + 1)(R_v + D_1)}{R_v^2 + D_1} = 0 \tag{17}$$

$$(\sum (R_v - R_i) \frac{R_v^2 R_i^2 + D_1(R_v^2 + R_v R_i + R_i^2) - D_2(R_v + R_i)}{R_v^3 + D_2} x_i) + D_1 + D_1^2 - \frac{D_2 - D_1^3}{R_v^3 + D_2}(R_v^2 + D_1) = 0 \tag{18}$$

Step 2 Assuming $R_v R_k - D_1 \neq 0$ and

$$(R_v^2 R_k^2 + D_1(R_v^2 + R_v R_k + R_k^2) - D_2(R_v + R_k)) \neq 0,$$

we do the followings.

1. Multiply equation 17 by $\dfrac{R_v^2 + D_1}{R_v(R_v R_k - D_1)}$ and subtract from the objective function 16.

2. Multiply equation 18 by

$$\frac{(R_v^3 + D_2)(R_v R_k - D_1)}{(R_v^2 + D_1)(R_v^2 R_k^2 + D_1(R_v^2 + R_v R_k + R_k^2) - D_2(R_v + R_k))}$$

and subtract it from equation 17.

This results in,

$$\text{Minimise } ((\sum_i \frac{(R_v - R_i)(R_k - R_i)}{R_v R_k - D_1} \times x_i) + D_1 \frac{(R_v + R_k + D_1 + 1)}{(R_v R_k - D_1)}), \tag{19}$$

$$\text{subject to } (\sum_i \frac{(R_v - R_i)(R_k - R_i)(R_k R_v R_i - D_1(R_v + R_k + R_i) + D_2)}{R_v^2 R_k^2 + D_1(R_v^2 + R_v R_k + R_k^2) - D_2(R_v + R_k)} x_i) + {} + F(R_v, R_k, D_1, D_2) = 0. \tag{20}$$

Step 3

Multiply equation 20 by

$$\frac{R_v^2 R_k^2 + D_1(R_v^2 + R_v R_k + R_k^2) - D_2(R_v + R_k)}{(R_v R_k - D_1)(R_k R_v R_\ell - D_1(R_v + R_k + R_\ell) + D_2)}$$

and subtract it from the objective function 19 which gives,

$$\text{Minimise } \Big(\sum_{i \neq v,k,\ell} \frac{q^3(v-i)(k-i)(l-i)}{-R_k R_v R_\ell + D_1(R_v + R_k + R_\ell) - D_2} x_i \Big) + F(R_v, R_k, R_\ell, D_1, D_2) \quad (21)$$

We note that if the coefficients of x_i's, $i \neq v, k, \ell$, are all positive then the expression 21 becomes minimum if $x_i = 0, \forall i,\ i \neq v, k, l$.

Now suppose there exists an $OA(3, n, q)$ which includes three non-zero distances, corresponding to the basic variables of **LP0** given by $\{v,\ v+1, n\}$. Then the coefficients of x_i's in 21 are all positive. This is true because in this case

$$R_k = R_{v+1} = R_v - q, R_\ell = R_n = -n$$

and the denominator of the coefficient of x_i reduces to

$$n((q-1)n - qv - q)^2 - n((q-1)n - qv - q)(q-2) + n(q-1)(n-2)$$

which is always positive if $n \geq 2 + \frac{q-2}{4}$. Moreover the numerator is $q^3(v-i)(v+1-i)(n-i)$ which is positive for all i's. Hence $F(R_v R_{v+1}, R_n, D_1, D_2) = F(v, n, q)$ is the minimum of the expression 21 and is achieved when $x_i = 0, \forall i \neq v, v+1, n$. and so $F(R_v R_k, R_\ell, D_1, D_2) = F(v, n, q)$ gives a lower bound on the number of rows in $OA(3, n, q)$.

Now suppose the orthogonal array has *only three* non-zero distances. Then the number of rows of this array achieves this bound and hence is minimum among all arrays $OA(3, n, q)$ (fixed value of n and q).

If we consider the case when the best $OA(3, n, q)$ has only 2 non-zero distances then our system of 3 equations becomes a system with 3 variables:(v, x_v, x_n). The solution in this case can be represented by the following expressions.

$$R_v = q - 2,$$

$$v = \frac{(q-1)n - (q-2)}{q}, \quad (22)$$

$$x_v = \frac{nq(n-1)(q-1)}{n+q-2}, \quad (23)$$

$$x_n = \frac{q^3 n - 3nq^2 + 3nq - n + 4q^2 - 5q - q^3 + 2}{n+q-2}. \quad (24)$$

This gives the lower bound $M \geq nq(q-1) - q(q-2)$ on the number of rows in the orthogonal array which coincides with the well known Rao bound [12].

□

A similar approach can be easily used for orthogonal arrays of strength 2 and 1. If $t = 2$ then we have the following results.

Proposition 9. *1. If $n \geq \frac{q^2}{4(q-1)}$ then the number of rows in an $OA(2, n, q)$ is lower bounded by*

$$F(v, n, q) + 1 = \frac{q^2 v(v+1)}{((q-1)n - qv)((q-1)n - qv - q) + (q-1)n},$$

where $0 < v < n$.

2. *Let C be an $OA(2,n,q)$ for which $W(C) \subseteq W_v = \{v, v+1\}$. If $n \geq \frac{q^2}{4(q-1)}$, then C has the minimum number of rows, given by $M = F(v,n,q)$ above. If the $OA(2,n,q)$ has only one non-zero distance we have*

$$R_v = -1, \;\; v = \frac{(q-1)n+1}{q}, x_v = (q-1)n, \;\; M \geq (q-1)n+1.$$

bound.

For the orthogonal array of strength 1 optimal arrays has only one non-zero weight n. In this case $v = n, R_v = -n, M = q, x_n = q$.

5 Optimal A-codes from E-codes

As noted earlier a q-ary (n, M, d) E-code with dual distance d' is an $OA(d' - 1, n, q)$.

Proposition 10. *Let C be a q-ary (n, M, d) E-code of dual distance $d' = 4$ and $W(C) \subset \mathcal{W}_v$. Then this code gives an A-code with 2-fold security and minimal E.*

If such an A-code exists then the following set of equations should be satisfied,

$$\begin{aligned} R_v x_v - n x_n &= -(q-1)n \\ R_v^2 x_v + n^2 x_n &= (x_v + x_n + 1)(q-1)n - (q-1)^2 n^2 \\ R_v^3 x_v + n^3 x_n &= (x_v + x_n + 1)(q-1)(q-2)n - (q-1)^3 n^3 \end{aligned}$$

The solution to this system of equations with the 3 variables (x_v, x_n, v), is given by expressions 22, 23, 24.

Hence we have $M = x_v + x_n + 1 = nq(q-1) - q(q-2)$.

We have two examples of E-codes that achieve this bound.

1. E-codes that is dual to $(q+2, q-1, 4)-$MDS codes with $q = 2^m$.
2. E-codes that is dual to $(\frac{q^m-1}{q-1} + 1, n-(m+1), 4)$ extended Hamming code.

In the following we briefly look at these E-codes.

5.1 Dual of $(q+2, q-1, 4)-$MDS code

Consider the dual of an $(q+2, q-1, 4)-$MDS code. This is an orthogonal array of strength 3, i.e., an $OA(3, q+2, q)$ with $\lambda = 1$ which is an MDS E-code generated by the generator matrix H_2 (page 242 [6]).

$$\begin{pmatrix} 1 & \cdots & 1 & 1\,0\,0 \\ \alpha_1 & \cdots & \alpha_{q-1} & 0\,1\,0 \\ \alpha_1^2 & \cdots & \alpha_{q-1}^2 & 0\,0\,1 \end{pmatrix}$$

where α_i, $\forall i$, are non-zero elements of $GF(q)$. This is a $(q+2, 3, q)$ MDS code with non-zero distances being $\{q, n = q+2\} = \mathcal{W}_v$[14].

5.2 Dual of the extended $(\frac{q^m-1}{q-1}+1, n-(m+1), 4)$ Hamming code

This is a $(\frac{q^m-1}{q-1}+1, m+1, q^{m-1})$ E-code with two non-zero distances q^{m-1} and $\frac{q^m-1}{q-1}+1$. The codewords of this code give an $OA(3, \frac{q^m-1}{q-1}+1, q)$ with $\lambda = q^{m+1}/q^3 = q^{m-2}$ which has minimum number of rows. This code exists only if $q = 2$.

We note that the parameters of this codes satisfy expressions 22, 23, 24.

6 Conclusion

In this paper we characterized A-codes (with and without secrecy) that provide r-fold security. We showed that these codes correspond to two well known combinatorial structures: t-designs and orthogonal arrays. We used Delsarte's approach to find a new linear programming bound for $OA(3, n, q)$ and $OA(2, n, q)$. The authors believe that this approach can be extended to the general $OA(t, n, q)$ with strength t, in which case, the MDS codes with $d' = t+1$ are the best candidates for optimal $OA(t, n, q)$ arrays as they have at most t non zero weights: $\{n-t+1, n-t+2, \ldots, n\}$.

References

1. D.R. Stinson, *The combinatorics of authentication and secrecy codes* , Journal Cryptology **2**, (1990), 23-49.
2. D.R. Stinson, *Combinatorial characterization of authentication codes,* Lecture Notes in Comput. Sci. **576** , Proceedings of Crypto 91, Springer-Verlag , 1992, 62-72.
3. P. Schobi, *Perfect authentication systems for data sources with arbitrary statistics,* presented at Eurocrypt '86.
4. J.H. Dinitz, D. Stinson, *Contemporary Design Theory. A Collection of Surveys,* A Wiley Interscience Publications, JOHN WILEY & SONS, INC, 1992.
5. J. MacWilliams, N. Sloane, *The theory of error correcting codes,* Noth Holland Publishing Company, 1978.
6. S. Roman, *Coding and Information Theory,* Springer Verlag, 1992.
7. L. Tombak, R. Safavi-Naini, *Authentication codes with perfect protection* Advances in Cryptology- AusCrypt'92, LNCS 718, Springer-Verlag, 1993, pp 15-26.
8. Ph. Delsarte, *An algebraic approach to the association schemes of coding theory,* Phillips Res. Rep. Suppl. 10,1973.
9. R.S. Rees, D.R. Stinson, *Combinatorial Characterization of Authentication Codes II,* personal communication.
10. C. Mitchell, M. Walker, P. Wild, *The combinatorics of perfect authentication schemes,* SIAM Journal of Discrete Mathematics, Vol 7, No 1, pp 102-107, 1994.
11. M. De Soete, K. Vedder, M. Walker, *Cartesian Authentication Schemes,* Advances in Cryptology, proc. of Eurocrypt '89, Lecture Notes in Computer Science, vol 434, Springer Verlag 1990, pp 476-490.

12. C.R. Rao, *Factorial experiments derivable from combinatorial arrangements of arrays*, J. Roy. Statist. Soc. 9, 128-139, 1947
13. A.Davydov, L.Tombak, *Number of minimal-weight words in block codes,* Problems of Information Transmission, Vol 24, No1, pp 11-24, 1988.
14. H.C.A van Tilborg, Uniformly packed Codes, Thesis, Eindhoven University of Technology (1976).
15. J. Bierbrauer, K. Gopalakrishnan and D. R. Stinson, *Bounds for resilient functions and orthogonal arrays*, Advances in Cryptology — Crypto '94, Proceedings (Lecture Notes in Computer Science 839), pp 247-256.

Meta-Message Recovery and Meta-Blind Signature Schemes Based on the Discrete Logarithm Problem and Their Applications

Patrick Horster · Markus Michels · Holger Petersen

Theoretical Computer Science and Information Security
University of Technology Chemnitz-Zwickau,
Straße der Nationen 62, D-09111 Chemnitz, Germany
email: {pho,mmi,hpe}@informatik.tu-chemnitz.de

Abstract. There have been several approaches in the past to obtain signature schemes with appendix and signature schemes giving message recovery based on the discrete logarithm problem. Most of them can be embedded into a Meta-ElGamal and Meta-Message recovery scheme. In this paper we present the Meta-blind signature schemes which have been developed from the ElGamal based blind signature scheme and the message recovery blind signature scheme discovered recently. From our Meta-scheme we get various variants from which some are more efficient than the already known ones. They can be recommended for practical use. Then we give interesting applications of the Meta-Message recovery and Meta-Blind signature schemes like authentic encryption schemes, key distribution protocols and authentication schemes. Again, we can extract highly efficient variants.

1 Introduction

There have been several approaches in the past to obtain signature schemes with appendix and signature schemes giving message recovery based on the discrete logarithm problem. Most of them can be embedded into a Meta-ElGamal and Meta-Message recovery scheme [HoP194, HMP294, HMP394, HMP494].

The concept of blind signature schemes was introduced by Chaum in 1982 [Chau82]. In a blind signature scheme an owner Alice wants to obtain a digital signature on a message chosen by herself from the notary Nancy, but Nancy shouldn't have any idea which message she signs. If she gets the message and the signature later, it must not be possible that Nancy can find a relationship between some blinded and unblinded parameters.

Recently blind ElGamal based signature schemes and blind message recovery signature schemes were introduced [CaPS94]. We show how to generalize them using the ideas of the Meta-ElGamal and the Meta-Message recovery signature scheme which results in Meta-Blind signature schemes. Note that not all variants can be used, e.g. there is no blind signature scheme for the original ElGamal signature scheme yet. Then we give some interesting applications of the Meta-Message recovery and Meta-Blind signature schemes like authentic encryption schemes, key distribution protocols and authentication schemes.

We first give a brief review of the Meta-ElGamal signature scheme and the Meta-Message recovery scheme. After this we present Meta-ElGamal blind signatures and Meta-Message recovery blind signatures. Then we discuss the most efficient variants of both blind Meta-schemes and continue with some useful applications of the Meta-Message recovery and Meta-Blind signature schemes.

2 The Meta-ElGamal signature scheme

The Meta-ElGamal signature scheme has been proposed in [HMP294, HMP494] and is based on the ideas of [HoP194].

The basic ElGamal signature scheme

For an ElGamal signature [ElGa84, ElGa85] the trusted authority chooses a large prime p and a generator $\alpha \in \mathbf{Z}_p^*$ with order $p-1$. p and α are public system parameters and authentically known to all users. The signer *Alice* chooses a random number $x_A \in \mathbf{Z}_{p-1}$ and computes $y_A := \alpha^{x_A} \pmod p$. She publishes y_A and keeps x_A secret. These values are constant for all messages to be signed. To sign a message $m \in \mathbf{Z}_{p-1}$ Alice chooses a random number $k \in \mathbf{Z}_{p-1}^*$. She computes $r := \alpha^k \pmod p$ and solves the congruence (1): $m \equiv x_A r + ks \pmod{p-1}$ for the parameter s. The triple $(m; r, s)$ is the signed message. It can be verified by checking the congruence $\alpha^m \equiv y_A^r r^s \pmod p$.

The Meta-ElGamal signature scheme

Instead of signature generation by the equation (1) we can also choose the general equation

$$A \equiv x_A B + kC \pmod q \qquad (2)$$

with $q \in \mathbf{P}$, $q|(p-1)$, and choose A, B, C as general functions $e, f, g : {\mathbf{Z}_q}^3 \to \mathbf{Z}_q$ with arguments m, r and s. As $m \in \mathbf{Z}_{p-1}$ we imply that m is reduced modulo q before it is used as an argument but in the following description we omit this for the sake of clearness.

The parameter s should either be used as argument in only one of the three functions or the functions have to be chosen carefully, such that the signature equation can be solved. Also all of the parameters m, r, s have to occur at least once. If two or three functions use exactly the same arguments, then they should be chosen as different operations. The occurrence of the insecure $rs-$ and $ms-$variants [HMP294], where the parameters r and s (m and s) occur exactly in one of the three functions e, f and g together but neither r nor s (m nor s) occurs in one of the two other, should be avoided. All four conditions apply also for equivalent variants, in which the signature equations can be transformed into each other. Furthermore none of the three functions should be equal to zero. To get efficient variants, in the functions should be chosen, such that s can be easily extracted (e.g. without inversions). It's also an advantage to choose one of the functions equal to one, to obtain an efficient signature verification. This verification is done by checking the equation

$$\alpha^A \equiv y_A^B r^C \pmod{p}.$$

As there are numerous variants, in the following we will only consider some efficient special cases of permutations, namely to choose A, B, C as a permutation of one of the following five types EG I – EG V, which have been analyzed in detail in [HMP494]:

$$\text{EG I: } (m,r,s), \text{EG II: } (f(m,r),s,1), \text{EG III: } (f(m,r),g(m,s),1),$$
$$\text{EG IV: } (f(m,r),g(r,s),1), \text{EG V: } (f(m,s),g(r,s),1).$$

The functions $f, g : \mathbf{Z}_q{}^2 \rightarrow \mathbf{Z}_q$ have to be invertible in the argument s to guarantee the solubility of the general signature equation (2) for the signature parameter s. For every type we get one of the following six permutations of the coefficients, which are enumerated by $No.$ 1 – 6:
$1: (a,b,c),\ 2: (a,c,b),\ 3: (c,b,a),\ 4: (c,a,b),\ 5: (b,c,a),\ 6: (b,a,c).$
For example $(a,b,c) = (m,r,s)$ in *Type* EG I and $(a,b,c) = (f(m,r),s,1)$ in *Type* EG II. Additionally we can generalize the computation of the parameter r by choosing $r' := \alpha^k \pmod{p}$ and computing $r := d(r', m)$ with a suitable function $d : \mathbf{Z}_p{}^2 \rightarrow \mathbf{Z}_p$. It also possible to vary the mode of operation that determines the group orders and the length of the parameters [HMP494]: XL is the ElGamal mode with $|p| = |q| = 512$, L the Schnorr mode [Schn89] with $|p| = 512$, $|q| = 160$, M the DSA mode [NIST91] with $|p| = 512$, $|q| = 160$, r reduced modulo q and S the small mode [Schn89, Knob94] with $|p| = 512$, $|q| = 160$ and a q_1 bit number $h(r)$ $(50 \leq |q_1| \leq 160)$ reduced by any hash function h.

All these generalizations can also be applied to the ElGamal signature scheme with two message blocks (*Type* EG VI – EG X) and the signature scheme with three message blocks (*Type* EG XI) [ElGa84, HMP494]. Combining the described variations we get the Meta-ElGamal signature scheme which can be written as $MEG = (Mode.Type.No., d, e, f, g)$.

In a simplified manner, we can also describe the Meta-ElGamal scheme by the tuple $(Mode, d, e, f, g)$ but then we loose useful structural information for the security analysis. Therefore we prefer the first notation even if it contains redundancy.

3 The Meta-Message recovery scheme

The Meta-Message recovery scheme has been proposed in [HMP394].

The basic Message recovery scheme

For a signature giving message recovery [NyRu93] the trusted authority chooses large primes p and q, where q is a large integer factor of $p-1$. She also chooses an element $\alpha \in \mathbf{Z}_p^*$ of order q. p, q and α are system parameters and authentically known to all users.

The signer Alice chooses x_A and y_A as in the ElGamal scheme. To sign a message $m \in \mathbf{Z}_{p-1}$ satisfying a suitable redundancy scheme, she chooses a random $k \in \mathbf{Z}_q^*$, computes $r' := \alpha^k \pmod p$, $r := (r')^{-1}m \pmod p$ and solves the congruence $s \equiv k - x_A r \pmod q$ for the parameter s. The signature is given by the tuple (r, s). The message can be recovered by computing $m := \alpha^s y_A^r r \pmod p$. The correctness of the signature can be checked by the given redundancy scheme.

The Meta-Message recovery scheme

We can apply the Meta-ElGamal scheme to this approach to obtain the Meta-Message recovery scheme [HMP394]. The general signature equation, which has to be solved for the parameter s is of the form

$$A \equiv x_A B + kC \pmod q \tag{3}$$

with A, B, C permutations of general functions $e, f, g : \mathbf{Z}_q{}^2 \to \mathbf{Z}_q$ with arguments r and s. The parameter r can be computed by $r' := \alpha^k \pmod p$ and $r := d(m, r')$ with a suitable function $d : \mathbf{Z}_p{}^2 \to \mathbf{Z}_p$, where $d^{-1}(r, r') = m$ exists. The signature is given by the tuple (r, s) and message recovery can be done by computing

$$m := d^{-1}(r, \alpha^{AC^{-1}} y_A^{-BC^{-1}} \pmod p).$$

The verification can be done by checking if m satisfies the redundancy scheme. If we look carefully on the necessary conditions on the functions e, f, g described in section 2, we see that we get the following ten types of permutations:

Type	(A, B, C) permutation of		
MR I	1	r	s
MR II	1	s	$f(r,s)$
MR III	1	r	$f(r,s)$
MR IV	1	$f(r,s)$	$g(r,s)$
MR V	r	r	$f(r,s)$

Type	(A, B, C) permutation of		
MR VI	r	s	$f(r,s)$
MR VII	s	s	$f(r,s)$
MR VIII	r	$f(r,s)$	$g(r,s)$
MR IX	s	$f(r,s)$	$g(r,s)$
MR X	$e(r,s)$	$f(r,s)$	$g(r,s)$

Among these only the types MR I, III and V are solvable for all choices of e, f, g. The most efficient types are the *Type* MR I – IV if we choose the parameter $C = 1$, because we need no inversion for message recovery. In *Type* MR II, IV, VI – X we have to choose suitable functions e, f, g to guarantee the solvability for the parameter s. In *Type* MR IV, we have to choose different functions f, g without homomorphic properties to guarantee the security of the signature scheme. It is argued in [HMP394] that *Mode* L is best suited for message recovery schemes. Furthermore the scheme can be extended for two and three message blocks, where one message block can be recovered.

4 Meta-ElGamal blind signatures

Here we present the Meta-ElGamal based blind signature scheme founded on the ElGamal based blind signature scheme in [CaPS94].

The basic blind signature scheme

For a blind signature [CaPS94] the trusted authority chooses large primes p and q, where q is a large integer factor of $p-1$. She also chooses an element $\alpha \in \mathbf{Z}_p^*$ of order q. p, q and α are system parameters and authentically known to all users.

The notary Nancy chooses $x_N \in \mathbf{Z}_{p-1}$ as her secret key and computes her public key $y_N := \alpha^{x_N} \pmod{p}$. To sign a message, she chooses a random $\tilde{k} \in \mathbf{Z}_q^*$, computes $\tilde{r} := \alpha^{\tilde{k}} \pmod{p}$, and transmits $\tilde{r}$ to the owner of the message $m \in \mathbf{Z}_{p-1}$ Alice. Alice chooses random $a, b \in \mathbf{Z}_q$, computes $r := \tilde{r}^a \alpha^b \pmod{p}$, $\tilde{m} := am\tilde{r}r^{-1} \pmod{q}$ and sends $\tilde{m}$ to Nancy. Nancy solves the congruence $\tilde{s} \equiv x_N \tilde{r} + \tilde{k}\tilde{m} \pmod{q}$ for the parameter $\tilde{s}$ and transmits $\tilde{s}$ to Alice, who computes $s := \tilde{s}r\tilde{r}^{-1} + bm \pmod{q}$. The signed message is given by the triple (m, r, s). The verification of the signature can be done by checking the congruence $\alpha^s \equiv y_A^r r^m \pmod{p}$.

The Meta-ElGamal blind signature scheme

For the sake of clearness the function d is chosen as $d(r, m) := r$ and we only focus on the *Mode* L. The adoption to the other modes is straightforward. Other choices for the function d will be discussed at the end of this section.

The idea is that notary Nancy chooses the blinded parameter $\tilde{r} := \alpha^{\tilde{k}} \pmod{p}$ herself with a random $\tilde{k} \in \mathbf{Z}_q^*$ and the owner Alice chooses the unblinded $r := \tilde{r}^a \alpha^b \pmod{p}$ with random $a, b \in \mathbf{Z}_q^*$. Nancy signs the blinded message $\tilde{m}$ using the equation (4): $\tilde{A} \equiv x_N \tilde{B} + \tilde{k}\tilde{C} \pmod{q}$, which is equivalent to $\tilde{k} \equiv \tilde{C}^{-1}(\tilde{A} - x_N \tilde{B}) \pmod{q}$ where x_N is the secret key of Nancy. The unblinded signed message is given by (m, r, s). Its validity is checked by the equation $\alpha^A \equiv y_N^B r^C \pmod{p}$. For the correctness of the signature scheme, it is necessary, that this equation is satisfied.

Thus we have $y_N^B r^C \equiv \alpha^{x_N B} \alpha^{(a\tilde{k}+b)C} \equiv \alpha^{x_N B + C(a\tilde{C}^{-1}(\tilde{A} - x_N \tilde{B})+b)} \equiv y_N^{(B - a\tilde{C}^{-1}\tilde{B}C)} \alpha^{a\tilde{C}^{-1}\tilde{A}C + bC} \pmod{p}$ and this must be equivalent to $\alpha^A \pmod{p}$. Hence we get the equations

$$A = a\tilde{A}C\tilde{C}^{-1} + bC \pmod{q}, \tag{5}$$
$$B = a\tilde{B}C\tilde{C}^{-1} \pmod{q}. \tag{6}$$

If the value s does not appear in C then it is possible to transform these two equations to get $\tilde{m} := \psi(a, b, m, r, \tilde{r})$ and $s := \theta(a, b, m, r, \tilde{m}, \tilde{r}, \tilde{s})$. Note that s or $\tilde{s}$ are not allowed in the equation for $\tilde{m}$. Furthermore we can transform the signature equation (4) to get $\tilde{s} := \rho(x_N, \tilde{k}, \tilde{m}, \tilde{r})$. Hence follows the Meta-ElGamal blind signature scheme:

Meta-ElGamal blind signature scheme		
parameter: p, q prime, α generator, m message		
Owner *Alice*		Notary *Nancy*
$a, b \in_R \mathbf{Z}_q^*$		$\tilde{k} \in_R \mathbf{Z}_p{}^*$
$\tilde{r}$	$\longleftarrow$	$\tilde{r} := \alpha^{\tilde{k}} \pmod p$
$r := \tilde{r}^a \alpha^b \pmod p$		
$\tilde{m} := \psi(a, b, m, r, \tilde{r})$	$\longrightarrow$	$\tilde{m}$
$\tilde{s}$	$\longleftarrow$	$\tilde{s} := \rho(x_N, \tilde{k}, \tilde{m}, \tilde{r})$
$s := \theta(a, b, m, r, \tilde{m}, \tilde{r}, \tilde{s})$		

The signed message is given by (m, r, s). Its verification can be done by checking the equation $\alpha^A \equiv y_N^B r^C \pmod p$. We illustrate the Meta-scheme by giving equations for some efficient variants in table 1.

No.	equation (5)	equation (6)
EB I.2	$m \equiv a\tilde{r}^{-1}\tilde{m}r + br$	$s \equiv a\tilde{r}^{-1}\tilde{s}r$
EB I.3	$s \equiv a\tilde{m}^{-1}\tilde{s}m + bm$	$r \equiv a\tilde{m}^{-1}\tilde{r}m$
EB I.4	$s \equiv a\tilde{r}^{-1}\tilde{s}r + br$	$m \equiv a\tilde{r}^{-1}\tilde{m}r$
EB I.5	$r \equiv a\tilde{m}^{-1}\tilde{r}m + bm$	$s \equiv a\tilde{m}^{-1}\tilde{s}m$
EB II.2	$1 \equiv af(\tilde{m}, \tilde{r})^{-1}f(m, r) + bf(m, r)$	$s \equiv af(\tilde{m}, \tilde{r})^{-1}\tilde{s}f(m, r)$
EB II.3	$s \equiv a\tilde{s} + b$	$f(m, r) \equiv af(\tilde{m}, \tilde{r})$
EB II.4	$s \equiv af(\tilde{m}, \tilde{r})^{-1}\tilde{s}f(m, r) + bf(m, r)$	$1 \equiv af(\tilde{m}, \tilde{r})^{-1}f(m, r)$
EB II.5	$f(m, r) = af(\tilde{m}, \tilde{r}) + b$	$s \equiv a\tilde{s}$

Table 1. Variants of the Meta-ElGamal blind signature scheme

Note that for those schemes in which the parameter s appears in C we can't get blind signature schemes for general functions f and g, because s and $\tilde{s}$ are not allowed as arguments in the function ψ. Thus we can't get a blind signature scheme using the basic ElGamal signature scheme.

A signature scheme is called blind, if all (blinded) parameters which are known by Nancy are statistically independent from the unblinded parameters of the signature. Generalizing Theorem 2 in [CaPS94] we can show that all variants are blind signature schemes:

Theorem 1: For any pair of triples $(\tilde{m}, \tilde{s}, \tilde{r})$, (m, s, r) with $m, r, \tilde{r} \in \mathbf{Z}_p^*$, $\tilde{r} \equiv \alpha^{\tilde{k}} \pmod p$, $\tilde{A} \equiv \tilde{B}x_N + \tilde{C}\tilde{k} \pmod q$, $\alpha^A \equiv y_N^B r^C \pmod p$ and A, B, C chosen as above, there exist unique $a, b \in \mathbf{Z}_q$ with $r \equiv \tilde{r}^a \alpha^b \pmod p$, $A = a\tilde{C}^{-1}\tilde{A}C + bC \pmod q$, $B = a\tilde{C}^{-1}\tilde{B}C \pmod q$.

The proof is straightforward adopting the proof in [CaPS94] and can be found in the full version of the paper [HMP594]. Hence the Meta-ElGamal blind signature scheme can be written as $MEB = (Mode.Type.No, d, e, f, g)$ similar to the Meta-ElGamal scheme (MEG). A security and efficiency analysis is given in the full paper [HMP594].

Generalized design

Instead of using $d(r,m) := r$ we can also use the general suitable function $d(r',m)$ where $r' := \tilde{r}^a\alpha^b \pmod p$ if m does not appear as argument in the functions e, f and g. The resulting Meta-scheme is given in the following table:

Meta-blind scheme for d-variants		
parameter: p, q prime, α generator, m message		
Owner *Alice*		Notary *Nancy*
$a, b \in_R \mathbf{Z}_q^*$		$\tilde{k} \in_R \mathbf{Z}_p{}^*$
$\tilde{r}'$	$\longleftarrow$	$\tilde{r}' := \alpha^{\tilde{k}} \pmod p$
$r' := \tilde{r}'^a\alpha^b \pmod p$		
$r := d(r', m)$		
$\tilde{r} := \psi(a, b, r)$	$\longrightarrow$	$\tilde{r}$
$\tilde{s}$	$\longleftarrow$	$\tilde{s} := \rho(x_N, \tilde{k}, \tilde{r})$
$s := \theta(a, b, r, \tilde{r}, \tilde{s})$		

Further, instead of using the equation $r' := (\tilde{r}')^a\alpha^b \equiv \alpha^{\tilde{k}a+b} \pmod p$ we can also use $r' := \tilde{r}' y_N^{-a}\alpha^b \equiv \alpha^{\tilde{k}-x_N a+b} \pmod p$ as suggested by Okamoto in [Okam92], $r' := (\tilde{r}')^a y_N^b \equiv \alpha^{\tilde{k}a+x_N b} \pmod p$ or $r' := (\tilde{r}')^a y_N \alpha^b \equiv \alpha^{\tilde{k}a+x_N+b} \pmod p$ which haven't been proposed before. This leads to slightly modified general equations (5), (6) from which we obtain many additional efficient variants.

5 Meta-Message recovery blind signatures

Now we present the Meta-Message recovery blind signature scheme based on the message recovery blind signature scheme [CaPS94]. The idea is that notary Nancy chooses the blinded parameter $\tilde{t} := \alpha^{\tilde{k}} \pmod p$ herself with a random $\tilde{k} \in \mathbf{Z}_q^*$ and the owner Alice chooses the unblinded $r := m\tilde{t}^a\alpha^b \pmod p$ with random $a, b \in \mathbf{Z}_q^*$. Nancy signs the blinded parameter $\tilde{r}$ using the equation (7): $\tilde{A} \equiv x_N\tilde{B} + \tilde{k}\tilde{C} \pmod q$, which is equivalent to $\tilde{k} \equiv \tilde{C}^{-1}(\tilde{A} - x_N\tilde{B}) \pmod q$, where x_N is the secret key of Nancy. The signature on the unblinded message m is given by (r, s). Its validity is checked by the message recovery equation $m := \alpha^{AC^{-1}} y_N^{-BC^{-1}} r \pmod p$.

For the correctness of the scheme it is necessary, that this equation is satisfied. Thus we have $\alpha^{AC^{-1}} y_N^{-BC^{-1}} r \equiv \alpha^{AC^{-1}-x_N BC^{-1}+a\tilde{k}+b} m \equiv \alpha^{AC^{-1}-x_N BC^{-1}+a(\tilde{C}^{-1}(\tilde{A}-x_N\tilde{B}))+b} m \equiv \alpha^{(C^{-1}A+a\tilde{C}^{-1}\tilde{A}+b)-x_N(C^{-1}B+a\tilde{C}^{-1}\tilde{B})} m$ and this should be equivalent to m modulo p. Hence we get the equations

$$A = -a\tilde{A}C\tilde{C}^{-1} - bC \pmod q, \tag{8}$$

$$B = -a\tilde{B}\tilde{C}^{-1}C \pmod q. \tag{9}$$

Note that we get nearly the same equations as in the Meta-ElGamal blind signature scheme. If the value s does not appear in C then it is possible to transform these two equations to get $\tilde{r} := \psi(a, b, r, \tilde{t})$ and $s := \theta(a, b, r, \tilde{r}, \tilde{s}, \tilde{t})$. Note that s and $\tilde{s}$ are not allowed in the equation for $\tilde{r}$. Furthermore we can transform the signature equation (7) to get $\tilde{s} := \rho(x_N, \tilde{k}, \tilde{r})$. From this the Meta-Message recovery blind signature scheme follows:

Meta-Message recovery blind signature scheme		
Parameter: p, q prime, α generator, m message		
Owner *Alice*		Notary *Nancy*
$a, b \in_R \mathbf{Z}_q$		$\tilde{k} \in_R {\mathbf{Z}_p}^*$
$\tilde{t}$	$\longleftarrow$	$\tilde{t} := \alpha^{\tilde{k}} \pmod{p}$
$r := m\tilde{t}^a \alpha^b \pmod{p}$		
$\tilde{r} := \psi(a, b, r, \tilde{t})$	$\longrightarrow$	$\tilde{r}$
$\tilde{s}$	$\longleftarrow$	$\tilde{s} := \rho(x_N, \tilde{k}, \tilde{r})$
$s := \theta(a, b, r, \tilde{r}, \tilde{s}, \tilde{t})$		

The signed message is given by (r, s). Message recovery is done by calculating

$$m := \alpha^{AC^{-1}} y_N^{-BC^{-1}} r \pmod{p}$$

and checking, if m satisfies the redundancy scheme. We summarize the equations for some efficient types in table 2.

No.	signature	equation(8)	equation(9)
MB I.2	$1 \equiv -x_N\tilde{s} + \tilde{k}\tilde{r}$	$1 \equiv -a\tilde{r}^{-1}r - br$	$s \equiv -a\tilde{r}^{-1}\tilde{s}r$
MB I.3	$\tilde{s} \equiv -x_N\tilde{r} + \tilde{k}$	$s \equiv -a\tilde{s} - b$	$r \equiv -a\tilde{r}$
MB I.4	$\tilde{s} \equiv -x_N + \tilde{k}\tilde{r}$	$s \equiv -a\tilde{r}^{-1}\tilde{s}r - br$	$1 \equiv -a\tilde{r}^{-1}r$
MB I.5	$\tilde{r} \equiv -x_N\tilde{s} + \tilde{k}$	$r \equiv -a\tilde{r} - b$	$s \equiv -a\tilde{s}$
MB II.1	$\tilde{s} \equiv -x_N f(\tilde{r}, \tilde{s}) + \tilde{k}$	$s \equiv -af(\tilde{r}, \tilde{s}) - b$	$f(r, s) \equiv -af(\tilde{r}, \tilde{s})$
MB II.6	$f(\tilde{r}, \tilde{s}) \equiv -x_N\tilde{s} + \tilde{k}$	$f(r, s) \equiv -a\tilde{s} - b$	$s \equiv -a\tilde{s}$
MB III.2	$\tilde{r} \equiv -x_N f(\tilde{r}, \tilde{s}) + \tilde{k}$	$r \equiv -a\tilde{r} - b$	$f(r, s) \equiv -af(\tilde{r}, \tilde{s})$
MB III.3	$f(\tilde{r}, \tilde{s}) \equiv -x_N + \tilde{k}\tilde{r}$	$f(r, s) \equiv -a\tilde{r}^{-1} f(\tilde{r}, \tilde{s})r - br$	$1 \equiv -a\tilde{r}^{-1}r$
MB III.4	$f(\tilde{r}, \tilde{s}) \equiv -x_N\tilde{r} + \tilde{k}$	$f(r, s) \equiv -af(\tilde{r}, \tilde{s}) - b$	$r \equiv -a\tilde{r}$
MB III.5	$1 \equiv -x_N f(\tilde{r}, \tilde{s}) + \tilde{k}\tilde{r}$	$1 \equiv -a\tilde{r}^{-1}r - br$	$f(r, s) \equiv -a\tilde{r}^{-1} f(\tilde{r}, \tilde{s})r$

Table 2. Efficient variants of the Message recovery blind signature scheme

Note that in the schemes listed in table 2 we can get the functions ψ and θ by transforming the equations (8) and (9) with a general function f. In any other variant of *Type* MB I – IV this is not possible for general functions f and g.

The proof of blindness is similar to the proof given for the Meta-ElGamal blind signature scheme above and can be found in [HMP594].

Hence we can define Meta-Message recovery blind signature scheme $MRB = (Mode.Type.No, d, e, f, g)$ similar to the Meta-Message recovery scheme (MMR) above. For the security and efficiency analysis we refer to the full version of this paper [HMP594].

6 Efficient variants

A detailed description of the most efficient variants which can be obtained from the scheme EG II.3 of the Meta-ElGamal signature scheme is given in the full version of this paper [HMP594]. Here we restrict to enumerate the most efficient variants.

Efficient Meta-ElGamal blind signatures

The most efficient variants of the Meta-ElGamal blind signature scheme are the variants EB II.3, EB II.4, EB III.3, EB III.4, EB IV.3, EB IV.4, EB V.3, EB V.4 where the addition is used for the functions f and g [HMP494]. Here Alice has to compute only two on-line exponentiations modulo p with a $|q|$ bit exponent and one off-line inverse modulo q. Notary Nancy needs just one off-line exponentiation with a $|q|$ bit exponent. Thus it is more efficient than the proposed scheme in [CaPS94] where the signature scheme (MEB I.3.$\sigma(1), r, s, r, m, id$) is used.

Efficient Meta-Message recovery blind signatures

The most efficient variants for the message recovery blind signature scheme are the variants MB I.3, MB I.5, MB II.1, MB II.6, MB III.2 and MB III.4. Here the owner needs one on-line and one off-line exponentiation modulo p with a $|q|$ bit exponent, the notary one off-line exponentiation modulo p with a $|q|$ bit exponent and the verifier two exponentiations modulo p with a $|p|$ bit exponent.

7 Applications of the Meta schemes

7.1 Authentic message encryption

The basic authentic encryption scheme has been derivated from a signature scheme giving message recovery [NyRu94] and the ElGamal encryption scheme [ElGa84]. In this scheme we have to submit three ciphertext blocks. An improvement of this scheme has been given in [HMP194] in which we need to transmit only two ciphertext blocks of length $|p| + |q|$ instead of $2|p| + |q|$ in the basic encryption scheme. This scheme can also be generalized for the Meta-Message recovery scheme.

The calculation of $r' := h(y_B^k \pmod p)$ and $r := d(r', m)$, where y_B is the public key of the recipient and h a one-way function, are the same in every variant. Furthermore the signature generation is like in the general equation (2). The message recovery can be done by the equation $m := d^{-1}(r, h(y_B^{AC^{-1}} y_A^{-x_B BC^{-1}} \pmod p)))$. The correctness of this equation is shown by the congruence $d^{-1}(r, h(y_B^{AC^{-1}} y_A^{-x_B BC^{-1}} \pmod p))) = d^{-1}(r, h(y_B^{(A - x_A B)C^{-1}} \pmod p))) = d^{-1}(r, h(y_B^{kCC^{-1}} \pmod p))) = m$. Note that the variants in [HMP194] which are based on the $rs-$variants are not authentic as pointed out by Lim [Lim 94]. His attack can be countermeasured if the receiver checks whether the session key $h(y_B^k \pmod p)$ has been used before. As this solution is not very practical we recommend not to use them.

7.2 Self-certified public keys

By applying the ideas described in [BaKn89, Guen89] we can create identity based certificates for the public keys of identified users with distinguished names, which results in the self-certified public keys [Gira91]. They have the following properties:

- The public key can be computed as a function of the identity, the public parameters (generator α, prime modul p, public key of the trusted authority y_Z) and the signature parameter r, which is not necessarily authentic. The secret key is computed by the trusted authority as the signature parameter s.
- The authenticity of the public key is not directly verified, but only the authorized user knows the corresponding secret key and thus can benefit of this public key.

In the following, we will describe the general approach to obtain the self-certified public key y_A of user *Alice*. For the sake of clearness we restrict the description to the *Mode* L.

Using the Meta-Message recovery scheme

The trusted authority Z, who uses his public key y_Z and his secret key x_Z signs the identity ID_A of Alice with the Meta-Message recovery scheme by choosing a random $k_A \in \mathbf{Z}_q$, computing $r'_A := \alpha^{k_A} \pmod p$, $r_A := d(r'_A, ID_A)$ and solving the general signature equation for the parameter x_A: $A \equiv x_Z B + k_A C \pmod q$ with $\pm A, \pm B, \pm C$ permutations of general functions $e, f, g : \mathbf{Z}_q{}^2 \rightarrow \mathbf{Z}_q$ and arguments r_A and x_A. This gives an equation of the form $x_A =: a_A(x_Z, k_A, r_A) b_A(x_Z, k_A, r_A)^{-1} \pmod q$, where the functions a_A and b_A are implicitly defined by the chosen variant. The tuple (r_A, x_A) is a signature on the message ID_A. The public key y_A can be computed as $y_A := \beta_A^{x_A} \pmod p$ with generator $\beta_A := \alpha^{b_A(x_Z, k_A, r_A)} =: v_A(\alpha, y_Z, r_A, ID_A) \pmod p$, such that the following congruence holds for y_A:

$$y_A \equiv \beta_A^{x_A} \equiv \alpha^{b_A(x_Z,k_A,r_A) a_A(x_Z,k_A,r_A) b_A(x_Z,k_A,r_A)^{-1}} \equiv$$

$$\alpha^{a_A(x_Z,k_A,r_A)} =: u_A(\alpha, y_Z, r_A, ID_A) \pmod p.$$

(Note, that $\alpha^{x_Z} \equiv y_Z \pmod p$ and $\alpha^{k_A} \equiv d^{-1}(r_A, ID_A) \pmod p$!) This means, that y_A can be computed as a function u_A of the authentic public parameters α, y_Z, ID_A and the parameter r_A, which doesn't need to be authentic. To guarantee, that the last equivalence holds, the functions e, f and g have to be chosen as a composition of arithmetic operations. The main drawback of this general approach is, that the trusted authority creates the secret keys of all users and therefore requires unconditional trust by the users.

Using Meta-Blind signature schemes

This drawback can be prevented by signing the secret key x_A with a hidden signature [HoKn91, HoP294], such that it can be modified by the user after signature generation without the trusted authority knowing it. It can also be signed with one of the two Meta-Blind signature schemes described above, to obtain a self-certified public key for one pseudonym of a user.

It should be mentioned that we can also compute identity-based public keys by signing the message $m := h(ID_A)y_A$ with a public hash function h to obtain a certificate (r, s) and recovering the public key as $y_A := mh(ID_A)^{-1} \pmod p$ by using the identity ID_A of the user [NyRu93]. This method can be applied to all Meta-Message recovery schemes.

Note that the computation of the self-certified public-keys is more efficient in some variants than in the previously known protocols. We refer to the full paper for a detailed analysis [HMP594].

7.2.1 Authentication schemes

In the authentication schemes, the user *Alice* who wants to authenticate herself to the verifier *Bob* proves the knowledge of the discrete logarithm x_A of her self-certified public key $y_A := u_A(\alpha, y_Z, r_A, ID_A)$ to the basis $\beta_A = t_A(\alpha, y_Z, r_A, ID_A)$ by the Zero-Knowledge-proof of Chaum, Evertse and van de Graaf [ChEG87]. Alice chooses a random number $v_A \in \mathbf{Z}_q^*$ and transmits $w_A := \beta_A^{v_A} \pmod p$ to Bob who chooses a random $c_A \in \mathbf{Z}_q$ and sends it to Alice. She calculates the response $z_A := v_A + x_A c_A \pmod p$. Bob accepts the proof if and only if $w_A \equiv \beta_A^{z_A} y_A^{-c_A} \pmod p$ is satisfied.

This can be done with all self-certified public keys obtained from the Meta-Message recovery scheme. It can also be applied to other authentication protocols, e.g. [ChEG87, BrMc90, Okam92].

7.2.2 Authenticated key exchange

To obtain a general authenticated key exchange protocol, we can apply the ideas from [BaKn89, Guen89] or the SELANE-protocols [HoKn91] which both use self-certified public keys.

The *first approach* combines mutual authentication and Diffie-Hellman key exchange [DiHe76] by using the (authentic) data exchanged during the authentication protocol to construct the session key. The session key can be computed from the authentic parameters w_A, w_B in the Meta-authentication scheme above and some exchanged, randomly chosen parameters $e_A := \beta_A^{d_A} \pmod p$, $e_B := \beta_B^{d_B} \pmod p$ in the following manner:

$$K := e_B^{v_A} w_B^{d_A} \equiv \beta_B^{v_A d_B + v_B d_A} \equiv \beta_A^{v_A d_B + v_B d_A} \equiv w_A^{d_B} e_A^{v_B} \pmod p.$$

Obviously this is only correct if $\beta_A = \beta_B$ and thus some variants can't be used.

In the *second approach* a Diffie-Hellman key is computed, which can only be known by the two parties. The key has to be verified after computation, to ensure that both sides know the same key. *Alice* computes $y_B := u_B(\alpha, y_Z, r_B, ID_B)$ and $\beta_B := t_B(\alpha, y_Z, r_B, ID_B)$. Then she chooses a random number $v_A \in \mathbf{Z}_q^*$ and computes $w_A := \beta_B^{v_A} \pmod p$. w_A is transmitted to *Bob* who computes $y_A := u_A(\alpha, y_Z, r_A, ID_A)$ and $\beta_A := t_A(\alpha, y_Z, r_A, ID_A)$. He chooses a random number $v_B \in \mathbf{Z}_q^*$ and computes $w_B := \beta_A^{v_B} \pmod p$, which he transmits to *Alice*. She computes her session key $K_A := w_B^{x_A} y_B^{v_A} \pmod p$ and *Bob* his session key $K_B := w_A^{x_B} y_A^{v_B} \pmod p$. If the transmission of the values w_A and w_B hasn't been disturbed by any attacker, the two session keys are identical as proven by the following congruence:

$$K_A = w_B^{x_A} y_B^{v_A} \equiv (\beta_A^{v_B})^{x_A} (\beta_B^{x_B})^{v_A} \equiv (\beta_B^{v_A})^{x_B} (\beta_A^{x_A})^{v_B} \equiv w_A^{x_B} y_A^{v_B} = K_B \pmod p.$$

Note, that both sides can use functions t_i and u_i related to different variants of the Meta-Message recovery scheme to compute their self-certified public keys y_i and the corresponding generators β_i $(i \in \{A, B\})$.

Both solutions are vulnerable to the triangle attack [Burm94] where under special circumstances the session key of two users can be calculated using eavesdropped information and additional information which is voluntarily given by the users to the attacker. This attack can be countermeasured, but the amortized security can't be proven [YaSh89].

A *third possibility* to exchange an authentic session key, is to sign as message m a random value $w_A := \alpha^{v_A} \pmod p$ by *Alice* with one of the Meta-Message recovery schemes and also a value $w_B := \alpha^{v_B} \pmod p$ by *Bob*. Both parties can exchange their signatures, recover the values w_A and w_B and compute the session key as in the Diffie-Hellman key exchange [DiHe76, NyRu94]:

$$K_A := w_B^{v_A} \equiv \alpha^{v_A v_B} \equiv w_A^{v_B} := K_B \pmod p.$$

7.3 Further applications

From the Meta-Message recovery scheme we can develop generalized hidden and weak blind signature schemes giving message recovery. Other applications of the Meta-Message recovery scheme are multisignatures, blind multisignatures and threshold cryptosystems.

8 Conclusion

Using the ideas of the Meta-ElGamal signature scheme and the Meta-Message recovery scheme we have shown how to generalize the ElGamal- and the Message recovery blind signature schemes and discussed the most efficient variants. Furthermore some interesting applications of the Meta-Message recovery signature scheme like Meta-authentic encryption schemes, identity based public keys used for authentication and authenticated key exchange have been described.

References

[BaKn89] F.Bauspieß, H.-J.Knobloch, "How to keep authenticity alive in a computer network", Lecture Notes in Computer Science 434, Advances in Cryptology: Proc. Eurocrypt '89, Berlin: Springer Verlag, (1990), pp. 38 – 46.

[BrMc90] E.F.Brickell, K.S.McCurley, "An Interactive Identification scheme based on discrete logarithms and factoring", Lecture Notes in Computer Science 473, Advances in Cryptology: Proc. Eurocrypt '90, Berlin: Springer Verlag, (1991), pp. 63 – 71.

[Burm94] M.Burmester, "On the risk of opening distributed keys", Lecture Notes in Computer Science 839, Advances in Cryptology: Proc. Crypto '94, Berlin: Springer Verlag, (1994), pp. 308 – 317.

[CaPS94] J.L.Camenisch, J.-M.Piveteau, M.A.Stadler, "Blind signature schemes based on the discrete logarithm problem", Preprint, presented at the Rump session of Eurocrypt '94, (1994), 5 pages.

[Chau82] D. Chaum, "Blind signatures for untraceable payments", Advances in Cryptology: Proc. Crypto '82, New York: Plenum Press, (1983), pp. 199–203.

[ChEG87] D.Chaum, J.H.Evertse, J.van de Graaf, "Demonstrating possession of a discrete logarithms and some generalizations", Lecture Notes in Computer Science 304, Advances in Cryptology: Proc. Eurocrypt '87, Berlin: Springer Verlag, (1988), pp. 127 – 141.

[DiHe76] W.Diffie, M.Hellman,"New directions in cryptography", IEEE Transactions on Information Theory, Vol. IT-22, No. 6, November, (1976), pp. 644 – 654.

[ElGa84] T.ElGamal, "Cryptography and logarithms over finite fields", Stanford University, CA., UMI Order No. DA 8420519, (1984), 119 pages.

[ElGa85] T.ElGamal, "A public key cryptosystem and a signature scheme based on discrete logarithms", IEEE Transactions on Information Theory, Vol. IT-30, No. 4, July, (1985), pp. 469 – 472.

[Gira91] M.Girault, "Self-Certified Public Keys", Lecture Notes in Computer Science 547, Advances in Cryptology: Proc. Eurocrypt '91, Berlin: Springer Verlag, (1991), pp. 490 – 497.

[Guen89] C.G.Günther, "An identity based key exchange protocol", Lecture Notes in Computer Science 434, Advances in Cryptology: Proc. Eurocrypt '89, Berlin: Springer Verlag, (1990), pp. 29 – 37.

[HoKn91] P.Horster, H.-J.Knobloch, "Discrete Logarithm based protocols", Lecture Notes in Computer Science 547, Advances in Cryptology: Proc. Eurocrypt '91, Berlin: Springer Verlag, (1992), pp. 399 – 408.

[HMP194] P.Horster, M.Michels, H.Petersen, "Authenticated encryption schemes with low communication costs", Electronics Letters, Vol. 30, No. 15, July, (1994), pp. 1230 – 1231.

[HMP294] P.Horster, M.Michels, H.Petersen, "Generalized ElGamal signature schemes for one message block", Proc. 2nd Int. Workshop on IT-Security, Vienna, Sep. 22.–23., (1994), 16 pages.

[HMP394] P.Horster, M.Michels, H.Petersen, "Meta signature schemes giving message recovery based on the discrete logarithm problem", Proc. 2. Int. Workshop on IT-Security, Wien, Sep. 22.–23., (1994), 12 pages.

[HMP494] P.Horster, M.Michels, H.Petersen, "Meta-ElGamal signature schemes", Proc. 2nd ACM conference on Computer and Communications security, Fairfax, Virginia, Nov. 2–4, (1994), pp. 96 – 107.

[HMP594] P.Horster, M.Michels, H.Petersen, "Meta-Message recovery and Meta-Blind signature schemes based on the discrete logarithm problem and their applications", (Full version), Technical Report TR-94-9, University of Technology Chemnitz-Zwickau, June, (1994), 22 pages[1].

[HoP194] P.Horster, H.Petersen, "Generalized ElGamal-signatures" (in German), Sicherheit in Informationssystemen, Proceedings of SIS '94, Zurich, March 10–11, 1994, Verlag der Fachvereine Zürich, (1994), pp. 89 – 106.

[HoP294] P.Horster, H.Petersen, "Classification of blind signature schemes and examples of hidden and weak blind signatures", Technical Report TR-94-1, University of Technology Chemnitz-Zwickau, Presented at the Rump Session of Eurocrypt '94, Perugia, Italy, (1994), 6 pages[1].

[Knob94] H.-J.Knobloch, "A remark on the size of ElGamal-type digital signatures", EISS Report 94/1, European Institute for System Security (EISS), University of Karlsruhe, (1994), 5 pages.

[Lim 94] C.H.Lim, E-mail to the authors, August 20, (1994).

[NIST91] National Institute of Standards and Technology, Federal Information Process. Standard, FIPS Pub XX: Digital Signature Standard (DSS), (1991).

[NyRu93] K.Nyberg, R.Rueppel, "A new signature scheme based on the DSA giving message recovery", Proc. 1st ACM Conference on Computer and Communications Security, Fairfax, Virginia, Nov. 3–5., (1993), 4 pages.

[NyRu94] K.Nyberg, R.Rueppel, "Message recovery for signature schemes based on the discrete logarithm problem", Pre-proceedings of Eurocrypt '94, University of Perugia, Italy, (1994), pp. 175 – 190.

[Okam92] T.Okamoto, "Provable secure and practical identification schemes and corresponding signature schemes", Lecture Notes in Computer Science 740, Advances in Cryptology: Proc. Crypto '92, Berlin: Springer Verlag, (1993), pp. 31 – 53.

[Schn89] C.P.Schnorr, "Efficient identification and signatures for smart cards", Lecture Notes in Computer Science 435, Advances in Cryptology: Proc. Crypto '89, Berlin: Springer Verlag, (1990), pp. 239 – 251.

[YaSh89] Y.Yacobi, Z.Shmuely, "On key distribution systems", Lecture Notes in Computer Science 435, Advances in Cryptology: Proc. Crypto '89, Berlin: Springer Verlag, (1990), pp. 344 – 355.

[1]Available via anonymous FTP in directory *ftp.tu-chemnitz.de/pub/Local/informatik/crypto*

A Digital Signature Scheme Based on Linear Error-correcting Block Codes

Mohssen Alabbadi
KACST
P.O.Box 6086
Riyadh - 11442, Saudi Arabia
alabbadi@sakacs00.bitnet

Stephen B. Wicker
Georgia Tech - Lorraine
2 et 3 Rue Marconi
57070 Metz, France
wicker@georgiatech-metz.fr

Abstract

A true trapdoor digital signature scheme is presented. The scheme uses linear error-correcting block codes in a manner similar to that of the McEliece public-key cryptosystem, the Rao-Nam private-key cryptosystem, and the three digital signature schemes proposed by Xinmei, Harn and Wang, and the authors. All these digital signature schemes have been shown to be susceptible to a number of attacks. The signature scheme described in this paper derives its security from the complexity of three problems: the decoding of general linear error-correcting block codes, the factoring of large matrices, and the derivation of a matrix from its right inverse. It is shown that the proposed scheme is resistant to the attacks that proved successful when used against the aforementioned digital signature schemes as well as other attacks. The required public key storage is about $3n^2$ bits. The complexity of the signature generation and validation algorithms are $O(n^2)$ and $O(nk)$ bit operations respectively, thus making the scheme amenable to use in high data rate applications.

1 Introduction

Diffie and Hellman introduced public-key cryptography in 1976 [1]. Two years later McEliece proposed a public-key encryption scheme based on linear error-correcting block codes [2]. McEliece's system derives its security from the intractibility of the general decoding problem, which has been shown to be NP-complete [3]. An efficient attack on McEliece's system has yet to be discovered, though several computationally intensive attacks have been discussed in the literature. In 1991, Xinmei [4] pursued the logical extension of McEliece's system and developed a digital signature scheme that is also based on linear error-correcting block codes. In Xinmei's scheme, signatures are generated in a manner similar to the way plaintext is encrypted in the Rao-Nam private-key cryptosystem [5].

Recently Xinmei's scheme has been shown to be susceptible to several different attacks. Harn and Wang showed in [6] that the combination of valid signatures of some messages yields a valid signature for another message. They modified Xinmei's scheme by introducing a nonlinear hashing function that precluded the threat of selective forgery. Futhermore, it was shown in [7] that the linearity of the code and knowledge of the error vectors can be exploited in a chosen-message attack that results in a total break of Xinmei's scheme. The Harn-Wang modified scheme was also shown to be totally breakable under known-message attack [8]. Finally, in [9] van Tilburg devised a direct attack that totally breaks the Xinmei scheme (a direct attack obtains the private key directly from the public key). This direct attack was also successfully extended to the Harn-Wang modified version of Xinmei's scheme. Another digital signature scheme was proposed in [10] that resisted the above attacks. This scheme was shown to be susceptible to universal forgery [11, 12]

All of the above attacks highlight weaknesses in the security of digital signature schemes based on linear error-correcting codes. In this paper these weaknesses are addressed and a digital signature scheme is presented that is impervious to the above attacks as well as other attacks. The proposed scheme derives its security from the complexity of three problems: the decoding of general linear error-correcting block codes, the factoring of large matrices, and the derivation of a matrix from its right inverse. The paper proceeds as follows. In section 2 the signature scheme is presented. The security of the scheme is evaluated in section 3, and section 4 examines the implementation of the scheme.

2 The Signature Scheme

2.1 Set-up

Each user, say user A, chooses a t_A-error correcting binary irreducible Goppa code C_A with length $n = 2^m$ and dimension k. The code is described by an irreducible polynomial $G_A(z)$ with degree t_A and coefficients in $GF(2^m)$. The user then selects a $k \times n$ binary generator matrix G_A and an $(n-k) \times n$ binary parity check matrix H_A for the code C_A. The generator matrix fixes the mapping between messages and code words in C_A. It should be noted that there is an extremely large number of generator and parity check matrices for a given (n,k) binary linear code. G_A can have as rows any set of k linearly independent code words from C_A placed in any order. There are thus $(2^k-1)(2^k-2)(2^k-4)\cdots(2^k-2^{k-1})$ possible generator matrices. A similar argument holds for the set of possible parity check matrices $\{H_A\}$, for the parity check matrix has as rows any basis set for the $(n-k)$ dimensional dual space of C_A arranged in any order. It follows that

$$G_A H_A^T = 0_{k\times(n-k)}, \tag{1}$$

where H_A^T is the transpose of H_A and $0_{k\times(n-k)}$ is the $k \times (n-k)$ all-zero matrix.

User A continues the set-up by finding two $k \times n$ binary matrices W_A and V_A such that

$$G_A = W_A \oplus V_A, \tag{2}$$

where the rank of W_A is k. There thus exists an $n \times k$ binary right-inverse W_A^{-R} such that

$$W_A W_A^{-R} = I_k, \tag{3}$$

where I_k is the $k \times k$ identity matrix. The matrix W_A is chosen such that $G_A W_A^{-R}$ has rank $k' \neq 0$, where $k' < k$ (the security considerations that impose this condition will be discussed in section 3. In section 4.1 a technique is presented for generating such W_A).

User A continues by generating a nonsingular $n \times n$ binary matrix P_A. The final step in setting up the signature scheme is the computation of the following matrices:

$$H'_A = P_A^{-1} H_A^T \tag{4}$$
$$W'_A = P_A^{-1} W_A^{-R} \tag{5}$$
$$W''_A = W_A^{-R} G_A W_A^{-R}. \tag{6}$$

User A publishes $G_A(z)$, W_A^{-R}, H'_A, W'_A, W''_A, t_A, and t'_A, where t'_A is an integer such that $t'_A < t_A$. This entire public key necessitates the storage of approximately $3n^2$ bits. The private key consists of the matrices V_A, W_A, G_A, $W_A^{-R} G_A$, and P_A.

It should be noted that the code C_A and the information necessary for error correction are made public, while the mapping between messages and code words is kept secret. The objective of the proposed scheme is to force the cryptanalyst to perform an exhaustive search of all possible mappings between messages and code words, which is equivalent to searching through all possible generator matrices for the code C_A.

As the final piece to the entire scheme, a system operator selects and publishes a function f that is used by all parties to the system. The function $f(\underline{x}, \underline{y})$ is a nonlinear noninvertible function such that $\underline{x} \in GF(2^k)$, $\underline{y} \in GF(2^n)$, and $f(\underline{x}, \underline{y}) \in GF(2^k)$. For example, $f(\underline{x}, \underline{y})$ can be implemented as the hashing of the concatenation of $\underline{x}$ and $\underline{y}$.

2.2 Signature Generation and Validation

A k-bit message $\underline{m}_j$ is signed by user A as follows. Two binary vectors are chosen at random: $\underline{e}_j$, an n-bit vector of weight t'_A, and $\underline{r}_j$, a k-bit vector of arbitrary (but nonzero) weight. The signature pair $(\underline{s}_j, \underline{x}_j)$ is then computed as follows:

$$\underline{x}_j = \{\underline{r}_j G_A \oplus f(\underline{m}_j, \underline{e}_j) V_A\} P_A \tag{7}$$
$$\underline{s}_j = \{\underline{e}_j \oplus f(\underline{m}_j, \underline{e}_j) W_A \oplus \underline{x}_j W_A^{-R} G_A\} P_A. \tag{8}$$

$\underline{x}_j$, $\underline{s}_j$, and $\underline{m}_j$ are transmitted. The destination user receives a possibly noise corrupted signature pair $(\underline{x}'_j, \underline{s}'_j)$ along with the possibly noisy message $\underline{m}'_j$. Signature validation is then performed in five steps.

1. The following expression is computed.

$$\begin{aligned} \underline{x}'_j \oplus \underline{s}'_j &= [\{\underline{r}_j G_A \oplus f(\underline{m}_j, \underline{e}_j) V_A \oplus \underline{e}_j \oplus f(\underline{m}_j, \underline{e}_j) W_A \oplus \underline{x}_j W_A^{-R} G_A\} P_A]' \\ &= [\{\underline{r}_j G_A \oplus f(\underline{m}_j, \underline{e}_j) G_A \oplus \underline{e}_j \oplus \underline{x}_j W_A^{-R} G_A\} P_A]' \end{aligned}$$

2. The syndrome of $\underline{x}'_j \oplus \underline{s}'_j$ is calculated.

$$\begin{aligned}(\underline{x}'_j \oplus \underline{s}'_j)H'_{\rm A} &= [\{\underline{r}_j G_{\rm A} \oplus f(\underline{m}_j, \underline{e}_j)G_{\rm A} \oplus \underline{e}_j \oplus \underline{x}_j W_{\rm A}^{-\rm R} G_{\rm A}\}P_{\rm A}]' P_{\rm A}^{-1} H_{\rm A}^{\rm T} \\ &= \underline{e}'_j H_{\rm A}^{\rm T}.\end{aligned}$$

3. The Berlekamp-Massey algorithm is applied to the above syndrome to obtain the error vector $\underline{e}'_j$. If $w_{\rm H}(\underline{e}'_j) \neq t'_{\rm A}$, then the receiver requests a retransmission of $\underline{x}_j$, $\underline{s}_j$, and $\underline{m}_j$. Otherwise the receiver continues the validation process under the assumption that $\underline{e}'_j = \underline{e}_j$, $\underline{x}'_j = \underline{x}_j$, and $\underline{s}'_j = \underline{s}_j$.

4. $f(\underline{m}_j, \underline{e}_j)$ is recovered from $\underline{x}_j$, $\underline{e}_j$, and $\underline{s}_j$ by computing the following expression.

$$\begin{aligned}\underline{s}_j W'_{\rm A} \oplus \underline{x}_j W''_{\rm A} \oplus \underline{e}_j W_{\rm A}^{-\rm R} &= \underline{s}_j P_{\rm A}^{-1} W_{\rm A}^{-\rm R} \oplus \underline{x}_j W_{\rm A}^{-\rm R} G_{\rm A} W_{\rm A}^{-\rm R} \oplus \underline{e}_j W_{\rm A}^{-\rm R} \\ &= \underline{e}_j W_{\rm A}^{-\rm R} \oplus f(\underline{m}_j, \underline{e}_j) \oplus \underline{x}_j W_{\rm A}^{-\rm R} G_{\rm A} W_{\rm A}^{-\rm R} \oplus \\ &\quad\ \underline{x}_j W_{\rm A}^{-\rm R} G_{\rm A} W_{\rm A}^{-\rm R} \oplus \underline{e}_j W_{\rm A}^{-\rm R} \\ &= f(\underline{m}_j, \underline{e}_j).\end{aligned}$$

5. Finally $f(\underline{m}_j, \underline{e}_j)$ is compared with $f(\underline{m}'_j, \underline{e}_j)$. If $f(\underline{m}_j, \underline{e}_j) = f(\underline{m}'_j, \underline{e}_j)$, then the signature pair is accepted.

2.3 Example

Consider the simple $(6, 3, 3)$ code $C_{\rm A}$, where

$$C_{\rm A} = \{000000, 100011, 010101, 001110, 110110, 101101, 011011, 111000\}.$$

The following are selected for the generator matrix $G_{\rm A}$ and the parity check matrix $H_{\rm A}$.

$$G_{\rm A} = \begin{bmatrix} 110110 \\ 101101 \\ 111000 \end{bmatrix} \quad H_{\rm A} = \begin{bmatrix} 011100 \\ 101010 \\ 110001 \end{bmatrix}$$

$W_{\rm A}$, $V_{\rm A}$, and $P_{\rm A}$ are selected as

$$W_{\rm A} = \begin{bmatrix} 101100 \\ 111101 \\ 111010 \end{bmatrix} \quad V_{\rm A} = \begin{bmatrix} 011010 \\ 010000 \\ 000010 \end{bmatrix} \quad P_{\rm A} = \begin{bmatrix} 100000 \\ 110000 \\ 000101 \\ 111101 \\ 100110 \\ 000001 \end{bmatrix}.$$

The following $W_{\rm A}^{-\rm R}$ and $P_{\rm A}^{-1}$ are then derived.

$$W_{\rm A}^{-\rm R} = \begin{bmatrix} 001 \\ 011 \\ 111 \\ 010 \\ 100 \\ 101 \end{bmatrix} \quad P_{\rm A}^{-1} = \begin{bmatrix} 100000 \\ 110000 \\ 011100 \\ 001001 \\ 101011 \\ 000001 \end{bmatrix}.$$

Finally H'_A, W'_A and W''_A are computed with the following result.

$$H'_A = \begin{bmatrix} 011 \\ 110 \\ 111 \\ 111 \\ 110 \\ 001 \end{bmatrix} \quad W'_A = \begin{bmatrix} 001 \\ 010 \\ 110 \\ 010 \\ 111 \\ 101 \end{bmatrix} \quad W''_A = \begin{bmatrix} 101 \\ 100 \\ 000 \\ 001 \\ 100 \\ 001 \end{bmatrix}$$

The message $\underline{m}_j = 001$ is signed as follows. $\underline{r}_j$ and $\underline{e}_j$ are chosen as 100 and 000001 respectively. Let $f(\underline{m}_j, \underline{e}_j) = 011$. Then eqns. 7 and 8 produce the signature pair $\underline{x}_j = 011101$ and $\underline{s}_j = 010111$. Each user validates the signature pair by using the public key. We shall assume here that the message and signature pair are received free of errors. Step 1 of the validation produces $\underline{x}_j \oplus \underline{s}_j = 001010$. Then the syndrome of $\underline{x}_j \oplus \underline{s}_j$ is computed to be 001, which indicates that the error vector $\underline{e}_j = 000001$. In the fourth step of the validation algorithm we find that $f(\underline{m}_j, \underline{e}_j) = f(\underline{m}'_j, \underline{e}_j) = 011$ and the signature pair is accepted.

3 Security of the scheme

In the following subsections several attacks, including those that have proven successful on the previous schemes, are used to characterize the security of the scheme proposed here.

3.1 Total Break

In any signature scheme based on block error-correcting codes, the public must have a valid parity check matrix (and thus know the code itself) in order to remove intentionally introduced error patterns during signature validation. The resistance of the signature scheme to a total break is thus solely dependent on the scheme's ability to hide the mapping from messages to code words (i.e., the generator matrix G_A). If G_A is known, then $W_A^{-R} G_A$ can be found (for W_A^{-R} is part of the public key). n signature pairs, each with the same $f(\underline{m}_j, \underline{e}_j)$, are then collected (this attack is similar to the one presented in [8]). Eqn. 8 is then used to form a system of n equations whose solution determines P_A. Once P_A is known, W_A and V_A can be obtained through a known-message attack.

In the proposed scheme, a total break appears to be infeasible, primarily because the public information does not completely describe G_A (the matrix $W''_A = W_A^{-R} G_A W_A^{-R}$ has rank $\leq k' < k$). The cryptanalyst is thus forced to perform an exhaustive search through all possible generator matrices for the code C_A.

3.2 Existential Forgery

3.2.1 Attack I

The cryptanalyst selects three n-bit vectors $\underline{x}_j$, $\underline{s}_j$, and $\underline{e}_j$ such that $(\underline{x}_j \oplus \underline{s}_j)H'_{\text{A}} = \underline{e}_j H^{\text{T}}_{\text{A}}$. This search has complexity $O(2^{n-k})$. The cryptanalyst then needs to find a k-bit $\underline{m}_j$ such that

$$f(\underline{m}_j, \underline{e}_j) = \underline{s}_j W'_{\text{A}} \oplus \underline{x}_j W''_{\text{A}} \oplus \underline{e}_j W^{-\text{R}}_{\text{A}}.$$

This requires an exhaustive search of $GF(2^k)$. The total complexity of this attack is thus

$$Comp(XF_I) = O(2^n). \tag{9}$$

3.2.2 Attack II

The cryptanalyst may try to combine valid signature pairs for two or more messages to produce a signature pair for another message. Let $(\underline{x}_1, \underline{s}_1), (\underline{x}_2, \underline{s}_2), \ldots, (\underline{x}_l, \underline{s}_l)$ be distinct valid signature pairs for the messages $\underline{m}_1, \underline{m}_2, \ldots, \underline{m}_l$ respectively, and let $\underline{e}_1, \underline{e}_2, \ldots, \underline{e}_l$ be the corresponding error vectors. Then $(\underline{x}', \underline{s}')$ is a valid signature pair for the message $\underline{m}'$ if $w_{\text{H}}(\underline{e}') = t'_{\text{A}}$, where $\underline{x}' = \underline{x}_1 \oplus \underline{x}_2 \oplus \cdots \oplus \underline{x}_l$, $\underline{s}' = \underline{s}_1 \oplus \underline{s}_2 \oplus \cdots \oplus \underline{s}_l$, and $\underline{e}' = \underline{e}_1 \oplus \underline{e}_2 \oplus \cdots \oplus \underline{e}_l$. The message $\underline{m}'$ is found by searching $GF(2^k)$ such that

$$f(\underline{m}', \underline{e}') = f(\underline{m}_1, \underline{e}_1) \oplus f(\underline{m}_2, \underline{e}_2) \oplus \cdots \oplus f(\underline{m}_l, \underline{e}_l).$$

The complexity of this attack is thus

$$Comp(XF_{II}) = O(2^k). \tag{10}$$

3.3 Universal Forgery

3.3.1 Attack I

Let X be a $k \times n$ binary matrix such that

$$XW'_{\text{A}} = I_k. \tag{11}$$

This matrix X can be found in polynomial time as follows. k linearlyindependent rows of W'_{A} are selected (this can be done by row reduction of the matrix W'_{A}, requiring $O(nk^2)$ bit operations). Let the k linearly independent rows be numbered as $l_1, l_2, \cdots, l_k$. The square submatrix formed by the k linearly independent rows is then inverted in $O(k^3)$ bit operations. The columns of the inverted matrix correspond to columns $l_1, l_2, \cdots, l_k$ of X and the other $n-k$ columns of X are filled with zeros.

$\underline{s}_j$ is obtained by computing

$$\underline{s}_j = [f(\underline{m}_j, \underline{e}_j) \oplus \underline{x}_j W''_{\text{A}} \oplus \underline{e}_j W^{-\text{R}}_{\text{A}}]X, \tag{12}$$

where $\underline{x}_j$ and $\underline{e}_j$ are chosen randomly with the constraint $w_{\text{H}}(\underline{e}_j) = t'_{\text{A}}$, and $\underline{m}_j$ is the message to be forged. The vectors $\underline{m}_j$, $\underline{x}_j$, $\underline{s}_j$, and $\underline{e}_j$ will be found acceptable in steps 4 and 5 of the validation procedure. Steps 1, 2, and 3, however, may not result in the syndrome corresponding to $\underline{e}_j$. There are 2^{n-k} distinct syndromes. It follows that the complexity of this attack is

$$Comp(UF_I) = O(2^{n-k}). \tag{13}$$

3.3.2 Attack II

In the validation procedure it is required that $\underline{x}_j$, $\underline{s}_j$, $\underline{e}_j$, and $f(\underline{m}_j, \underline{e}_j)$ satisfy the following equations:

$$\underline{s}_j H'_{\text{A}} \oplus \underline{x}_j H'_{\text{A}} = \underline{e}_j H^{\text{T}}_{\text{A}} \tag{14}$$
$$\underline{s}_j W'_{\text{A}} \oplus \underline{x}_j W''_{\text{A}} \oplus \underline{e}_j W^{-\text{R}}_{\text{A}} = f(\underline{m}_j, \underline{e}_j). \tag{15}$$

We can solve for $\underline{x}_j$, $\underline{e}_j$, or $\underline{s}_j$ given the other two, thus obtaining the following three expressions.

$$\underline{x}_j[H'_{\text{A}} \mid W''_{\text{A}}] = [\underline{s}_j H'_{\text{A}} \oplus \underline{e}_j H^{\text{T}}_{\text{A}} \mid \underline{s}_j W'_{\text{A}} \oplus \underline{e}_j W^{-\text{R}}_{\text{A}} \oplus f(\underline{m}_j, \underline{e}_j)] = \underline{x}_j Y_1. \tag{16}$$
$$\underline{e}_j[H^{\text{T}}_{\text{A}} \mid W^{-\text{R}}_{\text{A}}] = [\underline{s}_j H'_{\text{A}} \oplus \underline{x}_j H'_{\text{A}} \mid \underline{s}_j W'_{\text{A}} \oplus \underline{x}_j W''_{\text{A}} \oplus f(\underline{m}_j, \underline{e}_j)] = \underline{e}_j Y_2. \tag{17}$$
$$\underline{s}_j[H'_{\text{A}} \mid W'_{\text{A}}] = [\underline{x}_j H'_{\text{A}} \oplus \underline{e}_j H^{\text{T}}_{\text{A}} \mid \underline{x}_j W''_{\text{A}} \oplus \underline{e}_j W^{-\text{R}}_{\text{A}} \oplus f(\underline{m}_j, \underline{e}_j)] = \underline{s}_j Y_3. \tag{18}$$

where Y_1, Y_2, and Y_3 are $n \times n$ matrices such that

$$Y_1 = [H'_{\text{A}} \mid W''_{\text{A}}] \quad Y_2 = [H^{\text{T}}_{\text{A}} \mid W^{-\text{R}}_{\text{A}}] \quad Y_3 = [H'_{\text{A}} \mid W'_{\text{A}}]. \tag{19}$$

If one or more of these three matrices are full rank, then their inverses can be found and signatures are forged in polynomial time. The following lemmas show that this is not a problem.

Lemma 1 *The rank of Y_1 is ρ_1, where $n - k \leq \rho_1 < n$.*

Proof: $\rho_1 \geq n - k$ since H'_{A} has rank $n - k$. W''_{A} has rank $k' < k$ and $n - k + k' < n$, so $\rho_1 < n$. ∎

Lemma 2 *The rank of Y_2 is ρ_2, where $n - k \leq \rho_2 < n$.*

Proof: $\rho_2 \geq n - k$ since H^{T}_{A} has rank $n - k$. For the upper bound, let's assume that the rank of Y_2 is n. It follows that $Y_2 \underline{w} = 0_{n\times 1}$ (the n-bit all-zero column vector) iff $\underline{w} = 0_{n\times 1}$. Partition $\underline{w}$ into two column vectors, an $(n-k)$-bit vector $\underline{w}_1$ and a k-bit vector $\underline{w}_2$. Thus $Y_2 \underline{w} = H^{\text{T}}_{\text{A}} \underline{w}_1 \oplus W^{-\text{R}}_{\text{A}} \underline{w}_2 = 0_{n\times 1}$ iff $\underline{w}_1 = 0_{(n-k)\times 1}$ and $\underline{w}_2 = 0_{k\times 1}$. Premultiplying by G_{A}, we obtain $G_{\text{A}} Y_2 \underline{w} = G_{\text{A}} H^{\text{T}}_{\text{A}} \underline{w}_1 \oplus G_{\text{A}} W^{-\text{R}}_{\text{A}} \underline{w}_2$. Since G_{A} has rank k, $G_{\text{A}} Y_2$ must have an $(n-k)$-dimensional null space. Eqn. 1 shows that $G_{\text{A}} H^{\text{T}}_{\text{A}} \underline{w}_1 = 0_{k\times 1}$ for all $(n-k)$-bit vectors $\underline{w}_1$. Since all possible $\underline{w}_1$ span an $(n-k)$ dimensional space, the null space of $G_{\text{A}} Y_2$ must consist of all vectors of the form

$$\underline{w} \in \left\{ \begin{bmatrix} \underline{w}_1 \\ 0_{k\times 1} \end{bmatrix} \mid \underline{w}_1^{\text{T}} \in GF(2^{(n-k)}) \right\}. \tag{20}$$

It follows that $G_{\text{A}} W^{-\text{R}}_{\text{A}} \underline{w}_2 = 0_{k\times 1}$ if and only if $\underline{w}_2 = 0_{k\times 1}$ (otherwise the dimension of the null space of $G_{\text{A}} Y_2$ would exceed $(n-k)$). But in Section 2.1 we noted that the matrix W_{A} is chosen such that $G_{\text{A}} W^{-\text{R}}_{\text{A}}$ has rank k', where $k' < k$. The rank of Y_2 is thus less than n. ∎

Lemma 3 *The rank of Y_3 is the same as that of Y_2.*

Proof: Since $Y_3 = [H'_A \mid W'_A] = P_A^{-1} Y_2$ and P_A is a nonsingular $n \times n$ matrix, the result follows. ∎

To use equations 16, 17, and 18, the cryptanalyst must thus search $GF(2^n)$, making the complexity of this attack $Comp(UF_{II}) = O(2^{min(\rho_1, \rho_2)})$, with a lower bound on the complexity set at

$$Comp(UF_{II}) = O(2^{n-k}). \tag{21}$$

This shows the difficulty of this attack even if $\underline{s}_j$ or $\underline{r}_j$ are coming from a valid signature pair (i.e., it is difficult even obtaining another signature pair for a message using a valid signature pair of that message).

Furthermore, if the cryptanalyst wants to solve for $\underline{s}_j$ and $\underline{r}_j$ simultaneously using eqns. 14 and 15, he/she is faced with a system of n equations with $2n$ unknowns. It can be shown that the complexity of the solving this system is $O(2^{\rho_1 + \rho_2})$.

3.3.3 Attack III

We begin by observing that

$$\begin{aligned} \underline{x}_j &= \{\underline{r}_j G_A \oplus f(\underline{m}_j, \underline{e}_j) V_A\} P_A \\ &= \underline{r}'_j \oplus f(\underline{m}_j, \underline{e}_j) E'_A, \end{aligned} \tag{22}$$

where $\underline{r}'_j = \underline{r}_j G_A P_A$ and $E'_A = V_A P_A$. The known-message attack devised in [11] is not useful here because we do not have $\underline{r}'_j$. Furthermore, the chosen-message attack devised in [13, 14] requires a search of the domain of $f(\underline{m}_j, \underline{e}_j)$, making the complexity of the attack $O(2^k N_e)$, where $N_e = \begin{pmatrix} n \\ t'_A \end{pmatrix}$. Similarly

$$\begin{aligned} \underline{s}_j &= \{\underline{e}_j \oplus f(\underline{m}_j, \underline{e}_j) W_A \oplus \underline{x}_j W_A^{-R} G_A\} P_A \\ &= \underline{r}''_j \oplus f(\underline{m}_j, \underline{e}_j) E''_A, \end{aligned} \tag{23}$$

where $\underline{r}''_j = \{\underline{e}_j \oplus \underline{x}_j W_A^{-R} G_A\} P_A$ and $E''_A = W_A^{-R} G_A P_A$. Since $\underline{e}_j$ and $\underline{x}_j$ are known, the known-message attack devised in [11] can be attempted here. However, the number of messages required for this attack is $O(\sqrt{N})$, where N is the number of possible patterns for $\underline{r}''_j$. For the scheme proposed in this paper, $N = O(2^{k'} N_e)$.

4 Performance of the Scheme

4.1 Key Generation

The keys of the scheme can be easily generated assuming that a fast algorithm for generating nonsingular binary matrices is available. The matrix W_A should be generated such that its rank is k and the rank of $G_A W_A^{-R}$ is $k' < k$. The following algorithm generates the matrices W_A and W_A^{-R}.

Algorithm 1 *Generating W_A and W_A^{-R}. G_A is selected such that there is a row r_{min} with Hamming weight $w_{min} \leq n - k$. Let S_0 be the set of coordinates where r_{min} has value 0 and let S_1 be the set of coordinates corresponding to nonzero values.*

1. *An arbitrary $k \times k$ binary nonsingular matrix A is selected.*

2. *k coordinates of S_0 are selected. The $k \times n$ matrix $\tilde{W}_A$ is constructed by placing the columns of the matrix A in the positions corresponding to the selected coordinates of S_0. The rest of the matrix is filled with random values.*

3. *The $n \times k$ matrix $\tilde{W}_A^{-R}$ is constructed by placing the rows of A^{-1} in the rows corresponding to the k coordinates chosen in the previous step. The rest of the matrix is filled with zeros.*

4. *An $n \times n$ binary nonsingular matrix $\tilde{A}$ that hides the all-zero rows of $\tilde{W}_A^{-R}$ is then constructed by modifying the $n \times n$ identity matrix as follows.*

   (a) *The rows corresponding to the k coordinates chosen in step 2 are left unchanged.*

   (b) *Each row corresponding to one of the k coordinates in S_0 that were not selected in Step 2 is modified by changing (complementing) a random number (at least one) of the zeros in the positions corresponding to the k previously selected coordinates.*

   (c) *The rows corresponding to the coordinates in S_1 are modified as follows. $\omega_{min} - 1$ of the rows are randomly selected and each row is modified as described above. The modified bits for the $\omega_{min}-1$ rows form a $(\omega_{min}-1)\times k$ binary submatrix. The rows of this submatrix are added (bitwise addition), and the row in S_1 that was not selected before is modified according to the result of the addition of the submatrix.*

5. *The matrices W_A and W_A^{-R} are obtained through the computations $W_A = \tilde{W}_A \tilde{A}^{-1}$ and $W_A^{-R} = \tilde{A}\tilde{W}_A^{-R}$ respectively.*

This algorithm is guaranteed to work as long as there is a nonzero code word with Hamming weight $\leq n - k$ in the code. Any code that fails to satisfy this condition is by definition maximum distance separable (MDS) (e.g., the Reed-Solomon codes). Since the only known binary MDS codes have length 4 or less, the utility of the algorithm in constructing the signature scheme presented in this paper is virtually assured.

4.2 Signing and Validation

Eqn's. 7 and 8 show that the complexity of the signature generation procedure is $O(n^2)$ bit operations. It is assumed that a fast implementaion for the function f is available. The complexity of the validation procedure is $O(nk)$ bit operations.

4.3 Code Parameters

It is clear from eqn's. 9, 10, 13, and 21 that k and $n-k$ should be large to make the scheme secure. For example, for k, $n-k$ greater than 56, a 9-error-correcting binary Goppa code constructed over $GF(2^7)$ can be used, where $n = 2^7 = 128$ bits, $t_A = 9$ errors, and $k = 65$ bits (we are assuming equality in the Goppa code design equation $k \geq n - mt_A$). t'_A can be chosen to be 4 errors. The public key in this example requires about 48k bits. For k, $n-k$ greater than 100, a 13-error-correcting binary Goppa code constructed over $GF(2^8)$ can be used, where $n = 256$ bits and $k = 152$ bits. t'_A can once again be chosen to be 4 errors. The public key in this example requires about 140k bits.

5 Conclusion

A true trapdoor digital signature scheme has been presented. The proposed scheme is based on linear block error-correcting codes, and is thus capable of data transmission at high rates. It appears that the complexity of signature forgery is $O(2^{min(k,n-k)})$, where n and k are the length and dimension, respectively, of the code in use.

References

[1] W. Diffie and M. E. Hellman. New direction in cryptography. *IEEE Transactions on Information theory*, 22(11):644-654, November 1976.

[2] R. J. McEliece. Public-key cryptosystem based on algebraic coding theory. JPL DSN Progress Report 42-44, Jet Propulsion Laboratory, California Institute of Technology, Pasadena, CA, USA, January & February 1987, pages 114-116.

[3] E. R. Berlekamp, R.J. McEliece, and H. van Tilborg. On the inherent intractibility of certain coding problem. *IEEE Transactions on Information theory*, IT-24(3):384-386, May 1978.

[4] W. Xinmei. Digital signature scheme based on error-correcting codes. *Electronics Letters*, 26(13):898-899, 21st June 1990.

[5] T. R. N. Rao and K. Nam. Private-key algebraic-code encryption. *IEEE Transactions on Information theory*, 35(4):829-833, July 1989.

[6] L. Harn and D. -C. Wang. Cryptanalysis and modification of digital signature scheme based on error-correcting codes. *Electronics Letters*, 28(2):157-159, 16th January 1992.

[7] M. Alabbadi and S. B. Wicker. Security of Xinmei's digital signature scheme. *Electronics Letters*, 28(9):890-891, 23rd April 1992.

[8] M. Alabbadi and S. B. Wicker. Cryptanalysis of the Harn and Wang modification of the Xinmei digital signature scheme. *Electronics Letters*, 28(18):1756-1758, 27th August 1992.

[9] J. van Tilburg. Cryptanalysis of Xinmei digital signature scheme. *Electronics Letters*, 28(20):1935-1936, 24th September 1992.

[10] M. Alabbadi and S. B. Wicker. Digital signature schemes based on error-correcting codes. In *IEEE International Symposium on Information Theory*, page 199, San Antonio, Texas, USA, January 17-22 1993.

[11] M. Alabbadi and S. B. Wicker. Susceptiblity of digital signature schemes based on error-correcting codes to universal forgery. In *The Workshop on Information Protection*, Moscow, December 6-9 1993.

[12] J. van Tilburg. Cryptanalysis of the Alabbadi-Wicker digital signature scheme. In *Proceedings of the Fourteenth Symposium on Information Theory in the Benelux*, pages 114-119, Veldhoven, Netherlands, May 17-18 1993.

[13] R. Struik and J. van Tilburg. The Rao-Nam scheme is insecure against a chosen plaintext attack. In C. Pomeranc, editor, *Advances in Crypology-Crypto'87 Proceedings*, pages 445-457, Santa Barbara, CA, USA, August 16-20 1987, Springer-Verlag. (Lecture Notes in Computer Science # 239).

[14] J. Meijers and J. van Tilburg. On the Rao-Nam private-key cryptosystem using linear codes. In *IEEE International Symposium on Information Theory*, page 126, Budapest, Hungar, June 24-28 1991.

Secure acceleration of DSS signatures using insecure server

Philippe Béguin[*]

Philippe.Beguin@ens.fr
Laboratoire d'informatique [**]
Ecole Normale Supérieure
45, rue d'Ulm
F–75 230 Paris Cedex 05
FRANCE

Jean-Jacques Quisquater

Quisquater@dice.ucl.ac.be
Laboratoire DICE
Université Catholique de Louvain
Place du Levant, 3
B–1 348 Louvain-la-Neuve
BELGIUM

Abstract. Small units like chip cards (*smart card*) have the possibility of computing, storing and protecting data. Today such chip cards have limited computing power and some cryptoprotocols are too slow. Some new chip cards with secure coprocessors are coming but are not very reliable at the moment and a little bit expensive.

A possible alternative solution is to use an auxiliary unit in order to help the chip card. The known protocols are not very secure or are not efficient.

We show how to accelerate the computation of $a \times b \bmod c$ and of $a^t \bmod c$ where a, b, c, t are public. Next we show how to accelerate the discrete exponential modulo a prime number: this protocol is useful to accelerate DSS signatures and other schemes. This protocol is also the first one accelerating DSS signatures with the help of an insecure server: it is secure against both passive and active attacks (that is, when the server sends false values to get some information from the card). Moreover, this protocol is the first secure such a protocol which does not use precomputations in the card.

We describe a feasible version of these protocols, where the used RAM is small: with current chip cards it is thus possible to implement effectively such protocols.

1 Introduction

Small units like chip cards (another name is *smart card*) have the possibility of computing, storing and protecting data. Today such chip cards have limited computing power and some protocols are not executed in an efficient way (for instance, some protocols with public key cryptosystems). Some new chip cards with fast and secure coprocessors are coming but are not very reliable at the

[*] Part of this work was done while the author was visiting the Laboratoire de Microélectronique, Université Catholique de Louvain, Belgium.

[**] Supported by the Centre National de la Recherche Scientifique URA 1327.

moment (due to problems of auxiliary memory): another weak point is the associated cost.

A possible alternative solution is to use an auxiliary unit (a banking terminal, a card reader, ...) in order to help the chip card. In this paper we shall use the words *card* for the main unit and *server* for the auxiliary unit.

If the server is secure it is possible to imagine a secure link between the card and the server: the card sends the secret values to be used to the server; the server computes the result and sends it using again the secure link. The interesting (real life) case is working with an insecure server. This server may be under the influence of an opponent trying to obtain the secrets of the card or to cheat with a false result. The conclusion of this short analysis is that the card must protect its secrets and verify the computations received from the server.

Such protocols were first studied by Matsumoto, Kato and Imai [6] and Quisquater and De Soete [9]. Next Pfitzmann and Waidner [8] and Anderson [1] have shown that these protocols are not very secure. Then Yen and Laih [12], Matsumoto, Imai, Laih and Yen [5] and Kawamura and Shimbo [4] propose protocols using expensive precomputation and then not very efficient.

In this paper, we show how to accelerate the computation of $a \times b \bmod c$ and of $a^t \bmod c$ where a, b, c, t are public. Next we show how to accelerate the discrete exponential modulo a prime number: this protocol is useful to accelerate DSS signatures [7] and signature schemes based on the Schnorr's scheme [11]. We describe feasible version of these protocols, where the card does not need precomputations and where the used RAM is small: with current chip cards it is thus possible to implement effectively such protocols.

This protocol is secure against passive and active attacks: when the server sends false values to get some information from the card. Thus we can use this protocol with current chip cards to accelerate the DSS signatures without decreasing the security of this signature.

In this paper we denote multiplication $M \times N$ (*resp.* modulo $M \times N$) a multiplication of an M bits number by an N bits number (*resp.* a modulo of an M bits number by an N bits number). We call modular multiplication, a multiplication of two 512 bits numbers modulo a 512 bits number. We denote by $|a|$ the number of bits of a (i.e. $|a| = \lfloor \log_2 a \rfloor + 1$).

We count the number of computations done by the card in number of modular multiplications. Here we consider that the computation of $a \times b$ is about the equivalent of $\frac{1}{2} \times \frac{|a|}{512} \times \frac{|b|}{512}$ modular multiplications and $a \bmod b$ is about the equivalent of $\frac{\theta}{2} \times \frac{|a|}{1024} \times \frac{|b|}{512}$ modular multiplications. By θ we denote a constant near 1 varying with the implementations of the operation modulo. Here we use the practical value 1.25 for θ. In the context of the card we consider as equivalent the modular square and the modular multiplication.

2 Computation of $a \times b \bmod c$

Let a, b, c be non negative integers such that $a < c$ and $b < c$. The card gives a, b, c to the server. The goal is to obtain the result of $a \times b \bmod c$ and a proof that this result is correct with a high probability: here we hope that the probability for the card of accepting a false value is less than $\frac{1}{2^{20}}$ or $\frac{1}{2^{64}}$. The designer will choose the level of security depending on the context.

The protocol is the following one:

1. The card chooses k secret prime numbers $p_1, \ldots, p_k$ such that for all i, $|p_i| = N_v$.
2. The card sends to the server a, b, c.
3. The server computes and sends to the card
   $\alpha = \lfloor (a \times b)/c \rfloor$,
   $r = (a \times b) \bmod c$.
4. The card verifies:
   $\alpha < c$,
   $r < c$,
   for each number p_i: $(a \times b) \bmod p_i = (\alpha \times c + r) \bmod p_i$.
5. If during this former step the verification is correct, then the card accepts the result: $a \times b \bmod c := r$.

In order to minimize the computations during the verification $(a \bmod p_i) \times (b \bmod p_i) \bmod p_i = (\alpha \bmod p_i) \times (c \bmod p_i) + (r \bmod p_i) \bmod p_i$, the card computes:

1. $\alpha_i = \alpha \bmod p_i$,
2. $c_i = c \bmod p_i$,
3. $e_i = \alpha_i \times c_i$,
4. $a_i = a \bmod p_i$,
5. $b_i = b \bmod p_i$,
6. $d_i = a_i \times b_i$,
7. $f_i = (r + e_i - d_i) \bmod p_i$.

Next the card verifies $f_i = 0$. That is, for each number p_i, the card needs 5 modulo $512 \times N$ (steps 1, 2, 4, 5, 7) and 2 multiplications $N_v \times N_v$ (steps 3 and 6); thus, the card needs the equivalent of $5 \cdot \frac{\theta}{2} \frac{512}{1024} \frac{N_v}{512} + 2 \cdot \frac{1}{2} \frac{N_v}{512} \frac{N_v}{512}$ modular multiplications.

Now we study the possibility for the server of cheating, that is, the card accepts a false value r^* instead of r.

Theorem 2.1 *Let a, b, c be non negative integers such that $|a|, |b|, |c| \leq N$ and $a, b < c$. If the card chooses secretly k random prime numbers of length N_v, then the probability ϱ that the card accepts a false value satisfies*

$$\varrho \leq \frac{\binom{\lfloor \frac{2N}{N_v - 1} \rfloor}{k}}{\binom{M}{k}},$$

where M is the number of prime numbers of length N_v.

Proof. Let α, r such that

$$a \times b = \alpha \times c + r \qquad \text{where} \quad r < c. \tag{1}$$

Then α, r are uniquely determined and $\alpha < c$.
Suppose the card receives α^*, r^* such that $\alpha^* < c, r^* < c$ and $r^* \neq r$. By the unicity of (1),

$$a \times b \neq \alpha^* \times c + r^* \tag{2}$$

Let $p_1, \ldots, p_M$ the prime numbers of length N_v.
Let $I(\alpha^*, r^*) = \{i : (a \times b) \bmod p_i = (\alpha^* \times c + r^*) \bmod p_i\}$.
By the Chinese Remainder Theorem,

$$(a \times b) \bmod P = (\alpha^* \times c + r^*) \bmod P, \tag{3}$$

where $P = \prod_{i \in I} p_i$.
Since $|p_i| = N_v$, then $p_i \geq 2^{N_v - 1}$, hence $P \geq 2^{l(N_v-1)}$ where $l = |I|$.
Since $|a|, |b|, |c| \leq N$ and $r^*, \alpha^* < c$, then $(a \times b) < 2^{2N}$ and $\alpha^* \times c + r^* < (2^N - 1) * 2^N + 2^N = 2^{2N}$.
If $2^{l(N_v-1)} \geq 2^{2N}$ then $P > (a \times b)$ and $P > \alpha^* \times c + r^*$. By (3), we have $a \times b = \alpha^* \times c + r^*$, which contradicts (2).
Hence $2^{l(N_v-1)} < 2^{2N}$ then $l \leq \lfloor \frac{2N}{N_v - 1} \rfloor$.
The card chooses randomly k prime numbers $\{p_j\}_{j \in J}$ where $|J| = k$. The card accepts r^* if and only if $J \subset I$. Then the probability ϱ that the card accepts r^* satisfies

$$\varrho \leq \frac{\binom{|I|}{|J|}}{\binom{M}{|J|}} \leq \frac{\binom{\lfloor \frac{2N}{N_v-1} \rfloor}{k}}{\binom{M}{k}}.$$

□

To minimize the number of multiplications done by the card, we use

case a. one prime number of length 32 bits to obtain a probability of cheating $\leq 1/2^{20}$,
case b. one prime number of length 75 bits to obtain a probability of cheating $\leq 1/2^{64}$.

Hence, to obtain with the help of the server the result of $a \times b \bmod c$ where a, b, c are 512 bits numbers and $a, b < c$, with a probability $> 1 - \dfrac{1}{2^{20}}$ in the case a, and $> 1 - \dfrac{1}{2^{64}}$ in the case b the card

- computes the equivalent of around $\frac{1}{9.8}$ modular multiplication in the case a, and $\frac{1}{4}$ in the case b,
- exchanges 320 bytes with the server,
- needs 272 bytes of RAM in the case a, and 294 bytes in the case b,
- generates a random prime number with a size of 32 bits in the case a, and with a size of 75 bits in the case b.

Remark. If one wants to compute a modular multiplication and obtain a proof that the return value is correct with a probability $> 1 - \varrho$, one must change the prime number p used in the verification before each computation. Otherwise, the server could compute α^*, r^* satisfying $(a \times b) \bmod p_j = (\alpha^* \times c + r^*) \bmod p_j$ for a certain amount l_s of chosen p_j. Hence, if the card detects the error, for future computations, the server knows that the prime number chosen by the card does not belong to the chosen l_s. Then for the calculation of the probability, we must replace M by $M - l_s$ and so after some such rounds, the probability of cheating becomes $> \varrho$.

If the card uses a prime number of 75 bits then $|I| \leq 13$. Hence the server could not choose more than 13 prime numbers. Then after n verifications M could be replaced by $M - 13n$. Then if the number of verifications done by the card is less than 10^{18} the probability of cheating remains less than $\frac{1}{2^{64}}$. In this case the card could use a secret and unique prime number of 75 bits stored at the initialization.

If the card uses a prime number of 32 bits, the probability decreases much faster and the card must generate a new prime number before each computation. This can be done very efficiently using techniques developed by Couvreur and Quisquater [3].

3 Computation of $a^t \bmod c$

By repeated applications of the former protocol, the card is able to compute $a^t \bmod c$ in an efficient way. We suppose $a < c$.

We denote:

- $t = t_0 + t_1 2 + \cdots + t_k 2^k = 2^{i_1} + \cdots + 2^{i_\nu}$.
- VER$[a, b, \alpha, r, p_v]$ the verification: $(a \times b) \bmod p_v = (\alpha \times c + r) \bmod p_v$.

The protocol is the following one:

1. The card uses the randomly selected prime number p_v with $|p_v| = N_v$, computes and stores $c_p = c \bmod p_v$.
2. The card sends to the server a, t, c.
3. The server computes and sends to the card
   - $A = [\alpha_1, \ldots, \alpha_k]$, $R = [r_1, \ldots, r_k]$
   - $B = [\beta_2, \ldots, \beta_\nu]$, $S = [s_2, \ldots, s_\nu]$

   such that
   - for each $i \geq 1$
     $\alpha_i = \lfloor (r_{i-1} \times r_{i-1})/c \rfloor$,
     $r_i = (r_{i-1} \times r_{i-1}) \bmod c$,

     with $r_0 = a$,
   - for each $j \geq 2$
     $\beta_j = \lfloor (r_{i_j} \times s_{j-1})/c \rfloor$,
     $s_j = (r_{i_j} \times s_{j-1}) \bmod c$,

     with $s_1 = r_{i_1}$.

4. The card verifies $\forall i \geq 1 \quad \mathrm{VER}[r_{i-1}, r_{i-1}, \alpha_i, r_i, p_v]$,
$\forall j \geq 2 \quad \mathrm{VER}[r_{i_j}, s_{j-1}, \beta_j, s_j, p_v]$.
5. If there is no error during this last step, the card accepts: $a^t \bmod c := s_\nu$.

Theorem 3.1 *If a, c are non negative integers of length at most 512 bits such that $a < c$, then the probability of accepting a false value $a^t \bmod c$ is less than $1/2^{20}$ in the case a ($N_v = 32$) and less than $1/2^{64}$ in the case b ($N_v = 75$).*

Proof. Suppose $s_\nu \neq a^t \bmod c$. Hence, in the verification 4, there is at least one error. Then, according to theorem 2.1, the card detects this error with probability $> 1 - \frac{1}{2^{20}}$ in the case a, and $> 1 - \frac{1}{2^{64}}$ in the case b.

□

Let us suppose that a and c have a size of 512 bits. During the step 4, the card computes:

- $r_{0,p} = a \bmod p_v$
  for each $i \geq 1$, $d_{i,p} = r_{i-1,p} \times r_{i-1,p}$,
  $\alpha_{i,p} = \alpha_i \bmod p_v$,
  $e_{i,p} = \alpha_{i,p} \times c_p$,
  $r_{i,p} = r_i \bmod p_v$,
  $f_{i,p} = (r_{i,p} + e_{i,p} - d_{i,p}) \bmod p_v$,
  the card verifies $f_{i,p} = 0$,
- $s_{1,p} = r_{i_1} \bmod p_v$
  for each $j \geq 2$, $g_{j,p} = r_{i_j,p} \times s_{j-1,p}$,
  $\beta_{j,p} = \beta_j \bmod p_v$,
  $h_{j,p} = \beta_{j,p} \times c_p$,
  $s_{j,p} = s_j \bmod p_v$,
  $k_{j,p} = (s_{j,p} + h_{j,p} - g_{j,p}) \bmod p_v$,
  the card verifies $k_{j,p} = 0$.

The number of operations done by the card is the following one:

- 2 modulo $512 \times N_v$ (computations of c_p, $r_{0,p}$),
- for each $i \in \{1, \ldots, k\}$:
  - 2 modulo $512 \times N_v$ (computations of $\alpha_{i,p}$, $r_{i,p}$),
  - 2 multiplications $N_v \times N_v$ (computations of $d_{i,p}$, $e_{i,p}$),
  - 1 modulo $2N_v \times N_v$ (computation of $f_{i,p}$),
- for each $j \in \{2, \ldots, \nu\}$:
  - 2 modulo $512 \times N_v$ (computations of $\beta_{j,p}$, $s_{j,p}$),
  - 2 multiplications $N_v \times N_v$ (computations of $g_{j,p}$, $h_{j,p}$),
  - 1 modulo $2N_v \times N_v$ (computation of $k_{j,p}$).

Then the card needs the equivalent of around

$$(2k + 2\nu)\frac{\theta}{2}\frac{512}{1024}\frac{N_v}{512} + (2k + 2\nu - 2)\frac{1}{2}\frac{N_v}{512}\frac{N_v}{512} + (k + \nu - 1)\frac{\theta}{2}\frac{2N_v}{1024}\frac{N_v}{512} \qquad (4)$$

modular multiplications, that is, $\simeq \frac{k+\nu}{22}$ in the case a, and $\simeq \frac{k+\nu}{8}$ in the case b.

For the verification of vectors A, R, the card only needs memory for $r_{i-1,p}$, $\alpha_{i,p}$, $e_{i,p}$, $d_{i,p}$. Indeed $r_{i,p}$ uses the location for $r_{i-1,p}$, and $f_{i,p}$ is put instead of $\alpha_{i,p}$. The card stores $[r_{i_1,p}, \ldots, r_{i_\nu,p}]$; similarly for the verification of vectors B, S the card needs some RAM only for $s_{j-1,p}, \beta_{j,p}, h_{j,p}, g_{j,p}$ stored at the location of $r_{i-1,p}$, $\alpha_{i,p}$, $e_{i,p}$, $d_{i,p}$.

The card stores $a, c, t, p_v, c_p, A, R, B, S, r_{i-1,p}, \alpha_{i,p}, e_{i,p}, d_{i,p}, r_{i_1,p}, \ldots, r_{i_\nu,p}$; so it needs $(2k+2\nu) \times 64 + (8+\nu) \times \lceil \frac{N_v}{8} \rceil + \lceil \frac{k+1}{8} \rceil$ bytes of memory. It is possible to modify the protocol if the card has not enough memory. In this case, the server does not send the vectors A, R, B, S, but sends α_1, r_1, and after the verification of the two values by the card, the server sends α_2, r_2, aso. For this version of the protocol the card needs $4 \times 64 + (8+\nu) \times \lceil \frac{N_v}{8} \rceil + \lceil \frac{k+1}{8} \rceil$ bytes of memory.

Moreover there are $2(k+\nu) \times 64 + \lceil \frac{k+1}{8} \rceil$ exchanged bytes between the card and the server.

Thanks to the server, to obtain $a^t \bmod c$ where a, c are 512 bits numbers, with a probability $> 1 - \dfrac{1}{2^{20}}$ in the case a, and $> 1 - \dfrac{1}{2^{64}}$ in the case b, the card

- computes the equivalent of $\frac{k+\nu}{22}$ modular multiplications in the case a, and $\frac{k+\nu}{8}$ in the case b,
- exchanges $2(k+\nu) \times 64 + \lceil \frac{k+1}{8} \rceil$ bytes with the server,
- needs $256 + (8+\nu) \times \lceil \frac{N_v}{8} \rceil + \lceil \frac{k+1}{8} \rceil$ bytes of RAM,
- generates a random prime number with a size of 32 bits in the case a, and uses the secret prime number of 75 bits stored at the initialization in the case b.

These two protocols $a \times b \bmod c$ and $a^t \bmod c$ are very efficient to obtain the result with the corresponding proof of correctness; but all computations are public and are not convenient to produce a RSA signature or a signature using the discrete exponential. On the contrary, these protocols are very adequate to obtain fast verifications for RSA, DSS aso.

4 The discrete exponential

In this section, we show how the card can compute, thanks to a server, $a^x \bmod p$ with a a public and fixed integer, p a public and fixed prime number, and x secretly chosen by the card. Suppose that a, p are with a size of 512 bits such that $a < p$. Applications for this protocol are very important: signature of Schnorr [11], DSS signatures [7], aso. We use our previous protocol and the protocol of Brickell, Gordon, Mc Curley and Wilson [2].

The protocol BGCW

The goal of this protocol is to compute a^x for all $x \leq N$ using some precomputations.

If $x = \sum_{i=0}^{m-1} x_i b_i$ with $0 \leq x_i \leq h$, and if a^{b_i} is known for each i, then the algorithm for computing a^x is the following one:

$$
\begin{aligned}
& B \leftarrow \textstyle\prod_{x_i=h} a^{b_i} \\
& A \leftarrow B \\
& \text{for } d = h-1 \text{ to } 1 \text{ by } -1 \\
& \qquad B \leftarrow B \times \textstyle\prod_{x_i=d} a^{b_i} \\
& \qquad A \leftarrow A \times B \\
& \text{return(A)}
\end{aligned}
$$

In our protocol, multiplications are modular multiplications, the $a_i = a^{b_i}$ are computed by the server, and A is computed by the card. To avoid the observation of the used time for a computation by an opponent which could give some information about x, it is necessary that the card uses a constant time for each computation: a solution is an algorithm with a constant number of multiplications, using, if necessary, the simulation (same time, no operation) of some multiplications.

During the computations, the card does it using one of the two methods:

case 1. The card stores $a^{b_0}, \ldots, a^{b_{m-1}}$, next computes A. Let $k_d = \#\{x_i : x_i = d\}$; the number of multiplications done by the card during the algorithm is $(k_h - 1) + \sum_{d=1}^{h-1}(k_d + 1) = h - 2 + \sum_{d=1}^{h} k_d \leq h - 2 + m$. Some simulation of multiplications is needed; thus the card computes exactly the equivalent of $h - 2 + m$ multiplications.

case 2. Let $c_d = \prod_{x_i=d} a^{b_i}$. The card computes $c_1, \ldots, c_h$ while receiving the a^{b_i}'s. First $c_i = 1$ for each i, thus after receiving the first value there is no multiplication to do. But after this first step, in order to avoid to give any information to the server (or any opponent), if the received number has to be multiplied by 1, the card needs to simulate a complete multiplication. Thus the card needs exactly the equivalent of $m - 1$ multiplications to obtain $c_1, \ldots, c_h$. Next the card needs $2(h-1)$ multiplications to obtain A. The computations done by the card are exactly the equivalent of $2h - 3 + m$ multiplications.

Using $b_i = b^i$, we have $m = \lceil \log_b N \rceil$ and $h = b - 1$. The card computes a^x using:

case 1. $\lceil \log_b N \rceil + b - 3$ multiplications and storing $\lceil \log_b N \rceil - 1$ values $(a^{b_1}, \ldots, a^{b_{m-1}})$,

case 2. $\lceil \log_b N \rceil + 2b - 5$ multiplications and storing $b - 1$ values $(c_1, \ldots, c_h)$.

Our protocol is the following. Let x a number of the set $\{0, \ldots, N\}$. For example, for the DSS, N is a prime number of length 160 bits. And suppose

$$x = \sum_{i=0}^{m-1} x_i b^i,$$

where $x_i \in \{0, \ldots, b-1\}$.

1. The card uses the randomly selected prime number p_v of length N_v bits, computes and stores $p_0 = p \bmod p_v$.
2. The server sends to the card, the numbers $a_i = a^{b^i} \bmod p$. We have $a_i = a_{i-1}^b \bmod p$ for all $i = 1, \ldots, m-1$, with $a_0 = a$. Then the card knowing a can verify a_1 using the protocol of section 3, next it can verify a_2 aso. Then the card can calculate $a^x \bmod p$ with the protocol **BGCW**. It keeps in mind only the values it needs to compute $a^x \bmod p$.

Theorem 4.1 *If a, p are non negative integers of length at most 512 bits such that $a < p$, then the probability of accepting a false value $a^x \bmod p$ is less than $1/2^{20}$ in the case a and less than $1/2^{64}$ in the case b.*

Proof. Suppose $a^x \bmod p$ is not correct. Hence, at least one of the a_i is not correct. According to theorem 3.1, this would be detect with probability $> 1 - \frac{1}{2^{20}}$ in the case a or $> 1 - \frac{1}{2^{64}}$ in the case b.

□

Performances

Let $k = |b| - 1$ and $\nu = \nu(b)$. Knowing $a_{i-1}, a_{i-1} \bmod p_v, p_0$, by (4) the card must do the equivalent of $\text{mult}(k, \nu) = (2k + 2\nu - 2)\frac{\theta}{2}\frac{512}{1024}\frac{N_v}{512} + (2k + 2\nu - 2)\frac{1}{2}\frac{N_v}{512}\frac{N_v}{512} + (k + \nu - 1)\frac{\theta}{2}\frac{2N_v}{1024}\frac{N_v}{512}$ modular multiplications to obtain and verify a_i for all $i = 1, \ldots, m-1$. It must do $2\frac{\theta}{2}\frac{512}{1024}\frac{N_v}{512}$ modular multiplications to obtain $a \bmod p_v$ and $p_0 = p \bmod p_v$. Hence it must do the equivalent of $(m-1) * \text{mult}(k, \nu) + \frac{\theta N_v}{1024}$ modular multiplications to obtain all the a_i and a proof that they are correct with a high probability. Hence to obtain $a^x \bmod p$ the card must do

case 1. $\lceil \log_b N \rceil + b - 3 + (\lceil \log_b N \rceil - 1) * \text{mult}(|b| - 1, \nu(b)) + \frac{\theta N_v}{1024}$ modular multiplications.

case 2. $\lceil \log_b N \rceil + 2b - 5 + (\lceil \log_b N \rceil - 1) * \text{mult}(|b| - 1, \nu(b)) + \frac{\theta N_v}{1024}$ modular multiplications.

Here, a and p are fixed, so they can be stored in the ROM. Then, the card must store for the two cases 130 bytes in the ROM (the numbers b, m, a, p). In the case b, the card must also store p_v (10 bytes).

The card stores in the EEPROM

case 1. $(\lceil \log_b N \rceil - 1) * 64 + \lceil \frac{|x|}{8} \rceil$ bytes : the numbers $a^b \bmod p, \ldots, a^{b^{m-1}} \bmod p$ and x. It must write each number only one time for each signatures. Hence this is also the total number of bytes write in the EEPROM.

case 2. $(b-1) * 64 + \lceil \frac{|x|}{8} \rceil$ bytes : the numbers $c_1, \ldots, c_{b-1}$ and x. It must write each number c_i in average $\frac{m-1}{b-1}$ times for each signature and x only one time. Hence the total number of bytes write in the EEPROM is $(\lceil \log_b N \rceil - 1) * 64 + \lceil \frac{|x|}{8} \rceil$.

In the cases 1a and 2a the need RAM is $160 + 4 * \nu(b)$ bytes and in the cases 1b and 2b the need RAM is $208 + 10 * \nu(b)$

The exchange values between the card and the server are in the two cases $(\lceil \log_b N \rceil - 1) * 2 * (|b| + \nu(b) - 2) * 64$ bytes. Here we suppose that the server knows b, a, p, then the card does not send them to the server.

Security

The values given to the server are independent of x: then the protocol is secure against passive attacks.

If the server cheats to obtain some information, the card will see that with a probability $> 1 - \frac{1}{2^{20}}$ or $> 1 - \frac{1}{2^{64}}$. Then it will not use the value $a^x \bmod p$. Hence the server does not obtain any information. Then the protocol is secure against active attacks.

In conclusion, our protocol is secure against passive and active attacks and the card obtains the good result with a probability $> 1 - \frac{1}{2^{20}}$ or $> 1 - \frac{1}{2^{64}}$.

Performances of our protocol for the DSS

Here N is a number of length 160 bits. Without the help of the server the card must do 240 modular multiplications on the average. We use in the first case $b = 16, m = 40$ and in the second $b = 8, m = 54$.

The following table gives for the two cases, the number of modular multiplications done by the card, the needed RAM, EEPROM and ROM (in bytes), the number of bytes exchanged between the card and the server and the factor of acceleration by using our protocol. We also give the total number of bytes write in the EEPROM during the protocol and the maximal average times we must write in each bytes.

	case 1a	case 2a	case 1b	case 2b
security	$1/2^{20}$	$1/2^{20}$	$1/2^{64}$	$1/2^{64}$
multiplications	60.1	72.3	67.8	85.2
RAM (bytes)	164	164	218	218
EEPROM (bytes)	2516	468	2516	468
Write (bytes)	2516	3392	2516	3392
Number of writing	1	7.6	1	7.6
ROM (bytes)	130	130	140	140
data transfers (bytes)	19968	20352	19968	20352
factor of acceleration	4	3.3	3.53	2.8

Let us notice that smart cards with fast data transfers (> 15 kbytes/s) are coming.

5 Conclusion

This paper shows how to use an insecure server for accelerating some useful cryptographic protocols. We present a protocol to obtain the modular exponentiation of the DSS: it's the first protocol who accelerate the discrete exponential modulo a prime number, secure against passive attacks without using precomputations. And it is also the first one secure against active attacks. Using a card of small memory, our protocol accelerates the DSS modular exponentiation with a factor 4 in the average without decreasing the security of the DSS scheme: this protocol gives no information about the secret value.

If the values a, b, p are standardized for a group of cards, the server only needs to store values: in fact the server may be an insecure external ROM. In particular, we could have a card with a second external ROM which does not need to be secure.

References

1. Anderson, R. J.: Attack on server-assisted authentication protocols. Electronic Letters (1992) p. 1473.
2. Brickell, E., Gordon, D. M., McCurley, K. S., Wilson, D.: Fast exponentiation with precomputation. In Advances in Cryptology – Proceedings of Eurocrypt '92 (1993) vol. Lecture Notes in Computer Science 658 Springer-Verlag pp. 200–207.
3. Couvreur, C., Quisquater, J.-J.: An introduction to fast generation of large prime numbers. Philips Journal of Research (1982) pp. 231–264.
4. Kawamura, S., Shimbo, A.: Fast server-aided secret computation protocols for modular exponentiation. IEEE Journal on selected areas communications **11** (1993).
5. Matsumoto, T., Imai, H., Laih, C.-S., Yen, S.-M.: On verifiable implicit asking protocols for RSA computation. In Advances in Cryptology – Proceedings of Auscrypt' 92 (1993) vol. Lecture Notes in Computer Science 718 Springer-Verlag pp. 296–307.
6. Matsumoto, T., Kato, K., Imai, H.: Speeding up secret computation with insecure auxiliary devices. In Advances in Cryptology – Proceedings of Crypto '88 (1989) vol. Lecture Notes in Computer Science 403 Springer-Verlag pp. 497–506.
7. NIST: FIPS 186 for Digital Signature Standard (DSS).
8. Pfitzmann, B., Waidner, M.: Attacks on protocols for server-aided RSA computation. In Advances in Cryptology – Proceedings of Eurocrypt '92 (1993) vol. Lecture Notes in Computer Science 658 Springer-Verlag pp. 153–162.
9. Quisquater, J.-J., Soete, M. D.: Speeding up smart card RSA computation with insecure coprocessors. In Procedings of Smart Cards 2000 (1989) pp. 191–197.
10. Rivest, R., Shamir, A., Adleman, L.: A method for obtaining digital signatures and public-key cryptosystems. Communications of the ACM **21** (1978) pp. 120–126.
11. Schnorr, C.: Efficient identification and signatures for smart cards. In Advances in Cryptology – Proceedings of CRYPTO '89 (1990) vol. Lecture Notes in Computer Science 435 Springer-Verlag pp. 235–251.
12. Yen, S.-M., Laih, C.-S.: More about the active attack on the server-aided secret computation protocol. Electronic Letters (1992) p. 2250.

SESSION 6

CRYPTANALYSIS

Chair: Luke O'Connor

(Queensland University of Technology, Australia)

The Magic Words are Squeamish Ossifrage

Extended Abstract

Derek Atkins[1], Michael Graff[2], Arjen K. Lenstra[3], Paul C. Leyland[4]

[1] 12 Rindge Avenue, Cambridge, MA 02140, U. S. A.
E-mail: `warlord@mit.edu`

[2] Iowa State University, 215 Durham Center, Ames, IA 50010-2120, U. S. A.
E-mail: `explorer@iastate.edu`

[3] MRE-2Q334, Bellcore, 445 South Street, Morristown, NJ 07960, U. S. A.
E-mail: `lenstra@bellcore.com`

[4] Oxford University Computing Services, 13 Banbury Road, Oxford, OX2 6NN, U. K.
E-mail: `pcl@ox.ac.uk`

Abstract. We describe the computation which resulted in the title of this paper. Furthermore, we give an analysis of the data collected during this computation. From these data, we derive the important observation that in the final stages, the progress of the double large prime variation of the quadratic sieve integer factoring algorithm can more effectively be approximated by a quartic function of the time spent, than by the more familiar quadratic function. We also present, as an update to [15], some of our experiences with the management of a large computation distributed over the Internet. Based on this experience, we give some realistic estimates of the current readily available computational power of the Internet. We conclude that commonly-used 512-bit RSA moduli are vulnerable to any organization prepared to spend a few million dollars and to wait a few months.

1 Introduction

One of the earliest descriptions of the RSA public key cryptosystem appeared in Martin Gardner's column 'Mathematical Games' in the August 1977 issue of Scientific American. There, the inventors of RSA presented the following challenge. Let

$$r = 1\ 1438\ 1625\ 7578\ 8886\ 7669\ 2357\ 7997\ 6146\ 6120\ 1021\ 8296\ 7212\ 4236\ 2562\ 5618\ 4293$$
$$5706\ 9352\ 4573\ 3897\ 8305\ 9712\ 3563\ 9587\ 0505\ 8989\ 0751\ 4759\ 9290\ 0268\ 7954\ 3541$$

be the public modulus and let $e = 9007$ be the public exponent; find the plaintext English message which corresponds to the encrypted message

$$9686\ 9613\ 7546\ 2206\ 1477\ 1409\ 2225\ 4355\ 8829\ 0575\ 9991\ 1245\ 7431\ 9874\ 6951\ 2093$$
$$0816\ 2982\ 2514\ 5708\ 3569\ 3147\ 6622\ 8839\ 8962\ 8013\ 3919\ 9055\ 1829\ 9451\ 5781\ 5154,$$

where the original plaintext English message had been transformed into a decimal number using the transformation **A** = 01, **B** = 02, ..., **Z** = 26, with 00 indicating a space between words. It is readily verified that application of this transformation to the title of this paper, followed by an eth powering modulo r, results in the encrypted message. Here we describe how we reversed this process and found the title of this paper, thereby solving the 'RSA-challenge' and winning the US$100 prize. The prize has been donated to the Free Software Foundation.

The modulus r has 129 decimal digits and is, according to [6], the product of a 64-digit prime p and a 65-digit prime q such that both $p-1$ and $q-1$ are relatively prime to e. The primes p and q were kept secret. It is well known that the encrypted message can be decrypted by computing (encrypted message)^d mod r where d satisfies $d \cdot e \equiv 1 \bmod (p-1)(q-1)$. Because of the condition on p and q, finding d is straightforward if $(p-1)(q-1)$ is known. But knowing $(p-1)(q-1)$ is equivalent to knowing the secret primes p and q (cf. [21]).[5] It follows that the encrypted message can be decrypted by factoring r.

In the full paper, we will describe in detail how we managed to factor r. This extended abstract consists of a discussion of some historical remarks on the supposed difficulty of factoring r (Section 2), an outline of the method that we used to factor r (Section 3), an overview of the analysis that will appear in the full paper (Section 4), a view behind the scenes of this world-wide computing effort (Section 5), and some concluding remarks (Section 6).

2 Predicting the difficulty of factoring r

Back in 1976, Richard Guy wrote 'I shall be surprised if anyone regularly factors numbers of size 10^{80} without special form during the present century' [8]. In 1977, Rivest estimated in [20] that factoring a 125-digit number which is the product of two 63-digit prime numbers would *require* at least 40 quadrillion years using the best factoring algorithm known, assuming that $a * b \pmod{c}$ could be computed in 1 nanosecond, for 125-digit numbers a, b, and c.[6] Thus, it is not surprising that the inventors of RSA felt confident that 'with such a huge modulus the message will never be recovered' [23] and offered a $100 prize to the first successful decoder of the encrypted message. Interestingly, until the message was decoded, none of the parties involved remembered the expiration date of April 1, 1982, given in [20] but not in [6].

With 10^9 modular multiplications per second, about 1.3×10^{33} can be carried out in 40 quadrillion years. It is not clear why, back in 1977, it was believed that 1.3×10^{33} modular multiplications were required to factor a 125 or 126-digit number. Unfortunately, Rivest does not recall how he obtained his estimate. At that time, Pollard's 'rho method' was probably the fastest available factoring

[5] This does *not* imply that in order to decrypt the encrypted message it is necessary to find p and q but no faster way to decrypt an RSA-encryption has yet been published.

[6] A similar estimate can be found in [6].

method for which a run-time analysis had been published. To find a prime factor p it needs, on average, about $2\sqrt{p}$ iterations, where each iteration costs two modular multiplications. For a 63-digit prime factor this amounts to at most 1.3×10^{32} modular multiplications. This suggests that Rivest might have used the rho method but miscounted the number of zeros. In that case, the correct estimate should have been 4 quadrillion years, which still sounds sufficiently impressive to convince people of the infeasibility of breaking 125-digit RSA keys.

Since 1977 many new factoring algorithms have been invented and the availability and speed of computing resources has changed dramatically. Rivest's imaginary '1 nanosecond per modular multiplication' machine, however, still stretches the imagination. With pipelining and special purpose hardware with gate delays of about 10 picoseconds, it might just be feasible, even for 129-digit numbers. If we were to build such a machine, then we estimate that it has a fair chance to find the 64-digit factor of r after 5×10^{15} modular multiplications using the *elliptic curve method* (ECM). This would require two months: 240 quadrillion times faster than Rivest's estimate — progress that is due solely to improved factoring methods.

Today, finding 64-digit prime factors using ECM is believed to be infeasible. On a Sparc 10 workstation the 5×10^{15} modular multiplications on 129-digit numbers that would probably be needed for ECM would take well in excess of 15000 years. ECM uses mostly computations on local data which can be kept in the cache, and hardly any access to main memory. Consequently, the method runs x times faster on a machine whose 'mips rating' is x times better. Therefore, a statement of the kind 'finding a 64-digit prime factor of a 129-digit number using ECM would probably take more than half a million mips years' might make some sense. Here, we rate a Sparc 10 workstation at 35 mips; notice that this would imply a mips rating of about 3 million for Rivest's imaginary machine if it used ordinary 32-bit arithmetic.

For the quadratic sieve factoring algorithm (QS), the method that we used to factor r, run-times expressed in mips years are much harder to justify. Sieving algorithms spend most of their time accessing more or less random locations in memory. On most workstations, processor speed is poorly correlated with memory speed and, therefore, the mips rating of the processor is not a reliable measure of the expected performance of a sieving algorithm. To give some examples: on a Sparc 10 workstation QS would have taken about 120 years to factor r, which leads to an estimate of about 4000 mips years. On a Dec 5000/240, rated at 25 mips, we would have spent 237 years, which translates into almost 6000 mips years. On a Sun 3/50, however, rated at 1.5 mips, we would have spent about 1100 years but only 1700 mips years. Averaging over the machines that were used, and keeping in mind that we are indulging in energetic handwaving, we give a very approximate estimate of 4000 to 6000 mips years for the time spent on the factorization of r. If the ratio between memory and processor speed of Rivest's machine is not much worse than on current workstations, it could factor r in less than a day. Even though expressing run-times in mips years is far from ideal for memory-bound processes, it is common practice in factoring literature. It provides a convenient way to compare and predict run-times of factoring problems, and to check the accuracy of theoretical predictions.

Heuristically it can be argued that the expected run-time of QS behaves as

$$L(n) = \exp((1+o(1))\sqrt{\log n \log\log n}), \tag{1.1}$$

for $n \to \infty$, where n is the number to be factored. Often, one simply ignores the $o(1)$, and interprets the resulting $L(n)$ as the number of operations needed to factor n. Since the $o(1)$ is neither 0 nor constant, this practice hardly makes sense.

This naive approach was first used in [21: Section IX.A], where $L(n)$, without the $o(1)$, was given as the run-time of Schroeppel's linear sieve factoring algorithm (cf. [22]). This is a big improvement compared with Rivest's slightly earlier estimate in [6]. The run-time from [21] did not include the matrix elimination step, because this step was considered to be trivial compared to the sieving step (cf. [22]). Including it would have increased the run-time to

$$\exp((u/2+o(1))\sqrt{\log n \log\log n})$$

(cf. [18: Theorem 6.1]), where a linear dependency in an $(s+1)\times s$ bit-matrix can be found in time s^u. At the time of the publication of [21], the best one could do was $u \approx 2.795$. Although for small n the matrix step is in practice negligible compared to the sieving step, this is not the case for the larger n in [21: Table 1], thus making these values strictly speaking (and disregarding the $o(1)$-issue) incorrect, for 1978. It was later shown that the sparseness of the matrix can be exploited and that $u = 2 + o(1)$ can indeed be used.

This does not imply that there are any significant digits in [21: Table 1]. The table illustrates, however, the approximate growth rate of $L(n)$, which *can* be used in an attempt to predict run-times: if factoring n_1 takes time t for some QS-implementation and $|\log(n_2/n_1)|$ is reasonably small, then factoring n_2 using the same implementation can be expected to take time approximately $t \cdot L(n_2)/L(n_1)$, where both $o(1)$'s are simply omitted.

Using this method it was estimated in [2] that factoring a 120-digit number using QS would take about 950 mips years, based on the observation from [16] that factoring a 116-digit number took about 400 mips years. The actual 120-digit factorization took about 825 mips years, slightly less than the prediction, due to several improvements in the program and intentional suboptimality of the parameter choices for the 116-digit factorization. Similar extrapolation of the 120-digit result to r would lead to about 4200 mips years, which is on the low side of the 4000 to 6000 mips years that we spent. This may be due to a combination of two factors. In the first place, the effect of the unknown behavior of the $o(1)$ in the 9 digit jump from 120 to 129 digits is significantly bigger than in the jump from 116 to 120 digits. Apparently, neglecting the $o(1)$ leads to an overly optimistic estimate. Secondly, the effects of small (and relatively slow) memories should be even worse for r than for the 120-digit factorization from [2].

The reason why these deliberations are considered to be useful is that they might help us to assess the security of widely-used 512-bit RSA moduli. Since $L(2^{512})/L(10^{129}) \approx 92$ (without the two $o(1)$'s), we find that factoring a 512-bit RSA modulus using our current QS-implementation can probably not be done in less than 500 000 mips years. An upper bound is harder to give, but a million mips years is probably the right order of magnitude.

We should stress that this estimate might not be a good indication of the difficulty to break a 512-bit RSA modulus. It tells us how hard it would probably be for a fairly well understood, reliable and by now rather ancient algorithm. The newer *number field sieve* factoring algorithm (NFS) (cf. [13]) is asymptotically superior to QS. Recent experiments have suggested that the crossover point between QS and NFS lies well below 116 digits (cf. [5; 7]), but it remains to be seen how well the memory requirements of NFS for 512-bit numbers can be handled. In any case, we suspect that with the factorization of r we have seen the last big QS-factorization. Furthermore, given how hard it was, 17 years ago, to make a decent prediction about the difficulty of factoring r, it is probably better to avoid making any firm prediction about 512-bit numbers.

3 Factoring r

We used the double large prime multiple polynomial variation of the quadratic sieve factoring method (QS) to factor r. The goal of QS is to find pairs of integers x, y such that $x^2 \equiv y^2 \bmod r$. Because r divides $x^2 - y^2 = (x-y)(x+y)$, we find that $r = \gcd(r, x-y)\gcd(r, x+y)$. If the pairs are generated in a random fashion, then there is a probability of $1/2$ that this factorization is non-trivial (because r has only two distinct prime factors) [3]. In QS, pairs x, y are constructed in two steps, the *sieving step* and the *matrix step* [12: 4.16; 16; 18; 24]. We give an outline of these steps as applied to r. In the full paper we will give more details.

3.1 The sieving step

First, we select a *multiplier*, a small positive integer m such that mr is a quadratic residue modulo many small primes (cf. [9: 4.5.4]). Next, we compute the *factor base* P, consisting of -1 and the primes $p \leq B_1$ for which mr is a quadratic residue modulo p, for some bound B_1. In the sieving step we collect a set of *relations*: integer tuples $(v, q_1, q_2, (e_p)_{p\in P})$ such that

$$v^2 \equiv q_1 \cdot q_2 \cdot \prod_{p\in P} p^{e_p} \bmod r, \tag{3.2}$$

where each q_i is either 1 or a *large prime* $\in (B_1, B_2]$, for some *large prime bound* B_2. If $q_1 = q_2 = 1$ the relation is called *full*, if only one of the q_i equals 1 it is a *partial*, and a *double partial* otherwise. If the large primes match, the (double) partial relations can be combined into *cycles* [16]. The sieving step is complete as soon as #fulls+#cycles $> \#P$.

We used $m = 5$ as multiplier. Asymptotically, the factor base size in QS applied to n behaves as $\sqrt{L(n)}$, for $n \to \infty$. A factor base size of 245 810 elements was close to optimal for the 120-digit number RSA-120 factored in [2], with multiplier 7. Therefore a factor base of $245\,810\sqrt{L(mr)/L(7 \cdot \mathrm{RSA}-120)} \approx 554\,933$ (omitting both $o(1)$'s) elements should be reasonable but on the small side (because the $o(1)$ grows with n). After experiments with other values, we settled for $\#P = 524\,339 = 51 + 2^{19}$ (and $B_1 = 16\,333\,609$). Our choice is certainly within 20% of optimal, and probably slightly suboptimal. We felt that this was less undesirable than the memory-related problems caused by an even larger choice.[7] We used $B_2 = 2^{30}$.

Based on our experience with many other factorizations, we expected that we would need about 110 000 fulls before we had enough cycles to complete the sieving step. Experiments indicated that this would take less than 6000 mips years. More than 8 million relations would have to be collected (since only 1 out of every $\approx$ 75 is full), using a program which would need approximately 10.5 MBytes to run. We opted for the idle-cycle collection method from [15]. This sounds easier than it was, even though we could re-use the software, because our effort would need an order of magnitude more time, memory, and disk space to run the sieving program and to store the relations. We give more details of the resource management in Section 5. We estimate that we had approximately 600 contributors using more than 1600 machines and producing about 80% of the relations. The other 20% was contributed by several MasPars running the program from [4].

On March 21 1994 we had about 8.25 million relations, with more than 108 000 fulls and 417 000 cycles. Because $108\,000 + 417\,000 > 524\,339 = \#P$, the 'cease and desist' message was mailed out on March 22. The final counts, on March 26, were: 112 011 fulls, 1 431 337 partials, and 6 881 138 double partials, for a total of 8 424 486 relations after less than 220 days of sieving. The (double) partials that could occur in cycles were written to tape by the first author and sent to the third (by regular overnight mail). They resulted in 457 455 cycles, constructed using the method from [16]. With the fulls, which were `ftp`-ed from `hot-spare.mit.edu` to `flash.bellcore.com` via `tbird.cc.iastate.edu`, this led to 569 466 sparse 524 339-dimensional vectors $(e_p)_{p\in P}$ as in (3.2).

3.3 The matrix step

Here we find linear dependencies modulo 2 among the $> \#P$ bit-vectors $(e_p \bmod 2)_{p\in P}$. Each dependency corresponds to a set $W = \{(w, (e_p)_{p\in P}) : w^2 \equiv \prod_{p\in P} p^{e_p} \bmod r\}$ for which $\sum_W (e_p)_{p\in P} = (2w_p)_{p\in P}$ for integers w_p. Consequently, $x \equiv \prod_W w \bmod r$ and $y \equiv \prod_{p\in P} p^{w_p} \bmod r$ satisfy $x^2 \equiv y^2 \bmod r$.

---

[7] Because $\#P \equiv 51 \bmod 2^{14}$ we could use the QS-implementation from [4] on a 16K MasPar massively parallel computer. The choice is on the high side for this implementation, which performed noticeably worse than expected based on the experience from [2].

To find dependencies among the rows of the 569 466 × 524 339 bit-matrix with, on average, ≈ 47 bits per row, we intended to use the same approach as in previous large scale factorizations. The largest matrix processed so far, however, had less than half the number of rows and columns (252 222 × 245 810 with the same density, cf. [2]), making the present effort an order of magnitude more difficult. Using structured Gaussian elimination (cf. [10; 14; 19]) the matrix was reduced to a dense 188 614 × 188 160 bit-matrix. This took less than 12 CPU-hours on a Sparc 10 workstation, 97% of which was spent building the 4 436 201 280 byte dense matrix, in 268 separate files of about 16 MBytes each.

To find a dependency among the rows of the dense matrix, we used the incremental version from [1] of the MasPar dense matrix eliminator from [11]. The dense matrix was processed in 5 blocks. With a core size of 1GByte, 41 595 rows could be processed per block. Each new block was first eliminated with the pivots found in the previous blocks, then with the new pivots in the block itself, after which the result was written to disk. Each of the first four blocks resulted in a file of ≈ 980 MBytes. Notice that one wrong bit, either in the dense matrix or in the intermediate files, can render the entire computation worthless. For this reason, the dense matrix intentionally contained 268 spurious dependencies which were supposed to be found at regular intervals during the elimination process to signal possible errors.

The entire process took 45 hours on a 16K MasPar MP-1: 75 minutes to read the dense matrix, 100 minutes to write the first four blocks, and 42 hours for the eliminations. This is better than we had expected,[8] because, unlike previous eliminations, most pivot rows had to be read from disk before eliminating with them and they could not be stored in registers during the elimination. All 268 spurious dependencies were found at the right moment during the computation, and 205 'true' dependencies were found at the end. It took a few minutes to convert the 205 dependencies modulo 2 in the dense matrix to dependencies in the sparse one. Computing the pairs x, y with $x^2 \equiv y^2 \bmod r$ took a few minutes per dependency. The first three dependencies led to $r = 1 \cdot r$. At 18:15 UT on April 2 1994 the fourth one led to the factorization $r = p \cdot q$, with p the 64-digit prime

3490 5295 1084 7650 9491 4784 9619 9038 9813 3417 7646 3849 3387 8439 9082 0577

and q the 65-digit prime

3 2769 1329 9326 6709 5499 6198 8190 8344 6141 3177 6429 6799 2942 5397 9828 8533.

Five of the first ten dependencies were 'unlucky'. It might be interesting to note that $p-1 = 2^5 \cdot 3^2 \cdot \bar{p}$ for a 62-digit prime $\bar{p} = 1 + 2 \cdot 7^2 \cdot \hat{p}$ and a 60-digit prime $\hat{p}$; and that $q - 1 = 2^2 \cdot 41 \cdot \bar{q}$ for a 63-digit prime $\bar{q} = 1 + 2^2 \cdot 53 \cdot \hat{q}$ and another 60-digit prime $\hat{q}$. We suspect that $p - 1$ and $q - 1$ were consciously chosen to have large prime factors, so that r would withstand a Pollard $p - 1$ factoring

[8] The 4 hours for the 245 810 column matrix from [2] extrapolate to $4 \cdot (524\,339/245\,810)^3 \approx 39$ hours.

attack. The large prime factors of $\bar{p}-1$ and $\bar{q}-1$ might have been based on the widespread belief that they would be necessary to prevent a decryption attempt using iterated encryption [17]. The resistance of r against a Pollard $p+1$ attack, which had not yet been published by 1977, was probably a coincidence: $p+1 = 2 \cdot 1\,376\,164\,939\,307\,949\,996\,650\,933 \cdot \mathrm{p}40$, and $q+1 = 2 \cdot 3^4 \cdot 11 \cdot 79 \cdot 197 \cdot 227 \cdot \mathrm{p}55$, with $\mathrm{p}j$ denoting a j-digit prime.

4 Analysis of the data collected

Let $Q = \{q : q \text{ prime}, B_1 < q \leq B_2, (\frac{mr}{q}) = 1\}$ be the set of 26 679 473 large primes which can possibly occur in the (double) partial relations. Let $p(q)$ be the probability that $q \in Q$ occurs in a partial relation. In [16] it is shown that t partial relations can be expected to generate $c \cdot t^2$ cycles, where $c = (\sum_{q \in Q} p(q)^2)/2$. To be able to predict the number of cycles among partials it is therefore useful to get more insight in the behavior of $p(q)$. It has been suggested in [16] that $p(q)$ is proportional to $1/q^\alpha$, for some positive $\alpha < 1$. In the full paper we will analyse which α best fits our data, and discuss how well the theoretically estimated number of cycles among the partials agrees with our findings. Furthermore, we will present the α_1 and α_2 corresponding to $p_1(q)$ and $p_2(q)$, where $p_1(q)$ is the probability that $q \in Q$ occurs as smallest large prime in a double partial and $p_2(q)$ is the probability that it appears as largest large prime in a double partial relation.

Different factorizations with similar α's usually have similar cycle-yields, which makes the α's good indicators of the cycle-yield. Because the behavior of the α's can be derived long before the factorization is complete, this might be helpful to predict the cycle-yield in other factorizations. The behavior of the cycle-yield is of particular interest for future NFS factorizations where relations can have more than 2 large primes (cf. [7]). Understanding their cycle-yield is crucial to be able to predict the run-times (cf. [5]).

The estimates that were sent to the contributors (cf. Section 5) were based on extrapolations of the cycle-curve. Initially a quadratic curve gave a good fit, and was therefore used to extrapolate. We lost our confidence in quadratic extrapolation in late December 1993, when the extrapolation predicted that we would need more than 13 million relations. Fortunately, we noticed in January that a quadratic no longer gave a close fit, and that the cycle-curve was showing stronger than quadratic growth. Experiments indicated, quite unexpectedly, that a quartic function gave a very good approximation. However the residuals, although small, were quite well serially correlated, which probably implies that the cycle-curve does *not* behave as a quartic. Since the error terms were relatively small, and because the first few extrapolations turned out to be unusually accurate, we kept using the quartic anyway. We predicted in early February that 8.15 million relations would suffice. The quartic extrapolation proved to be very slightly optimistic — it turned out that we actually needed 8.2 million relations. In the full paper we will provide more details and graphs of the actual yields and of the quadratic and quartic extrapolations.

5 Resource management

To factor r we assembled the largest collaboration yet seen in computational number theory and, possibly, performed the largest single computation ever completed. In several important respects, the resources we had available were barely adequate for the task. Consequently, ingenuity and diplomacy were required for the successful completion of the project. Full details of the resource management aspects of the computation will be given in the full paper; here we give a summary of the salient points.

Based on experience with earlier factorizations, especially those in [15] and [2], we could make reasonably precise estimates of the disk space, amount of computation and memory usage which would be required. Before we started, we estimated that we would need about 8 million relations, each of which would take about 350 bytes to store. We knew that a few mips-millenia would be required. We also estimated that the factor base would need to have about 400 000 to 600 000 elements, implying that the sieving programs would take over 8 MBytes of active memory. We did not know, before we started, how many machines and of what power would be available to us but we did have some encouraging offers of support. It was clear, however, that an unusually large number of people and machines would be involved with the project.

The first action was to settle the size of the factor base. As explained in 3.1, a figure of about half a million primes was close to optimal. A somewhat larger number would have reduced the theoretical amount of computation required, but we were already using 10.5 MBytes of active virtual memory. Given that most of the machines on the Internet have less than 16 MBytes of physical memory, and many have 8 or less, even 10.5 MBytes is uncomfortably large and would seriously restrict the number of people capable of helping us.

Before going public, the first and fourth authors ported the software to as many different kinds of workstations and PCs as were available to us. The first author persuaded MIT to lend us a file server for the duration. This machine was a DEC 5000/240 with 32 MBytes RAM and two (later three) 975 MBytes disks. MIT systems staff also agreed to perform regular backups of the information on disk. For these reasons MIT was chosen as collection site.

Also before the computations started, the second and fourth authors wrote documents explaining what we were proposing to do, how we were going to do it, and how to get further information should the reader wish to join in. The second author set up several mailing lists and email aliases for communications to and from our workers and the four coordinators; he also took on the role of front-line contact person, dealing with virtually all the 600 contributors and many others who expressed an interest but did not join in for whatever reason.

The postings to potential contributors went out on August 19 1993 to the 'number theory net', on August 23 to the 'cypherpunks' and the 'PGP development group', and on August 24 to the following newsgroups: alt.hackers, alt.security, alt.security.pgp, alt.security.ripem, comp.arch, comp.security.misc, sci.crypt, and sci.math. The initial response to our postings and the number of incoming relations was sufficiently encouraging to conclude that the project would be feasible.

Once contributors started offering their services, we had to port our software to their platforms, if we had not already done so. Although one Unix box is very much like another, there are sufficient differences that we often had to ask our contributors to perform the port for us and to send back the modifications so that we could pass them on to others with the same platform. Our code was run successfully on machines as disparate as 16MHz 80386sx PCs and Cray C90s. An attempted port to a Thinking Machines CM-5 failed, but one US corporation managed to get the sieving code running on a couple of fax machines!

The relatively severe memory requirements and the commonness of 8 MBytes machines gave us a strong incentive to produce memory-frugal variants of the siever. By reducing the sieve batch size and by reading the roots of mr mod the p's from a file, we were able to reduce the space required from the default 10.5 MBytes to 6.5 MBytes, albeit at a cost of running over twice as slowly. However, half a computer is better than none and by allowing more people to take part, we shortened the overall time taken for the sieving phase. Even so, 6.5 MBytes does not leave much room for an operating system and most of our contributors with 8 MBytes machines were only able to run our code overnight.

Once we were up to speed we received on average about 40 thousand relations per day, with peaks of over 50 thousand during the holiday seasons. Daily, all newly received relations that satisfied (3.2) were sorted and merged with older data; faulty or duplicate relations were thrown out. This took at most a few hours per day, even when the accumulated data had reached a couple of GBytes. About one relation in ten thousand received was unacceptable in some way. Of these, many had suffered in transit through mail gateways but we also received a number of relations intended for another factoring-by-email computation being run at the same time — these relations were sent on to the correct destination, together with a polite note to suggest that their contributors be informed of their error.

About half-way through the computation, it became clear that we would run out of disk space if we continued to store the relations in plain text. Accordingly, the fourth author wrote a simple but efficient compressor, and the bulk of the data was kept in a more compact format. Each day's data was left as ASCII for convenience (fewer processing programs had to be re-written) and a combined uncompress-sort-merge-compress of the total data set performed every few weeks as the disk began to get uncomfortably full. Unfortunately, we did not notice the disk overflowing in early January 1994. About three weeks' data had been corrupted; fortunately, the outputs from the daily runs of the email processor were still on disk so we were able to recover relatively easily.

To monitor the progress, the fourth author adapted the cycle-counting software from [16] to the relatively small workstation we had at MIT. Towards the end of the project this became a challenging task, with several GBytes of compressed data; a graph containing several million nodes, edges and components and a few hundred thousand cycles; no disk space to decompress or to write intermediate files; and only a 25 mips processor with 32 MBytes of physical memory. Details will be given in the full paper.

We have already described in Section 4 how the quadratic extrapolation began to indicate that we would need many more relations than we had predicted at the start of the project. We became seriously concerned at this point that we would have difficulty in maintaining the interest of our contributors for several months longer than anticipated. Further, although we had enough disk space (just!) to process 9 million relations, an extra 50% would have caused us significant problems. Luckily, our discovery of the much more accurate quartic prediction was made before we told our contributors, saving us from worrying them with a false alarm.

The resulting counts were mailed to the contributors each month, along with an estimate of how much more would be needed. These reports were also posted to Usenet, as it was found that they were very effective at attracting new contributors. The estimates were based on extrapolation of the cycle-curve (cf. Section 4).

Some substantial effort had to be devoted to problem solving. As our program had not previously run on certain platforms, its portability had not been *proven*. Two examples will suffice. One unfortunate contributor discovered that his disk had filled with over 300 MBytes of error messages overnight after our program had run wild. We discovered rather bizarre behavior of a particular compiler for the Intel 80x86 — unless the value of a certain variable was printed out, the program would crash unpredictably.

6 Conclusion

Our Internet contributors were exclusively volunteers, donating spare computer time from overnight and weekend running. Although 600 people and 1600 machines constitute the largest *ad hoc* multiprocessor so far assembled, it is only a tiny fraction of the size and power of the entire Internet. It is difficult to get even a rough estimate of the potential power available. At the time of writing (October 1994) it is thought that there are between 3 and 4 million machines on the Internet; it is currently growing at about 10-20% per month. If we assume, conservatively, that there are 3 million machines, each of which can average 5 mips (i.e., a typical 10 mips workstation with 50% availability) the potential power available is around 1.5×10^7 mips — about five times the power of Rivest's hypothetical machine. In principle, the Internet could have factored r in three hours! The implementation details are left as an exercise for the reader.

Let us attempt to give a more plausible estimate. We believe that we could acquire 100 thousand machines without superhuman or unethical efforts. That is, we would *not* set free an Internet worm or virus to find resources for us. Many organizations have several thousand machines each on the net. Making use of their facilities would require skilful diplomacy, but should not be impossible. Assuming the 5 mips average power, and a one year elapsed time, it is not too unreasonable to embark on a project which would require half a million mips years. We conclude that 512-bit RSA keys are on the brink of vulnerability to a venerable but robust algorithm. However, we believe that solving the RSA-challenge is probably the last gasp of an elderly workhorse. A credible attack on a 512-bit key would almost certainly use an NFS implementation.

However, even using NFS to factor a 512-bit number would be a non-trivial undertaking. Without falling into the trap of making over-precise estimates of run-times, we can say that the resources required will be well in excess of what we used to factor a 426-bit key. If the open Internet were to be used, the resource management would be tricky. If an organization were to purchase the hardware necessary to give an average power of 500 000 mips, — 5000 processors, each rated at 100 mips — an outlay of several million dollars would be needed. Assuming that NFS can be implemented on those machines and assuming that the matrix step can be performed, 512-bit keys would take a few months to factor. Nonetheless, organizations exist with annual budgets in excess of ten million dollars and which might regard it to be cost-effective to break 512-bit RSA keys protecting information of particular interest.

Acknowledgments. In the first place we want to thank everyone who donated their time to this project. Here is a list of all contributors to the sieving step, in the following format: a number indicating the percentage of the contribution, followed by one or more names of the persons or institutions responsible for that contribution. Some contributors confirmed that they wanted to remain anonymous ('Confirmed Anonymous'), some contributors did not respond when we asked their permission to include their name in this paper ('Unclaimed'), and for some we only have an email address. We apologize for any omissions, or spelling errors.

8.348 Arjen K. Lenstra, 5.022 Magnus Y. Alvestad, 4.412 Brian A. LaMacchia, 4.126 Mats Lofkvist, 3.855 Tage Stabell-Kulo, 3.704 Clem Taylor, 3.579 Case Larsen, 3.295 Electronic Data Systems, Research & Development, 2.490 Harald Hanche-Olsen, 2.459 Germano Caronni, 1.988 Daniel R. Oelke, 1.883 Derek Atkins, 1.445 Edesio Costa e Silva, 1.250 Jonathan Bertoni, 1.219 Mark Shand, 1.161 Robin Humble, 1.148 David DiGiacomo, 1.115 Allan Sherman, 0.976 Robert J. Harley, 0.974 Brick Verser, 0.970 Lucien Van Elsen, 0.934 Andrew Loewenstern, 0.927 Paul Leyland, 0.819 Scott Logan, 0.810 Pekka Jarvelinen, 0.748 Michael Graff, 0.733 Unclaimed, 0.717 Shaun Case, Jim Garlick, 0.680 Teun Nijssen, 0.666 Walter Lioen, Herman te Riele, Dik Winter, 0.666 J.P.M. de Vreught, 0.616 Mark S. Manasse, 0.594 Unclaimed, 0.561 Steven Leikeim, 0.558 Bruce K. Martin Jr., 0.556 John ffitch, 0.538 Jack Repenning, 0.521 Jeffrey Blohm, 0.515 Jim Castleberry, 0.514 John Kohl, 0.497 Billy Barron, 0.472 Andrew Odlyzko, 0.471 Boris Hemkemeier, 0.468 Bruce Rossiter, 0.458 Nur Serinken, 0.445 Peter Conrad, 0.443 Ken Rose, 0.442 Christer Berg, 0.429 Bob Devine, 0.428 Dana Jacobsen, 0.423 olson@lxt.com, 0.414 Lee Nave, 0.409 Unclaimed, 0.370 Paul Hodgkinson, 0.367 Unclaimed, 0.365 Sylvestre Matuschka, 0.354 Bill Rea, 0.353 Confirmed Anonymous, 0.349 David Crowley, 0.347 Hugh D. Gamble, 0.333 Bruce Dodson, 0.333 Herb Savage, 0.326 Andrew Mossberg, 0.321 Eric Postpischil, 0.310 Unclaimed, 0.304 Daniel L. Carroll, 0.296 Unclaimed, 0.295 Ian T. M. Flanigan, 0.284 Confirmed Anonymous, 0.281 Mitchell Perilstein, 0.270 Confirmed Anonymous, 0.268 Eric Prestemon, 0.257 Michael J. Griffin, 0.257 Dan Nachbar, Applied Computing Systems Institute of Massachusetts, Center for Intelligent Information Retrieval, 0.253 Roland Kaltefleiter, 0.250 Richard A. Lethin, 0.248 Erik Schoenfelder, 0.245 Michael K. Cepek, 0.244 Alan Bawden, 0.243 Chris Claborne, AT&T Global Information Systems, 0.240 Dave Sill, 0.238 Jeff Hayward, 0.237 Mark Eichin, 0.236 Bill Broadley, 0.236 Confirmed Anonymous, 0.227 Lee Richardson, 0.223 Toma's Oliveira e Silva, 0.222 Theodore Ts'o, 0.214 R. Loader, 0.213

Mark V. Shaney, 0.212 Roger M. Levasseur, 0.212 Keith Bostic, 0.211 Peter Widow, 0.210 David Hollenberg, 0.198 Richard P. Brent, 0.198 James R. Fowler, 0.197 Leo Broukhis, 0.196 Bill Sommerfeld, 0.194 David Lee, 0.190 Unclaimed, 0.189 Chris Siebenmann, 0.189 Brian P. Fitzgerald, 0.186 David Buckley, 0.180 Jeff Woolsey, 0.174 Nick Holloway, 0.173 Brad Jones, 0.169 Andreas Steffen, 0.169 Serge Pachkovsky, 0.167 Peter Ilieve, 0.165 Stefan Gaertner, 0.165 Henri Cohen, 0.164 Tatu Mannisto, 0.160 Will Gilbert, 0.158 Andrew S. Krzywdzinski, 0.155 David J. Wright, 0.155 Henry Ellingworth, 0.154 root@cse.nau.edu, 0.151 Marc Brett, 0.150 Alan Barrett, 0.147 Scott Bennett, 0.146 anonymous grad student at New York University, 0.145 Mike Olson, 0.143 Alfred Wassermann, 0.142 Janne Himanka, 0.141 David L. Black, 0.136 Matthew Martin, 0.135 Jim McKim, 0.134 Craig Steinberger, 0.133 Ross Finlayson, 0.132 Confirmed Anonymous, 0.129 Narin Suphasindhu, 0.129 Woody Weaver, 0.129 Lloyd Miller, 0.127 Confirmed Anonymous, 0.126 Thomas Denny, 0.125 Roy Goodman, Digital Equipment Corporation, 0.124 Michael G. Reed, 0.123 Lance Cottrell, 0.123 David Comay, 0.123 Ronald M. Sorli, 0.123 Archie L. Cobbs, 0.121 Jim Hutchins, 0.120 Kelly Hall, 0.118 Unclaimed, 0.118 Allan Gottlieb, 0.116 Tomas Tengling, 0.116 Otto J. Makela, 0.114 Matthew Lyle, 0.113 Bret Ketchum, 0.113 Unclaimed, 0.111 Milt Mallory, Lincoln Ong, Ron Roberts, 0.111 Jeffrey I. Schiller, 0.110 Paul Rouse, 0.110 Mikko Siren, 0.105 John Oswalt, 0.102 Mike Chang, 0.101 Gary Oberbrunner, 0.097 Richard Doty, 0.095 Confirmed Anonymous, 0.095 Donald Nichols, 0.095 Bill Danielson, 0.094 Matthew Jackson, 0.094 Timothy A. Ramsey, 0.092 Unclaimed, 0.092 Olivier Bonaventure, 0.088 Felipe Castro A., 0.088 D.J. James, 0.087 Paul Zimmermann, 0.085 rps@ch.hp.com, 0.085 Hoyt A. Stearns jr., 0.083 Mansour Esmaili, 0.083 Durval Menezes (and others), 0.079 Dominik Gaillardetz, 0.077 Chuck Fee, 0.076 Unclaimed, 0.070 Robert Kulagowski, 0.069 Len Adleman, Dhiren Patel, 0.069 Geoffrey Baehr, 0.068 Jim Kirkpatrick, 0.068 Adam S. Nealis, 0.067 Frank Zizza, Samuel Hall, 0.066 Edward Mehlschau, 0.066 Richard Tobin, 0.064 Jonathan A. Jones, 0.060 Eng. Carmine Di Biase, 0.060 Aaron J. Heller, 0.060 Warren Gish, 0.058 Confirmed Anonymous, 0.058 Confirmed Anonymous, 0.057 Glenn Crocker, 0.057 Matthew J. Kidd, 0.056 Roy Kipp, 0.055 Renate Scheidler, 0.053 Jyri J. Virkki, 0.053 Michael D. Ernst, 0.053 Eric Johnson, 0.051 Jean-Pierre Szikora, 0.050 Jeff Murphy, 0.049 Gary A. Delong, 0.048 Wayne Schlitt, 0.048 Robin O'Leary, 0.048 Bryan Olson, 0.047 Greg Menounos, 0.047 Dave Madden, 0.046 Antonio Lioy, 0.046 Unclaimed, 0.046 Glenn Hollinger, 0.046 Jim Hickstein, 0.045 Confirmed Anonymous, 0.045 Unclaimed, 0.045 Mark Riordan, 0.045 Dirk Weigenand, 0.045 Richard Pinch, 0.044 Johannes Gronvall, 0.044 Russ Pagenkopf, 0.041 Robert Spellman, 0.040 Shawn Instenes, 0.038 Erol Basturk, 0.037 Christopher B. Moore, 0.037 Patrick Demichel, 0.036 Anish Mathuria, 0.036 Bob Clements, 0.036 Neil C. Kenneally, 0.036 Eugene W. Stark, 0.035 Unclaimed, 0.034 Marc Evans, The Destek Group, Inc., 0.034 Tom Epperly, 0.033 Unclaimed, 0.033 Peter Broadwell, 0.032 Geoffrey D. Bennett, 0.032 Daniel Tauber, 0.032 Mike Rose, 0.031 Christopher M. Conway, 0.031 James S. Vera, 0.031 Charles E. Spurgeon, 0.030 Manu Iyengar, 0.030 Peter Gutmann, 0.029 Bill Wade, 0.027 Pace Willisson, 0.027 Blair Zajac, 0.027 Larry Gadallah, 0.026 Tim Shepard, 0.025 Unclaimed, 0.025 Michael Brandmaier, 0.025 Andries E. Brouwer, 0.024 Alan Klietz, 0.024 Noam Shomron, 0.024 Thomas von Kamptz, 0.024 UBC IEEE Student Branch, 0.024 Unclaimed, 0.023 Carl Schott, 0.022 Paul J. Murphy, 0.022 Derek Clegg, 0.022 George M. Sipe, 0.021 Hugh D.R. Evans, 0.021 Confirmed Anonymous,, 0.020 Chris Davey, 0.020 Dave Ihnat, 0.020 Unclaimed, 0.020 Alan Fothergill, 0.020 Unclaimed, 0.020 Tilman Enss, 0.019 Kevin Hood, 0.019 Steve Uurtamo, 0.019 Andres Kruse, NIKHEF, 0.018 Unclaimed, 0.018 Unclaimed, 0.018 Jeffrey C. Ollie, 0.018 Mike Griffin, 0.018 James Leinweber, 0.018 Christian Weisgerber, 0.017 Markus Lamminmaki, 0.016 Bob Proulx, 0.016 Mark Edward Stahl, 0.016 Uwe Hollerbach, 0.016 Matthias Rosenberger, 0.016 Stewart A. Levin, 0.015 Mike Pearce, 0.015 Cornelis van der Laan, 0.015 Unclaimed, 0.014 Robert A. Hayden, 0.013 Jerome Abela, 0.013 Kenneth S.A. Oksanen, 0.013 David Metcalfe, 0.013 Unclaimed, 0.013 Lance M. Cottrell, 0.013 Allen Condit, 0.012 Claude Barbe, 0.012 Unclaimed, 0.012 David L. Johnson, 0.012 Dave Mitchell, 0.011 Bob Kupiec, 0.011 Juergen Hannken-Illjes, 0.011 John Cownie, 0.011 Peter Clark, 0.011 Stefan Larsson, 0.011 Ken Hardy, 0.010 Nelson Bolyard, 0.010 Unclaimed, 0.010 Timo Suhonen, 0.010 Andrew Gray, 0.010 Unclaimed, 0.010 Malcolm Beattie, 0.009 James Beal, 0.009 Simon Foley, 0.009 Seth Finkelstein, 0.009 John Oswalt, 0.009 Unclaimed, 0.009 Richard G. von Blucher, 0.009 Don Hejna, 0.008 Craig Groeschel, 0.008 Per Bojsen, 0.008 Carl Witty, 0.008 D.J. James, 0.007 Patrick Wendt, 0.007 Unclaimed, 0.007 Jason Yanowitz, and 0.007 Mark Delany.

Acknowledgements are due to Bruce Dodson for factoring $p+1$ using Peter Montgomery's ECM program, to Allen McIntosh for his assistance with our initial curve-fitting experiments, to Ron Rivest for his permission to quote from [20], and to Rich Schroeppel for his helpful comments on the run-times in [21].

We are particularly grateful to Jeff Schiller at MIT, who made available to us computing resources, GBytes of disk space and frequent backups of our hard-earned data. The fourth author is especially thankful for being permitted to log in to `hot-spare.mit.edu` in order to monitor progress and to test and install new software to handle the ever-increasing torrent of incoming data.

References

1. D. J. Bernstein, A. K. Lenstra, *A general number field sieve implementation*, 103–126 in: [13].
2. T. Denny, B. Dodson, A. K. Lenstra, M. S. Manasse, *On the factorization of RSA-120*, Advances in Cryptology, Crypto '93, Lecture Notes in Comput. Sci. **773** (1994) 166–174.
3. J. D. Dixon, *Asymptotically fast factorization of integers*, Math. Comp. **36** (1981) 255–260.
4. B. Dixon, A. K. Lenstra, *Factoring integers using SIMD sieves*, Advances in Cryptology, Eurocrypt '93, Lecture Notes in Comput. Sci. **765** (1994) 28–39.
5. B. Dodson, A. K. Lenstra, *NFS with four large primes: an explosive experiment*, in preparation.
6. M. Gardner, *Mathematical games, A new kind of cipher that would take millions of years to break*, Scientific American, August 1977, 120–124.
7. R. Golliver, A. K. Lenstra, K. S. McCurley, *Lattice sieving and trial division*, Algorithmic number theory symposium, Lecture Notes in Comput. Sci. **877** (1994) 18–27.
8. R. K. Guy, *How to factor a number*, Proc. Fifth Manitoba Conf. Numer. Math., Congressus Numerantium **16** (1976) 49–89.
9. D. E. Knuth, *The art of computer programming*, volume 2, *Seminumerical algorithms*, second edition, Addison-Wesley, Reading, Massachusetts, 1981.
10. B. A. LaMacchia, A. M. Odlyzko, *Computation of discrete logarithms in prime fields*, Designs, Codes and Cryptography **1** (1991) 47–62.
11. A. K. Lenstra, *Massively parallel computing and factoring*, Proceedings Latin'92, Lecture Notes in Comput. Sci. **583** (1992) 344–355.
12. A. K. Lenstra, H. W. Lenstra, Jr., *Algorithms in number theory*, Chapter 12 in: J. van Leeuwen (ed.), *Handbook of theoretical computer science*, Volume A, *Algorithms and complexity*, Elsevier, Amsterdam, 1990.
13. A. K. Lenstra, H. W. Lenstra, Jr. (eds), *The development of the number field sieve*, Lecture Notes in Math. **1554**, Springer-Verlag, Berlin, 1993.
14. A. K. Lenstra, H. W. Lenstra, Jr., M. S. Manasse, J. M. Pollard, *The factorization of the ninth Fermat number*, Math. Comp. **61** (1993) 319–349.
15. A. K. Lenstra, M. S. Manasse, *Factoring by electronic mail*, Advances in Cryptology, Eurocrypt '89, Lecture Notes in Comput. Sci. **434** (1990) 355–371.
16. A. K. Lenstra, M. S. Manasse, *Factoring with two large primes*, Advances in Cryptology, Eurocrypt '90, Lecture Notes in Comput. Sci. **473** (1990) 72–82; Math. Comp., to appear.

17. U. M. Maurer, *Fast generation of prime numbers and secure public-key cryptographic parameters*, Journal of Cryptology, to appear.
18. C. Pomerance, *Analysis and comparison of some integer factoring algorithms*, pp. 89–139 in: H. W. Lenstra, Jr., R. Tijdeman (eds), *Computational methods in number theory*, Math. Centre Tracts **154/155**, Mathematisch Centrum, Amsterdam, 1983.
19. C. Pomerance, J. W. Smith, *Reduction of huge, sparse matrices over finite fields via created catastrophes*, Experiment. Math. **1** (1992) 89–94.
20. R. L. Rivest, letter to Martin Gardner, 1977.
21. R. L. Rivest, A. Shamir, L. Adleman, *A method for obtaining digital signatures and public-key cryptosystems*, Comm. ACM **21** (1978) 120–126.
22. R. C. Schroeppel, personal communication, May 1994.
23. A. Shamir, personal communication, April 1994.
24. R. D. Silverman, *The multiple polynomial quadratic sieve*, Math. Comp. **48** (1987) 329–339.

Cryptanalysis of Multiple Modes of Operation

Eli Biham
Computer Science Department
Technion - Israel Institute of Technology
Haifa 32000, Israel

Abstract

In recent years, several new attacks on DES were introduced. These attacks have led researchers to suggest stronger replacements for DES, and in particular new modes of operation for DES. The most popular new modes are triple DES variants, which are claimed to be as secure as triple DES. To speed up hardware implementations of these modes, and to increase the avalanche, many suggestions apply several standard modes sequentially. In this paper we study these *multiple* (cascade) modes of operation. This study shows that many multiple modes are much weaker than multiple DES, and their strength is comparable to a single DES.

We conjecture that operation modes should be designed around an underlying cryptosystem without any attempt to use intermediate data as feedback, or to mix the feedback into an intermediate round. Thus, in particular, triple DES used in CBC mode is more secure than three single DES's used in triple CBC mode. Alternatively, if several encryptions are applied to each block, the best choice is to concatenate them to one long encryption, and build the mode of operation around it.

1 Introduction

The Data Encryption Standard[12] has several modes of operation[13] in which it can be used. These modes were devised to have a limited error propagation, to allow synchronization in data communications, to hide patterns in the plaintexts and to protect against chosen plaintext attacks on the underlying cryptosystem and against dictionary attacks. In the Cipher Block Chaining (CBC) mode and the Cipher Feedback (CFB) mode, each ciphertext block depends on all the previous plaintext blocks, by using the previous ciphertext block during encryption. The Output Feedback (OFB) mode was designed to allow precomputation of a major part of the encryption process, and to act as a pseudo-random bit generator. In this mode, a chosen plaintext attack does not let an attacker more information than a known plaintext attack. The CFB and OFB modes also allow encryption with a variety of blocksizes.

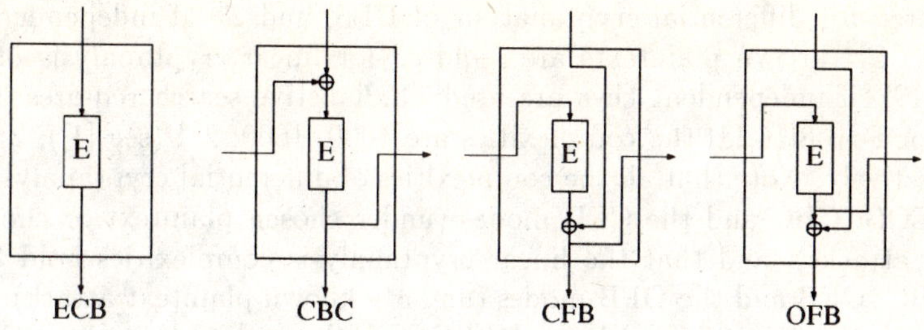

Figure 1. DES Modes of Operation.

Although these modes were designed to protect against chosen plaintext attacks, there is no attempt to protect against known plaintext attacks. In the modes of operation of DES, if an attacker knows both the plaintext blocks and the ciphertext blocks, he can calculate the values of actual inputs and outputs of the underlying cryptosystem, and can mount any known plaintext attack.

Since the DES modes of operation were introduced (they are described in Figure 1), many new non-standard modes were suggested. The first of which is the counter mode in which a counter is incremented and used as a feedback, while there is no feedback from other plaintext blocks. Other examples of suggested modes are PCBC, which was also used as a MAC function in the Kerberos system, and PFF (Plaintext Feed Forward)[6], which is similar to decryption under CBC (except that it uses encryption rather than decryption internally). All these modes are designed around one encryption function, without inner-feedbacks. We will call such modes *single modes*.

In the recent years, several new attacks on DES were introduced[3,9,17,5,2]. These attacks have led many people in the cryptographic community to suggest stronger replacements to the DES, which can be either new cryptosystems or new modes of operation for the DES. The most popular new modes are the *multiple modes*, which are combined from several consecutive applications of single modes[6,8]. In particular, *triple modes* combined from three consecutive applications of single modes were suggested. These triple modes were claimed to be as secure as triple DES, although they do not have triple DES as a building block. An advantage of the triple modes and multiple modes when implemented in hardware is that their speed is just the same as of single modes, since the single modes can be pipelined.

In this paper we cryptanalyze many multiple modes of operation. In particular, we show that many triple modes are much weaker than triple DES, and that some triple modes are not much more secure than a single DES.

Our attacks may be based upon any known attack on the underlying cryptosystems, and in particular differential cryptanalysis[3], linear cryptanalysis[9], improved Davies' attack[2], and exhaustive search. For reference we assume that the following complexities are required by these attacks: 2^{47} chosen plaintexts are required for differential cryptanalysis of DES, and 2^{61} if independent keys are used. 2^{43} known plaintexts are required for linear cryptanalysis of DES, and 2^{60} (?) if independent keys are used. Exhaustive search requires 2^{55}–2^{56} steps. For Feal-8[16,11] the complexities are 1000, 1000, 2^{24} (see [1]), 2^{24}, and 2^{64} respectively. Note that all the complexities of differential cryptanalysis hold for the ECB, CBC and the CFB modes (under chosen plaintext or chosen ciphertext attacks), and that the linear cryptanalysis complexities hold for the ECB, CBC, CFB and the OFB modes (under a known plaintext attack). (Note that an attack on the 8-bit CFB mode of DES with a reduced number of rounds was described in [15]). The best full-round differential characteristic of DES has probability about 2^{-63} and the best full-round differential characteristic of Feal has probability 2^{-16}. Unless otherwise indicated, we assume that DES is the underlying cryptosystem of the attacked modes. Throughout this paper, whenever we refer to the CFB and the OFB modes, we actually mean their full feedback variants, i.e., the 64-bit CFB and the 64-bit OFB, respectively.

Our attacks are of three major kinds: Chosen plaintext attacks are applicable to the ECB mode and potentially to other modes which were not designed to be immune to chosen plaintext attacks. We concentrate on chosen ciphertext attacks which are applicable to many of the modes which are immune to chosen plaintext attacks. For example, the CBC and the CFB modes are vulnerable to chosen ciphertext attacks (with attacks much simpler than the ones described in this paper).

The third kind of attacks (which we do not actually apply in this paper) generalizes the chosen plaintext and chosen ciphertext attacks into chosen plaintext and ciphertext attacks, in which the attacker can decide for each block whether he chooses the plaintext or the ciphertext. These attacks are not adaptive: the attacker can choose all the plaintext/ciphertext blocks before he receives the first encrypted/decrypted block. This model is very strong, since in practice no encryption chip or software allows changing direction from encryption to decryption and vice versa during the process of encryption/decryption. We can slightly reduce this demand by viewing an equivalent model which does not require changing encryption/decryption direction for each block. In this model, two chips loaded with the same key are required: one of them always encrypts and the other always decrypts. In this model, the attacks are adaptive chosen plaintext on one chip and an adaptive chosen ciphertext on the other chip, both executed in parallel. Whenever in the original attacks we have to encrypt a block, we feed the encrypting chip with the plaintext block, and feed the decrypting chip with the resultant ciphertext. Whenever in the original attacks we have to decrypt a block, we feed the decrypting chip with the ciphertext block, and feed the encrypting chip with the resultant plaintext. This model is more realistic in the sense that each chip either encrypts or decrypts, but the adaptive attack requirement causes this attack to work almost only when two such loaded chips may be directly manipulated by the attacker. The chosen plaintext and ciphertext attacks are particularly applicable to double modes. They can cryptanalyze many modes that cannot be attacked by the simpler attacks and can attack other modes with a smaller complexity than other attacks.

We show that many multiple modes are weaker than the corresponding multiple ECB mode, when chosen plaintext, chosen ciphertext or chosen plaintext and ciphertext attacks are applicable. If a multiple mode combines several single modes, in which in each of them a different cryptosystem is used, and in which the keys of the various single modes are independent, the strength of the multiple mode might not exceed the strength of the strongest single mode component. If the various keys are not independent, the strength of the multiple mode might even be the same as of its weakest component. Two-key triple DES (triple ECB mode) is such an (already known) example [14].

We conjecture that operation modes should be designed around an underlying cryptosystem without any attempt to use intermediate data as feedback, or to mix the feedback into an intermediate round. Alternatively, if several encryptions are applied in each block, the best choice is to concatenate them to one long encryption, and build the mode of operation around the result.

This paper is divided to the following sections: In Section 2 we show that multiple modes are at least as strong as the strongest single mode contained within, when the keys of all the various single modes are independent. In Section 3 we analyse many multiple modes and describe our analysis techniques. In Section 4 we summarize the results.

2 The Strength of Multiple Modes

In this section we show that multiple modes of operation are not less secure than their strongest single mode component, whenever the keys of the various components are independent. This result holds in models in which the attacker has access to the plaintexts (and not only to their statistics). This result was already proved in the context of cascade ciphers in [7][1].

Let A and B be two modes and let C be the combined double mode C=AB, whose component keys K_A and K_B are chosen independently. The following theorem shows that C is not weaker than either of its components. It is similar to Theorem 5 in [7], whose proof holds in our case as well.

Theorem 1 The cracking problem of either A or B is efficiently reducible to the cracking problem of C=AB.

Conclusion 1 A multiple mode may not be weaker than its strongest component, if the component keys are chosen independently.

We show that this theorem holds *only* if the various components' keys are independent. In particular it does not hold for two-key triple modes (such as encrypt with K_1, encrypt (or decrypt) with K_2, and encrypt with K_1 again), since it might be that one key (K_1) is used both in the strongest component and the weakest component, and then we might find it by attacking the weakest

[1]It does not hold when the attacker has access only to the statistics of the plaintexts[10]. In our model the attacker always knows both the plaintexts and the ciphertexts.

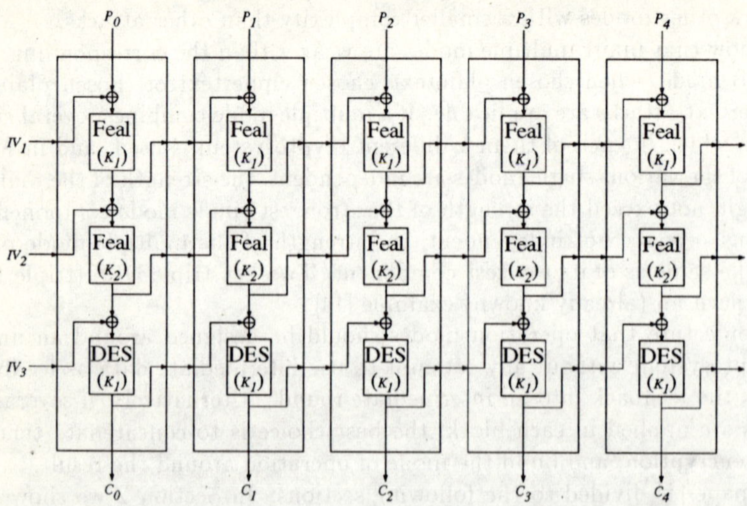

Figure 2. The triple CBC mode, using Feal, Feal and DES.

component. For example, we study the case of a triple CBC mode which uses Feal[16,11] in its first two components, and DES[12] in the third, while the same key K_1 is used in both the first component and the third component (see Figure 2). By methods described in the next section, we can find the key K_1 of the first component using 2^{18} chosen ciphertexts. The key of the third component is the same as the key of the first component. The key of the second component can then be easily found using 1000 chosen ciphertexts (or 2^{24} known plaintexts). Therefore, the whole secret key of the multiple mode is found using about 2^{18} chosen ciphertexts within a few minutes. Note that the third component (which uses DES) by itself is much more resistant than the whole system, and cannot be attacked successfully by any known method with complexity smaller than 2^{43}.

3 Analysis

For the cryptanalysis of the modes of operation, we use several techniques. Most of these techniques select one of the encryption boxes in the modes of operation, inside one of the single modes, and feed it with the data required for differential or linear cryptanalysis. After the key of the encryption box is found, other (or the same) techniques are used to find the remaining keys (one at a time).

In the following sections we describe six cryptanalysis techniques, which introduce the most useful principles used to cryptanalyze multiple modes. Additional techniques can be developed using these principles. Each of the techniques finds one key. Unless otherwise indicated, the complexities quoted in the descriptions of these techniques are the complexities to find this one key. The total complexities of the attacks on the various modes are described in the summary. A few of the full attacks might become adaptive; however, in most cases the attacks remain non-adaptive.

We refer the encryption operations used in the modes of operation as *encryption boxes*, and number them with the index of the mode during the multiple encryption. The encryption boxes can actually apply decryption operations in particular single modes (in which during mode decryption, an encryption operation is to be used). In our discussion we use the terms input and output of the encryption boxes to be their input/output during mode encryption, regardless of whether we talk about mode encryption or mode decryption, and regardless of the particular operation in the encryption box (i.e., encryption or decryption). We keep the words plaintext and ciphertext to be the plaintext/ciphertext of the multiple mode, rather than to be the input/output of the encryption boxes. We also assume that the keys entering the encryption boxes are independent. We denote the key entering encryption box i by K_i, and the initial value of the ith single mode (if any) by IV_i (See Figure 2).

3.1 Technique A: The Basic Technique

Our basic technique for analyzing multiple modes of operation is to feed one of the underlying encryption boxes (in one of the single modes) with the data required for differential cryptanalysis. This may be done by choosing pairs of tuples of blocks in such a way that most blocks are the same in both pairs, and these blocks cause many internal values to be fixed when both tuples are encrypted/decrypted. One block should differ by the difference required for differential cryptanalysis, and it should cause this difference to appear in the input (or output) of one of the encryption boxes. In addition, we should be able to collect the output (or input) of this encryption block, up to XOR with some of the fixed internal values. This situation allows us to attack the encryption box by the regular differential attacks to which it is vulnerable (if it is vulnerable). This basic technique can be based on any differential cryptanalytic attack, and any successful *R-attack (either 0R, 1R, 2R or 3R-attack) can be applied.

One of the simplest forms of this technique attacks the ECB|CBC|CBC mode (see Figure 3) using a chosen ciphertext attack. Our aim is to feed the output of encryption box 1 (in the single ECB component) with pairs differing by the differences required for differential cryptanalysis. After these pairs are decrypted, the inputs of the encryption box are just the plaintexts we receive from the decryption of the triple mode. Thus, the regular differential cryptanalytic techniques (such as counting) can be applied. Note that due to the symmetry of DES (and most blockciphers), there is no technical difference between a chosen plaintext and a chosen ciphertext attack. Note also that if the same value of two successive ciphertext blocks is repeated twice in different positions in a ciphertext message (encrypted under the same keys with the ECB|CBC|CBC mode), the same feedbacks result in both positions, and any third block is decrypted into the same plaintext in both positions.

For the attack, the attacker chooses many pairs of tuples of blocks (C_0, C_1, C_2) and ($C_0 \oplus \Omega_T$, C_1, C_2), where C_0, C_1, and C_2 are some arbitrary block values,

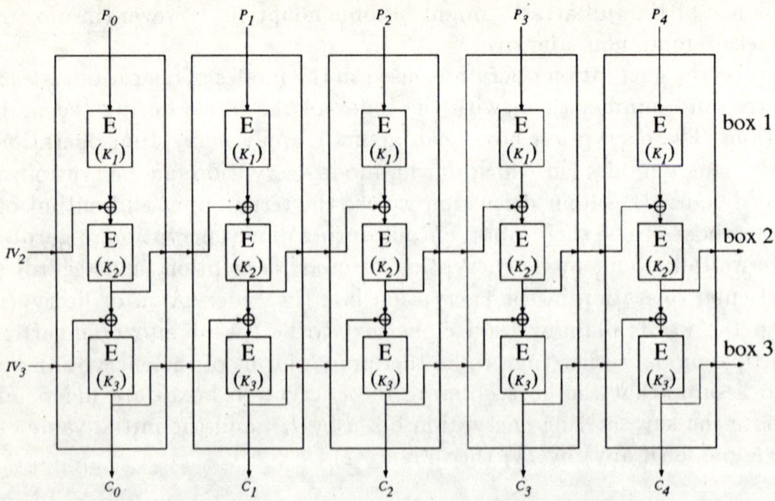

Figure 3. The triple mode: ECB|CBC|CBC.

and Ω_T is the difference required for differential cryptanalysis. If a differential attack with Ω_T requires n pairs to attack an ECB mode, the attacker should choose n tuples (C_0, C_1, C_2) and request to decrypt the $6n$ blocks consisting of all the pairs (C_0, C_1, C_2) and ($C_0 \oplus \Omega_T$, C_1, C_2).

It is evident that the difference of the tuples is (Ω_T, 0, 0) for each pair. Due to the structure of the triple mode, the differences 0 cause differences 0 in the input of box 3, and after XORing these differences with the differences of the feedbacks, we result with differences (–, Ω_T, 0) in the output of box 2, where '–' denotes an unpredictable value. Similarly, the differences at the output of box 1 are (–, –, Ω_T). Therefore, in the third blocks of the tuples, the differences of the output of box 1 are Ω_T, just as chosen by the attacker. Since the input of box 1 is the plaintext received by decryption of the triple mode, all the requirements for differential cryptanalysis of box 1 are satisfied. As a result, we can find the key used in box 1 by applying differential cryptanalytic attacks.

The attack described above assumes that the characteristic is set in the last rounds of box 1, and that the *R-attack is done on the first rounds. This attack can use quartets, octets or structures of any size by fixing C_1 and C_2 and playing with structures of C_0.

This technique, as described above, does not apply to the differential attack on the full 16-round DES[4,3], since the later requires the knowledge of actual plaintext (in our case: ciphertext) bits, and not only their differences. However, the 14 plaintext (ciphertext) bits required by the attack, are not known to the attacker just because they are XORed with a 14-bit constant. This constant can be found together with the key using a more extensive analysis.

Since the analysis phase of the attack on the full 16-round DES is faster by a

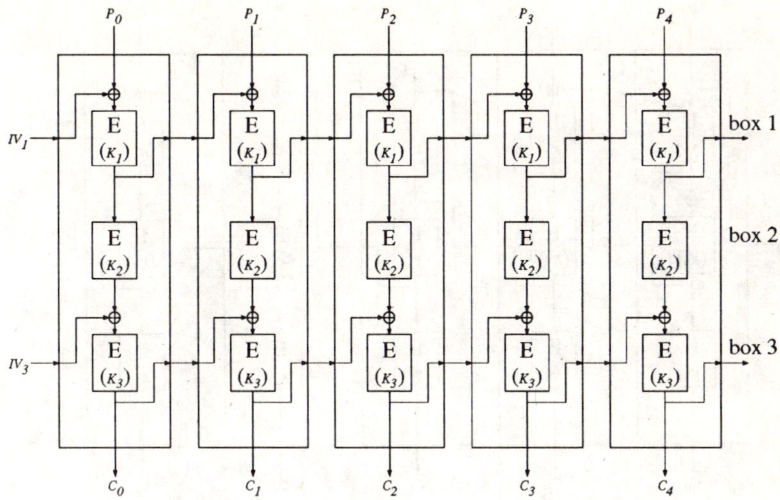

Figure 4. The triple mode: CBC|ECB|CBC.

factor of 2^{10} from the data collection phase, and since in our case the encryption times of the data collection phase costs $3 \cdot 3 = 9$ times more DES encryptions than the attack on the ECB mode, we conclude that the data analysis in our case takes about the same time as the data collection phase. Therefore, the complexity of a differential cryptanalytic attack on the first key of this triple mode is $3 \cdot 2^{47}$ chosen ciphertexts (2^{47} chosen ciphertext tuples). Using auxiliary structuring techniques, the number of chosen ciphertexts can be reduced to 2^{47}.

3.2 Technique B: Enhancement of the Basic Technique

An enhancement of the basic technique allows attacking modes whose plaintexts are mixed with feedbacks before they are fed into the first encryption box. Examples of such modes are CBC|ECB|CBC and CBC|CBC|ECB. These modes are described in Figures 4 and 5. This enhanced technique may also use any *R-attack, but requires finding more than one subkey. Thus, the number of required plaintexts is similar to the number of plaintexts required by the independent key variant of the differential cryptanalytic attack.

In these modes, we choose the differences of the tuples just as we do in the basic technique, but we receive less information from the received plaintexts. In the basic technique the inputs of encryption box 1 are known to the attacker. In the generalized modes attacked by this enhanced technique, the inputs of the encryption box in the ECB mode (boxes 2 and 3, respectively) are not known to the attacker. However, the value of this input XORed with an unknown fixed value (same in both members of the pair) is known. This fixed value may be mixed to the subkeys to form actual subkeys[3]. The independent-key variant of

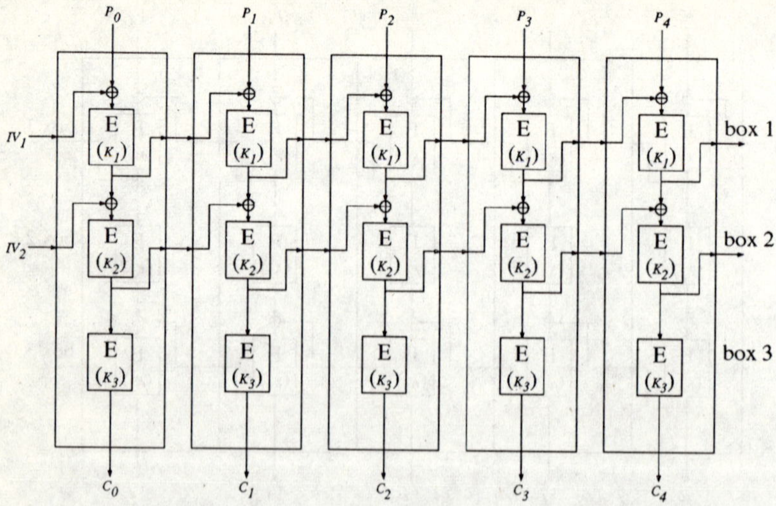

Figure 5. The triple mode: CBC|CBC|ECB.

the differential cryptanalytic attack can now find all the actual subkeys (actually only three actual subkeys are required). By analyzing the actual subkeys, we can find 55 independent parity bits of the DES key, 63 bits of the fixed value and one additional parity bit of both. By trying the two values of the unknown bit of the key we can find the complete key. The complexity of this attack is similar to the complexity of the independent key variant of the original attack on the ECB mode.

Whenever this enhancement uses a counting method to find the key (rather than the method used in the attack on the full 16-round DES), we must ensure that the fixed value is the same in all the tuples. For this, we have to choose the same C_1's and C_2's in all the pairs.

In the CBC|CBC|ECB mode, the other keys can be found by technique D (as in the attack on the triple CBC mode described later). In the CBC|ECB|CBC mode, K_3 can be found easily, since the input of box 3 can be easily calculated; then, K_1 can also be completed.

3.3 Technique C: A Technique using Linear Cryptanalysis

The basic technique can also be applied using linear cryptanalysis. In this technique, we do not choose pairs of messages and study their differences, as we do when differential cryptanalysis is used. Instead, we fix many blocks which are mixed with the inputs/outputs of the attacked encryption box, and we end up with the knowledge of the inputs and the outputs of the attacked encryption box XORed with some unknown fixed values. Since linear cryptanalysis is not affected by the combination of such fixed values, we can do the whole linear cryptanalysis, just as is done in the regular model (i.e., single ECB mode) — we just end up with parity bits combining key bits and bits of the fixed values. Since linear cryptanalysis can find the subkeys also when independent keys are used (i.e., when all the subkeys are independent), we can complete the encryption keys even in this more complex case, after we find several subkeys, rather than just one or two.

This technique can be applied to the modes attacked by techniques A and B. For example, to attack the CBC|ECB|CBC mode, it requires choosing many tuples of ciphertexts (C_0, C_1, C_2) where C_1 and C_2 should be fixed in all the tuples, and C_0 can be chosen at random. The resultant plaintext block P_2 is of the form $D_{K_2}(C_0 \oplus V_1) \oplus V_2$, where V_1 and V_2 are fixed values depending on the choice of the fixed ciphertext blocks C_1 and C_2. Linear cryptanalysis can find the key K_2 and the fixed values V_1 and V_2 (except one bit due to the complementation property: simultaneous complementation of K_2, V_1 and V_2 does not change the results). Then, attacks to find K_1 and K_3 can be mounted (even exhaustive search for each of them requires now only 2^{55}–2^{56} steps, and faster attacks *are* feasible).

This technique requires 2^{60} chosen tuples of ciphertext to find the key of the ECB component. The other keys of the CBC|ECB|CBC mode can be found even by exhaustive search with complexity about 2^{55}. The other keys of the ECB|CBC|CBC and the CBC|CBC|ECB modes should be found by techniques D or F.

A similar technique can use the improved Davies' attack[5,2], but its complexity is expected to be higher than with linear cryptanalysis.

3.4 Technique D

In technique B we used the single ECB component within the multiple mode to allow a fixed value to be XORed to the input pairs of the ECB component, and thus we could handle the additional mixing of the plaintexts before they are entered to the encryption boxes. Whenever we do not have a single ECB component in our mode, like in the triple CBC mode (CBC|CBC|CBC), we can use another enhancement of the basic technique, that allows to find the keys of the encryption boxes.

For the triple CBC mode, we choose the pairs of four-block tuples (C_0, C_1, C_2, C_3) and (C_0, $C_1 \oplus \Omega_T$, C_2, C_3) (with the difference (0, Ω_T, 0, 0)), with the same C_0, C_1 and C_2 in all the pairs. The various pairs differ only in the values of C_3, while the two members of a single pair differ only in the value of C_1. Thus, the differences are developed during decryption to (–, A, Ω_T, 0) at the output of encryption box 2, and to (–, –, B, Ω_T) at the output of encryption box 1, where A and B are some fixed differences in all the pairs (since they depend only on C_0, C_1, C_2 and Ω_T which are the same in all the pairs). As a result, encryption box 1 has difference Ω_T in the output of the fourth block, and its input is known to the attacker (as a plaintext block) XORed with the unknown fixed value B. Once we find the value of B, technique B can be used to find the key K_1.

The value of B can be found using a full-round characteristic of encryption box 1. If DES is used, it has probability about 2^{-63}, which (for many keys) will allow identifying the expected difference of the input to this box. Since the known plaintext block P_3 is XORed with the feedback from the previous block to form the input to the box, the differences satisfy $B = P_3' \oplus \Omega_P$, and B can be calculated for any right pair (P_3' is the difference between the plaintext block P_3 and its counterpart). The true value of B should be the most frequent resulting value, if the probability of the characteristic is not too low, and thus it can be identified (possibly using a huge memory of 2^{64} one-byte counters). This identification can be somewhat easier if we use the observation that we can find 52 bits of B even if we use only a 15-round characteristic, whose probability is about 2^{-55}, since we can predict the behavior of five S boxes in the 16th round (which have zero input differences).

This enhanced technique requires about 2^{66} chosen ciphertext tuples to find B, both feedbacks to P_3 (whose XOR is B) and the key K_1. It requires full-length characteristics, whose number of rounds is the same as the number of rounds of the attacked encryption box (sometimes characteristics with one round less can be used), and thus the number of required plaintexts is similar to the number of plaintexts required by a 0R-attack (1R-attack). This technique cannot use linear cryptanalysis.

One could also design modes with many feedbacks, that would seem more secure than modes with a small number of feedbacks. If we would take this suggestion to extreme, we could CBC-feedback every round of the triple-encryption, resulting with 48 feedbacks. This would make the intermediate data during the triple encryption be more dependent on the previous blocks, and would increase the avalanche of the previous blocks. However, as we conclude from the triple CBC mode above, any multiple CBC mode is not more secure that its basic box against 0R-attacks. In this suggestion, the basic box is just one round, which is trivial to break. Thus, this extreme suggestion is also trivial to break. An attack requires only few chosen ciphertexts to find all the subkeys, even if independent keys are used.

3.5 Technique E: Using Exhaustive Search

The best example of this technique analyzes the CBC|CBC|ECB mode. This technique finds the key of the last (ECB) encryption box using exhaustive search.

The attacker chooses one pair of ciphertext tuples (C_0, C_1, C_2) and (C_0^*, C_1, C_2) in which $C_0 \neq C_0^*$. For this pair, $P_2 \oplus P_2^*$ equals the difference of the input of the last encryption box of block 0. Thus, we can exhaustively search all values of K_3 by decrypting C_0 and C_0^* and verifying that the difference of the results equals $P_2 \oplus P_2^*$.

Unlike most of the techniques that we describe, this technique has a known plaintext variant. Given about 2^{65} known plaintexts, the birthday paradox predicts the existence of two tuples (C_0, C_1, C_2) and (C_0^*, C_1^*, C_2^*) in which $C_1 = C_1^*$, $C_2 = C_2^*$. The same technique might be applied on this pair.

3.6 Technique F: The Birthday Technique

This technique has several variants, of which only one is described in this section. All these variants use the birthday paradox to find good samples for cryptanalysis, and they can use differential cryptanalysis, linear cryptanalysis and exhaustive search for finding the key of a single component. The variant we describe in this section cryptanalyzes the last encryption box of the triple CBC mode (or any multiple CBC/ECB mode whose last component is CBC), and it finds the key of the last component by exhaustive search.

This variant requires the attacker to choose 2^{33} ciphertext tuples of the form (C, C, C, C), where C is chosen at random, and to receive the corresponding plaintexts (P_0, P_1, P_2, P_3), of which only the P_3's are actually required.

The CBC decryption of the third single CBC mode of a tuple (C, C, C, C) results in $(?, H, H, H)$, where $H = C \oplus \mathrm{DES}_{k_3}^{-1}(C)$. H is a pseudo-random function of C (and not a permutation of the values of C). Thus, given 2^{33} random C's, with a high probability two of the C's result with the same H. Therefore, for these two C's, the same value of P_3 is expected. False alarms can result from the first two single CBC modes (due to the same property), and thus the following analysis should be repeated three times on average until K_3 is found.

Given the 2^{33} P_3's resulting from triple CBC decryption of the (C, C, C, C) tuples, we search for pairs of C and C^* for which $P_3 = P_3^*$. For such pairs we assume that both C and C^* satisfy

$$C \oplus \mathrm{DES}_{k_3}^{-1}(C) = C^* \oplus \mathrm{DES}_{k_3}^{-1}(C^*).$$

Then, we exhaustively evaluate this equation for all the 2^{56} possible values of K_3. The equation is satisfied for a fraction of about 2^{-64} of the wrong keys, and thus we can be quite sure that a key satisfying this equation is the right key. (To decrease the false alarm probability, we can select only keys which satisfy the equation using two different pairs of tuples). Note that after we find K_3, the same technique can find K_2 using the same data. Then, K_1 can be found by exhaustive search, differential cryptanalysis or linear cryptanalysis.

A more sophisticated variant of this technique can attack the more complex CBC|CBC^{-1}|CBC (CBC encrypt, CBC decrypt, CBC encrypt) mode with 2^{66} chosen ciphertexts and complexity.

4 Summary

We studied the strength of multiple modes of operation. We showed that in many cases, these modes are weaker than the corresponding multiple ECB mode. In several cases, these modes are not more secure than just one single encryption using the same cryptosystem. For example, the triple CBC mode (CBC|CBC|CBC – whose components encrypt using a single DES) and the modes CBC|CBC|ECB, CBC|ECB|CBC and ECB|CBC|CBC are weaker than triple DES, and their strength is comparable to the strength of a single DES.

Mode	Cryptanalysis Using Technique					
	A	B	C	D	E	F
ECB|CBC|CBC	2^{47}		2^{60}			2^{58}
CBC|ECB|CBC		2^{61}	2^{60}			2^{58}
CBC|CBC|ECB		2^{61}	2^{60}		2^{56}	
CBC|CBC|CBC				2^{66}		2^{58}
CBC|CBC^{-1}|CBC						2^{66}
CBC feedback every round				Few		

Table 1. Summary of the easiest-key (chosen ciphertext) attacks on multiple modes of DES.

Mode	Cryptanalysis Using Technique					
	A	B	C	D	E	F
ECB|CBC|CBC	1000		2^{24}			2^{66}
CBC|ECB|CBC		1000	2^{24}			2^{66}
CBC|CBC|ECB		1000	2^{24}		2^{64}	
CBC|CBC|CBC				2^{17}		2^{66}
CBC|CBC^{-1}|CBC						2^{66}
CBC feedback every round				Few		

Table 2. Summary of the easiest-key (chosen ciphertext) attacks on multiple modes of Feal-8.

The triple mode CBC|CBC^{-1}|CBC, where CBC^{-1} is CBC decryption, is not much stronger.

Tables 1 and 2 summarize the results obtained for the multiple modes of operation when the underlying cryptosystems are DES and Feal-8 respectively. All the attacks are chosen ciphertext attacks. The complexities quoted are the complexities of finding one key of one of the single modes (i.e., the easiest key to find), in terms of the number of tuples required or the complexity of the analysis (the largest of them). To find the other keys the complexity might be higher. Table 3 summarizes the total complexities of attacking the multiple modes of operation, and finding all their keys. In the full paper we will describe results on multiple modes incorporating additional single modes (such as CFB).

We conclude that strong modes of operation should not be based on combining simpler modes, nor use internal feedbacks. We suggest to use single modes, and to incorporate multiple encryption as the underlying cryptosystems of the single modes. Alternatively, whenever we have a multiple mode or any other mode which uses internal feedbacks, it can be strengthened by eliminating the use of the internal feedbacks.

Mode	Complexity E=DES	Complexity E=Feal-8
ECB|CBC|CBC	2^{58}	2^{17}
CBC|ECB|CBC	2^{58}	2^{17}
CBC|CBC|ECB	2^{58}	2^{17}
CBC|CBC|CBC	2^{59}	2^{18}
CBC|CBC^{-1}|CBC	2^{66}	2^{66}
CBC feedback every round	Few	Few

Table 3. Total complexities of the attacks on the multiple modes.

Acknowledgments

I would like to acknowledge Ross Anderson whose ideas motivated this research, and to Carl Ellison and Burt Kaliski whose valuable remarks and suggestions improved the quality of this paper. Shimon Even has pointed me to [7] and [10]. Acknowledgment: This research was supported by the fund for the promotion of research at the Technion.

References

[1] Eli Biham, *On Matsui's Linear Cryptanalysis*, Lecture Notes in Computer Science, Advances in Cryptology, proceedings of EUROCRYPT'94, to appear.

[2] Eli Biham, Alex Biryukov, *An Improvement of Davies' Attack on DES*, Lecture Notes in Computer Science, Advances in Cryptology, proceedings of EUROCRYPT'94, to appear.

[3] Eli Biham, Adi Shamir, *Differential Cryptanalysis of the Data Encryption Standard*, Springer-Verlag, 1993.

[4] Eli Biham, Adi Shamir, *Differential Cryptanalysis of the full 16-round DES*, Lecture Notes in Computer Science, Advances in Cryptology, proceedings of CRYPTO'92, pp. 487–496, 1992.

[5] D. W. Davies, *Investigation of a Potential Weakness in the DES Algorithm*, 1987, private communication.

[6] Carl Ellison, private communications, 1993.

[7] Shimon Even, Oded Goldreich, *On the Power of Cascade Ciphers*, ACM Transactions on Computer Systems, Vol. 3, NO. 2, pp. 108–116, May 1985.

[8] Burt Kaliski, *Triple-DES: A Brief Report*, RSA laboratories, private communication, October 29, 1993.

[9] Mitsuru Matsui, *Linear Cryptanalysis Method for DES Cipher*, Lecture Notes in Computer Science, Advances in Cryptology, proceedings of EUROCRYPT'93, pp. 386–397, 1993.

[10] Ueli M. Maurer, James L. Massey, *Cascade Ciphers: The Importance of Being First*, Journal of Cryptology, Vol. 6, No. 1, pp. 55–61, 1993.

[11] Shoji Miyaguchi, Akira Shiraishi, Akihiro Shimizu, *Fast Data Encryption Algorithm FEAL-8*, Review of electrical communications laboratories, Vol. 36, No. 4, pp. 433–437, 1988.

[12] National Bureau of Standards, *Data Encryption Standard*, U.S. Department of Commerce, FIPS pub. 46, January 1977.

[13] National Bureau of Standards, *DES Modes of Operation*, U.S. Department of Commerce, FIPS pub. 81, December 1980.

[14] Paul C. van Oorschot, Michael J. Wiener, *A Known Plaintext Attack on Two-Key Triple Encryption*, Lecture Notes in Computer Science, Advances in Cryptology, proceedings of EUROCRYPT'90, pp. 318–325, 1990.

[15] Bart Preneel, Marnix Nuttin, Vincent Rijmen, Johan Buelens, *Cryptanalysis of the CFB Mode of the DES with a Reduced Number of Rounds*, Lecture Notes in Computer Science, Advances in Cryptology, proceedings of CRYPTO'93, pp. 212–223, 1993.

[16] Akihiro Shimizu, Shoji Miyaguchi, *Fast Data Encryption Algorithm FEAL*, Lecture Notes in Computer Science, Advances in Cryptology, proceedings of EUROCRYPT'87, pp. 267–278, 1987.

[17] Michael J. Wiener, *Efficient DES Key Search*, technical report TR-244, School of Computer Science, Carleton University, Ottawa, Canada, May 1994. Presented at the Rump session of CRYPTO'93, August 1993.

Linear Cryptanalysis of LOKI and s^2DES

Toshio Tokita   Tohru Sorimachi   Mitsuru Matsui

Computer & Information Systems Laboratory
Mitsubishi Electric Corporation
5-1-1, Ofuna, Kamakura, Kanagawa, 247, Japan
tokita@mmt.isl.melco.co.jp   sori@mmt.isl.melco.co.jp   matsui@mmt.isl.melco.co.jp

Abstract. This paper discusses linear cryptanalysis of LOKI89, LOKI91 and s^2DES. Our computer program based on Matsui's search algorithm has completely determined their best linear approximate equations, which tell us applicability of linear cryptanalysis to each cryptosystem. As a result, LOKI89 and LOKI91 are resistant to linear cryptanalysis from the viewpoint of the best linear approximate probability, whereas s^2DES is breakable by a known-plaintext attack faster than an exhaustive key search. Moreover, our search program, which is also applicable to differential cryptanalysis, has derived their best differential characteristics as well. These values give a complete proof that characteristics found by Knudsen are actually best.

1 Introduction

LOKI is a DES-like cryptosystem that was proposed by Brown *et al.* [5] in 1990. It has four 12-bit input/8-bit output S-boxes, all of which are the same. The first version of LOKI was redesigned due to a weakness of its key schedule part found by Knudsen *etc.* [6][8][9]. Knudsen also showed that neither of the first version, called LOKI89, nor the second version, called LOKI91, has any differential characteristics whose probability is high enough for successful differential cryptanalysis [9][10].

s^2DES was proposed by Kim [7] in 1991, which has the same structure as DES except its S-box tables. Knudsen [11] found that s^2DES has several iterative characteristics which lead to successful differential cryptanalysis. However, the best differential characteristics of LOKI89, LOKI91 and s^2DES are unknown, while those of DES have been recently calculated [3]. Moreover, as far as we know, there has been no discussion about applicability of linear cryptanalysis to these cryptosystems.

This paper for the first time discusses linear cryptanalysis of LOKI89, LOKI91 and s^2DES. We begin by studying statistical properties of their S-boxes, and then using Matsui's search algorithm [3], completely determine their best linear approximate equations. We also take into consideration, for comparison, DES variants whose S-boxes are reordered so that they are stronger in regard to differential or linear cryptanalysis [3]. As a result, we show that LOKI89 and LOKI91 are resistant to linear cryptanalysis from the viewpoint of the best linear approximate probability and even stronger than the modified DES whose

S-boxes are rearranged in the strongest order against linear cryptanalysis. On the other hand, s^2DES is just slightly stronger than the original DES, and hence breakable by a known-plaintext attack faster than an exhaustive key search.

We have implemented a computer program for breaking LOKI91 reduced to six round to estimate the number of known-plaintexts required for successful linear cryptanalysis of LOKI with arbitrary number of rounds. Our experimental results suggest that the strength of n-round LOKI89/91 corresponds to $2n$-round DES in regard to linear cryptanalysis.

Our search program has also derived the best differential characteristics of these cryptosystems, which give us a complete proof that characteristics found by Knudsen *etc.* [1][6][9][10][11] are actually best. We also show that LOKI89 and LOKI91 are even stronger than the modified DES such that the order of its S-boxes is the strongest choice in regard to differential cryptanalysis.

2 Preliminaries

2.1 Notations

Figure 1 shows the data randomization part and F-function of DES-like cryptosystems, which are the scope of this paper. We omit the initial and final permutations. Throughout this paper, the notations described here are used unless otherwise mentioned.

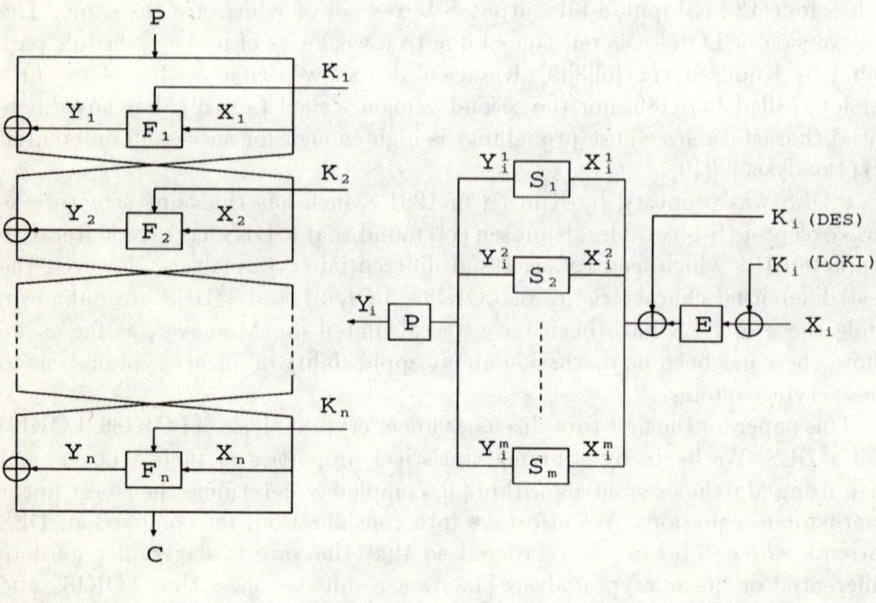

Figure 1: The data randomization part and F-function of DES-like cryptosystem.

We will discuss differential cryptanalysis and linear cryptanalysis in parallel, and for this purpose, we define the best probability of n-round cipher depending on the context as described in [3]:

[In the case of Differential Cryptanalysis]

- ▷ $P(\Delta X_i^j, \Delta Y_i^j) \stackrel{\text{def}}{=} Prob\{X_i^j \oplus \Delta X_i^j = Y_i^j \oplus \Delta Y_i^j\}$,
- ▷ $P(\Delta X_i, \Delta Y_i) \stackrel{\text{def}}{=} Prob\{F_i(X_i \oplus \Delta X_i, K_i) = Y_i \oplus \Delta Y_i\}$,
- ▷ $BEST_n^{DC} \stackrel{\text{def}}{=} \max_{\Delta X_i = \Delta X_{i-2} \oplus \Delta X_{i-1} (3 \leq i \leq n), (\Delta P, \Delta C) \neq (0,0)} \{ \prod_{i=1}^{n} P(\Delta X_i, \Delta Y_i) \}$,

[In the case of Linear Cryptanalysis]

- ▷ $P(\Gamma Y_i^j, \Gamma X_i^j) \stackrel{\text{def}}{=} |\ Prob\{\ Parity(X_i^j \bullet \Gamma X_i^j) = Parity(Y_i^j \bullet \Gamma Y_i^j)\ \} - 1/2\ |$,
- ▷ $P(\Gamma Y_i, \Gamma X_i) \stackrel{\text{def}}{=} |\ Prob\{\ Parity(X_i \bullet \Gamma X_i) = Parity(Y_i \bullet \Gamma Y_i)\ \} - 1/2\ |$,
- ▷ $BEST_n^{LC} \stackrel{\text{def}}{=} \max_{\Gamma O_i = \Gamma O_{i-2} \oplus \Gamma I_{i-1} (3 \leq i \leq n), (\Gamma P, \Gamma C) \neq (0,0)} \{\ 2^{n-1} \prod_{i=1}^{n} P(\Gamma Y_i, \Gamma X_i)\ \}$,

where X_i^j, X_i and K_i are randomly given, and the symbol $\bullet$ represents a bitwise AND operation.

2.2 LOKI89/91 and s^2DES

LOKI is a 64-bit key/64-bit block cryptosystem similar to DES. The main difference between LOKI and DES is the F-function and the key-scheduling part. The input of the F-function of LOKI is XORed with the 32-bit subkey, and expanded to 48 bits, which enter into four 12-bit input/8-bit output S-boxes. The 12-bit input of the S-box is partitioned into two segments: a 4-bit row value '*row*' and an 8-bit column value '*col*'. The row value '*row*' is used to select one of 16 S-functions $Sfn(row, col)$, which then take as input the column value '*col*' and produce an 8-bits output value. The structure of $Sfn(row, col)$ depends on versions of LOKI as follows [6]:

$$[LOKI89] : Sfn(row, col) = (col \oplus row)^{31} mod\ g_{row},$$
$$[LOKI91] : Sfn(row, col) = (col + ((row * 17) \oplus ff_{16}) \& ff_{16})^{31} mod\ g_{row},$$

where g_{row} is an irreducible polynomial over $GF(2^8)$, which is used in forming the $\{row\}$-th S-box. We omit the detail of their key-scheduling part and the initial and final permutations, since our analysis is independent of them. (Note: ROL12 and ROL13 shown in Figure 5 in [6] must be exchanged.) s^2DES is a 56-bits key/64-bits block cryptosystem, which has the same structure as DES except its S-box tables. They are based on Boolean functions satisfying the Strict Avalanche Criterion (SAC) [7].

3 Statistical Properties of LOKI and s^2DES

3.1 Differential and Linear Characteristics of the S-boxes

In this section, we discuss the strength of LOKI and s^2DES in regard to differential and linear cryptanalysis from viewpoints of differential and linear characteristics of their S-boxes, respectively.

Figure 2 illustrates frequency distribution of differential characteristics of the S-boxes using a line graph, where the ordinate axis denotes probability p and the abscissa axis shows the ratio of the number of pairs $(\Delta X_i^j, \Delta Y_i^j)$ such that $p=P(\Delta X_i^j, \Delta Y_i^j)$. To normalize the size of the S-boxes, we have considered, in the case of DES and s^2DES, a 12-bit input/8-bit output table that consists of two neighboring S-boxes: S_1 and S_2.

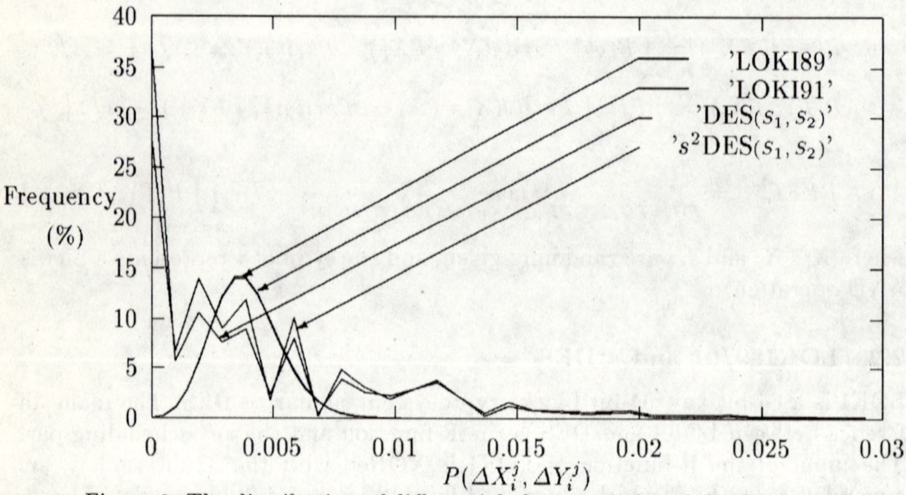

Figure 2: The distribution of differential characteristics of the S-boxes.

Characteristics of the S-boxes of LOKI89 and LOKI91 are densely distributed from $p = 0$ to $p \cong 2^{-5}$, while those of DES and s^2DES are widely distributed from $p = 0$ to $p \cong 2^{-2}$ and have many '0' entries. Note that though the distribution of LOKI89 is almost the same as that of LOKI91, their maximum values are different.

Table 1 shows the best differential characteristics of the S-boxes. The best probability of LOKI91 is lower than that of LOKI89, as the designers intended. Each of LOKI89 and LOKI91 has a unique characteristic that attains the best probability, whereas DES and s^2DES have 60 and 9 best characteristics, respectively.

	LOKI89	LOKI91	DES	s^2DES
The best probability	1.00×2^{-4}	1.03×2^{-5}	1.00×2^{-2}	1.00×2^{-2}
The best characteristic $(\Delta X_i^j, \Delta Y_i^j)$	$(004_{16}, 01_{16})$	$(004_{16}, 01_{16})$	$(34_{16}, 2_{16})$ *of* $S1$ *etc.*	$(0C_{16}, D_{16})$ *of* $S5$ *etc.*

Table 1. The best differential characteristic of the S-boxes.

Figure 3 illustrates frequency distribution of linear characteristics of the S-boxes using a line graph, where the ordinate axis denotes probability p and the abscissa axis shows the ratio of the number of pairs $(\Gamma Y_i^j, \Gamma X_i^j)$ such that $p = P(\Gamma Y_i^j, \Gamma X_i^j)$.

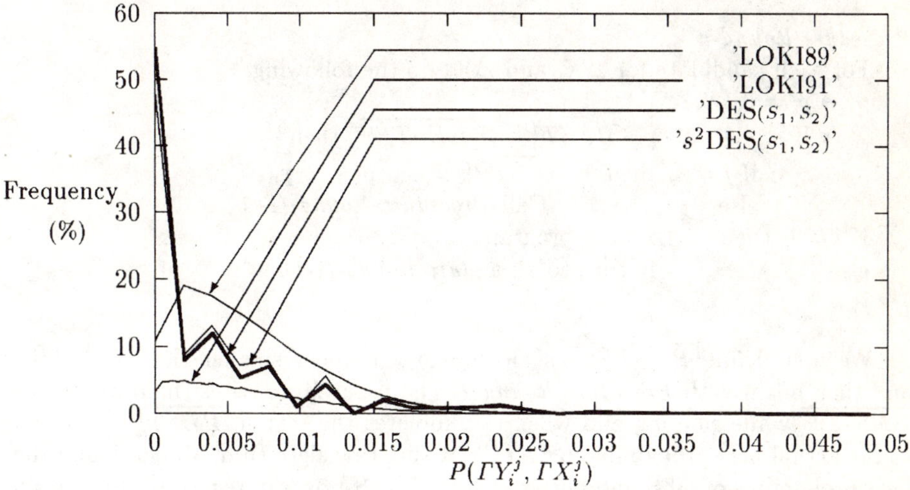

Figure 3: The distribution of linear characteristics of S-box.

Linear characteristics of the S-boxes of DES and s^2DES are widely distributed and again have many '0' entries. However, as opposed to the case of differential characteristics, the distribution of linear characteristics of LOKI89 is different from that of LOKI91, while their maximum values are almost the same.

Table 2 shows the best linear characteristics of the S-boxes. Each cryptosystem has a unique characteristic that attains the best probability. LOKI89 and LOKI91 are hence expected to be resistant to linear cryptanalysis from the viewpoint of the characteristics of their S-boxes.

	LOKI89	LOKI91	DES	s^2DES
The best probability	$\frac{1}{2} + 1.25 \times 2^{-5}$	$\frac{1}{2} - 1.28 \times 2^{-5}$	$\frac{1}{2} - 1.25 \times 2^{-2}$	$\frac{1}{2} + 1.13 \times 2^{-2}$
The best characteristic $(\Gamma Y_i^j, \Gamma X_i^j)$	$(61_{16}, F4A_{16})$	$(8D_{16}, 41F_{16})$	$(F_{16}, 10_{16})$ of S5	$(E_{16}, 1F_{16})$ of S5

Table 2. The best linear characteristic of the S-boxes.

3.2 The Best Probabilities of LOKI and s^2DES

In this section, we discuss the strength of LOKI and s^2DES in regard to differential and linear cryptanalysis from viewpoints of the best differential characteristic probability and the best linear approximate probability, respectively.

In [3] Matsui has proposed a practical algorithm for determining the best differential characteristic and linear approximate expression of DES-like cryptosystems on the basis of duality between differential cryptanalysis and linear cryptanalysis. His program works by induction of the number of rounds n. In other words, it derives the best n-round probability $BEST_n$ from knowledge of the best i-round probability $(1 \leq i \leq n-1)$. The framework of the algorithm is established by the following procedure including essentially recursive routines [3]:

Procedure Round-i:

For each candidate for ΔX_i and ΔY_i, do the following:

- $p_i = (\Delta X_i, \Delta Y_i)$,
- If $p_1 \cdot p_2 \cdot ... \cdot p_i \cdot BEST^{DC}_{n-i} \geq \overline{BEST^{DC}_n}$ then
  - If $i = n$ then $\overline{BEST^{DC}_n} = p_1 \cdot p_2 \cdot ... \cdot p_n$,
  - else Call *Procedure Round-(i+1).*

If $i = 1$, then Exit the program,
else Return to *Procedure Round-(i-1).*

We first define $\overline{BEST^{DC}_n}$ as any positive number smaller than $BEST^{DC}_n$ and then begin with *Procedure Round-1.* The program rewrites the initial value $\overline{BEST^{DC}_n}$ while running and when it completes the search, $\overline{BEST^{DC}_n}$ is equal to the actual best probability $BEST^{DC}_n$. Using this algorithm, Matsui found the best probability of DES and better orders of its S-boxes in regard to differential and linear cryptanalysis.

We have implemented this algorithm to determine the best differential characteristic probability of LOKI89, LOKI91, s^2DES and dcDES, where dcDES is a DES-variant whose S-boxes are rearranged in the strongest order against differential cryptanalysis [3]. Figure 4 summarizes our computational results.

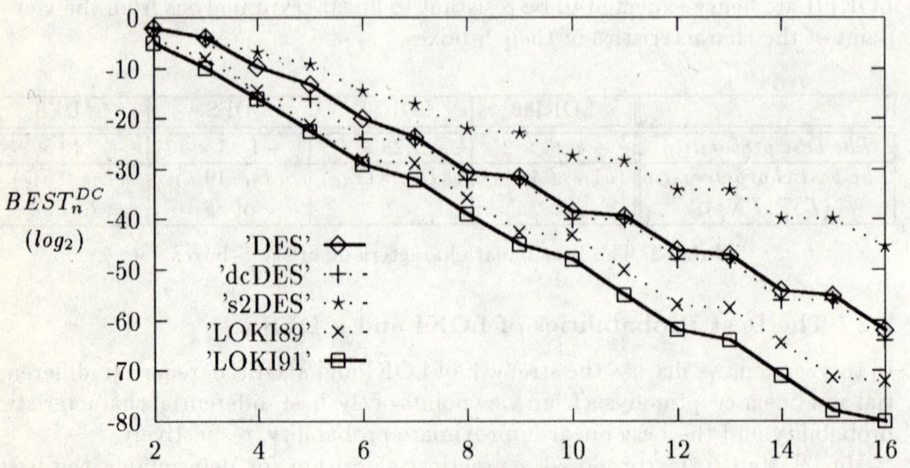

Figure 4: The best probability of differential cryptanalysis.

Though various characteristics of LOKI89, LOKI91 and s^2DES have been studied in recent works [1][9][10][11], our results first give a complete proof that some of them are actually best. For instance, the best 13-round probability of LOKI91 is 2^{-64}, which corresponds to four time repetitions of type B characteristic showed in [10]. Figure 4 indicates that LOKI91 is stronger than LOKI89, and s^2DES is weak in regard to differential cryptanalysis, as stated in [9][10][11].

The program for deriving the best differential characteristics is also applicable to calculating the best linear approximate equations. We have then derived the best linear approximate probabilities of LOKI89, LOKI91 and s^2DES, which are showed in Figure 5 with those of the original DES and lcDES, where lcDES is a DES-variant whose S-boxes are rearranged in the strongest order against linear cryptanalysis [3].

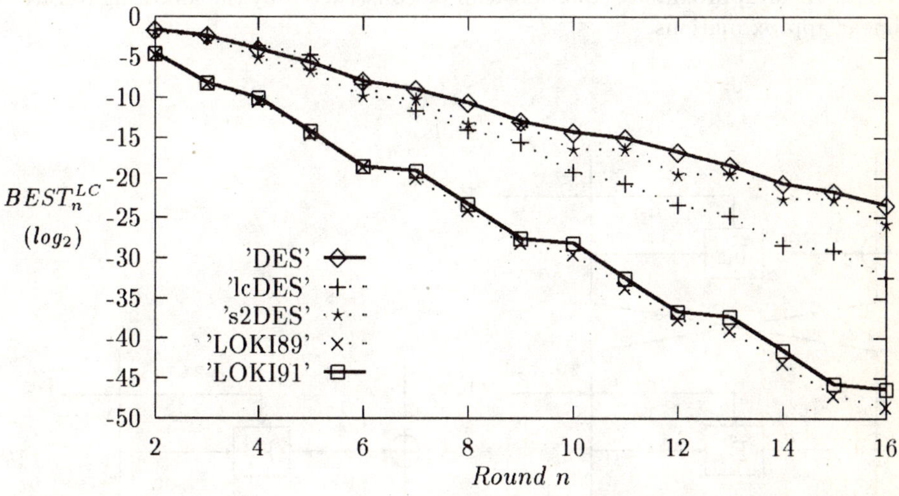

Figure 5: The best probability of linear cryptanalysis.

Figure 5 shows that LOKI89 and LOKI91 are much stronger than lcDES, and hence resistant to linear cryptanalysis. Note that LOKI89 is slightly better than LOKI91. Since s^2DES is slightly stronger than DES, it is breakable by a known-plaintext attack. Therefore, we conclude that LOKI is resistant to both differential and linear cryptanalysis from viewpoints of the best differential and linear probabilities, respectively.

The following is the best 16-round linear approximate equation of each cryptosystem, where we omit the initial and final permutations (see [2] for notations):

The best 16-round linear expression of LOKI89 holds with $BEST_{16}^{LC} = 1.37 \times 2^{-49}$:

$$P_L[30] \oplus C_L[19]$$
$$= K_2[19] \oplus K_3[30] \oplus K_5[19] \oplus K_6[30] \oplus K_8[19]$$

$$\oplus K_9[30] \oplus K_{11}[19] \oplus K_{12}[30] \oplus K_{14}[19] \oplus K_{15}[30]. \quad (1)$$

The best 16-round linear expression of LOKI91 holds with $BEST_{16}^{LC} = 1.51 \times 2^{-47}$:

$$\begin{aligned} &P_L[18,22,26] \oplus C_L[18,22,26] \\ &\quad = K_2[18,22,26] \oplus K_3[18,22,26] \oplus K_5[18,22,26] \oplus K_6[18,22,26] \\ &\qquad \oplus K_8[18,22,26] \oplus K_9[18,22,26] \oplus K_{11}[18,22,26] \oplus K_{12}[18,22,26] \\ &\qquad \oplus K_{14}[18,22,26] \oplus K_{15}[18,22,26]. \end{aligned} \quad (2)$$

The best 16-round linear expression of s^2DES holds with $BEST_{16}^{LC} = 1.19 \times 2^{-26}$:

$$\begin{aligned} &P_L[5,10,11] \oplus C_H[5,10,11] \\ &\quad = K_2[4,5,6,7] \oplus K_4[4,5,6,7] \oplus K_6[4,5,6,7] \oplus K_8[4,5,6,7] \\ &\qquad \oplus K_{10}[4,5,6,7] \oplus K_{12}[4,5,6,7] \oplus K_{14}[4,5,6,7] \oplus K_{16}[4,5,6,7]. \end{aligned} \quad (3)$$

These linear approximate equations can be constructed by the following iterative linear approximations:

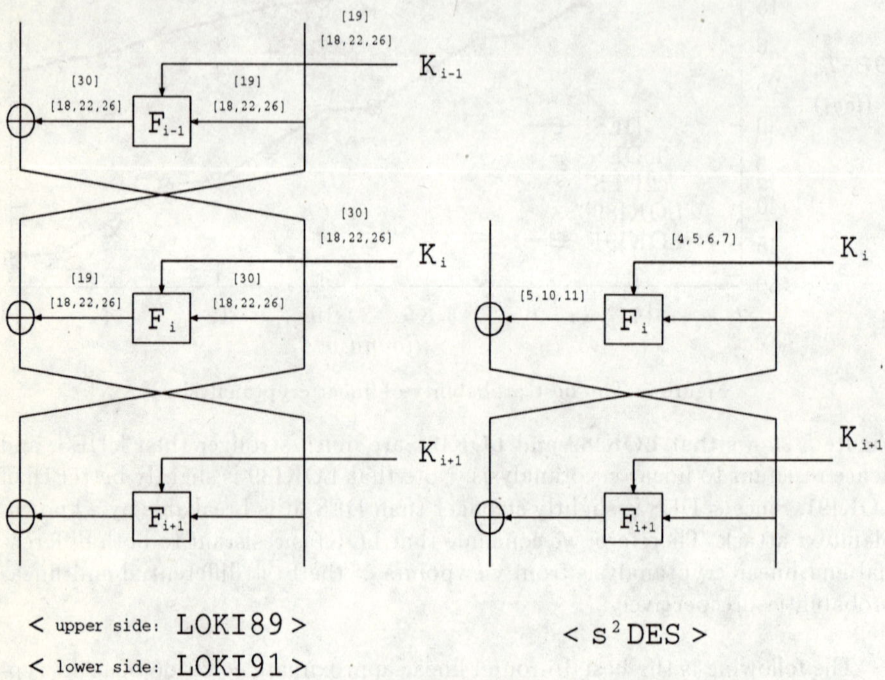

Figure 6: Iterative linear approximations establishing the best 16-round probability.

4 Experimental Results

This chapter describes our experimental results of linear cryptanalysis of 6-round LOKI91 to estimate the number of known-plaintexts required for breaking LOKI with arbitrary number of rounds.

Matsui has introduced two versions of known-plaintext attacks of n-round cryptosystems: the first method uses key equations based on the best $(n-1)$-round linear approximate expression [2], and the latter applies key equations based on the best $(n-2)$-round linear approximate expression [4].

The $(n-2)$-round method is better than the $(n-1)$-round method from the viewpoint of the probability, whereas the $(n-1)$-round method is better than the $(n-2)$-round method from a viewpoint of the size of counters and memory for the effective text/key bits. Since LOKI91 has 12-bit input/8-bit output S-boxes, the effective text/key bits are at least 12 bits in the $(n-1)$-round method, whereas they are at least 24 bits in the $(n-2)$-round method. Due to memory constraint, we have adopted the $(n-1)$-round method for linear cryptanalysis of LOKI91.

We now begin by describing 6-round LOKI91 using the following 5-round best linear approximate expression:

$$\begin{aligned} &P_L[18,22,26] \oplus C_H[18,22,26] \oplus C_L[18,19,21,23,24] \\ &= K_2[18,22,26] \oplus K_3[18,22,26] \oplus K_5[18,19,21,23,24]. \end{aligned} \tag{4}$$

It follows that we have the following expression of 6-round LOKI91 which holds with the best 5-round probability $1/2 - 1.60 \times 2^{-15}$:

$$\begin{aligned} &P_H[18,22,26] \oplus C_H[18,22,26] \oplus C_L[18,19,21,23,24] \oplus F_1(P_L, K_1)[18,22,26] \\ &= K_3[18,22,26] \oplus K_4[18,22,26] \oplus K_6[18,19,21,23,24], \end{aligned} \tag{5}$$

where the following 25 bits essentially affect its left–hand side:

- (Known) text information(13bits):
  $P_L[16] \sim P_L[27]$, $P_H[18,22,26] \oplus C_H[18,22,26] \oplus C_L[18,19,21,23,24]$,
- (Unknown) subkey information(12bits):
  $K_1[16] \sim K_1[27]$.

Note that $P_H[18,22,26] \oplus C_H[18,22,26] \oplus C_L[18,19,21,23,24]$ represents one-bit information. We hence obtain a total of 13 secret key bits — unknown 12 subkey bits and one bit of the right–hand side of equation (5) — using information on known 13 text bits by the following algorithm [2]:

Data Counting Phase

(Step 1) Prepare 2^{13} counters $U_i (0 \leq i < 2^{13})$ and initialize them by zeros, where i corresponds to each value on 13 known text bits of equation (5).

(Step 2) For each plaintext P and the corresponding ciphertext C, compute the value 'i' of Step 1, and count up the U_i by one.

Key Counting Phase

(Step 3) Prepare 2^{12} counters $T_j (0 \leq j < 2^{12})$ and initialize them by zeros, where j corresponds to each value on 12 unknown subkey bits of equation (5).

(Step 4) For each j of Step 3, let T_j be the sum of U_i's such that the left side of equation (5), whose value can be uniquely determined by i and j, is equal to zero.

(Step 5) Let T_{max} be the maximal value and T_{min} be the minimal value of all T_j'.
- If $|T_{max} - N/2| > |T_{min} - N/2|$, then adopt the subkey value 'j' corresponding to T_{max} and guess that the right side of equation (5) is 0.
- If $|T_{max} - N/2| < |T_{min} - N/2|$, then adopt the subkey value 'j' corresponding to T_{min} and guess that the right side of equation (5) is 1.

Table 3 shows the success rate of our attack, where each entry shows an average of 30 trials. Generally speaking, the number of known-plaintexts required for successful linear cryptanalysis is described as $C|p - 1/2|^{-2}$, where C is constant value. Table 3 tells us that we can estimate $C = 8$.

N	$2\|p-1/2\|^{-2}$	$4\|p-1/2\|^{-2}$	$6\|p-1/2\|^{-2}$	$8\|p-1/2\|^{-2}$
Success Rate	17%	53%	83%	100%

Table 3. The success rate of our experiments.

Table 4 summarizes the estimate of the number of known-plaintexts required for breaking n-round LOKI. We have applied the $(n-2)$-round method with C=8 [2] to DES and s^2DES. The sign $(-)$ shows that the number of required known-plaintexts exceeds 2^{64}.
It follows that LOKI89 and LOKI91 are resistant to linear cryptanalysis, and the strength of n-round LOKI89/91 corresponds to $2n$-round DES.

Rounds	4	5	6	7	8	9	10	11	12	13	14	15	16
LOKI89	$2^{19.7}$	$2^{24.0}$	$2^{32.2}$	$2^{40.2}$	$2^{43.0}$	$2^{51.2}$	$2^{59.2}$	$2^{62.0}$	$(-)$	$(-)$	$(-)$	$(-)$	$(-)$
LOKI91	$2^{19.6}$	$2^{23.2}$	$2^{31.7}$	$2^{40.1}$	$2^{41.3}$	$2^{49.8}$	$2^{58.3}$	$2^{59.5}$	$(-)$	$(-)$	$(-)$	$(-)$	$(-)$
DES	$2^{6.4}$	$2^{7.7}$	$2^{11.1}$	$2^{14.4}$	$2^{19.1}$	$2^{21.1}$	$2^{24.4}$	$2^{29.1}$	$2^{31.8}$	$2^{33.1}$	$2^{36.5}$	$2^{39.9}$	$2^{44.5}$
s^2DES	$2^{6.6}$	$2^{8.3}$	$2^{13.1}$	$2^{16.5}$	$2^{22.7}$	$2^{23.6}$	$2^{29.8}$	$2^{29.8}$	$2^{35.9}$	$2^{35.9}$	$2^{42.1}$	$2^{42.1}$	$2^{48.3}$

Table 4. The required number for known-plaintext attack of LOKI89,LOKI91 and s^2DES.

NOTE:

Recent researches [12] [13] have revealed that multiple differential/linear paths should be taken into consideration for strict evaluation of block ciphers. Though their effects do not seem to be 'visible' in our cases, more detailed investigation is a future topic.

References

1. Biham,E.,Shamir,A.: Differential Cryptanalysis of the Data Encryption Standard. Springer Verlag (1993)
2. Matsui,M.: Linear Cryptanalysis Method for DES cipher. Advances in Cryptology – Eurocrypt'93, Lecture Notes in Computer Science, Springer-Verlag **765** (1993) 386–397
3. Matsui,M.: On correlation between the order of S-boxes and the strength of DES. Pre-proceedings of Eurocrypt'94 (1994) 375-387
4. Matsui,M.: The First Experimental Cryptanalysis of the Data Encryption Standard. Advances in Cryptology – Crypto'94, Lecture Notes in Computer Science, Springer-Verlag **839** (1994) 1–11
5. Brown,L.,Pieprzyk,J.,Seberry,J.: LOKI–A Cryptographic Primitive for Authentication and Secrecy Applications. Advances in Cryptology – Auscrypt'90, Lecture Notes in Computer Science, Springer-Verlag **453** (1990) 229–236
6. Brown,L.,Kwan,M.,Pieprzyk,J.,Seberry,J.: Improving Resistance to Differential Cryptanalysis and the Redesign of LOKI. Advances in Cryptology – Asiacrypt'91, Lecture Notes in Computer Science, Springer-Verlag **739** (1993) 36–50
7. Kim,K.: Construction of DES-like S-boxes Based on Boolean Functions Satisfying the SAC. Advances in Cryptology – Asiacrypt'91, Lecture Notes in Computer Science, Springer-Verlag **739** (1993) 59–72
8. Biham,E.,Shamir,A.: Differential Cryptanalysis of Snefru, Khafre, REDOC-II, LOKI and Lucifer. Advances in Cryptology – Crypto'91, Lecture Notes in Computer Science, Springer-Verlag **576** (1992) 156–171
9. Knudsen,L.: Cryptanalysis of LOKI. Advances in Cryptology – Asiacrypt'91, Lecture Notes in Computer Science, Springer-Verlag **739** (1993) 22–35
10. Knudsen,L.: Cryptanalysis of LOKI91. Advances in Cryptology – Auscrypt'92, Lecture Notes in Computer Science, Springer-Verlag **718** (1993) 196–208
11. Knudsen,L.: Iterative Characteristics of DES and s^2-DES. Advances in Cryptology – Crypto'92, Lecture Notes in Computer Science, Springer-Verlag **740** (1993) 497-511
12. Lai,X.,Massey,J.,Murphy,S.: Markov ciphers and differential cryptanalysis. Advances in Cryptology – Eurocrypt'91, Lecture Notes in Computer Science, Springer-Verlag **547** (1991) 17–38
13. Nyberg,K.: Linear Approximation of Block Ciphers. Presented at Rump Session in Eurocrypt'94

SESSION 7

HUSH FUNCTIONS

Chair: Tsutomu Matsumoto

(Yokohama National University, Japan)

Collisions and Inversions for Damgård's Whole Hash Function

Jacques Patarin

Bull CP8, 68 route de Versailles - B.P.45 - 78430 Louveciennes, France

Abstract. Ivan Damgård gave a great theorem about hash functions in [2] : if there is a computationally collision free function f from m bits to t bits where $m > t$, then there exists a computationally collision free hash function h mapping messages of arbitrary polynomial lenghts to t-bit strings. Moreover the construction of h from f is very efficient. Then, he suggested, among others, to choose for f a knapsack scheme. However, in [1] and [4] it was shown that it is possible to find collisions on f, and even to find a preimage for f with an algebraic algorithm. Nevertheless, it was not shown how to find collision, or a preimage for h. (We call h Damgård's "whole" Hash function). Then, in [3] it was shown how to find a collision on h with the LLL Algorithm.
Here we will show how to find collision, and also how to find a preimage for h with an algebraic algorithm. A quick comparison of the two techniques (LLL and Algebraic) will be given.
For example, in about 2^{33} operations and 2^{24} storage it will be possible to find a collision for h. And with about 2^{48} operations and 2^{32} storage we will be able to find a preimage for h. (This is better than the previously known algorithm for a preimage given in [5] p. 202 which needs 2^{64} in time and 2^{32} in memory). Then we will study how to construct from f two new candidate hash functions $H1$ and $H2$ by slightly modifying Damgård's scheme in order to make the search of collisions more difficult, and in order to have a theorem showing why it looks "more difficult".

1 Introduction and Notations

function f

Let $a_1, \ldots, a_s$ be fixed integers of 120 binary digits, randomly selected, where $s = 256$. If x is a string of $s = 256$ binary symbols, $x = x_1, \ldots, x_s$, then f is (by definition) the function of 256 bits $\rightarrow$ 128 bits such that : $f(x) = \sum_{i=1}^{s} x_i a_i$.
Throughout this paper, we will denote by $b_i = a_{i+128}, i = 1, \ldots, 128$.

function h_1

Let p be a constant string of 128 bits, and let x be any string of 128 bits. We will define $h_1(x)$ by : $h_1(x) = f(p, x) = \sum_{i=1}^{128} p_i a_i + \sum_{i=1}^{128} x_i b_i$.

So h_1 is the function of 128 bits $\rightarrow$ 128 bits such that : $h_1(x) = C_0 + \sum_{i=1}^{128} x_i b_i$, where C_0 is a constant.

function h_2

By definition, we will denote by h_2 the function of 256 bits $\rightarrow$ 128 bits such that, if x and y are two strings of 128 bits : $h_2(x, y) = f[f(p, x), y]$.

So we have : $h_2(x, y) = \sum_{i=1}^{128} (h_1(x))_i a_i + \sum_{i=1}^{128} y_i b_i$, where $(h_1(x))_i$ denotes the bit number i of $h_1(x)$.

We will denote $\sum_{i=1}^{128} (h_1(x))_i a_i$ by $\lambda(x)$. So $h_2(x, y) = \lambda(x) + \sum_{i=1}^{128} y_i b_i$.

In [2], I. Damgård has defined a hash function h and a hash function h' based on function f.

h mapps strings of arbitrary lenghts to 128 bits strings. h' maps strings of lenghts multiple of 128 bits to 128 bits strings. Function h is the main hash function but in [2], I. Damgård writes also that in many applications we can use h' instead of h. We will consider h and h' in the particular case of an input of 256 bits. In this case, if x and y are two strings of 128 bits, and if 0_{128} is a string of 128 zeros, then

$$h(x, y) = f[h_2(x, y), 0_{128}] \tag{1}$$

$$\text{and } h'(x, y) = h_2(x, y). \tag{2}$$

In this paper we will study how to find collisions for h_2 (in paragraph 2), and how to find a preimage for h_2 (in paragraph 3). Clearly finding a collision for h_2 will give us a collision for h' and for h. And clearly if we can find a preimage for h_2 we will be able to find a preimage for h'.

Moreover, if we are able to find a preimage for h_2, then if (x_0, y_0) is a known message such that $h(x_0, y_0) = \alpha$, then we will be able to find another message $(x_1, y_1) \neq (x_0, y_0)$ such that $h(x_1, y_1) = h(x_0, y_0) = \alpha$.

This is because if we denote by $\beta = h_2(x_0, y_0)$, then if we are able to find a preimage $(x_1, y_1) \neq (x_0, y_0)$ such that $h_2(x_1, y_1) = \beta$, then $h(x_1, y_1) = h(x_0, y_0)$ as claimed.

Note : This is not exactly the same problem as finding a preimage for h (because here we use (x_0, y_0) and not only α in order to find (x_1, y_1)) but in most applications where a one way hash function is required it is in fact the property of not finding another (x_1, y_1) with the same value than (x_0, y_0) that is needed.

2 How to find collisions for h_2

Our algorithm will be mainly a variation of the algorithms described in [1] and [4] in order to find a collision on f or to invert f. (In this paper we will quickly explain all the ideas needed in our algorithms, but the knowledge of papers [1] and [4] could be useful because in [1] and [4] some of these ideas are explained with more details).

A collision on f is called a "pseudo-collision" and a collision on h_2 is called a "real collision" because our algorithm for a collision on h_2 gives easilly an algorithm for a collision on the hash function h suggested by Damgård in [2]. However the first idea to find real collisions could be to use exactly the same algorithms as in [4] : in order to find a collision for h_1, or h_2, it is clearly sufficient to know how to find a collision for the 128 → 128 knapsack. And in [4] paragraph 3, such an algorithm is given : it needs 2^{32} operations and 2^{32} storage. Nevertheless, we will see here that it's possible to find a collision for h_2 with less power : 2^{33} operations and 2^{24} storage will be sufficient. (Or 2^{29} operations and 2^{29} storage for another time/memory trade off).

Note : Another idea is to use the algorithm LLL to find collisions. Then the algorithm LLL is also used in order to find a collision for the 128 → 128 knapsack. However here we will only describe algebraic algorithms, and a quick comparison of both techniques will be given in paragraph 4.

In order to have a general view of our algorithm, the general diagram given below shows the general interactions of the operations that will be carried out. (This diagram is very similar to the diagrams given in [1] and [4]).

General Diagram for collisions (Steps 3, 4, 5, 6 will be done 2^9 times)

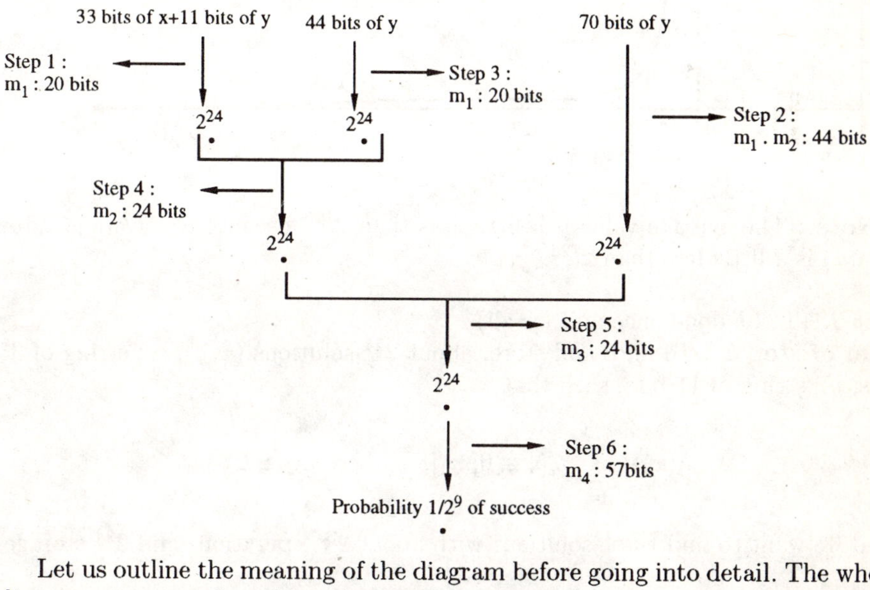

Let us outline the meaning of the diagram before going into detail. The whole diagram gives an algorithm which gives a collision on h_2 with a probability of success of $1/2^9$ when each step is done once. However, steps 1 and 2 are done once and for all, but we will do steps 3, 4, 5, 6 again with other parametrable values 2^9 times, in order to find a collision with a high probability. The complete algorithm is then in 2^{24} storage and 2^{33} operations. Each black dot represents a step of the algorithm. The number 2^{24} associated with the black dot represents the evaluation of the number of partial solutions that we will have to store for this step.

Let m_1, m_2, m_3, m_4 be integers such that :

1. The m_i are pairwise coprime.
2. $m_1 \simeq 2^{20}, m_2 \simeq 2^{24}, m_3 \simeq 2^{24}, m_4 \simeq 2^{57}$. So we have : $m_1 m_2 m_3 m_4 \simeq 2^{125}$.
3. $m_1 = \mu_1 \mu_2$, where μ_1 and μ_2 are integers pairwise coprime, and $\mu_1 \simeq 2^{11}$.

The aim of our Algorithm is to find $(x, y) \neq (x', y')$ such that $h_2(x, y) \equiv h_2(x', y')$ modulo $m_1.m_2.m_3.m_4$. (1).

Since $m_1.m_2.m_3.m_4 \simeq 2^{125}$, it is possible to see that (1) implies with a very high probability that $h_2(x, y) = h_2(x', y')$. (A precise calculation shows that the probability is $\geq 90\%$).

This comes from the fact that $h_2(x, y)$ is not equidistributed.

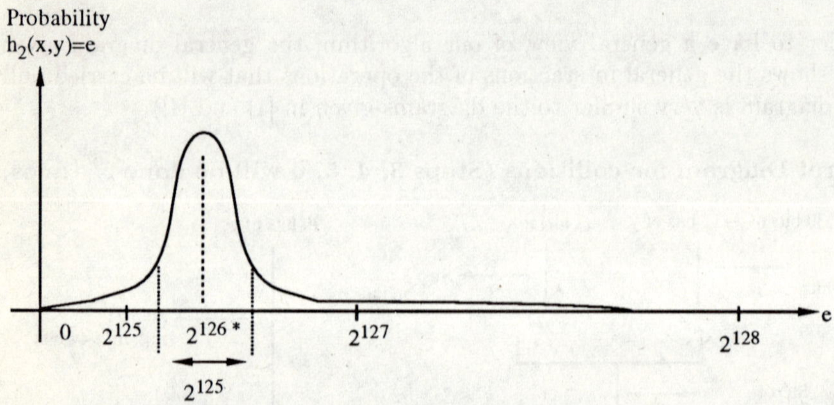

***Note** : The average value is a little less than 2^{126} because the average value of $\lambda(x)$ is a little less than 2^{125}.

Step 1. (To be done once and for all).
Aim of step 1 : To find, and store, about 2^{24} solutions (x, y), x : string of 33 bits, y : string of 11 bits, such that :

$$\lambda(x) + \sum_{i=1}^{11} y_i b_i \equiv 0[m_1], \quad \text{where } m_1 \simeq 2^{20}.$$

And we want to find these solutions with about 2^{33} operations and 2^{24} storage.

Algorithm for step 1

• First, the 2^{11} values $\sum_{i=1}^{11} y_i b_i$ modulo m_1 are computed and stored in such a way that we will have easy access to all the sequences y such that $\sum_{i=1}^{11} y_i b_i$ has a given value modulo m_1.

• Then, for all the values x, one by one, we calculate $-\lambda(x)$ modulo m_1 and we see if there is a corresponding y stored at that value. The probability that it appends for a given x is about $2^{11}/2^{20} = 1/2^9$. Thus, since we have 2^{33} value for x, it will append about 2^{24} times. And we find, and store, like this the 2^{24} solutions wanted with 2^{33} operations and 2^{24} storage.

Step 2. (To be done once and for all).

Aim of step 2 : To find, and store, about 2^{24} solutions y, y : string of 70 bits, $y = y_{56}, y_{57}, \ldots, y_{125}$, such that :

$$\sum_{i=56}^{125} y_i b_i \equiv 0[m_1.m_2], \quad \text{where } m_1.m_2 \simeq 2^{44}.$$

And we want to find these solutions with about 2^{33} computations and 2^{24} storage.

Algorithm for step 2

Since $m_1 = \mu_1\mu_2$, we have $m_1 m_2 = \mu_1(\mu_2.m_2)$ where $\mu_1 \simeq 2^{11}$, and $\mu_2 m_2 \simeq 2^{33}$. Before going into detail, a small diagram describing the "basic operations" for the Algorithm of step 2 is shown below :

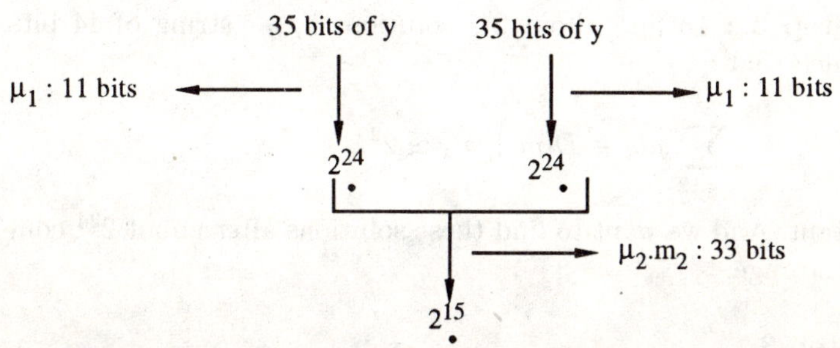

Small diagram for step 2 (to be done 2^9 times) These "basics operations" will give 2^{15} solutions after 2^{24} computations and 2^{24} storage. However, we will do them 2^9 times, in order to find $2^9 \times 2^{15} = 2^{24}$ solutions with 2^{33} computations and 2^{24} storage.

We now give details for the "basic operations" of the small diagram.

– First, all the solutions such that $\sum_{i=56}^{90} y_i b_i \equiv C[\mu_1]$ (2), where C is a constant, are found and stored modulo $\mu_2 m_2$. We have about $2^{35}/2^{11} \simeq 2^{24}$

such solutions. (These solutions are found as usual by computing and storing $\sum_{i=56}^{66} y_i b_i$ modulo μ_1 (3), and then computing one by one the values $C - \sum_{i=67}^{90} y_i b_i$ modulo μ_1 (4) and seeing if such a value has been obtained in (3). In this way all the solutions of (2), for a given C, are found after at most 2^{24} computations and storage.

– Then, for the same constant C, all the solutions such that $\sum_{i=91}^{125} y_i b_i \equiv -C[\mu_1]$ (5) are found. Such a solution S is computed modulo $\mu_2 m_2$, and we see if the opposite value of S modulo $\mu_2 m_2$ is a value reached for the solutions obtained for (2). The probability that it is the case is about $2^{24}/2^{33} = 1/2^9$. Since we found 2^{24} solutions, this will so append about $2^{24}/2^9 = 2^{15}$ times. Thus in this way we will obtain 2^{15} solutions y such that $\sum_{i=56}^{90} y_i b_i \equiv -\sum_{i=91}^{125} y_i b_i [\mu_1]$ and $\sum_{i=56}^{90} y_i b_i \equiv -\sum_{i=91}^{125} y_i b_i [\mu_2 m_2]$.

So $\sum_{i=56}^{125} y_i b_i \equiv 0[\mu_1 \mu_2 m_2]$ as required. These 2^{15} solutions have been found after 2^{24} computations and 2^{24} storage. By doing it again with 2^9 different values for C, we will finally obtain $2^9 \times 2^{15} = 2^{24}$ solutions after 2^{33} computations and 2^{24} storage as claimed.

Step 3. **Aim of step 3 :** To find about 2^{24} solutions y, y : string of 44 bits, $y = y_{12}, \ldots, y_{55}$, such that :

$$\sum_{i=12}^{55} y_i b_i \equiv D[m_1],\ m_1 \simeq 2^{20},$$

where D is a constant. And we want to find these solutions after about 2^{24} computations and 2^{24} storage.

Algorithm for step 3

As usual, these solutions are found first by computing and storing the value $\sum_{i=12}^{33} y_i b_i$ modulo m_1 (6), then by computing the values $D - \sum_{i=34}^{55} y_i b_i$ and see all the solutions such that this value has been obtained in (6).

Step 4. **Aim of step 4 :** To find about 2^{24} solutions (x, y), x : string of 33 bits, y : string of 11+44=55 bits, such that :

$$\lambda(x) + \sum_{i=1}^{55} y_i b_i \equiv K[m_1 m_2],$$

where K is constant. And we want to find these solutions after about 2^{24} computations and 2^{24} storage.

Algorithm for step 4
All the solutions found in step 1 are stored modulo m_2, in such a way that we will have easy access to all the solutions of step 1 with a given value modulo m_2.

Then, one by one, we compute modulo m_2 the opposite value of the solutions of step 3, and we see if this value has been obtained with a solution of step 1. If it is the case, we merge the two corresponding strings y and we obtain in this way a solution for this step 4, because we will have $\lambda(x) + \sum_{i=1}^{55} y_i b_i \equiv D[m_1]$ and $\lambda(x) + \sum_{i=1}^{55} y_i b_i \equiv 0[m_2]$. On average we will find 2^{24} such solutions (because $m_2 \simeq 2^{24}$ and we found about 2^{24} solutions in step 1 and in step 3).

Step 5. **Aim of step 5** : To find 2^{24} solutions y, y : string of 55+70=125 bits, such that :

$$\lambda(x) + \sum_{i=1}^{125} y_i b_i \equiv K'[m_1 m_2 m_3],$$

where K' is a constant. And we want to find the solutions with about 2^{24} computations and 2^{24} storage.

Algorithm for step 5
By combining the solutions found in step 2 and step 4, we obtain exactly that.

Step 6. **Aim of step 6** : To see if, from the 2^{24} solution found in step 5, two of them have the same value mod m_4, $m_4 \simeq 2^{57}$.

Algorithm for step 6
We simply have to compute and store all the solutions found in step 5 modulo m_4. In this way we will see if we have two solutions with the same value after doing at most 2^{24} computations, and with 2^{24} storage. The probability of such an event is about

$$2^{24} \times 2^{24} \times 1/2^{57} \simeq 1/2^9.$$

If this doesn't happen, then we will try steps 3, 4, 5, 6 again with differents values for the constants D, K and K'. After 2^9 such tries, we will find a collision with a good probability.

Conclusion

The first idea to find a collision for h_2 could be to fix the 128 bits of x so that h_2 is then just a $128 \to 128$ knapsack, and to find a collision on that $128 \to 128$ knapsack. Nevertheless, here the main new idea in our algorithm is the fact that we were able to use 33 bits of x in step 1. Finally, our algorithm needs on average about 2^{33} computations and 2^{24} in storage. Since this is clearly realistic, we can conclude that the (complete) hash function suggested at Crypto'89 is not collision free.

Moreover, it is possible to design variations of our algorithm in order to obtain different time/memory trade off.

A precise study can show that if we have 2^t computations and 2^m storage, we can design such an algorithm to find collisions for h if :

$$\begin{cases} t \geq m \geq 0 \\ 6m + 7t \geq 372 \\ 3m + 2t \geq 125. \end{cases}$$

For example, with 2^{43} computations and 2^{13} storage,
or with 2^{33} computations and 2^{24} storage,
or with 2^{29} computations and 2^{29} storage.

Note. This is the power needed to find a collision with our Algorithms. However as soon as we have found one collision, it is very easy to find a lot of collisions : let x, y, z, t be strings such that $h_2(x, y) = h_2(z, t)$ and $(x, y) \neq (z, t)$. Now let i be an index such that $y_i = 0$ and $t_i = 0$. Then let y' be the string y except that $y'_i = 1$ and let t' be the string t except that $t'_i = 1$. Then $h_2(x, y') = h_2(z, t')$. (In average by iterating this idea on more than one such index i, this idea will give immediatly about 2^{32} collisions for h_2).

3 How to invert h_2

When e is an (average) given value for h_2, we will now see how to find a solution (x, y) such that $h_2(x, y) = e$.

In [5] p. 202 it is written that such a preimage "could be found directly with the Schroeppel-Shamir attack in 2^{64} operations and 2^{32} storage". This is the best algorithm published so far. However, here we will see that it's possible to use less power (for example 2^{48} operations and 2^{32} storage).

Before going into more detail, we will first give the general diagram of the algorithm. (This diagram uses the same notation as the diagram of paragraph 2, and the diagrams of [1] and [4]). This general diagram gives a probability of success of $1/2^{16}$ when each step is done once. However, steps 3, 4 and 5 will be done 2^{16} times in order to find a solution (x, y) with a high probability after 2^{48} operations and 2^{32} storage.

General Diagram for inversion (Steps 3, 4, 5 will be done 2^{16} times) :

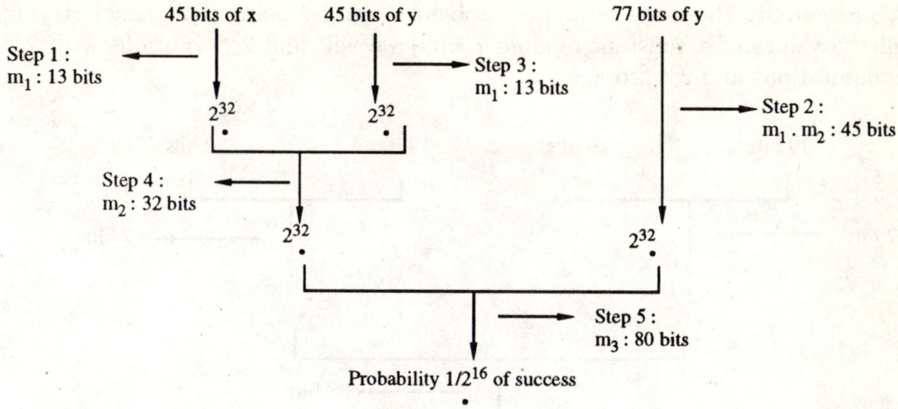

We will now go through each step in more detail :
Let m_1, m_2, m_3 be integers such that :

1. The m_i are pairwise coprime
2. $m_1 \simeq 2^{13}, m_2 \simeq 2^{32}, m_3 \simeq 2^{80}$.

The aim of our algorithm is to find a (x, y) such that $h_2(x, y) = e$ modulo $m_1.m_2.m_3$ (1), where e is a given constant.

We will suppose that e is such that $|e - 2^{126}| < 2^{124}$ since this is the case with a probability $\geq 90\%$ for an output $h_2(x, y)$. So, since $m_1.m_2.m_3 \simeq 2^{125}$ and since $|h_2(x, y) - 2^{126}| < 2^{124}$ with a probability $\geq 90\%$ it is possible to see that (1) will implies with a probability $\geq 90\%$ that $h_2(x, y) = e$.

Step 1. **Aim of step 1** : To find, and store, about 2^{32} solutions x, x : string of 45 bits such that $\lambda(x) \equiv C[m_1]$, where C is a given constant.

And we want to find these solutions in 2^{45} operations and 2^{32} storage.

Algorithm for step 1

Just compute all the 2^{45} values $\lambda(x)$ and store the solution values. Since $m_1 \simeq 2^{13}$, we will obtain about $2^{45}/2^{13} = 2^{32}$ solutions, as required.

Step 2. **Aim of step 2** : To find, and store, about 2^{32} solutions y, y : string of 77 bits, $y = y_{46}, y_{47}, \ldots, y_{122}$, such that :

$$\sum_{i=46}^{122} y_i b_i \equiv D[m_1 m_2],$$

where D is a given constant. And we want to find these solutions in 2^{39} operations and 2^{32} storage.

Algorithm for step 2

The "small diagram" below shows how to find 2^{25} such solutions with 2^{32} computations and 2^{32} storage. (We don't go into all the details of the steps because it's essentially the same technique as before). So by doing it 2^7 times (trying all the values of a constant modulo 7 bits) we will find 2^{32} solutions with 2^{32} computations and 2^{32} storage.

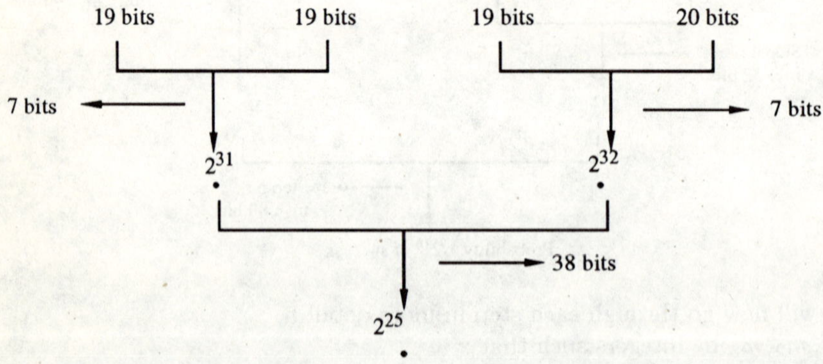

Small diagram for step 2 (to be done 2^7 times)

Step 3. **Aim of step 3 :** To find, and store, about 2^{32} solutions y, y : string of 45 bits such that $\sum_{i=1}^{45} y_i b_i \equiv e - C - D[m_1]$, where e is the value for which we want to find a preimage,, C is the constant of step 1, and D is the constant of step 2.

And we want to find these solutions in 2^{32} computations and storage.

Algorithm for step 3
We proceed as usual :

1. Computing and storing all the values $-\sum_{i=1}^{13} y_i b_i + e - C - D$ modulo m_1.

2. Computing one by one all the 2^{32} values $\sum_{i=14}^{45} y_i b_i$ modulo m_1 and see if this value has been found in 1.

In this way we obtain about $2^{13} \times 2^{32}/2^{13} = 2^{32}$ solutions as required.

Step 4. **Aim of step 4 :** To find, and store, about 2^{32} solutions (x, y), x : string of 45 bits, y : string of 45 bits, such that $\lambda(x) + \sum_{i=1}^{45} y_i b_i \equiv e - D[m_1 m_2]$, where e and D are as before.

And we want to find these solutions after 2^{32} computations and 2^{32} storage.

Algorithm for step 4
These solutions are obtained as usual from the solutions found in steps 1 and 3.

Step 5. **Aim of step 5 :** To find a solution (x, y), x : string of 45 bits, y : string of 45+77=122 bits, such that $\lambda(x) + \sum_{i=1}^{122} y_i b_i \equiv e[m_1 m_2 m_3]$, with a probability of success of about $1/2^{16}$ with 2^{32} computations and 2^{32} storage.

Algorithm for step 5

By combining as usual the solutions found in steps 2 and 4, we will obtain such a solution with a probability of success of about $2^{32} \times 2^{32}/2^{80} = 1/2^{16}$ as required.

Finding a solution with a high probability

In 2^{48} computations and 2^{32} storage, we can do again 2^3 times Step 1, and we can do again 2^9 times Step 2.

So we can have $2^3 \times 2^9 = 2^{12}$ possible values for the pair of constants (C, D). Now when such (C, D) is fixed, steps 3, 4 and 5 can be done 2^4 times. In fact, it is possible to do these steps 2^4 times in order to find more solutions because 122 bits are used for y so we have 6 bits of y that we can fix with different values in order to find some other solutions in step 3.

Finally, step 5 will be done $2^4 \times 2^{12} = 2^{16}$ times, (since we try 2^{12} possible values for (C, D)).

Conclusion

We will obtain a (x, y) such that $h_2(x, y) = e$ after such a step 5 with a high probability.

The complete algorithm needs 2^{48} for computations and 2^{32} for storage.

Moreover, it is possible to design variations of our algorithm in order to obtain different time/memory trade off.

A precise study can show that if we have 2^t computations and 2^m storage, we can design such an algorithm to find a preimage for h if :

$$\begin{cases} t \geq m \geq 0 \\ 9t + 6m \geq 619. \end{cases}$$

For example with 2^{55} computations and 2^{21} storage.

Or with 2^{48} computations and 2^{32} storage.

Or with 2^{42} computations and 2^{41} storage.

4 Comparisons between algebraic algorithms and LLL algorithms

In [3] a practical implementation of the LLL algorithm is given in order to find collisions in the function h. This was exactly our problem in paragraph 2, but we used an algebraic algorithm instead of the LLL algorithm.

Both algorithms give collisions and are practical. No real implementation of our algebraic algorithm has been done, so it's difficult to compare the two algorithms.

However, as explained in [5] it seems clear that the LLL algorithm is much better when the knapsack function f (from which h is made) has a "small" compression factor (for example when f hashes 192 bits in 128 bits the "compression factor" is only 1.5 and LLL will be better). And it is also clear that when the compression factor is high the algebraic method will be better (for example when f hashes 512 bits in 128 bits, or when f hashes 640 bits in 160 bits, the "compression factor" is 4, and the algebraic method will be better).
Here, in Damgård's example the compression factor for f is 2, and LLL is perhaps better to find collisions for h. Nevertheless our algebraic algorithm is the best algorithm published to find a preimage for h. However in [6] C.P. Schnorr suggested an algorithm combining LLL and the "birthday paradox" in order to find a preimage for f (but not for h). So it could be an interesting study to try to design such an algorithm for h and to compare it with our algebraic algorithms.
In conclusion both Algorithms are useful, but for collisions on h LLL seems better when f is a function with small compression, and our algorithm seems better when f is a function with high compression.

5 Two candidates to design a better hash function

In [4] some ideas where given in order to design a better hash function. However all these ideas failed. Here we will give some ideas which seems to be useful (and we will be able to prove that our candidates hash functions will be at least as strong as the basic function, and probably much stronger).

Candidate 1 : Hash function $H1$

Let f be, as usual, the $256 \rightarrow 128$ knapsack : that is so say, if $x = x_1, \ldots, x_{256}$ is a string of 256 bits, we have : $f(x) = \sum_{i=1}^{256} x_i \alpha_i$, where α_i, $1 \leq i \leq 256$, are 256 constants of 120 bits, randomly chosen.

And let g be a $256 \rightarrow 256$ knapsack : that it so say : $g(x) = \sum_{i=1}^{256} x_i \beta_i$, where β_i, $1 \leq i \leq 256$, are 256 constants of 248 bits, randomly chosen.
We will now define the function $h = f \circ g$.
So h is a function from strings of 256 bits to strings of 128 bits. And we will denote by $H1$ the function designed from h with Damgård's construction in order to obtain a hash function. So $H1$ can hash a string of arbitrary length to a string of 128 bits. From Damgård's theorem, we can prove that finding a collision for $H1$ is at least as difficult as finding a collision for h.
If we can find a collision for h, we can find two strings x and x' of 256 bits, $x \neq x'$, such that : $f(g(x)) = f(g(x'))$.
Let $y = g(x)$ and let $y' = g(x')$.
If $y = y'$ then we have found a collision for g, but this is very difficult because

g is a $256 \rightarrow 256$ knapsack. So we will suppose $y \neq y'$. Then we have found four strings x, x', y, y', of 256 bits, $x \neq x'$ and $y \neq y'$ such that :

$$\begin{cases} \sum_{i=1}^{256} y_i \alpha_i = \sum_{i=1}^{256} y'_i \alpha_i & (1) \\ g(x) = y & (2) \\ g(x') = y' & (3) \end{cases}$$

Equation (1), when $y \neq y'$, shows that we have a collision for f. So finding a collision for h is at least as difficult as finding a collision for f (or a collision for g, if $y = y'$, but finding a collision for g is much more difficult than for f). And in fact, it seems much more difficult, because we also have to find two strings x and x' such that (2) and (3) are satisfied. For example our algebraic algorithm seems to fail for h, and the LLL algorithm does not seem to be useful either. So we leave as an open problem to find a collision for h.

Note 1 : Here to compute $H1$ we need about three times more computations than for f. So our modification has a cost.

Note 2 : Instead of a $256 \rightarrow 256$ knapsack function for g, any function g of 256 bits $\rightarrow$ 256 bits "hard" to invert can be chosen. (Note that it is probably easier to find a function of 256 bits $\rightarrow$ 256 bits "hard" to invert than to find a function of 256 bits $\rightarrow$ 128 bits "hard" to invert. So our construction can be useful).
If a bijection is chosen for g, then when $x \neq x'$ we will be sure that $g(x) \neq g(x')$. So a bijection "hard to invert" can be an interesting choice. Another idea can be to design the composition of three (or more) functions instead of two (one function $256 \rightarrow 128$ and the other functions $256 \rightarrow 256$).

Candidate 2 : Hash function H_2

Let f be, as usual the $256 \rightarrow 128$ knapsack.
In [2], I. Damgård explained how to construct a hash function from h from f. Here we will slitly modify this construction : the idea is to design a different padding in order to obtain a hash function $H2$ probably more secure than h.
Let X be a string of arbitrary lenght.
X is split in groups $x_1, \ldots x_f$ or lenght 128 bits. For that some 0's are padded in the last bloc x_f. Then, another bloc x_{f+1} is created with the value of the number of 0's padded in base 2. (All this is exactly the same that what was done in [2]).
Let p_0 be a given and public string of 128 bits.
Let

$$\begin{aligned} h_1(X) &= f(p_0, x_1) \\ h_2(X) &= f(h_1(X), x_1) \\ &\vdots \\ h_{f+1}(X) &= f(h_f(X), x_{f+1}) \end{aligned}$$

In the construction of [2], $h_{f+1}(X)$ was the Hash value of X.
But here, let $H2(X) = f(h_{f+1}(X), x_1 \oplus x_2 \oplus \ldots \oplus x_{f+1})$, where $\oplus$ denotes the XOR function. $H2(X)$ will be the Hash value of our new function $H2$.
If we are able to find a collision for $H2$, then we are able to find two strings X and X', $X \neq X'$, such that

$$f(h_{f+1}(X), x_1 \oplus x_2 \ldots x_{f+1}) = f(h_{f'+1}(X'), x'_1 \oplus x'_2 \oplus \ldots \oplus x'_{f'+1}). \quad (1)$$

Then, one of these two cases has to be true.

First case. $h_{f+1}(X) \neq h_{f'+1}(X')$ or $x_1 \oplus \ldots \oplus x_{f+1} \neq x'_1 \oplus \ldots \oplus x'_{f'+1}$.
Then (1) shows that a collision on f has been found. So we have found some strings a, b, c, d of lenght 128 bits, $(a, b) \neq (c, d)$, and two strings X and X' such that :

$$\begin{cases} f(a,b) = f(c,d) \\ h_{f+1}(X) = a \\ h_{f'+1}(X') = c \\ x_1 \oplus \ldots \oplus x_{f+1} = b \\ x'_1 \oplus \ldots \oplus x'_{f'+1} = d \end{cases}$$

So this seems more difficult than just finding a collision for f.

Second case. $h_{f+1}(X) = h_{f'+1}(X')$ (1) and $x_1 \oplus \ldots \oplus x_{f+1} = x'_1 \oplus \ldots \oplus x'_{f'+1}$ (2).
Then since $X \neq X'$, (1) shows that we have found a collision on exactly the Hash function h of [2], and in [2] it was proved that this is at least as difficult as to found a collision on f. Moreover here we have the extra condition (2), so this seems more difficult than just finding a collision for h.

Note 1 : Instead of the XOR function $\oplus$, any group operation for 128 bits can be chosen, or even any function of all the bits of X. The general idea is to have 128 bits of redundancy in the strings where collisions can be found.

Note 2 : It is possible to suggest 256 bits of redundancy (or more). For example $H2'(X) = f(H2(X), x_1 * \ldots * x_{f+1})$, where $*$ is another group operation on 128 bits.

Note 3 : Here to compute $H2$ we will need asymptotically for large strings only about 1% more computations than for f (because we have to compute an extra XOR for each block of 128 bits, instead of about 128 additions). So $H2$ is almost exactly as efficient as the initial function h of Damgård. So it is easy to see that $H2$ will be quiet efficient on 32 bits computers (but still probably slower than $MD4$ for example) and also very efficient on 64 bit and 128 bit computers (where it may be quicker than $MD4$). Note also that if we have enough memory, it is possible to store all the values a_i, $1 \leq i \leq 256$, and all the values $a_{2i-1} + a_{2i}$, $1 \leq i \leq 128$, it order to compute two times quicker. We can also store all the values $\varepsilon_1 a_{4i-3} + \varepsilon_2 a_{4i-2} + \varepsilon_3 a_{4i-1} + \varepsilon_4 a_{4i}, \varepsilon_j \in \{0,1\}, j = 1,2,3,4, 1 \leq i \leq 64$, in order to compute four times quicker etc.

6 Conclusion

The complete hash function h suggested in [2] is not collision free. Collisions can be found with the LLL algorithm or with an algebraic algorithm. Moreover with an algebraic algorithm it is also possible to find a preimage for this function h. Furthermore with these algorithms, various time/memory trade-offs are possible. However, we suggest two new candidates Hash Functions $H1$ and $H2$. We think that these Hash Functions avoid these attacks so they are hash functions with a very simple mathematical definition which seems to be secure. Moreover we can prove that these functions are at least as secure as the basic Knapsack function, and probably much more secure.

References

1. P. Camion and J. Patarin, *"The Knapsack Hash Function proposed at Crypto'89 can be broken"*, Proceedings of Eurocrypt'91, pp. 39-53, Springer Verlag.
2. I. Damgård, *"A Design Principles for Hash Functions"*, Proceedings of Crypto'89, pp. 416-427, Springer Verlag.
3. A. Joux and L. Granboulan, *"A practical attack against Knapsack based Hash Functions"*, Proceedings of Eurocrypt'94.
4. J. Patarin, *"How to find and avoid collisions for the Knapsack Hash Function"*, Proceedings of Eurocrypt'93, pp. 305-317.
5. B. Preneel, *"Analysis and Design of Cryptographic Hash Functions"*, Katolieke Universiteit Leuven.
6. C.P. Schnorr, unpublished communication, 1991.

Attacking the SL_2 Hashing Scheme

Chris Charnes and Josef Pieprzyk *

Center for Computer Security Research
Department of Computer Science
University of Wollongong
Northfields Ave. Wollongong
NSW 2522, Australia
e-mail: charnes@cs.uow.edu.au
e-mail: josef@cs.uow.edu.au

Abstract. Tillich and Zémor proposed a definition of a new hash function which uses $SL_2(2, 2^n)$, the group of unimodular two-dimensional matrices with entries in $GF(2^n)$, to compute the hash values of binary strings. This hashing scheme has several attractive features; hash values can be computed quickly and small modifications to the input text can be detected. However, this scheme is weak. Using a group theoretic argument we are able to produce two distinct binary strings of small length which hash to the same value in $SL_2(2, 2^n)$ for the range specified by Tillich and Zémor.

1 Introduction

Tillich and Zémor in [6], proposed a hashing scheme based on $SL_2(2, 2^n)$, the group of two-dimensional unimodular matrices with entries in the Galois field $GF(2^n)$. The current scheme replaces a previous hashing scheme of Zémor based on the groups $SL_2(2, Z_p)$, and which was broken by a 'density' attack, see [6]. The new hashing scheme is attractive. Hashing is fast, as the arithmetic is done in $GF(2^n)$. It has the provable property that small modifications of input text can be detected. The set of hashcodes is large, and in the specified range, probabilistic attacks such as the birthday paradox are computationally infeasible. The condition for finding a pair of clashing messages is equivalent to the problem of finding short factorizations in the groups $SL_2(2, 2^n)$, a problem known to be potentially difficult, see [5]. It is proved in [6] that the hash function is immune to the density attack. Other desirable properties of the hash function are described in [6]. The rationale underlying the use of the two-dimensional unimodular groups to design hashing functions is discussed in [7].

* Support for this project was provided in part by the Australian Research Council under the reference number A49131885

Despite these provable properties, we show that the scheme described by Tillich and Zémor [6] is weak. We devise a new attack on the hash function which uses a group theoretic argument to derive a condition for clashing in $SL_2(2, F_2[X])$, see section 2. From this we derive a condition for the existence of colliding messages in the groups $SL(2, 2^n)$. We observe that this condition is satisfied, in the range specified by Tillich and Zémor, by the group $SL(2, 2^{131})$. Thereby producing two binary strings of small length which hash to the same value in $SL(2, 2^{131})$.

We begin by reviewing the hashing algorithm proposed by Tillich and Zémor [6].

Definition 1. (Tillich and Zémor). Choose a Galois field $GF(2^n)$, where n is in the range $130 - 170$. The defining parameter is an irreducible polynomial $P_n(X)$ (over $F_2 = GF(2)$) of degree n, where n is in the above mentioned range.

The hashing algorithm consists of the following.

Definition 2. (Tillich and Zémor). Let A and B be the following elements of the group $SL_2(2, F_2[X])$ – the group of two-dimensional unimodular matrices with entries in the polynomial ring $F_2[X]$

$$A = \begin{pmatrix} X & 1 \\ 1 & 0 \end{pmatrix}, \quad B = \begin{pmatrix} X & X+1 \\ 1 & 1 \end{pmatrix}.$$

π is the mapping $\pi : \{0, 1\} \to \{A, B\}$ which takes 0 to A and 1 to B.

The Hashcode of a binary string $x_1 x_2 \dots x_k$ is the matrix product

$$\pi(x_1)\pi(x_2)\dots\pi(x_k).$$

Where this product is computed in the Galois field $F_{2^n} = GF(2^n)$ defined by $P_n(X)$, or more formally, the quotient $GF(2^n) = F_2[X]/ < P_n(X) >$.

Let $G =< A, B >$ be the subgroup of $SL_2(2, F_2[X])$ generated by A and B. Reducing the entries of A and B modulo $P_n(X)$ (by the Euclidean algorithm) defines a homomorphism from G into $SL_2(2, F_{2^n})$, a group of order $q^2(q+1)(q-1)$ where $q = 2^n$. It is proved in [6] that the images of A and B, under this mapping, generate the full group $SL_2(2, F_{2^n})$. It follows from this that the homomorphic image of G is $SL_2(2, F_{2^n})$. Thus the hashcode of a binary message $x_1 x_2 \dots x_k$ is the product $\pi(x_1)\pi(x_2)\dots\pi(x_k)$ reduced modulo $P_n(X)$, and is an element of the group $SL_2(2, F_{2^n})$.

2 Preliminary to the attack

Firstly we derive a relation in the group G, i.e., two words in the alphabet $\{A, B\}$ – products of the A and B and their inverses, which are equal in G. To do this we define two *involutions* (elements of order two) in G.

Lemma 3. *Let $\alpha = A^{-1}B$, then α is an involution in G.*

Proof. In G, $A^{-1} = \begin{pmatrix} 0 & 1 \\ 1 & X \end{pmatrix}$, hence $\alpha = A^{-1}B$ equals

$$\begin{pmatrix} 0 & 1 \\ 1 & X \end{pmatrix}\begin{pmatrix} X & X+1 \\ 1 & 1 \end{pmatrix} = \begin{pmatrix} 1 & 1 \\ 0 & 1 \end{pmatrix}.$$

In G, $\alpha^2 = \begin{pmatrix} 1 & 0 \\ 0 & 1 \end{pmatrix}$, so α is an involution.

Lemma 3 gives us another involution in G. Namely β, which is defined as:

$$\beta = A\alpha A^{-1} = BA^{-1}.$$

Lemma 4. *Let $\beta = A\alpha A^{-1}$. Then β is an involution in G, and $\alpha\beta \neq \beta\alpha$.*

Proof. That β is an involution follows from lemma 3. We show that α does not commute with β.

By definition, $\beta = A(A^{-1}B)A^{-1} = BA^{-1}$. Substituting for A^{-1}, B and matrix multiplication gives

$$\beta = \begin{pmatrix} X+1 & X^2 \\ 1 & X+1 \end{pmatrix}.$$

So

$$\alpha\beta = \begin{pmatrix} X & X^2+X+1 \\ 1 & X+1 \end{pmatrix}.$$

Similarly,

$$\beta\alpha = \begin{pmatrix} X+1 & X^2+X+1 \\ 1 & X \end{pmatrix}.$$

Thus α does not commute with β.

It is well known that a non-commuting pair of involutions in any group generates a *Dihedral* non-abelian subgroup of the group. Hence by lemmas 3 and 4, we have that

$$D = <\alpha, \beta>$$

is a Dihedral subgroup of G. The only part of this that we need is the following.

Lemma 5. *The involutions α and β satisfy the following relation in G*

$$\alpha(\alpha\beta)\alpha = \beta\alpha. \tag{1}$$

Proof. By associativity,

$$\alpha(\alpha\beta)\alpha = (\alpha\alpha)\beta\alpha,$$

and $\alpha^2 = \beta^2 = \begin{pmatrix} 1 & 0 \\ 0 & 1 \end{pmatrix}$, hence the result.

Using relation (1), we can derive a pair of words in the alphabet $\{A, B\}$ which are equal in G.

Theorem 6. *The following relation holds in G*

$$A^{-1}B(A^{-1}B^2A^{-1})A^{-1}B = BA^{-2}B. \tag{2}$$

Proof. Lemma 5 states that $\alpha(\alpha\beta)\alpha = \beta\alpha$. Substituting for $\alpha = A^{-1}B$ and $\beta = BA^{-1}$ in relation (1), we obtain

$$A^{-1}B(A^{-1}B(BA^{-1}))A^{-1}B = (BA^{-1})(A^{-1}B). \tag{3}$$

Using associativity, this expression simplifies to

$$A^{-1}B(A^{-1}B^2A^{-1})A^{-1}B = BA^{-2}B. \tag{4}$$

It is easy now to check directly that (4) is a valid relation in G. This relation gives rise to clashing strings in the groups $SL_2(2, F_{2^n})$. We pursue this theme in the next section.

3 Determining the order of A

We have previously remarked that each irreducible polynomial $P_n(X)$ of degree n, defines a homomorphism of the group $G =< A, B >$ onto the group $SL_2(2, F_{2^n})$. The image of an element

$$\begin{pmatrix} E(X) & F(X) \\ H(X) & G(X) \end{pmatrix}$$

of G, under this homomorphism is obtained by reducing $E(X), F(X), G(X)$ and $H(X)$ modulo $P_n(X)$. We denote by this $\tilde{E}(X), \tilde{F}(X)$, etc.

Reducing both sides of relation (4) modulo $P_n(X)$, gives a relation in the group $SL_2(2, F_{2^n})$. However, the reduced relation cannot be used directly (by substituting for A and B according to [6]), to produce a pair of clashing binary messages.

Our problem is that relation (4) involves the inverse powers A^{-1} and A^{-2}. The homomorphic image of an inverse of an element in a group, is the inverse of the image of the element. Thus these inverse powers of A also occur in the reduced relation. This problem could be solved if we knew the order of the homomorphic image of A, for then A^{-1} could be expressed as a positive power of A. Thus the problem of constructing a pair of clashing strings is reduced to the problem of determining the order of the homomorphic image of A. We study this problem.

The conjugacy classes of the groups $SL_2(2, F_{2^n})$ are well known (see for example [3]). Besides the two single classes containing the identity and the involutions, the other conjugacy classes contain elements of two types:

- $(q-2)/2$ classes of elements whose order divides $q-1$.
- $q/2$ classes of elements whose order divides $q+1$.

These classes contain respectively: $q(q+1)$ and $q(q-1)$ elements.

It is evident that for the specified range of the hash function, i.e., $130 \leq n \leq 170$, that the order of the homomorphic image of A in $SL_2(2, F_{2^n})$ as defined by any irreducible $P_n(X)$, is not two. Hence the order of such an image of A must divide either $q-1$ or $q+1$. Moreover, there is nothing in the specification of the hashing algorithm which forces A to have the full order, i.e. $q \pm 1$. In the specified range this would produce only impractically long clashing strings. (But shorter length strings than that given by *trivial factorization*, see [6]). It turns out that we can choose an appropriate $P_n(X)$ so that the order of A is reasonable.

3.1 Choosing the right $P_n(X)$

The key to determining the right irreducible polynomial $P_n(X)$ is the special form of A. The following holds.

Proposition 7. *For all n such that $n \geq 1$, A^n is a symmetric matrix in $SL_2(2, F_2[X])$ which has the following form*

$$A^n = \begin{pmatrix} E_n(X) & F_{n-1}(X) \\ F_{n-1}(X) & G_{n-2}(X) \end{pmatrix}, \tag{5}$$

where $E_n(X)$, $F_{n-1}(X)$, etc. denote elements of $F_2[X]$ of degree n, $n-1$, etc. Moreover, for odd n and $n > 1$ the least degree term of $F_{n-1}(X)$ is 1.

Proof. Taking the transpose of A^n, we have

$$(A^n)^T = (A^T)^n,$$

and the right hand side equals A^n since A is a symmetric matrix. Thus A^n is a symmetric matrix. The second part is proved by induction on n.

Assume the off-diagonal term has the form as asserted for powers up to $n-1$ for $n > 1$. Then

$$A^{n+1} = A^{n-1}A^2 = A^{n-1}\begin{pmatrix} X^2+1 & X \\ X & 1 \end{pmatrix},$$

which is

$$\begin{pmatrix} E_{n-1}(X) & F_{n-2}(X) \\ F_{n-2}(X) & G_{n-3}(X) \end{pmatrix}\begin{pmatrix} X^2+1 & X \\ X & 1 \end{pmatrix}.$$

So the off-diagonal entry of A^{n+1} is $E_{n-1}(X) \cdot X + F_{n-2}$. The polynomial $E_{n-1}(X) \cdot X$ has degree n and its least degree term is not 1. By the induction hypothesis the least degree term of F_{n-2} is 1. Hence the off-diagonal term of A^{n+1} has the right form. The remaining assertions follow similarly.

Consider now the powers A^{m+1} as in Proposition 7, and suppose that $F_m(X)$ – the off-diagonal term of A^{m+1} is an irreducible polynomial of degree m over F_2. Suppose further that $(m+1)$ divides either $q-1$ or $q+1$, where $q = 2^m$. Then we have the following result.

Proposition 8. *Suppose that $F_m(X)$ is an irreducible polynomial of degree m over F_2 which satisfies the above hypothesis, and $(m+1)$ is a proper divisor of either $q-1$ or $q+1$, where $q = 2^m$. Then the probability that the order of the homomorphic image of A (defined by $F_m(X)$), does not equal $q-1$ or $q+1$ is respectively: $\phi(q-1)/(q-1)$ or $\phi(q+1)/(q+1)$.*

Proof. Let $GF(2^m)$ be the Galois field defined by $F_m(X)$.

By Proposition 7, we have that

$$A^{m+1} = \begin{pmatrix} E_{m+1}(X) & F_m(X) \\ F_m(X) & G_{m-1}(X) \end{pmatrix}.$$

Consider first the case that the order of the image of A (defined by $F_m(X)$), divides $q-1$ and furthermore that $(m+1)$ is a proper divisor of $q-1$. We will determine the probability that the order of the homomorphic image of A is $q-1$. Assume that this is the case. Then $q-1 = (m+1)n$, so

$$A^{(q-1)} = A^{(m+1)n} = \begin{pmatrix} E_{m+1}(X) & F_m(X) \\ F_m(X) & G_{m-1}(X) \end{pmatrix}^n.$$

Reducing $A^{(q-1)}$ modulo $F_m(X)$, we have that

$$\begin{pmatrix} 1 & 0 \\ 0 & 1 \end{pmatrix} = \begin{pmatrix} \tilde{E}_{m+1}(X) & 0 \\ 0 & \tilde{G}_{m-1}(X) \end{pmatrix}^n.$$

In other words, the order of

$$k = \begin{pmatrix} \tilde{E}_{m+1}(X) & 0 \\ 0 & \tilde{G}_{m-1}(X) \end{pmatrix}$$

divides n, which is less than $q-1$. Unimodularity implies that k belongs to some cyclic subgroup C_{q-1} of $SL_2(2, 2^m)$. But there are $\phi(q-1)$ elements in C_{q-1} whose order does not divide $q-1$. So the probability that a random element such as k is one of these is $\phi(q-1)/(q-1)$, and hence the probability that the order of k is less than $q-1$, is $1 - \phi(q-1)/(q-1)$.

The assumption that the order of A is $q-1$ produces an element in C_{q-1} whose order is less that $q-1$, but the probability of finding such an element is $1 - \phi(q-1)/(q-1)$. Hence with probability

$$1 - (1 - \phi(q-1)/(q-1)) = \phi(q-1)/(q-1),$$

the order of A is less than $q-1$.

The argument is the same when the order of the homomorphic image of A divides $q+1$, except that $q+1$ replaces $q-1$.

4 Calculations

The search for the right $P_n(X)$ depends on Propositions 7 and 8 of the previous section.

Under the hypothesis of these two propositions, we searching for an irreducible polynomial $F_m(X)$ of degree m, such that $m+1$ is a proper divisor of $q-1$ or $q+1$, where $q=2^m$. Proposition 7 ensures us that the off-diagonal term of A^{m+1} satisfies the necessary condition for $F_m(X)$ to be irreducible.

Now we do some calculations with GAP [4].

We find that when $m=100$, the off-diagonal term $F_{100}(X)$ of A^{101} is not an irreducible polynomial. However, it does factorize into two irreducible polynomials as

$$F_{100}(X) = I_{50}(X)^2, \tag{6}$$

where $I_{50}(X)$ is irreducible over $GF(2)$ of degree 50. This pattern of factorization holds for other odd powers of A, see [2]. Another example occurs when $m=105$, here the off-diagonal term $F_{210}(X)$ of A^{211} factorizes as

$$F_{210}(X) = I_{105}(X)^2, \tag{7}$$

where $I_{105}(X)$ is irreducible $GF(2)$ of degree 105.

If we define $GF(2^{50})$ using $I_{50}(X)$ and reduce A^{101} modulo $I_{50}(X)$ we find, in accordance with Proposition 8, that

$$A^{101} = \begin{pmatrix} 1 & 0 \\ 0 & 1 \end{pmatrix}.$$

Thus the order of the homomorphic image of A in $SL_2(2, 2^{50})$, as defined by $I_{50}(X)$ is 101.

Consider now Galois fields $GF(2^n)$ for $130 \leq n \leq 170$, the range specified in [6]. We find that the first field which satisfies our hypothesis is $GF(2^{131})$.

The factorization of $2^{131}-1$ into prime factors is:

$$263 \cdot 10350794431055162386718619237468234569.$$

So 263 divides $2^{131}-1$, and has the form $263 = 2 \cdot 131 + 1$. (In the previous examples, 101 is a prime factor of $2^{50}+1$ and $101 = 2 \cdot 50 + 1$. Similarly 211 is a factor of $2^{105}+1$.)

Raising A to the 263-th power, we find again that the off-diagonal term of A^{263}, F_{262} satisfies the following relation

$$F_{262}(X) = I_{131}(X)^2, \tag{8}$$

where $I_{131}(X)$ is an irreducible polynomial over $GF(2)$ of degree 131.

We can now define $GF(2^{131})$ using the irreducible polynomial $I_{131}(X)$ and reduce A^{263} modulo $I_{131}(X)$. We find that

$$A^{263} = \begin{pmatrix} 1 & 0 \\ 0 & 1 \end{pmatrix},$$

and since 263 is a prime we have proved the following.

Theorem 9. *The order of the homomorphic image of A (as defined by $I_{131}(X)$) in $SL(2, 2^{131})$ is 263.*

We finish this section by giving the irreducible polynomial we used to define $GF(2^{131})$.

Definition 10. $I_{131}(X)$ is an irreducible polynomial over $GF(2)$ of degree 131, which has the form:

$$\begin{aligned} I_{131}(X) = \; & X^{131} + X^{130} + X^{128} + X^{124} + X^{123} + X^{122} \\ & + X^{120} + X^{115} + X^{114} + X^{112} + X^{99} + X^{98} \\ & + X^{96} + X^{67} + X^{66} + X^{64} + X^{3} + X^{2} + 1. \end{aligned}$$

4.1 Clashing messages

We can now construct a pair of binary messages which hash to the same value in $SL(2, 2^{131})$.

We work in the Galois field $GF(2^{131})$ defined by the irreducible polynomial $I_{131}(X)$ given in Definition 10. By Theorem 9, the order of the homomorphic image of A in $SL(2, 2^{131})$ is 263. Hence the order of the inverse image A^{-1} is $263 - 1 = 262$, and the order of the image of A^{-2} is $263 - 2 = 261$. Reducing relation (4) modulo $I_{131}(X)$ gives the following relation in $SL(2, 2^{131})$:

$$A^{262}B(A^{262}B^{2}A^{262})A^{262}B = BA^{261}B. \tag{9}$$

We now substitute 0 for A and 1 for B in (9), and obtain the following

Theorem 11. *The binary string*

$$(0^{262}, 1, 0^{262}, 1, 1, 0^{262}, 0^{262}, 1)$$

and the string

$$(1, 0^{261}, 1)$$

hash to the same value in the group $SL(2, 2^{131})$, where $GF(2^{131})$ is defined by $I_{131}(X)$. (Here, 0^{262} denotes 262 consecutive zeros, etc.)

5 Conclusion

We have found a pair of clashing binary messages for the hash function proposed by Tillich and Zémor [6], thereby showing a weakness in this function. Our attack relies on the structural properties of the groups $SL(2, 2^n)$ and is not restricted to the group $SL(2, 2^{131})$. If $q - 1$ and $q + 1$ are both primes (twin-primes), then our attack fails, since the length of the putative colliding messages would be impractically long. However, there are no twin-primes in the specified range of the hash function, see [1]. Similarly, if the factorization of both $q - 1$ and $q + 1$ involves large primes our attack fails. In [2] we examine the factorizations of $q - 1$ and $q + 1$ ($q = 2^n$) in the range $130 \leq n \leq 170$, and determine the powers of two for which the SL_2 hash function is vulnerable to our attack.

The authors had access to the results which are attacked in this paper, after an announcement of a preliminary program of Crypto'94, stating that the results were accepted as a paper for presentation at Crypto'94. We realize that this was not consistent with IACR rules, and apologize for that.

References

1. J. Brillhart et al. Factorizations of $b^n \pm 1$ $b = 2, 3, 5, 6, 7, 10, 11, 12$ up to high powers. Contemp. Math. Vol. 22, 2nd ed. 1988 Amer. Math. Society.
2. C. Charnes and J. Pieprzyk. The Dihedral subgroup attack on the SL_2 hash function. (In preparation.)
3. L. Dornhoff. Group Representation Theory Vol. 1. 1971 Marcel Dekker, Inc., New York.
4. M. Schönert et al. GAP Groups, Algorithms and Programming 3.3. Lehrstuhl D für Mathematik, RWTH Aachen, 1993.
5. L. Babai, W.M. Kantor, and A. Lubotsky. Small-diameter Cayley graphs for finite simple groups. *Europ. J. of Combinatorics*, Vol. 10, pp. 507–552, 1989.
6. J-P. Tillich and G. Zémor. Hashing with SL_2. *Proceedings of CRYPTO'94, Yvo G. Desmet (Ed.)* LNCS Vol. 839, Springer-Verlag, pp. 40–49, 1994.
7. G. Zémor. Hash Functions and Cayley Graphs. *Designs, Codes and Cryptography* Vol. 4, pp. 381–394, 1994.

SESSION 8

KEY DISTRIBUTION

Chair: Tatsuaki Okamoto

(NTT Laboratories, Japan)

Security of the Center in Key Distribution Schemes

Kaoru KUROSAWA[1], Koji OKADA[1], Keiichi SAKANO[2]

[1] Department of Electrical and Electronic Engineering,
Faculty of Engineering, Tokyo Institute of Technology
2-12-1 O-okayama, Meguro-ku, Tokyo 152, Japan
[2] Matsushita Electric Industrial Co., LTD.
1006, Kadoma, Kadoma-shi, Osaka, 571, Japan

Abstract. This paper studies the security of the trusted center in a b-secure t-group key distribution scheme in which the center issues a private information $v_i \in V$ to each user i based on the center secret $s \in S$. User i can obtain the common key $k \in K$ with $t-1$ other users from v_i so that any dishonest b users cannot learn any key they should not know. First, we show how to distribute the power of the center to m centers so that, even if $l-1$ centers and b users collaborate, they cannot learn any key that b users should not know. Next, we prove that $\log_2 |S| \geq \binom{b+t}{t} \log_2 |K|$.

1 Introduction

Key distribution is a major problem in network security [1] $\sim$ [7]. If users of a group (a conference) wish to communicate in a network using symmetric encryption, they must share a common key. A t-group key distribution scheme is a method to distribute initial private pieces of information among a set of users, so that each group of t users can compute a common key for secure conference non-interactively. This information is generated and distributed by a trusted center. We say that the scheme is b-secure if any bad coalition of b users does not gain any information on any key they should not know.

Blom was the first who considered such schemes [1]. He showed a scheme for $t = 2$ by using a symmetric matrix. (It was studied further by [5].) Blundo et al. showed a scheme for any t by using a symmetric polynomial [2]. In such schemes, however,

1. The center knows every communicaiton.
2. If the center gets down, no new participant cannot join the system.

Therfore, we should distribute the power of the center. In other words, there should be m centers.

In this paper, we present a (m, l)-threshold scheme on centers such as follows.

(1) Even if $l-1$ centers collaborate, they have no information on any common key.

(2) Even if $l-1$ centers and b users collaborate, they have no information on any common key which the b users should not know.
(3) If at least l centers are active (even if $m-l$ centers are down), they can issue a private piece of information to a user.

Actually, we show how to modify any one center scheme to our (m, l)-threshold scheme. Then, (1) and (2) are proved by using entropy.

Further, we consider the size of the center's secret in one center schemes. Let $|K|$ denote the cardinality of a set of common keys. Let V_i be the domain of a private piece of a user i. [2] showed that $\log_2 |V_i| \geq \binom{b+t-1}{t-1} \log_2 |K|$. We prove that $\log_2 |S| \geq \binom{b+t}{t} \log_2 |K|$. Consider a system such that some users join the system today and some users join the system a year later. Then, the size of S is an important issue because, if the center must keep a large amount of information secret, the security of the system degrade. Our bound is best possible because schemes of [1] and [2] meet the equality.

2 Model and Definitions

We denote the cardinality of a set A by $|A|$. $A \backslash B = \{a | a \in A, a \notin B\}$. For a random variable X, $H(X)$ denotes the entropy. See [9] for the details of entropy.

Definition 1. We define a t-group key distribution scheme $(I, \hat{S}, V, K, f, g)$ as follows. In the system, there is a trusted center C and a set of users. I denotes the set of identities of users. S denotes a set of secrets of C.

(step 1) $\hat{S}$ is a random variable distributed over S. C chooses $s \in S$ according to $\hat{S}$ and keeps it secret.
(step 2) f is a mapping from $S \times I$ to V, where V is the domain of a private piece of a user. When a user $i \in I$ joins the system, C computes $f(s, i)$ and gives it to i secretly. We denote $f(s, i)$ by v_i.
(step 3) g is a mapping from $V \times I^{t-1}$ to K, where K is a set of common keys of t users. We denote a common key of the user i and $t-1$ users $i_1, i_2, \ldots, i_{t-1}$ by $k_{(i,i_1,\ldots,i_{t-1})} \in K$. The user i obtains the key non-interactively by using v_i as follows

$$k_{(i,i_1,\ldots,i_{t-1})} = g(v_i, i_1, \ldots, i_{t-1}) . \tag{1}$$

Let V_i and $K_{(i,i_1,\ldots,i_{t-1})}$ denote the random variables induced by v_i and $k_{(i,i_1,\ldots,i_{t-1})}$, respectively.

Definition 2. A t-group key distribution scheme $(I, \hat{S}, V, K, f, g)$ is b-secure if

(1) Each t users share a common key:
For $\forall s \in S$, $\forall (i, i_1, \ldots, i_{t-1}) \in I^t$ and any permutation π on $(i, i_1, \ldots, i_{t-1})$,

$$k_{(i,i_1,\ldots,i_{t-1})} = k_{\pi(i,i_1,\ldots,i_{t-1})} .$$

(2) Any b users have no information on any key they should not know:
For $\forall\{j_1,\ldots,j_b\} \subset I$, $\forall\{i_1,\ldots,i_t\} \subset I$ such that $\{j_1,\ldots,j_b\} \cap \{i_1,\ldots,i_t\} = \phi$, it holds that

$$\Pr(k_{(i_1,\ldots,i_t)}|v_{j_1}\cdots v_{j_b}) = \Pr(k_{(i_1,\ldots,i_t)}) \ .$$

Remark.

(a) ¿From eq.(1) and Def. 2 (1), we have

$$\Pr(k_{(i,i_1,\ldots,i_{t-1})}|v_i) = \cdots = \Pr(k_{(i,i_1,\ldots,i_{t-1})}|v_{i_{t-1}}) = 1 \ , \text{ or}$$
$$H(K_{(i,i_1,\ldots,i_{t-1})}|V_i) = \cdots = H(K_{(i,i_1,\ldots,i_{t-1})}|V_{i_{t-1}}) = 0 \ .$$

(b) Def.2 (1) allows us to write $k_{(i,i_1,\ldots,i_{t-1})}$ as k_A for $A = \{i, i_1, \ldots, i_{t-1}\}$.
(c) Def. 2 (2) is restated as follows.
For $\forall\{j_1,\ldots,j_b\} \in I$ and $\forall A$ such that $|A| = t$, $A \cap \{j_1,\ldots,j_b\} = \phi$,

$$H(K_A|V_{j_1}\cdots V_{j_b}) = H(K_A) \ .$$

(d) Note that $k_{(i,i_1,\cdots,i_{t-1})} = g(v_i, i_1, \cdots, i_{t-1}) = g(f(s,i), i_1, \cdots, i_{t-1})$. Define $e_{(i,i_1,\cdots,i_{t-1})}(s) \triangleq g(f(s,i), i_1, \cdots, i_{t-1})$. Then, for $A = \{i, i_1, \cdots, i_{t-1}\}$,

$$k_A = e_A(s) \ . \tag{2}$$

3 Distributing the Power of the Center

3.1 Overview

In this section, we distribute the power of the trusted center to m centers $C_1, \cdots, C_m$. We present a (m,l)-threshold b-secure t-group key distribution scheme such that

(A1) If at least l centers are active (even if $m-l$ centers are down), they can issue a private piece of information to each user.
(A2) Even if any $l-1$ centers collaborate, they have no information on any key.
(A3) Even if any b users and any $l-1$ centers collaborate, they have no information on a key they should not know.

Actually, we show how to modify any one center scheme $(I, \hat{S}, V, K, f, g)$ satisfying the following properties to our (m,l)-threshold scheme. The schemes given by [1] and [2] satisfy these properties:

(a) S is a set of vectors of a vector space over $GF(q)$.
(b) V is also a set of vectors of a vector space over $GF(q)$.
(c) $f(s,i)$ is linear on s. That is, for $\forall\alpha, \forall\beta \in GF(q)$,

$$f(\alpha s_1 + \beta s_2, i) = \alpha f(s_1, i) + \beta f(s_2, i) \ .$$

(d) $e_A(s)$ (see eq.(2)) is an element of $GF(q)$. Further, for $\forall\alpha, \forall\beta \in GF(q)$,

$$e_A(\alpha s_1 + \beta s_2) = \alpha e_A(s_1) + \beta e_A(s_2) \ .$$

Our scheme consists of a preprocessing phase, a participation phase and a key generation phase. Suppose that a dealer distributes a secret s_0 to m centers by Shamir's (m, l)-threshold scheme. The preprocessing phase is a simple unconditionally secure multiparty protocol which executes this Shamir's scheme without the dealer. All m centers participate in this phase.

In the participation phase, suppose that $C_1 \sim C_l$ are active and $C_{l+1} \sim C_m$ are down. When a user i joins the system, C_j $(j = 1, 2, \cdots, l)$ gives the user i

$$v_{ij} = f(x_j, i) \ . \tag{3}$$

where x_i is the share of C_i given in the preprocessing phase.

In the key generation phase, user i computes $v_i = f(s_0, i)$ by applying Lagrange formula [8] to $\{v_{i1} \sim v_{il}\}$.

Let $\hat{k_A}$ denote the common key of a set A of our (m, l)-threshold scheme. Then, $\hat{k_A} = e_A(s_0)$.

3.2 Proposed scheme

Preprocessing phase

(step 1) Each center C_j chooses $s_j \in S$ independently and secretly according to $\hat{S}$.

(step 2) Each C_j chooses a vector polynomial $h_j(z)$ over $GF(q)$ of order $l-1$ such that $h_j(0) = s_j$ randomly. C_j sends $h_j(u)$ to C_u secretly for $\forall u \neq j$.

Let

$$h(z) \triangleq \sum_{i=1}^{m} h_i(z) \ , \quad s_0 \triangleq \sum_{i=1}^{m} s_i \ (= h(0)) \ , \quad x_j \triangleq h(j) \ .$$

At step 2, C_j can obtain x_j.

Participation phase

For simplicity, suppose that only $C_1, \cdots, C_l$ are active.

(step 3) When a user i joins the system, C_j $(j = 1, 2, \cdots, l)$ gives the user i

$$v_{ij} = f(x_j, i) \ .$$

Key generation phase

(step 4) The user i computes

$$v_i = \sum_{j=1}^{l} \alpha_j v_{ij} \qquad \text{where } \alpha_j = \prod_{w=1, w\neq j}^{l} \frac{-w}{j-w} \ . \tag{4}$$

Then, i executes step 3 of Def.1 to obtain a common key with $(i_1, \cdots, i_{t-1})$, $\hat{k}_{i,i_1,\cdots,i_{t-1}}$.

Lemma 3.

(1) $\sum_{j=1}^{l} \alpha_j x_j = s_0$.

(2) $\sum_{j=1}^{l} \alpha_j v_{ij} = f(s_0, i)$.

(3) $\hat{k}_{(i,i_1,\cdots,i_{t-1})} = g(\sum_{j=1}^{l} \alpha_j v_{ij}, i_1, \cdots, i_{t-1}) = e_{(i,i_1,\cdots,i_{t-1})}(s_0)$.

Proof.
(1) Lagrange formula [8] gives us

$$h_u(x) = \sum_{j=1}^{l} \prod_{w=1, w\neq j} \frac{x-w}{j-w} h_u(j) .$$

So,

$$s_u = h_u(0) = \sum_{j=1}^{l} \prod_{w=1, w\neq j} \frac{-w}{j-w} h_u(j) = \sum_{j=1}^{l} \alpha_j h_u(j) .$$

Therefore,

$$s_0 = \sum_{u=1}^{m} s_u = \sum_{u=1}^{m} \sum_{j=1}^{l} \alpha_j h_u(j) = \sum_{j=1}^{l} \alpha_j x_j .$$

(2)

$$\sum_{j=1}^{l} \alpha_j v_{ij} = \sum_{j=1}^{l} \alpha_j f(\sum_{u=1}^{m} h_u(j), i) = f(\sum_{j=1}^{l} \alpha_j x_j, i) = f(s_0, i) \quad \text{(from (1))} .$$

(3)

$$\begin{aligned} g(\sum_{j=1}^{l} \alpha_j v_{ij}, i_1, \cdots, i_{t-1}) &= g(f(s_0, i), i_1, \cdots, i_{t-1}) \qquad \text{(from (2))} \\ &= e_{(i,i_1,\cdots,i_{t-1})}(s_0) \qquad \text{(from eq.(2))} . \end{aligned}$$

□

3.3 Security

In this subsection, we show (A2) and (A3). We assume that all centers are semi-honest. They behave correctly. They, however, try to compute something after the protocol execution. $\hat{K}_A$ denotes the random variable induced by $\hat{k}_A$.

(A2) is proved first.

Lemma 4. *Suppose that* $H(P|Q) = 0, H(Q|R) = H(Q)$. *Then,*

$$H(P|R) = H(P) \ . \tag{5}$$

Proof. Note that $H(Q|R) = H(Q)$ is equivalent to $H(R|Q) = H(R)$. Then

$$\begin{aligned} I(PQ;R) = H(R) - H(R|PQ) &= H(R|Q) - H(R|PQ) \\ = I(R;P|Q) &= H(P|Q) - H(P|QR) = 0 \ . \end{aligned}$$

Hence,

$$0 = I(PQ;R) = I(P;R) + I(Q;R|P) \geq 0 \ .$$

Thus $I(P;R) = 0$, eq.(5) holds. □

Let $z_1 = (h_1(z), \cdots h_{l-1}(z))$, $z_2 = (h_l(1), \cdots, h_l(l-1), \cdots h_m(1), \cdots h_m(l-1))$. Let Z_1 and Z_2 be the random variables induced by z_1 and z_2, respectively. Note that z_1 and z_2 are everything that $C_1, \cdots, C_{l-1}$ know.

Theorem 5. *Even if any* $l-1$ *centers collaborate, they have no information on any key.*

Proof. For simplicity, suppose that $C_1, \ldots, C_{l-1}$ collaborate. Let S_0 be the random variable induced by s_0.

For $\forall A \subset I$ such that $|A| = t$, $\hat{k_A}$ is determined from s_0 from Lemma 3. Therefore

$$H(\hat{K_A}|S_0) = 0 \ . \tag{6}$$

On the other hand, $h_l(x)$ is a random vector polynomial of order $l-1$. Therefore, $H(S_l|Z_1Z_2) = H(S_l)$. Hence,

$$H(S_0|Z_1Z_2) = H(S_0) \ . \tag{7}$$

Then, from eq.(6), eq.(7) and Lemma 4, we have

$$H(\hat{K_A}|Z_1Z_2) = H(\hat{K_A}) \ . \tag{8}$$

□

Next, we prove (A3). We prove (A3) even if all centers $C_1, \cdots, C_m$ issue private information to each user. Let $u = (f(x_l,1), \cdots, f(x_l,b), \cdots, f(x_m,1), \cdots, f(x_m,b))$, where $x_j = \sum_{i=1}^{m} h_i(l)$ $(j = l, \cdots, m)$. u is everything that user $1 \cdots b$ received from C_j $(j = l, \cdots, m)$. Thus, (u, z_1, z_2) is everything that user $1 \cdots b$ and $C_1 \cdots C_{l-1}$ know. Let U be the random variable induced by u.

Theorem 6. *Even if any* b *users and any* $l-1$ *centers collaborate, they have no information on any key they should not know.*

Proof. For simplicity, suppose that $C_1, \cdots, C_{l-1}$ and user $1, \cdots, b$ collaborate. Consider A such that $A \bigcap \{1, \cdots, b\} = \phi$. Our goal is to show that $H(\hat{K_A}|Z_1 Z_2 U) = H(\hat{K_A})$.

Suppose that

$$H(\hat{K_A}|U Z_1 Z_2) < H(\hat{K_A}) \ . \tag{9}$$

Then, we will show that

$$H(K_A|V_1 \cdots V_b) < H(K_A) \ . \tag{10}$$

which is a contradiction (see Remark (c) in Section 2).

Suppose that $v_1, \cdots, v_b$ are given, where

$$v_i = f(s, i) \tag{11}$$

from step 2 of Def.1. Now, choose z_1 and z_2 such that

$$\begin{aligned} z_1 &= (h_1(z), \cdots, h_{l-1}(z)) \ , \\ z_2 &= (h_l(1), \cdots, h_l(l-1), \cdots, h_m(1), \cdots h_m(l-1)) \end{aligned}$$

at random. From z_1 and z_2, we can compute

$$x_i = \sum_{j=1}^{m} h_j(i) \qquad 1 \le i \le l-1 \ . \tag{12}$$

It is clear that $h_l(l), \cdots, h_m(l)$ are independent of z_1 and z_2. Therefore, we can consider that

$$s = \sum_{j=l}^{m} h_j(l) \tag{13}$$

in eq.(11). Then, from eq.(11) and z_1, we can compute

$$\begin{aligned} v_i + f(\sum_{j=1}^{l-1} h_j(l), i) &= f(\sum_{j=l}^{m} h_j(l), i) + f(\sum_{j=1}^{l-1} h_j(l), i) \\ &= f(\sum_{j=1}^{m} h_j(l), i) \\ &= f(x_l, i) \ . \end{aligned} \tag{14}$$

Further, from z_1 and eq.(14), Lagrange formula [8] gives us

$$f(x_\delta, i) = \sum_{j=1}^{l} \prod_{w=1, w \ne j}^{l} \frac{\delta - w}{j - w} f(x_j, i) \tag{15}$$

$(\delta = l+1, \cdots, m, \ i = 1, \cdots, b)$. Thus, from eq.(12) eq.(14) and eq.(15), we have obtained $x_1, \cdots, x_{l-1}$ and $u = (f(x_l, 1), \cdots, f(x_l, b), \cdots, f(x_m, 1), \cdots, \ f(x_m, b))$ which are consistent with $\{v_i\}$, z_1 and z_2. Let $\hat{k_A}$ be a common key of A which is determined from $x_1, \cdots x_l$ (see Lemma 3 (1)). ¿From our assumption, we obtain some information on $\hat{k}_A$ from z_1 , z_2 and u. On the other hand,

$$\begin{aligned}\hat{k}_A &= e_A(\sum_{i=1}^{l} \alpha_i x_i) \\ &= e_A(\sum_{i=1}^{l-1} \alpha_i x_i) + \alpha_l e_A(\sum_{j=1}^{m} h_j(l)) \\ &= e_A(\sum_{i=1}^{l-1} \alpha_i x_i) + \alpha_l e_A(\sum_{j=1}^{l-1} h_j(l)) + \alpha_l e_A(\sum_{j=l}^{m} h_j(l)) \\ &= e_A(\sum_{i=1}^{l-1} \alpha_i x_i) + \alpha_l e_A(\sum_{j=1}^{l-1} h_j(l)) + \alpha_l e_A(s)\end{aligned}$$

from Lemma 3 (1) and eq.(13). We know $x_1, \cdots, x_{l-1}$ and $h_1(l), \cdots h_{l-1}(l)$ from eq.(12) and z_1. This means that we have some information on $e_A(s)$. Now, we have derived eq. (10) since $k_A = e_A(s)$ (see eq.(2)). □

4 Lower Bound on the Size of the Center's Secret

For a b-secure t-group ID-based cryptosystem $(\hat{S}, I, V, K, f, g)$, [2] showed a lower bound of $|V|$. In this section, we show a lower bound of $|S|$.

Proposition 7. *[2] Suppose that* A, E, $B_i \subseteq I$ $(i = 1, 2, \cdots, m)$, $|A| = |B_i| = t$, $|E| = b$, $A \bigcap E = \phi$, $B_i \bigcap E \neq \phi$ $(i = 1, 2, \cdots, m)$. *Then* $H(K_A | K_{B_1} \cdots K_{B_m}) = H(K_A)$.

Let all t subsets of $\{1, 2, \cdots, t+b\}$ be $D_1, D_2, \cdots, D_l$, where $l = \binom{t+b}{t}$.

Lemma 8. $H(K_{D_l} | K_{D_1}, \cdots, K_{D_v}) = H(K_{D_l})$ *for* $\forall v \leq l-1$.

Proof. Let $A = D_l$, $E = \{1, 2, \cdots, t+b\} \backslash D_l$, $B_i = D_i (i = 1, 2, \cdots, v)$. Then, it is easy to see that these A, $\{B_i\}$ and E satisfy the condition of Proposition 7. □

Theorem 9. *Let all* t *subsets of* $\{1, 2, \cdots, t+b\}$ *be* $D_1, D_2, \cdots, D_l$, $l = \binom{t+b}{t}$. *Then*

$$\log_2 |S| \geq H(\hat{S}) \geq \sum_{i=1}^{l} H(K_{D_i}) \ .$$

Proof. Once $s \in S$ is chosen, $k_{D_1}, \cdots, k_{D_l}$ are all determined (see eq.(2)). Therefore $H(K_{D_1} \cdots K_{D_l} | \hat{S}) = 0$. Then,

$$\begin{aligned} H(\hat{S}) &= H(\hat{S}|K_{D_1} \cdots K_{D_l}) + H(K_{D_1} \cdots K_{D_l}) - H(K_{D_1} \cdots K_{D_l}|\hat{S}) \\ &= H(\hat{S}|K_{D_1} \cdots K_{D_l}) + H(K_{D_1} \cdots K_{D_l}) \\ &\geq H(K_{D_1} \cdots K_{D_l}) \\ &= H(K_{D_1}) + H(K_{D_2}|K_{D_1}) + \cdots H(K_{D_l}|K_{D_1} \cdots K_{D_{l-1}}) \\ &= H(K_{D_1}) + H(K_{D_2}) + \cdots H(K_{D_l}) \qquad \text{(from Lemma 8)} \\ &= \sum_{i=1}^{l} H(K_{D_i}) \ . \end{aligned}$$

□

Corollary 10. *If $g(v_i, i_1, \ldots, i_{t-1})$ is uniformly distributed over K for $\forall(i, i_1, \ldots, i_{t-1}) \in I^t$, then $\log_2 |S| \geq H(\hat{S}) \geq l \cdot \log_2 |K|$.*

References

1. R.Blom : An Optimal Class of Symmetric Key Generation Systems. Eurocrypt'84, pp.335-338 (1984)
2. C.Blundo, A.De Santis, A.Herzberg, S.Kutten, U.Vaccaro and M.Yung : Perfectly-Secure Key Distribution for Dynamic Conferences. Crypto'92 (1992)
3. A.Beimel and B.Chor : Interaction in Key Distribution Schemes. Crypto'93 (1993)
4. L.Gong and D.J.Wheeler : A matrix Key-Distribution Scheme. Journal of Cryptology, 2, pp.51-59 (1990)
5. T.Matsumoto and I.Imai : On the Key Predistribution Systems: A Practical Solution to the Key Distribution Problem. Crypto'87, pp.185-193 (1988)
6. E.Okamoto and K.Tanaka : Key Distribution System Based on Identification Information. IEEE J. on Selected Areas in Communications, 7(4), pp.481-485 (1989)
7. S.Tsujii and J.Chao : A New ID-based Key Sharing Scheme. Crypto'91, pp.288-299 (1991)
8. Y.Desmedt and Y.Frankel : Shared Generation of Authenticators and Signatures. In Advances in Cryptology. Proc. of Crypto'91, pp.11-15 (1991)
9. R.G.Gallager : Information Theory and Reliable Communications. John Wiley & Sons, New York, NY (1968)

Incidence Structures for Key Sharing
— Extended Abstract —

Tsutomu Matsumoto*

Division of Electrical and Computer Engineering
Yokohama National University
156 Tokiwadai, Hodogaya, Yokohama, 240 Japan
Email: tsutomu@mlab.dnj.ynu.ac.jp Fax: +81-45-338-1157

Abstract. Assuming a set of v entities and a set $\mathbf{B}$ of b key-sharing systems, this paper proposes a way of assigning each entity a subset of $\mathbf{B}$ so that any two entities have at least one common key-sharing system with which they can share an h-bit common key. Such an assignment is nothing but a cohesive incidence structure. If an entity is assigned a subset $\{S_0, \cdots, S_{r-1}\} \subset \mathbf{B}$ then by the system centers for $S_0 \cdots, S_{r-1}$, respectively, the entity is supplied r tamper-resistant modules (TRMs) containing data depending on the entity's identifier and the secret information for the corresponding system. The use of plural TRMs per entity can be sound with respect to the status of micro-electronics. Assume that every key-sharing system in $\mathbf{B}$ cannot be completely broken unless at least m TRMs are successfully attacked to infer m pieces of $h \times m$-bit data inside them. Then each entity has r TRMs which contain $r \times h \times m$-bit data in total while the minimum number of TRMs to attack for complete breaking is $b \times m$. The *gain* defined by (minimum number of TRMs to attack)/(total memory per key-bit per entity), is thus b/r. Gain 1 is attained by the (trivial) method using $r = b$ TRMs per entity with $b(\geq 1)$ key-sharing systems. A larger gain will save memory per entity to yield the same security level measured by the tamper-resistance required for complete breaking. This paper also provides a method to generate desirable assignments yielding gain $b/r > 2$ with large v exponential in r, by introducing a novel binary operation on incidence structures which preserves cohesiveness and constant-weight properties.
Keywords. Binary Matrix, Combinatorial Design, Cryptography, Identifier, Key Distribution, Key Sharing, Tactical Configuration, Tamper Resistant Module.

1 Introduction

Background. In large network systems, one of the prerequisites for efficiently utilizing confidential/ authenticated communications by common-key cryptography is to develop superior *key sharing* schemes which ensure conveniently sharing

* This work was done while the author was a Visiting Professor at Institute for Algorithms and Cognitive Systems, University of Karlsruhe, Am Fasanengarten 5, D-76128 Karlsruhe, Germany.

cryptographic keys among communication partners. The KPS (Key Predistribution Systems) [1] is a large class of such key sharing schemes covering several variants of concrete schemes in [2, 3, 4, 5] as well as the *linear schemes* [1] a version of which has been realized using one-chip IC cards [6]. The remarkable property of KPS is that for the purpose of key sharing there are no need to send messages between the entities who will make a cryptographic communication using the obtained key. Each of the entity should just input the partner's identifier to its *tamper-resistant module* (TRM) containing a common algorithm and an individual data provided by one or plural system center(s).

Motivation. The total security of KPS would be based on lack of information, physical infeasibility, and computational infeasibility. By *completely broken* we mean a state that an attacker has gotten sufficient information to produce every individual data in the system. There exists a KPS which cannot be completely broken unless extracting m individual data from at least m TRMs. And this is proved optimal. More precisely, the ratio (minimum number of TRMs to attack)/(memory per key-bit per entity) is one. Can the ratio become larger if plural TRMs can be used by each user ? In other words, is a concurrent use of a set of key-sharing systems meaningful? The scenario would be acceptable when an IC chip could provide a number of regions which can exhibit enough tamper resistance. Seeing current status of micro-electronics we assume that the use of multiple TRMs per entity is reasonable.

Methodology. Assigning several key-sharing systems to each entity can be interpreted as making an *incidence structure*, or equivalently, constructing a (0, 1)-matrix having certain desirable properties. Thus, combinatorics can serve a reasonable tool to apply.

Results. We observe that the desirable incidence structures are represented by *normal*, *cohesive*, *constant-row-weight* matrices having exponential number of rows in terms of row-dimension and greater ratio (row-dimension)/(row-weight) > 1. (Each technical term will be explained in the body of the paper.) Then we propose a binary operation over the set of all binary matrices and show that it is very helpful to provide concrete incidence structures desirable for our application. In particular, we give several examples achieving the ratio greater than 2. The results obtained are independent from concrete key-sharing systems.

Organization. Section 2 clearly describes our method using terminology of incidence structures and what are desirable for the method. Section 3 shows incidence structures known so far and their insufficiency for our application. Section 4 proposes and analyzes a binary operation to produce new incidence structures with preserving desirable properties for our application. Section 4 also provides several concrete incidence structures. Section 5 concludes the paper.

2 A Way of Using Plural Key-Sharing Systems

2.1 Primitive Key-Sharing Systems

Environment. By an *entity* we denote what processes/sends/receives information, like a person/a group of persons, an equipment/a set of devices, or, a program/a set of programs. Let $\mathcal{E} = \{\text{entity}0, \cdots, \text{entity}v-1\}$ be the set of all entities to be considered. Let $\mathcal{I}$ be a set and assume that each entity, say, entity i, has its own *identifier* (ID) ID_i ($\in \mathcal{ID}$) such that entity i and entity j coincide if $ID_i = ID_j$.

Model Key-Sharing System. When entity i joins the system, by a single system center or a set of plural system centers, entity i is supplied a *tamper resistant module* (TRM) which stores (after some preparatory interaction with the system center(s)) an individual data x_i ($\in \{0,1\}^{h \times m}$) and a common algorithm *alg*, where h and m are positive integers. The hm-bit data x_i depends on ID_i and the secret of the system center(s). Algorithm *alg* acts as follows. On input x_i and $ID_j \in \mathcal{I}$, *alg* outputs $k_{ij} = alg(x_i, ID_j)$ ($\in \{0,1\}^h$), the master-key for the pair of entities i and j, where *alg* and every x_i, x_j are designed so that $alg(x_a, ID_b) = alg(x_b, ID_a)$ holds for any entities a, $b \in \mathcal{E}$. The TRM is designed so that entity i can input ID_j and execute *alg* inside the TRM and obtain the output k_{ij} but for anybody even entity i it is physically and logically very hard to read out or infer hidden x_i correctly from the TRM. This system is a typical implementation of Key Predistribution System (KPS). Note that for the purpose of key sharing there are no need to send messages between the entities. Note also that the above mentioned idea can be readily modified to cope with the key sharing among three or more entities.

Security. By *completely broken* we mean a state that an attacker has gotten sufficient information to produce every individual data in the system. And to attain such a state is called *complete breaking*. There exists such a KPS which cannot be completely broken unless extracting m individual data (x_i's) from at least m TRMs. And this is proved optimal.

2.2 Incidence Structures

Notation 1. For positive integers v and b, let $I(v,b)$ denote the set of all $(0,1)$-matrices each of which has v rows and b columns.

Definition 1. A finite *incidence structure* is a triple $\mathbf{D} = (\mathcal{V}, \mathbf{B}, F)$ where $\mathcal{V}$ and $\mathbf{B}$ are any two disjoint finite sets and F is a binary relation between $\mathcal{V}$ and $\mathbf{B}$, i.e., $F \subset \mathcal{V} \times \mathbf{B}$ [7]. The elements of $\mathcal{V}$ are called *points*, those of $\mathbf{B}$ *blocks* and those of F *flags*. Let label the points as $p_0, \cdots, p_{v-1}$ and the blocks $B_0, \cdots, B_{b-1}$. Then the matrix $D = [D_{ij}]_{0 \le i < v, 0 \le j < b} \in I(v,b)$ defined by

$$D_{ij} = \begin{cases} 1 & \text{if } (p_i, B_j) \in F, \\ 0 & \text{otherwise,} \end{cases}$$

is called an *incidence matrix* for **D**. D depends on the labeling used, but it is unique up to column and row permutations. Conversely, every (0, 1)-matrix determines an incidence structure.

Definition 2. Let $D = [D_{ij}] \in I(v, b)$ and **D** be the incidence structure determined by D. The ith row's weight of D, or the ith point's degree of **D**, is defined as $R_i(D) = \sum_{j=0}^{b-1} D_{ij}$. The jth column's weight of D, or j^{th} block's degree, of **D** is defined as $K_j(D) = \sum_{i=0}^{v-1} D_{ij}$. The meeting number of the ith row and the jth row of D, or the meeting number of the ith point and the jth point of **D**, is defined as $\Lambda_{ij}(D) = \sum_{f=0}^{b-1} D_{if} D_{jf}$.

1) D and **D** are called *normal* if $R_i(D) < b$ and $K_j(D) < v$ for every i and j.
2) D and **D** are called *cohesive* if $\Lambda_{ij}(D) \geq 1$ for every i and j.
3) D is called *constant-row-weight* with $R(D)$ and **D** is called *constant-point-degree* with $R(D)$ if $R_i(D) = R(D)$ for every i.
4) D is called *constant-column-weight* with $K(D)$ and **D** is called *constant-block-degree* with $K(D)$ if $K_j(D) = K(D)$ for every j.
5) D and **D** are called *tactical* with $R(D)$ and $K(D)$ if $R_i(D) = R(D)$ and $K_j(D) = K(D)$ for every i and j.

Notation 2. If $D \in I(v, b)$ is tactical with $R(D) = r$ and $K(D) = k$, we denote this fact by $D \in T(v, b, r, k)$.

Example 1. All of the following matrices are normal, cohesive, and tactical.

$$P = \begin{bmatrix} 1 & 1 & 0 \\ 1 & 0 & 1 \\ 0 & 1 & 1 \end{bmatrix} \in T(3,3,2,2), \qquad Q = \begin{bmatrix} 1 & 1 & 1 & 0 \\ 1 & 1 & 0 & 1 \\ 1 & 0 & 1 & 1 \\ 0 & 1 & 1 & 1 \end{bmatrix} \in T(4,4,3,3),$$

$$R = \begin{bmatrix} 1 & 1 & 1 & 0 & 0 \\ 1 & 1 & 0 & 0 & 1 \\ 1 & 0 & 0 & 1 & 1 \\ 0 & 0 & 1 & 1 & 1 \\ 0 & 1 & 1 & 1 & 0 \\ 1 & 1 & 0 & 1 & 0 \\ 1 & 0 & 1 & 0 & 1 \\ 0 & 1 & 0 & 1 & 1 \\ 1 & 0 & 1 & 1 & 0 \\ 0 & 1 & 1 & 0 & 1 \end{bmatrix} \in T(10,5,3,6), \; S = \begin{bmatrix} 1 & 1 & 0 & 1 & 0 & 0 & 0 \\ 1 & 0 & 1 & 0 & 0 & 0 & 1 \\ 0 & 1 & 0 & 0 & 0 & 1 & 1 \\ 1 & 0 & 0 & 0 & 1 & 1 & 0 \\ 0 & 0 & 0 & 1 & 1 & 0 & 1 \\ 0 & 0 & 1 & 1 & 0 & 1 & 0 \\ 0 & 1 & 1 & 0 & 1 & 0 & 0 \end{bmatrix} \in T(7,7,3,3).$$

Observation 1. Given a normal cohesive tactical matrix $C \in T(v, b, r, k)$, for any integer $V \leq v$ we can construct a normal cohesive constant-row-weight matrix $D \in I(V, b)$ with $R(D) = r$ by selecting any V rows from C.

2.3 Assigning Plural Systems Using Incidence Structures

Tamper Resistance. The use of plural key-sharing systems per entity can be sound with respect to the current status of micro-electronics because a single IC chip can provide a number of different tamper-resistant regions.

Environment. Assume a set $\mathcal{E}$ of v entities each of which (say entity i) has unique identifier ($ID_i \in \mathcal{I}$) as before and a set of b key-sharing systems $\mathbf{B} = \{B_0, \cdots, B_{b-1}\}$. Let $\mathcal{V} = \{p_0, \cdots, p_{v-1}\}$ be a set of v elements and $\mathbf{H}$ an 1-to-1 one-way function from $\mathcal{I}$ to $\mathcal{V}$.

The Method. We propose a way of assigning each entity a subset of $\mathbf{B}$ so that any two entities have at least one common key-sharing system with which they can share an h-bit common key. This is nothing but determining a cohesive incidence structure with point set $\mathcal{V}$ and block set $\mathbf{B}$. We denote its incidence matrix by

$$D = \begin{bmatrix} D(0) \\ \vdots \\ D(v-1) \end{bmatrix} \in I(v, b)$$

with $D(i) \in I(1, b)$. We assume that there is an efficient algorithm A_D to compute a row in D given an index for the row.

Procedure. Let entity a and entity b be the entities of concern. Firstly entity a and b independently compute $i = \mathbf{H}(ID_a)$ and $j = \mathbf{H}(ID_b)$ and find $D(i) = A_D(i)$ and $D(j) = A_D(j)$. Of course entity a and entity b can record $D(i)$ and $D(j)$, respectively. Secondary, they calculate the common key-sharing system(s) indicated by both $D(i)$ and $D(j)$.

Memory per Entity. If row $D(i)$ shows a subset $\{S_0, \cdots, S_{r-1}\} \subset \mathbf{B}$ then by the system centers for $S_0 \cdots, S_{r-1}$, respectively, entity i is supplied r tamper-resistant modules (TRMs) containing data depending on the entity's identifier, ID_i, and the secret information for the corresponding key-sharing system. As described in **2.1** since there is a key-sharing system which cannot be completely broken unless at least m TRMs are successfully attacked to infer m pieces of $h \times m$-bit data inside them, assume that every system in $\mathbf{B}$ has such a property. Then if D is constant-row-weight with $R(D) = r$ then each entity has r TRMs which contain $r \times h \times m$-bit data in total, while the minimum number of TRMs to attack for complete breaking is $b \times m$. Thus, the ratio (minimum number of TRMs to attack)/(total memory per key-bit per entity) is b/r. Generally we adopt the following definition.

Definition 3. For matrix $D \in I(v, b)$ and its corresponding incidence structure $\mathbf{D}$, the *gain* $\Gamma(D)$ of D and $\mathbf{D}$ is defined as

$$\Gamma(D) = \frac{b}{\frac{1}{v}\sum_i R_i(D)} = \frac{vb}{\sum_i R_i(D)}.$$

Proposition 1. If D is constant-row-weight with $R(D) = r$ we have $\Gamma(D) = b/r$.

Observation 2. The conventional method using a single key-sharing system corresponds to matrix $J_1 \in I(v, 1)$ each of which entry is 1. Thus its gain is $\Gamma(J_1) = 1$. The same gain is attained by the method using $r = b$ TRMs per entity with b key-sharing systems. This is corresponding to matrix $J_b \in I(v,b)$ each of which entry is 1. The proposed assignment using a larger gain will save memory per entity to yield the same security level measured by the tamper-resistance required for complete breaking. For example, matrices R and S in Example 1 yield $\Gamma(R) = 5/3$ and $\Gamma(S) = 7/3$, respectively.

Desirable Incidence Structures. Let D be a cohesive incidence matrix defining our assignment. If there is an all-one column in D then the key-sharing system corresponding to the column can be always used. This is somewhat redundant, so we prefer to let D be normal. And the situation where every entity uses the same number of TRMs is easy to treat in theory and in practice, we prefer to let D be constant-row-weight. Another important condition to D is that it must have a lot of rows so that the method can be applied to large networks containing a lot of entities. Summing up all the conditions we have the following criterion:

Matrix $D \in I(v,b)$
- should be normal, cohesive, constant-row-weight,
- should yield a large gain, $\Gamma(D)$,
- should have v which is exponential in r,
- should have an efficient algorithm A_D to compute a row from its index.

3 Examining Available Incidence Structures

3.1 All Constant-Weight Vectors of Fixed Dimension

Fact 1. For any positive integer n, a matrix W_{2n+1} which has $\binom{2n+1}{n+1}$ rows of dimension $2n+1$ and weight $n+1$ is normal, cohesive, and tactical with $W_{2n+1} \in T(\binom{2n+1}{n+1}, 2n+1, n+1, \binom{2n}{n})$. Similarly, for any integer $n \geq 2$, a matrix W_{2n} which has $\binom{2n}{n+1}$ rows of dimension $2n$ and weight $n+1$ is normal, cohesive, and tactical with $W_{2n} \in T(\binom{2n}{n+1}, 2n, n+1, \binom{2n-1}{n})$.

Example 2. Three matrices in Example 1 can be interpreted as $P = W_3$, $Q = W_4$, and $R = W_5$. An enumeration of small examples for odd b is given below.

v	b	r	k	b/r
3	3	2	2	1.50
10	5	3	6	1.66
35	7	4	20	1.75
126	9	5	70	1.80
462	11	6	252	1.83
1,716	13	7	924	1.85
6,435	15	8	3,432	1.87
24,310	17	9	12,870	1.88
92,378	19	10	48,620	1.90
...	...	...	...	...
1.16×10^9	33	17	6.01×10^8	1.94
4.53×10^9	35	18	2.33×10^9	1.94
...	...	...	...	...

Observation 3. The above construction can achieve large values of v and k with keeping b and r small. However, there is a limitation; $b/r < 2$. Namely, the incidence structures defined by the all r-out-of-b vectors can be used for our application, but the gain b/r attained is always upper-bounded by two.

3.2 Finite Projective Planes

Fact 2. For any prime power q, there exists a projective plane $PG(2,q)$ of order q [7]. In fact, by letting W be the vector space of dimension 3 over $GF(q)$, all 1-dimensional subspaces of W as the points, and all 2-dimensional subspaces of W as the blocks, constitute an incidence structure $PG(2,q)$, which is normal, cohesive, and tactical with incidence matrix
$G_q \in T(q^2+q+1, q^2+q+1, q+1, q+1)$.

Example 3. Matrix S in Example 1 determines $PG(2,2)$. The following shows parameters of G_q for small q.

q	v	b	r	k	b/r
2	7	7	3	3	2.33
3	13	13	4	4	3.25
4	21	21	5	5	4.20
5	31	31	6	6	5.16
7	57	57	8	8	7.12
8	73	73	9	9	8.11
9	91	91	10	10	9.10
11	133	133	12	12	11.08
13	183	183	14	14	13.07
⋮	⋯	⋯	⋯	⋯	⋯

Observation 4. If a normal cohesive tactical matrix $D \in T(v,b,r,k)$ shows another regularity that $\Lambda_{ij}(D) = 1$ for every pair of different rows of D, then D defines an incidence structure called a ***block design*** [7]. Projective planes are examples of block designs. For any incidence matrix for any block design, we have a famous restriction on the parameters; $v \le b$, known as Fisher's inequality [7]. For this reason, the block designs cannot serve as a good source of incidence structures desirable for our application. Nevertheless, since the above table shows large gain b/r values, projective planes could be used as seeds with which generate desirable incidence structures.

4 Constructing Desirable Incidence Structures

4.1 A Binary Operation

Definition 4a. Let v, b, B be positive integers and $C \in I(v,b)$, $D \in I(1,B)$ be matrices such that

$$C = \begin{bmatrix} C(0) \\ \vdots \\ C(v-1) \end{bmatrix}, \quad C(i) \in I(1,b), \qquad D = [D_0, \cdots, D_{B-1}], \quad D_j \in \{0,1\}.$$

Let $w_0(D) = 0$ and $w_j(D) = \sum_{g=0}^{j-1} D_g$ for $j = 1, \cdots, B$.
If $v > 1$ let $i(f)$ $(\in \{0, \cdots, v-1\})$ denote the fth $(\in \{0, \cdots, w_B(D) - 1\})$ digit of the radix-v expression of integer i $(\in \{0, \cdots, v^{w_B(D)} - 1\})$.
Then $C\%D$ is defined as the matrix

$$E = [E_{ij}]_{0 \le i < v^{w_B(D)}, 0 \le j < B} \in I(v^{w_B(D)}, b \cdot B)$$

such that
1) when $v = 1$,

$$E_{ij} = \begin{cases} [0, \cdots, 0] \in I(1, b) & \text{if } D_j = 0, \\ C(0) \in I(1, b) & \text{if } D_j = 1, \end{cases}$$

2) when $v > 1$,

$$E_{ij} = \begin{cases} [0, \cdots, 0] \in I(1, b) & \text{if } D_j = 0, \\ C(i(w_j(D))) \in I(1, b) & \text{if } D_j = 1. \end{cases}$$

Definition 4b. Let v, b, V, B be positive integers and $C \in I(v, b)$, $D \in I(V, B)$ be matrices such that

$$D = \begin{bmatrix} D(0) \\ \vdots \\ D(V-1) \end{bmatrix}, \quad D(j) \in I(1, B).$$

Then $C\%D$ is defined by

$$C\%D = \begin{bmatrix} C\%D(0) \\ \vdots \\ C\%D(V-1) \end{bmatrix}.$$

Proposition 2. For matrices $C \in I(v, b)$ and $D \in I(V, B)$ we have $C\%D \in I(\sum_{i=0}^{V-1} v^{R_i(D)}, b \cdot B)$. In particular, if D is constant-row-weight with $R(D)$, we have $C\%D \in I(v^{R(D)} \cdot V, b \cdot B)$.

Proof) Straightforward from the definition of $C\%D$.

Proposition 3. Operation % is associative, *i.e.*, for matrices C, D, E we have $(C\%D)\%E = C\%(D\%E)$.

Proof) Omitted.

Example 4.

$$\begin{bmatrix} 1\,1\,0 \\ 1\,0\,1 \end{bmatrix} \% \begin{bmatrix} 1\,0\,1\,0 \\ \hline 0\,1\,1\,1 \end{bmatrix} = \left[\begin{array}{c|c|c|c} 1\,1\,0 & 0\,0\,0 & 1\,1\,0 & 0\,0\,0 \\ 1\,0\,1 & 0\,0\,0 & 1\,1\,0 & 0\,0\,0 \\ 1\,1\,0 & 0\,0\,0 & 1\,0\,1 & 0\,0\,0 \\ 1\,0\,1 & 0\,0\,0 & 1\,0\,1 & 0\,0\,0 \\ \hline 0\,0\,0 & 1\,1\,0 & 1\,1\,0 & 1\,1\,0 \\ 0\,0\,0 & 1\,0\,1 & 1\,1\,0 & 1\,1\,0 \\ 0\,0\,0 & 1\,1\,0 & 1\,0\,1 & 1\,1\,0 \\ 0\,0\,0 & 1\,0\,1 & 1\,0\,1 & 1\,1\,0 \\ 0\,0\,0 & 1\,1\,0 & 1\,1\,0 & 1\,0\,1 \\ 0\,0\,0 & 1\,0\,1 & 1\,1\,0 & 1\,0\,1 \\ 0\,0\,0 & 1\,1\,0 & 1\,0\,1 & 1\,0\,1 \\ 0\,0\,0 & 1\,0\,1 & 1\,0\,1 & 1\,0\,1 \end{array}\right],$$

$$
\begin{bmatrix} 1\,1\,0 \\ 1\,0\,1 \\ 0\,1\,1 \end{bmatrix} \% \begin{bmatrix} 1\,1\,0 \\ \hline 1\,0\,1 \\ \hline 0\,1\,1 \end{bmatrix} = \left[\begin{array}{c|c|c}
1\,1\,0 & 1\,1\,0 & 0\,0\,0 \\
1\,0\,1 & 1\,1\,0 & 0\,0\,0 \\
0\,1\,1 & 1\,1\,0 & 0\,0\,0 \\
1\,1\,0 & 1\,0\,1 & 0\,0\,0 \\
1\,0\,1 & 1\,0\,1 & 0\,0\,0 \\
0\,1\,1 & 1\,0\,1 & 0\,0\,0 \\
1\,1\,0 & 0\,1\,1 & 0\,0\,0 \\
1\,0\,1 & 0\,1\,1 & 0\,0\,0 \\
0\,1\,1 & 0\,1\,1 & 0\,0\,0 \\
\hline
1\,1\,0 & 0\,0\,0 & 1\,1\,0 \\
1\,0\,1 & 0\,0\,0 & 1\,1\,0 \\
0\,1\,1 & 0\,0\,0 & 1\,1\,0 \\
1\,1\,0 & 0\,0\,0 & 1\,0\,1 \\
1\,0\,1 & 0\,0\,0 & 1\,0\,1 \\
0\,1\,1 & 0\,0\,0 & 1\,0\,1 \\
1\,1\,0 & 0\,0\,0 & 0\,1\,1 \\
1\,0\,1 & 0\,0\,0 & 0\,1\,1 \\
0\,1\,1 & 0\,0\,0 & 0\,1\,1 \\
\hline
0\,0\,0 & 1\,1\,0 & 1\,1\,0 \\
0\,0\,0 & 1\,0\,1 & 1\,1\,0 \\
0\,0\,0 & 0\,1\,1 & 1\,1\,0 \\
0\,0\,0 & 1\,1\,0 & 1\,0\,1 \\
0\,0\,0 & 1\,0\,1 & 1\,0\,1 \\
0\,0\,0 & 0\,1\,1 & 1\,0\,1 \\
0\,0\,0 & 1\,1\,0 & 0\,1\,1 \\
0\,0\,0 & 1\,0\,1 & 0\,1\,1 \\
0\,0\,0 & 0\,1\,1 & 0\,1\,1
\end{array}\right] .
$$

4.2 The Operation Preserves Useful Properties

Theorem 1. For matrices $C \in I(v, b)$ and $D \in I(V, B)$, we have the following properties.

1) $C\%D$ is non-zero if C and D are non-zero.
2) $C\%D$ is normal if C and D are normal.
3) $C\%D$ is cohesive if C and D are cohesive.
4) $C\%D$ is constant-row-weight if C and D are constant-row-weight. Moreover, $R(C\%D) = R(C) \cdot R(D)$.
5) $C\%D$ is tactical if C and D are tactical. Moreover, $K(C\%D) = v^{R(D)-1} \cdot K(C) \cdot K(D)$.

Proof). Proving 1), 2), and 4) is straightforward from the definition of $C\%D$. Since property 3) is important for our application its proof is given here. A proof of 5), which is similar to those of 3) and 4), is omitted here. Assume that

$$C = \begin{bmatrix} C(0) \\ \vdots \\ C(v-1) \end{bmatrix}, \quad C(s) \in I(1,b),$$

$$D = \begin{bmatrix} D(0) \\ \vdots \\ D(V-1) \end{bmatrix}, \quad D(p) = [D_{p,0}, \cdots, D_{p,B-1}] \in I(1,B),$$

$$C\%D = \begin{bmatrix} E(0) \\ \vdots \\ E(\nu-1) \end{bmatrix}, E(i) = [E_{i,0}, \cdots, E_{i,B-1}], \; E_{i,j} \in I(1,b), \; \nu = \sum_{i=0}^{V-1} v^{R_i(D)}.$$

Proof of 3). For any i, $j \in \{0, \cdots, \nu-1\}$, by definition we have $\Lambda_{ij}(C\%D) = \sum_{f=0}^{B-1} E_{i,f} \cdot E_{j,f}^{\mathrm{T}}$. By the definition of $C\%D$, there exist p, $q \in \{0, \cdots, V-1\}$ such that $D(p)$ and $D(q)$ are respectively adopted to produce $E(i)$ and $E(j)$. If D is cohesive, then $\Lambda_{pq}(D) \geq 1$, which implies the existence of $g \in \{0, \cdots, B-1\}$ such that $D_{p,g} = D_{q,g} = 1$. Then, by the definition of $C\%D$, there exist s, $t \in \{0, \cdots, v-1\}$ such that $E_{i,g} = C(s)$ and $E_{j,g} = C(t)$. Thus, if D is cohesive we have

$$\Lambda_{ij}(C\%D) \geq E_{i,g} \cdot E_{j,g}^{\mathrm{T}} = C(s) \cdot C(t)^{\mathrm{T}} = \Lambda_{st}(C).$$

Therefore, if C is cohesive we have $\Lambda_{ij}(C\%D) \geq \Lambda_{st}(C) \geq 1$, which means that $C\%D$ is cohesive.

4.3 Recursively Constructing Desirable Structures

Definition 5. For a positive integer n and a binary matrix D, we define

$$D^{(n)} = \begin{cases} D & \text{if } n = 1, \\ D^{(n-1)}\%D & \text{if } n \geq 2. \end{cases}$$

Theorem 2. For $C \in T(v,b,r,k)$ and $D \in T(V,B,R,K)$, we have

$$C\%D \in T(v^R \cdot V, b \cdot B, r \cdot R, v^{R-1} \cdot k \cdot K),$$
$$C^{(n)} \in T(v^{\frac{r^n-1}{r-1}}, b^n, r^n, v^{\frac{r^n-1}{r-1}-n} \cdot k^n).$$

Proof) Follows directly from Theorem 1.

Example 5. The followings are normal, cohesive, and tactical matrices constructed by operation %.

$W_a\%W_b \in T(v,b,r,k)$ with

a b	v	b	r	k	b/r
11 3	640,332	33	12	232,848	2.75
13 3	8,833,968	39	14	3,171,168	2.78
9 5	20,003,760	45	15	6,667,920	3.00
15 3	142,227,675	45	16	44,169,840	2.81
17 3	1,772,928,300	51	18	625,739,400	2.83
⋮ ⋮	⋯	⋯	⋯	⋯	⋯

$W_3{}^{(n)} \in T(v,b,r,k)$ with

n	v	b	r	k	b/r
1	3	3	2	2	1.50
2	27	9	4	12	2.25
3	2,187	27	8	648	3.37
4	14,348,907	81	16	2,834,352	5.06
5	6.17×10^{14}	243	32	8.13×10^{13}	7.59
6	1.14×10^{30}	729	64	1.00×10^{29}	11.39
⋮	⋯	⋯	⋯	⋯	⋯

$W_5{}^{(n)} \in T(v,b,r,k)$ with

n	v	b	r	k	b/r
1	10	5	3	6	1.66
2	10,000	25	9	3,600	2.77
3	10^{13}	125	27	2.16×10^{12}	4.62
4	10^{40}	625	81	1.29×10^{39}	7.71
⋮	⋯	⋯	⋯	⋯	⋯

$G_2{}^{(n)} \in T(v,b,r,k)$ with

n	v	b	r	k	b/r
1	7	7	3	3	2.33
2	2,401	49	9	441	5.44
3	9.68×10^{10}	343	27	7.62×10^{9}	12.70
4	6.36×10^{33}	2,401	81	2.14×10^{32}	29.64
⋮	⋯	⋯	⋯	⋯	⋯

Observation 5. We can see that several of above examples almost meet the criterion for desirable incidence structures. As stated in Observation 1, from these we can derive a lot of desirable normal cohesive constant-row-weight matrices.

5 Discussion and Conclusion

1) For the key sharing problem, we have shown a way of using plural tamper-resistant modules per entity to achieve the same level of security with reduced memory.
2) We have set the criterion for the desirable incidence structure for this purpose and constructed several nice candidates.
3) A remaining problem in this article is to devise efficient row calculating algorithms for the obtained incidence structures. The property of operator % can be effectively used to construct such algorithms [8].
4) Another remaining problem is to analyze the resistance of the proposed method against attempts of *partial breaking*.
5) The newly introduced approach for assigning key-sharing systems is promising and worth while to further develop theoretically and practically.

Acknowledgment

The author would like to thank Thomas Beth, Hans-Joachim Knobloch, Peer Wichmann, and other co-workers in University of Karlsruhe for their valuable discussions and warm support.

References

[1] T. Matsumoto and H. Imai, "On the Key Predistribution System: A practical solution to the key distribution problem," Advances in Cryptology: Proceedings of CRYPTO'87, Lecture Notes in Computer Science No. 293, pp. 185-193, Springer-Verlag, 1987.

[2] R. Blom, "An optimal class of symmetric key generation systems," Advances in Cryptology: Proceedings of EUROCRYPT'84, Lecture Notes in Computer Science No. 209, pp. 335-338, Springer-Verlag, 1985.

[3] L. Gong and D. J. Wheeler, "A matrix key-distribution scheme," Journal of Cryptology, Vol. 2, pp. 51-59, Springer-Verlag, 1990.

[4] C. Blundo, A. De Santis, A. Herzberg, S. Kutten, U. Vaccaro, and M. Yung, "Perfectly-secure key distribution for dynamic conferences," Advances in Cryptology: Proceedings of CRYPTO'92, Lecture Notes in Computer Science No. 740, pp. 471-486, Springer-Verlag, 1993.

[5] W.-A. Jackson, K. M. Martin, and C. M. O'Keefe, "Multisecret threshold schemes," Advances in Cryptology: Proceedings of CRYPTO'93, Lecture Notes in Computer Science No. 773, pp. 126-135, Springer-Verlag, 1994.

[6] T. Matsumoto, "A novel IC card for KPS-based cryptography," IFIP WG10.5 Workshop on Secure Design and Test of Crypto-Chips, Abstract, Gmunden, Austria, 1991.

[7] T. Beth, D. Jungnickel, and H. Lenz, Design Theory, B.I.-Wissenschaftsverlag, 1985.

[8] T. Matsumoto, "Efficient algorithms for recursively defined incidence structures," in preparation.

SESSION 9

PUBLIC KEY CRYPTOGRAPHY

Chair: Yuliang Zheng

(University of Wollongong, Australia)

A public-key cryptosystem and a digital signature system based on the Lucas function analogue to discrete logarithms

Peter Smith
LUC Encryption Technology, Ltd
25 Lawrence St
Herne Bay
Auckland
New Zealand

Christopher Skinner
LUC Encryption Technology, Ltd
4/29B Nelson St
Woollahra NSW 2025
Australia

Abstract: Since 1975 many new cryptosystems have been based on elementary number theory, but until now it has not been recognised that they have been just as much grounded in the process of exponentiation. Lucas functions can be used to replace exponentiation to produce alternative cryptosystems that are not susceptible to attacks which rely on the fact that multiplication is closed under exponentiation, since Lucas functions do not exhibit this closure.

0. Introduction

In this paper we show that El Gamal public-key encryption and El Gamal digital signature [Elg] can be implemented using Lucas functions instead of exponentiation. Using Lucas functions instead of exponentiation was first done with LUC, a public-key cryptosystem and digital signature; and LUCDIF, the Lucas function version of Diffie-Hellman key negotiation [Smi]. The implementations described here are not without storage and timing overheads, but they can be shown to be asymptotically as fast; and, more importantly, they appear to be cryptographically much stronger than their exponentiation-based precursors. Since elliptic curve-based cryptosystems share this cryptographic strength, we show that these are inherently less efficient to calculate with than Lucas functions.

1. Lucas functions

Lucas functions are an example of higher order linear recurrences. If P_1, P_2, P_3, ..., P_m are integers, then we can define a sequence of integers $\{T_n\}$ by:

$$T_n = P_1 T_{n-1} + P_2 T_{n-2} + \ldots + P_m T_{n-m}.$$

We must define $T_0, T_1, T_2, \ldots, T_{m-1}$ independently, in order to be able to use the defining equation. This equation is called an m'th order linear recurrence relation. It can be easily seen that a sequence defined by a first-order linear recurrence relation is made up of numbers which are a constant (T_0) times successive powers of P_1. Sequences satisfying higher order linear relations can be thought of as generalisations of powers, so it is not surprising that generalisations of exponentiation-based cryptosystems to some of these sequences is possible.

The general second-order linear recurrence relation, in the form in which we will use it, is:

$$T_n = PT_{n-1} - QT_{n-2}. \qquad 1.0$$

We will always take P and Q to be relatively prime integers. If we take $P = 1 = -Q$, then the sequence of integers obtained by setting $T_0 = 0$ and $T_1 = 1$ is the well known Fibonacci sequence.

It is straightforward to find the general form of a sequence obtained from a second-order linear recurrence. Let and be the roots of the quadratic equation

$$x^2 - Px + Q = 0. \qquad 1.1$$

If c_1 and c_2 are any numbers, then the sequence $\{c_1\alpha^n + c_2\beta^n\}$ has the property that

$$P(c_1\alpha^{n-1} + c_2\beta^{n-1}) - Q(c_1\alpha^{n-2} + c_2\beta^{n-2}) = c_1\alpha^{n-2}(P\alpha - Q) + c_2\beta^{n-2}(P\beta - Q)$$

$$= c_1\alpha^{n-2}(\alpha^2) + c_2\beta^{n-2}(\beta^2) \quad \text{by 1.1}$$
$$= c_1\alpha^n + c_2\beta^n.$$

So this sequence satisfies the second-order linear recurrence relation 1.0, and it is not hard to see that any sequence $\{T_n\}$ satisfying 1.0 must be of the form $\{c_1\alpha^n + c_2\beta^n\}$, where $T_0 = c_1 + c_2$, and $T_1 = c_1\alpha + c_2\beta$.

Note that if T_0 and T_1 are integers, then by 1.0, all the terms in the sequence will be integers, even though α, β, c_1 and c_2 are probably not integers, and may not even be real.

Two particular solutions of the general second-order linear recurrence relation are of particular interest. They are denoted by $\{U_n\}$ and $\{V_n\}$, and are defined by:

$$U_n = \frac{\alpha^n - \beta^n}{\alpha - \beta}, \text{ so } c_1 = \frac{1}{\alpha - \beta} = -c_2$$

$V_n = \alpha^n + \beta^n$, so $c_1 = 1 = c_2$

These will both be sequences of integers, since we have:

$U_0 = 0, U_1 = 1, V_0 = 2$, and $V_1 = P$.

These sequences depend only on the integers *P* and *Q*, and the terms are called the Lucas functions of *P* and *Q*. They are sometimes written $U_n(P,Q)$ and $V_n(P,Q)$, to emphasize their dependence on *P* and *Q*. They were first discussed by Lucas [Luc], but their theory was considerably extended by Lehmer [Leh].

Note that if *N* is any number, then

$$U_n(P \bmod N, Q \bmod N) \equiv U_n(P,Q) \bmod N,$$

because this result is certainly true when *n* is 0 or 1, and for every *n* which is 2 or greater,

$$U_n(P,Q) \bmod N \equiv (P \bmod N)(U_{n-1}(P,Q) \bmod N) - (Q \bmod N)(U_{n-2}(P,Q) \bmod N)$$

so the stated result follows by induction. Similarly

$$V_n(P \bmod N, Q \bmod N) \equiv V_n(P,Q) \bmod N \qquad 1.2$$

Since the roots of 1.1, and , satisfy the equations

$$\alpha + \beta = P, \alpha\beta = Q$$

it is not difficult to find many relationships between the Lucas functions U_n and V_n, and the coefficients of the recurrence relation, 1.0, *P* and *Q*. The discriminant of 1.1, $D = P^2 - 4Q$, can be expressed in terms of the roots of the quadratic, and by:

$$D = (\alpha - \beta)^2.$$

Consider the linear recurrence relation created by using $V_k(P,Q)$ for *P* and Q^k for *Q*:

$$T_n = V_k(P,Q)\,T_{n-1} - Q^k T_{n-2}.$$

The roots of the corresponding quadratic equation, ′ and ′, must satisfy

$$\alpha' + \beta' = V_k(P,Q) = \alpha^k + \beta^k \text{ and } \alpha'\beta' = Q^k = \alpha^k\beta^k,$$

so we must have $\alpha' = \alpha^k$ and $\beta' = \beta^k$. This means that

$$V_n(V_k(P,Q),Q^k) = (\alpha^k)^n + (\beta^k)^n = \alpha^{nk} + \beta^{nk} = V_{nk}(P,Q).$$

This composition result is crucial; it is a clear generalisation of the rule for composition of powers, with the subscript of a Lucas function playing the role of a power. If we take $Q = 1$, then we get the simple relationship

$$V_{nk}(P,1) = V_n(V_k(P,1),1) \qquad 1.3$$

A further relation for the addition of powers follows easily as well:

$V_nV_m = (\alpha^n + \beta^n)(\alpha^m + \beta^m) = \alpha^{n+m} + \beta^{n+m} + \alpha^n\beta^m + \alpha^m\beta^n$, since adding this to

$$DU_nU_m = \frac{(\alpha^n - \beta^n)(\alpha^m - \beta^m)(\alpha - \beta)^2}{(\alpha - \beta)(\alpha - \beta)} =$$

$\alpha^{n+m} + \beta^{n+m} - \alpha^n\beta^m - \alpha^m\beta^n$,

we get $2V_{n+m} = V_nV_m + DU_nU_m = 2(\alpha^{n+m} + \beta^{n+m})$. 1.4

2. LUCELG PK

To set up LUCELG PK public-key encryption, the receiver publishes a prime p, ensuring that $(p + 1)$ is not composed of only small primes, a generator, , such that

$V_{(p+1)/t}(\lambda,1) \neq 2 \bmod p$, for all $t > 1$ dividing $(p + 1)$, and their public key, y, which is equal to $V_x(\lambda,1) \bmod p$ (x is the receiver's private key).

Assume the sender wants to send a message, M, to the receiver (M is greater than zero and less than p. A message longer than p can be sent by splitting it into blocks which are less than p). The sender first finds a different secret number, k, which is greater than zero, and less than p, for each message M - or message block - and calculates G, where

Encryption

$$G \equiv V_k(y,1) \bmod p.$$

The two halves of the cryptogram are then computed:

$$d_1 \equiv V_k(\lambda, 1) \bmod p, d_2 \equiv GM \bmod p.$$

Decryption

The receiver deciphers the cryptogram by first calculating G, since $G \equiv V_x(d_1, 1) \bmod p$, by 1.3, and only the receiver knows x. The multiplicative inverse (G^{-1}) of G can be calculated, modulo p, using the extended Euclidean algorithm, and the message is recovered by 1.3

$$M \equiv d_2(G^{-1}) \bmod p.$$

3. LUCELG DS

Lucas functions have formulae for multiplying (1.3) and adding (1.4) subscripts, so an equivalent of El Gamal's digital signature system is obtainable.

Two public-key values are necessary with LUCELG DS:

$$y \equiv V_x(\lambda, 1) \bmod p \text{ and } y' \equiv U_x(\lambda, 1) \bmod p.$$

Similarly, two values for part of the signature are necessary. As in LUCELG PK, a secret value, k, should be chosen for each message (or message block), m.

$$r \equiv V_k(\lambda, 1) \bmod p \text{ and } r' \equiv U_k(\lambda, 1) \bmod p.$$

The s component of the signature is calculated similarly to El Gamal [Elg], except that the equation is solved modulo $(p + 1)$ rather than modulo $(p - 1)$. Using the extended Euclidean algorithm we can solve for s by using

$$s \equiv k^{-1}(m - xr) \bmod (p+1).$$

To verify a LUCELG DS (m, r, r', s) signature, we first calculate the left hand side (LHS):

$$\text{LHS} \equiv V_m(\lambda, 1) \bmod p.$$

The right hand side (RHS) is a little more complicated than in El Gamal (1.4):

$$\text{RHS} \equiv \{V_r(y,1)V_s(r,1) + Dy'U_r(y,1)r'U_s(r,1)\}/2 \bmod p,$$ where $D \equiv \lambda^2 - 4 \bmod p$.

If RHS = LHS then the quadruple (m, r, r', s) is an authentic LUCELG DS signature.

The formula for the addition of subscripts, 1.4, involves the Lucas $\{U_i\}$ 'sister' series, so subsequently our Lucas function alternative to El Gamal involves the doubling of the public-key size - because two Lucas function values (*U* and *V*) have to be given - as well as increasing the size of the signature, because two '*r*' (*U* and *V*) values are necessary.

4. Cryptographic strength

If there are no weaknesses *per se* in the structure of the algorithms themselves which leads to easy cryptanalysis [Elg], we can assume that breaking them is equivalent to solving for *x* in the equation $V_x(M,1) \equiv C \bmod p$, where *M*, *C* and *p* are known. (In structure they are the same as the El Gamal ciphers from which they are adapted, and these have resisted attempts at breaking based on their structure.)

The best algorithms for solving the Discrete Logarithm (DL) problem rely on combining congruences multiplicatively [Bac]. This cannot be done with Lucas functions, because they are not closed under multiplication. Hence these sub-exponential algorithms cannot be applied to the Lucas function DL analogue.

The fastest exponential-time algorithm to solve the Lucas function equivalent of the Discrete Logarithm may take time proportional to $p^{1/5}$, where p is the modulus. (This is a conservative, 'worst case' estimate. In fact, the best exponential attack is probably much slower than this: two sources state that it is about $p^{1/2}$ [Bac] and [Men].)

We evaluate $Lp[a,b] = e^{((b+o(1))(\ln p)^a(\ln \ln p)^{1-a})}$ for a given p (this function counts the work in computer operations of the index calculus attacks), and then equate this to $p^{1/5}$ in order to find the size of p that takes equivalent effort to solve the Lucas function analogue of the Discrete Logarithm.

5. Methods for solving the Exponential Discrete Logarithm and the Lucas function analogue to the Discrete Logarithm

In the following figure, the Y-axis is the logarithm to the base ten of the number of computer operations; the X-axis is the bit-size of the modulus.

a	Gaussian Integer method	Lp[1/2,1]
b	Special number field sieve	Lp[2/5,1.00475]
c	General number field sieve	Lp[1/3, $3^{2/3}$]
d	Coppersmith number field sieve	Lp[1/3, 1.902]
e	Lenstra-Adelman number field sieve	Lp[1/3, 1.92]
f	Lucas function logarithm calculation time	$p^{1/5}$

Where $Lp[a, b] = e^{((b+o(1))(\ln p)^a(\ln \ln p)^{1-a})}$, with 0 < a < 1 [Men].

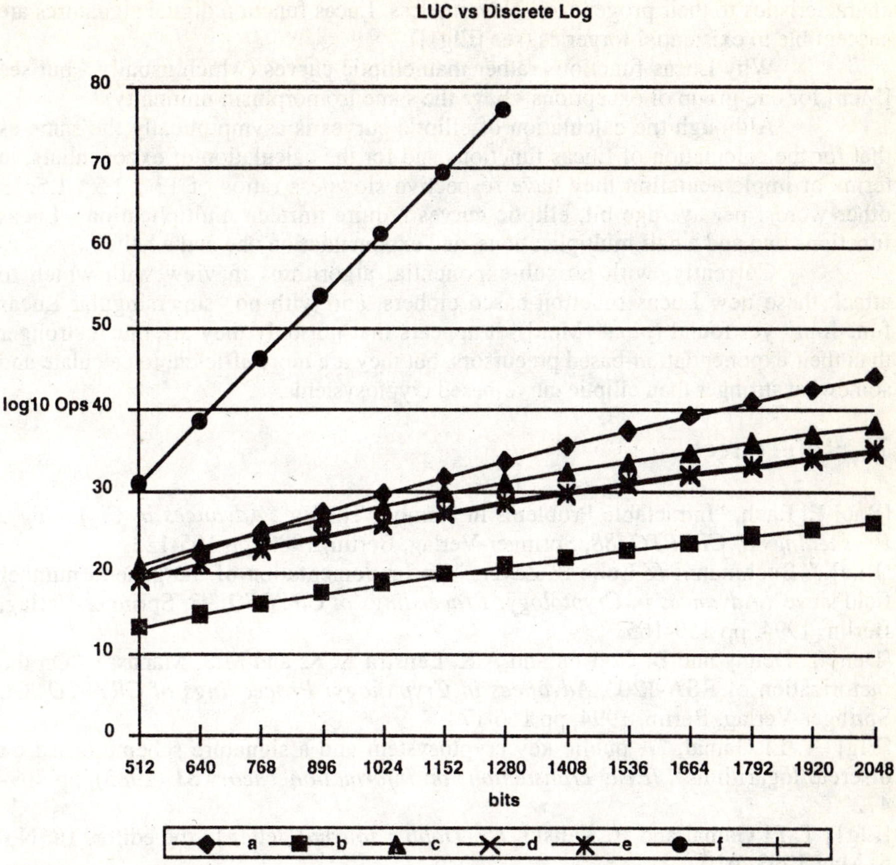

LUCDIF key negotiation at 512 bits is as hard to break as Diffie-Hellman key negotiation attacked by method **a**) with a 1024-bit modulus, **c**) with a 1152-bit modulus, **d**) with a 1512-bit modulus, and **e**) with a 1448-bit modulus.

6. Conclusion

The calculation of the *n*th Lucas function can be done in O(log*n*) operations, which is the same order as the computation of similar exponentials. Heuristics to speed up modular exponentiation can be brought over to the calculation of Lucas functions, if in more complicated form (witness the formula for adding subscripts). These new ciphers can be assured of having similar performance characteristics to their progenitors. Nevertheless, Lucas function digital signatures are susceptible to existential forgeries (see [Elg1]).

Why Lucas functions rather than elliptic curves (which usually - but see [Men] for one group of exceptions - have the same isomorphism immunity)?

Although the calculation of elliptic curves is asymptotically the same as that for the calculation of Lucas functions and for the calculation of exponentials, in terms of implementation they have respective slowness ratios of 13 : 2.5 : 1.5. In other words, per average bit, elliptic curves require thirteen multiplications, Lucas functions two and a half multiplications, and exponentiation one and a half.

Currently, with no sub-exponential algorithms in view with which to attack these new Lucas function-based ciphers, and with no "supersingular Lucas functions" yet found (*pace* [Men]), it appears that not only they are much stronger than their exponentiation-based precursors, but they are more efficient to calculate and somewhat stronger than elliptic curve-based cryptosystems.

7. References

[Bac] E. Bach, "Intractable Problems in Number Theory", *Advances in Cryptology: Proceedings of CRYPTO '88*, Springer-Verlag, Berlin, 1989, pp 105-122.

[Buc] J. Buchmann & Loho & Zayer, "An Implementation of the general number field sieve", *Advances in Cryptology: Proceedings of CRYPTO '93*, Springer-Verlag, Berlin, 1994, pp 159-165.

[Den] T. Denny and B. Dodson and A.K. Lenstra A. K. and M.S. Manasse, "On the factorization of RSA-120", *Advances in Cryptology: Proceedings of CRYPTO '93*, Springer-Verlag, Berlin, 1994, pp 166-174.

[Elg] T. El Gamal, "A public-key cryptosystem and a signature scheme based on discrete logarithms", *IEEE Transactions on Information Theory* **31** (1985), pp 469-472.

[Elg1] T. El Gamal and B. Kaliski, *Dr. Dobb's Journal*, letter to the editor, **18**, No. 5, May 1993, p10.

[Gor] D.M. Gordon, "Discrete Logarithms in GF(p) using the Number Field Sieve", *Siam J Disc Math* **6** No. 1, Feb 1993, pp 124-138.

[Leh] D. H. Lehmer, "An extended theory of Lucas' functions", *Annals of Math.,***31** (1930) pp 419-448.

[Luc] F. E. A. Lucas, "Théorie des fonctions numériques simplement périodiques", *American Jnl Math,* **1** (1878) pp 184-240, 289-321.

[Men] A. J. Menezes, T. Okamoto, S. A. Vanstone, "Reducing Elliptic Curve Logarithms to Logarithms in a Finite Field", *IEEE Transactions on Information Theory* **39** (1993), pp 1639-1646.

[Pom] C. Pomerance, "Fast Factorization & Discrete Logarithm Algorithms", *Discrete Algorithms & Complexity*, W. Rheinboldt et al, *Proceedings 1986 Kyoto Conference on Algorithms and Complexity.*

[Smi] P. Smith and M. Lennon, "LUC: A new public-key system", *Proceedings of IFIP/Sec '93*, Elsevier Science Publications, 1994.

Higher Radix Nonrestoring Modular Multiplication Algorithm and Public-key LSI Architecture with Limited Hardware Resources

Masayuki Abe Hikaru Morita

NTT Information and Communication Systems Laboratories
1-2356 Take Yokosuka-shi Kanagawa, Japan

Abstract. Security applications to be installed in small size hardware such as cellular phones and smart cards need a small and practical LSI for key distribution or authentication. This paper describes an improved modular multiplication algorithm and LSI architecture for public-key schemes with the goal of limiting hardware resources. The algorithm, which employs higher radix arithmetic, eliminates the slow restoring which occurs in modular multiplication. The proposed architecture is based on the use of RAM and low operation frequency. The LSI is designed to calculate 512 bit modular exponentiation within 0.1 seconds at the frequency of 17 MHz. This requires only 13 Kgates and six 512bit RAMs.

1 Introduction

Public-key schemes such as DH [DH76] and RSA [RSA78] provide key distribution and authentication functions. One big obstacle to the introduction of these schemes is their massive calculations (512 bit or longer number modular exponentiation), and many researchers have been trying to improve calculation speed. Some algorithms such as addition chain [Knu81] [BC89] or precomputation [BGMW92], have been introduced, but they still require a very large storage capacity. The lavish use memory and CPU power can make C language programs calculate 512 bit modular exponentiation in about 2.5 seconds [BGV93]. More efficient results are obtained by using assembly languages [MY93] or DSPs [DK90]. Therefore, the software implementation of public-key schemes for key distribution and authentication is practically achieved with recent powerful PCs or WSs.

Many research activities on hardware implementation have also been done to introduce many methods such as radix 2 based high speed algorithm or systolic array architecture [Bri89][HDVG88] [IWMD92] [IMI92]. Some results show that it is possible to achieve 512 bit modular exponentiation in 0.008 s (64 kbps). However, their primary goal was to achieve speeds high enough to perform line encryption which is much faster than key distribution, so that the proposed architectures do not lay emphasis on the hardware amount and thus demand excessive hardware resources or sophisticated implementation technology such as very high frequency (150 MHz), high power consumption (400 mA x 5V), and many gates (50K).

Security applications to be installed in small size hardware such as cellular phones and smart cards need public-key schemes for key distribution or authentication. However, because of their physical constraints, these handy systems allow only small amounts of software and inexpensive hardware. Also, due to severe power constraints, this type of handy small systems can permit only low instruction operation frequencies, and space for additional functions such as security is very limited. For example, some cellular phones operate at about 15 MHz and a smart card has only 5x5 mm^2 area and operates at about 4 MHz. Recently, small and low power RISC devices are available for use of handy applications. However, according to our experiment, they calculate modular exponentiation in 4 seconds (on ARM6 development board). So they are insufficient for key distribution.

Accordingly, the hardware must:

(1) be small enough to be integrated with other circuits on a small chip,

(2) operate at a low operation frequency, and

(3) achieve practical speed for key distribution or authentication.

There has been little research for implementing this kind of small and practical public-key hardware [Bri89]. Unfortunately, their details were not reported so that it is difficult to offer a valid comparison.

Our goal is to develop an LSI that satisfies the above requirements. This paper introduces a RAM based architecture which achieves a very small number of gates by eliminating the use of a long accumulator. An efficient algorithm is proposed for the modular multiplication suitable for the RAM based architecture. The algorithm is based on higher radix arithmetic and eliminates slow restoring which is needed in the existing algorithms to deal with overflow. Finally, the paper applies the proposed algorithm and architecture to a prototype modular exponentiation LSI designed with a logic synthesizer [NONN90] and 0.8 μ CMOS library [VLSI92].

Section 2 investigates several approaches from the viewpoint of memory and frequency requirements. Section 3 explains in detail the algorithm proposed. Section 4 discusses the characteristics of the parameters described in section 3 and applies our architecture to the design of a public-key scheme LSI.

2 Approaches

High-speed modular exponentiation LSIs usually use long carry save adders that are based on radix 2 arithmetic. The adders need to access 512 bit buffers at one time, so that the buffers must use registers or very high operation frequency is required for the RAMs to load data into the accumulators. Moreover, the carry save adders require twice as many registers as the ordinary adders.

Since registers occupy about 10 gates/bit and RAMs take about 1.4 gates/bit, it is very efficient to use RAMs instead of registers for 512 bit buffers. However, the use of RAMs and a low single phase frequency makes high-speed architectures impractical because loading data into the accumulator takes too many clock cycles. Although radix 2 arithmetic has a very short critical path, it is wasted if the operating frequency is low. Thus we adopt higher radix arithmetic and the RAM based architecture to meet the severe requirements.

3 Algorithm and architecture

3.1 Modular exponentiation

Public-key schemes mainly use modular exponentiation which is calculated by repeating modular multiplications. The main idea to speed up modular exponentiation is reducing the number of repetitions. Based on this idea, the addition chain was introduced. The method needs one or more extra buffers whose size are the same as the modulus, however, its upper bound is just a 17% reduction in the number of repetitions. Thus we adopted the traditional binary method requiring the least buffers. Necessary memory size is discussed in 4.3.

3.2 Modular multiplication

Modular multiplication $R = AB \bmod N$ is done by dividing multiplier B into n parts of k bit B_i as follows.

$$R = (((AB_{n-1} \bmod N)\, 2^k + AB_{n-2}) \bmod N)\, 2^k + \ldots.)\, 2^k + AB_0) \bmod N \quad (1)$$

Equation (1) is done by repeating the next procedure from i=0 to n where B_{-1}= 0.

$$R_{(i+1)} = (R_{(i)} - \hat{q}_{(i)} N)\, 2^k + AB_{n-1-i} \quad (2)$$

$\hat{q}_{(i)}$ is the estimated quotient which approximates $\lfloor R_{(i)}/N \rfloor$ for modular reduction. Detailed description about $\hat{q}_{(i)}$ will be given later.

Equation (2) is tough to calculate with small buffers because R, N and A are long numbers. R, N, and A are also divided into m parts of l bits each. When $k=l$, carry processing can be easily realized as shown in Fig.1. The j th carries $cr1_j$ and $cr2_j$ are handed over to the least bit position of the j+2 th addition or subtraction stage. If $k \neq l$, the j th carries must be inputted to the middle of the adder or subtracter in the j+1 th step, and the adder and subtracter become complicated. Accordingly, we discuss only the case $k=l$ hereafter.

In Fig.1 it is assumed that $\hat{q}_{(i)}$ and R are expressed in k bits and $(m+1)k$ bits respectively. However, if $\hat{q}_{(i)}$ is equal to $q_{(i)}$ which is an exact quotient obtained by dividing R by N, because of $0 \leq \hat{q}_{(i)}, B_{n-1-i} \leq 2^k - 1$ and $A \leq N - 1$, $R_{(i+1)}$ has the range of $0 \leq R_{(i+1)} \leq (2^{k+1} - 1)(N - 1)$ and $\hat{q}_{(i+1)}$ lies in the range of $0 \leq \hat{q}_{(i+1)} \leq 2^{k+1} - 1$. Therefore, $\hat{q}_{(i+1)}$ and $R_{(i+1)}$ need k+1 and $(m+1)k$+1 bits long respectively. The extended $\hat{q}_{(i+1)}$ makes $\hat{q}_{(i)} N_j$ k+1 bit long. Therefore $R_{j+1(i)} \| R_{j(i)} - \hat{q}_{(i)} N_j$ yields 2 bit carry, and succeeding calculation needs complicated adder or subtracter. So $R_{(i+1)}$ should be restored into $0 \leq R_{(i+1)} \leq 2^k N$ by performing $R_{(i+1)} - 2^k N$. This unexpected restoring takes at least m clocks by using k bit subtracter.

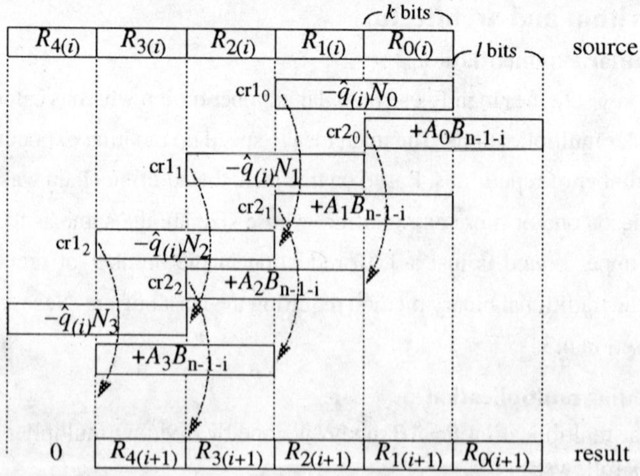

Fig. 1. Processing $R_{(i+1)} = (R_{(i)} - \hat{q}_{(i)} N) 2^k + AB_{n-1-i}$ at m=4, k=l

Similar overflow can be seen in ordinary division. In that case, the SRT method [Hw79] can give a solution by applying redundant expressions to R and $\hat{q}_{(i)}$ and using an adder/subtracter instead of a subtracter for $R_{(i)} - \hat{q}_{(i)} N$. However, SRT can not eliminate the overflow in modular multiplication where AB_{n-1-i} is added.

We have two ideas to avoid the restoring. The first idea is employing redundant expression not only for $R\,\hat{q}$ but also for B_{n-1-i}. The absolute range of AB_{n-1-i} then shrinks into $|AB_{n-1-i}| \le 2^{k-1}(N-1)$. The second idea is to predict the effect of $+AB_{n-1-i}$ and control $q_{e(i)}$ beforehand. If $+AB_{n-1-i}$ increases $R_{(i+1)}$, then $\hat{q}_{(i)}$ should be increased by 1 to obtain the same result as doing $R_{(i+1)} - 2^k N$ against upcoming overflow. Procedure 1 shows the method of avoiding overflow in the case of $\hat{q}_{(i)} = q_{(i)}$ for all i.

[Procedure 1]

(1) Add a sign bit to $R_{(i)}$ and B_{n-1-i}.

(2) Shift B_{n-1-i}'s range into $-2^{k-1} < B'_{n-1-i} \le 2^{k-1}$.

(3) Increment $\hat{q}_{(i)}$ as $\hat{q}'_{(i)} = \hat{q}_{(i)} + \delta_{(i)}$.

where $\delta_{(i)} = 1$ if $Sign(R_{(i)}) = Sign(B_{(i)})$ or $\delta_{(i)} = 0$ otherwise.

According to Procedure 1, the range of $R_{(i+1)}$ is $-2^k N \le R_{(i+1)} \le 2^k N$ so that $\hat{q}'_{(i+1)}$

results in $-2^k \leq \hat{q}'_{(i+1)} \leq 2^k$ (details are shown in appendix 1). This means $\hat{q}'_{(i+1)}$ is k+1 bits long. However, since $N_j \leq 2^k - 1$, $|\hat{q}'_{e(i+1)} N_j|$ can be expressed in 2k bits and the processing shown in Fig. 1 is possible.

The problem is that the estimated quotient sometimes has an error. Here, we assume that the estimation function returns $\hat{q}_{(i)}$ whose range is $q_{(i)} \leq \hat{q}_{(i)} \leq q_{(i)} + 1$. A simple way to realize this is as follows.

$$\hat{q}_{(i)} = \begin{cases} 2^k - 1 & \text{if} |R_{n(i)} \| R_{n-1(i)}| = N_{n-1} \| N_{n-2} \\ \left\lfloor \dfrac{|R_{n(i)} \| R_{n-1(i)} \| R_{n-2(i)}|}{N_{n-1} \| N_{n-2}} \right\rfloor & \text{otherwise} \end{cases} \quad (3)$$

This is straightforward but the equivalent method which does not use long division is shown in [Knu81]. There are also other algorithms that avoid trial division with extra inputs (e.g. 1/N).

When $\hat{q}_{(i)} = q_{(i)} + 1$, the range of $R_{(i+1)}$ may be expanded and overflow can occur. However, as long as we use Eq. (3) for estimation, we can still get $\hat{q}_{(i+1)} N_j$ within 2k bits by using $\hat{c}_{(i)}$ defined in Eq. (4).

$$\hat{c}_{(i)} = |R_{ni} \| R_{n-1i} \| R_{n-2i}| - \hat{q}(N_{n-1} \| N_{n-2}) \quad (4)$$

Obviously, $\hat{c}_{(i)}$ is the remainder of division defined in Eq.(3) and can be easily and rapidly obtained with a few extra circuits.

$\hat{c}_{(i)}$ indicates the upcoming effect by the estimation error. When $\hat{c}_{(i)} \geq 2^k$, $\hat{q}_{(i)} = q_{(i)}$ accurately. When $\hat{c}_{(i)} < \hat{q}_{(i)}$, $\hat{q}_{(i)}$ may have been already equal to $q_{(i)} + 1$ so that $\delta_{(i)}$ must be zero. In this case, even if $\hat{q}_{(i)}$ is equal to $q_{(i)}$, $R_{(i+1)}$ lies into $|R_{(i+1)}| \leq 2^k N$ that is small enough not to cause overflow. Thus modified algorithm 1 eliminates any restoring and complicated carry processing. A more detailed observation is given in appendix 2. The modified procedure (3) by using $\hat{c}_{(i)}$ is shown in Procedure 2.

[Procedure 2]

(3) Increment or decrement $\hat{q}_{(i)}$ as $\hat{q}'_{(i)} = \hat{q}_{(i)} + \delta$ where $\delta_{(i)} = 1$

if $Sign(R_{(i)}) = Sign(B_{(i)})$ <u>and</u> $\hat{c} \geq \hat{q}_{(i)}$ else $\delta_{(i)} = 0$ otherwise.

Since $2^k \geq \hat{q}_{(i)}$, the condition $\hat{c} \geq \hat{q}_{(i)}$ can be replaced to $\hat{c} \geq 2^k$. Then the comparator can become simple. The final algorithm for modular multiplication is algorithm 1.

[Algorithm 1: R=AB mod N]

$$2^{kn-1} \le N < 2^{kn};\ 0 \le A < N;\ 0 < B < N;\ B_{-1} = 0;$$

$$B'_{n-1-i} = \begin{cases} 2^k - B_{n-1-i} + \mathrm{MSB}\,(B_{n-2-i}) & \text{if}\,\mathrm{MSB}\,(B_{n-1-i}) = 1 \\ B_{n-1-i} + \mathrm{MSB}\,(B_{n-2-i}) & \text{otherwise} \end{cases}$$

$$\hat{q}_{(i)} = \left\lfloor \frac{\left|R_{n(i)} \| R_{n-1(i)} \| R_{n-2(i)}\right|}{N_{n-1} \| N_{n-2}} \right\rfloor$$

$$\hat{c}_{(i)} = \left(\left|R_{n(i)} \| R_{n-1(i)} \| R_{n-2(i)}\right|\right) \bmod \hat{q}_{(i)}$$

$$\delta_{(i)} = \begin{cases} 1 & \text{if}\ (Sign\,(R_{(i)}) \oplus Sign\,(B_{(i)}))\ \&\ (\hat{c}_{(i)} \ge 2^k) \\ 0 & \text{otherwise} \end{cases}$$

$$\hat{q}'_{(i)} = \hat{q}_{(i)} + \delta_{(i)}$$

$$R_{(0)} = \begin{cases} A & \text{if}\,\mathrm{MSB}\,(B_{n-1}) = 1 \\ 0 & \text{otherwise} \end{cases}$$

for i=0 to n
  buf1 = $R_{0(i)}$; buf2 = 0; buf3 = 0; $\mathrm{cr1}_{-1}$= $\mathrm{cr1}_{-2}$=0; $\mathrm{cr2}_{-1}$= $\mathrm{cr2}_{-2}$=0;
  for j=0 to m

$$\mathrm{cr1}_j \| \mathrm{buf1} \| \mathrm{buf2} = R_{j(i)} \| \mathrm{buf1} + (-1)^{Sign\,(R_{(i)})} (\hat{q}'_i N_j) + \mathrm{cr1}_{j-1}$$

$$\mathrm{cr2}_j \| \mathrm{buf3} \| R_{j-1(i+1)} = \mathrm{buf2} \| \mathrm{buf3} + A_{j-1} B'_{n-1-i} + \mathrm{cr2}_{j-2}$$

  next j
next i

4 Implementation

4.1 Parallel processing and data flow

Figure 2 shows the pipeline block performing $R_{(i+1)} = (R_{(i)} \mp \hat{q}'N)\,2^k \pm A\left|B_{n-1-i}\right|$. As shown in Fig.1, $\mp\hat{q}_{(i)}N_j$ and $\pm A\left|B_{n-1-i}\right|$ can be performed in parallel. Vertically overlapped areas in Fig.1 are passed from buf1 to buf2, and to buf3 in sequence and finally stored to R in Fig.2. Cr1 and cr2 are the shift registers where carries are stored and output one clock later. As shown in section 3, though $\hat{q}'_{(i)}$ and N_j are k+1 and k bits long respectively, $\hat{q}'_{(i)}N_j$ can be expressed with $2k$ bits. Accordingly, the MSB of Mul1 can be disregarded and only $2k$ bits are passed to Asb1. The sign bit of R switches the operation in Asb1. Similarly, the sign bit of B'_{n-1-i} controls Asb2 and is not put into Mul2.

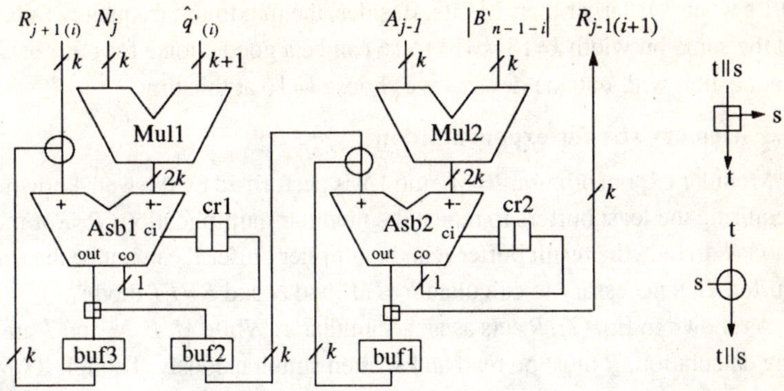

Fig. 2. The pipeline block

4.2 Optimal radix

In trial division, the larger k becomes, the longer the division time becomes. On the other hand, increasing k reduces the number of trial divisions. Moreover, k can strongly influence the maximum frequency and the number of gates so there exists the optimal size of k.

Figure 3 shows the relationship between k and the number of gates and calculation time with 512 bit modulus at the maximum operating frequency of each k. The number of gates is estimated by considering the number of gates in RAMs, multipliers, adder-subtracters, buffers, quotient estimation block, and selectors. The quotient estimation block is assumed to consist of register transfer logic using $2k$ bit wide adder-subtracters. The calculation time is estimated by counting the clocks needed for algorithm 2 and overhead for exponentiation.

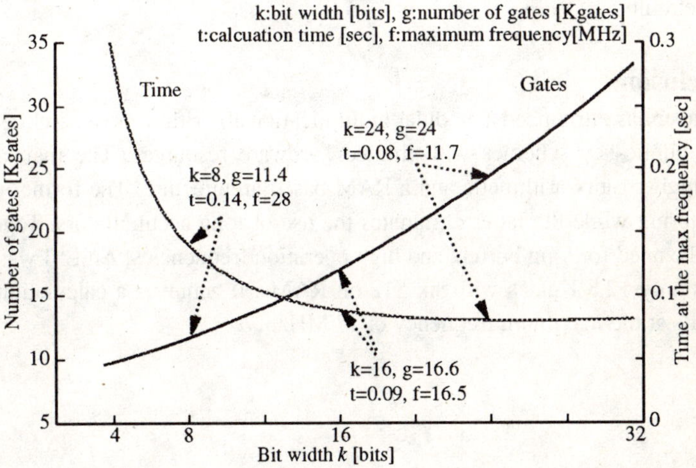

Fig. 3. Estimated calculation time and gate size against arithmetic bit width k

Although the decrease in calculation time becomes smaller around k=16 and beyond, the number of gates continues to increase. The estimated calculation time become shorter than

0.1 s when k is larger than 13 bits. Besides, the maximum frequency falls under 20 MHz at the same bit width k=13. k=13 to 16 can be a good choice for our goal. To get smooth connection with outside devices we choose k=16 at this time.

4.3 Memory size for exponentiation

Modular exponentiation $R=M^E$ mod N is performed by the well-known binary method requiring the least buffers to repeat the modular multiplications $R=RM$ mod$N$ and $R=RR$ mod N. In fact, the result buffer R and multiplier buffer R can not be the same. So another buffer, T, is necessary to calculate $R=TM$ mod N and $R=TT$ mod N.

As shown in Eq. (2), R acts as an accumulator. While M, E, N, and T are only read during calculation, R must be read and written simultaneously. Though RAM can't be read and written at the same time, alternating between buffers $R1$ and $R2$ for reading and writing gives us the easiest solution. Since a register occupies about 10 gates/bit and RAM takes about 1.4 gates/bit or so, doubled RAM remains advantageous. That is, we take six RAMs for exponentiation.

4.4 LSI Design and Results

A modular exponentiation LSI was designed by using a logic synthesizer and the 0.8μ CMOS process. High density macro cells were used for the adder/subtracter-multipliers because they contain critical paths. The synthesized data show that the number of gates used by exponentiation logic is less than 12.8 K and approximately 4.7 K extra gates are needed for the six 512 bit RAMs. The calculation time for 512 bit exponentiation is shorter than 0.1 s at the maximum frequency of 17MHz. Layout shows that modular exponentiation occupies about 10 mm^2, 6 mm^2 for standard cell random logic and 4 mm^2 for the two adder/subtracter-multipliers. This LSI is now being integrated with other security circuits.

5 Conclusion

This paper has introduced a modular multiplication algorithm and an architecture suitable for public-key schemes with limited hardware resources. The main idea is to employ higher radix arithmetic and a RAM based architecture. The former eliminates slow restoring while the latter eliminates the use of long accumulators. Together they obviate the need for long buffers and high operation frequencies. An LSI was designed that uses only 12.8 Kgates with six 512 bit RAMs. It achieves a calculation speed of about 0.1 s at the maximum frequency of 17 MHz.

Acknowledgments

We would like to thank our colleagues at NTT Laboratories, especially Mr. Aoyama, for support of designing and producing the LSI.

References

[BC89] J. Bos and M. Coster: "Addition Chain Heuristics," *Advances in Cryptology-CRYPTO'89, LNCS 435*, Springer-Verlag, pp.400-407, 1989

[BGMW92] E.F. Brickell, D.M. Gordon, K.S. McCurley, and D.B. Wilson: "Fast Exponentiation with Precomputation (Extended Abstract)," *Advances in Cryptology - EUROCRYPT '92, LNCS 658*, Springer-Verlag, pp.200-207, 1992

[BGV93] A. Bosselaers, R. Govaerts, and J. Vandewalle: "Comparison of three modular reduction functions," *Advances in Cryptology-CRYPTO'93, LNCS 773*, Springer-Verlag, pp.175-186, 1993

[Bri89] E. F. Brickell: "A Survey of Hardware Implementations of RSA," *Advances in Cryptology - CRYPTO'89, LNCS 435*, Springer-Verlag, pp.368-370, 1989

[Bri82] E.F. Brickell: "A Fast Modular Multiplication Algorithm with Application to Two Key Cryptography," *Advances in Cryptology-CRYPTO'82*, pp.51-60,Plenum, 1982.

[DH76] W. Diffie and M.E. Hellman: "New Directions in Cryptography," *IEEE Transaction of Information Theory*, vol.IT-22, no.6,pp.644-654, Nov.1976

[DK90] S.R. Dusse and B.S. Kaliski Jr.: "A Cryptographic Library for the Motorola DSP56000," *Advances in Cryptology-EUROCRYPT'90, LNCS 473*, pp.230-244, Springer-Verlag, 1991

[HDVG88] F. Hoornaert, M. Decroos,J. Vandewalle, and R. Govaerts: "Fast RSA-Hardware: Dream or Reality?" *Advances in Cryptology-EUROCRYPT '88, LNCS 330*, Springer-Verlag, pp.257-264, 1988

[Hw79] K.Hwang: *Computer Arithmetic: Principles, Architecture and Design*, John Wiley & Sons, 1979

[IMI92] K. Iwamura, T. Matumoto, and H.Imai: "High-Speed Implementation Methods for RSA Scheme," *Advances in Cryptology-EUROCRYPT'92, LNCS 658*, Springer-Verlag, pp.221-238

[IWMD92] P. Ivey, S. Walker, J. Stern, and S. Davidson: "An Ultra-High Speed Public Key Encryption Processor," *IEEE 1992 Custom Integrated Circuits Conference*, 1992

[Knu81] D. E. Knuth: *The Art of Computer Programming - Seminumerical Algorithms*, vol.2, Addison - Westley, second edition, 1981.

[MY93] H.Morita, C.H.Yang: "A Modular-Multiplication Algorithm Using Lookahead Determination," *IEICE Transaction of fundamentals*, vol.E76-A, no.1, pp.70-77, Jan.1993

[NONN90] Y.Nakamura, K.Oguri, A.Nagoya, and R.Nomura: "A Hierarchical Behavioral Description Based CAD System," *Proceedings of IFIP EURO ASIC '90*, pp.282-287, May. 1990

[RSA78] R.L. Rivest, A. Shamir, and L. Adleman: "A Method of Obtaining Digital signatures and Public Key Cryptosystems," *Comm. of ACM*, vol. 21, no.2, pp.120-126, Feb. 1978.

[VLSI92] VLSI Technology, Inc. "VSC470 Library," VSD13881, and "0.8-Micron Datapath Library (VCC4DP3)," VSD13940, 1992

Appendix 1

[Proposition]

According to algorithm 1, if $\hat{q}_{(i)} = q_{(i)}$, $\hat{q}'_{(i)} N_j < 2^{2k}$.

[Proof]

In the beginning, let $R_{(i)} \geq 0$. When $\hat{q}_{(i)} = q_{(i)}$, $0 \leq R_{(i)} - \hat{q}_{(i)} N \leq N - 1$.

Case 1) $\delta_{(i)} = 0$

In this case, $\hat{q}'_{(i)} = \hat{q}_{(i)} = q_{(i)}$. Therefore, $0 \leq R_{(i)} - \hat{q}'_{(i)} N \leq N - 1$. The range of AB'_{n-1-i} is $-2^{k-1}(N-1) \leq AB'_{n-1-i} \leq 0$. Thus,

$$-2^{k-1}(N-1) < R_{(i+1)} \leq 2^k (N-1). \tag{A-1}$$

Case 2) $\delta_{(i)} = 1$

In this case $\hat{q}' = \hat{q} + 1 = q + 1$, $-N \leq R_{(i)} - \hat{q}'_{(i)} N \leq -1$. The range of AB_{n-1-i} is $0 \leq AB_{n-1-i} \leq 2^{k-1}(N-1)$. Thus,

$$-2^k N \leq R_{(i+1)} \leq -2^k + 2^{k-1}(N-1). \tag{A-2}$$

According to Eq.(A-1) and Eq.(A-2),

$$-2^k N \leq R_{(i+1)} \leq 2^k (N-1). \tag{A-3}$$

In the same way, when $R_{(i)} < 0$,

$$-2^k (N-1) \leq R_{(i+1)} \leq 2^k N. \tag{A-4}$$

According to (A-3) and (A-4), generally,

$$-2^k N \leq R_{(i+1)} \leq 2^k N. \tag{A-5}$$

From Eq.(A-5), Eq.(3) and Procedure 1, $0 \leq \hat{q}'_{(i+1)} \leq 2^k$. Besides, $N_j \leq 2^k - 1$. Thus,

$$\hat{q}'_{(i+1)} N_j \leq 2^{2k} - 2^k < 2^{2k} \tag{A-6}$$

[End]

Appendix 2

[Proposition 1]

If $\hat{c}_{(i)} \geq \hat{q}_{(i)}$, then $\hat{q}_{(i)} = q_{(i)}$.

[Proof]

Let $R_{(i)} \geq 0$.

$$R_{(i)} - \hat{q}_{(i)} N = \sum_{j=0}^{n} 2^{kj} R_{j(i)} - \hat{q}_{(i)} \sum_{j=0}^{n-1} 2^{kj} N_j \tag{A-7}$$

$$= 2^{k(n-2)} \hat{c}_{(i)} + \sum_{j=0}^{n-3} 2^{kj} R_{j(i)} - \hat{q}_{(i)} \sum_{j=0}^{n-3} 2^{kj} N_j \tag{A-8}$$

In the case of $0 \leq R_{i(j)}$, when $\hat{c}_{(i)} \geq \hat{q}_{(i)}$, Eq.(11) is larger than or equal to zero. According to [Knu81], $\hat{q}_{(i)}$ is equal to $q_{(i)}$ or $q_{(i)} + 1$. Therefore, if $R_{(i)} - \hat{q}_{(i)} N \geq 0$, $\hat{q}_{(i)} = q_{(i)}$.

Similarly, in the case of $R_{(i)} \leq 0$, if $\hat{c}_{(i)} \leq \hat{q}_{(i)}$ we find $\hat{q}_{(i)} = q_{(i)}$.

[End]

[Proposition 2]

If $\hat{c}_{(i)} < \hat{q}_{(i)}$ and $\hat{q}_{(i)} = q_{(i)}$ and $\delta_{(i)} = 0$, then $\hat{q}'_{(i+1)} \leq 2^k$.

[Proof]

When $R_{(i)} \geq 0$, the lower bound of $R_{(i+1)}$ is as follows.

$$R_{(i+1)} = (R_{(i)} - \hat{q}'_{(i)} N) 2^k + AB_i \tag{A-9}$$

$$\geq -\hat{q}'_{(i)} \sum_{j=0}^{n-3} 2^{kj} N_j - 2^k (N-1) \tag{A-10}$$

If $\hat{q}'_{(i)} \leq 2^k$, then $R_{(i+1)} \geq -2^k N$ in Eq.(A-10). This is true for all n and k. Similarly, the upper bound is obtained in the case of $R_{(i)} < 0$. Thus, we obtain

$$-2^k N \leq R_{(i+1)} \leq 2^k N. \tag{A-11}$$

According to Eq.(A-11) and Eq.(3), $\hat{q}'_{(i+1)} \leq 2^k$. Since $R_{(0)} = 0$ or A, $\hat{q}'_{(0)} \leq 2^k$. Thus, $\hat{q}'_{(i)} \leq 2^k$ is true for all i.

[End]

Low Exponent Attack against Elliptic Curve RSA

Kaoru KUROSAWA[1], Koji OKADA[1], Shigeo TSUJII[2]

[1] Department of Electrical and Electronic Engineering,
Faculty of Engineering, Tokyo Institute of Technology
2–12–1 O-okayama, Meguro-ku, Tokyo 152, JAPAN
[2] Department of Information Systems Engineering, Chuo University
1–13–27 Kasuga, Bunkyo-ku, Tokyo 112, JAPAN

Abstract. Hastad showed that low exponent RSA is not secure if the same message is encrypted to several receivers. This is true even if time-stamp is used for each receiver. For example, let $e = 3$. Then if the number of receivers = 7, the eavesdropper can find the plaintext from the seven ciphertexts of each receiver.
This paper shows that elliptic curve RSA is not secure in the same scenario. It is shown that the KMOV scheme and Demytko's scheme are not secure if $e = 5, n \geq 2^{1024}$ and the number of receivers = 428. In Demytko's scheme, e can take the value of 2. In this case, this system is not secure if the number of receiver = 11 for $n \geq 2^{175}$.

1 Introduction

Hastad showed that low exponent RSA is not secure if the same message is encrypted to several receivers [1]. This is true even if time-stamp is used for each receiver. For example, let $e = 3$. Then if the number of receivers = 7, the eavesdropper can find the plaintext from the seven ciphertexts of each receiver.

On the other hand, elliptic curve RSA were proposed recently [2][3]. Low exponent attack is not known against elliptic curve RSA [2], although it is much more complicated than usual RSA.

This paper shows a low exponent attack against elliptic curve RSA. It is shown that the KMOV scheme and Demytko's scheme are not secure if $e = 5, n \geq 2^{1024}$ and the number of receivers = 428. In Demytko's scheme, e can take the value of 2. In this case, this system is not secure if the number of receiver = 11 for $n \geq 2^{175}$. (Even though, each receiver has a different times-stamp and a different elliptic curve.)

2 Elliptic curve RSA

2.1 Elliptic curve [4]

Let $p > 3$ be a prime. Suppose that

$$4a^3 + 27b^2 \neq 0 \mod p .$$

Define

$$E_p(a,b) \triangleq \{(x,y)|\ y^2 = x^3 + ax + b \bmod p,\ 0 \le x < p,\ 0 \le y < p\} \cup \{P_\infty\} .$$

$E_p(a,b)$ forms an Abelian group under a certain addition.

1. P_∞ serves as the identity element.
2. If $P = (x_1, y_1) \in E_p(a,b)$, $-P = (x_1, -y_1)$.
3. If $Q = (x_2, y_2) \in E_p(a,b), Q \ne -P$, then $P + Q = (x_3, y_3)$, where

$$x_3 = \lambda^2 - x_1 - x_2 ,$$
$$y_3 = \lambda(x_1 - x_3) - y_1 ,$$

and

$$\lambda = \begin{cases} (y_2 - y_1)/(x_2 - x_1) & \text{if } P \ne Q , \\ (3x_1^2 + a)/2y_1 & \text{if } P = Q . \end{cases}$$

Lemma 1. *Let p be an odd prime satisfying $p = 2 \bmod 3$. Then, for $0 < b < p$, $E_p(0,b)$ is a cyclic group of order $|E_p(0,b)| = p + 1$.*

Lemma 2. *kP denotes k times addition of P, that is,*

$$kP \triangleq P + P + \cdots + P .$$

Let $P = (x,y)$, and $kP = (x_k, y_k)$. If $y_i \ne 0 \bmod p$, then

$$x_{2i} = \frac{(x_i^2 - a)^2 - 8bx_i}{4(x_i^3 + ax_i + b)} \quad \bmod p .$$

If $x_i \ne x_{i+1}$ and $x \ne 0$, then

$$x_{2i+1} = \frac{(a - x_i x_{i+1})^2 - 4b(x_i + x_{i+1})}{x(x_i - x_{i+1})^2} \quad \bmod p . \tag{1}$$

Unfortunately eq.(1) cannot be used if $x = 0 \bmod p$. However, it can be shown [3] that the equation can be rearranged to give

$$x_{2i+1} = \frac{4b + 2(a - x_i x_{i+1})(x_i + x_{i+1})}{(x_i - x_{i+1})^2} - x \quad \bmod p \tag{2}$$

which is valid for all $0 \le x \le p-1$ (and consequently for all $0 \le x \le n-1$ when computations are performed modulo n).

2.2 KMOV scheme [2]

This method utilizes Lemma 1. In other words, p and q must be a special form.

Step 0 (Key Generation) User U chooses large prime p and q such that

$$p = q = 2 \mod 3 .$$

U computes the product $n = pq$ and $N_n = lcm(\sharp E_p(0,b), \sharp E_q(0,b)) = lcm(p+1, q+1)$.
U chooses an integer e which is co-prime to N_n and computes an integer d such that

$$ed = 1 \mod N_n .$$

Summarizing, U's secret key is $d, (p, q, \sharp E_p(0,b), \sharp E_q(0,b)), N_n)$, and U's public key is n, e.

Step 1 (Encryption) A plaintext $M = (m_x, m_y)$ is an integer pair, where $m_x \in Z_n, m_y \in Z_n$. Let $M = (m_x, m_y)$ be a point on the elliptic curve $E_n(0,b)$, where b is determined by m_x and m_y.
Sender A encrypts the point M by encryption function $E(\cdot)$ with the receiver's public key e and n as

$$C = E(M) = eM \text{ over } E_n(0,b) ,$$

and sends a ciphertext pair $C = (c_x, c_y)$ to a receiver B.

Step 2 (Decryption) Receiver B decrypts a point C by decryption function $D(\cdot)$ with his secret key d and public key n as

$$M = D(C) = dC \text{ over } E_n(0,b) .$$

2.3 Demytko's RSA [3]

This method utilize Lemma 2. p and q can be arbitrary. Let

$$\overline{E_p(a,b)} \triangleq \{(x,y) | y^2 v = x^3 + ax + b \bmod p\} \cup \{P_\infty\} ,$$

where v is a fixed quadratic non-residue modulo p. Then, $\overline{E_p(a,b)}$ also forms an Abelian group.

For $\forall x \in Z_p$,

$$\exists y \quad (x,y) \in E_p(a,b) \quad \text{or}$$
$$\exists y \quad (x,y) \in \overline{E_p(a,b)} .$$

Let $P = (x,y)$. we write $kP = (k*x, k*y)$. Then, $k*x$ can be computed without knowing y by using Lemma 2 in either case.

Step 0 (Key Generation) Let p and q be large primes. Let $n = pq$. Choose a and b such that $gcd(4a^3 + 27b^2, n) = 1$, arbitrarily. Let

$$N_1 \triangleq |E_p(a,b)| \ ,$$
$$N_2 \triangleq |\overline{E_p(a,b)}| \ ,$$
$$N_3 \triangleq |E_q(a,b)| \ ,$$
$$N_4 \triangleq |\overline{E_q(a,b)}| \ .$$

Choose e such that

$$gcd(e, N_1) = gcd(e, N_2) = gcd(e, N_3) = gcd(e, N_4) = 1 \ .$$

The public key is (n, e, a, b). Let $d_1, \ldots, d_4$ be

$$ed_1 = 1 \mod lcm(N_1, N_3) \ ,$$
$$ed_2 = 1 \mod lcm(N_1, N_4) \ ,$$
$$ed_3 = 1 \mod lcm(N_2, N_3) \ ,$$
$$ed_4 = 1 \mod lcm(N_2, N_4) \ .$$

Step 1 (Encryption) Let $x \in Z_n$ be a plaintext. Compute $e * x \in Z_n$ by using Lemma 2 and eq.(2). Then the ciphertext is $c = e * x$.

Step 2 (Decryption) Compute $w = c^3 + ac + b \bmod n$. Let

$$i = \begin{cases} 1 & \text{if } (w/p) = (w/q) = 1 \ , \\ 2 & \text{if } (w/p) = 1, (w/q) = -1 \ , \\ 3 & \text{if } (w/p) = -1, (w/q) = 1 \ , \\ 4 & \text{if } (w/p) = (w/q) = -1 \ . \end{cases}$$

The plaintext is obtained by computing $d_i * c$ by using Lemma 2.

3 Hastad's attack [1]

Let (n_i, e) be an RSA public key of user U_i $(i = 1, 2, \ldots)$, where e is common and $\{n_i\}$ are relatively prime. Hastad showed that, if e is small, broad cast encryption is not secure. Suppose that A wants to send the same message x to user $U_1, U_2, \ldots, U_k$. Let t_i be the time-stamp for U_i. She will compute and send

$$y_i = (2^{|t_i|}x + t_i)^e \mod n_i \ .$$

y_i is a polynomial of x with degree e. Hastad proved the following Proposition.

Proposition 3. *Given a set of equations $\sum_{j=0}^{h} a_{ij}x^j = 0 \bmod n_i, i = 1, 2, \ldots, k$ where $x < n$ and $gcd(\langle a_{ij} \rangle_{j=0}^{h}, n_i) = 1$ for all i. Then it is possible to recover x in time polynomial in e, k and $\log n_i$ if*

$$N > n^{\frac{h(h+1)}{2}} (k + h + 1)^{\frac{k+h+1}{2}} 2^{\frac{(k+h+1)^2}{2}} (h+1)^{(h+1)} \ . \tag{3}$$

As before $N = \prod_{i=1}^{k} n_i$, $n = \min n_i$, h is the degree of the equation and k is the number of equations.

This Proposition means that, if $e = 3$ and $k \geq 7$, the attacker can find x from $y_1, y_2, \ldots, y_k$.

4 Low exponent attack against elliptic curve RSA

Suppose that A wants to send the same message x to $U_1, U_2, \ldots, U_k$. Let the public key of U_i of Demytko's RSA scheme be

$$(n_i, e, a_i, b_i) \; .$$

In the KMOV scheme, $a_i = 0$ and b_i is computed from the ciphertext. Assume that $\{n_i\}$ are relatively prime. A computes and send the ciphertexts $c_1, c_2, \ldots, c_k$.

For simplicity, we omit time-stamps in the following discussion. However, Theorem 4 and 9 hold even if time-stamps are used as in [1].

4.1 $e = 2$ (attack against Demytko)

In Demytko's scheme, e can be 2 if each N_i is odd.

Theorem 4. *Suppose that $n \geq 2^{175}$. In Demytko's scheme, if $e = 2$ and $k \geq 11$, then x can be found from $c_1, \ldots, c_k$ in polynomial time.*

Proof. ¿From Lemma 2,

$$c_i = \frac{(x^2 - a_i)^2 - 8b_i x}{4(x^3 + a_i x + b_i)} \mod n_i \; .$$

Let

$$F_i(x) \triangleq 4c_i(x^3 + a_i x + b_i) - (x^2 - a_i)^2 + 8b_i x \mod n_i \; .$$

Then,

$$F_i(x) = 0 \mod n_i$$

and $\deg F_i(x) = 4$. In Proposition 3, $h = 4$. Then, $n^{\frac{h(h+1)}{2}} = n^{10}$. Further, if $k = 11$,

$$(k + h + 1)^{\frac{k+h+1}{2}} 2^{\frac{(k+h+1)^2}{2}} (h + 1)^{(h+1)} = 16^8 \cdot 2^{128} \cdot 5^5 < 2^{175} \; .$$

Thus, the right hand side of eq.(3)

$$< 2^{175} \cdot n^{10} \; .$$

Therefore, if $k = 11$ and $n \geq 2^{175}$, eq.(3) holds. □

4.2 $e = 3$ (attack against Demytko)

Theorem 5. *Suppose that $n \geq 2^{482}$. If $e = 3$ and $k \geq 61$, then x can be found from $c_1, \ldots, c_k$ in polynomial times in Demytko's scheme.*

Proof. ¿From Lemma 2,

$$x_2^{(i)} = \frac{(x^2 - a_i)^2 - 8b_i x}{4(x^3 + a_i x + b_i)} \mod n_i \ , \tag{4}$$

$$c_i = \frac{(a_i - x x_2^{(i)})^2 - 4b(x + x_2^{(i)})}{x(x - x_2^{(i)})^2} \mod n_i \ . \tag{5}$$

By substituting eq.(4) into eq.(5), we have

$$c_i = \frac{h_i(x)}{g_i(x)} \mod n_i$$

for some polynomials $h_i(x)$ and $g_i(x)$, where $\deg h_i(x) = 10$ and $\deg g_i(x) = 9$. Let

$$F_i(x) = c_i g_i(x) - h_i(x) \ .$$

Then $F_i(x) = 0$ and $\deg F_i(x) = 10$. In Proposition 3, we have $h = 10$. Then, $n^{\frac{h(h+1)}{2}} = n^{55}$. Further, if $k = 61$,

$$(k + h + 1)^{\frac{k+h+1}{2}} 2^{\frac{(k+h+1)^2}{2}} (h+1)^{(h+1)} \leq 2^{2888} < (2^{482})^6 \ .$$

Thus, the right hand side of eq.(3)

$$< (2^{482})^6 \cdot n^{55} \ .$$

Therefore, if $k = 61$ and $n \geq 2^{482}$, eq.(3) holds. □

After a preliminary version of this paper [5], it has turned out that this bound can be tighter [6]. Namely, $k \geq 49$.

4.3 $e = 5$ (attack against KMOV and Demytko)

Theorem 6. *Suppose that $n \geq 2^{723}$. If $e = 5$ and $k \geq 664$, then x can be found from $c_1, \ldots, c_k$ in polynomial times for both the KMOV scheme and Demytko's scheme.*

Proof. First, we show a proof for Demytko's scheme. By the similar argument as the case $e = 3$, we have

$$c_i = \frac{h_i(x)}{g_i(x)} \mod n_i$$

for some polynomials $h_i(x)$ and $g_i(x)$, where $\deg h_i(x) = 25$ and $\deg g_i(x) = 24$. Let

$$F_i(x) = c_i g_i(x) - h_i(x) \ .$$

Then $F_i(x) = 0$ and $\deg F_i(x) = 25$. In Proposition 3, we have $h = 25$. Then, $n^{\frac{h(h+1)}{2}} = n^{325}$. Further, if $k = 664$,

$$(k+h+1)^{\frac{k+h+1}{2}} 2^{\frac{(k+h+1)^2}{2}} (h+1)^{(h+1)} \leq 2^{241630} < (2^{723})^{339} \ .$$

Thus, the right hand side of eq.(3)

$$< (2^{723})^{339} \cdot n^{325} \ .$$

Therefore, if $k = 664$ and $n \geq 2^{723}$, eq.(3) holds.

Next, we show a proof for the KMOV scheme. In the KMOV scheme, a plaintext is $M = (m_x, m_y)$ and the ciphertext is $C = (c_x, c_y)$. That is, x coordinate but also y coordinate are used for encryption. m_x is found from $\{c_x\}$ in the same way as the above discussion. We show how to find m_y.

Lemma 7. *Let $kP = (x_k, y_k)$. Note that $(x_{2i}, y_{2i}) = (x_i, y_i) + (x_i, y_i)$, $(x_{2i+1}, y_{2i+1}) = (x_i, y_i) + (x_{i+1}, y_{i+1})$. If $y_i \neq 0$, then*

$$y_{2i} = \frac{3x_i^2 + a}{2y_i}(x_i - x_{2i}) - y_i \mod p \ .$$

If $x_i \neq x_{i+1}$, then

$$y_{2i+1} = \frac{y_{i+1} - y_i}{x_{i+1} - x_i}(x_i - x_{2i+1}) - y_i \mod p \ .$$

Lemma 8.

$$m_y = \frac{f(m_x, x_2, x_3, c_x) - g(m_x, x_2, x_3, c_x)}{2c_y(x_2 - m_x)(x_3 - x_2)} \mod n \ , \tag{6}$$

where

$$f(m_x, x_2, x_3, c_x) = 3m_x^2(m_x - x_2)\{(m_x - x_3)(x_2 - c_x) + (m_x - x_2)(x_3 - c_x)\} \ ,$$
$$g(m_x, x_2, x_3, c_x) = 2(m_x^3 + b)\{2(m_x - x_3)(x_2 - c_x) + (m_x - x_2)(x_3 - x_2)\} \ .$$

Proof. In the KMOV scheme, $(x_1, y_1) = (m_x, m_y), (x_5, y_5) = (c_x, c_y)$ and $a = 0$. Therefore, form Lemma 7,

$$y_2 = \frac{3m_x^2}{2m_y}(m_x - x_2) - m_y \mod n \ , \tag{7}$$

$$y_3 = \frac{y_2 - m_y}{x_2 - m_x}(m_x - x_3) - m_y \mod n \ , \tag{8}$$

$$c_y = \frac{y_3 - y_2}{x_3 - x_2}(x_2 - c_x) - y_2 \mod n \ . \tag{9}$$

By substituting eq.(7) and eq.(8) into eq.(9), and note that $m_y^2 = m_x^3 + b \mod n$, we have

$$c_y = \frac{f(m_x, x_2, x_3, c_x) - g(m_x, x_2, x_3, c_x)}{2m_y(x_2 - m_x)(x_3 - x_2)} \mod n \ .$$

Hence, eq.(6) holds. □

At this moment, we know all parameters of the right hand side of eq.(6). Therefore, we can find m_y from Lemma 8 □

Theorem 9. *Suppose that $n \geq 2^{1024}$. If $e = 5$ and $k \geq 428$, then x can be found from $c_1, \ldots, c_k$ in polynomial times for both the KMOV scheme and Demytko's scheme.*

Further, Theorem 6 can be extended to any small e.

References

1. J.Hastad : On using RSA with low exponent in a public key network. Proc. of Crypto'85, pp.403-408 (1985)
2. K.Koyama, U.M.Maurer, T.Okamoto and S.A.Vanstone : New public-key schemes based on elliptic curves over the ring Z_n. Proc. of Crypto'91 (1991)
3. N.Demytko : A new elliptic curve based analogue of RSA. Proc. of Eurocrypt'93, pp.39-48, May 24 (1993)
4. D.M.Bressoud : Factorization and primality testing. Springer-Verlag (1989)
5. K.Kurosawa and S.Tsujii : Low exponent attack against elliptic curve RSA. Technical Report of IEICE, ISEC94-2, pp.11-17 (1994)
6. H.Kuwakado and K.Koyama : On the security of RSA-type schemes over cubic curves against the Hastad attack. Technical report of IEICE, ISEC94-10, pp.23-30 (1994)

SESSION 10

BLOCK CIPHER ALGORITHMS

Chair: Rei Safavi-Naini

(University of Wollongong, Australia)

A Unified Markov Approach to Differential and Linear Cryptanalysis

Luke O'Connor [⋆,1,2] and Jovan Dj. Golić [⋆⋆,2,3]

[1] Distributed Systems Technology Centre (DSTC), Brisbane, Australia
[2] Information Security Research Centre, Queensland University of Technology
GPO Box 2434, Brisbane Q 4001, Australia
[3] School of Electrical Engineering, University of Belgrade

Abstract. Differential and linear cryptanalysis are two attacks on product ciphers that use approximations of the round function **F** to derive information about the secret key. For the case of differential cryptanalysis, it is well-known that the probability of differentials can be modeled by a Markov chain, and it is known, for example, that the chain for DES converges to the uniform distribution. In this paper, a Markov chain for linear cryptanalysis is introduced as well and it is proved that both chains converge to the uniform distribution for almost all round functions **F**. This implies that in the independent random subkey model, almost all product ciphers become immune to both differential and linear cryptanalysis after a sufficient number of rounds.

1 Introduction

Differential and linear cryptanalysis [2, 8] are two attacks on iterated mappings that use approximations of the round function **F** to derive information about the secret key used in the mapping. The round function **F** is considered to be fixed since the nonlinear components of the round functions are fixed (such as the S-boxes), even though a varying subkey is also taken as input at each round. Differential and linear cryptanalysis proceed by approximating **F** at several rounds, and then combine these local approximations to form a global approximation of the plaintext in terms of the ciphertext. In the case of differential cryptanalysis the local approximation is derived from the distribution of differences in the XOR table, while for linear cryptanalysis the local approximation is derived from

⋆ The work reported in this paper has been funded in part by the Cooperative Research Centres program through the Department of the Prime Minister and Cabinet of Australia. Email: `oconnor@dstc.edu.au`.

⋆⋆ The research was supported in part by the Science Fund of Serbia, grant #0403, through the Institute of Mathematics, Serbian Academy of Arts and Sciences. Email `golic@fit.qut.edu.au`.

linearities in the round function. Design of iterated mappings that are resistant to differential cryptanalysis was simplified by the observation that the distribution of differentials can be modeled as a Markov chain [7]. We say 'model' since the probabilities derived from the Markov chain approach assume that the subkeys are random and independent. In particular, if this chain converges to the uniform distribution, this is considered to be strong evidence that the cipher becomes resistant to differential attacks, which is true for DES [5] and most likely for IDEA [6]. Knudsen and Nyberg [11] have derived a general upper bound on the probability of a differential in terms of the most likely one-round difference.

Extending the Markov approach, we will show that almost all round functions $\mathbf{F}$ have corresponding Markov chains for differentials that converge to the uniform distribution, proving that almost all product ciphers are resistant to this attack given a sufficient number of rounds. Similarly, we define a Markov chain based on correlation coefficients that models the probability of linearizations used in linear cryptanalysis, and show that almost all round functions $\mathbf{F}$ have corresponding chains that converge to the uniform distribution. For both chains these results are proved under the assumptions that the subkeys are random and independent. More precisely, using several results from the theory of random graphs, we show that the chain converges with probability close to one if the number of nonzero entries in the $N \times N$ transition matrix $\mathbf{P}$ is at least $N \log N$. Our main result is then to prove that this is true for the chains corresponding to both differential and linear cryptanalysis for almost all round functions $\mathbf{F}$.

The paper is organized as follows. In Section 2 we provide some basic definitions for Markov chains, and introduce probabilistic arguments for demonstrating convergence based on the random graph theory. In Section 3 we consider the Markov chain for differential cryptanalysis, and in Section 4 the Markov chain for linear cryptanalysis. Section 3 is short as compared to section 4 as many of the concepts related to Markov chains for differentials have been developed.

2 Finite Markov Chains and Random Graphs

A stochastic process described by an $N \times N$ transition matrix $\mathbf{P} = [P_{ij}]$, $1 \leq i, j \leq N$,

$$\mathbf{P} = \begin{bmatrix} P_{11} & P_{12} & \cdots & P_{1N} \\ P_{21} & P_{22} & \cdots & P_{2N} \\ \vdots & \vdots & \ddots & \vdots \\ P_{N1} & P_{N2} & \cdots & P_{NN} \end{bmatrix} \tag{1}$$

is called a finite markov chain when N is finite. Let $\mathbf{P}^{(r)} = [P_{ij}^{(r)}]$, $1 \leq i, j \leq N$, be the rth power of $\mathbf{P}$. State i communicates with state j if there exist integers

r_1, r_2 such that $P_{ij}^{(r_1)}, P_{ji}^{(r_2)} > 0$, denoted $i \leftrightarrow j$. It can be verified that '$\leftrightarrow$' is an equivalence relation, and if **P** has only one equivalence class (all states communicate), then **P** is said to be *irreducible.* State i has period $d_i = \min\{k \mid P_{ii}^{(k)} > 0\}$, and is said to *aperiodic* if $d_i = 1$. The period of **P** is defined as $d = \gcd(d_1, d_2, \cdots, d_N)$, and **P** is said to be aperiodic if $d = 1$. Finite, irreducible and aperiodic chains are called *ergodic*. This class of chains is important because their asymptotic properties can be derived. The following well-known theorem may be found in Feller [3], for example.

Theorem 1. If **P** is ergodic, then there exists a unique distribution $\Pi = (\pi_1, \pi_2, \ldots, \pi_N)$ such that

$$\pi_j = \lim_{r \to \infty} P_{ij}^{(r)}. \tag{2}$$

The distribution Π is said to the *limiting distribution* for **P**. □

Observe that $\sum_j P_{ij} = 1$ by definition, and if in addition $\sum_i P_{ij} = 1$, then **P** is said to be *doubly stochastic*. As will be shown, the transition matrices of interest are doubly stochastic, and in this case a more precise statement concerning the limiting distribution can be made (see Ash [1] for a proof).

Theorem 2. If **P** is ergodic and doubly stochastic, then the uniform distribution $\Pi = (1/N, 1/N, \cdots, 1/N)$ is the limiting distribution for **P**. □

As has been observed by many authors, **P** can be considered as the adjacency matrix of a directed graph $\mathbf{G} = (V, E)$, where $V = \{v_1, v_2, \ldots, v_N\}$ and there is a directed edge from v_i to v_j if and only if $P_{ij} > 0$. We will call **G** the *underlying graph* of **P**. A directed graph **G** is called strongly connected if for all v_i, v_j, there is a directed path from vertex v_i to vertex v_j. Then the matrix **P** is irreducible if and only if **G** is strongly connected. Also observe that if **G** has a loop (an edge from v_i to itself), then **P** is aperiodic. It is is clear that as the number of edges in **G** is increased, the more likely **G** is to be strongly connected and to possess a loop. We will investigate the conditions under which the number of edges in a graph guarantees these properties with high probability.

We will say that almost all graphs with N vertices and $m(N)$ edges possess a certain property if the fraction of graphs with such property tends to one when $N \to \infty$. Using simple combinatorial arguments, it can be shown that almost all directed graphs G with N vertices and m edges have a loop when $m = N \cdot \gamma_N$, $\gamma_N \to \infty$. Further, Palásti [12] has shown that almost all directed graphs G with m edges are strongly connected when $m = N(\log N + \gamma_N)$, $\gamma_N \to \infty$. Here γ_N is any function that tends to ∞ as N does such as $\log N$ or $\log\log N$.

Theorem 3. Let $m = N(\log N + \gamma_N)$ where $\gamma_N \to \infty$. Then almost all directed graphs G are both aperiodic and strongly connected.

Proof. For any two events α_1, α_2, we have $\Pr(\alpha_1, \alpha_2) \geq \Pr(\alpha_1) + \Pr(\alpha_2) - 1$. If the events of interest are 'G is aperiodic' and 'G is strongly connected', then the joint probability tends to one when $N \rightarrow \infty$. □

In the analysis to follow we are interested in the more general case when the number of edges m is a random variable for any N. As before, it is assumed that for each N and m, a graph is chosen uniformly at random. Then we have the following corollary to Theorem 3.

Corollary 1 Let G be a directed graph with m edges. Let $\Pr\{m \geq N(\log N + \gamma_N)\} \rightarrow 1$ where $\gamma_N \rightarrow \infty$. Then when $N \rightarrow \infty$

$$\Pr\{G \text{ is aperiodic and strongly connected}\} \rightarrow 1. \tag{3}$$

□

We will use Corollary 1 to argue that the Markov chains defined for differential and linear cryptanalysis are both ergodic with high probability as their respective transition matrices contain a large number of nonzero entries. In particular, we will prove that the number of nonzero entries in both transition matrices dominates $N \log N$ for almost all round functions $\mathbf{F}$, implying that the underlying graph satisfies the conditions of Corollary 1.

3 Differential Cryptanalysis

Let '+' denote a difference operation such that ΔX is said to be the difference of X and X' if $\Delta X = X + X'$. The difference operation is often taken as XOR, and is related to operation used to mix the key with the ciphertext. For ciphers such as DES, FEAL and LOKI the natural difference operation is XOR while for IDEA it is a combination of modular addition and multiplication. In this paper we will assume that XOR is the difference operation. Let ΔP be a difference of plaintexts (plaintext difference) and let ΔC_k be the difference of ciphertexts (ciphertext difference) after round k, $0 \leq k \leq r$, for an r-round cipher. It has been observed that for certain ciphers

$$\Pr\{\Delta C_k = j \mid \Delta P = i\} = P_{ij}^{(k)} \tag{4}$$

for an appropriately defined stochastic matrix $\mathbf{P} = [P_{ij}]$, when *it is assumed that the subkeys of these ciphers are independent and uniformly distributed*. Such ciphers are called Markov ciphers [7], and include DES, FEAL, LOKI and IDEA. The belief that $P_{ij}^{(k)}$ is approximately equal to $\Pr(\Delta C_k = j \mid \Delta P = i)$ when the subkeys are dependent is known as the Hypothesis of Stochastic Equivalence [6].

The $\mathbf{P}$ matrix is directly obtained from the XOR table for the round function $\mathbf{F}$, which must be bijective since the cipher is invertible. Note that for a Feistel cipher, $\mathbf{F}$ includes the swapping operation of the halves. For an n-bit round function $\mathbf{F}$, for each input difference $\Delta X = i$ and output difference $\Delta Y = j$, $1 \leq i, j \leq 2^n - 1$, P_{ij} is defined as

$$P_{ij} = 2^{-n} \cdot \sum_{\substack{X, X' \in Z_2^n \\ \Delta X = X + X'}} [\mathbf{F}(X) + \mathbf{F}(X') = \Delta Y] \tag{5}$$

where $[\cdot]$ is a boolean predicate evaluating to 0 or 1. Here $N = 2^n - 1$ since we do not consider the degenerate cases where $i = 0$ or $j = 0$ (that is, the states of the chain correspond to the $2^n - 1$ nonzero n-bit vectors). The transition matrix $\mathbf{P}$ is doubly stochastic since the round function $\mathbf{F}$ is bijective.

Theorem 4. Let $\mathbf{F} : Z_2^n \to Z_2^n$ be a round function with an ergodic transition matrix $\mathbf{P}$. Then for any nonzero plaintext difference ΔP and any nonzero ciphertext difference ΔC_r, when the number of rounds $r \to \infty$

$$\Pr\{\Delta C_r = j \mid \Delta P = i\} \to \frac{1}{N}. \tag{6}$$

□

Thus ciphers with ergodic transition matrices are immune to differential cryptanalysis after a sufficient number of rounds. Let $\Lambda(\mathbf{P})$, or simply, Λ denote the number of nonzero entries in $\mathbf{P}$. If $\mathbf{F}$ is selected uniformly at random, then Λ is an integer random variable. Our objective is to show that Λ dominates $N \log N$ with probability tending to one thus implying that $\mathbf{P}$ is ergodic for almost all $\mathbf{F}$.

Theorem 5. For a uniformly distributed function $\mathbf{F}$,

$$\Pr\{\Lambda \geq N^2/(2\log(N+1))\} = 1 - o\left(N^{-\log\log N + 5.5}\right). \tag{7}$$

□

Consequently, for any number of vertices N and any given number of edges Λ, under the plausible assumption that the underlying graph of the transition matrix is uniformly distributed, Theorem 5 and the random graph theory result of Corollary 1 imply

Corollary 2 For uniformly distributed function $\mathbf{F}$, the probability that the Markov chain for differential cryptanalysis is ergodic tends to one when $N \to \infty$. □

4 Linear Cryptanalysis

Linear cryptanalysis was introduced recently by Matsui [9, 8], and is currently the best known non-exhaustive attack on the Data Encyption Standard (DES). The basis of the attack is finding linear relationships between certain bits of the plaintext P, ciphertext C and key K, expressed as $\sum P + \sum C = \sum K$. More formally, the attack derives an approximation of the form

$$\sum_{i=1}^{n} a_{1i}p_i + \sum_{i=1}^{n} a_{2i}c_i = \sum_{i=1}^{m} a_{3i}k_i \pmod 2 \tag{8}$$

where $a_{ij} \in \{0,1\}$ and $P = p_1, \ldots, p_n$, $C = c_1, \ldots, c_n$ and $K = k_1, \ldots k_m$. Matsui has shown that $\sum K$ can be determined accurately using the maximum likelihood method if a sufficient amount N_L of known ciphertext is available. In particular, if the approximation in (8) is correct with probability q^*, the attack is expected to be successful 98% of the time when $N_L \approx |q^* - 1/2|^{-2}$. The result of the attack is the knowledge of one bit of information concerning the key, namely the value of $\sum K$.

We will assume that at each round a subkey is XORed with the current ciphertext. Let $Y_i = y_{i,1}, y_{i,2}, \ldots, y_{i,n}$ be a binary n-vector for $0 \le i \le r$. Also let the intermediate ciphertext at round i be denoted as $C_i = c_{i,1}, c_{i,2}, \ldots, c_{i,n}$, with the subkey denoted as $K_i = k_{i,1}, k_{i,2}, \ldots, k_{i,n}$. The approximation used at round i will be

$$\sum_{j=1}^{n} y_{ij}(c_{ij} + k_{ij}) = \sum_{j=1}^{n} y_{i+1,j}c_{i+1,j} \tag{9}$$

which is true with some probability q_i. Then Y_i denotes the sum of the input variables used in the approximation at round i, and also the sum of the output variables used in the approximation at round $i-1$, for $i > 1$. When these r approximations are added modulo 2, the two terms involving Y_i will cancel, leaving an approximation with probability q^* in terms of a sum of plaintext bits $Y_0 = \sum P$, a sum of the ciphertext bits $Y_r = \sum C$ and a sum of key bits $\sum K$, which is of the same form as in (8). All the linearizations of iterated block ciphers under consideration can be derived in this manner.

When the keys bits are assumed to be random and independent, the approximations in (9) for different i are independent, due to the way the subkey and the current ciphertext are combined at each round. In this case, Gallager [4] has shown that

$$q^* = \frac{1}{2} + 2^{r-1} \cdot \prod_{i=1}^{r} \left(q_i - \frac{1}{2} \right) \tag{10}$$

referred to as the Piling-Up lemma by Matsui. It is more convenient to reformulate the probability q^* in terms of correlation coefficients. If f and g are two

n-bit boolean functions then the correlation coefficient, or simply, the correlation of f and g, denoted by $c(f,g)$, is defined as

$$c(f,g) = 2^{-n} \cdot \sum_X (-1)^{f(X)}(-1)^{g(X)} = \Pr(f = g) - \Pr(f \neq g).$$

But if for each i we view Y_{i-1} and Y_i as boolean functions $\sum_{j=1}^{n} y_{i-1,j}c_{i-1,j}$ and $\sum_{j=1}^{n} y_{ij}c_{i,j}$, respectively, then

$$q_i - \frac{1}{2} = \frac{c(Y_{i-1}, Y_i)}{2}.$$

The next lemma shows that any correlation between the plaintext, ciphertext and key can be expressed as a product of correlation coefficients involving the linearizations defined by the Y_i.

Lemma 6. Let $Y_0 = \sum P$ and $Y_r = \sum C$ represent linear combinations of the plaintext and ciphertext, respectively, in an r-round cipher using independent subkeys $K_1, K_2, \ldots, K_r$. Let q^* be the probability of the approximation $Y_0 = Y_r + \sum K$. If we consider Y_r as a function of the plaintext and all the subkeys, then $c(Y_0, Y_r + \sum K) = \prod_{i=1}^{r} c(Y_{i-1}, Y_i)$ and hence

$$q^* = \frac{1}{2} + \frac{1}{2} \cdot \prod_{i=1}^{r} c(Y_{i-1}, Y_i). \tag{11}$$

□

4.1 A Chain for Linear Cryptanalysis

The round function $\mathbf{F} : Z_2^n \rightarrow Z_2^n$ is bijective, and let $f_i : Z_2^n \rightarrow Z_2$ be the boolean function that describes the ith bit of $\mathbf{F}$, $1 \leq i \leq n$. Let $X = x_1 x_2 \cdots x_n$ denote the vector of input variables. For $N = 2^n - 1$, define an $N \times N$ matrix $\mathbf{P} = [P_{ij}], 1 \leq i,j \leq N$, where $i = (i_1 i_2 \cdots i_n)_2, j = (j_1 j_2 \cdots j_n)_2$ in base 2, and

$$P_{ij} = c^2 \left(\sum_k i_k x_k, \sum_k j_k f_k \right). \tag{12}$$

That is, P_{ij} is the square of the correlation between a particular linear combination of the x_i and a linear combination of the f_i. Note that the chain excludes the trivial values of $i = j = 0$. Call $\mathbf{P}$ the correlation matrix. We will show that $\mathbf{P}$ has each row and column summing to one (i.e. doubly stochastic) which has strong implications for the limiting distribution of the powers of $\mathbf{P}$ (if it exists). Consider the columns of $\mathbf{P}$ first. The sum of a given column corresponds to the total correlation between $f = \sum_k j_k f_k$ and the set of all nontrivial linear functions. Since f is balanced this is also the total correlation to all the linear functions which is known to be one for any boolean function [10]. On the other hand, since $\mathbf{F}$ is bijective, input variables can be expressed as a bijective function $\mathbf{F}^{-1}$ of the output variables. By the same argument one then obtains that each row of $\mathbf{P}$ also sums to one. Hence we have

Lemma 7. For a function $\mathbf{F}$, the correlation matrix $\mathbf{P}$ is doubly stochastic. □

Let $Y = (Y_0, Y_1, \cdots, Y_r)$ denote an r-round approximation of a block cipher. Let $\mathbf{P}^{(r)} = [P_{ij}^{(r)}]$ be the rth power of $\mathbf{P}$. By definition of the chain we have that

$$P_{ij}^{(r)} = \sum_{\substack{\sum i_k p_k = Y_0 \\ \sum j_k c_k = Y_r}} \prod_{t=1}^{r} c^2(Y_{t-1}, Y_t). \tag{13}$$

Now, since the square of the overall correlation is, by virtue of Lemma 6, upper bounded by $P_{ij}^{(r)}$, Theorem 2.2 results in

Theorem 8. For a round function $\mathbf{F} : Z_2^n \to Z_2^n$ with an ergodic correlation matrix $\mathbf{P}$, the correlation between any linear function Y_0 of the plaintext P and any linear function Y_r of the ciphertext C for a large number of rounds r, asymptotically satisfies

$$|2q^* - 1| = \left| \prod_{i=1}^{r} c(Y_{i-1}, Y_i) \right| \leq \frac{1}{\sqrt{N}}. \tag{14}$$

□

Thus under an assumption similar to the Hypothesis of Stochastic Equivalence, Theorem 8 indicates that ciphers with ergodic correlation matrices are immune to linear cryptanalysis after a sufficient number of rounds.

4.2 Ergodicity for Random Round Functions

As with differential cryptanalysis, let $\Lambda(\mathbf{P})$, or simply Λ, denote the number of nonzero entries in the correlation matrix $\mathbf{P}$. Assuming that $\mathbf{F}$ is chosen uniformly at random, Λ then becomes an integer random variable which can be expressed as an integer sum $\Lambda = \sum_{i=1}^{N} \sum_{j=1}^{N} \lambda_{ij}$ of binary random variables where λ_{ij} is equal to one if $P_{ij} > 0$ and to zero otherwise. Our objective is to derive the expectation and variance of Λ. By using the well-known expressions [3] it is easy to show that

$$\mathbf{E}[\Lambda] = \sum_{1 \leq i,j \leq N} (1 - p_{ij}) \tag{15}$$

$$\mathbf{Var}[\Lambda] = \sum_{1 \leq i,j \leq N} (p_{ij} - p_{ij}^2) + \sum_{1 \leq i,j \leq N} \sum_{\substack{1 \leq i'j' \leq N \\ (i',j') \neq (i,j)}} (p_{ij,i'j'} - p_{ij} p_{i'j'}) \tag{16}$$

where $p_{ij} = \Pr(\lambda_{ij} = 0)$ and $p_{ij,i'j'} = \Pr(\lambda_{ij} = 0, \lambda_{i'j'} = 0)$. We now determine these probabilities and their asymptotic behaviour when 2^n is large, as is the case in practice.

Lemma 9. For any i, j

$$p_{ij} = P_1 \stackrel{\text{def}}{=} \frac{\binom{2^{n-1}}{2^{n-2}}^2}{\binom{2^n}{2^{n-1}}} \sim \sqrt{\frac{8}{\pi 2^n}}. \tag{17}$$

□

It is much more difficult to derive the pairwise probabilities $p_{ij,i'j'}$. There are three possible cases: (1) $i' = i$ and $j' \neq j$, (2) $i' \neq i$ and $j' = j$ and (3) $i' \neq i$ and $j' \neq j$. They are settled by the following two lemmas.

Lemma 10. For any $i' = i$, $j' \neq j$ or $i' \neq i$, $j' = j$

$$p_{ij,i'j'} = P_2 \stackrel{\text{def}}{=} \frac{\sum_{k=0}^{2^{n-2}} \binom{2^{n-2}}{k}^4}{\binom{2^n}{2^{n-1}}} \sim \frac{8}{\pi 2^n}. \tag{18}$$

□

Lemma 11. For any $i' \neq i$ and $j' \neq j$

$$p_{ij,i'j'} = P_3 \stackrel{\text{def}}{=} \frac{1}{\binom{2^n}{2^{n-1}}^2 \binom{2^{n-1}}{2^{n-2}}^4} \cdot \sum_{\mathcal{M}} \frac{2^n!}{\prod_{l=0}^{15} m(l)} \sim \frac{8}{\pi 2^n} \tag{19}$$

where $\mathcal{M}$ is the set of all the non-negative integer solutions $(m(0), \ldots, m(15))$, with alternative notation (l_1, l_2, l_3, l_4) for $l = (l_1, l_2, l_3, l_4)_2$, to the system of 16 linear equations of the form

$$\sum_{l_{s_3}, l_{s_4}} m(l_1, l_2, l_3, l_4) = 2^{n-2}, \qquad \forall l_{s_1}, l_{s_2} \tag{20}$$

for $(s_1, s_2) = (1, 2), (3, 4), (1, 3)$ and $(2, 4)$, respectively, where (s_1, s_2, s_3, s_4) is a permutation of (1, 2, 3, 4). □

Lemmas 9–11 essentially show the asymptotic pairwise independence of the zero entries in the correlation matrix when 2^n is large. Consequently, in light of (15), (16) and Chebyshev's inequality Lemmas 9–11 result in

Theorem 12. For uniformly distributed function **F**, the expectation and variance of the number Λ of nonzero entries in the correlation matrix satisfy

$$\mathbf{E}[\Lambda] = N^2(1 - P_1) \sim N^2 \left(1 - \sqrt{\frac{8}{\pi N}}\right) \sim N^2$$

$$\mathbf{Var}[\Lambda] = N^2 P_1(1 - P_1) + 2N^2(N-1)(P_2 - P_1^2) + N^2(N-1)^2(P_3 - P_1^2) = o(N^3)$$

where $N = 2^n - 1$. For any $\gamma_N = o(N)$,

$$\Pr\{\Lambda \geq N(\log N + \gamma_N)\} = 1 - o\left(\frac{1}{N}\right). \tag{21}$$

□

Consequently, for any number of vertices N and any given number of edges Λ, under the plausible assumption that the underlying graph of the transition matrix is uniformly distributed, Theorem 12 and the random graph theory result of Corollary 1 imply

Corollary 3 For uniformly distributed function $\mathbf{F}$, the probability that the Markov chain for linear cryptanalysis is ergodic tends to one when $N \to \infty$. □

5 Conclusion

The Markov approach to product cipher design has been discussed with respect to two cryptographic attacks. The convergence of these chains to the uniform distribution suggests that the iterative structure of product ciphers is a good design principle for generating mappings for which certain measures of strength should tend to be distributed uniformly. The main difficulty with the Markov approach is to demonstrate the ergodicity of the transition matrix $\mathbf{P}$: that is, demonstrate that $\mathbf{P}$ is finite, aperiodic and irreducible. In most cases the dimensions of $\mathbf{P}$ will make a direct inspection of its entries infeasible, as for DES where $\mathbf{P}$ has approximately $2^{64} \times 2^{64}$ entries. This then suggests that a probabilistic approach must be taken in proving the ergodicity of of a large class of transition matrices $\mathbf{P}$. We have proven results for 'almost all' round functions $\mathbf{F}$, but it appears difficult to say something meaningful about a given round function, say that of IDEA. A new design principle for round functions is to guarantee the ergodicity of the $\mathbf{P}$ matrix for both differential and linear cryptanalysis. This has been possible for DES with respect to differental cryptanalysis [5].

The next step in the Markov approach is to evaluate the rate of convergence of the chain to its stationary distribution. Advanced techniques, possibly based on estimating the second largest eigenvalue of the transition matrix, are available to determine the convergence rate of ergodic chains. Since the number of nonzero entries in the transition matrices for both differential and especially linear cryptanalysis is large, it should be expected that for most round functions the convergence is exponential and rapid.

References

1. R. B. Ash. *Information Theory.* New York: Dover Publications, 1965.
2. E. Biham and A. Shamir. Differential cryptanalysis of DES-like cryptosystems. *Journal of Cryptology,* 4(1):3–72, 1991.
3. W. Feller. *An Introduction to Probability Theory and its Applications.* New York: Wiley, 3rd edition, Volume 1, 1968.
4. R. G. Gallager. *Low Density Parity Check Codes.* MIT Press, Cambridge. Mass., 1963.
5. G. Hornauer, W. Stephan, and R. Wernsdorf. Markov ciphers and alternating groups. *Advances in Cryptology, EUROCRYPT 93, Lecture Notes in Computer Science, vol. 765, T. Helleseth ed., Springer-Verlag,* pages 453–460, 1994.
6. X. Lai. *On the design and security of block ciphers.* ETH Series in Information Processing, editor J. Massey, Hartung-Gorre Verlag Konstanz, 1992.
7. X. Lai, J. Massey, and S. Murphy. Markov ciphers and differential analysis. In *Advances in Cryptology, EUROCRYPT 91, Lecture Notes in Computer Science, vol. 547, D. W. Davies ed., Springer-Verlag,* pages 17–38, 1991.
8. M. Matsui. Linear cryptanalysis of DES cipher (I). (version 1.03) private communication.
9. M. Matsui. Linear cryptanalysis method for DES cipher. *Advances in Cryptology, EUROCRYPT 93, Lecture Notes in Computer Science, vol. 765, T. Helleseth ed., Springer-Verlag,* pages 386–397, 1994.
10. W. Meier and O. Staffelbach. Nonlinearity criteria for cryptographic functions. *Advances in Cryptology, EUROCRYPT 89, Lecture Notes in Computer Science, vol. 434, J.-J. Quisquater, J. Vandewalle eds., Springer-Verlag,* pages 549–562, 1990.
11. K. Nyberg and L. R. Knudsen. Provable security against differential cryptanalysis. *Advances in Cryptology, CRYPTO 92, Lecture Notes in Computer Science, vol. 740, E. F. Brickell ed., Springer-Verlag,* pages 566–574, 1993.
12. I. Palásti. On the strong connectedness of random graphs. *Studia Sci. Math. Hungar.,* 1:205–214, 1966.

How to Strengthen DES Using Existing Hardware

Eli Biham* Alex Biryukov**

Abstract. Differential, linear and improved Davies' attacks are capable of breaking DES faster than exhaustive search, but are usually impractical due to enormous amounts of data required. In [20] Wiener designed a million dollar special purpose computer capable of breaking DES in 3.5 hours in average by exhaustive search. In this paper we describe methods of strengthening DES against exhaustive search, differential attacks, linear attacks and improved Davies' attacks that can be applied on existing DES hardware. We use the fact that there are DES chips in the market that permit replacement of the S-boxes. We introduce the concept of key-dependent invariant S-box transformations. Differential and linear properties of the cipher are invariant under these transformations. We show how to expand the key using such transformations. Possible reorderings of S-boxes are discussed; we present orders of the original DES S-boxes which are slightly stronger than the standard order of S-boxes. Finally we suggest a concrete scheme to strengthen DES which uses the methods described above. This modified DES can be used with existing DES hardware and is much stronger than the standard DES.

1 Introduction

Since the Data Encryption Standard was introduced [17], its 56-bit key size was subject to criticism of the research community [10, 9]. It was considered to be too short to withstand exhaustive search attack on a special purpose computer. Recent results [20] show that with todays technology such computer will cost about a million US$ and will be able to find a key in 3.5 hours in average.

In parallel, many researches invested a great effort to cryptanalyze DES. Their work lead to development of two powerful methods of cryptanalysis of iterative ciphers: differential cryptanalysis [2] and linear cryptanalysis [14]. Recently Davies' attack [8] has been improved to be capable of breaking DES faster than exhaustive search [3]. Those are the only known methods of breaking DES faster than half of exhaustive search; they require huge amounts of 2^{47},2^{43} and 2^{50} plaintexts, respectively.

These attacks are very important for our understanding of the design principles of good cryptosystems. The fact that these attacks on DES are impractical

* Computer Science Department, Technion - Israel Institute of Technology, Haifa 32000, Israel.

** Applied Mathematics Department, Technion - Israel Institute of Technology, Haifa 32000, Israel.

(due to the enormous amounts of data required) is a result of a careful design. Still the real threat to the practical use of DES is its short secret key.

Several suggestions were made in the last two decades in order to strengthen DES: increase of the number of rounds from 16 to 32, 64 or even more [10], multiple encryption or larger key size[9], independent subkeys (768 bits) [1], dramatic increase of the key scheduling complexity [13, 19] and others. Not considering security features of these solutions we note that most of them either require the design of new hardware or decrease encryption speed considerably.

The standard of DES[17] requires hardware implementation. During the last two decades many different DES chips were developed. All these chips will become useless if the standard is to be modified or substituted. Some of these chips were designed with this fact in mind, and they allow the user to choose his favorite S-boxes as a replacement to the standard S-boxes (for example see [18]).

In this paper we describe new methods to strengthen DES against the attacks mentioned above. These methods require no hardware replacement, whenever the existing hardware can load alternative S-boxes. Our changes to DES are based on loading new S-boxes. We introduce the concept of key-dependent invariant S-box transformation. These transformations preserve the properties of the S-boxes related to differential and linear attacks. We show how to increase the key size using these transformations, resulting in a dramatical increase of the complexity of exhaustive search. Possible reorderings of the S-boxes are discussed. In [2] it is shown that some modified orders of the S-boxes weaken DES; we present several modified orders of the S-boxes of DES that slightly increase strength against both differential and linear attacks. We give an example of an order for which linear attacks require 2^{58} known plaintexts and differential attacks require 2^{48} chosen plaintexts.

Recently Kim, Park and Lee suggested a new set of DES-like S-boxes (which they call – s^3DES). We believe that this set is more secure than the original set against differential and linear attacks (when the order of $S1$ and $S2$ is reversed). We use this set to strengthen our modified DES. We also show that random key dependent S-boxes (as in Khufu [16]) might weaken DES.

Finally we suggest a concrete scheme, which uses s^3DES S-boxes and has a longer key. This modified DES can be used with existing DES hardware and is claimed to be stronger than DES in a view of linear and differential attacks. Exhaustive search of the whole key space is infeasible in this suggested scheme, due to the longer key size.

2 Notations

Throughout this paper, the following notations are used.

n_b A binary number n is denoted with the subscript b (e.g. $110000_b = 48$).
n_x A hexadecimal number n is denoted with the subscript x (e.g. $10_x = 16$).
$E_K(P)$ The encryption of 64-bit plaintext block P under the key K.

K_d A 56-bit subkey (of our scheme) which is entered to the (original) DES key scheduling algorithm.
K_i The i-th round 48-bit subkey of K_d.
$E(\cdot)$ The expansion operation of DES.

3 Possible Directions

Our aim is to develop methods that can strengthen DES (against exhaustive search, and differential and linear attacks) that require no additional investments in hardware. We also do not want to slow down the performance of encryption. Since some hardware implementations of DES permit to change S-boxes, we suggest several ways to change them with a positive effect on the security of DES. It is clear that these changes should be made very carefully since the S-boxes are a vital part of DES and the strength of the algorithm crucially depends on their choice. For example in [2] it was shown how even negligible changes to the S-boxes of DES can make differential attacks much more successful. Most previous attempts to suggest alternative S-boxes for DES actually weakened the resultant cryptosystem, since the designers of the new S-boxes were not aware of crucial design principles of DES. We suggest three approaches to reach this goal.

3.1 Key-Dependent S-Box Transformations

Our first suggestion is to create a new S-box by a transformation of an existing S-box by XORing a six-bit key material $K_a[s]$ before the S-box substitution and XORing a four-bit key material $K_b[s]$ to the output of the S-box (see Figure 1). An equivalent description of the same suggestion XORs a 48-bit subkey K_a to the expanded input of the F-function, and XORs a 32-bit subkey K_b to the result of the S-boxes, before the P permutation. Note that the same K_a and K_b are used in all the rounds during encryption. It is clear that this operation is XOR-linear and does not influence differential or linear cryptanalysis. The improved Davies' attack can become only more complicated. Constant K_a has no influence on the attack, since inputs are considered to be random. Constant K_b has no influence on even distributions and produces 16 variations of the odd distributions (permutation of rows and columns), like D_7 (which is used for the improved attack). This way one can gain up to 80 new key bits (In the following subsections we discuss the number of effective key bits that can be gained this way).

These additional XORs with constant keys induce some transformations of S-boxes, so the new set of S-boxes must be calculated from an old set of S-boxes when a new key is chosen. Consider the following transformation of some abstract S-box $\mathcal{S}$, where $K_a[s]$ is the value of the six bits of K_a which enter $\mathcal{S}$ and $K_b[s]$ is the value of the four bits of K_b which are XORed to the output of $\mathcal{S}$:

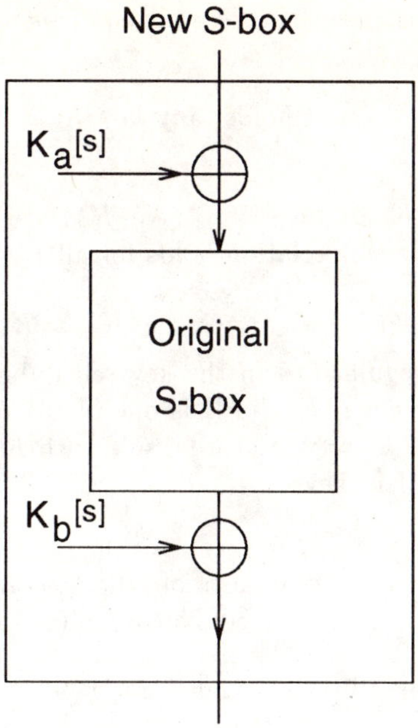

Fig. 1. New S-box.

$$(T_{K_a[s]K_b[s]}\mathcal{S})(x) = \mathcal{S}(x \oplus K_a[s]) \oplus K_b[s] \tag{1}$$

The effect of $K_a[s]$ on $\mathcal{S}$ is a transposition of rows according to the value of the two outmost bits of $K_a[s]$ and a transposition of columns according to the four inner bits of $K_a[s]$. The effect of $K_b[s]$ on $\mathcal{S}$ is an independent transposition of each row. In order to get a new set of S-boxes one must perform the operation described in equation (1). This approach does not influence differential and linear attacks. Thus it cannot make the cipher stronger or weaker against these attacks. The approach marginally strengthens the cipher against the improved Davies' attack. However, it increases the key size considerably in order to thwart exhaustive search. In the following subsections, we study several important properties of the resultant cipher.

Equivalent Keys

Definition 1 Two keys K_1 and K_2 are equivalent if $E_{K_1}(P) = E_{K_2}(P)$ for any P.

Assumption 1 If two keys $K = (K_a, K_b, K_d)$, $K^* = (K_a^*, K_b^*, K_d^*)$ are equivalent, then

$$K_i \oplus K_a = K_i^* \oplus K_a^*, \quad i = 1 \ldots 16 \quad \text{and} \quad K_b = K_b^*. \tag{2}$$

Clearly, if (2) holds, then the two keys are equivalent. The question is whether there are equivalent keys.

Theorem 1 If the assumption holds, any key $K = (K_a, K_b, K_d)$ has exactly three equivalent keys.

Proof If two triplets (K_a, K_b, K_d), (K_a^*, K_b^*, K_d^*) are equivalent, according to the assumption, the following relation holds for all 16 subkeys:

$$K_1 \oplus K_1^* = K_2 \oplus K_2^* = \ldots = K_{16} \oplus K_{16}^* = K_a \oplus K_a^* = Const \qquad (3)$$

Due to the known regularities in the key scheduling algorithm of DES [7], equation (3) holds only when $K_d \oplus K_d^*$ is one of the four known weak keys. If $K_d \oplus K_d^* = 0$ then $K_a \oplus K_a^* = 0$, and we result with $K = K^*$. Thus, any key K has exactly three equivalent keys.
Q.E.D.

Corollary 1 For any pair of weak keys of DES K_d, K_d^* and for any K_a, there exists K_a^* such that (K_a, K_b, K_d) is equivalent to (K_a^*, K_b, K_d^*), for any K_b.

Proof Equation (3) holds since the weak keys produce sets of constant subkeys.
Q.E.D.

Corollary 2 For any pair of the semi-weak keys of DES K_d, K_d^* and for any K_a, there exists K_a^* such that (K_a, K_b, K_d) is equivalent to (K_a^*, K_b, K_d^*), for any K_b.

Proof A pair of semi-weak keys suits (3) since if a key K_d generates the set of subkeys:

$$K_1 \ldots K_{16} = s, t, t, t, t, t, t, t, s, s, s, s, s, s, s, t.$$

then its counterpart K_d^* generates the set:

$$K_1^* \ldots K_{16}^* = t, s, s, s, s, s, s, s, t, t, t, t, t, t, t, s.$$

Thus $K_i \oplus K_i^* = s \oplus t = K_a \oplus K_a^* = Const \neq 0$ for any $i = 1 \ldots 16$.
Q.E.D.

The key space is divided into equivalence sets of size four: each key has three equivalents. These key equivalences cancel the effect of two key bits.

Since DES S-boxes are nonlinear, set of all transformations $T_{K_a K_b}$ contains 2^{80} different transformations, or in other words no two pairs (K_a,K_b) and (K_a^*,K_b^*) generate the same set of S-boxes. This is proved by the following corollary of Theorem 1.

Corollary 3 If the assumption holds, no two different pairs (K_a, K_b) and (K_a^*, K_b^*) are equivalent.

Proof If there are two equivalent pairs (K_a, K_b) and (K_a^*, K_b^*), then for any K_d, (K_a, K_b, K_d) is equivalent to (K_a^*, K_b^*, K_d^*), and by the proof of Theorem 1, no two equivalent keys have the same K_d.
Q.E.D.

Complementation Property In this section we show that the method of invariant S-box transformations possesses a strong complementation property, which cancels the effect of 32 out of the 48 bits of K_a.

Consider a pair of keys (K_a, K_b, K_d) and (K_a^*, K_b, K_d). K_a can be divided into two keys: 16 bit internal key K_a^i and 32 bit external key K_a^e, where $K_a = E(K_a^e) \oplus E^*(K_a^i)$, E is the expansion of DES, and E^* takes bits indexed $2j, 2j+1$ in K_a^i ($j \in [0,7]$) into bits $6j, 6j+1$ while all the other 32 bits are set to zero. Thus, we receive an equivalent description of our scheme that contains the short internal key K_a^i on each round and K_a^e is XORed to both halves of data entering the cipher after IP and leaving the cipher before IP^{-1}. This external key is ineffective since it does not take part in the encryption process. As a result of this and of the equivalences described in the previous section, (K_a, K_d, K_b) can be searched 2^{34} times faster than full exhaustive search with a chosen plaintext attack similar to the attack on the complementation property of DES (factor 2^{32} due to the complementation property and factor 2^2 due to equivalent keys).

For this shortcut we need 2^{32} chosen plaintexts representing all possible values of $P_i = P \oplus (i,i)$ encrypted into C_i under the unknown key. P is encrypted under all keys $K = (K_a, K_b, K_d)$ where $K_a = E^*(K_a^i)$ (i.e., $K_a^e = 0$), and two fixed bits of K_d (one in each half) are zero. Then we search for P_i for which $C_i = C \oplus (i,i)$ (this can be done efficiently with a lookup table). Such a P_i suggests the key $(E(i) \oplus E^*(K_a^i), K_b, K_d)$. Since the key is longer then the blocksize, we need to verify this suggested key with additional ciphertexts. This attack described above uses 32 complementation properties and two key equivalences (see section 3.1). The complementation property of DES is included in these 34 redundancies. Thus, the number of the additional effective key bits is 47 rather than 80.

Weak and Semi-Weak Keys

Definition 2 A key K is called a weak key if $E_K(E_K(P)) = P$ for any P.

Definition 3 A pair of keys K_1 and K_2 are called semi-weak keys if $E_{K_1}(E_{K_2}(P)) = E_{K_2}(E_{K_1}(P)) = P$ for any P.

All the known weak keys of DES have symmetric subkeys, st. $K_1 = K_{16}$, $K_2 = K_{15}$, etc. (actually $K_1 = K_2 = \ldots = K_{16}$). All the known pairs of semi-weak keys of DES have: $K_1 = K_{16}^*$, $K_2 = K_{15}^*$,…,$K_{16} = K_1^*$.

Lemma 1 Let K_d be a weak (or semi-weak) key of DES of the form described above. Then, for any K_a, and K_b, the key $K = (K_a, K_b, K_d)$ is a weak (semi-weak) key of our scheme.

Lemma 2 For any two semi-weak keys of DES (not necessarily from one pair) for which $K_d \oplus K_d^*$ is a weak key, and for any K_a, there exists K_a^* such that for any K_b the pair of keys (K_a, K_b, K_d) and (K_a^*, K_b, K_d^*) is a pair of semi-weak keys of our scheme.

Related Keys Consider a pair of new keys with difference $(\triangle K_a, \triangle K_b, 0)$, where $\triangle K_a^i = 0$. The maximal probability of $\triangle K_a \to \triangle K_b$ by the F-function of DES is 1/4. Then if the plaintext difference is $(\triangle K_a^e, \triangle K_a^e)$, the ciphertext difference will be the same with probability $\frac{1}{2^{32}}$. Though the keys used are unknown the relation between them leaks relation between possible ciphertexts. We estimate that there are no relations with probability higher than $\frac{1}{2^{32}}$. In order to use this property for an attack, the attacker must be able to choose relations between keys, making such an attack to be of theoretical interest only. There are several ways to avoid weak choices of related keys in this scheme. One of them is to hash the key with a hash function in order to create K_a and K_b. Then, an attacker will not be able to find a pair of keys with the required relation.

Equivalent Representations of Our Scheme This scheme is equivalent to the following scheme which has no K_b, but has two different K_a's used in different rounds: No XOR with the key is performed after the S-boxes. In rounds 1,4,5,8,9,12,13,16 there is a XOR with K_a^1 = original K_a before the S-boxes and in rounds 2,3,6,7,10,11,14,15 there is a XOR with $K_a^2 = E(P(\text{original } K_b)) \oplus K_a^1$ before the S-boxes.

3.2 Key-Dependent Reorderings of the S-Boxes

In this section we show that more than 256 good reorderings of DES S-boxes exist. We suggest to increase the key size by 8 bits using these reorderings.

In [2] it was shown that many changes to the order of the S-boxes can make DES much weaker. One can ask the question whether the standard order of the S-boxes is optimal. In [6] it is stated that somewhat reduced probability p of $\psi \to 0$ in case of three active S-boxes was designed into DES (design rule S-8 in [6]).

In order to find good orders, we must solve an optimization problem, finding the maximal probability p for each possible order of the eight S-boxes ($7! = 5040$ orders, rather than 8!, since the analysis is invariant for cyclic reorderings). The characteristics $\psi \to 0$ with only three adjacent active S-boxes takes place in DES if the input differences of these S-boxes are of the forms $00xy11_b \to 0$, $11xy10_b \to 0$, $10xy00_b \to 0$ respectively. Table 1 describes the standard order of the S-boxes in terms of the maximal entries in the difference distribution tables for each pattern. Table 2 shows the maximal probabilities of the two-round iterative characteristics for the standard order of the S-boxes. We can see that p is reached when the first three S-boxes are active, with $p = \frac{1120}{64^3}$. From Table 1 we can see also that the order $S1, S7, S4, \ldots$ [2] (the order of the remaining S-boxes is irrelevant) is the worst, giving the highest probability of two round iterative characteristic ($p = \frac{14 \cdot 16 \cdot 16}{64^3} \approx \frac{1}{73}$). Clearly, any rotation of the order of the S-boxes does not change p, thus, the orders come in sets of eight orders.

A program was written to solve the described optimization problem. It found $136 \cdot 8$ orders for which the maximal probability of a two-round iterative characteristic is as in DES or smaller. Among those, $32 \cdot 8 = 256$ orders have probability

S box	$00xy11_b$	$11xy10_b$	$10xy00_b$
1	14	6	12
2	6	8	10
3	8	8	10
4	8	16	16
5	8	4	8
6	6	8	10
7	8	16	14
8	8	8	10

Table 1. Maximal values corresponding to the entries $00xy11_b \to 0$, $11xy10_b \to 0$, $10xy00_b \to 0$ in difference distribution tables of DES S-boxes.

Active S-boxes	$Prob(\psi \to 0)(\cdot 2^{-18})$
1,2,3	1120
2,3,4	768
3,4,5	1024
4,5,6	320
5,6,7	896
6,7,8	960
7,8,1	768
8,1,2	480

Table 2. Standard order of the S-boxes, maximal probabilities of two-round iterative characteristic for pattern $\psi \to 0$.

lower than in DES: $p = \frac{1024}{64^3} = \frac{1}{256}$. We performed extensive analysis for one of these *best* orders. Table 3 describes the order: $S1, S5, S6, S7, S8, S2, S4, S3$.

This order has two characteristics with maximal probability: $00007940_x \to 0$ and $00007B40_x \to 0$ both with probability $\frac{1}{256}$. For this particular order the complexity of differential attack becomes $(\frac{1}{256})^6 = 2^{-48}$ instead of $(\frac{1}{234})^6 = 2^{-47.2}$. This is not a major gain against differential attack; however, quite surprisingly this order of S-boxes makes Matsui's linear attack infeasible since it requires 2^{58} known plaintexts.

The improved Davies' attack suggests that $32 \cdot 8$ orders out of $136 \cdot 8$ are weaker than the original order of the S-boxes by a factor of 4–5 in terms of required known plaintexts and complexity of the attack. These are all the orders where S_8 comes after S_2 or S_4. Among the $32 \cdot 8$ *best* differential orders $18 \cdot 8$ are weaker under Davies' attack. These results can be verified easily by looking at Figure 9 in [8].

Several papers study the influence of reorderings of the S-boxes in the view of linear cryptanalysis [4, 15]. It is stated that the current order of the S-boxes is relatively weak against linear cryptanalysis, and that most of the orders strengthen DES against this attack. We estimate that we can choose out of the pool of

Active S-boxes	$Prob(\psi \to 0)(\cdot 2^{-18})$
1,5,6	560
5,6,7	896
6,7,8	960
7,8,2	640
8,2,4	1024
2,4,3	960
4,3,1	768
3,1,5	384

Table 3. New order of the S-boxes: $S1, S5, S6, S7, S8, S2, S4, S3$, maximal probabilities of two-round iterative characteristic for pattern $\psi \to 0$.

$104 \cdot 8$ orders that are strong as DES or better against differential and improved Davies' attacks, at least 256 orders *strong* against differential, linear and improved Davies' cryptanalysis and add 8 new bits to the key which will decide the order of S-boxes in use. This increases the complexity of exhaustive search by a factor of 256. A variant of the attack on the full 16-round DES described in [2] can be performed for this modification of DES with metastructures covering $15 \cdot 8 = 120$ different characteristics which suffice for the all orders. It requires about 2^{51} chosen plaintexts.

The approach described in this section strengthens marginally against linear, differential, improved Davies' and exhaustive search attacks.

3.3 Using Alternative DES-Like S-Boxes

One can compute several different sets of S-boxes according to the design principles of DES, and use additional key bits to control which set is used. The key size is increased by $\log(\mathcal{N}_{sets})$ bits. The problem with this approach is that we need to perform a thorough check for each set of S-boxes against all known attacks. The storage of the S-boxes is increased by the factor of $\mathcal{N}_{sets}$, but the scheme is strengthened by a smaller factor.

Another approach is to add new design principles to DES. This was already done in [11]. Their s^3DES S-boxes suit all the published design principles of DES plus one more — two inputs with difference $11xy10_b$ cannot have the same output. This property prohibits three adjacent active S-boxes to cause zero output difference (in DES this is possible with probability about $\frac{1}{234}$ — which was intentionally lowered by the designers [6]). Moreover, in s^3DES all the eight S-boxes should be active in order to have such effect. This lowers the probability of the two-round iterative characteristic used to attack the full 16-round DES to 2^{-96} (independent of the order of the S-boxes). Knudsen[12] found a four-round iterative characteristic of s^3DES. The iteration of this characteristic to 13 rounds has probability about $2^{-66.5}$, but there is a 16-round linear approximation of s^3DES with probability about $\frac{1}{2} \pm 2^{-26}$, for which an attack requires about 2^{43} known plaintexts. However, if we reverse the order of $S1$ and $S2$ of s^3DES, then the best known differential characteristic has probability about $2^{-63.6}$ and the best linear approximation has probability $\frac{1}{2}+2^{-33.7}$ [5]. In [3] it is shown that s^3DES is immune to the improved Davies' attack. Thus, it is predicted that this variant of the s^3DES S-boxes is much more secure than the standard set of S-boxes of DES.

The properties of the S-boxes that we used in sections 3.1 and 3.2 also hold for the S-boxes of s^3DES, and thus this suggestion can be used simultaneously with the previous ones.

3.4 Random Key-Dependent S-Boxes

S-boxes are probably the most studied and still the most mysterious parts of DES. Since most attacks start from an analysis of the S-boxes, one of the methods, that makes cryptanalysis more complex is to hide the S-boxes, and to make them key-dependent. For example, Khufu [16] is more secure than Khafre [16, 2] although they are very similar, only because of the hidden key-dependent S-boxes.

In [2] a study of DES with known random S-boxes is described. It is shown that 97% of the random sets of S-boxes are vulnerable to differential attack with only 2^{21} chosen plaintexts. Here we analyze a more general case of unknown random S-boxes in which the S-boxes are key-dependent. We will show that approximately 10% of the resultant sets of S-boxes are breakable with only 2^{26} chosen plaintexts.

Table 4 describes approximate distribution of patterns of type $00xy00_b \rightarrow 0$ in random S-boxes. This table is a result of testing 100000 sets of eight random S-boxes. We see that patterns $00xy00_b \rightarrow 0$ with probability $\frac{1}{4}$ or better take place only in 1.7% of all the sets and with probability $\frac{1}{8}$ or better in 97% of all sets (as shown in [2]). Thus, in 97% of the sets, some two-round iterative characteristic with pattern $00xy00_b \rightarrow 0$ has probability higher or equal to $\frac{1}{8}$, and the corresponding 13-round characteristic has probability higher or equal to 2^{-18}. However, we do not know exactly which pattern succeeds. There are 24 different patterns of this type (three for each S-box). Therefore, we should use all the 24 characteristics that cover all the possible patterns.

Using the first round trick of the full 16-round attack on DES [2], we get a 2R-attack with 2^{13} structures, each structure contains 2^6 chosen plaintexts producing 2^9 different pairs of each of the three patterns $00xy00_b \neq 000000_b$. Each structure contains a right pair for each pattern with probability $2^{-18} \cdot 2^5 = 2^{-13}$. The plaintext difference is of the form (v, ψ) where ψ is some input difference in two middle bits to a particular S-box and v is some output difference of this S-box (at most four bits differ). This attack has a very high S/N since 36 bits of the ciphertext XOR must be zero (or easily predictable) so we can discard almost all wrong pairs.

The attack is as follows: In the first phase of the attack on DES with key-dependent S-boxes we find all the patterns with probability $\frac{1}{8}$ or higher using $8 \cdot 2^{13} \cdot 2^6 = 2^{22}$ chosen plaintexts. During the attack, we do not know a-priori the actual probability of the characteristics. However, after we identify the right

Number of occurrences	Percentage of random S-box sets for which pattern $00xy00_b \to 0$ takes place with probability as below or better					
	6/64	8/64	10/64	12/64	14/64	16/64
0	100.0	100.0	100.0	100.0	100.0	100.0
1	100.0	97.1	68.4	27.8	7.5	1.7
2	99.9	85.7	30.9	4.0	0.3	0.0
3	99.4	65.2	10.0	0.4	0.0	0.0
4	97.5	41.7	2.5	0.0	0.0	0.0
5	92.9	22.2	0.5	0.0	0.0	0.0
6	83.6	10.0	0.1	0.0	0.0	0.0
7	69.9	3.8	0.0	0.0	0.0	0.0
8	53.0	1.3	0.0	0.0	0.0	0.0
9	36.0	0.3	0.0	0.0	0.0	0.0
10	21.7	0.1	0.0	0.0	0.0	0.0
11	11.6	0.0	0.0	0.0	0.0	0.0
⋮	⋮	⋮	⋮	⋮	⋮	⋮
24	0.0	0.0	0.0	0.0	0.0	0.0

Table 4. Distribution of patterns $00xy00_b \to 0$ in random S-boxes.

pairs, we can find an approximation of the probability of the pattern $00xy00_b \to 0$ for each S-box by the formula:

$$P(00xy00_b \to 0) = \sqrt[6]{\frac{N_{rightpairs}}{N_{allpairs}}}. \tag{4}$$

In the second phase, we perform a massive attack on the concrete patterns which were found in the first phase in which we find most values of the active S-box, which we denote by S. We use the right pair(s) that we already identified and continue the 2R-attack described above in order to find more right pairs. In the first round we have $\psi \to v$. Since we do not know both the S-box S and the key, we will hide the XOR with K_1 on the first round inside the S-box S. Denote by P_L and P_R left and right halves of the plaintext. Then we obtain the following formula for the active S-box:

$$S(P_R[s]) \oplus S(P_R^*[s]) = P_L[s] \oplus P_L^*[s] = v \tag{5}$$

Only the S-box S is unknown in (5), thus we get four bits of this S-box. There can be 32 different right pairs suggesting new S-box bits. We organize these 32 pairs with their v in a table. Thus we get $32 \cdot 4$ bits of particular S-box out of total $64 \cdot 4$. In order to find bits of the key we need to know another pattern of type $\psi \to \phi$ from the last round. Such pattern can be found in a 1R-attack. With the same data which we used to find 32 right pairs ($2 \cdot 32 \cdot 2^{18} = 2^{24}$ chosen plaintexts) we expect to find about four right pairs for a 1R-attack. Now by hiding K_{16} in S-box on the last round we can get a part of another table for the same S-box. These two tables can be used in order to find 5 key bits of $K_1 \oplus K_{16}$. In the last 16th round $\phi \rightarrow \eta$, where ϕ is the output difference of the F-function on the 15th round ($\psi \rightarrow \phi$). Since ϕ differs in inputs to at most six S-boxes, using the same 32 right pairs we can gain up to $6 \cdot 4 \cdot 32$ bits of these S-boxes.

If we have two patterns $\psi_1 \rightarrow \phi_1$ and $\psi_2 \rightarrow \phi_2$ for the same S-box then we can find $48 \cdot 4$ bits of this S-box and a sixth bit of the key $K_1 \oplus K_{16}$. In general each new pattern for S-box reduces the number of the unknown S-box bits by a factor of two. So we need about six different patterns to find all the bits of the S-box except four bits which cannot be found with this method. As seen from Table 4, the chances for several patterns with probabilities greater or equal than $\frac{1}{8}$ are very high. For example, for about 10% of the keys we can find all the bits of the S-boxes except four for each and about 30–40 bits of $K_1 \oplus K_{16}$ using 2^{26} chosen plaintexts and for about 84% it can be found using 2^{29} chosen plaintexts. Later we can complete the key using other auxiliary techniques.

Due to this weakness of the key-dependent random S-boxes of DES, we do not recommend to use this method in our proposed scheme.

4 Modified DES Scheme

In this section we present our concrete scheme of modified DES. We suggest to use s^3DES S-boxes with a reversed order of $S1$ and $S2$, instead of the standard DES S-boxes, since they are more resistant to differential cryptanalysis. It is also possible to use our scheme with the standard DES S-boxes. Our scheme uses keys of the form (K_a, K_b, K_c, K_d) where:

K_a Consists of 16 bits. It is expanded by E^* (described in section 3.1) to 48 bits and is then XORed to the input of the S-boxes in all the rounds.

K_b Consists of 32 bits. It is XORed to the output of the S-boxes in all the rounds.

K_c Consists of 8 bits if DES S-boxes are used and consists of 15 bits if s^3DES S-boxes are used. These bits decide the order in which the S-boxes are loaded. Each combination of bits corresponds to one of the *strong* orders of the S-boxes.

K_d Consists of 56-bits. It is loaded to the DES key scheduling algorithm.

Remark: The choice of a 16-bit K_a (rather than 48-bit) eliminates key equivalences and most complementation properties discussed in sections 3.1, 3.1. Two complementation properties still remain — one is the famous complementation property of DES and another is of the following type: Let

$$\tilde{P} = P \oplus 7FFF80007FFF8000_x,$$
$$\tilde{K}_a = K_a \oplus C00000C00000_x,$$
$$\tilde{K}_i = K_i \oplus FFFFFF000000_x.$$

Then

$$C = E_K(P) \Rightarrow \tilde{C} = E_{\tilde{K}}(\tilde{P}).$$

The E expansion prohibits existence of this complementation property in DES (see also [10]). In order to eliminate the two complementation properties in our scheme, we can fix one bit of each half of K_d, effectively reducing its size to 54 bits.

The key in our scheme (K_a,K_b,K_c,K_d) consist of $16+32+8+56=112$ bits in case of DES S-boxes and $16+32+15+56=119$ bits for s^3DES S-boxes. In order to change the keys during encryption, it is now required not only to change the 56-bit DES key. We should also compute the S-boxes and load them to the hardware. The following algorithm generates the S-boxes:

1. Take s^3DES S-boxes (or standard DES S-boxes) and reorder them according to K_c (using K_c as an index to a table of strong orders).
2. For each S-box S_i, $i = 1 \ldots 8$ in the received order, perform the transformation under the two bits $(2i-2, 2i-1)$ of K_a that are XORed to the input of $\mathcal{S}_i$ and the four bits of K_b XORed to the output of $\mathcal{S}_i$ according to the following formula ($K_a[s]$ is used to denote the two bits of K_a padded with four zero bits and $K_b[s]$ is used to denote the four bits of K_b which correspond to the input and the output of the S-box $\mathcal{S}$ respectively):

$$\mathcal{S}_{new}(x) = \mathcal{S}_{original}(x \oplus K_a[s]) \oplus K_b[s] \tag{6}$$

3. The resultant S-boxes are loaded into the hardware and K_d is loaded into DES keys scheduling algorithm.

Those who prefer to simplify key processing slightly (and reduce the space, required for keeping the table of orders), can eliminate the reorderings and ignore K_c, thus using keys of the form (K_a,K_b,K_d). We suggest to use in such case the s^3DES S-boxes, with the reversed order of $S1$ and $S2$.

We claim that our scheme is more secure than s^3DES or DES against differential, linear and improved Davies' attacks and that an exhaustive search requires more than trillion years on Wiener's machine [20]. Its main advantage is that organizations can increase the security of their systems which use DES in hardware, with the same hardware they use today. An additional advantage is the backward compatibility to the standard DES, that can be achieved by choosing $K_a = K_b = 0$ and K_c which does not modify the order of the S-boxes. Table 5 compares the security of the variants of our scheme and the standard DES.

5 Summary

In this paper we described methods of strengthening DES against exhaustive search, differential, and linear attacks that can use existing hardware, without slowing encryption speed. We used the fact that there are DES chips on the market that allow the user to load S-boxes of his choice (for example [18]).

The concept of key-dependent invariant S-box transformation was introduced. We showed several ways to expand the key of DES. Possible reorderings

Scheme	Number of Key Bits	Complexity of Attack: Exhaustive	Differential	Linear	Im.Davies'
DES	56	2^{55}	2^{47}	2^{43}	2^{50}
Our scheme with:					
DES S-boxes	112	2^{110}	2^{51}	2^{53}	2^{52}
s^3DES S-boxes	119	2^{117}	2^{66}	2^{64}	∞
s^3DES w/o reorders	104	2^{102}	2^{66}	2^{64}	∞

Table 5. Comparison of our scheme with DES.

of S-boxes were discussed, and orders that are better than the standard order of the S-boxes were shown. We gave an example of better orders for which a linear attack needs 2^{58} plaintexts. We discussed s^3DES S-boxes. We claimed that this set of S-boxes is far more secure than the standard set. We have also shown that the replacement of the standard S-boxes by random key dependent S-boxes might weaken DES.

Finally we suggested a concrete scheme which uses s^3DES S-boxes and has a longer key. This scheme can be used with existing DES hardware and is claimed to be stronger than DES in view of differential, linear and improved Davies' attacks, and especially in view of exhaustive search.

References

1. Thomas A. Berson, *Long key variants of DES*, Advances in Cryptology, Proceedings of CRYPTO'82, pp. 311 – 313, 1982.
2. Eli Biham, Adi Shamir, *Differential Cryptanalysis of the Data Encryption Standard*, Springer-Verlag, 1993.
3. Eli Biham, Alex Biryukov, *An Improvement of Davies' Attack on DES*, Proceedings of EUROCRYPT'94, to appear.
4. Eli Biham, Alex Biryukov, Uwe Blöcher, Markus Dichtl, *Modifications of DES and their Effect on Differential and Linear Cryptanalysis*, unpublished paper, 1994.
5. Ishai Ben-Aroya, Eli Biham, *A Systematic Method to Find Characteristics*, unpublished paper, 1993.
6. Don Coppersmith, *The Data Encryption Standard (DES) and its Strength Against Attacks*, IBM Journal of Research and Development, Vol. 38, No. 3, pp. 243–250, May 1994.
7. D.W. Davies, *Some Regular Properties of the 'Data Encryption Standard' Algorithm*, Advances in Cryptology, Proceedings of CRYPTO'82, pp. 89 – 96, 1982.
8. D.W. Davies, *Investigation of a Potential Weakness in the DES Algorithm*, private communications, 1987.
9. Whitfield Diffie, Martin Hellman, *Exhaustive Cryptanalysis of the NBS Data Encryption Standard*, IEEE Computer, Vol. 10, No. 6, pp. 74 – 84, June 1977.
10. M. Hellman, R. Merkle, R. Schroeppel, L. Washington, W. Diffie, S. Pohlig, P. Schweitzer, *Results of an Initial Attempt to Cryptanalyze the NBS Data Encryption Standard*, Information Systems Laboratory Report, Stanford University, November 1976.

11. Kwangjo Kim, Sangjun Park, Sangjin Lee, *Reconstruction of s^2DES S-boxes and their Immunity to Differential Cryptanalysis*, Proceedings of JW-ISC93 – Korea-Japan Joint Workshop on Information Security and Cryptology, Seoul, Korea, October 24–26, 1993.
12. Lars Knudsen, *An Analysis of Kim, Park and Lee's DES-like S-boxes*, private communication, June 1993.
13. Lars Knudsen, *On the Design of Secure Block Ciphers*, Fast Software Encryption, Proceedings of Cambridge security workshop, pp. 9 – 11, December 1993.
14. Mitsuru Matsui, *Linear Cryptanalysis Method for DES Cipher*, Proceedings of EUROCRYPT'93, pp. 386 – 397, 1993.
15. Mitsuru Matsui, *On Correlation Between the Order of S-boxes and the Strength of DES*, Proceedings of EUROCRYPT'94, to appear.
16. Ralph C. Merkle, *Fast Software Encryption Functions*, Lecture Notes in Computer Science, Advances in Cryptology, Proceedings of CRYPTO'90, pp. 476 – 501, 1990.
17. National Bureau of Standards, *Data Encryption Standard*, Federal Information Processing Standards Publication 46, January 1977.
18. SuperCrypt, *High Speed Cryptographic Data Security Element*, Preliminary Data Sheet.
19. J.-J. Quisquater, Y. Desmedt, M. Davio, *The Importance of 'Good' Key Scheduling Schemes*, Proceedings of CRYPTO'85, pp. 537 – 542, 1985.
20. M. J. Wiener, *Efficient DES Key Search*, technical report TR-244, School of Computer Science, Carleton University, Ottawa, Canada, May 1994. Presented at the Rump session of CRYPTO'93, August 1993.

RUMP SESSION

Chair: Rei Safavi-Naini

(University of Wollongong, Australia)

Some Cryptographic Properties of exponential Functions

Xingong Chang[1], Zong-Duo Dai[2] and Guang Gong[3]

[1] Dept. of Math., University of Science and Technology of China, Hefei, China
[2] State Key Lab. of Information Security, Dept. of Math., Graduate School, Academia Sinica, 100039-08, Beijing, China, E-Mail: lois.@bepc2.ihep.ac.cn
[3] Dept. of App. Math., University of Chengdu Electronic Science and Technology, Chengdu, Sichuan, China

Abstract. Some cryptographic properties such as linear structure, SAC and nonlinearity of Exponential boolean functions and permutations on $GF(2)^n$ are studied in this paper.
Keywords: exponential permutation, linear structure, SAC, nonlinearity

1 Introduction

Exponential permutations on n dimensional linear space $GF(2)^n$ with proper cryptographic properties have important applications in cryptology. In this paper we study some cryptographic properties such as linear structure, SAC and nonlinearity of exponential boolean functions and exponential permutations on $GF(2)^n$. The main results are: 1. The exponential boolean functions with linear dimension being equal to zero are completely classified. 2. A class of exponential permutations satisfying SAC is found. 3. A lower bound of the nonlinearities of boolean functions is given. 4. A relation between the nonlinearities of exponential boolean functions and the periodic cross correlations of two m-sequences is given, and the nonlinearities of the exponential permutations for some options of exponents are given.

2 Definitions

Let $x = (x_1, x_2, \cdots, x_n)$, and let $f(x)$ and $f_i(x)$ be boolean functions on $GF(2)^n$. Let $\mathbf{f} = (f_1(x), f_2(x), \cdots, f_n(x))$ be a transformation on $GF(2)^n$. A point $\alpha = (a_1, a_2, \cdots, a_n)$ is called a linear structure [5] of $f(x)$, if $f(x) + f(x+\alpha)$ is a constant. The set of all linear structures of f, denoted by $\mathcal{L}_f$, is a linear subspace of $GF(2)^n$, and the dimension of $\mathcal{L}_f$, denoted by $dim(\mathcal{L}_f)$, is called linear dimension of f. The function f satisfies the propagation criterion(PC) [5] with respect to the point α if the function $f(x+\alpha)+f(x+\alpha)$ is balanced; and f satisfies strict avalanche criterion(SAC) [7] if f satisfies PC with respect all points α with $w(\alpha) = 1$; and $\mathbf{f}$ satisfies SAC if $f_i(x)'s$ satisfy SAC. Let $\mathcal{R}_f$ be the set of all points α with respect to which the function f does not satisfy PC. The size of $\mathcal{R}_f$, denoted by $|\mathcal{R}_f|$, is unchanged under the affine transformations. The integer $N(f) = \min_\varphi\{w(f+\varphi)\}$ ($N(\mathbf{f}) = min\{N(\sum_{i=1}^n a_i f_i(x))|a_i \in GF(2)\}$) is called the nonlinearity of f ($\mathbf{f}$), where φ runs over all possible affine functions on $GF(2)^n$. The boolean function f can be uniquely represented in the form of a polynomial as follows

$$f(x) = \sum a_{i_1,i_2,\cdots,i_n} x_1^{i_1} x_2^{i_2} \cdots x_n^{i_n}$$

where $(i_1, i_2, \cdots, i_n)$ runs over all binary n-tuples, $a_{i_1,i_2,\cdots,i_n} \in GF(2)$, $x_i^0 = 1, x_i^1 = x_i$, the integer $N_a(f) = \max\{\sum_{j=1}^n i_j | a_{i_1,i_2,\cdots,i_n} = 1\}$ ($N_a(\mathbf{f})$ =min $\{N_a(\sum_{i=1}^n a_i f_i)|a_i \in GF(2)\}$) is called the algebraic nonlinear degree of f ($\mathbf{f}$).

3 Main Results

Let c be an integer, $1 \leq c \leq 2^n - 1$, $\gcd(c, 2^n - 1) = 1$, and let $\beta \in GF(2^n)$, and let $\alpha^* = \{\alpha_i | 1 \leq i \leq n\}$ and $\beta^* = \{\beta_i | 1 \leq i \leq n\}$ be two bases of $GF(2^n)$ over $GF(2)$, and let $Tr(x)$ be the trace function from $GF(2^n)$ to $GF(2)$. Let $x^c_{\beta,\alpha}(x)$ and $\mathbf{x}^c_{\beta^*,\alpha^*}(x)$ be defined as follows:

$$x^c_{\beta,\alpha^*}(x) = Tr(\beta(\sum_{i=1}^n x_i\alpha_i)^c) \tag{1}$$

$$\mathbf{x}^c_{\beta^*,\alpha^*}(x) = (\mathbf{x}^c_{\beta_1,\alpha^*}(x), \mathbf{x}^c_{\beta_2,\alpha^*}(x), \cdots, \mathbf{x}^c_{\beta_n,\alpha^*}(x)) \tag{2}$$

which will be called the exponential boolean function and the exponential permutation on $GF(2)^n$, respectively.

Theorem 1. *Let $c = 1 + 2^k$, $d = \gcd(k, n)$. For the exponential permutation $\mathbf{x}^c_{\beta^*,\alpha^*}(x)$ on $GF(2)^n$, we have*

1. *$\mathbf{x}^c_{\beta^*,\alpha^*}(x)$ satisfies SAC if and only if $\beta_j \alpha_i^{1+2^k} \notin GF(2^d)\ \forall i, j$.*
2. *With k and α^* fixed, the number of distinct permutations of the form $\mathbf{x}^c_{\beta^*,\alpha^*}(x)$ satisfying SAC is not less than $\prod_{i=0}^{n-1}(2^n - 2^i - n(2^d - 1))$.* □

The exponential permutations x^c with $w(c) = 2$ are studied in literature (e.g. [4].)

Theorem 2. *For the exponential boolean function $x^c_{\beta,\alpha^*}(x)$, we have*

1. *$\dim(\mathcal{L}_{x^c_{\beta,\alpha^*}}) = 0$ if and only if $w(c) > 2$.*
2. *If $c = 1 + 2^k$, then $\mathcal{L}_{x^c_{\beta,\alpha^*}} = \mathcal{R}_{x^c_{\beta,\alpha^*}} = (\beta^{-1}GF(2^d))^e$ and $\dim(\mathcal{L}_{x^c\beta,\alpha^*}) = d$, where $e(1+2^k)^{-1} \equiv 1 \pmod{2^n - 1}, d = \gcd(k, n)$.* □

Theorem 3. *Let $f(x_1, x_2, \cdots, x_n)$ be a boolean function, then*

1. *$N(f) \geq 2^{n-1} - \sqrt{|R_f|2^{\frac{n}{2}-1}}$*
2. *If f is balanced and satisfying SAC, then $N(f) \geq \max\{2^{n-2}, 2^{n-1} - \sqrt{|R_f|2^{\frac{n}{2}-1}}\}$* □

Table 1.

c	$N(\mathbf{x}^c_{\beta^*,\alpha^*})$	$N_a(\mathbf{x}^c_{\beta^*,\alpha^*})$	n
2^k+1	$2^{n-1}-2^{\frac{n+e}{2}-1}$	2	$e=\gcd(k,n)$ n/e odd
$\frac{2^{k(n+1)}-1}{2^{2k}-1}$ $*_1$,	$2^{n-1}-2^{\frac{n+e}{2}-1}$	$\frac{n+1}{2}$	$\gcd(k,n)=1$ n odd
$2^{2k}-2^k+1$	$2^{n-1}-2^{\frac{n+e}{2}-1}$	$k+1$	$e=\gcd(k,n)$ n/e odd
$\frac{2^{mk}+1}{2^k+1}$	$2^{n-1}-2^{\frac{n+e}{2}-1}$	$k\frac{m-1}{2}+1$	$e=\gcd(k,n)$ n/e , m odd
$2^{n/2+1}-1$	$2^{n-1}-2^{n/2}$	$n/2+1$	$n\equiv 0 \pmod 4$
$\frac{1}{3}(2^{n+1}+2^{n/2+1}-1)$ $*_2$	$2^{n-1}-2^{n/2}$	$n/2+1$	$n\equiv 0 \pmod 4$
$(2^m-1)(2^{2m}+1)+2$	$2^{4m-1}-2^{3m-1}$	$m+2$	$n=4m$
$2^{n/2}+3$	$2^{n-1}-32^{n/2-1}$	3	$n=4m$ $(n>4)$
$\frac{1}{3}(2^n-1)+2^i$	$2^{n-1}-\frac{2^{n-1}+2^{n/2+\delta(r)}}{3}$ $*_3$	$n/2+1$	n even $r\equiv 0,1 \pmod 3$, $*_3$
$2^{n-1}-1$	$\geq 2^{n-1}-2^{n/2}$	$n-1$	

$*_1$: $\frac{2^{k(n+1)}-1}{2^{2k}-1}\equiv(2^k+1)^{-1} \pmod{2^n-1}$

$*_2$: $\frac{1}{3}(2^{n+1}+2^{n/2+1}-1)\equiv(2^{n/2+1}-1)^{-1} \pmod{2^n-1}$

$*_3$: $r\equiv\frac{2^{-i}(2^n-1)}{3}$ or 1 (mod 3), and

$$\delta(r)=\begin{cases}0, & r\equiv 0 \pmod 3 \ \textit{or}\ r\equiv 1 \pmod 3\ \textit{and}\ n/2\equiv 0 \pmod 2\\ 1, & r\equiv 1 \pmod 3\ \textit{and}\ n/2\equiv 1 \pmod 2\end{cases}$$

Remark: The first part of Theorem 3 is stimulated by Theorem 1 of [5].

Let γ be a primitive element of $GF(2^n)$, and let $\mathbf{u}=\{u_k\}$ and $\mathbf{v}=\{v_k\}$ be two m-sequences of period 2^n-1 whose elements are given by $u_k=Tr(\gamma^k)$ and $v_k=Tr(\gamma^{ck})$ respectively. Let $C_c(\tau)=\sum_0^{2^n-2}(-1)^{v_k+u_{k+\tau}}$, and let $M_0=\max\{C_c(\tau)\mid C_c(\tau)\geq 0\}$, and $M_1=\max\{-C_c(\tau)\mid C_c(\tau)\leq 0\}$, and $P_c=\max_{0\leq\tau<2^n-1}|C_c(\tau)|$.

Theorem 4. *1.* $N(\mathbf{x}^c_{\beta^*,\alpha^*})=\begin{cases}2^{n-1}-\frac{M_0+1}{2}, & M_0+2\geq M_1\\ 2^{n-1}-\frac{M_1-1}{2}, & M_0+2<M_1\end{cases}$

2. $N(\mathbf{x}^c_{\beta^*,\alpha^*})=2^{n-1}-\frac{P_c+\delta}{2}$, *with* $\delta=0$ *or* 1 *or* -1. □

In terms of Theorem 4 and the well-known results on the values of $C_c(\tau)$ [1], [2], [3], [6], we can obtain the following

Theorem 5. *The nonlinearities of the exponential permutations* $\mathbf{x}^c_{\beta^*,\alpha^*}(x)$ *on* $GF(2)^n$ *for some options of exponents is written in Table 1.*

Acknowledgment: This extended abstract was finished while Zong-Duo Dai was a visitor of the Centre for Computer Security Research at the Department of Computer Science, University of Wollongong, NSW, Australia in December 1994.

References

1. Tor Helleseth, Some Results about the Cross-Correlation Function between Two Maximal Linear Sequences, Discrete Mathematics, Vol.16, 1976, pp.209-232.
2. Y.Niho, Multi-values Cross-Correlation Function between Two Maximal Linear Recursive Sequences, Ph.D. Dissertation, Univ. of Southern California, Los Angeles, CA(1972).
3. K.Nyberg, Differentially Uniform Mappings for Cryptography, Lecture Notes in Computer Science, Advances in Cryptology, Proceedings of EUROCRYPT'93, 1993.
4. Josef P.Pieprzyk, Non-Linearity of Exponent Permutations, Lecture Notes in Computer Science, Advances in Cryptology, Proceedings of EUROCRYPT'89, pp.80-92, 1989.
5. J.Seberry, X.M.Zhang, and Y.Zheng, Structure of cryptographic functions with strong avalanche characteristics, Pre-proceedings of AISACRYPT'94, pp.96-106.
6. M.K.Simmon, J.K.Omura, R.A.Scholtz, B.K.Levitt, Spread Spectrum Communication, Vol.I, Computer Science Press, Inc., 1985, Chapter 5.
7. A.F.Webster and S.E.Tavares, On the design of S-boxes, Lecture Notes in Computer Science 219, Advances in Cryptology, Proceedings of CRYPTO'85, pp.523-534, 1986.

Factoring: The DNA Solution

Donald Beaver

Penn State University, State College, PA 16802, USA

Abstract. We consider molecular models for computing and derive a DNA-based mechanism for solving intractable problems through massive parallelism. In principle, such methods might reduce the effort needed to solve otherwise difficult tasks, such as factoring large numbers. We investigate the application of such techniques to cryptography.

1 Introduction

Until recently, most computer scientists regarded computational devices as being essentially the same: according to a complexity-theoretic strengthening of the Church-Turing thesis, it seemed not only that computational devices are capable of computing the same class of results (recursive ones) but moreover they do so with roughly the same efficiency (polynomial differences in running time). Building on the work of others, Shor recently gave algorithms for factoring and discrete logarithm using a quantum computer, a probabilistic Turing machine whose state transitions follow quantum-mechanical laws [Sho94]. These transitions are such that, roughly speaking, an exponential number of paths are followed, but only certain paths, each corresponding to a solution, are ultimately observable. The question arises whether other computational models might escape the "polynomial bonds" of Turing-like devices.

Adleman suggested a positive answer [A94], showing how a series of molecular reactions could solve a 7-node Hamiltonian Path problem.[1] Since Hamiltonian Path is an NP-complete problem and hence outside the known range of polynomial-time computational devices, a solution to this problem suggests that molecular computers might also escape polynomial bounds.

We construct a polynomial-step molecular experiment to illustrate how the massive parallelism supplied by molecular-scale miniaturization might help solve intractable problems. We discuss the application of our techniques to the well-known cryptographic problem of factoring large numbers and discuss whether molecular-scale computing is indeed a fundamentally new model, a threat to current cryptographic key sizes, or merely a pleasant curiosity (from the viewpoint of a cryptographer).

---

[1] The Hamiltonian Path problem is to find a simple path that visits every node of a graph precisely once – or alternatively, at least to report whether such a path exists.

2 Computing with DNA

As usual, evolution has beaten us to the punch, having translated "CPU" as "DNA" millions of years ago. DNA, or deoxyribonucleic acid, encodes our genes and much (if not all) of the operation of our cells, using a four-letter alphabet of bases, abbreviated A, C, T, and G. As a long string of characters (*e.g.* ACTTAGACCATG), a strand of DNA bears strong similarity to a Turing machine's tape. Unfortunately, many simple and desirable operations on such strings are nontrivial from a molecular and chemical standpoint.

Fortunately, many other simple operations are feasible. Life reproduces its DNA by copying, and the polymerase chain reaction (PCR) duplicates this feat on a massive scale. DNA is normally double-stranded, with a complementary sequence running along the opposite strand according to pairing rules: A is paired with T, and C with G. Thus ATTGTC will line up with its Watson-Crick complement, TAACAG. One can heat DNA to separate double strands into single strands, and after attaching suitable "primers," one can use DNA polymerase to copy single strands by synthesizing their complements. In a single such reaction, the number of copies of a strand can be doubled; with repetition, an exponential number of strands can be made.

Other tools follow Nature's lead as well. For example, bacteria wage biological warfare using restriction enzymes (RE's), which can cut up foreign DNA containing certain patters – a sort of anti-password. For example, Eco RI finds the sequence $\begin{smallmatrix}\text{GAATTC}\\\text{CTTAAG}\end{smallmatrix}$ and cuts it into two: $\begin{smallmatrix}\text{G}\phantom{\text{TTAA}}\\\text{CTTAA}\end{smallmatrix}$ $\begin{smallmatrix}\text{AATTC}\\\phantom{\text{AATT}}\text{G}\end{smallmatrix}$ Notice that Eco RI does not cut straight through: it leaves two short ends with single-stranded DNA flailing about. These bare ends can later realign with their original partner or some other complementary end floating about in solution. (DNA ligase is used to seal the "nick" in the DNA backbone that remains even after the complementary portions pair up.)

The art of recombinant DNA is based on such operations: permit DNA with rough ends to seek out partners and combine. The vast numbers of DNA molecules in a solution allow a myriad of combinations to occur, including those in which a new gene is inserted – or those in which a string representing a random pair of factors or a solution to an NP-complete problem is generated.

Unfortunately, RE's seldom recognize sequences longer than 6 bases, meaning that only a small finite number of short patterns can be found and cut. Fortunately, DNA sequences (oligonucleotides) can be synthesized to order, permitting the recombination of bare ends to occur without needing RE's to produce the ends in the first place.

The sequence of DNA in a given strand can be determined, although this is infeasible to do for all the molecules in a given solution (unless they are identical). Molecules can be separated by length by placing them on an agarose gel and applying electrical current to draw them through; smaller molecules travel faster and end up in bands (according to length) further down along the gel.

Thus, we can imagine we have the following primitives at hand: (1) duplication and amplification of a strand; (2) creation of polynomial-length strands (oligonucleotides); (3) large-scale recombination of bare, complementary single strands; (4) separation by length.

3 NP Complete Problems

If all you have is a hammer, everything looks like a nail. Since DNA is linear and the set of tools to manipulate it is limited, some problems are more suitable than others for computation using DNA chemistry. Granted, any string can be written in the 4-letter language of DNA. But how is one to take two base-4 strings of DNA, each representing a number, and then come up with another base-4 string representing their product? Such a goal is quite nontrivial, both abstractly (using only the given primitives) and chemically (at the lab bench).

The Hamiltonian Path problem is a natural candidate, since its solution is merely a line through a graph. No costs are associated with the edges or vertices, and no abstract logical or mathematical manipulation is needed. Given a candidate solution, we need only check whether (1) it is of the proper length and whether (2) it visits any vertex twice.

If we encode edges as DNA, we can use the massive parallelism of molecular interactions to generate many combinations of edges, and then select and amplify those which encode a path visiting each vertex exactly once. If no such path exists, no such molecule will be found. We sketch a solution derived without reference to [A94].

Assume a standard encoding ϕ of numbers and strings into the four-letter alphabet {A,C,T,G}, and let $\overline{\phi}$ be the Watson-Crick complement of the encoding.[2]

Given graph $G = (V, E)$ with $V = \{v_1, \ldots, v_n\}$, source v_1 and destination v_n, do the following. Let $Z(i, j, s)$ be the oligonucleotide:

$$\underline{\overline{\phi}(\text{“step } s,\ v_i,\ v_i\text{”})\qquad\qquad}$$
$$\qquad\qquad\overline{\qquad\qquad\phi(\text{“step } s+1,\ v_j,\ v_j\text{”})}$$

(The reason for repeating vertices will be clear in a moment.) Let L and R be the following oligonucleotides, containing short random primer sequences LP and RP for the PCR reaction:

$$L\text{: }\ \overline{\text{LP}\ \phi(\text{“step } 1,\ v_1,\ v_1\text{”})} \qquad\qquad R\text{: }\ \underline{\overline{\phi}(\text{“step } n-1,\ v_n,\ v_n\text{”})\ \text{RP}}$$

For each edge $(i, j) \in E$ and for each $s \in \{1, \ldots, n-1\}$, synthesize $Z(i, j, s)$. Synthesize L and R. Mix these fragments and allow the ends to anneal (seal nicks with ligase). It is not hard to see that the only molecules containing both LP and RP will be those consisting of exactly n fragments, encoding a *path* from v_1 to v_n. Use PCR to amplify them.

We now extract those molecules that encode a *Hamiltonian* path, namely those containing exactly one occurence of each vertex. This is not so trivial with our limited toolbox. For each v_i, do the following. Lengthen every molecule by, say, 20 bases for each occurrence of "v_i, v_i", by denaturing and incubating

[2] Some care is needed for practical reasons: single strands can interact with themselves to form loops, or mildly with other strands that are not fully complementary. Suitable designs or simple randomization reduces this probability.

with single-stranded $\phi(v_i)$ATATATATATATATATATAT$\phi(v_i)$. The ends anneal with occurrences of "v_i, v_i", effectively inserting a loop[3] of 20 bases. After sealing nicks and amplifying with PCR, the results are separated by length, and only those molecules having increased by exactly 20 bases are retained.

After these n operations, the only surviving molecules are those which encode a Hamiltonian path.[4] Since the path may not be unique, this answers only the question of existence. Additional simple manipulations to discover a path are possible, however.

(In Adleman's experiment [A94], "step numbers" are not used. Instead, initial candidates of varying length are generated, and then separated by length to retain paths of length $n-1$. Moreover, selection of *Hamiltonian* paths uses a primitive not included here, essentially by grabbing on to paths containing v_i, using $\overline{\phi}(v_i)$ attached to magnetic beads. As in our independently derived method above, this requires n repetitions, one for each vertex.)

4 Cryptography

Rough calculations show that these methods for solving NP-complete problems are not likely to pose a threat to cryptography in the near future. Consider factoring a 1000-bit number by any standard reduction to Hamiltonian Path (*cf.* [CLR90], pp. 954-959). This gives a graph with at least 10^6 nodes. It is probably safe to underestimate the number of possible paths at 2^{10^6}. Thus, on the order of $2^{10^6} \approx 10^{300,000}$ candidate molecules are needed. Vastly underestimating the size of DNA as that of H_2O, we have:

$$\frac{10^3\text{g/l} \cdot 6.02 \cdot 10^{23}\text{molec/mol}}{18.0\text{g/mol}} << 10^{30} molec/l.$$

Thus, far more than $10^{300000}/10^{30} >> 10^{200000}$ liters of solution would be needed, an amount that perhaps would have unsettled the biblical Noah.

What is easily overlooked is the fact that such methods will not scale well. Unless and until a constructive proof that P=NP is found, the "solution" of an NP-complete problem is highly misleading. Even in the case of factoring, if every path in a superpolynomial computation is assigned a molecule, then a superpolynomial number of molecules will be needed. Merely fitting these molecules into a polynomial volume is an impossible task, but a necessary one: if the molecules are going to have enough time to mix and react, then light must be able to pass from one side of the test tube to the other within polynomial time. This impossible task does fortunately expose new avenues for further research, leaving open the question of whether black-hole algorithms for factoring exist.

[3] A palindrome is suggested to stabilize the unpaired single-strand portion as a loop, but it is not necessary. Other minor biochemical modifications may be helpful.

[4] Using loops of cleverly chosen, different lengths, the repetitions can be avoided.

References

[A94] L. Adleman. "Molecular Computation of Solutions to Combinatorial Problems." *Science* **266** (November 1994), 1021–1024.

[CLR90] T. Cormen, C. Leiserson, R. Rivest. Introduction to Algorithms. New York: McGraw Hill, 1990.

[Sho94] P. Shor. "Algorithms for Quantum Computation: Discrete Logarithms and Factoring." *Proceedings of the* 35th *FOCS,* IEEE, 1994, 124–134.

Can one design a signature scheme based on error-correcting codes?

Jacques Stern

Laboratoire d'Informatique, École Normale Supérieure

Abstract. In this note, we show that the signature scheme based on error-correcting codes which has been proposed during the ASIACRYPT'94 conference and appears in this volume (see [1]) is not secure. The attack involves gathering a few hundred signatures. ¿From then on, only elementary linear algebra is used.

1 The Use of Error-Correcting Codes in Cryptography.

Since the appearance of public key cryptography, there has been a continuous line of research aiming at the discovery of alternatives to the standard techniques based on arithmetical properties of large numbers. In order to achieve such a program, error-correcting codes seemed quite attractive. As soon as 1978, a public key cryptosystem based on the use of Goppa codes was proposed by Mc Eliece in [3]. This cryptosystem is still standing. Concerning the problem of identification, a scheme was proposed by the author in [4]. This time, random codes with no specific structure were used. It is of course possible to turn our authentication scheme into a signature scheme by the standard technique that replaces queries from the verifier by values suitably obtained from the message to sign together with the initial commitments of the prover (see [2]). Unfortunately, this yields rather long and therefore a bit unpractical signatures. All attempts to design a signature scheme based on error-correcting codes and having reasonable signature length have failed (see the references of [1]). We will show that the same is true with the scheme proposed in the present volume ([1]).

2 The Attack.

The scheme appearing in [1] is a bit intricate. Actually, it is not really necessary to understand the technical details of key generation, signature generation and signature check in order to follow our attack. We will focus on the weak part of the scheme which lies in the following equation, litterally taken from [1].

$$\underline{s}_j = \{\underline{e}_j \oplus f(\underline{m}_j, \underline{e}_j)W_A \oplus \underline{x}_j W_A^{-R} G_A\} P_A$$

In the above, W_A and G_A are secret $(k \times n)$ matrices, and P_A is a secret $(n \times n)$ matrix. W_A^{-R} is a known $(n \times k)$ matrix. Also, $\underline{s}_j$, $\underline{e}_j$, $\underline{x}_j$ and $f(\underline{m}_j, \underline{e}_j)$ are known row vectors, the first three of dimension n and the last one of dimension k. $\underline{s}_j$,

$\underline{x}_j$ are part of the signature and $\underline{e}_j$ is computed during signature check, as well as $f(\underline{m}_j, \underline{e}_j)$.

We write $\underline{y}_j$ in place of $\underline{x}_j W_A^{-R}$. Of course all matrices and vectors are over the two element field.

Now, the above equation provides a known linear equation between the coefficients of the unknown matrices P_A, $W_A P_A$ and $G_A P_A$. More precisely, each signature gives n scalar equations since both sides of the equation are n-bit vectors. Since there are $n(2n + k)$ unknowns, it should take something like $2k + n$ signatures to solve the system. Once this is done, P_A, $W_A P_A$ and $G_A P_A$ are known and new signatures can be easily manufactured.

It turns out that the above argument is not completely correct. In order to get the requested conclusion, we need to have a sample of vectors $\mathbf{z}_j = \{\underline{e}_j, f(\underline{m}_j, \underline{e}_j), \underline{y}_j\}$ that generate the whole $2k+n$-dimensional space. There is a subtle point here: although the row vectors $\underline{y}_j$ and $f(\underline{m}_j, \underline{e}_j)$ are basically random, the vectors $\underline{e}_j$, are randomly chosen among n-bit vectors with a prescribed number t of ones (error patterns). Thus, if t is even, there is no way the $\mathbf{z}_j$ can generate the whole space since they are all included in the hyperplane consisting of vectors with an even number of ones among the first n bits.

Let F_N be the space generated by the $\mathbf{z}_j$ after N signatures have been collected. If F_N is not the entire space, let H_N be a hyperplane containing F_N and let $h = 0$ be a cartesian equation of this hyperplane. Now if the linear functional h has some non zero coefficient among the last $2k$ ones, then, it is easily seen that with probability $1/2$, the next signatures takes you outside H_N. This shows that we will very quickly come up with a situation where h has its $2k$ trailing coefficients equal to zero. We call such a situation *favourable*. At this point, the $\mathbf{z}_j$ generate a subspace of the form $E \times F_2^{2k}$ and the linear application corresponding to the matrix obtained by appending the blocks P_A, $W_A P_A$ and $G_A P_A$ is known on this subspace. Especially P_A is known on E and $W_A P_A$ and $G_A P_A$ are completely determined.

Note that, in the above situation, it is already possible to sign whenever a vector of weight t can be found in E: this can be easily checked by going into the construction of [1]. Also note that, if no such vector can be found in E the next signature will provide one. This enables us to estimate an upper bound on the numbers of signatures required in order to issue a new unauthorized signature. After N signatures, the probability that a favourable situation has not been reached is bounded above by the probability of getting less than $2k+n$ heads after tossing a fair coin N times. Using classical estimates on binomial coefficients, this is equivalent to $2^{N(H_2(\lambda)-1)}$, where $\lambda = \frac{2k+n}{N}$ and H_2 is the entropy function defined by $H_2(x) = -x \log_2 x - (1-x)\log_2(1-x)$. This upper bound quickly decreases when N increases. In [1] the following dimensions are suggested

- $n = 128$ and $k = 65$ in which case$2k + n = 258$. The above probability is bounded by 0.0027 for $N = 600$.
- $n = 256$ and $k = 152$ in which case$2k + n = 560$. The above probability is bounded by 0.069 for $N = 1200$.

Thus, as announced, a few hundred signatures are enough to break the scheme. Furthermore, our analysis is overly pessimistic and a favourable situation is presumably reached much earlier than what is suggested by the bounds.

3 Can the Scheme be Rescued?

We do not think the scheme can be rescued. Of course, suggestions can be made in order to make the attack slightly more difficult: for example the error vector $\underline{e}_j$ could be computed from say $\underline{m}_j$ by deterministic hashing. Note that this suggestion does not appear in [1] (the same way the discussion about odd and even weights was not present in the paper included in the preproceedings). For this reason, we will only offer a qualitative analysis.

As the numbers of known signatures increases, the vector space denoted by E in our above analysis grows. We distinguish two cases

1. if t (the weight of error vectors) is odd, then E ultimately covers the whole space
2. if t is even, then E ultimately covers the whole hyperplane consisting of vectors of even weight

In both cases, any message can ultimately be signed, even for the tentatively "repaired" version of the scheme. Note that, in some unlucky cases, the convergence can be a bit slow, for example if we get "stuck" in some hyperplane whose equation is a linear functional with a single variable. Then, it will take an average of n/t signatures to get out. Again, a quantitative worst-case analysis based on these unlucky cases would be overly pessimistic and the generic case should converge fast enough.

References

1. M. Alabbadi and S. B. Wicker, A digital signature scheme based on linear error-correcting block codes, this volume.
2. A. Fiat and A. Shamir, How to prove yourself: Practical solutions to identification and signature problems, *Proceedings of Crypto 86*, Lecture Notes in Computer Science 263, 181-187.
3. R. J. McEliece, Public key cryptosystem based on algebraic coding theory, JPLDSN Progress Report 42-44, Jet Propulsion Laboratory, California Institute of Technology, Pasadena, CA, USA, January and February 1978, 114-116.
4. J. Stern, A new identification scheme based on syndrome decoding. *Proceedings of Crypto 93*, Lecture Notes in Computer Science 773, 13-21.

DESV-1: A Variation of the Data Encryption Standard (DES)

G.Carter[2] A.Clark[1] and L.Nielsen[1]

[1] Information Security Research Centre
[2] School of Mathematics
Queensland University of Technology

Abstract. This paper introduces a variation of the Data Encryption Standard (DES), called DESV-1, describes its implementation, and analyses it using the principles of differential cryptanalysis, showing its resistance to this attack. Indications are that as few as eight rounds of DESV-1 will give the same security as sixteen rounds of the DES, but the question is still open.

1 Description and Implementation of DESV-1

Whilst most modifications of the DES [3] involve increasing the key size, DESV-1 has the same structure and key size as the DES with the exception that the exclusive-or (XOR) operation used is replaced by an operation denoted $\otimes$ which has as input, the output of the S-boxes, called A, and the right half of the previous round, called a, where A and a are 32-bit blocks. Each can be thought of as eight successive 4-bit subblocks labelled ${}_1A$, ${}_2A$, ..., ${}_8A$ and ${}_1a$, ${}_2a$, ..., ${}_8a$. The operation $\otimes$ is defined on these subblocks as ${}_jA \otimes {}_ja \equiv [{}_jA]_{10} \times [{}_ja]_{10}(modulo 17), 1 \leq j \leq 8$, where $\times$ denotes ordinary integer multiplication, and $[{}_jA]_{10}$ and $[{}_ja]_{10}$ are the decimal representation of the 4-bit blocks ${}_jA$ and ${}_ja$. The resulting eight 4-bit outputs of the operation $\otimes$ are concatenated and the result is the right half of the next round. Note that if ${}_jA$ or ${}_ja$ is the all-zero block, then $[{}_ja]_{10}$ (or $[{}_jA]_{10}$) is sixteen for the purpose of the operation $\otimes$. This same device was used in the cipher IDEA [2]. In one round of DESV-1 $L_i = R_{i-1}, 1 \leq i \leq n-1$ and $R_i = F(R_{i-1}, K_i) \otimes L_{i-1}, 1 \leq i \leq n-1$. The modulo 17 multiplication is performed by means of a look-up table, and the required inverses are similarly obtained. When compared to the DES in software implementation, there is approximately a 20% increase in the time taken for encryption and decryption. Complete mixing of bits occurs faster in DESV-1 than in the DES. Analysis of the plaintext avalanche effects of both ciphers indicates that, at worst, complete mixing of bits occurs in one fewer round in DESV-1. DESV-1 is also more resistant than the DES to differential cryptanalysis, as will be shown in Section 2.

2 Differential Cryptanalysis of DESV-1

The notion of difference will be as for the DES; that is, given X and X^*, the difference, $X' = X \oplus X^*$ where $\oplus$ indicates the XOR operation [1]. The initial attempt to define the difference X' to be $X \otimes (X^*)^{-1}$ where $\otimes$ is the modulo 17 multiplication and $(X^*)^{-1}$ is the multiplicative inverse (modulo 17) of X^* failed, as the principles of differential cryptanalysis require expressions of the type $(X \oplus K) \otimes (X^* \oplus K)^{-1}$ to eliminate the key, leaving $X \otimes (X^*)^{-1}$. This does not happen, hence the original notion of difference as it is used in the attack on the DES, is applied to the attack on DESV-1. Let a_i and a_i^* be 32-bit blocks which, after expanding and XORing with key K_i, are inputs to the F-function in round i of DESV-1. Let $a_i' = a_i \oplus a_i^*$. Let A_i and A_i^* be the respective outputs of F (after the permutation) for inputs $a_i \oplus K_i$ and $a_i^* \oplus K_i$. Let $A_i' = A_i \oplus A_i^*$. Thus, in round i, the 4-bit input differences to the operation $\otimes$ are ${}_jA_i'$ and ${}_ja_{i-1}', 1 \leq j \leq 8$. For given differences, a_i', Biham and Shamir determined A_i' with certain probability as per the so-called XOR tables [1]. In the DES, ${}_ja_{i+1}' = {}_jA_i' \oplus {}_ja_{i-1}'$ for *all* pairs $({}_jA_i, {}_jA_i^*)$ and $({}_ja_{i-1}, {}_ja_{i-1}^*)$. However, in DESV-1, in most cases, ${}_ja_{i+1}' \neq {}_jA_i' \otimes {}_ja_{i-1}'$. In fact, ${}_ja_{i+1}'$ will vary depending on the pairs $({}_jA_i, {}_jA_i^*)$ and $({}_ja_{i-1}, {}_ja_{i-1}^*)$. Thus, given ${}_jA_i'$ and ${}_ja_{i-1}'$, ${}_ja_{i+1}'$ can be determined only probabilistically. Such probabilities can be determined and can be tabulated in an XOR table which we will refer to as the XMOD table. It follows that the input difference to round $i+1$ can only be determined probabilistically from a knowledge of A_i' and a_{i-1}'. This probability is called a *cro ss probability*. The largest cross probability is $\frac{72}{256}$. If we define a characteristic in a similar manner to Biham and Shamir, its probability must incorporate such cross probabilities.

2.1 The Differential Attack on DESV-1

We have developed a theoretical attack that will work on any number of rounds of DESV-1 provided a characteristic of suitably high probability can be found. In the XMOD table we exploit the fact that, if the input differences to the operation $\otimes$ are 0 and 13, then the output difference will be 1, 9 or 13 with probability $\frac{148}{256} > 0.5$. Consider the last two rounds of an n-round version of DESV-1. The attack requires some of the 4-bit subblocks ${}_ja_{n-1}'$, $1 \leq j \leq 8$ to be zero blocks. This, generally, can be arranged with good probability by choosing a suitable characteristic. So we may suppose that such a zero block exists. Generate enough pairs so that the left ciphertext output difference, ${}_jC_L'$ equals thirteen. By examining all input pairs $({}_ja_{n-1}, {}_ja_{n-1}^*)$ to the operation $\otimes$ such that ${}_ja_{n-1}'$ equals zero, and all the output pairs $({}_jC_L, {}_jC_L^*)$ such that ${}_jC_L'$ equals thirteen, we can determine the other input difference to $\otimes$, ${}_jA_n'$. Note that if the pair $({}_jC_L, {}_jC_L^*) \in S$, where $S = \{(2,15),(3,14),(6,11),(7,10)\}$ then ${}_jA_n'$ equals 1, 9 or 13 with probability one rather than $\frac{148}{256}$; that is, ${}_jA_n'$ equals 0001, 1001 or 1101 always. Thus we can say that the first bit of ${}_jA_n'$ is one with probability $\frac{12}{16}$, the second bit is one with probability one half, the third bit is zero always, and the fourth bit is one always. The task is to generate enough pairs such that $({}_jC_L, {}_jC_L^*) \in S$. If this can be done, then certain bits of A_n' are known with high probability and the principles of differential cryptanalysis can be applied to find those keys which are involved in generating the first, third and fourth bits of ${}_jA_n'$. This attack has been successfully used on a four-round version of DESV-1, the characteristic being the one used by Biham and Shamir to break six rounds of the DES, $4008\,0000\,0400\,0000_x$, [1]. Generate enough pairs so that $({}_1C_L, {}_1C_L^*)$ and $({}_6C_L, {}_6C_L^*) \in S$. Thus, for such pairs, ${}_1A_4'$ and ${}_6A_4'$ will be 0001, 1001 or 1101 since ${}_1a_3'$ and ${}_1a_6'$ equals zero. Now, allowing for the permutation, this implies (using the bit numbering system 1,2,3,..,32) that bits 16 and 32 of the output difference of the F-function will each be one with probability $\frac{12}{16}$, bits 3 and 20 will have a difference of zero always, and bits 9 and 21 will have a difference of one always. Applying the differential cryptanalysis method, we find the keys to S-boxes 1,3,4,5,6 and 8 in the last round; that is thirty-six bits of the last-round key. If a minimum of 100,000 pairs are used then in all our trials all thirty-six bits of the key were found correctly. The characteristic with the highest probability is a compromise between the F-function probabilities and the cross probabilites. We have not yet found a method which yields the best compromise. The probability of this characteristic in the attack on DESV-1 is made up as follows: $\frac{1}{4} \times (\frac{24}{256} \times \frac{32}{256}) \times \frac{1}{32} \approx 2^{-13}$. The first factor in the above expression is the F-function probability from the XOR tables. The second factor, $(\frac{24}{256} \times \frac{32}{256})$, is the cross probability from Round 1 to Round 2 from the XMOD table. The last factor is the probability that, given ${}_ja_3'$ equals zero then $({}_jC_L, {}_jC_L^*) \in S$. Note that the cross probability from Round 2 to Round 3 is not required as it does not matter what the non-zero component of a_3' is. We only require some of the ${}_ja_3'$ to be zero.

2.2 Remarks on the Differential Attack

If we use Biham and Shamir's iterative characteristic, $1960\,0000\,0000\,0000_x$ [1] to attack any number of rounds, we can make some comparisons with the DES in regards to the complexity of the attack. To break n rounds of the DES this characteristic probability is given by $(\frac{14\times8\times10}{64^3})^{\frac{n-2}{2}}$ while for DESV-1 the corresponding probability is given by $\frac{1}{32}(\frac{14\times8\times10}{64^3})^{\frac{n-2}{2}}(\frac{40^2\times20}{256^3})^{\frac{n-2}{2}}$. These results are produced below in Table 1 for $n = 4, 8, 12, 16$ rounds. The iterative characteristic may not be the one with highest probability, so one cannot draw the conclusion that eight rounds of DESV-1 is as secure from a differential attack as fifteen rounds of the DES. However, it appears certain that fewer than sixteen rounds of DESV-1 will be as secure from a differential attack as the full sixteen round DES. This helps offset the loss of speed in encryption and decryption. The

$n =$	4	8	12	16
DES	2^{-8}	2^{-24}	2^{-40}	2^{-56}
DESV-1	2^{-22}	2^{-56}	2^{-90}	2^{-124}

Table 1. Probabilities of the Iterative Characteristics

iterative characteristic may not be the one with the best 16-round probability, but we can show that the probability of the best 16-round characteristic is at most 2^{-60} and, hence differential cryptanalysis is worse than exhaustive search. The figure of 2^{-60} is obtained by realising

that the best possible scenario for a characteristic path through sixteen round s of DESV-1 is that in any round, the middle two bits of the input difference ${}_j a_i'$ should be non-zero and the output difference ${}_k A_i'$ should contain only one non-zero bit. In this case, the largest crossing probability is $\frac{32}{256}$ and the largest S-box probability is $\frac{1}{4}$, hence the probability associated with each round is at best $(\frac{1}{4} \times \frac{32}{256})$. Using a 13-round characteristic in a 3R-attack, the best characteristic probability is given by $(\frac{1}{4} \times \frac{32}{256})^{12} \sim 2^{-60}$.

3 Conclusions and Further Research

As indicated earlier we have broken a four-round version of DESV-1 using differential cryptanalysis with 100,000 plaintext-ciphertext pairs. However, to date we have been unable to extend this attack past four rounds. Indications are that linear cryptanalysis will prove less efficient than differential cryptanalysis. We are investigating this. The fact that fewer rounds of DESV-1 will give the same security as sixteen rounds of the DES in relation to differential cryptanalysis, will more than offset the loss of speed in encryption and decryption. In the future, it is planned to investigate the extension of our attack to more than four rounds. We also plan

to look at replacing $\otimes$ with other Latin squares of order 16 or larger to see if they are cryptographically stronger than the one used, and, if so, by how much.

References

[1] E.Biham and A.Shamir. *Differential Cryptanalysis of DES- like Cryptosystems* Journal of Cryptology, 4(1):3-72, 1991.

[2] X.Lai and J.Massey. *A Proposal for a New Block Encryption Standard*, Advances in Cryptology: Proceedings of EUROCRYPT '90, Springer-Verlag, Berlin, pp 389-404, 1991.

[3] National Bureau of Standards (U.S.). *Data Encryption Standard (DES)*, tech.rep., Federal Information Processing Standards, 1977. Publication 46.

Author Index

Springer-Verlag and the Environment

We at Springer-Verlag firmly believe that an international science publisher has a special obligation to the environment, and our corporate policies consistently reflect this conviction.

We also expect our business partners – paper mills, printers, packaging manufacturers, etc. – to commit themselves to using environmentally friendly materials and production processes.

The paper in this book is made from low- or no-chlorine pulp and is acid free, in conformance with international standards for paper permanency.

Lecture Notes in Computer Science

For information about Vols. 1–840
please contact your bookseller or Springer-Verlag

Vol. 841: I. Prívara, B. Rovan, P. Ružička (Eds.), Mathematical Foundations of Computer Science 1994. Proceedings, 1994. X, 628 pages. 1994.

Vol. 842: T. Kloks, Treewidth. IX, 209 pages. 1994.

Vol. 843: A. Szepietowski, Turing Machines with Sublogarithmic Space. VIII, 115 pages. 1994.

Vol. 844: M. Hermenegildo, J. Penjam (Eds.), Programming Language Implementation and Logic Programming. Proceedings, 1994. XII, 469 pages. 1994.

Vol. 845: J.-P. Jouannaud (Ed.), Constraints in Computational Logics. Proceedings, 1994. VIII, 367 pages. 1994.

Vol. 846: D. Shepherd, G. Blair, G. Coulson, N. Davies, F. Garcia (Eds.), Network and Operating System Support for Digital Audio and Video. Proceedings, 1993. VIII, 269 pages. 1994.

Vol. 847: A. L. Ralescu (Ed.) Fuzzy Logic in Artificial Intelligence. Proceedings, 1993. VII, 128 pages. 1994. (Subseries LNAI).

Vol. 848: A. R. Krommer, C. W. Ueberhuber, Numerical Integration on Advanced Computer Systems. XIII, 341 pages. 1994.

Vol. 849: R. W. Hartenstein, M. Z. Servít (Eds.), Field-Programmable Logic. Proceedings, 1994. XI, 434 pages. 1994.

Vol. 850: G. Levi, M. Rodríguez-Artalejo (Eds.), Algebraic and Logic Programming. Proceedings, 1994. VIII, 304 pages. 1994.

Vol. 851: H.-J. Kugler, A. Mullery, N. Niebert (Eds.), Towards a Pan-European Telecommunication Service Infrastructure. Proceedings, 1994. XIII, 582 pages. 1994.

Vol. 852: K. Echtle, D. Hammer, D. Powell (Eds.), Dependable Computing – EDCC-1. Proceedings, 1994. XVII, 618 pages. 1994.

Vol. 853: K. Bolding, L. Snyder (Eds.), Parallel Computer Routing and Communication. Proceedings, 1994. IX, 317 pages. 1994.

Vol. 854: B. Buchberger, J. Volkert (Eds.), Parallel Processing: CONPAR 94 – VAPP VI. Proceedings, 1994. XVI, 893 pages. 1994.

Vol. 855: J. van Leeuwen (Ed.), Algorithms – ESA '94. Proceedings, 1994. X, 510 pages.1994.

Vol. 856: D. Karagiannis (Ed.), Database and Expert Systems Applications. Proceedings, 1994. XVII, 807 pages. 1994.

Vol. 857: G. Tel, P. Vitányi (Eds.), Distributed Algorithms. Proceedings, 1994. X, 370 pages. 1994.

Vol. 858: E. Bertino, S. Urban (Eds.), Object-Oriented Methodologies and Systems. Proceedings, 1994. X, 386 pages. 1994.

Vol. 859: T. F. Melham, J. Camilleri (Eds.), Higher Order Logic Theorem Proving and Its Applications. Proceedings, 1994. IX, 470 pages. 1994.

Vol. 860: W. L. Zagler, G. Busby, R. R. Wagner (Eds.), Computers for Handicapped Persons. Proceedings, 1994. XX, 625 pages. 1994.

Vol: 861: B. Nebel, L. Dreschler-Fischer (Eds.), KI-94: Advances in Artificial Intelligence. Proceedings, 1994. IX, 401 pages. 1994. (Subseries LNAI).

Vol. 862: R. C. Carrasco, J. Oncina (Eds.), Grammatical Inference and Applications. Proceedings, 1994. VIII, 290 pages. 1994. (Subseries LNAI).

Vol. 863: H. Langmaack, W.-P. de Roever, J. Vytopil (Eds.), Formal Techniques in Real-Time and Fault-Tolerant Systems. Proceedings, 1994. XIV, 787 pages. 1994.

Vol. 864: B. Le Charlier (Ed.), Static Analysis. Proceedings, 1994. XII, 465 pages. 1994.

Vol. 865: T. C. Fogarty (Ed.), Evolutionary Computing. Proceedings, 1994. XII, 332 pages. 1994.

Vol. 866: Y. Davidor, H.-P. Schwefel, R. Männer (Eds.), Parallel Problem Solving from Nature - PPSN III. Proceedings, 1994. XV, 642 pages. 1994.

Vol 867: L. Steels, G. Schreiber, W. Van de Velde (Eds.), A Future for Knowledge Acquisition. Proceedings, 1994. XII, 414 pages. 1994. (Subseries LNAI).

Vol. 868: R. Steinmetz (Ed.), Multimedia: Advanced Teleservices and High-Speed Communication Architectures. Proceedings, 1994. IX, 451 pages. 1994.

Vol. 869: Z. W. Raś, Zemankova (Eds.), Methodologies for Intelligent Systems. Proceedings, 1994. X, 613 pages. 1994. (Subseries LNAI).

Vol. 870: J. S. Greenfield, Distributed Programming Paradigms with Cryptography Applications. XI, 182 pages. 1994.

Vol. 871: J. P. Lee, G. G. Grinstein (Eds.), Database Issues for Data Visualization. Proceedings, 1993. XIV, 229 pages. 1994.

Vol. 872: S Arikawa, K. P. Jantke (Eds.), Algorithmic Learning Theory. Proceedings, 1994. XIV, 575 pages. 1994.

Vol. 873: M. Naftalin, T. Denvir, M. Bertran (Eds.), FME '94: Industrial Benefit of Formal Methods. Proceedings, 1994. XI, 723 pages. 1994.

Vol. 874: A. Borning (Ed.), Principles and Practice of Constraint Programming. Proceedings, 1994. IX, 361 pages. 1994.

Vol. 875: D. Gollmann (Ed.), Computer Security – ESORICS 94. Proceedings, 1994. XI, 469 pages. 1994.

Vol. 876: B. Blumenthal, J. Gornostaev, C. Unger (Eds.), Human-Computer Interaction. Proceedings, 1994. IX, 239 pages. 1994.

Vol. 877: L. M. Adleman, M.-D. Huang (Eds.), Algorithmic Number Theory. Proceedings, 1994. IX, 323 pages. 1994.

Vol. 878: T. Ishida; Parallel, Distributed and Multiagent Production Systems. XVII, 166 pages. 1994. (Subseries LNAI).

Vol. 879: J. Dongarra, J. Waśniewski (Eds.), Parallel Scientific Computing. Proceedings, 1994. XI, 566 pages. 1994.

Vol. 880: P. S. Thiagarajan (Ed.), Foundations of Software Technology and Theoretical Computer Science. Proceedings, 1994. XI, 451 pages. 1994.

Vol. 881: P. Loucopoulos (Ed.), Entity-Relationship Approach – ER'94. Proceedings, 1994. XIII, 579 pages. 1994.

Vol. 882: D. Hutchison, A. Danthine, H. Leopold, G. Coulson (Eds.), Multimedia Transport and Teleservices. Proceedings, 1994. XI, 380 pages. 1994.

Vol. 883: L. Fribourg, F. Turini (Eds.), Logic Program Synthesis and Transformation – Meta-Programming in Logic. Proceedings, 1994. IX, 451 pages. 1994.

Vol. 884: J. Nievergelt, T. Roos, H.-J. Schek, P. Widmayer (Eds.), IGIS '94: Geographic Information Systems. Proceedings, 1994. VIII, 292 pages. 19944.

Vol. 885: R. C. Veltkamp, Closed Objects Boundaries from Scattered Points. VIII, 144 pages. 1994.

Vol. 886: M. M. Veloso, Planning and Learning by Analogical Reasoning. XIII, 181 pages. 1994. (Subseries LNAI).

Vol. 887: M. Toussaint (Ed.), Ada in Europe. Proceedings, 1994. XII, 521 pages. 1994.

Vol. 888: S. A. Andersson (Ed.), Analysis of Dynamical and Cognitive Systems. Proceedings, 1993. VII, 260 pages. 1995.

Vol. 889: H. P. Lubich, Towards a CSCW Framework for Scientific Cooperation in Europe. X, 268 pages. 1995.

Vol. 890: M. J. Wooldridge, N. R. Jennings (Eds.), Intelligent Agents. Proceedings, 1994. VIII, 407 pages. 1995. (Subseries LNAI).

Vol. 891: C. Lewerentz, T. Lindner (Eds.), Formal Development of Reactive Systems. XI, 394 pages. 1995.

Vol. 892: K. Pingali, U. Banerjee, D. Gelernter, A. Nicolau, D. Padua (Eds.), Languages and Compilers for Parallel Computing. Proceedings, 1994. XI, 496 pages. 1995.

Vol. 893: G. Gottlob, M. Y. Vardi (Eds.), Database Theory – ICDT '95. Proceedings, 1995. XI, 454 pages. 1995.

Vol. 894: R. Tamassia, I. G. Tollis (Eds.), Graph Drawing. Proceedings, 1994. X, 471 pages. 1995.

Vol. 895: R. L. Ibrahim (Ed.), Software Engineering Education. Proceedings, 1995. XII, 449 pages. 1995.

Vol. 896: R. N. Taylor, J. Coutaz (Eds.), Software Engineering and Human-Computer Interaction. Proceedings, 1994. X, 281 pages. 1995.

Vol. 897: M. Fisher, R. Owens (Eds.), Executable Modal and Temporal Logics. Proceedings, 1993. VII, 180 pages. 1995. (Subseries LNAI).

Vol. 898: P. Steffens (Ed.), Machine Translation and the Lexicon. Proceedings, 1993. X, 251 pages. 1995. (Subseries LNAI).

Vol. 899: W. Banzhaf, F. H. Eeckman (Eds.), Evolution and Biocomputation. VII, 277 pages. 1995.

Vol. 900: E. W. Mayr, C. Puech (Eds.), STACS 95. Proceedings, 1995. XIII, 654 pages. 1995.

Vol. 901: R. Kumar, T. Kropf (Eds.), Theorem Provers in Circuit Design. Proceedings, 1994. VIII, 303 pages. 1995.

Vol. 902: M. Dezani-Ciancaglini, G. Plotkin (Eds.), Typed Lambda Calculi and Applications. Proceedings, 1995. VIII, 443 pages. 1995.

Vol. 903: E. W. Mayr, G. Schmidt, G. Tinhofer (Eds.), Graph-Theoretic Concepts in Computer Science. Proceedings, 1994. IX, 414 pages. 1995.

Vol. 904: P. Vitányi (Ed.), Computational Learning Theory. EuroCOLT'95. Proceedings, 1995. XVII, 415 pages. 1995. (Subseries LNAI).

Vol. 905: N. Ayache (Ed.), Computer Vision, Virtual Reality and Robotics in Medicine. Proceedings, 1995. XIV, 567 pages. 1995.

Vol. 906: E. Astesiano, G. Reggio, A. Tarlecki (Eds.), Recent Trends in Data Type Specification. Proceedings, 1995. VIII, 523 pages. 1995.

Vol. 907: T. Ito, A. Yonezawa (Eds.), Theory and Practice of Parallel Programming. Proceedings, 1995. VIII, 485 pages. 1995.

Vol. 908: J. R. Rao Extensions of the UNITY Methodology: Compositionality, Fairness and Probability in Parallelism. XI, 178 pages. 1995.

Vol. 909: H. Comon, J.-P. Jouannaud (Eds.), Term Rewriting. Proceedings, 1993. VIII, 221 pages. 1995.

Vol. 910: A. Podelski (Ed.), Constraint Programming: Basics and Trends. Proceedings, 1995. XI, 315 pages. 1995.

Vol. 911: R. Baeza-Yates, E. Goles, P. V. Poblete (Eds.), LATIN '95: Theoretical Informatics. Proceedings, 1995. IX, 525 pages. 1995.

Vol. 912: N. Lavrač, S. Wrobel (Eds.), Machine Learning: ECML – 95. Proceedings, 1995. XI, 370 pages. 1995. (Subseries LNAI).

Vol. 913: W. Schäfer (Ed.), Software Process Technology. Proceedings, 1995. IX, 261 pages. 1995.

Vol. 914: J. Hsiang (Ed.), Rewriting Techniques and Applications. Proceedings, 1995. XII, 473 pages. 1995.

Vol. 915: P. D. Mosses, M. Nielsen, M. I. Schwartzbach (Eds.), TAPSOFT '95: Theory and Practice of Software Development. Proceedings, 1995. XV, 810 pages. 1995.

Vol. 916: N. R. Adam, B. K. Bhargava, Y. Yesha (Eds.), Digital Libraries. Proceedings, 1994. XIII, 321 pages. 1995.

Vol. 917: J. Pieprzyk, R. Safavi-Naini (Eds.), Advances in Cryptology - ASIACRYPT '94. Proceedings, 1994. XII, 431 pages. 1995.

Vol. 918: P. Baumgartner, R. Hähnle, J. Posegga (Eds.), Theorem Proving with Analytic Tableaux and Related Methods. Proceedings, 1995. X, 352 pages. 1995. (Subseries LNAI).